THE ROUGH GUIDE TO

Belgium &
Luxembourg

This sixth edition updated by

Martin Dunford, Phil Lee and Emma Thomson

ROUGH
GUIDES

roughguides.com

Contents

Introduction to
Belgium &
Luxembourg

We bet you a beer – hell, make that two – that Belgium will exceed your expectations. Rumours of a drab, flat land famous only for its fries and EU bureaucracy are false. The country's highlights range from the ancient and quirky to the oh-so-cool: you can bank on centuries-old castles and boisterous carnivals as well as home-grown haute couture, comic book museums and cutting-edge art. And thanks to its compact geography, travellers can flit from the historic to the hip with a quick train ride. You might spend the morning touring one of Flanders' culture-rich cities – Brussels, Bruges, Antwerp and Ghent – and lunching in a Michelin-starred restaurant, before whiling away the afternoon exploring a time-forgotten Ardennes village, where the pubs – known as estaminets – dish up hearty dinners of beer-soaked rabbit stews.

If you overindulge, no matter – you'll be able to work it off cycling poplar-lined **canals**, hiking hilly **moors** and canoeing or kayaking along jinking **rivers**, all the while trying to wrap your tongue around the country's **three official languages** – French, Dutch and German. What's more, the country is one vast, immersive history lesson: it was here that Napoleon was finally defeated at the **Battle of Waterloo**, and here too that some of the bloodiest battles of **World Wars I and II** were played out. Indeed, a trip to Belgium is especially poignant in the lead up to 2018, when the centenary of the **Great War** will be commemorated with numerous special events, "lest we forget".

Meanwhile, **Luxembourg** isn't reserved for bankers and diplomats. Its **UNESCO**-listed capital, perched on a plateau above green gorges, will instantly charm travellers; its regional **wines** will tickle the taste buds; and its **thermal spas** unwind every last knot. So much more than convenient targets for a weekend-break or cross-Channel booze-run, Belgium and Luxembourg are central to Europe's cultural identity – EU or no EU.

ABOVE DAMME-BRUGES CANAL **RIGHT** MAS, ANTWERP

Where to go

The beauty of bijou Belgium is that you can see a lot in a short amount of time. Divided into **three regions** – Flanders, the Dutch-speaking north; Wallonia, the French-speaking south; and Brussels, a bilingual island stranded in the south of Flanders – almost all the major towns are connected by a speedy and compact **rail network**.

Brussels has myriad personalities thanks to the numerous nationalities that now call the city home. This demographic mix is as fascinating as the capital's odd blend of modern business districts, characterful **old town** and open green spaces. The huge selection of hotels – from boutique to budget – make Brussels a good base to explore surrounding towns on day-trips, but be sure to allocate a good few days to the capital itself, particularly for its **world-class museums** and countless cosy and atmospheric **bars**.

Northern **Flanders** – made up of the provinces of West and East Flanders,

FACT FILE

Belgium may be one of Europe's smallest nations, but it packs a lot in:

• It has three official **languages**

• The world's first weekly **newspaper** was printed in Antwerp in 1605

• Belgium has more **castles** per square kilometre than any other country and the lowest number of McDonalds

• The Belgian coastal **tram** is the longest in the world at 68 kilometres

• It's home to the **smallest town in the world**: Durbuy has just 500 inhabitants

The tiny Grand Duchy of Luxembourg does its best to compete:

• Most Luxembourgers speak **Luxembourgish** – a dialect of German – yet all official business is carried out in French

• It has won the **Eurovision Song Contest** five times

• Of a **population** of just 531,400, over 40 per cent are immigrants

• Tax haven-ites can choose from over 155 **banks**

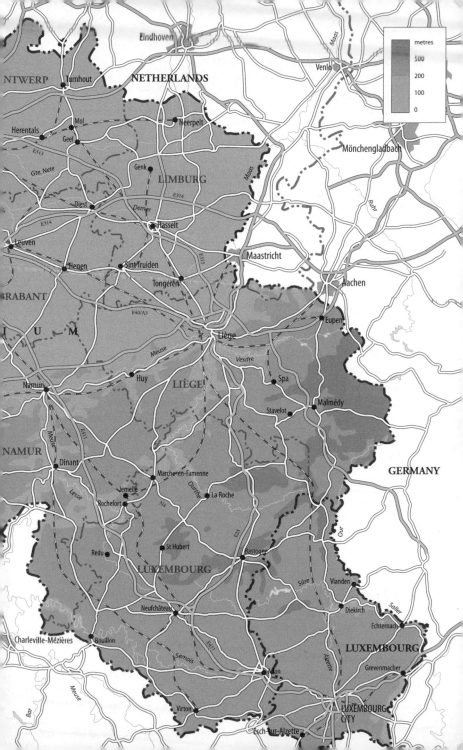

CHOCOLATE: A BELGIAN ART FORM

The Belgians picked up their love of **chocolate** via the most circuitous of historical routes. The Aztecs of Mexico were drinking chocolate, which they believed gave them wisdom, when Hernando Cortéz's Spanish conquistadors turned up in 1519. Cortéz took a liking to the stuff and brought cocoa beans back to Spain as a novelty gift for the **Emperor Charles V** in 1528. Within a few years its consumption had spread across Charles's empire, including today's Belgium and Luxembourg. At first the making of chocolate was confined to a few Spanish monasteries, but eventually Belgians got in on the act and they now produce what are generally regarded as the world's finest chocolates. Even the smallest town will have at least one **chocolate shop** and although some brands are everywhere – Leonidas, Godiva and Neuhaus are three big players – try to seek out **independent producers** such as Wittamer or Pierre Marcolini in Brussels (see p.94), or The Chocolate Line in Bruges (see p.123), as their chocolates are usually that bit better.

Antwerp, Limburg and the top half of Brabant – is mainly flat, but features a wealth of vibrant, forward-thinking cities. At the helm is **Antwerp**, a bustling old port famed for its nightlife and high fashion, but try and build in time to visit **Mechelen**, which lies just to the south – hugely underrated, the city has a burgeoning café culture and superb local brewery. Further west are the great medieval cloth towns of **Bruges** and **Ghent**, with a stunning concentration of Flemish art, listed architecture and winding canals. Bruges is undoubtedly touristy in summer, but you shouldn't miss it on any account. Beyond lies the Belgian **coast**, its sandy shores serviced by the world's longest tramline and its restaurants dishing up excellent seafood. The North Sea is too cold for anything other than a brave toe dip, but the rolling dunes near the resorts of **De Haan** and **Ostend** make for a lovely walk. Back inland, it's worth spending a couple of days based in **Ieper** (Ypres), heart of the World War I battlefields and an ideal base from which to explore the vast, sad acreages of cemeteries and first-class museums dedicated to the conflict.

To the east of Brussels lies the old university city of **Leuven**, where you'll find Belgium's largest *begijnhof* (a type of convent where the nuns retain to the right to return to a secular life). Moving south, the Walloon province of **Hainaut** is dominated by industrial **Charleroi** – currently busy reinventing itself – and the more obviously appealing **Mons**, but it's also home to handsome **Tournai**, with its magnificent cathedral. To the east lies Belgium's most scenic region, the **Ardennes**, spread across the three provinces of **Namur**, **Liège** and **Luxembourg**, the first two of which are also cities – try to visit both, as they're rich in history and good eating. The Ardennes is an area of deep, wooded valleys and heath-laden plateaus, often very wild and excellent for hiking, cycling and canoeing. Both Namur and Luxembourg City are good bases, or try smaller **Bouillon** or **La Roche-en-Ardenne**.

The Ardennes reaches across the Belgian border into the northern part of the **Grand Duchy of Luxembourg**, a landscape of hills and wooded ravines topped with tumbledown castles overlooking rushing rivers. The two best centres for touring the countryside are the quiet little towns of **Vianden** and **Echternach**, featuring an extravagantly picturesque castle and a splendid abbey respectively. Indeed, despite its feeble reputation, the Duchy

SHEER BEER BLISS

No other country in the world produces more beers than Belgium – around **eight hundred** and counting. There are strong, dark brews from a handful of **Trappist monasteries**, light wheat beers perfect for a hot summer's day, fruity **lambic beers** bottled and corked like champagne (see box, p.77), and unusual concoctions that date back to medieval times. In the Basics section (see box, p.30), we've listed a selection of the best and most common to get you started, but really the joy is in experimenting with new brews. Any decent establishment will have a beer menu, as well as the **glasses** to go with them – no Belgian bar worth its salt would dare to serve a beer in anything other than its proper glass.

– or rather its northern reaches – packs more scenic highlights into its tight borders than many other, more renowned holiday spots, and is perfect for hiking and, at a pinch, mountain-biking. The Ardennes fizzles out into the **Moselle Valley**, whose slopes are lined with vines, while in the south UNESCO-listed **Luxembourg City**'s bastions and bulwarks recall the days when this was one of the strongest fortresses in Europe.

When to go

Weather-wise, Belgium and Luxembourg are on par with the **south of England**: they're both temperate countries, with warm summers and moderately cold winters – with the occasional brutal blast of snow and ice appearing in January and even February. The threat of **rain** is undeniably omnipresent, but at least it keeps things green. Generally speaking, **temperatures** rise the further south you go, with Wallonia a couple of degrees warmer than Flanders for most of the year.

Both countries can be visited year round, but are at their best from spring to late summer (**April to September**) when the weather is calmer and the nights longer. However, there are a few **exceptions**: Bruges is inundated with tourists during August, so it's best to book a bed and enjoy the town after 6pm when the buses depart en masse; Ghent is a ghost town the first two weeks of August because everyone is recovering from the two-week Gentse Feesten blowout; and Wallonia, especially the Ardennes, tends to go into hibernation in winter with many sites closing. Finally, December and early January can also be a lovely time to visit thanks to the legendary **Christmas markets** that crop up in all the major towns.

MONTHLY TEMPERATURES AND RAINFALL

	Jan	Feb	Mar	Apr	May	Jun	Jul	Aug	Sep	Oct	Nov	Dec
BRUSSELS												
max/min (°C)	6/-1	8/0	11/4	14/6	19/10	22/11	23/14	23/14	21/11	15/8	9/3	6/0
rainfall (mm)	66	61	53	60	55	76	95	80	63	83	75	88
LUXEMBOURG CITY												
max/min (°C)	2/-2	4/-2	8/1	12/3	17/7	20/10	23/12	22/12	19/10	13/6	7/1	3/-1
rainfall (mm)	71	62	70	61	81	82	68	72	70	75	83	80

Author picks

Our authors have scaled belfry towers, hiked hidden paths and slurped on bowls of *paling in 't groen* (a sort of eel soup) to bring you the very best recommendations. Here are some of their personal favourites.

A beer pilgrimage Take a tour of Brussels' last working brewery, Cantillon (see p.76). Over a hundred years old, it gives fascinating insights into the brewing of Gueuze beer – and there's the all-important taste test at the end too.

Rural bike ride Come springtime the fruit-growing region of Haspengouw, in Limburg province, is alive with blossoms. Rent a bike and pedal beneath the floral boughs, stopping off at Zoutleeuw's pretty hamlet church (see box, p.217).

Sample unusual chocolates Pop into The Chocolate Line (see p.123), Bruges' best chocolatier, famed for its lip-smackingly unusual flavours, such as tequila chocolate shots.

Strike a pose Visit the boutiques of Antwerp's leading clothes designers (see box, p.187) and don't miss the superb exhibitions at MoMu (see p.186).

A theme park like no other The marvellously inventive gardens and zoo of Pairi Daiza (see p.233) are situated in an old monastery's grounds, yet its themed zones are truly Disney-esque.

Taste boulets-frites A visit to Liège wouldn't be complete without lunch or dinner at *Café Lequet* (see p.269), a bonhomie haunt serving the city's best meatballs doused in sweet *sirop de Liège*.

Beer ... and then some Seek out Délices et Caprices (see p.94), a tiny shop just off Brussels' touristy rue des Bouchers, which sells rare brews and all sorts of Belgian goodies to go with.

Max out your memory card Take postcard-worthy photos of Luxembourg's prettiest hamlet by climbing the hill above Esch-Sur-Sûre (see p.312) – locals can point you towards the trail.

Toast your trip Take a vineyard tour and stock up on bottles of Luxembourg's sparkling crémant (see p.321) – a great alternative to champagne, and at a quarter of the price.

> Our author recommendations don't end here. We've flagged up our favourite places – a perfectly sited hotel, an atmospheric café, a special restaurant – throughout the guide, highlighted with the ★ symbol.

FROM TOP ESCH-SUR-SÛRE; DÉLICES ET CAPRICES; THE CHOCOLATE LINE

18

things not to miss

It's not possible to see everything that Belgium and Luxembourg have to offer in one trip – and we don't suggest you try. What follows, in no particular order, is a selective and subjective taste of the two countries' highlights, from wonderful food and striking Gothic architecture to handsome forested hills. Each entry has a page reference to take you straight into the Guide, where you can find out more. Coloured numbers refer to chapters in the Guide section.

1

1 ADORATION OF THE MYSTIC LAMB, GHENT

Page 155

One of the medieval world's most astonishing paintings and Ghent's pride and joy.

2 MOSELLE VALLEY, LUXEMBOURG

Page 321

Sip your way through a glass or three of crémant, Luxembourg's incredibly quaffable, sparkling white wine.

3 GRAND-PLACE, BRUSSELS

Page 46

Take a seat at a café terrace, order a beer and admire the intricate UNESCO-listed guildhouses of this world-famous, cobbled square.

4 THE HAUTES FAGNES, ARDENNES

Page 275

The Ardennes' windswept expanse of moorland and woodland offers fabulous hiking.

12

13

14

Itineraries

Belgium and Luxembourg may be small, but they're jam-packed with things to do. The urban centres are a major draw, and our Grand Tour is a fast-paced two-week route covering the main cities. The other itineraries are themed with a particular interest in mind: one marks the centenary of the Great War; and the third celebrates the region's wealth of outdoor activities.

THE GRAND TOUR

Allow two weeks for this highlights tour, which takes in the capitals as well as a section of the North Sea coastline and the rugged Ardennes.

Brussels Kick off the trip by spending a few days touring the dynamic capital. Sip a beer in a time-forgotten *estaminet*, visit the world-class art galleries and take your photo with the diminutive Manneken Pis. **See p.55**

Antwerp Head north for Belgium's best nightlife, cutting-edge restaurants and all things related to the painter Rubens. **See p.182**

Ghent Cut across country to the buzzing university town of Ghent – filled with waterways and ancient architecture and home to the lauded *Adoration of the Mystic Lamb* masterpiece. **See p.155**

Bruges Belgium's second-most famous city mustn't be missed. Get lost amid her medieval maze of cobbled streets, visit the UNESCO-listed *begijnhof* and wander the canals. **See p.101**

Ostend Use up-and-coming Ostend as your base to explore the North Sea coastline. Ride the world's longest tramline and tuck into a plate of ultra-fresh *moules-frites*. **See p.125**

Bouillon Hop on a train headed south for French-speaking Wallonia and visit Bouillon's impossibly pretty hilltop castle amid the verdant, rolling hills of the Ardennes region. **See p.287**

Luxembourg City Explore one of Europe's most spectacularly sited capitals, from the underground casemates hidden beneath the Old Town to the laid-back bars of the leafy Grund. **See p.300**

WORLD WAR I SITES

2014–2018 marks the centenary of the Great War. Travellers planning a pilgrimage might trace the following route, which is best done at a relaxed pace. Alternatively, Luxembourg has numerous World War II museums associated with the Battle of the Bulge.

Mons Start in this Wallonian city where the Battle of Mons played out and learn about the Angels of Mons legend. **See p.230**

Ieper (Ypres) At the heart of Belgium's World War I region, this picturesque town is home to the In Flanders Fields Museum and moving Menin Gate, and is the departure point for bus or bike tours of the Ypres Salient. **See p.138**

Diksmuide Journey north to unassuming Diksmuide, famous for its Ijzertoren – a towering monument to peace – and the nearby Dodengang (Trench of Death). **See p.136**

ABOVE EU PARLIAMENT, BRUSSELS

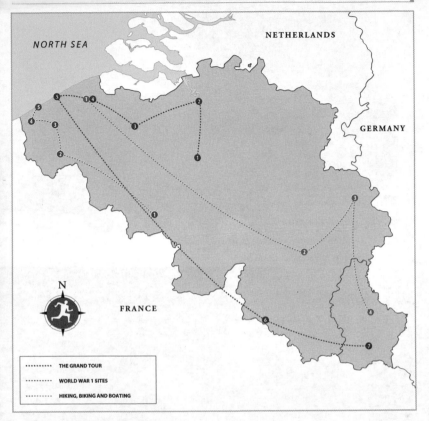

Veurne Head towards the coast, stopping off to visit Veurne's medieval stadhuis – site of King Albert I's WWI headquarters. **See p.133**

Nieuwpoort Finish up in Nieuwpoort to see the sluices that saved Belgium from total occupation. **See p.132**

HIKING, BIKING AND BOATING

Flat in the north, hilly in the south and riddled with rivers, Belgium and Luxembourg are an outdoor enthusiast's playground. This route combines a bit of everything.

Bruges Get warmed up with a gentle boat ride through the winding canals of Bruges' medieval centre then rent bikes and pedal along the canal to the picture-perfect village of Damme. **See p.120 & p.124**

La Roche-en-Ardenne Visit this popular Ardennes town for a family-friendly kayaking session along the River Lesse. **See p.285**

The Hautes Fagnes Head westwards to the wild Hautes Fagnes national park and hike to Belgium's highest point – Signal de Botrange. **See p.275**

Mullerthal Trail Lace up the hiking boots once more and cross the border into Luxembourg to tackle this 112km trail littered with impressive rock formations. **See p.323**

TRADITIONAL SWEET WAFFLES, BRUSSELS

Basics

Getting there

UK travellers are spoilt for choice when it comes to getting to Belgium. There are flights to Brussels from London and a string of regional airports; Eurostar trains direct from London St Pancras to Brussels; ferries from Hull to Zeebrugge, near Bruges; Eurotunnel services from Folkestone to Calais, a short drive from the Belgian coast; and frequent international buses from London to Brussels and Antwerp. Buses are usually the least expensive means of transportation, but the train is faster and often not that much pricier, and there are all sorts of great deals on flights too. Luxembourg is also easy to get to: there are flights from London but it's also just three hours from Brussels to Luxembourg City by train.

For travellers arriving from North America, the main decision is whether to fly direct to Brussels – though the options are limited – or via another European city, probably London. Australians, New Zealanders and South Africans have to fly via another city – there are no nonstop flights.

Flights from the UK

From the **UK**, Belgium's major airport – **Brussels** – is readily reached from London and a large number of regional airports. There's also Brussels-Charleroi airport, whose name is somewhat deceptive – it's actually on the edge of Charleroi, about 50km south of the capital. **Luxembourg City** airport, the third choice, is just a short bus ride from Luxembourg City. Airlines flying from the UK to Belgium include British Airways, Brussels Airlines (Ⓦ brusselsairlines.com), easyJet, Flybe, bmi regional (Ⓦ bmiregional.com) Lufthansa, KLM and Ryanair (to Brussels Charleroi). Luxair (Ⓦ luxair.lu) has flights to Luxembourg City from London City, British Airways flies there from

Heathrow, and easyJet from London Gatwick. **Flying times** are insignificant: no more than 1.5hr from London or regional airports to Brussels and Luxembourg.

Whichever route and carrier you choose, it's hard to say precisely what you'll pay at any given time – there are just too many variables. That said, flying to Brussels from the UK with one of the low-cost airlines, a reasonable **average fare** would be about £170 return (including taxes), though you can pay as little as £70 and as much as £400.

Flights from Ireland

Flying from **Ireland**, Aer Lingus has daily flights to Brussels from Dublin and Cork; Scandinavian Airlines flies from Dublin to both Brussels and Luxembourg City; and Ryanair has flights from Dublin to Brussels-Charleroi. **Prices** for flights vary considerably, but begin at about €170 return from Dublin to Brussels. Flying **times** are modest: Dublin to Brussels takes about 1hr 40min.

Flights from the US and Canada

From the **US**, you can **fly direct** to Brussels from New York City (United or Delta), Philadelphia (US Airways; American; British Airways), Atlanta (Delta), KLM, Washington (United) and Chicago (United; Lufthansa), but you'll often find **cheaper deals** if you're prepared to stop once, either in the US or mainland Europe. **Return fares** to Brussels from New York can be found for as little as $900, but $1500 is a more normal fare. There are no direct flights from the **West Coast**, but plenty of carriers will get you to Brussels with one stop for as little as $1200 return. There are no direct flights from the US to Luxembourg.

From **Canada**, Jet Airways (Ⓦ jetairways.com) flies direct from Toronto to Brussels, while Air Canada flies nonstop to London Heathrow, with onward connections to Brussels. From Toronto to Brussels, **return fares** start at around Can$1400; from Vancouver it's more like Can$1700.

A BETTER KIND OF TRAVEL

At Rough Guides we are passionately committed to travel. We believe it helps us understand the world we live in and the people we share it with – and of course tourism is vital to many developing economies. But the scale of modern tourism has also damaged some places irreparably, and climate change is accelerated by most forms of transport, especially flying. All Rough Guides' flights are carbon-offset, and every year we donate money to a variety of environmental charities.

Flights from Australia and New Zealand

There are no direct flights from **Australia** or **New Zealand** to Brussels or Luxembourg City. Most itineraries will involve **two changes**, one in the Far East – Singapore, Bangkok or Kuala Lumpur – and then another in the gateway city of the airline you're flying with (most commonly Paris, Amsterdam or London). **Fares** to Brussels from Sydney or Melbourne are in the Aus$1500–2000 range; from Auckland figure on NZ$2000–2500.

Flights from South Africa

There are no direct flights from **South Africa** to Belgium or Luxembourg City, but KLM does offer direct/nonstop flights to **Amsterdam**, a short train ride away from Belgium, from both Cape Town and Johannesburg. With other airlines, you will have to change at a gateway city – for example Lufthansa via Frankfurt – but this can often be more economical. As for sample **fares**, direct/nonstop return flights with KLM from South Africa begin at about R7000. The **flight time**, direct, is about 11 hours.

By train from the UK

Eurostar trains (Ⓦeurostar.com) departing from London St Pancras (plus Ebbsfleet and Ashford in Kent) reach Brussels via the Channel Tunnel in a couple of hours. In Brussels, trains arrive at **Bruxelles-Midi/Brussel-Zuid** station. Eurostar operates around **ten services a day** and **fares** are largely defined by ticket flexibility: the least flexible returns cost around £160; the most flexible, whose times and dates can be changed at will, work out at about £400. However, advance booking – at least two weeks ahead – can cut the cost of the cheapest return ticket dramatically, and Eurostar also offers myriad special deals and discounts. Eurostar tickets from London to Brussels are also **common rated** for Belgium as a whole, which means, for example, that you can travel onto Bruges via Brussels at no extra cost; this common rating system may come to an end if and

when other train companies start using the Channel Tunnel (see box below).

Rail passes

If you're visiting Belgium and/or Luxembourg as part of a longer European trip, it may be worth considering a **pan-European rail pass**. There are lots to choose from and **Rail Europe** (Ⓦraileurope.com), the umbrella company for all national and international passes, operates a comprehensive website detailing all the options with prices. Note in particular that some passes have to be bought before leaving home, others can only be bought in specific countries.

Driving from the UK

To reach Belgium by car or motorbike from the **UK**, you can either take a **car ferry** (see below) or use **Eurotunnel**'s (Ⓦeurotunnel.com) shuttle train through the Channel Tunnel from Folkestone to Calais. Eurotunnel **fares**, which are charged per vehicle including passengers, depend on the time of year, time of day and length of stay; the journey takes about **35min**. As an example, a five-day return fare in the summer costs in the region of £100. Advance booking is strongly advised. Note that Eurotunnel only carries cars (including occupants) and motorbikes, not foot passengers. From the Eurotunnel exit in Calais, it's just 50km or so to De Panne, on the Belgian coast, 120km to Bruges and 200km to Brussels.

By ferry from the UK

At time of writing, there's only one **car ferry** operating between the UK and Belgium. This links Hull and Zeebrugge, a few kilometres from Bruges, and is operated by **P&O** (Ⓦpoferries.com). The sailing time is about 13hr. **Tariffs** vary enormously, depending on when you leave, how long you stay, what size your vehicle is and how many passengers are in it; there is also the cost of a cabin to consider. As a sample fare, a five-day return ticket for two adults and two children in a standard-size car with cabin will cost £300 and up; booking ahead is strongly recommended, and essential in summer.

EUROSTAR'S MONOPOLY

Eurostar was allowed a monopoly of train travel through the Channel Tunnel from its opening in 1994 to January 2010. Since then, several rail companies have expressed an interest in running services through the tunnel, especially Germany's **Deutsche Bahn** (Ⓦbahn.com), but nothing has happened yet.

By train from continental Europe

Belgium and Luxembourg have borders with France, Germany and the Netherlands. A raft of rail lines runs into Belgium from its neighbours – and Luxembourg has good international connections too. **Ordinary trains** operated by France's SNCF (Ⓦsncf .com), Germany's Deutsche Bahn (Ⓦbahn.com) and the Netherlands' NS (Ⓦns.nl) link many cities and towns and there is also a somewhat confusing range of high-speed **express trains**, including ICE (mainly to and from Germany; Ⓦbahn.com) and Thalys (Ⓦthalys.com). The hub of the Thalys network is Brussels, from where there are trains to (among many destinations) Rotterdam, Amsterdam, Paris and Cologne. Predictably, express trains are almost always **more expensive** than ordinary services.

By bus from the UK

Travelling by **long-distance bus** is generally the cheapest way of reaching Belgium from the UK, but it is very time-consuming. **Eurolines** (Ⓦeurolines .co.uk), part of National Express, has four daily departures from London's Victoria coach station to Brussels, with a journey time of around seven hours. Return tickets cost about £50. There are also regular Eurolines buses to several other Belgian cities, including Bruges, Ghent and Antwerp.

Getting around

Travelling around Belgium is almost always easy: it's a small country, and there's an extremely well-organized – and reasonably priced – public transport system, with an extensive train network supplemented by (and tied in with) a plethora of local bus services. Luxembourg is, of course, even smaller, but here matters are not quite so straightforward: the train network is limited, and public transport is largely based around buses, whose timetables can demand careful scrutiny.

Travel **between Belgium and Luxembourg** is a seamless affair – with no border controls and with routine through-ticketing by train and bus. **Two main rail lines** link the two countries: the first runs from Brussels to Luxembourg City via Namur and Arlon, the second links Liège with Luxembourg City. **Journey times** are insignificant –

Brussels to Luxembourg City takes under three hours – and services are frequent. Note also that in addition to the domestic deals and discounts described below, there is a host of pan-European rail passes (see p.22).

By train

Belgium

The best way of getting around Belgium is by train. The system, operated by the **Société Nationale des Chemins de Fer Belges/Belgische Spoorwegen** (Belgian Railways; Ⓦbelgianrail.be), is one of the best in Europe: trains are fast, frequent and very punctual; the network of lines is comprehensive; and **fares** are relatively low. For example, a standard, second-class ticket (*billet ordinaire/gewone biljet*) from Bruges to Arlon, one of the longest domestic train journeys you can make, costs just €21.10 one-way, while the 40min trip from Ghent to Brussels costs €8.90. Standard return tickets are twice the cost of a single, but same-day return tickets knock about ten percent off the price. First-class fares cost about fifty percent on top of the regular fare. There are substantial **discounts** for children and seniors (65+) and other discount tickets and deals that reward off-peak travelling and repeat journeys. Best of all are the **special weekend returns**, which can knock up to fifty percent off. With any ticket, you're free to **break your journey** anywhere en route and continue later that day, but you're not allowed to backtrack. You can **buy tickets** via the company's compendious website and at any train station, either at the ticket office or at the automatic ticket machines installed at all major stations, though note that these only accept credit cards (not debit cards).

Luxembourg

In Luxembourg, trains are run by the **Société Nationale des Chemins de Fer Luxembourgeois** (CFL; Ⓦwww.cfl.lu). The network comprises just a handful of lines, with the principal route cutting north-south down the middle of the country from Belgium's Liège to Luxembourg City via Clervaux and Ettelbruck. Trains are fast and efficient, and most operate hourly. A free **diagrammatic plan** of the country's bus and train network is available at most train stations, as are individual train and bus **timetables**, or you can purchase a countrywide bus and train timetable from all major train stations at minimal cost. A **network ticket** (*billet réseau*), valid for train and bus travel across the whole of the Grand Duchy, is very reasonably priced, with a one-day pass costing €4, or €16 for a pack of five. These are valid from the first time you use them (you must punch them in the machines provided to record the time) until 8am the following day. Another option, available between Easter and October, is the **Luxembourg Card** (see p.298), which permits free travel on the country's buses and trains and also gives discounted admission to many tourist attractions.

By bus

Belgium

With so much of the country covered by the rail network, Belgian buses are mainly of use for travelling **short distances**, and wherever there's a choice of transportation the train is quicker and not that much more expensive. Indeed, to all intents and purposes Belgium buses essentially supplement the trains, with services radiating out from the train station and/or connecting different rail lines. That said, local buses are invaluable in some parts of rural Belgium, like the **Botte de Hainaut** and **the Ardennes**, where the train network fizzles out. Three bus companies provide nationwide coverage: **De Lijn** (Ⓦdelijn.be) in the Flemish-speaking areas; **STIB** (Ⓦwww.stib-mivb.be) in Brussels; and **TEC** (Ⓦinfotec.be) in Wallonia.

Luxembourg

In Luxembourg, the sparseness of the rail system means that buses are much more important than in Belgium, though again bus and train services are **fully integrated**. A free diagrammatic plan of the Grand Duchy's bus and train network is available at major bus and train stations, as are individual bus timetables; alternatively, for a few euros, you can purchase a countrywide bus and train **timetable** from all major train stations or you can get detailed information online (Ⓦcfl.lu).

By car

For the most part, **driving** around Belgium and Luxembourg is pretty much what you would hope: smooth, easy and quick. Both countries have a good road network, with most of the major towns linked by some kind of motorway or dual carriageway, though snarl-ups are far from rare, especially in Belgium. That said, big-city driving, where congestion and one-way systems are the norm, is almost always problematic, particularly as drivers in Belgium are generally considered some of the most pugnacious in Europe. One problem peculiar to Belgium, however, is **signage**. In most cases the French and Flemish names are similar – or at least mutually

recognizable – but in others they do not resemble each other at all (see box, p.25). In Brussels and its environs, all the road signs are bilingual, but elsewhere it's either French or Flemish and, as you cross **Belgium's language divide** (see p.341), the name you've been following on the road signs can simply disappear, with, for example, "Liège" suddenly transformed into "Luik". Whatever you do, make sure you've got a good road map (see p.36).

Rules of the road are straightforward: you drive on the right, and speed limits are 50km/h in built-up areas, 90km/h outside, 120km/h on motorways; note that speed cameras are commonplace. Drivers and front-seat passengers are required by law to wear seatbelts, and penalties for drunk driving are always severe. Remember also that trams have right of way over any other vehicle, and that, unless indicated otherwise, motorists must give way to traffic merging from the right. There are no toll roads, and although **fuel** is expensive, at €1.60 per litre (diesel €1.40) in Belgium and slightly less in Luxembourg, the short distances involved mean this isn't too much of an issue.

Most **foreign driving licences** are honoured in Belgium and Luxembourg, including all EU/EEA, Australian, New Zealand, US and Canadian ones. If you're **bringing your own car**, you must have adequate insurance, preferably including coverage for legal costs, and it's advisable to have an appropriate breakdown policy from your home motoring organization too.

Renting a car

All the major **international car rental agencies** are represented in Belgium and Luxembourg. To rent a car, you'll have to be 21 or over (and have been driving for at least a year), and you'll need a credit card – though some local agencies will accept a hefty cash deposit instead. **Rental charges** are fairly reasonable, beginning around €250 per week for unlimited mileage in the smallest vehicle, and (should) include collision damage waiver and vehicle (but not personal) insurance. To cut costs, book in advance and online. If you go to a **smaller, local company** (of which there are many), you should proceed with care: in particular, check the policy for the excess applied to claims and ensure that it includes a collision damage waiver (applicable if an accident is your fault) as well as adequate levels of financial cover. If you **break down** in a rented car, you'll get roadside assistance from the particular repair company the rental firm has contracted. The same principle works with your own vehicle's breakdown policy providing you have coverage abroad.

FRENCH AND FLEMISH PLACE NAMES

The list below provides the **French and Flemish names** of some of the more important towns in Belgium where the difference may cause confusion. The official name comes first, the alternative afterwards, except in the case of Brussels where both languages are of equal standing.

FRENCH–FLEMISH

Bruxelles – Brussel
Ath – Aat
Liège – Luik
Mons – Bergen
Namur – Namen
Nivelles – Nijvel
Soignies – Zinnik
Tournai – Doornik

FLEMISH–FRENCH

Antwerpen – Anvers
Brugge – Bruges
De Haan – Le Coq

Gent – Gand
Ieper – Ypres
Kortrijk – Courtrai
Leuven – Louvain
Mechelen – Malines
Oostende – Ostende
Oudenaarde – Audenarde
Ronse – Renaix
Sint Truiden – St-Trond
Tienen – Tirlemont
Tongeren – Tongres
Veurne – Furnes
Zoutleeuw – Léau

By bike

Belgium

Cycling is something of a national passion in Belgium, and it's also – given the short distances and largely flat terrain – a viable and fairly effortless way of getting around. But you do have to be selective: cycling in most of the big cities and on the majority of trunk roads – where separate cycle lanes are far from ubiquitous – is precarious, verging on the suicidal. On the other hand, once you've reached the countryside, there are dozens of **clearly signposted cycle routes** to follow – and local tourist offices will invariably have maps and route descriptions, which you can supplement with the relevant **IGN (NGI) map** (see p.36). The logic of all this means that most Belgian cyclists – from Eddy Merckx lookalikes to families on an afternoon's pedal – carry their bikes to their chosen cycling location by car or train (though not by bus – it's not usually allowed). Belgian Railways transports bicycles with the minimum of fuss and at minimal cost.

If you haven't brought your own, you can **rent bikes** from forty train stations nationwide (mostly in Flanders) under the **Blue Bike** scheme (Ⓦ blue-bike .be) at just €3 per day plus an initial registration of €10. It's a good idea to reserve your bike ahead of time during the summer. Otherwise, local bike rental shops are commonplace – reckon on €15 for basic/ no-frills models.

Luxembourg

Luxembourg is popular with cyclists and has over 500km of **cycle tracks**, many of them following old

railway lines. You can **rent bikes** at an assortment of campsites, hostels, hotels and tourist offices for around €15 a day (€25–30 for a mountain-bike); tourist offices also have comprehensive lists of local bike rental outlets. Bear in mind also that you can take your bike on trains (but not buses) anywhere in the country at minimal cost. For further details, consult the website of the Luxembourg National Tourist Office (see p.39).

Accommodation

Inevitably, hotel accommodation is one of the major expenses you'll incur on a trip to Belgium and Luxembourg – indeed, if you're after a degree of comfort, it's going to be the costliest factor by far. There are budget alternatives, however, beginning with the no-frills end of the hotel market and also B&Bs – though note that these are effectively rented rooms in private houses rather than the British-style bed-and-breakfast. Even more of a bargain are the youth hostels, be they Hostelling International-affiliated or "unofficial" (private) ones, which are located in the larger cities and/or main tourist spots of both countries.

It is advisable to **book in advance** no matter where you're going, but most tourist offices do operate an on-the-spot reservation service for same-night accommodation, either free or at minimal charge.

TOP FIVE CHARACTER HOTELS·

Both Belgium and Luxembourg have a battery of **charming hotels**, from chi-chi lodgings in ancient canal houses to Art Nouveau villas. Here are five of the best.
Adornes, Bruges. See p.120.
Le Dixseptième, Brussels. See p.83
Erasmus, Ghent. See p.167.
Hôtel Hors Château, Liège. See p.269
Rubens Grote Markt, Antwerp. See p.194

Hotels

All **hotels** in Belgium and Luxembourg are graded via the star system of the **Benelux Hotel Classification** scheme. By necessity, this scheme measures easily identifiable criteria – lifts, toilets, room service, etc – rather than aesthetics, specific location or even cost. **Prices** fluctuate wildly with demand and not necessarily with the season – indeed, summer is bargain time in Brussels. One-star and no-star hotels are rare, and prices for two-star establishments start at around €80 for a double room without private bath or shower, €90 with en-suite facilities. Three-star hotels cost upwards of about €95; for four- and five-star places you'll pay €125-plus. Generally, the stated price includes **breakfast**, except in the very cheapest of places. Note also that hotel foyers can be deceptively plush compared with the rooms beyond, and you only begin to hit the real comfort zone at three stars. You can book ahead easily either online or by calling the hotel direct – English is almost always spoken.

B&Bs

In recent years, the number of **Belgian B&Bs** (*chambres d'hôtes/gastenkamers*) has increased rapidly, though "B&B" is perhaps something of a misnomer as guests rarely have much contact with their hosts – it's more like a **rented room in a private house**. The **average rate** for a B&B in both Belgium and Luxembourg works out at €50–80 per double per night, a tad more in Brussels and Bruges.

The only common snag is that many B&Bs are **inconveniently situated** far from the respective town or city centre – be sure to check out the location before you accept a room. Note too that as the owners don't usually live on the premises, access often has to be arranged beforehand. In most places, the tourist office has a list of local B&Bs, which it will issue to visitors, but in the more popular destinations – for instance Bruges and Ghent – B&Bs are publicized alongside hotels. In **Luxembourg**, B&Bs are less of a feature, though again local tourist offices have the details. Wherever the arrangements are more formalized – again as in Bruges – the B&B premises are inspected and awarded stars in accordance with the Benelux Hotel Classification scheme (see above).

Hostels

If you're travelling on a tight budget, a **hostel** may well be your accommodation of choice – whether you're youthful or not. They can often be extremely good value, and offer clean and comfortable **dorm beds** as well as a choice of **private rooms** (doubles and sometimes singles) at rock-bottom prices. Both city and country locations can get very full between June and August, when you should book in advance. If you're planning on spending several nights in **HI-affiliated** hostels, it makes sense to join your home HI organization before you leave to avoid paying surcharges, though you can join at the first local hostel you stay at instead.

Belgium

Belgium has around thirty HI-affiliated hostels (*auberges de jeunesse/jeugdherbergen*) operated by two separate organizations, **Vlaamse Jeugdherbergen** (Ⓦ www.vjh.be), covering the Flemish region, and **Les Auberges de Jeunesse de Wallonie** (Ⓦ lesaubergesdejeunesse.be) for Wallonia. Both run hostels in Brussels. **Dorm beds** cost about €25 per person per night including breakfast; there are no age restrictions. Most hostels have single- and double-bedded rooms in which prices rise to €25–30 per person per night. **Meals** are often available and in some hostels there are

self-catering facilities too. Some of Belgium's larger cities – primarily Antwerp, Bruges and Brussels – have several **private hostels** (sometimes referred to as *logements pour jeunes/jeugdlogies*), offering dormitory accommodation and, invariably, double- and triple-bedded rooms, at broadly similar prices, though standards vary enormously.

Luxembourg

Luxembourg has nine youth hostels, all members of the **Centrale des Auberges de Jeunesse Luxembourgeoises** (CAJL; ⓦyouthhostels.lu). **Prices** for HI members are around €20 per person for a dorm bed, €25 per person in a double room, both with breakfast included; some places also serve meals.

Camping

Camping is a popular pastime in both Belgium and Luxembourg. In **Belgium**, there are literally hundreds of campsites to choose from, anything from a field with a few pitches through to extensive complexes with all mod cons. The country's campsites are regulated by two governmental agencies – one for Flanders and one for Wallonia – and each produces its own camping booklets and operates a **website**: ⓦcamping.be for Flanders, ⓦcampingbelgique.be for Wallonia. Many Belgian campsites are situated with the motorist in mind, occupying key locations beside main roads, and they are all classified within the **Benelux one- to five-star matrix** (see box below). The majority are one- and two-star establishments, for which a family of two adults, two children, a car and a tent can expect to pay between €20 and €40 per night. Prices are comparable in **Luxembourg**,

which has around ninety registered campsites, all detailed on ⓦcamping.lu. Luxembourg does not now enforce the Benelux star system (though individual campsites can register if they wish), and the best campsites are now awarded the **Luxembourg Quality Label**; environmentally friendly sites can opt for the **Luxembourg EcoLabel** instead.

Farm and rural holidays

In both Belgium and Luxembourg, the tourist authorities coordinate **farm and rural holidays**, ranging from family accommodation in a farmhouse to the renting of rural apartments and country dwellings. In Wallonia and Luxembourg, there are also **gîtes d'étapes** – dormitory-style lodgings situated in relatively remote parts of the country – which can house anywhere between ten and one hundred people per establishment. You can often choose to rent just part of the gîte d'étape or stay on a bed-and-breakfast basis. Some of the larger gîtes d'étape (or gîtes de groupes) cater for large groups only, accepting bookings for a minimum of 25 people.

In all cases, advance booking is essential and **prices**, naturally enough, vary widely depending on the quality of accommodation, the length of stay and the season. As examples, a high-season (mid-June to Aug), week-long booking of a pleasantly situated and comfortable farmhouse for four adults and three children might cost you in the region of €350–450, whereas a ten-person gîte d'étape might cost €300–400. For further details, check out ⓦlogereninvlaanderenvakantieland.be for Flanders; ⓦgitesdewallonie.net for Wallonia; and ⓦgites.lu for Luxembourg.

Food and drink

Belgian cuisine, particularly that of Brussels and Wallonia, is held in high regard worldwide, and in most of Europe is seen as second only to French in quality – indeed, many feel it's of equal standing. For such a small country, there's a surprising amount of provincial diversity, but it's generally true to say that pork, beef, game, fish and seafood – especially mussels – are staple items, often cooked with butter, cream and herbs, or sometimes beer – which is, after all, Belgium's national drink. Soup is also common, a hearty stew-like affair offered in a huge tureen from which you can help yourself – a satisfying and reasonably priced meal in itself. The better Belgian chefs are often eclectic, dipping into many other cuisines, especially those of the Mediterranean, and also borrowing freely from across their own country's cultural/linguistic divide.

Luxembourg cuisine doesn't rise to quite such giddy heights, though it's still of an excellent standard. The food here borrows extensively from the **Ardennes** but, as you might expect, has more Germanic influences, with sausages and sauerkraut featuring on menus alongside pork, game and river fish. As for **drink**, one of the real delights of Belgium is its **beer**, and Luxembourg produces some very drinkable **white wines** from the vineyards along the west bank of the River Moselle.

For a **menu reader** in both French and Flemish (Dutch), see pp.355–357 & pp.360–362.

Food

In both Belgium and Luxembourg, the least expensive places to eat are **cafés** and **bars** – though the distinction between the two is typically blurred, hence the large number of **café-bars**. A number of these establishments will flank the main square of every small and medium-sized town you visit, offering basic dishes such as pasta, soups, *croque-monsieurs* (a toasted ham and cheese sandwich served with salad) and chicken or steak with chips. **Prices** are usually reasonable – reckon on about €15 for the more modest dishes, €20 for the more substantial – though of course you will often pay more in the most popular tourist destinations. In general – and especially in Wallonia – the quality of these dishes will regularly be excellent and portions characteristically substantial. In the big cities, these café-bars play second fiddle to more specialist – and equally inexpensive – places: primarily pasta and pizza joints, cafés that cater for the shopper (and specialize in cakes and pastries), ethnic café-restaurants and so forth.

Though there's often a thin dividing line between the café and the **restaurant**, the latter are mostly a little more formal and, not surprisingly, rather more expensive. Even in the cheapest restaurant a main course will rarely cost under €17, with a more usual figure being between €20 and €25. Restaurants are usually open at lunch time (noon–2pm), but the main focus is in the evening. In addition, many restaurants close one day a week, usually Monday or Tuesday, and in the smaller towns kitchens start to wind down around 9.30/10pm. Many bars, cafés and restaurants offer a good-value *plat du jour/dagschotel*, usually for around €15, and frequently including a drink. **Vegetarians** may, however, not be so enamoured: Belgian and Luxembourg cuisine is largely fish- and meat-based, which means vegetarians can be in for a difficult time, though all of the larger towns do have at least a couple of vegetarian places, even if these tend to operate limited opening hours.

Breakfast, lunch and snacks

In most parts of Belgium and Luxembourg you'll **breakfast** in routine fashion with a cup of coffee and a roll or croissant, though the more expensive hotels usually offer sumptuous banquet-like breakfasts with cereals, fruit, hams and cheeses. Everywhere, **coffee** is almost always first-rate – aromatic and strong, but rarely bitter; in Brussels and the

---

FRITES

They may be known almost everywhere as **French fries**, but the fact is **frites** are a Belgian invention, and nowhere in the country are you far from a *frietkot* or *friture* stall. To be truly authentic, *frites* must be made with Belgian potatoes and parboiled before being deep-fried. They're also not quite the same unless eaten with a wooden fork out of a large paper cone, preferably with a large dollop of **mayonnaise** on top – or one of the many different toppings available, ranging from **curry** to **goulash** sauce.

WAFFLES

Everywhere there are stands selling **waffles** (*gaufres/wafels*), a mixture of butter, flour, eggs and sugar grilled on deep-ridged waffle irons and served up steaming hot with jam, honey, whipped cream, ice cream, chocolate or fruit. There are two main types of waffle – the **Liège version**, sweet, caramelized and with the corners squared off; and the **Brussels waffle**, larger, fluffier and needing a topping to give added flavour.

south it's often accompanied by hot milk (*café au lait*), but throughout Belgium there's a tendency to serve it in the Dutch fashion, with a small tub of evaporated rather than fresh milk.

Later in the day, the most common **snack** is *frites* (chips) – served everywhere in Belgium from *friture/ frituur* stands or parked vans, with salt or mayonnaise, or more exotic dressings (see box, p.28). More wholesome are the filled **baguettes** (*broodjes*) that many bakeries and cafés prepare on the spot – imaginative, tasty creations that make a meal in themselves. Many fish shops, especially on the coast, also do an appetizing line in seafood baguettes, while **street vendors** in the north sell various sorts of toxic-looking sausage (*worst*), especially black pudding (*bloedworst*).

Mussels – *moules/mosselen* – cooked in a variety of ways and served with chips, is a national favourite at **lunch or dinner** – indeed it's effectively Belgium's national dish. Traditionally, mussels are only served in season – i.e. when there is an "r" in the month (September to April) – and are best eaten the time-honoured way, served in a vast pot with chips and mayonnaise on the side, either *à la marinière* (steamed with white wine, shallots and parsley or celery), or *à la crème* (steamed with the same ingredients but thickened with cream and flour).

Wallonian cuisine

Wallonian cuisine is broadly similar to French, based upon a fondness for rich sauces and fresh ingredients. From the Walloons come *truite à l'Ardennaise* (trout cooked in a wine sauce); *chicorées gratinées au four* (chicory with ham and cheese); *fricassée Liègeoise* (basically, fried eggs, bacon and sausage or blood pudding); *fricadelles à la bière* (meatballs in beer); and *carbonnades de porc Bruxelloises* (pork with a tarragon and tomato sauce).

The **Ardennes**, in particular, is well known for its cured **ham** (similar to Italian Parma ham) and, of course, its **pâté**, made from pork, beef, liver and kidney – though it often takes a particular name from an additional ingredient, for example *pâté de faisan* (pheasant) or *pâté de lièvre* (hare). Unsurprisingly, game (*gibier*) features heavily on most Ardennes menus. Among the many **salads** you'll find are *salade de Liège*, made from beans and potatoes, and *salade wallonie*, a warm salad of lettuce, fried potatoes and bits of bacon.

Flemish cuisine

In **Flanders**, the food is akin to that of the Netherlands, characteristically plainer and simpler than that of Wallonia. Indeed, for decades traditional Flemish cuisine was regarded with much disdain as crude and unsubtle, but in recent years there's been a dramatic revival of its fortunes, and nowadays Flemish specialities appear on most menus in the north and there are dozens of speciality Flemish restaurants too. **Common dishes** include *waterzooi*, a soup-cum-stew consisting of chicken or fish boiled with fresh vegetables; *konijn met pruimen*, an old Flemish standby of rabbit with prunes; *paling in 't groen* (eel braised in a spinach sauce with herbs); *stoofvlees* (beef marinated in beer and cooked with herbs and onions); *stoemp* (mashed potato mixed with vegetable and/or meat purée); and *hutsepot* (literally hotchpotch, a mixed stew of mutton, beef and pork).

Luxembourg cuisine

Favourite dishes in **Luxembourg** include pike in green sauce (*hiecht mat kraïderzooss*); jugged hare (*huesenziwwi*); black pudding (*boudin*) served with apple sauce and mashed potatoes; tripe (*kuddelfleck*); nettle soup (*brennesselszopp*); buckwheat dumplings (*stäerzelen*) and smoked collar of pork with broad beans (*judd mat gaardebou'nen*), which is virtually the national dish. Along the **Moselle River** many restaurants serve *friture de la Moselle*, small fried fish. At many annual celebrations and fairs, lots of restaurants serve *fesch* – whole fish fried in batter.

Cakes, pastries and chocolate

Belgium and Luxembourg heave with **patisseries**, where you can pick up freshly baked bread, plus cakes and pastries – from mousse slices through to raspberry tarts and beyond. Belgium is, of course, famous for its **chocolates** (see box, p.8), and on average each Belgian eats a prodigious 12.5kg of the stuff annually. The big Belgian **chocolatiers** – for example Neuhaus, Godiva and Leonidas – have stores in all the main towns and cities, but many consider their products too sugary – one of the reasons why all of Belgium's cities now boast at least a couple of small, **independent chocolate makers**. These almost invariably charge more than their bigger rivals, but few would deny the difference in taste.

Drink

No trip to **Belgium** would be complete without sampling its **beer**, which is always good, almost always reasonably priced and comes in an amazing variety of brews (see box below). There's a **bar** on almost every corner and most serve at least twenty types of beer; in some the "menu" runs into the hundreds. Traditionally, Belgian bars are cosy, unpretentious places, the walls stained brown by years of tobacco smoke, but in recent years many have been decorated in anything from a sort of potty medievalism (wooden beams etc) through to Art Nouveau and a frugal post-

BELGIAN BEER: SOME TASTING NOTES

What follows is a handful of tasting notes to help you through the (very pleasurable) maze that is Belgian beer. There'll doubtless be some familiar names here, but others are bound to surprise – and quite possibly send you more than a little giddy.

Brugse Zot (Blond 6%, Brugse Zot Dubbel 7.5%) Huisbrouwerij De Halve Mann, a small brewery located in the centre of Bruges, produces zippy, refreshing ales with a dry, crisp aftertaste. Their Blond is a light and tangy pale ale, whereas the Bruin – Brugse Zot Dubbel – is a classic brown ale with a full body.

Bush Beer (7.5% and 12%) A Walloon speciality. At 12%, it's claimed that the original version is the strongest beer in Belgium, and it's actually more like a barley wine, with a lovely golden colour and an earthy aroma. The 7.5% Bush is a tasty pale ale with a hint of coriander.

Chimay (red top 7%, blue top 9%) Made by the Trappist monks of Forges-les-Chimay, in southern Belgium, Chimay beers are widely regarded as among the best in the world. Of the several brews they produce, these two are the most readily available, fruity and strong, deep in body, and somewhat spicy with a hint of nutmeg and thyme.

La Chouffe (8%) Produced in the Ardennes, this distinctive beer is instantly recognizable by the red-hooded gnome *chouffe* that adorns its label. It's a refreshing pale ale with a peachy aftertaste – very palatable indeed, but also very strong.

Gouden Carolus (8%) Named after – and allegedly the favourite tipple of – the Habsburg emperor Charles V, Gouden Carolus is a full-bodied dark brown ale with a sour and slightly fruity aftertaste. Brewed in the Flemish town of Mechelen.

Hoegaarden (5%) The role model for all Belgian wheat beers, Hoegaarden, from east of Leuven, is light and extremely refreshing, despite its cloudy appearance. The ideal drink for a hot summer's day, it's brewed from equal parts of wheat and malted barley.

De Koninck (5%) Antwerp's leading brewery, De Koninck, is something of a Flemish institution. Its standard beer is a smooth pale ale that's very drinkable, with a sharp aftertaste; better on draught than in the bottle.

Kriek (Cantillon Kriek Lambic 5%, Belle Vue Kriek 5.2%, Mort Subite Kriek 4.3%) A type of beer rather than a particular brew, Kriek is made from a base lambic beer to which are added cherries or, in the case of the more commercial brands, cherry juice and perhaps even sugar. Other fruit beers are available too – such as Framboise – but Kriek is perhaps the happiest blend, and the better versions (including the three mentioned above) are not too sweet and taste wonderful. Kriek is decanted from a bottle with a cork, like a sparkling wine.

Kwak (8%) This Flemish beer, the main product of the family-run Bosteels brewery, is not all that special – it's an amber ale sweetened by a little sugar – but it's served in dramatic style, poured into a distinctive hourglass that's placed in a wooden stand.

Orval (6.2%) One of the world's most distinctive malt beers, Orval is made in the Ardennes at the Abbaye d'Orval, founded in the twelfth century by Benedictine monks from Calabria. Refreshingly bitter, the beer is a lovely amber colour and makes a great aperitif.

Rochefort (Rochefort 6 7.5%, Rochefort 8 9.2%, Rochefort 10 11.3%) Produced at a Trappist monastery in the Ardennes, Rochefort beers are typically dark and sweet and come in three main versions: Rochefort 6, Rochefort 8 and the extremely popular Rochefort 10, which has a deep reddish-brown colour and a delicious fruity palate.

Rodenbach (Rodenbach 5% and Rodenbach Grand Cru 6.5%) Located in the Flemish town of Roeselare, the Rodenbach brewery produces a reddish-brown ale in several forms, with the best brews aged in oak containers. Their widely available Rodenbach is a tangy brown ale with a hint of sourness. The much fuller – and sourer – Rodenbach Grand Cru is more difficult to get hold of, but delicious.

Westmalle (Westmalle Dubbel 7%, Tripel 9%) The Trappist monks of Westmalle, just north of Antwerp, claim their beers not only cure loss of appetite and insomnia, but reduce stress by half. Whatever the truth, the prescription certainly tastes good. Their most famous beer, Westmalle Tripel, is deliciously creamy and aromatic, while the popular Westmalle Dubbel is dark and supremely malty.

modernist style, which is especially fashionable in the big cities. Many bars serve simple **food** too, while a significant percentage pride themselves on first-rate food served from a small but well-conceived menu.

Luxembourg also has a good supply of bars, with imported Belgian beers commonplace alongside the fairly modest lagers of the country's three dominant **breweries** – Diekirch, Mousel and Bofferding – and the white wines from the west bank of the River Moselle.

Wines and spirits

In **Belgium**, beer very much overshadows **wine**, but the latter is widely available, with French vintages being the most popular. In **Luxembourg**, the duchy's pleasant whites are worth sampling, fruitier and drier than the average French wine and more akin to the vintages of Germany. A Luxembourg speciality is **crémant**, sparkling, Champagne-like wine – very palatable and reasonably priced: try the St-Martin brand, which is excellent and dry. To guarantee quality, all the premium Luxembourg wines are marked with the appellation "Marque Nationale".

There's no one national Belgian **spirit**, but the Flemings have a penchant – like their Dutch neighbours – for **jenever**, which is similar to gin, made from grain spirit and flavoured by juniper berries. It's available in most ordinary as well as specialist bars, the latter selling as many as several hundred varieties. Broadly speaking, jenever comes in **two types**: young (*jonge*) and old (*oude*), the latter characteristically pale yellow and smoother than the former; both are served ice-cold. In Luxembourg, you'll come across locally produced bottles of **eau de vie** – distilled from various fruits and around fifty percent alcohol by volume – head-thumping stuff.

Festivals and events

Belgium and Luxembourg are big on festivals and special events – everything from religious processions through to cinema, fairs and contemporary music binges. These are spread right throughout the year, though as you might expect, most tourist-oriented events and festivals take place in the summer.

Belgium

Belgium's annual **carnivals** (*carnavals*), held in February and early March, are original, colourful and boisterous in equal measure. One of the most renowned is held in February at Binche, in Hainaut, when there's a procession involving some 1500 extravagantly dressed dancers called Gilles. There are also carnivals in Ostend and Aalst, and in Eupen, where the action lasts over the weekend before Shrove Tuesday and culminates with **Rosenmontag** on the Monday – a pageant of costumed groups and floats parading through the town centre. Most remarkable is Stavelot's carnival, where the streets are overtaken by so-called **Blancs Moussis**, townsfolk clothed in white hooded costumes and equipped with long red noses.

Nominally commemorating the arrival by boat of a miraculous statue of the Virgin Mary from Antwerp in the fourteenth century, the **Brussels Ommegang** is the best known of the festivals with a religious inspiration; a largely secular event these days, it's held on the first Tuesday and Thursday of July. If you want to see anything on the Grand-Place, however, where most of the action is, you have to reserve seats months in advance. Among the other religious events perhaps the most notable is the **Heilig-Bloedprocessie** (Procession of the Holy Blood), held in Bruges on Ascension Day, when the shrine encasing the medieval phial, which supposedly contains a few drops of the blood of Christ, is carried solemnly through the streets.

Among any number of folkloric events and fairs, one of the biggest is the **Gentse Feesten**, a big nine-day knees-up held in Ghent in late July, with all sorts of events from music and theatre through to fireworks and fairs.

Luxembourg

Carnival is a big deal in Luxembourg, too, with most communities having some kind of celebration – if nothing else, almost every patisserie sells small doughnut-like cakes, *knudd*, during the days beforehand. On Ash Wednesday, a great straw doll is set alight and then dropped off the Moselle bridge in **Remich** with much whooping-it-up, while on the first Sunday after Carnival bonfires are lit on hilltops all over the country on **Buurgbrennen**. Mid-Lent Sunday sees **Bretzelsonndeg** (Pretzel Sunday), when pretzels are sold in all the Duchy's bakeries and there are lots of processions. At **Easter**, no church bells are rung in the whole of the country between Maundy Thursday and Easter Saturday – folklore asserts that

FESTIVAL VAN VLAANDEREN (MARCH–OCT)

The extraordinarily ambitious **Festival van Vlaanderen** (Flanders Festival; ⓦfestival.be) offers over five hundred concerts of classical music in churches, castles and other historic venues in over eighty Flemish towns, cities and villages. Each of the big **Flemish-speaking cities** – Antwerp, Mechelen, Ghent and Bruges – gets a fair crack of the cultural whip, as does Brussels, with the festival celebrated for about two weeks in each city before moving on to the next.

the bells fly off to Rome for confession – and their place is taken by children, who walk the streets with rattles announcing the Masses from about 6am onwards. On Easter Monday morning, with the bells "back", the children call on every house to collect their reward – brightly coloured Easter eggs.

Every village in Luxembourg has an annual fair – **kermess** – which varies in scale and duration according to the size of the village, ranging from a stand selling fries and hot dogs to a full-scale funfair. The **Schueberfouer** in Luxembourg City – over the first three weeks of September – is one of the biggest mobile fairs in Europe, held since 1340 (it started life as a sheep market) and traditionally opened by the royal family. On the middle Sunday, in the **Hammelsmarsch**, shepherds bring their sheep to town, accompanied by a band, and then proceed to work their way round the bars.

Luxembourg's **National Day** is on June 23, and on the previous evening, at 11pm or so, there is an enormous fireworks display off the Pont Adolphe in the capital and all the bars and cafés are open through most of the night. On June 23 itself there are parades and celebrations across most of the country.

Festival and events calendar

FEBRUARY

Luxembourg: Carnival, Sunday preceding Shrove Tuesday; ⓦ visitluxembourg.com. Carnival parades take place in several Luxembourg towns, including Diekirch and Remich.

Eupen: Carnival, Shrove Tuesday and the preceding four or five days; ⓦ opt.be. Eupen Carnaval kicks off with the appearance of His Madness the Prince and climaxes with the Rosenmontag (Rose Monday) procession.

Malmédy: Carnival, Shrove Tuesday and the preceding four or five days; ⓦ opt.be. In Malmédy carnival is called Cwarme, and on the Sunday groups of Haguètes, masked figures in red robes and plumed hats, wander around nipping passers-by with wooden pincers.

Aalst: Carnival, Shrove Tuesday and the preceding two days; ⓦ opt.be. Aalst Carnaval begins on the Sunday with a parade of the giants – locals on stilts hidden by elaborate costumes – and floats, often with a contemporary/satirical theme.

Binche: Carnival, Shrove Tuesday and the preceding two days; ⓦ opt.be. Binche Carnaval builds up to the parade of the Gilles, locals dressed in fancy gear complete with ostrich-feather hats. See p.235.

Luxembourg: Buurgbrennen (Bonfire Day), first Sunday after Carnival (between late Feb and early March); ⓦ visitluxembourg .com. Bonfires plus hot-food stalls all over Luxembourg, but especially in Luxembourg City.

MARCH

Brussels: Ars Musica, all month; ⓦ arsmusica.be. This contemporary classical music festival has an impressive international reputation and regularly features world-renowned composers. Performances are held in numerous venues around the city – and there are concerts in Bruges, Antwerp, Mons and Liège too.

Brussels: Anima, the International Animation Film Festival, ten days in early March; ⓦ animatv.be. First-rate animation festival, which screens over 100 new and old cartoons from around the world at the Flagey Centre in Ixelles.

Ostend: Bal Rat Mort (Dead Rat Ball), first Saturday of March; ⓦ balratmort.com. Held in the kursaal *casino*, this is a lavish, fancy-dress carnival ball with a different theme each year. The venue holds some 2,500 revellers, but you still need to book early.

Stavelot: Carnival, Refreshment Sunday (fourth Sunday in Lent); ⓦ opt.be. Stavelot Carnaval features the famous parade of the Blancs Moussis, all hoods and long red noses. See p.272.

APRIL

Brussels: International Fantastic Film Festival, two weeks in the middle of April; ⓦ bifff.net. This well-established festival is a favourite with cult-film lovers, and has become the place to see all those entertainingly dreadful B-movies, as well as more modern sci-fi classics, thrillers and fantasy epics.

Sint-Truiden: Bloesemfeesten (Blossom festival), late April; ⓦ bloesemfeesten-haspengouw.be. Blessing of the blossoms in Sint-Truiden, at the heart of the Haspengouw fruit-growing region.

MAY

Brussels: Concours Musical International Reine Elisabeth de Belgique, early to late May; ⓦ cmireb.be. A world-famous classical music competition that was established over fifty years ago by Belgium's violin-playing Queen Elisabeth. The categories change annually, rotating piano, voice and violin, and the winners perform live in the Grand-Place in July. Tickets can be difficult to get hold of and can cost an arm and a leg, but the venues do include the splendid Palais des Beaux Arts and the Conservatoire Royal de Musique.

Mechelen: Hanswijkprocessie (Procession of our Lady of Hanswijck), Sunday before Ascension Day; ⓦ hanswijkprocessie.be. Large and ancient procession held in the centre of Mechelen. Traditionally focused on the veneration of the Virgin Mary, but more a historical pageant today.

Bruges: Heilig Bloedprocessie (Procession of the Holy Blood), Ascension Day, forty days after Easter; ⓦ holyblood.com. One of medieval Christendom's holiest relics, the phial of the Holy Blood, is carried through the centre of Bruges once every year. Nowadays, the procession is as much a tourist attraction as a religious ceremony, but it remains a prominent event for many Bruggelingen (citizens of Bruges). See p.106.

Echternach, Luxembourg: Springprozession, Whit Tuesday; ⓦ springprozession.com. Ancient and rather eccentric dancing procession commemorating the eighth-century English missionary St Willibrord.

Brussels: Jazz Marathon, three days in May; ⓦ www .brusselsjazzmarathon.be. Hip cats can listen to nonstop jazz around the city for three whole days (which change each year – check the website), and although most of the seventy-plus bands are perhaps less familiar names, the quality of the music is usually very high. Entrance fees vary depending on the venue, but you can buy a three-day pass from the tourist office and there are a number of free jazz concerts too.

JUNE

Tournai: Les journées des quatre cortèges (Days of the Four Processions), second Saturday & Sunday; ⓦ tournai.be. Lively carnival mixing modern and traditional themes, from fifteen folkloric giants representing historic figures with local connections, such as Louis XIV and the Merovingian king Childeric, to flower-decked floats, fireworks and military bands.

Luxembourg: Luxembourg National Day, June 23. Expect fireworks in the capital and celebrations – including much flag-waving – all over the Grand Duchy.

Brussels: Brussels Festival of European Film, eight days in late June; ⓦ brff.be. Something of a moveable feast, this festival promotes the work of young film directors from across Europe. It's not one of Europe's better-known film festivals, but the organizers have worked hard to establish a solid reputation and it's a great opportunity to catch up on some of the latest European (and Belgian) films. The festival takes place in the capital's Flagey arts centre, in Ixelles.

JULY

Knokke-Heist: Internationaal cartoon festival, early July to mid-Sept; ⓦ cartoonfestival.be. Established in the 1960s, this summer-season festival in the seaside resort of Knokke-Heist showcases several hundred world-class cartoons drawn from every corner of the globe.

Brussels: Ommegang, first Tuesday & Thursday of July; ⓦ ommegang.be. This grand procession, cutting a colourful course from place du Grand Sablon to the Grand-Place, began in the fourteenth century as a religious event, celebrating the arrival of a miracle-working statue of the Virgin from Antwerp; nowadays it's almost entirely secular with a whole gaggle of locals dressed up in period costume. It all finishes with a traditional dance on the Grand-Place and has proved so popular that it's now held twice a year, when originally it was just once. To secure a seat on the Grand-Place for the finale, you'll need to reserve at the Brussels tourist office (see p.82) at least six months ahead.

Werchter, near Leuven: Rock Werchter Festival, four days in early July; ⓦ rockwerchter.be. Belgium's premier rock and pop festival and one of the largest open-air music events in Europe. There are special festival buses from Leuven train station to the festival site.

Bruges: Cactusfestival, three days over the second weekend of July; ⓦ cactusmusic.be. Going strong for over twenty years, the Cactusfestival is something of a classic. Known for its amiable atmosphere, it proudly pushes against the musical mainstream with rock, reggae, rap, roots and R&B all rolling along together, from both domestic and foreign artists. It's held in Bruges' city centre, in the park beside the Minnewater.

Ghent: Gentse Feesten (Ghent Festival), mid- to late July, but always including July 21; ⓦ gentsefeesten.be. For ten days every July, Ghent gets stuck into partying, pretty much round the clock. Local bands perform free open-air gigs throughout the city and street performers turn up all over the place – fire-eaters, buskers, comedians, actors, puppeteers and so forth. There's also an outdoor market selling everything from jenever (gin) to handmade crafts.

Bruges: Moods, two weeks, usually from the last weekend of July; ⓦ moodsbrugge.be. Bruges' biggest musical knees-up (formerly called Klinkers), devoted to just about every type of music you can think of. There are big-time concerts on the Markt and the Burg, the city's two main squares, plus more intimate performances in various bars and cafés. It's Bruges at its best – and most of the events are free.

Veurne: Boetprocessie (Penitents' Procession), last Sunday in July; ⓦ boetprocessie.be. Although this event is now a good deal cheerier, with lots of townsfolk dressed up in fancy historical gear, it's still got a gloomy heart with a couple of hundred participants dressed in the brown cowls of the Capuchins, some dragging heavy crosses behind them. See box, p.135.

Boechout, Antwerp: Sfinks, last weekend in July; ⓦ sfinks.be. Sfinks is Belgium's best world-music festival, held outdoors in the suburb of Boechout, about 10km southeast of downtown Antwerp.

AUGUST

Malmédy: August 15. Once every year, the chefs and cooks of Malmédy rustle up a giant omelette using ten thousand eggs and then distribute it among the keen and hungry.

Bruges: Musica Antiqua, ten days in early Aug; ⓦ musica-antiqua.be. Part of the Festival van Vlaanderen (see box, p.32), this well-regarded festival of medieval music offers an extensive programme of live performances at a variety of historic venues in Bruges. Tickets go on sale in February and are snapped up fast.

Zeebrugge and the coast: Sand sculptures, Aug to late Sept. Sand sculpture competitions are popular along the Belgian coast throughout the summer, and Zeebrugge features some of the best, with everything from the bizarre to the surreal and beyond. It's certainly not bucket-and-spade stuff – participants are allowed to use heavy-plant diggers and bulldozers.

Kiewit, just outside Hasselt: Pukkelpop, three days in the middle of Aug; ⓦ pukkelpop.be. Large-scale progressive music festival running the gamut from indie through r'n'b to house.

Ath: La Ducasse, four days at the end of Aug; ⓦ ducasse-ath.be. Dating back to the thirteenth century, this festival has all sorts of parades and parties, but the star turn is the giant figures – or goliaths – that make their ungainly way round town, representing historical and folkloric characters.

Luxembourg City: Schueberfouer, three weeks from the last week of August; ⓦ fouer.lu. A former shepherds' market, this is now the capital's largest funfair.

SEPTEMBER

Nivelles: Le Tour Sainte-Gertrude de Nivelles, last Sunday in Sept or first Sunday in Oct; ⓦ tourisme-nivelles.be. Beginning in the centre of Nivelles, this is a religious procession in which the reliquary of St Gertrude is escorted on a circular, 15km route out into the countryside surrounding the town. The jollity gets going when locals dressed in historical gear and several goliaths join the last leg of the procession.

Tournai: La Grande Procession de Tournai, second Sun in Sept. Part secular shindig in historical costume, part religious ceremony involving the carrying of the reliquary of St Eleuthère through the city's streets, this procession dates back to the eleventh century.

OCTOBER

Ghent: Ghent Film Festival, twelve days in Oct; ⓦ filmfestival .be. The Ghent Film Festival is one of Europe's foremost cinematic events. Every year, the city's cinemas combine to present a total of around two hundred feature films and a hundred shorts from all over the world, screening Belgian films and the best of world cinema well before they hit the international circuit. There's also a special focus on music in film.

NOVEMBER

Vianden, Luxembourg: Miertchen (St Martin's Fire), mid-Nov. A celebration of the end of the harvest (and formerly the payment of the levy to the feudal lord), with bonfires and a big open-air market.

DECEMBER

Nationwide: The Arrival of St Nicholas (aka Santa Klaus), Dec 6. The arrival of St Nicholas from his long sojourn abroad is celebrated by processions and the giving of sweets to children right across Belgium and Luxembourg. In Luxembourg, he's traditionally accompanied by "Père Fouettard" (the bogey-man), dressed in black and carrying a whip to punish naughty children.

Travel essentials

Addresses

In the French–speaking part of **Belgium** and in **Luxembourg**, addresses are usually written to a standard format. The first line begins with the category of the street or thoroughfare (rue, boulevard etc), followed by the name and then the number; the second line gives the area – or zip – code, followed by the town or area. Common abbrevations include "bld" or "bd" for *boulevard*, "av" for *avenue*, "pl" for *place* (square) and "ch" for *chaussée*. An exception is the hyphenated Grand-Place (main square), written in full. In the **Flemish-speaking** areas, the first line gives the name of the street which is followed by (and joined to) its category – hence Krakeelplein is Krakeel square, Krakeelstraat is Krakeel street; the number comes next. The second line gives the area – or zip – code followed by the town or area. Consequently, Flemish abbreviations occur at the end of words: thus "Hofstr" for *Hofstraat*. An exception is Grote Markt (main square), which is not abbreviated. Common categories include *plein* for square, *plaats* for place, *laan* or *weg* for avenue, *kaai* for quay, and *straat* for street. In bilingual **Brussels**, all signs give both the French and Flemish versions. In many cases, this is fairly straightforward as they are either the same or similar, but sometimes it's extremely confusing (see box, p.79), most notoriously in the name of one of the three principal train stations – in French, Bruxelles-Midi; in Flemish Brussel-Zuid.

Concessions

Concessionary rates apply at almost every sight and attraction as well as on public transport. Rates vary, but usually children under 5 go free and kids over 5 and under 15/16 get a substantial discount. There are senior discounts too, with the age of eligibility being 65, though at some point this will no doubt rise. Family ticket deals are commonplace.

Crime and personal safety

By comparison with other parts of Europe, both Belgium and (even more so) Luxembourg are relatively free of **crime**, so there's little reason why you should ever come into contact with either country's police force. However, there is more street crime in Belgium than there used to be, especially in Brussels (the area around the Gare du Midi is especially dodgy) and Antwerp, and it's advisable to be on your guard against petty theft. Using **public transport**, even late at night, isn't usually a problem, but if in doubt take a taxi. If you are robbed, you'll need to go to a **police station** to report it, not least because your insurance

BELGIAN EMBASSIES ABROAD

For further information, consult Ⓦ diplomatie.belgium.be.

Australia Ⓦ diplomatie.belgium.be/australia
Canada Ⓦ diplomatie.be/ottawa
Ireland Ⓦ diplomatie.belgium.be/ireland
Luxembourg Ⓦ diplomatie.be/luxembourg
Netherlands Ⓦ diplomatie.belgium.be/netherlands

New Zealand No embassy – see Australia – plus consular representation in Auckland, Wellington and Christchurch.
South Africa Ⓦ diplomatie.be/pretoria
UK Ⓦ diplomatie.belgium.be/united_kingdom
US Ⓦ diplobel.us

LUXEMBOURG EMBASSIES ABROAD

For further information, consult Ⓦ www.mae.lu

Belgium Ⓦ bruxelles.mae.lu/fr
UK 27 Wilton Crescent, London SW1X 8SD ☎ 020 7235 6961, Ⓦ londres.mae.lu/en, Ⓔ embassy@luxembourg.co.uk

US 2200 Massachusetts Ave NW, Washington DC 20008 ☎ 202 265 4171, Ⓦ washington.mae.lu/en, Ⓔ info@luxembourg-usa.org

company will require a police report; remember to make a note of the report number – or, better still, ask for a copy of the statement itself. Don't expect a great deal of concern if your loss is relatively small – and don't be surprised if the process of completing forms and formalities takes ages.

Electricity

The **current** is 220 volts AC, with standard European-style two-pin plugs. British equipment needs only a plug adaptor; American apparatus requires a transformer and an adaptor.

Entry requirements

Citizens of the EU/EEA, including the UK and Ireland, plus citizens of Australia, New Zealand, Canada and the US do not need a **visa** to enter either Belgium or Luxembourg if staying for ninety days or less, but they do need a current **passport** (or **EU national identity card**), whose validity exceeds the length of their stay by at least three months. Travellers from **South Africa**, on the other hand, need a passport and a tourist visa for visits of less than ninety days; visas must be obtained before departure and are

available from the appropriate embassy (see above).

For stays of **longer than ninety days**, EU/EEA residents will have few problems, but everyone else needs a mix of **visas** and **permits**. In all cases, consult the appropriate embassy at home before departure.

Gay and lesbian travellers

Gay and **lesbian** life in both Belgium and Luxembourg does not have a high international profile, especially in comparison with the Netherlands next door. Nonetheless, there's a vibrant gay scene in **Brussels** (see p.93) and **Antwerp** (see p.197) and at least a couple of gay bars and clubs in every major town. In both countries the gay/lesbian scene is left largely unmolested by the rest of society, a pragmatic tolerance – or intolerance soaked in indifference – that has provided opportunities for **legislative change**. In 1998 Belgium passed a law granting certain rights to cohabiting couples irrespective of their sex, and civil unions for same-sex couples were legalized, after much huffing and puffing by the political right, in 2003; Luxembourg legalized same-sex civil unions in 2004. The legal **age of consent** for men and women is 16 in both Belgium and Luxembourg.

ROUGH GUIDES TRAVEL INSURANCE

Rough Guides has teamed up with WorldNomads.com to offer great travel insurance deals. Policies are available to residents of over 150 countries, with cover for a wide range of adventure sports, 24hr emergency assistance, high levels of medical and evacuation cover and a stream of travel safety information. Roughguides.com users can take advantage of their policies online 24/7, from anywhere in the world – even if you're already travelling. And since plans often change when you're on the road, you can extend your policy and even claim online. Roughguides.com users who buy travel insurance with WorldNomads.com can also leave a positive footprint and donate to a community development project. For more information, go to Ⓦ roughguides.com/shop.

Health and insurance

Under reciprocal health-care arrangements, all citizens of the **EU** and **EEA** (European Economic Area) are entitled to free, or at least subsidized, **medical treatment** within the public health-care system of both Belgium and Luxembourg. With the exception of **Australians**, whose government has a reciprocal health agreement with Belgium, **non-EU/EEA** nationals are not entitled to any free treatment and should, therefore, take out their own medical insurance. If you're seeking treatment under reciprocal health arrangements, it's worth double-checking that the medic you see is working within (and seeing you as) a patient of the public system. Technically you should have your passport and your **European Health Insurance Card (EHIC)** to hand to prove that you are eligible for EU/EEA health care, but often no one bothers to check. EU/EEA citizens may also want to consider **private health insurance**, both to cover the cost of items not within the EU/EEA scheme, such as dental treatment and repatriation on medical grounds, and to enable them to seek treatment within the private sector. Note also that the more worthwhile insurance policies promise to sort matters out before you pay (rather than after) in the case of major expense; if you do have to pay upfront, get and keep the receipts.

English-speaking medical staff are common-place in Brussels, Luxembourg City and the Flemish-speaking parts of Belgium, but elsewhere, you'll be struggling unless you have some rudimentary grasp of French. Your hotel will usually be able to arrange – or help to arrange – an appointment with a doctor, but note that he/she will almost certainly see you as a private patient.

Minor ailments can often be remedied at a **pharmacy** (French *pharmacie*, Flemish *apotheek*): pharmacists are highly trained, able to give advice (often in English), and authorized to dispense many drugs which would only be available on prescription in many other countries. Pharmacies are ubiquitous. No **inoculations** are currently required for either Belgium or Luxembourg. Note, however, that **mosquitoes** thrive in the country's canals and can be a real handful (or mouthful) if you are camping. An antihistamine cream such as Phenergan Is the best antidote, although this can be difficult to find – in which case preventative sticks (Autan; Citronella) are the best bet.

Other than for medical matters, it's a good idea to take out travel insurance to cover against **theft and loss**. Note that some all-risks home insurance policies may cover your possessions when overseas.

Internet

In both Belgium and Luxembourg, almost all hotels, B&Bs and hostels provide wi-fi and/or **internet access** for their guests either free or at minimal charge, as do many cafés. Every major library offers internet access too – free but almost invariably time-limited.

Mail

Both Belgium and Luxembourg have an efficient postal system. **Post offices** are fairly plentiful and mostly open Monday to Friday 9am to 4pm or 5pm, though some big-city branches also open on Saturday from 9am to 3pm. **Stamps** are sold at a wide range of outlets including many shops and hotels. Mail to the US takes seven days or so, within Europe two to three days. **Mail boxes** are painted red in Belgium and yellow in Luxembourg.

Maps

The **maps** provided in this Guide should be suffi-cient for most purposes, but drivers will need to buy a good road map and prospective hikers will need specialist hiking maps. One very good-value **national road map** is the clear and easy-to-use Michelin (Ⓦmichelintravel.com) *Belgium and Luxembourg* (1:350,000) map, which comes complete with an index. Michelin also publishes an excellent **Benelux road map** in book form at 1:150,000; this comes with 74 city maps, though the **free city maps** issued by the tourist offices in all the major towns are even better and have more detail.

Belgium's Institut Géographique National/ Nationaal Geografisch Instituut (IGN/NGI; Ⓦngi .be) produces the most authoritative **hiking maps** (1:10,000, 1:20,000, 1:50,000) covering the whole of the country. The equivalent organization in Luxembourg, Luxembourg Survey (Ⓦact.public .lu), does a similarly thorough job in Luxembourg with two series of Ordnance Survey maps, one at 1:50,000 (two sheets), the other at 1:20,000 (thirty sheets).

All the maps mentioned should be easy enough to track down in Belgium or Luxembourg, but to be sure (and to check what's currently on the market) you might consider ordering from a leading **bookseller** before departure – Ⓦstanfords.co.uk is hard to beat. Finally, in both countries, **GPS navigation** is easy and straightforward both for hikers and drivers.

Media

British **newspapers** and **magazines** are easy to get hold of in both Belgium and Luxembourg and neither is there much difficulty in finding American publications. As far as **British TV** is concerned, BBC1 and BBC2 television channels are on most hotel-room TVs in Belgium and on one in Luxembourg too. Access to cable and satellite channels is commonplace in hotels and bars across both countries. **Domestic TV** is largely uninspiring, though the Flemish-language TV1 and Kanaal 2 usually run English-language films with subtitles, whereas the main Wallonian channels – RTBF 1 and ARTE – mostly dub; Luxembourg's RTL channel does both. As for **radio**, frequencies and schedules for the BBC World Service (@ bbc.co.uk/worldservice), Radio Canada (@ rcinet.ca) and Voice of America (@ voanews.com) are listed on their respective websites.

Money and exchange

In both Luxembourg and Belgium, the currency is the **euro** (€). Each euro is made up of 100 cents. There are seven euro **notes** – in denominations of €500, €200, €100, €50, €20, €10 and €5 – and eight different **coins**, specifically €2 and €1, then 50, 20, 10, 5, 2 and 1 cents. Euro notes and coins feature a common EU design on one face, but different country-specific designs on the other. Note also that many retailers will not touch the €500 and €200 notes with a bargepole – you'll have to break them down into smaller denominations at the bank. At the time of writing the **rate of exchange** for €1 is £0-82; US$1.37; Can$1.52; Aus$1.49; NZ$1.59; ZAR14.67. For the most up-to-date rates, check the currency converter website @ oanda.com. You can change **foreign currency** into euros at most banks, which are ubiquitous; **banking hours** are usually Monday to Friday from 9am to 3.30/4pm, with a few banks also open on Saturday mornings.

ATMs are liberally distributed around every city, town and major village in both Belgium and Luxembourg – and they accept a host of **debit cards** without charging a transaction fee. **Credit cards** can be used in ATMs too, but in this case transactions are treated as loans, with interest accruing daily from the date of withdrawal.

Opening hours

Business hours (ie office hours) normally run from Monday to Friday 9.30/10am to 4.30/5pm. Normal **shopping hours** are Monday through Saturday 10am to 5.30/6pm, though many smaller shops open late on Monday morning and/or close a tad earlier on Saturdays. In addition, in some of the smaller towns and villages many places close at lunch time (noon–2pm) and for the half-day on Wednesdays or Thursdays. At the other extreme, larger establishments – primarily supermarkets and department stores – are increasingly likely to have extended hours, often on Fridays when many remain open till 9pm. In the big cities, a smattering of **convenience stores** (magasins de nuit/avondwinkels) stay open either all night or until 1am or 2am daily; other than these, only die-hard money-makers – including some **souvenir shops** – are open late or on Sunday.

In Belgium, there are ten national **public holidays** (see box, p.38) per year and two regional holidays, one each for Wallonia and Flanders. Luxembourg has pretty much the same public holidays with a couple of exceptions. For the most part, these holidays are keenly observed, with most businesses and many attractions closed and public transport reduced to a Sunday service.

Phones

All but the remotest parts of Belgium and Luxembourg are on the **mobile phone** (**cell phone**)

INTERNATIONAL CALLS

PHONING HOME FROM BELGIUM AND LUXEMBOURG

To make an international phone call from Belgium or Luxembourg, dial the appropriate international access code as below, then the number you require, omitting the initial zero where there is one.
Australia ☎ 0061
Canada ☎ 001
Republic of Ireland ☎ 00353
New Zealand ☎ 0064
South Africa ☎ 0027
UK ☎ 0044
US ☎ 001

PHONING BELGIUM AND LUXEMBOURG FROM ABROAD

To call a number in Belgium or Luxembourg, dial the local international access code, then ☎ 32 for Belgium or ☎ 352 for Luxembourg, followed by the number you require, omitting the initial zero where there is one.

network at GSM900/1800, the band common to the rest of Europe, Australia and New Zealand. Mobile/cell phones bought in North America will need to be able to adjust to this GSM band. If you intend to use your own mobile/cell phone in Belgium and Luxembourg, note that **call** and data roaming charges can be excruciating – particularly irritating is the supplementary charge that you often have to pay on incoming calls – so check your with your provider before you depart. You may find it cheaper to buy a **local SIM card**, though this can get complicated: many mobiles/cells will not permit you to swap SIM cards and the connection instructions for the replacement SIM card may not be in English. If you overcome these problems, you can buy local SIM cards at high-street phone companies, which offer myriad deals beginning at about €5 per SIM card. **Text messages**, on the other hand, are normally charged at ordinary or at least bearable rates – and with your existing SIM card in place. And, of course, you can use the free text and photo service available on **Whatsapp** on local wifi.

There are **no area codes** in either Belgium or Luxembourg, but Belgian numbers mostly begin with a zero, a relic of former area codes, which have now been incorporated into the numbers themselves. Telephone numbers beginning ☎0900 or 070 are premium-rated, ☎0800 are toll-free. Within both countries, there's no distinction between local and long-distance calls – in other words, calling Ostend from Brussels costs the same as calling a number in Brussels.

Useful telephone numbers

Belgium Domestic directory enquiries Flemish ☎ 1207; French ☎ 1307.
Belgium International directory enquiries Flemish ☎ 1204; French ☎ 1304.
Luxembourg Domestic, international directory enquiries and International operator assistance ☎ 12410.

Shopping

When it comes to **shopping**, chocolates (see p.8) and beer (see p.30) are the apple of the tourists' eye, but it's worth seeking out the local open-air **markets**: most towns and large villages have a market day once a week and it's here you can sample all manner of **local delicacies**. In the cities, there are fresh produce markets too, but there are also sprawling flea markets, flower markets, antique markets and bird markets (though these are not to everyone's taste).

Sports and outdoor activities

Most visitors to Belgium confine their exercise to **cycling** and **walking**, both of which are ideally suited to the flatness of the terrain and, for that matter, the excellence of the public transport system. The same applies to Luxembourg, except that the land is much hillier and often more scenic. Both also offer all the sporting facilities you would expect of prosperous, European countries, from golf to gyms, swimming pools to horseriding. More distinctive offerings include **korfbal** (🌐korfbal.be), a home-grown sport popular in the Netherlands and Flemish-speaking Belgium, cobbled together from netball, basketball and volleyball, and played with mixed teams and a high basket; **canal ice skating**, again in the Flemish-speaking areas, though this is of course dependent on the weather being cold enough; and, in the Ardennes, **canoeing**, **kayaking** and **mountaineering**.

The chief spectator sport is **football** and the 34 teams that make up the two leading divisions of the country's national league attract a fiercely loyal following. Big-deal clubs include RSC Anderlecht of Brussels (🌐rsca.be), Club Brugge (🌐clubbrugge .be), and Standard Liège (🌐standard.be). The football season runs from early August to May with a break over the Christmas period.

PUBLIC HOLIDAYS IN BELGIUM AND LUXEMBOURG

Note that if any of the below falls on a Sunday, the next day becomes a holiday

New Year's Day
Easter Monday
Labour Day (May 1)
Ascension Day (forty days after Easter)
Whit Monday
Luxembourg National Day (June 23)
Flemish Day (Flemish-speaking Belgium only; July 11)
Belgium National Day (July 21)

Assumption (mid-August)
Walloon Day (French-speaking Belgium only; September 27)
All Saints' Day (November 1)
Armistice Day (Belgium only; November 11)
Christmas Day
St Stephen's Day/Boxing Day (only an official holiday in Luxembourg; December 26)

Time zones

Both Belgium and Luxembourg are on **Central European Time** (CET): one hour ahead of Greenwich Mean Time; six hours ahead of US Eastern Standard Time; nine hours ahead of US Pacific Standard Time; nine hours behind Australian Eastern Standard Time; and eleven hours behind New Zealand. There are, however, minor variations during the changeover periods involved in **daylight saving**. Both Belgium and Luxembourg operate daylight saving time, moving their clocks forward one hour in the spring and one hour back in the autumn.

Tipping

There's no need to **tip** when there's a service charge – as there often is – but when there isn't, restaurant waiters will anticipate a ten to fifteen percent tip. In taxis, tipping is neither necessary nor expected, but often people will simply round up the fare.

Toilets

Public toilets remain comparatively rare in both Belgium and Luxembourg, but a few big-city cafés and bars operate what amounts to an ablutionary sideline, charging a €0.40–1 fee for the use of their toilets whether you're a customer or not; you'll spot the plate for the money as you enter.

Tourist information

Belgium has two official tourist boards, one covering the French-speaking areas, the other the Flemish-speaking regions; they share responsibility for Brussels. These boards are respectively the **Office de Promotion du Tourisme de Wallonie et Bruxelles** (OPT; ⓦ belgiumtheplaceto.be and ⓦ opt.be), and **Toerisme Vlaanderen** (Visit Flanders; ⓦ visitflanders.com). Their websites cover everything from hotels and campsites to forthcoming events. Both also publish a wide range of glossy, free booklets of both a general and specific nature, available at tourist offices throughout Belgium. A similarly excellent set of services is provided by the **Office National du Tourisme Luxembourg** (Luxembourg National Tourist Office; ⓦ visitluxembourg.com).

In both Belgium and Luxembourg, there are **tourist offices** in every large village, town and

> ## BRUSSELS BLOGS
> For an alternative take on the Belgian capital, take a peek at one of these regularly updated blogs.
> **My Secret Brussels**
> ⓦ mysecretbrussels.com
> **Tastes of Brussels** ⓦ tastesofbrussels .wordpress.com
> **Why I Am Not Skinny**
> ⓦ whyiamnotskinny.wordpress.com/ about

city, and most are located on or near the main square.

Travelling with children

In general terms at least, Belgian/Luxembourg society is sympathetic to its **children** and the tourist industry follows suit. Extra beds in hotel rooms are usually easy to arrange; many restaurants (but not the smartest) have children's menus; concessions for children are the rule (see p.34), from public transport to museums; and baby-changing stations are commonplace.

Pharmacists carry all the kiddy stuff you would expect – nappies, baby food and so forth. Certain hotels, particularly the better ones on the coast, offer a **babysitting** service, and a few resorts operate a municipal service of registered babysitters.

Travellers with disabilities

In all the major cities, the most obvious difficulty facing people with **mobility problems** is in negotiating the cobbled streets and narrow, often broken pavements of the older districts, where the key sights are mostly located. Similarly, provision for people with disabilities on the **public transport** system is only average, although improving – many new buses, for instance, are now wheelchair accessible. And yet, while it can be difficult simply to get around, practically all **public buildings**, including museums, theatres, cinemas, concert halls and hotels, are obliged to provide access, and do. Hotels, hostels and campsites that have been certified wheelchair-accessible carry the **International Accessibility Symbol** (ISA). Bear in mind, however, that a lot of the older, narrower **hotels** are not allowed to install lifts for reasons of conservation, so check first.

Brussels

THE GRAND-PLACE, BRUSSELS

1

Brussels

Wherever else you go in Belgium, allow time for Brussels, which is anything but the dull centre of EU bureaucracy some would have you believe: in postwar years, the city has become a thriving, cosmopolitan metropolis, with top-flight museums and architecture, a superb restaurant scene and an energetic nightlife. Moreover, most of the key attractions are crowded into a well-preserved late seventeenth-century centre that is small enough to be absorbed over a few days, its boundaries largely defined by a ring of boulevards – the "petit ring" or, less colloquially, the "petite ceinture".

First-time visitors to Brussels are often surprised by the raw vitality of the **city centre**. It isn't neat and tidy, and many of the old tenement houses are shabby, but there's a buzz about the place that's hard to resist. The larger, westerly portion of the centre comprises the **Lower Town**, fanning out from the marvellous **Grand-Place**, with its exquisite guildhouses and town hall, while up above, on a ridge to the east, lies the much smaller **Upper Town**, home to the finest art collection in the country at the **Musées Royaux des Beaux Arts**.

Since the eleventh century, the ruling elite has lived in the Upper Town – a state of affairs that still in part remains, though in recent times this class division has been complicated by discord between Belgium's two main linguistic groups, the **Walloons** (the French-speakers) and the **Flemings** (the Dutch- or Flemish-speakers). To add to the communal stew, these two groups now share their city with many others, including EU civil servants and **immigrants** from North and Central Africa, Turkey and the Mediterranean. Brussels' compact nature heightens the contrasts: in five minutes you can walk from a chichi shopping mall into an African bazaar, or from a depressed slum quarter to a resplendent square of antique shops and exclusive cafés. This is something that increases the city's allure, not least by way of the sheer variety of affordable **cafés** and **restaurants** – Brussels is a wonderful place to eat, its gastronomic reputation perhaps exceeding that of Paris these days. It's also a great place to drink, with **bars** ranging from designer chic to rough-and-ready, plus everything in between.

The city's **specialist shops** are another pleasure. Everyone knows about Belgian chocolates, but here in the capital there are also huge open-air markets, contemporary art galleries and shops devoted to anything from comic books to costume jewellery and club-land fashion. Furthermore, Belgium is such a small country, and the rail network so fast and efficient, that Brussels also makes the perfect base for a wide range of **day-trips** – to Ghent, Bruges, and the French-speaking cities to the south, Tournai and Mons.

Brief history

Brussels takes its name from Broekzele, or "village of the marsh", a community which grew up beside the wide and shallow River Senne in the sixth century, allegedly around

BRÜSEL COMIC SHOP

Highlights

❶ The Grand-Place Extraordinarily beautiful, this is one of Europe's most perfectly preserved Gothic-Baroque squares. **See p.46**

❷ Éditions Jacques Brel Devotees of *chanson* should make a beeline for the Éditions to hear Brel in full, very anguished, voice. **See p.56**

❸ The Musée d'Art Ancien Holds an exquisite sample of early Flemish paintings. **See p.60**

❹ Musée Victor Horta A fascinating museum set in the old house and studio of Victor Horta, the leading exponent of Art Nouveau. **See p.73**

❺ Bars Brussels has some wonderful bars; two of the oldest and most atmospheric are *À l'Imaige de Nostre-Dame* and *Au Bon Vieux Temps*. **See p.87**

❻ Comic strips The Belgians love their comics and the Brüsel comic shop has the best range in the city. **See p.93**

❼ Flea markets The pick of the bunch is held daily on place du Jeu de Balle. **See p.94**

HIGHLIGHTS ARE MARKED ON THE MAPS ON P.47, PP.52–53 AND PP.74–75

1

BILINGUAL BRUSSELS

As a cumbersome compromise between Belgium's French- and Flemish-speaking communities, Brussels is the country's only officially **bilingual region**. This means that every instance of the written word, from road signs and street names to the *Yellow Pages*, has by law to appear in both languages. Visitors soon adjust, but for simplicity we've used the **French version** of street names, sights, etc throughout this chapter.

---

a chapel built here by St Géry, a French bishop turned missionary. An insignificant part of Charlemagne's empire at the end of the eighth century, it was subsequently inherited by the dukes of **Lower Lorraine** (roughly Wallonia and northeast France), who constructed a fortress here in 979. Protected, the village benefited from its position on the trade route between Cologne and the burgeoning towns of Bruges and Ghent to become a significant trading centre in its own right. The surrounding marshes were drained to allow for further expansion, and in 1229 the city was granted its first charter by the **dukes of Brabant**, the feudal overlords who controlled things here, on and off, for around two hundred years. In the early fifteenth century, marriage merged the interests of the Duchy of Brabant with that of Burgundy, whose territories passed to the **Habsburgs** in 1482.

The first Habsburg rulers had close ties with Brussels, and the **Emperor Charles V** ran his vast kingdom from the city for over a decade, making it wealthy and politically important in equal measure. By contrast, his successor **Philip II** lived in Spain and ruled through a governor resident in Brussels. Horrified by the Protestant leanings of many of his Low Country subjects, the king imposed a series of anti-Protestant edicts, and when these provoked extensive **rioting**, he dispatched an army of ten thousand men – led by a hardline reactionary, the Duke of Albe – to crush his opponents in Brussels absolutely. Albe quickly restored order, and then, with the help of the Inquisition, set about the rioters with gusto, his Commission of Civil Unrest soon nicknamed the "**Council of Blood**" after its habit of executing those it examined. Brussels, along with much of the Low Countries, exploded in revolt, and in 1577, the one-time protégé of the Habsburgs, **William the Silent**, made a triumphant entry into the city and installed a Calvinist government. Protestant control lasted for just eight years, before Philip's armies recaptured Brussels. Seeing which way the religious wind was blowing, hundreds of Protestants left the city and the economy slumped, though complete catastrophe was averted by the conspicuous consumption of the (Brussels-based) Habsburg elite, whose high spending kept hundreds of workers in employment. Brussels also benefited from the digging of the **Willebroek Canal**, which linked it to the sea for the first time in its history in 1561.

By the 1580s, the Habsburgs had lost control of the northern part of the Low Countries (now the Netherlands) and Brussels was confirmed as the capital of the remainder, the **Spanish Netherlands** – broadly modern Belgium. Brussels prospered more than the rest of the country, but it was always prey to the dynastic squabbling between France and Spain: in 1695, for example, **Louis XIV** bombarded Brussels for 36 hours merely to teach his rivals a lesson, though the **guilds**, those associations of skilled merchants and workers who were crucial to the economy of Brussels, rebuilt their devastated city in double time, and it's this version of the Grand-Place that survives today.

In 1700 Charles II, the last of the Spanish Habsburgs, died without issue. The ensuing **War of the Spanish Succession** dragged on for over a decade, but eventually the Spanish Netherlands was passed to the Austrian Habsburgs, who ruled – as had their predecessors – through a governor based in Brussels. It was during this period as capital of the **Austrian Netherlands** (1713–94) that most of the monumental buildings of the Upper Town were constructed and its Neoclassical avenues and boulevards laid out

1

– grand extravagance in the context of an increasingly industrialized city crammed with a desperately poor working class.

The **French Revolutionary army** brushed the Austrians aside in 1794, and the Austrian Netherlands became part of France until the defeat of Napoleon, when it was absorbed into the new **Kingdom of the Netherlands**. Brussels took turns with The Hague as the capital, but the experiment was short-lived, and in 1830 a Brussels-led rebellion removed the Dutch and led to the creation of an **independent Belgium** with Brussels as capital.

BRUSSELS AND AROUND

1

The **nineteenth century** was a period of modernization and expansion, during which the city achieved all the attributes of a modern European capital under the guidance of Burgomaster Anspach and **King Léopold II**. New boulevards were built; the Senne – which by then had become an open sewer – was covered over in the city centre; many slum areas were cleared; and a series of grand buildings was erected. The whole enterprise culminated in the golden jubilee exhibition celebrating the founding of the Belgium state in the newly inaugurated Parc du Cinquantenaire. Following the **German occupation** of Belgium in World War II, the modernization of Brussels has proceeded inexorably, with many major development projects refashioning the city and reflecting its elevated status as the headquarters of both NATO and the EU.

The Grand-Place

The obvious place to begin any tour of Brussels is the **Grand-Place**, one of Europe's most beautiful squares, which sits at the centre of the Lower Town. Originally marshland, the Grand-Place was drained in the twelfth century, and became a market, cementing its role as the commercial hub of the emergent city when the city's guilds built their headquarters on the square. In the fifteenth century it also assumed a civic and political function, with the construction of the **Hôtel de Ville**. The ruling dukes visited the square to meet the people or show off in tournaments, and it was here that official decrees and pronouncements were proclaimed. During the religious wars of the sixteenth century, the Grand-Place became as much a place of public execution as of trade, but thereafter it resumed its former role as a marketplace. Of the square's medieval buildings, however, only parts of the Hôtel de Ville and one or two **guildhouses** have survived, the consequence of an early example of the precepts of total war, a 36-hour **French artillery bombardment** which pretty much razed Brussels to the ground in 1695. After the French withdrew, the city's guildsmen dusted themselves down and speedily had their headquarters rebuilt, adopting the distinctive and flamboyant **Baroque style** that characterizes the square today – a set of slender, gilded facades swirling with exuberant, self-publicizing carvings and sculptures. Each guildhouse has a name, usually derived from one of the statues, symbols or architectural quirks decorating its facade. Inevitably, such an outstanding attraction draws tourists and expats in their droves, but there's no better place to get a taste of Brussels' past and Eurocapital present.

Hôtel de Ville

Guided tours only: in French Wed 2pm, Sun noon & 3pm; in Dutch Wed 1pm, Sun 11am & 4pm; in English Wed 3pm, Sun 10am, 11am & 4pm • €5

On the south side of the Grand-Place, the scrubbed and polished **Hôtel de Ville** (town hall) dominates the square, its 96m **spire** soaring high above two long series of robust windows, whose straight lines are mitigated by fancy tracery and an arcaded gallery. The building dates from the beginning of the fifteenth century, when the town council decided to build itself a mansion that adequately reflected its wealth and power. The

---

THE BRUSSELS CARD

The good-value **Brussels Card** (⊕ brusselscard.be) provides free access to most of the city's key museums, unlimited travel on the STIB public transport network, and discounts of up to 25 percent at specified restaurants and bars. There are **three versions** – 24hr (€24), 48hr (€36), and 72hr (€43) – and each is valid from the first time it is used, rather than the day of issue. The card is on sale **online** via the website and at both main **tourist offices** (see p.82); there are no concessionary rates for seniors or children. It's issued with a free city map and a booklet detailing all the benefits.

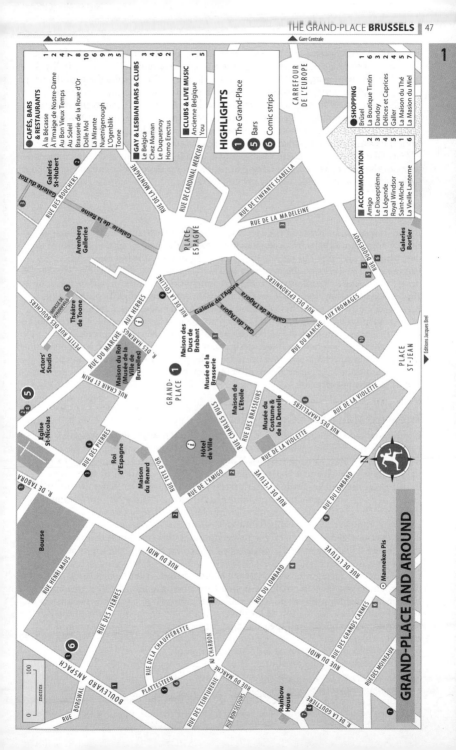

GRAND-PLACE AND AROUND

CAFÉS, BARS & RESTAURANTS
- A la Bécasse 1
- A l'Imaige de Nostre-Dame 2
- Au Bon Vieux Temps 4
- Au Soleil 7
- Brasserie de la Roue d'Or 8
- Dolle Mol 10
- La Mirante 6
- Nuetnigenough 9
- L'Ogenblik 3
- Toone 5

GAY & LESBIAN BARS & CLUBS
- Le Belgica 3
- Chez Maman 4
- Le Duquesnoy 6
- Homo Erectus 2

CLUBS & LIVE MUSIC
- Ancienne Belgique 1
- You 5

HIGHLIGHTS
- ① The Grand-Place
- ⑤ Bars
- ⑥ Comic strips

SHOPPING
- Brüsel 1
- La Boutique Tintin 6
- Dandoy 3
- Délices et Caprices 2
- Galler 4
- La Maison du Thé 5
- La Maison du Miel 7

ACCOMMODATION
- Amigo 2
- Le Dixseptième 3
- La Légende 4
- Royal Windsor 5
- Saint-Michel 1
- La Vieille Lanterne 6

Cathedral

Gare Centrale

CARREFOUR DE L'EUROPE

RUE DE CARDINAL MERCIER

RUE DE L'INFANTE ISABELLA

RUE DE LA MADELEINE

RUE DE LA MONTAGNE

Galeries St-Hubert

Galerie du Roi

RUE DES BOUCHERS

Galerie de la Reine

Arenberg Galleries

PLACE ESPAGNE

RUE DES EPERONNIERS

RUE DUQUESNOY

Galeries Bortier

Galerie de l'Agora

Gal. de l'Agora

RUE DE LA COLLINE

AUX HERBES

PETITE RUE DES BOUCHERS

IMPASSE DE SCHUDDEVELD

Théâtre de Toone

Actors' Studio

R. DES HARENGS

RUE DU MARCHE AUX HERBES

Maison des Ducs de Brabant

Maison du Roi (Musée de la Ville de Bruxelles)

RUE CHAIR ET PAIN

GRAND-PLACE

Musée de la Brasserie

RUE DU MARCHE AUX FROMAGES

PLACE ST-JEAN

Maison de L'Étoile

RUE DES CHAPELIERS

Musée du Costume & de la Dentelle

RUE DE LA VIOLETTE

RUE DE LA VIOLETTE

RUE DES BRASSEURS

Eglise St-Nicolas

RUE DES PIERRES

Roi d'Espagne

RUE TÊTE D'OR

Maison du Renard

Hôtel de Ville

RUE CHARLES BULS

RUE DE L'AMIGO

R. DE TABORA

Bourse

RUE HENRI MAUS

RUE DU MIDI

RUE DE L'ETUVE

RUE DU LOMBARD

Manneken Pis

RUE DES PIERRES

RUE DE LA CHAUFFERETTE

AU CHARBON

BOULEVARD ANSPACH

RUE BORGVAL

PLATTESTEEN

RUE DES TEINTURERIE

RUE DU MARCHE

RUE DE BON SECOURS

Rainbow House

R. DE LA GOUTTIÈRE

RUE DU LOMBARD

RUE DU MIDI

RUE DES GRANDS CARMES

RUE DES MOINEAUX

N

0   100
metres

Editions Jacques Brel

1

first part to be completed was the **east wing** – the original entrance is marked by the twin lions of the Lion Staircase, though the animals were only added in 1770. Work started on the **west wing** in 1444 and continued until 1480. Despite the gap, the wings are of very similar style, and you have to look hard to notice that the later one is slightly shorter than its neighbour, allegedly at the insistence of Charles the Bold who, for some unknown reason, refused to have the adjacent rue de la Tête d'Or narrowed. The niches were left empty and the **statues** seen today, which represent leading figures from the city's past, were added as part of a nineteenth-century refurbishment.

Visits take in a string of lavish official rooms used for receptions and council meetings (but not the tower), with **tours** starting at the reception desk off the interior quadrangle – be prepared for the guides' overly reverential script.

The tower
No public access

By any standard, the **tower** of the Hôtel de Ville is quite extraordinary, its remarkably slender appearance the work of **Jan van Ruysbroeck**, the leading spire specialist of the day, who also played a leading role in the building of the cathedral (see p.58). Ruysbroeck had the lower section built square to support the weight above, choosing a design that blended seamlessly with the elaborately carved facade on either side – or almost: look carefully and you'll see that the **main entrance** is slightly out of kilter. Ruysbroeck used the old belfry porch as the base for the new tower, hence the misalignment, a deliberate decision rather than the miscalculation which (according to popular legend) prompted the architect's suicide. Above the **cornice** protrudes an octagonal extension where the basic design of narrow windows flanked by pencil-thin columns and pinnacles is repeated up as far as the pyramid-shaped **spire**, a delicate affair surmounted by a gilded figure of **St Michael**, protector of Christians in general and of soldiers in particular.

The west side of the Grand-Place

On the west side of the Grand-Place, at the end of the row, the **Roi d'Espagne** is a particularly fine building which was once the headquarters of the guild of bakers; it's named after the bust of King Charles II of Spain (see box, p.49) on the upper storey, flanked by a Moorish and a Native American prisoner, symbolic trophies of war. Balanced on the balustrade are allegorical statues of Energy, Fire, Water, Wind, Wheat and Prudence, presumably meant to represent the elements necessary for baking the ideal loaf. The guildhouse now holds the most famous of the square's bars, *Le Roy d'Espagne*, though more appealing is the café next door, *La Brouette*, in **La Maison de la Brouette** at **nos. 2–3**, once the tallow makers' guildhouse – though it takes its name from the wheelbarrows etched into the cartouches. The figure at the top is St Gilles, the guild's patron saint.

Next door, the three lower storeys of the **Maison du Sac**, at **no. 4**, were constructed for the carpenters and coopers, with the upper storeys being appropriately designed by a cabinet-maker, and featuring pilasters and caryatids which resemble the ornate legs of Baroque furniture. The **Maison de la Louve**, at **no. 5**, was originally home to the influential archers' guild, and the pilastered facade is studded with sanctimonious representations of concepts like Peace and Discord, and the medallions just beneath the pediment carry the likenesses of four Roman emperors set above allegorical motifs indicating their particular attributes. Thus, Trajan is shown above the Sun, a symbol of Truth; Tiberius with a net and cage for Falsehood; Augustus with the globe of Peace; and Julius Caesar with a bleeding heart for Disunity. Above the door, there's a charming if dusty bas-relief of the Roman she-wolf suckling Romulus and Remus, while the pediment holds a relief of Apollo firing at a python; right on top, the Phoenix rises from the ashes.

1

> ## THE HEALTH OF CHARLES II
> Philip IV of Spain (1605–65) had no fewer than fourteen children, but only one of his sons
> – **Charles II** (1661–1700) – reached his twenties. With women banned from the succession,
> the sickly Charles became king aged just four and, much to everyone's surprise, survived to
> adulthood. After his first marriage in 1679, there were great hopes that he would sire an **heir**,
> but none arrived. A second marriage, twenty years later, was equally fruitless, and, as it became
> increasingly clear that Charles was unable to procreate, Europe focused on what was to
> happen when Charles died and the Spanish royal line died out. Every ambassador to the
> Spanish court wrote long missives home about the health of Charles, none more so than the
> English representative, **Stanhope**, who painted an especially gloomy picture: "He (Charles) has
> a ravenous stomach and swallows all he eats whole, for his nether jaw stands out so much that
> his two rows of teeth cannot meet." In the autumn of 1700, it was clear that Charles was dying
> and his doctors went to work in earnest, replacing his pillows with freshly killed pigeons and
> covering his chest with animal entrails. Not surprisingly, this didn't work and Charles died on
> November 1, an event which triggered the **War of the Spanish Succession** (see p.44).

At **no. 6**, the **Maison du Cornet** was the headquarters of the boatmen's guild and is a
fanciful creation of 1697, sporting a top storey resembling the stern of a ship. Charles
II makes another appearance here too – it's his head in the medallion, flanked by
representations of the four winds and of a pair of sailors. Finally the house of the
haberdashers' guild, **Maison du Renard** at **no. 7**, displays animated cherubs in bas-relief
playing at haberdashery on the ground floor, while a scrawny gilded fox – after which
the house is named – squats above the door. Up on the second storey a statue of Justice,
flanked by figures symbolizing the four continents, suggests the guild's designs on
world markets – an aim to which St Nicholas, patron saint of merchants, glinting
above, clearly gives his blessing.

The south side of the Grand-Place
Beside the Hôtel de Ville, the arcaded **Maison de l'Étoile**, at **no. 8**, is a nineteenth-
century rebuilding of the medieval home of the city magistrate. In the arcaded
gallery, the exploits of city magistrate **Everard 't Serclaes** are commemorated: in
1356 the Francophile Count of Flanders attempted to seize power from the Duke of
Brabant, occupying the magistrate's house and flying his standard from the roof.
't Serclaes scaled the building, replaced the count's standard with that of the Duke
of Brabant, and went on to lead the recapturing of the city, events represented in
bas-relief above a reclining **statue** of 't Serclaes. His effigy is polished smooth from
the long-standing superstition that good luck will come to those who stroke it
– surprising really, as 't Serclaes was hunted down and hacked to death by the
count's men in 1388.

Next door, the **Maison du Cygne**, at **no. 9**, takes its name from the ostentatious swan
on the facade, but is more noteworthy as the place – it was once a bar – where **Karl
Marx** regularly met up with Engels during his exile in Belgium. It was in Brussels in
February 1848 that they wrote the *Communist Manifesto*, before they were deported as
political undesirables the following month. Appropriately enough, the Belgian
Workers' Party was founded here in 1885, though nowadays the building shelters one
of the city's more exclusive restaurants.

The adjacent **Maison des Brasseurs**, at **no. 10**, is the only house on the Grand-Place
still to be owned by a guild – the brewers' – not that the equestrian figure stuck on top
gives any clues: the original effigy (of one of the city's Habsburg governors) dropped
off, and the present statue, picturing the eighteenth-century aristocrat Charles of
Lorraine, was moved here simply to fill the gap. Inside is a small and mundane brewery
museum, the **Musée de la Brasserie** (daily 10am–5pm; €6).

1

The east side of the Grand-Place

The seven guildhouses (**nos. 13–19**) that fill out the east side of the Grand-Place have been subsumed within one grand facade, whose slender symmetries are set off by a curved pediment and narrow pilasters, sporting nineteen busts of the dukes of Brabant. More than any other building on the Grand-Place, this **Maison des Ducs de Brabant** has the flavour of the aristocracy – as distinct from the bourgeoisie – and, needless to say, it was much admired by the city's Habsburg governors.

The north side of the Grand-Place

Other than the **Maison du Roi** (see below), the guildhouses and private mansions (**nos. 20–39**) running along the north side of the Grand-Place are not as distinguished as their neighbours, though the **Maison du Pigeon** (**nos. 26–27**), the painters' guildhouse, is of interest as the house where **Victor Hugo** spent some time during his exile from France – he was expelled for his support of the French insurrection of 1848. The house also bears four unusual masks in the manner of the "green man" of Romano-Celtic folklore. The adjacent **Maison des Tailleurs** (**nos. 24–25**) is appealing too, the old headquarters of the tailors' guild, adorned by a pious bust of St Barbara, their patron saint.

Maison du Roi: Musée de la Ville de Bruxelles

Grand-Place • Tues–Sun 10am–5pm • €4 • ⓦ www.museedelavilledebruxelles.be

Much of the north side of the Grand-Place is taken up by the late nineteenth-century **Maison du Roi**, a fairly faithful reconstruction of the palatial Gothic structure commissioned by Charles V in 1515. The emperor had a point to make: the Hôtel de Ville was an assertion of municipal independence, and Charles wanted to emphasize imperial power by constructing his own building directly opposite. Despite its name, no sovereign ever lived here permanently, though this is where the Habsburgs held their more important **prisoners** – the counts of Egmont and Hoorn (see p.66) spent their last night here before being beheaded just outside. The building now holds the **Musée de la Ville de Bruxelles**, comprising a wide-ranging collection whose best sections feature medieval fine and applied art.

The ground floor

Inside, the **first room** to the right of the entrance boasts several superb **retables**, altarpieces that were a speciality of the city from the end of the fourteenth century until the economic slump of the 1640s – most of them comprised of a series of mini-tableaux illustrating biblical scenes, with the characters wearing medieval gear in a medieval landscape. It's the extraordinary detail that impresses: look closely at the niche carvings on the whopping **Saluzzo** altarpiece (aka *The Life of the Virgin and the Infant Christ*) of 1505 and you'll spy the candlesticks, embroidered pillowcase and carefully draped coverlet of Mary's bedroom in the *Annunciation* scene. Up above and to the right, in a swirling, phantasmagorical landscape of what look like climbing toadstools, is the *Shepherds Hear the Good News*. Also in this room is **Pieter Bruegel the Elder**'s *Wedding Procession*, a good-natured scene with country folk walking to church to the accompaniment of bagpipes. The **second room** to the right is devoted to another municipal speciality: large and richly coloured **tapestries**, dating from the sixteenth and seventeenth centuries and depicting folkloric events and tales of derring-do.

The upper floors

Upstairs, the first floor has scale models of the city and various sections on aspects of its history, and the second continues in the same vein. Also on the second floor is a goodly sample of the **Manneken Pis'** (see p.55) vast wardrobe: around one hundred saccharine costumes ranging from Mickey Mouse to a maharajah, all of them gifts from various visiting dignitaries.

The Lower Town

Cramped and populous, the **Lower Town** fans out from the Grand-Place in all directions, bisected by one major **north-south boulevard**, variously named Adolphe Max, Anspach and Lemonnier. Setting aside the boulevard – which was ploughed through in the nineteenth century – the **layout** of the Lower Town remains essentially medieval, a skein of narrow, cobbled lanes and alleys in which almost every street is crimped by tall and angular town houses. There's nothing neat and tidy about any of this, and it's this that gives Brussels its appeal – dilapidated terraces stand next to prestigious mansions and the whole district is dotted with **superb buildings**, everything from beautiful Baroque churches through to Art Nouveau department stores.

These days arguably the most attractive part of the area is **northwest** of the Grand-Place, where the church of **Ste-Catherine** stands on its own café-table-covered square, and not far away **place St-Géry** is a secondary hub of activity. The streets immediately **north** of the Grand-Place are of less immediate appeal, with dreary **rue Neuve** – a pedestrianized main drag that's home to the city's mainstream shops and stores – leading up to the clumping skyscrapers that surround the **place Rogier** and the **Gare du Nord** – although relief is at hand in the precise Habsburg symmetries of the **place des Martyrs** and the Art Nouveau **Centre Belge de la Bande Dessinée**. You'll also want to take a stroll in the elegant **Galeries St-Hubert**, though nearby **rue des Bouchers** is not the restaurant haven it cracks itself up to be. To the **south** of the Grand-Place, almost everyone makes a beeline for the city's mascot, the **Manneken Pis**, but more enjoyable is the museum dedicated to Belgium's most celebrated chansonnier, **Jacques Brel**, and the lively, increasingly gentrified but still resolutely working-class **Marolles** district.

St-Nicolas

rue au Beurre 1 • Daily: July–Aug 10am–6pm; Sept–June 9am–6pm

Walking **northwest** out of the Grand-Place along rue au Beurre, you soon reach the church of **St-Nicolas**, dedicated to St Nicholas of Bari, the patron saint of sailors or, as he's better known, Santa Claus. The church dates from the twelfth century, but has been heavily restored on several occasions, most recently in the 1950s when parts of the outer shell were reconstructed in a plain Gothic style. The **interior** hardly sets the pulse racing, although – among a scattering of objets d'art – there is a handsome **reliquary shrine** near the entrance. Of gilded copper, the shrine was made in Germany in the nineteenth century to honour a group of Catholics martyred by Protestants in the Netherlands in 1572.

Bourse

place de la Bourse

Opposite the church of St-Nicolas rises the grandiose **Bourse**, formerly the home of the city's stock exchange, a Neoclassical structure of 1873 caked with fruit, fronds, languishing nudes and frolicking putti. This breezily self-confident structure sports a host of allegorical figures (Industry, Navigation, Asia, Africa, etc) that both reflect the preoccupations of the nineteenth-century Belgian bourgeoisie and, in their easy self-satisfaction, imply that wealth and pleasure are synonymous. Nowadays the building hosts temporary exhibitions while it's made ready as the venue of the new **Belgian Museum of Beer**, due to open in 2018.

Rue Antoine Dansaert and Place St-Géry

In front of the Bourse, **place de la Bourse** is little more than a traffic-heavy knot in boulevard Anspach, but the streets beyond have more appeal, especially **rue Antoine Dansaert**, where several of the most innovative and stylish of the city's fashion designers

1

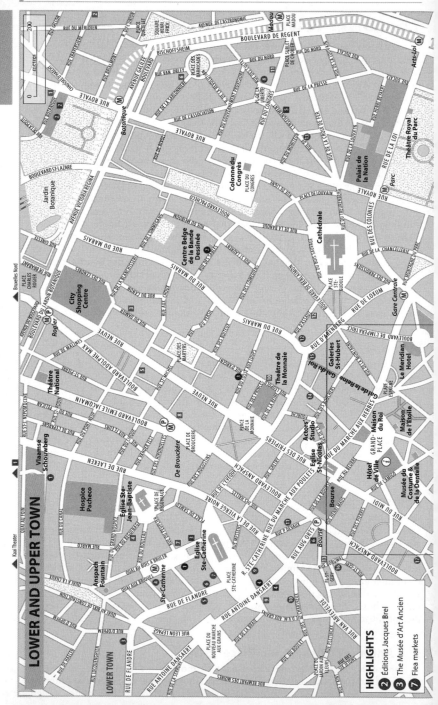

LOWER AND UPPER TOWN

LOWER TOWN

HIGHLIGHTS

2 Éditions Jacques Brel

3 The Musée d'Art Ancien

7 Flea markets

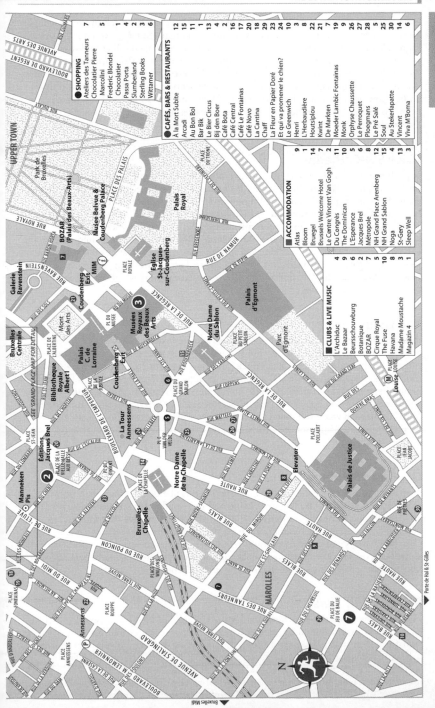

● SHOPPING

Ateliers des Tanneurs	7
Chocolatier Pierre Marcolini	5
Frederic Blondel Chocolatier	1
Passa Porta	4
Slumberland	2
Sterling Books	3
Wittamer	6

● CAFÉS, BARS & RESTAURANTS

A la Mort Subite	12
Arcadi	15
Au Bon Bol	11
Bar-Bik	1
Le Bier Circus	13
Bij den Boer	4
Café Bota	2
Café Central	16
Café Le Fontainas	17
Café Novo	20
La Cantina	18
Chaff	29
La Fleur en Papier Doré	23
Et qui va promener le chien?	24
Le Greenwich	10
Henri	3
L'Herbaudière	8
Houtsiplou	22
Kwint	21
De Marken	7
Moeder Lambic Fontainas	19
Monk	9
Orphyse Chaussette	26
Le Perroquet	27
Ploegmans	28
Le Pré Salé	5
Soul	25
Au Stekerlapatte	30
Vincent	14
Viva M'Boma	6

■ ACCOMMODATION

Atlas	9
Bloom	1
Bruegel	14
Brussels Welcome Hotel	7
Le Centre Vincent Van Gogh	2
Du Congrès	11
The Dominican	10
L'Esperance	6
Jacques Brel	8
Métropole	12
NH Grand Place Arenberg	5
NH Grand Sablon	15
Noga	4
St-Géry	13
Sleep Well	3

■ CLUBS & LIVE MUSIC

L'Archiduc	4
Le Bazaar	9
Beursschouwburg	6
Botanique	2
BOZAR	7
Cirque Royal	5
The Fuse	10
Havana	3
Madame Moustache	8
Magazin 4	1

1

have set up shop among the dilapidated old town houses that stretch up to place du Nouveau Marché aux Grains. Off its left side is tiny **place St-Géry**, which is crowded by high-sided tenements whose stone balconies and wrought-iron grilles hark back to ritzier days. The square is thought to occupy the site of the sixth-century chapel from which the medieval city grew, and has one specific attraction in the refurbished, late nineteenth-century covered market, the **Halles St-Géry**, an airy glass, brick and iron edifice now used for temporary exhibitions of art and photography. The square is also home to some of the trendiest **bars** and most boisterous terraces in town, such as *Café Central* (see p.88).

Place Ste-Catherine

Just off rue Antoine Dansaert, tree-shaded **place Ste-Catherine** lies at the heart of one of the city's most fashionable districts. It's named for the large **church of Ste-Catherine** (daily 8.30am–5.30pm), a battered nineteenth-century replacement for the Baroque original, of which the creamy, curvy **belfry** beside the west end of the church is the solitary survivor. Venture inside the church and, behind the glass screen that closes off most of the nave, you'll spy a fourteenth-century **Black Madonna and Child**, a sensually carved stone statuette that was chucked into the Senne by Protestants but fished out while floating on a fortuitous clod of peat. The real attraction here and on the adjacent **place du Vieux Marche-aux-Grains**, though, is the buzzy **cafés** which spread their tables out across the two squares.

The Quais

Quai aux Briques and the parallel **quai au Bois à Brûler** extend northwest from place Ste-Catherine on either side of a wide and open area that was, until it was filled in, the most central part of the city's main **dock**. Strolling along this open area, you'll pass a motley assortment of old houses, warehouses, shops and restaurants which together maintain an appealing canal-side feel – an impression heightened in the early morning when the streets are choked with lorries bearing trays of fish for local restaurants. The fanciful **Anspach water fountain** at the end of the old quays, with its lizards and dolphins, honours Burgomaster Anspach, a driving force in the 1880s move to modernize the city.

Galeries St-Hubert

Northeast corner of the Grand-Place lie the **Galeries St-Hubert**, whose handsome glass-vaulted galleries – **du Roi**, **de la Reine** and the smaller **des Princes** – date from 1847, making this one of Europe's first indoor **shopping arcades**. Even today, it's a grand place to escape the weather or have a coffee, and the pastel-painted walls, classical pilasters and cameo sculptures retain an air of genteel sophistication. Try *Arcadi* (see p.85) at the far end for snacks and lunches, while *l'Ogenblik* (see p.85), just off the main gallery, is good for high-end slap-up dinners.

Rue des Bouchers

Halfway down, **rue des Bouchers** divides the Galeries St-Hubert in two and is the city's best-known restaurant ghetto, where the narrow cobblestone lanes are transformed at night into fairy-lit tunnels flanked by elaborate displays of dull-eyed fish and glistening molluscs; it's all very tempting, but these restaurants have a reputation for charging way over the odds, and are best avoided. A small side alley, **Impasse de la Fidélité**, is home to a number of rowdy drinking joints centred on the *Delirium Café*, the heart of the Brussels drinking scene for young tourists. It's far better, though, to head for the rather wonderful bar (see p.90) of the nearby puppet theatre **Théâtre Royal de Toone**.

La Monnaie

It's a short walk from rue de Bouchers to the **place de la Monnaie**, a dreary modern square that's overshadowed by the huge shopping and office complex of Centre Monnaie and the Théâtre Royal de la Monnaie (nowadays simply known as **La Monnaie**) – Brussels' prestigious opera house, a Neoclassical structure built in 1819 with an interior added in 1856 to a design by Poelaert, the architect of the Palais de Justice (see p.67). The theatre's real claim to fame, however, is as the starting point of the revolution against the Dutch in 1830: a nationalistic libretto in Auber's *The Mute Girl of Portici* sent the audience wild, and they poured out into the streets to raise the flag of Brabant, signalling the start of the rebellion. The opera told the tale of an Italian uprising against the Spanish, and with such lines as "To my country I owe my life, to me it will owe its liberty", one of the Dutch censors – of whom there were many – should really have seen what was coming, as a furious King William I pointed out.

Rue Neuve and the Place des Martyrs

From place de la Monnaie, Brussels' principal shopping street, pedestrianized **rue Neuve**, forges north as far as the boulevards of the petit ring. About halfway up, on the right, the **place des Martyrs** is a cool, rational square superimposed on the city by the Habsburgs in the 1770s. There's no mistaking the architectural elegance of the ensemble, though the **imposing centrepiece** was added later: it comprises a stone plinth surmounted by a representation of the Fatherland Crowned and rising from an arcaded gallery inscribed with the names of those 445 rebels who died in the Belgian revolution of 1830.

Centre Belge de la Bande Dessinée

rue des Sables 20 • Tues–Sun 10am–6pm • €8 • ⓦ cbbd.be

Just east of the place des Martyrs, Brussels' only surviving **Horta**-designed department store, the **Grand Magasin Waucquez**, dating from 1906, exhibits all the classic features of Victor Horta's work (see p.73), from the soft lines of the ornamentation to the metal grilles, exposed girders and balustrades, and is worth a visit for just that. It's now home to the **Centre Belge de la Bande Dessinée**, which incorporates a café, reference library and bookshop downstairs and the enjoyable **comic-strip museum** on the floors above. The labelling of the displays is almost exclusively in French and Dutch, but a free and very thorough English guidebook is available at the ticket desk. Among much else, there are examples of work from all the leading practitioners: **Tintin** creator Georges Remi; Jijé; Peyo (best known for the Smurfs); and Edgar P. Jacobs, whose theatrical compositions and fluent combination of genres – science fiction, fantasy and crime – are seen to good effect in his *Blake and Mortimer* series.

Manneken Pis

Walking south from the Grand-Place, it's the briefest of strolls to Brussels' best-known tourist sight, the **Manneken Pis**, a diminutive statue of a pissing urchin stuck high up in a shrine-like affair that's protected from the crowds by an iron fence. There are all sorts of folkloric tales about the origins of the lad, from lost aristocratic children recovered when they were taking a pee to peasant boys putting out dangerous fires and – least likely of the lot – kids slashing on the city's enemies from the trees and putting them to

1

flight. More reliably, it seems that Jerome Duquesnoy, who cast the original bronze statue in the 1600s, intended the Manneken to embody the "irreverent spirit" of the city; certainly, its popularity blossomed during the sombre, priest-dominated years following the Thirty Years' War. The statue may have been Duquesnoy's idea, or it may have replaced an earlier stone version of ancient provenance, but whatever the truth it has certainly attracted the attention of thieves, notably in 1817 when a French ex-convict swiped it before breaking it into pieces. The thief and the smashed Manneken were apprehended, the former publicly branded on the Grand-Place and sentenced to a life of forced labour, while the fragments of the latter were used to create the mould in which the present-day Manneken was cast. It's long been the custom for visiting VIPs to donate a **costume**, and the little chap is regularly kitted out in different tackle – often military or folkloric gear, but occasionally stetsons and chaps, golfers' plus fours and Mickey Mouse outfits, which you can see in the city's historical museum (p.50). You can also see the Manneken's equally irreverent though rather more modern sister – **Jeanneke Pis** – squatting in a niche opposite *Delirium Café* (p.54).

Éditions Jacques Brel

place de la Vieille-Halle aux Blés 11 • Tues–Fri 10am–6pm, Sat & Sun noon–6pm, plus July & Aug Mon 10am–6pm • €5 • ⓦ jacquesbrel.be

A five-minute walk from the Grand-Place, **Éditions Jacques Brel** is a small but inventive museum celebrating the life and times of the Belgian singer Jacques Brel (1929–78), who was born and raised in Schaarbeek, a suburb of Brussels, although he lived much of his life in France. A legend in his own musical lifetime, Brel became famous in the 1960s as the gravelly voiced singer of mournful *chansons* about death, loss, desire and love, all of which he wrote himself (see box below). He died in 1978 at the age of 49 in Paris (having spent his final years in the Marquesas Islands, where he is buried), but he was a proud Belgian to the end, and this museum goes some way to explaining the man and his relationship with his homeland through family reminiscences, film and music, with the help of a free audio tour: Brel's monologue on the charms and tedium of Belgian life – "The Doctor" – is hilarious. You can also don another headset and set off on a Jacques Brel city-centre tour, which was put together – like the museum – by the songwriter's widow and daughters, strolling the streets of Brussels to his songs and

---

JACQUES BREL PLAYLIST

If you like what you hear at the **Éditions Jacques Brel**, you might want to check out some songs from the **playlist** below, which covers the very best of Brel's work.

Amsterdam This deliberately repetitive, climactic tale of sailors in seedy ports is a fantastically evocative song, and one of Brel's most intense live numbers.

Au suivant A typically satirical, biting rant against war, militarism and middle-class bourgeois values.

Les Bonbons Brel at his wittiest and most unforgiving, poking fun at 1960s hippies.

La Chanson de Jacky The songwriter in autobiographical mode, looking back in fantastically rumbustious fashion on his career, and forward to his future.

Je suis un soir d'été This late and very atmospheric study of summer ennui in small-town Belgium is one of Brel's most beautiful creations.

Mathilde One of Brel's greatest love songs, brilliantly covered by Scott Walker.

Le Moribond The tormented and yet curiously upbeat lament of a dying man that gave rise to the Terry Jacks hit of 1974.

Ne me quitte pas A truly anguished love song – perhaps one of the most affecting ever written – that was memorably covered by Nina Simone.

Quand on n'a que l'amour One of Brel's earliest songs, *When love is all you have* was his first hit single.

La Quête *The Impossible Dream* has been covered by just about everyone and is quite rightly one of Brel's best-known songs, but his version stands out.

stopping off at sights meaningful to Brel along the way, such as the spot on the Grand-Place where he conceived the song *Jef*.

1

Notre Dame de la Chapelle
place de la Chapelle 15 • Daily 9am–6pm

Founded in 1134, the sprawling, broadly Gothic **Notre Dame de la Chapelle** is the city's oldest church, though the attractive Baroque bell tower was only added after the French artillery bombardment of 1695. Inside, heavyweight columns with curly capitals support a well-proportioned **nave**, whose central aisle is bathed in light from the soaring windows. Among the assorted furniture and fittings, the **pulpit** is the most arresting, an intricately carved hunk of wood featuring the Old Testament prophet Elijah stuck out in the wilderness. The prophet looks mightily fed up, but then he hasn't realized that there's an angel beside him with a loaf of bread (manna). The church's main claim to fame is the **memorial to Pieter Bruegel the Elder**, high up on the wall of the south aisle's fourth chapel. The painting – a copy of a Rubens showing St Peter being given the keys to heaven – is the work of Pieter's son Jan, while the other plaque and bronze effigy in the chapel were added in the 1930s. Pieter is supposed to have lived and died just down the street at rue Haute 132.

The Quartier Marolles

South of Notre Dame de la Chapelle, **rue Blaes**, together with the parallel **rue Haute**, form the double spine of the **Quartier Marolles**, which was home to artisans working on the nearby mansions of the Sablon (see p.66) in the seventeenth century. Industrialized in the eighteenth century, it remained a thriving working-class district until the 1870s, when the paving-over of the Senne led to the riverside factories closing down and moving to the suburbs. The workers and their families followed, initiating a long process of decline, which turned the district into an impoverished **slum**. Things finally started to change in the late 1980s, when outsiders began to snaffle up property here, and although the *quartier* still has its rougher moments, the two main streets – **rue Haute** and **rue Blaes** (or at least those parts from Notre Dame de la Chapelle to place du Jeu de Balle) – are now lined with antique and interior-design shops, and the odd decent restaurant (see pp.85–87). Place du Jeu de Balle, at the heart of Marolles, is also the appropriately earthy location of the city's most famous **flea market** (daily 7am–2pm), which is at its hectic best on Sunday mornings.

It's worth knowing that a free **public elevator** (daily 7am–midnight), just off rue Haute on rue Notre-Dame de Graces, can whisk you up to the Palais de Justice in the Upper Town – a useful short cut.

The Upper Town

From the heights of the **Upper Town**, the Francophile ruling class long kept a beady eye on the proletarians down below. It was here they built their mansions and palaces, and the wide avenues and grand architecture of this aristocratic quarter – the bulk of which dates from the late eighteenth and nineteenth centuries – have survived pretty much intact, lending a stately, dignified feel that's markedly different from the tatty confusion of the Lower Town.

The Upper Town begins at the foot of the sharp slope which runs north to south from one end of the city centre to the other, its course marked – in general terms at least – by a wide **boulevard** that's variously named Berlaimont, L'Impératrice and L'Empereur. Above here the **rue Royale** and **rue de la Régence** together make up the Upper Town's spine, on and around which is the outstanding **Musées Royaux des Beaux**

1

Arts, the pick of Belgium's many fine art collections; the low-key **Palais Royal**; and the entertaining **Musée des Instruments de Musique** (MIM). A short walk south, rue de la Régence soon leads to the well-heeled **Sablon** neighbourhood, whose antique shops and chic bars and cafés fan out from the medieval church of **Notre Dame du Sablon**. Beyond this is the monstrous late nineteenth-century **Palais de Justice**, traditionally one of the city's most disliked buildings.

Cathedral of St Michael and Ste Gudule

place Ste-Gudule • Mon–Fri 7am–6pm, Sat & Sun 8.30am–6pm • Free • ⓦ www.cathedralestmichel.be

It only takes a couple of minutes to walk from the Grand-Place to the east end of rue de la Montagne, where a short slope climbs up to the city's **cathedral**, a splendid Gothic edifice whose commanding position is only slightly compromised by the modern office blocks either side. Begun in 1215, and three hundred years in the making, the cathedral is dedicated jointly to the **patron and patroness of Brussels**, respectively St Michael the Archangel and Ste Gudule, the latter a vague seventh-century figure whose reputation was based on her gentle determination: despite all sorts of shenanigans, the devil could never make her think an uncharitable thought.

The cathedral sports a striking, twin-towered, **white stone facade**, with the central double doorway trimmed by fanciful tracery as well as statues of the Apostles and – on the central column – the Three Wise Men. The facade was erected in the fifteenth century in High Gothic style, but the intensity of the decoration fades away inside with the cavernous triple-aisled **nave**, completed a century before. Other parts of the interior illustrate several phases of Gothic design, the **chancel** being the oldest part of the church, built in stages between 1215 and 1280 in the Early Gothic style.

The interior is short on **furnishings and fittings**, reflecting the combined efforts over the years of Protestants and the French Republican army, but the massive oak **pulpit** survives, an extravagant chunk of frippery by the Antwerp sculptor Hendrik Verbruggen, featuring Adam and Eve being chased from the Garden of Eden, while up above the Virgin Mary and some helpful cherubs stamp on the head of the serpent-dragon.

The stained-glass windows

The cathedral also boasts some superb sixteenth-century **stained-glass windows**, beginning above the main doors with the hurly-burly of the Last Judgement. Look closely and you'll spy the donor in the lower foreground with an angel on one side and a woman with long blonde hair (symbolizing Faith) on the other. Each of the main colours has a symbolic meaning, green representing hope, yellow eternal glory and light blue heaven. There's more remarkable work in the transepts – in the **north transept** Charles V kneels alongside his wife beneath a vast triumphal arch as their patron saints present them to God the Father, and in the **south transept** Charles V's sister, Marie, and her husband, King Louis of Hungary, play out a similar scenario. Both windows were designed by **Bernard van Orley** (1490–1541), long-time favourite of the royal family and the leading Brussels artist of his day.

Chapel of the Blessed Sacrament and treasury

Mon–Fri 10am–12.30pm & 2–5pm, Sat 10am–12.30pm & 2–3.45pm, Sun 2–5pm • €1

Just beyond the north transept, flanking the choir, is the Flamboyant Gothic **Chapel of the Blessed Sacrament**, named after an anti-Semitic legend that featured a Jew from a small Flemish town stealing the consecrated Host from his local church and seeing it stabbed with daggers by his fellow Jews, before being rescued by his wife and brought to the cathedral, thereby saving her soul – the chapel was built to display the retrieved Host in the 1530s. The four **stained-glass windows** of the chapel retell the tale in a strip cartoon that unfolds above representations of the aristocrats who paid for the windows. The workmanship, based on designs by van Orley (see p.58) and his one-time apprentice Michiel van Coxie (1499–1592), is delightful. The highlight of the cathedral **treasury** – also displayed in the chapel – is a splendid Anglo-Saxon reliquary of the **True Cross**, recently winkled out of the ornate, seventeenth-century, gilded silver reliquary Cross (Item 4) that was made to hold it. There are also two flowing sixteenth-century **altar paintings** to look out for in the chapel – *The Legend of Ste Gudule* and *The Last Supper* by Michiel van Coxie – and, behind the chapel's high altar, the ghoulish **skull** of St Elizabeth of Hungary (1207–31), a faithful wife, a devoted mother and a loyal servant of the church – hence her beatification.

Galerie Ravenstein and the Palais des Beaux Arts

Across the road from **Gare Centrale**, dug deep into the slope where the Lower and Upper Town meet, the **Galerie Ravenstein** shopping arcade (ⓦwww.galerieravenstein.com) clambers up to rue Ravenstein – a classic piece of 1950s design, sporting bright and cheerful tiling and an airy atrium equipped with a (defunct) water fountain. At the far end, on rue Ravenstein, stands the **Palais des Beaux Arts** or **BOZAR** (see p.92), a severe, low-lying edifice designed by Horta during the 1920s (see box, p.73). The building holds a theatre and concert hall and hosts numerous temporary exhibitions, mostly of contemporary art and photography. From here, you can either climb the steps up to rue Royale or follow the street along to the top of the Mont des Arts and the Musée des Instruments de Musique.

Mont des Arts

The most prominent feature of the slope between the Lower and Upper Towns is the **Mont des Arts**, a name bestowed by Léopold II in anticipation of a fine art museum he intended to build. However, the project was never completed, and the land was only properly built upon in the 1950s. At the bottom, **place de l'Albertine** is overlooked by a large and imposing equestrian statue of Belgium's most popular king, **Albert I** (1875–1934), gazing out at a modest statue of Albert's popular queen, Elizabeth, across the street. From here a wide stone **stairway** clambers up to a **piazza** equipped with water fountains, footpaths and carefully manicured shrubbery, and eventually to the Upper Town proper and the Musée des Instruments and Musique Musées Royaux des Beaux Arts. Not surprisingly, there are nice views from the top and a decent restaurant – *Kwint* (see p.87) – from which to enjoy them.

Musée des Instruments de Musique (MIM)

rue Montaigne de la Cour 2 • Tues–Fri 9.30am–5pm, Sat & Sun 10am–5pm • €12 • ⓦ mim.fgov.be

Near the top of the Mont Des Arts, the **Old England building** is a whimsical Art Nouveau confection – all glass and wrought iron – that started life as a store built by the eponymous British company as its Brussels headquarters in 1899. Cleverly recycled, it now houses the entertaining **Musée des Instruments de Musique**, whose permanent collection, featuring several hundred musical instruments, spreads over four main floors. The special feature here is the **infrared headphones**, which are cued to play music to match the type of instrument you're looking at. This is really good fun, especially in the folk-music section on **Floor 1**, where you can listen, for example, to a Tibetan temple trumpet, Congolese drums, a veritable battery of bagpipes and a medieval Cornemuse, as featured in the paintings of Pieter Bruegel the Younger. One word of caution, however: middle-aged parents will no doubt spot the dreaded ocarina, a slug-shaped instrument that was once popular with children and drove many an adult to despair.

1

Place Royale

Composed and self-assured, **place Royale** forms a fitting climax to rue Royale, the dead-straight backbone of the Upper Town, which runs the 2km north to the Turkish neighbourhood of St-Josse. Precisely symmetrical, the square is framed by late eighteenth-century mansions, each an exercise in architectural restraint, though there's no mistaking their size or the probable cost of their construction.

St-Jacques-sur-Coudenberg

place Royale • Tues–Sat 1–5.30pm, Sun 9am–5.30pm

The indifferent church of **St-Jacques-sur-Coudenberg** is a fanciful 1780s version of a Roman temple, with a colourfully frescoed pediment representing Our Lady as Comforter of the Depressed. Indeed, the building was so secular in appearance that the French Revolutionary army had no hesitation in renaming it a Temple of Reason. The French destroyed the statue of a Habsburg governor that once stood in front of the church; its replacement – a dashing equestrian representation of **Godfrey de Bouillon**, one of the leaders of the First Crusade – dates from the 1840s. It was an appropriate choice, as this was the spot where Godfrey is supposed to have exhorted his subjects to enlist for the Crusade, rounding off his appeal with a thunderous "*Dieu li volt*" (God wills it).

Experience Brussels

rue Royale 2–4 • Daily 10am–6pm • Free

Experience Brussels is an interactive walk-through exhibition of what makes Brussels what it is today – an international multicultural city that arguably has little to do with the rest of Belgium. It's full of population statistics and is really targeted more at Belgian school kids than casual tourists, but the pictures and recordings of ordinary Brussels residents, and a large interactive map of the city's neighbourhoods, give a nice insight into the city beyond the tourist attractions.

Musées Royaux des Beaux Arts

rue de la Régence 3 • Tues–Sun 10am–5pm • €8 for each museum, €13 for all three • Ⓦ fine-arts-museum.be

On the edge of place Royale, the **Musées Royaux des Beaux Arts** holds Belgium's best all-round collection of fine art, a vast hoard that is exhibited in three interconnected museums: the **Musée d'Art Ancien**, with art from the Renaissance to the early nineteenth century; the **Musée Magritte**, devoted solely to the work of the Belgian surrealist; and the new **Musée Fin-de-Siècle** which covers art from the mid-nineteenth to the early twentieth century. The museums also host a prestigious programme of **temporary exhibitions** for which a supplementary admission fee is usually required.

Musée d'Art Ancien

The galleries of the **Musée d'Art Ancien** surround the main hall, with the paintings of the fifteenth and sixteenth centuries, including the Flemish primitives and the Bruegels, on the left as you come in, and later work – principally paintings of the seventeenth and eighteenth centuries, including the work of Rubens and his contemporaries – on the right.

The fifteenth century

The museum's collection begins with several paintings by **Rogier van der Weyden** (1399–1464), who moved to Brussels from his home town of Tournai in the 1430s, becoming the city's official painter shortly afterwards. When it came to portraiture, Weyden's favourite technique was to highlight the features – and tokens of rank – of his

"...Depuis vingt ans,
je parle en tout cas,
si pas de la Belgique,
je parle des Belges."

1

subject against a black background. His *Portrait of Antoine de Bourgogne* is a case in point, with Anthony, the illegitimate son of Philip the Good, casting a haughty, tight-lipped stare to his right while wearing the chain of the Order of the Golden Fleece and clasping an arrow, the emblem of the guild of archers.

Weyden's contemporary, Leuven-based **Dieric Bouts** (1410–75), is well represented by the two panels of his *Justice of the Emperor Otto*. The story was well known: in revenge for refusing her advances, the empress accuses a nobleman of attempting to seduce her. He is executed, but the man's wife remains convinced of his innocence and subsequently proves her point by means of an ordeal by fire – hence the red-hot iron bar she's holding. The empress then receives her just desserts, being burnt on the hill in the background.

Moving on, the anonymous artist known as the **Master of the Legend of St Lucy** weighs in with a finely detailed, richly allegorical *Madonna with Saints* where, with the city of Bruges in the background, the Madonna presents the infant Jesus for the adoration of eleven holy women. Decked out in elaborate medieval attire, the women have blank, almost expressionless faces, but each bears a token of her sainthood, which would have been easily recognized by a medieval congregation: St Lucy, whose assistance was sought by those with sight problems, holds two eyeballs in a dish.

Beyond here is a beautifully coloured, clear and precise Lamentation by Petrus Christus (1410–75), and several fine portraits by **Hans Memling** (1430–94), plus his softly hued *Martyrdom of St Sebastian*, which was commissioned by the guild of archers in Bruges around 1470 and shows the trussed-up saint serenely indifferent to the arrows of the firing squad.

The sixteenth century

One of the museum's most interesting paintings is a copy of *Temptations of St Anthony*, the original of which, by **Hieronymus Bosch** (1450–1516), is in Lisbon's Museu Nacional. No one is quite sure who painted this triptych – it may or may not have been one of Bosch's apprentices – but it was certainly produced in Holland in the late fifteenth or early sixteenth century and shows an inconspicuous saint sticking desperately to his prayers surrounded by all manner of fiendish phantoms. On the right panel, Anthony is tempted by lust and greed; on the left, his companions help him back to his shelter after he's been transported through the skies by weird-looking demons. Another leading Flemish artist, **Quinten Matsys** (1465–1530), is well represented, not only by his *Triptych of the Holy Kindred*, which abandons the realistic interiors and landscapes of his Flemish predecessors in favour of the grand columns and porticoes of the Renaissance, and a loving and sensitive *Virgin and Child*. There's also a beautifully composed *Adoration of the Magi* by **Gerard David** (1460–1523).

Beyond here are paintings by the German painters **Lucas Crach the Younger** and **Elder** and the museum's superb collection of works by the Bruegel family, notably **Pieter the Elder** (1527–69), who moved to Brussels in the early 1560s. He preferred to paint in the Netherlandish tradition and his works often depict crowded Flemish scenes in which are embedded religious or mythical stories, a sympathetic portrayal of everyday life that revelled in the seasons and was worked in muted browns, greys and bluish greens with red or yellow highlights. Typifying this approach are two particularly absorbing works, the *Adoration of the Magi* and the *Census at Bethlehem* – a scene that **Pieter** (1564–1638), his son, repeated on several occasions. The versatile Pieter the Elder also dabbled with the lurid imagery of Bosch, whose influence is seen most clearly in the *Fall of the Rebel Angels*, a frantic panel painting which had actually been attributed to Bosch until Bruegel's signature was discovered hidden under the frame. The *Fall of Icarus* is, however, his most haunting work, its mood perfectly captured by Auden in his well-known poem *Musée des Beaux Arts*.

The seventeenth century

The larger works of the museum's other major painter, **Peter-Paul Rubens** (1577–1640), are gathered together in one room, as are the works of his contemporary **Jacob Jordaens** (1593–1678), whose big and brassy canvases perfectly suit the space. Like Rubens, Jordaens had a bulging order book, and for years he and his apprentices churned out paintings by the cartload. His best work is generally agreed to have been completed early on – between about 1620 and 1640 – and there's evidence here in the two versions of the *Satyr and the Peasant*, the earlier work clever and inventive, the second a hastily cobbled-together piece that verges on buffoonery. As for Rubens, the museum holds a wide sample of his work, including the *Ascent to Calvary*, an intensely physical painting, capturing the confusion, agony and strain as Christ struggles on hands and knees under the weight of the cross; and the bloodcurdling *Martyrdom of St Lieven*, whose cruel torture – his tongue has just been ripped out and fed to a dog – is watched from on high by cherubs and angels. In another room there are more paintings by Rubens, among them depictions of the Archdukes Albert and Isabella and the wonderfully observed *Four Studies of the Head of a Negro*, a preparation for the black magus in the *Adoration of the Magi*, a luminous work that hangs in the same room. From the same era there are also works by the skilled portraitist **Anthony van Dyck** (1599–1641), who is well represented by depictions of St Anthony and St Francis and figures of an old man and an old woman, and there are also portraits by the Dutchmen **Rembrandt** and **Frans Hals**, among a variety of other Dutch works.

The eighteenth century

The museum has a scattering of eighteenth-century paintings, the main highlight of which by far is the much celebrated *Death of Marat* by **Jacques-Louis David** (1748–1825), a propagandist piece of 1793 showing Jean-Paul Marat, the French Revolutionary hero, dying in his bath after being stabbed by Charlotte Corday. David has given Marat a perfectly proportioned, classical torso and a face, which, with its large hooded eyes, looks almost Christ-like, the effect heightened by the flatness of the composition and the emptiness of the background. The dead man clasps a quill in one hand and the letter given him by Corday in the other, inscribed "my deepest grief is all it takes to be entitled to your benevolence". As a counterpoint, to emphasize the depth of Corday's betrayal, David has added another note, on the wooden chest, written by Marat and beginning, "You will give this warrant to that mother with the five children, whose husband died for his country". The painting was David's paean to a fellow revolutionary, for, like Marat, he was a Jacobin – the deadly rivals of the Girondins, who were supported by Corday. David was also a leading light of the Neoclassical movement and became the new regime's Superintendent of the Fine Arts. He did well under Napoleon, too – until Waterloo, after which he was exiled, along with all the other regicides, ending his days in Brussels.

Musée Magritte

From the ground floor of the Musée d'Art Ancien, a passageway leads through to Level -2 of the **Musée Magritte**, whose four floors are devoted to the life, times and work of **René Magritte** (see box, p.64). Beginning on the top floor, the museum trawls through Magritte's life chronologically, with original documents, old photos and snatches of film, quotations and a decent sample of his paintings (though sadly not many of his most famous works, which are scattered around the galleries of the world). There is an early sketch of his wife Georgette, early Cubist efforts and the later surrealist works he became best known for – often perplexing pieces, whose weird, almost photographically realized images and bizarre juxtapositions aim to disconcert. There are posters by Magritte, too (he was an accomplished graphic artist), advertising drinks, films and commercial products, as well as a selection of the more Impressionistic works he produced in the 1940s. All in all it gives a good sense of his restless intelligence, skill and, above all, wit, which shines through in everything on display.

1

RENÉ MAGRITTE

René Magritte (1898–1967) is easily the most famous of Belgium's modern artists, his disconcerting, strangely haunting images a familiar part of popular culture. Born in a small town just outside Charleroi, he entered the Royal Academy of Fine Arts in Brussels in 1915, and was a sporadic student there until 1920. Initially, Magritte worked in a broadly **Cubist** manner, but in 1925, influenced by the Italian painter Giorgio de Chirico, he switched over to Surrealism and almost immediately stumbled upon the themes and images that would preoccupy him for decades to come. His work incorporated startling comparisons between the ordinary and the extraordinary, with the occasional erotic element thrown in. **Favourite images** included men in bowler hats, metamorphic figures, enormous rocks floating in the sky and juxtapositions of night and day. He also dabbled in word paintings, mislabelling familiar forms to illustrate the arbitrariness of linguistic signs. His canvases were devoid of emotion, deadpan images that were easy to recognize but perplexing because of their setting. He broke with this characteristic style at times, most famously in 1948 to revenge long years of neglect by the French artistic establishment. Hundreds had turned up to see Magritte's first **Paris exhibition**, but were confronted with crass and crude paintings of childlike simplicity. These so-called **Vache** paintings created a furore, and Magritte beat a hasty artistic retreat. Despite this, Magritte was picked up and popularized by an American art dealer, Alexander Iolas, who made him very rich and very famous.

Magritte and his family lived in Jette, a suburb of Brussels, until the late 1950s, and the house is now the **Musée René Magritte** (see p.63). He died in 1967, shortly after a major retrospective of his work at the Museum of Modern Art in New York cemented his reputation as one of the great artists of the twentieth century.

Musée Fin-de-Siècle

From Level -2 of the Musée Magritte, a stairway proceeds down to the six subterranean half-floors of the **Musée Fin-de-Siècle**, a strong and well-presented selection of works from the nineteenth and early twentieth centuries. There are decadent high society scenes by **Félicien Rops** (see p.73) and, at the other end of the spectrum, paintings by Belgium's Social Realists, including **Charles de Groux** (1825–70) and **Eugene Laermans** (1864–1940), who shifted from the Realist style into more Expressionistic works, as in the overtly political *Red Flag* and *The Emigrants*. Look out too for Leon Frederic's (1856–1940) *The Chalk Sellers*, and the paintings of the ultimate chronicler of nineteenth-century working-class life, **Constantin Meunier** (1831–1905; see p.76), who is well represented here by a number of paintings, for example the *Banks of the Sambre*, which hangs near **Van Gogh**'s *The Peasant*. There are works by French Impressionists and Post-Impressionists – **Monet**, **Seurat**, **Gauguin** among them – and also paintings by the Belgian Impressionists, such as **Théo van Rysselberghe** (1862–1926), a Brussels artist whose most interesting canvases – as in his *The Promenade* – exhibit a studied pointillism; **Émile Claus** (1849–1924), who produced the charmingly rustic *Trees Beside the River Leie*; and the versatile **Henry van de Velde** (1863–1957), who also came under the influence of Seurat – hence the similarly pointillist-style *Girl Darning*.

Among the **Symbolists**, look out for the disconcerting canvases of **Fernand Khnopff** (1858–1921), who painted his sister, Marguerite, again and again, using her refined, almost plastic beauty to stir a vague sense of passion. His haunting *Memories of Lawn Tennis* is typical of his oeuvre, a work without narrative, a dream-like scene with each of the seven women bearing the likeness of Marguerite. In *The Caress*, Marguerite pops up once more, this time with the body of a cheetah pawing sensually at an androgynous youth. **Antoine Wiertz**, who has a museum all to himself near the EU Parliament building (see p.70), pops up too, his *La Belle Rosine* a typically disagreeable painting in which the woman concerned faces a skeleton.

There is also a superb sample of the work of **James Ensor** (1860–1949; see p.346). Ensor, the son of a Flemish mother and an English father, spent nearly all of his long life working in Ostend, his home town. His first paintings were impressionistic portraits and landscapes, delicately picking out his colours, as in *Sombre Lady and Drunkards*. Later, he became fascinated by **masks**, and painted them repeatedly, along with images of death and perversity. His *Scandalized Masks* of 1883 was his first mask painting, a typically unnerving canvas that works on several levels, while his *Skeletons Quarrelling for a Kipper* (1891) is one of the most macabre paintings you'll see.

Palais Royal

Late July to mid-Sept Tues–Sun 10.30am–4.30pm • Free • ⓦ www.monarchie.be

Around the corner from place Royale, the long and rather cumbersome **Palais Royal** is something of a disappointment, consisting of a stodgy nineteenth-century conversion of late eighteenth-century town houses, begun by King William I, the Dutch royal who ruled both Belgium and the Netherlands from 1815 to 1830. The Belgian rebellion of 1830 polished off the joint kingdom, and since then the kings of independent Belgium haven't spent much time here. Indeed, although it remains their official residence, the royals have lived in Laeken (see p.77) for decades and it's hardly surprising, therefore, that the **palace interior** is formal and unwelcoming. It comprises little more than a predictable sequence of opulent rooms, all gilt trimmings, parquet floors and endless royal portraits, though three features make a visit (just about) worthwhile: the tapestries designed by **Goya**; the magnificent chandeliers of the **Throne Room**; and the Mirror Room's *Heaven of Delight* **iridescent ceiling**, a contemporary work by the Belgian artist Jan Fabre, made up of more than a million wing cases of the Thai jewel beetle.

Musée BELvue

Tues–Fri 10am–5pm, Sat & Sun 10am–6pm • €6; combined ticket with Coudenberg Palace €10 • ⓦ BELvue.be

The **Hôtel Bellevue**, at the corner of place des Palais and rue Royale, was once part of the palace, but has been turned into the **Musée BELvue**, which tracks through the brief history of independent Belgium. It's all very professionally done, with the **corridor displays** concentrating on the country's kings, and the **rooms** on Belgium as a whole. Juicing up the displays is a wide range of original artefacts – documents, letters, costumes and so forth, including the corduroy mountaineering jacket that Albert I was wearing when he died in 1934. But it's the old **photographs** that really catch the eye: one particularly interesting display focuses on those Flemish nationalists who collaborated with the Germans during the World War II occupation; another is devoted to the protracted conflict between the Catholics and the anticlericalists that convulsed the country for much of the nineteenth century. It's an appropriate location for the museum too, as it was in this building that the rebellious Belgians fired at the Dutch army, which was trying to reach the city centre across the Parc de Bruxelles (see p.66) in 1830.

Coudenberg Palace

Tues–Fri 10am–5pm, Sat & Sun 10am–6pm • €6; combined ticket with Musée BELvue €10 • ⓦ belvue.be

Dating from the 1770s, the Hôtel Bellevue was built on top of the subterranean remains of the **Coudenberg Palace**, which stretched right across to what is now place Royale. A castle was first built on this site in the eleventh century and was enlarged on several subsequent occasions, but it was badly damaged by fire in 1731 and the site was cleared forty years later, leaving only the foundations. These have recently been cleared

1

of debris, revealing a labyrinth of tunnels that can only be reached from the Musée BELvue. Visitors can wander round these foundations, the most notable feature of which is the **Magna Aula**, or great hall, built by Philip the Good in the 1450s. A small display of excavated items, including a pair of helmets, does put some flesh on the historical bones and a map of the layout of the palace is provided at Musée BELvue reception. You emerge on the other side of the street at the so-called **Hoogstraten House**, which displays a collection of objects found on the site, and then exit onto an alley next door to the Musical Instruments Museum.

Parc de Bruxelles

Set between the Palais Royal and the Belgian Parliament building, the **Parc de Bruxelles** is the most central of the city's main parks, along whose tree-shaded footpaths civil servants and office workers stroll at lunch time, or race to catch the métro in the evenings. They might well wish the greenery was a bit more interesting. Laid out in the **formal French style** in 1780, the park undoubtedly suited the courtly – and courting – rituals of the times, but today the straight footpaths and long lines of trees seem a little tedious, though the classical statues and large **fountain** in the centre do cheer things up a tad.

Place du Trône

From the east side of the royal palace, rue Ducale leads to **place du Trône**, where the conspicuous equestrian statue of Léopold II was the work of Thomas Vinçotte, whose skills were much used by the king – look out for Vinçotte's chariot on top of the Parc du Cinquantenaire's triumphal arch (see p.71).

Place du Petit Sablon

Just off the eastern side of busy rue Royale, the peaceful rectangle of **place du Petit Sablon** was laid out as a public garden in 1890 after previous use as a horse market. The wrought-iron fence surrounding the garden is decorated with 48 **statuettes** representing the medieval guilds; inside, near the top of the slope, are ten slightly larger statues honouring some of the country's leading sixteenth-century figures. The ten are hardly household names in Belgium, never mind anywhere else, but one or two may ring a few bells – Mercator, the sixteenth-century geographer and cartographer responsible for the most common representation of the earth's surface, and William the Silent (see p.44), to all intents and purposes the founder of the Netherlands. Here also, on top of the fountain, are the figures of the counts **Egmont and Hoorn**, beheaded on the Grand-Place for their opposition to the Habsburgs in 1568.

Notre Dame du Sablon

place du Grand Sablon • Daily 9am–6pm

The fifteenth-century church of **Notre Dame du Sablon** began life as a chapel for the guild of archers in 1304. Its fortunes were, however, transformed when a **statue of Mary**, purportedly with healing powers, was brought here from Antwerp in 1348. The chapel soon became a centre of pilgrimage, and a proper church – in High Gothic style – was built to accommodate its visitors. The church endured some inappropriate tinkering at the end of the nineteenth century, but remains a handsome structure, the sandy hues of its exterior stonework enhanced by slender buttresses and a forest of prickly pinnacles. The **interior** no longer holds the statue of Mary – the Protestants chopped it up in 1565 – but two carvings of a boat with its passengers and holy cargo recall its story, one located in the nave, the other above the inside of the rue de la Régence door. The woman in the boat is one Béatrice Sodkens, the pious creature whose visions prompted her to procure the statue and bring it here. The occasion of its arrival in Brussels is still celebrated annually in July by the **Ommegang** historic-heritage procession from the Sablon to the Grand-Place.

Place du Grand Sablon

Behind the church of Notre-Dame du Sablon, the sloping wedge of the **place du Grand Sablon** serves as the centre of the **Sablon** neighbourhood, which is one of the city's wealthiest districts – as evidenced by the luxury stores and chocolate shops (see p.94) that sit around its fringes. The square is busiest at weekends, when it hosts an **antiques market** (see p.95), and many of the shops hereabouts are devoted to antiques and art. You could easily spend an hour or so browsing the market and surrounding shops, or just soak up the atmosphere in one of Sablon's several cafés.

Palais de Justice

From place du Grand Sablon, it's a brief walk south to place Poelaert, named after the architect who designed the immense **Palais de Justice** which anchors the end of rue de la Régence, a monstrous Greco-Roman wedding cake of a building that dwarfs the square and everything around it. It's possible to wander into the building's sepulchral **main hall**, but it's the size alone that impresses – not that it pleased the several thousand townsfolk who were forcibly evicted so that the place could be built. Poelaert became one of the most hated men in the capital and, when he went insane and died in 1879, it was widely believed a *steekes* (witch) from the Marolles had been sticking pins into an effigy of him.

Place Louise

A stone's throw from the Palais de Justice, **place Louise** – part square, part traffic junction – heralds the edge of perhaps the city's most exclusive shopping district, home to a good proportion of Brussels' designer boutiques, jewellers and glossy shopping malls, which spread east along boulevard de Waterloo and south down the first part of avenue Louise.

The EU quarter and Le Cinquantenaire

By no means does Brussels end at the **petit ring**. King Léopold II pushed the city limits out beyond the course of the old walls, grabbing land from the surrounding *communes* to create the irregular boundaries that survive today. To the **east**, he sequestered a rough rectangle of land, across which he ploughed two wide boulevards to link the city centre with **Le Cinquantenaire**, a self-glorifying and markedly grandiose monument erected to celebrate the golden jubilee of Belgian independence, and one that now houses three sprawling museums, including the large **Musées Royaux d'Art et d'Histoire**. In recent decades the grandeur of Léopold's design has been overlaid with the uncompromising office blocks of the EU, which coalesce on and around rue de la Loi to form the loosely defined **EU quarter** – not a particularly enjoyable area to explore, although there are a handful of appealing parks and squares, while the flashy **EU Parliament** building is of passing interest, as are the other EU institutions.

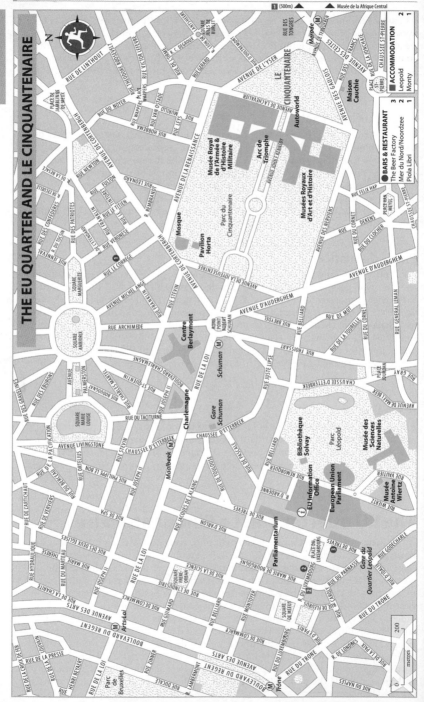

THE EU QUARTER AND LE CINQUANTENAIRE

ACCOMMODATION
Leopold	2
Monty	1

BARS & RESTAURANT
The Beer Factory	3
Mer du Nord/Noordzee	2
Piola Libri	1

1 (500m) ▲

▲ Musée de la Afrique Central

Musée Royal de l'Armée & d'Histoire Militaire

Arc de Triomphe

Autoworld

Maison Cauchie

Mosque

Pavillon Horta

Parc du Cinquantenaire

Musées Royaux d'Art et d'Histoire

LE CINQUANTENAIRE

Centre Berlaymont

Schuman

Gare Schuman

Charlemagne

Maelbeek

Bibliothèque Solvay

Parc Léopold

Musée des Sciences Naturelles

EU Information Office

European Union Parliament

Musée Antoine Wiertz

Parliamentarium

Gare du Quartier Leopold

Parc de Bruxelles

0   200
metres

EU Parliament

1

Parliamentarium Mon 1–6pm, Tues–Fri 9am–6pm, Sat & Sun10am–6pm • **Parliamentary chamber tours** Sept–June Mon–Thurs 10am & 3pm, Fri 10am; July & Aug Mon–Thurs 10am, 11am, 2pm, 3pm, Fri 10am, 11am; report to the visitors' entrance 15min in advance and be sure to take photo ID • Both free • **Information office** Mon–Thurs 9am–5pm, Fri 9am–1pm

The **EU Parliament** complex fronts onto the busy rectangle of **place du Luxembourg**, a wide and attractive square framed on three sides by late nineteenth-century town houses. The Parliament's central structure, the **Spaak building**, was completed in 1997, a glass, stone and steel behemoth equipped with a horseshoe-shaped debating chamber and a curved glass roof that rises to a height of 70m. It has its admirers, but is known locally as the "*caprice des dieux*", a wry comment on the EU's sense of its own importance. Behind, the **Spinelli building**, connected by a footbridge, was completed in 1992 and houses MEPs' offices and those of the various political groupings. The free thirty-minute **tours** of the Spaak building are fairly cursory affairs, more or less a look at the debating chamber and the stairwell outside, with the aid of headphones that take you through the whole thing and explain how the EU works. It's not exactly essential viewing, but you do learn something of the purpose of the building – which, amazingly enough, is here less for the debating chamber than to house the Parliament's various committees.

The other way to get the lowdown on the EU Parliament is in the new **Parliamentarium** exhibition, housed in a separate building on the left side of the main plaza. This is a series of interactive displays, around which you're guided by **audio guide**,

THE EU IN BRUSSELS

The three main institutions of the **European Union** operate mainly, though not exclusively, from Brussels. The **European Parliament** carries out its committee work and the majority of its business in Brussels, heading off for Strasbourg for around a dozen three-day plenary sessions per year. It's the only EU institution to meet and debate in public, and has been directly elected since 1979. There are currently 751 **MEPs** and they sit in political blocks made up of like-minded parties rather than national delegations; members are very restricted on speaking time, and debates tend to be well-mannered, consensual affairs controlled by the **President**, who is elected for a five-year period by Parliament itself – although this mandate is often split in two and shared by the two biggest political groups. The **Conference of Presidents** – the President of the Parliament and Leaders of all the political groups – meet to plan future parliamentary business. Supporting and advising this political edifice is a complex network of committees from agriculture to human rights.

The **European Council** consists of the heads of government of each of the member states and the President of the European Commission; they meet twice every six months in the much-publicized "European Summits". However, in between these meetings, ministers responsible for different issues meet in the **Council of the European Union**, the main decision-making structure alongside the European Parliament. There are complex rules regarding decision-making: some subjects require only a simple majority, others need unanimous support, some can be decided by the Council alone, others need the agreement of Parliament; and overall, in a bid to make the EU more democratic, the power of the Parliament has been strengthened in recent years. This political structure is underpinned by scores of Brussels-based committees and working parties, made up of both civil servants and political appointees.

The **European Commission** acts as the EU's executive arm and board of control, managing funds and monitoring all manner of agreements. The 28 Commissioners are political appointees, nominated by their home countries, but their tenure has to be agreed by the European Parliament and they remain accountable to the MEPs. The president of the Commission is elected by the European Parliament for a five-year period of office. Over twenty thousand civil servants work for the Commission, whose headquarters are in Brussels, mainly in the Berlaymont and adjacent Charlemagne building on rue de la Loi as well as other buildings in the area.

1

that trace the origins of the European vision, taking you through the EU's evolution from the Schuman Agreement of 1950 to its current 28 member states. It's a slick presentation, and free (EU citizens have already paid for it, after all) and gives a crash course on the workings of the EU Parliament and its other institutions, with screens on which you can find out about any of the 751 MEPs, displays on the various political groupings and their agendas and a mock parliamentary chamber that takes you through the excruciating decision-making processes by way of a series of short films. You can also take a mini-tour around the continent, listening to various European initiatives, and sit in comfy chairs and listen to European citizens describing their daily lives. Good stuff, all of it, but inevitably a touch worthy – and above all a giant slice of propaganda for the EU.

Musée Wiertz

rue Vautier 62 • Tues–Fri 10am–noon & 1–5pm • Free • ⓦ www.fine-arts-museum.be/en/museums/musee-wiertz-museum

There couldn't be a greater contrast to the squeaky-clean buildings of the EU Parliament than the **Musée Wiertz**, a small museum devoted to the works of one of the city's most distinctive nineteenth-century artists, **Antoine-Joseph Wiertz** (1806–65). Though little known now, Wiertz was a popular painter in his day (so much so that Thomas Hardy could write of "the staring and ghastly attitudes of a Wiertz museum"), and this museum is housed in his former **studio**, built for him by the Belgian state on the understanding that on his death he bequeath both it and his oeuvre to the nation. Wiertz painted mainly religious and mythological canvases, featuring gory hells and strapping nudes, as well as fearsome scenes of human madness and suffering. There are a number of elegantly painted quasi-erotic pieces featuring coy nudes, a colossal *Triumph of Christ*, a small but especially gruesome *Suicide* – not for the squeamish – and macabre works such as *The Thoughts and Visions of a Severed Head* and *Hunger, Folly, Crime* – in which a madwoman is pictured shortly after hacking off her child's leg and throwing it into the cooking pot. Mercifully, there is some relief, with a few conventional portraits and various saucy girls in states of undress. But whether Wiertz was really one of the greatest painters who ever lived – as he believed – only time will tell.

Muséum des Sciences Naturelles

rue Vautier 29 • Tues–Fri 9.30am–5pm, Sat & Sun 10am–6pm • €7 • ⓦ naturalsciences.be

Follow rue Vautier up the hill from the Wiertz museum and you soon reach the **Musée des Sciences Naturelles**, which holds the city's natural history collection. It's a large, sprawling and somewhat disorientating museum, whose wide-ranging displays are lodged in a mixture of late nineteenth-century and 1960s galleries. There are sections devoted to crystals and rocks; rodents and mammals; insects and crustaceans; a whale gallery featuring the enormous remains of a blue whale; and, most impressive of the lot, a capacious **dinosaur gallery** with a superb selection of dinosaur fossils discovered in the coal mines of Hainaut in the late nineteenth century. The most striking are those of a whole herd of iguanodons, whose skeletons are raised on two legs, though in fact these herbivores may well have been four-legged. An excellent multilingual text explains it all.

Parc Léopold

On rue Vautier, almost opposite the Musée Wiertz, a back entrance leads into the rear of **Parc Léopold**, a green and hilly enclave landscaped around a **lake**. The park is pleasant enough, but its open spaces were encroached upon years ago when the industrialist Ernest Solvay began constructing the educational and research facilities of

1

a prototype science centre here. The end result is a string of big, old buildings that spread along the park's western periphery. The most interesting is the **Bibliothèque Solvay** (no set opening times), a splendid barrel-vaulted structure with magnificent mahogany panelling overlaying a cast-iron frame.

Parc du Cinquantenaire

The wide and leafy lawns and tree-lined avenues of the **Parc du Cinquantenaire** slope up towards a gargantuan arch surmounted by a huge and bombastic bronze entitled *Brabant Raising the National Flag*. The arch, along with the two heavyweight stone buildings it connects, comprise **Le Cinquantenaire**, which was erected by Léopold II for an exhibition to mark the golden jubilee of the Belgian state in 1880. The buildings themselves contain three extensive collections – art and applied art; weapons; and cars – displayed in separate museums.

Musées Royaux d'Art et d'Histoire

South side of south wing of Cinquantenaire complex • Tues–Fri 9.30am–5pm, Sat & Sun 10am–5pm • €5 • ⓦ mrah.be

The **Musées Royaux d'Art et d'Histoire** bring together the city's main archeological, anthropological and decorative arts museums into one. The collection spans the world and the centuries, and there's too much to absorb on one visit, with galleries of Greek, Egyptian and Roman artefacts, Far Eastern art and textiles, medieval and Renaissance carving and religious artefacts, and a decent collection of glasswork and ceramics from all eras.

To the right of the entrance hall and set in part around the museum's neo-Gothic cloister, the **European decorative arts** galleries have perhaps the most immediacy. Highlights include some striking fifteenth- and sixteenth-century altarpieces from Antwerp, a prime collection of Brussels tapestries dating from the middle of the sixteenth century (the heyday of the city's tapestry industry), and an intriguing selection of scientific and precision instruments from the sixteenth century onwards.

On the other side of the entrance hall, the European collection continues with turn-of-the-twentieth-century furnishings, and an **Art Nouveau** section where the display cases were designed by Victor Horta for a firm of jewellers and now accommodate the celebrated *Mysterious Sphinx*, an ivory bust of archetypal Art Nouveau design – the work of Charles van der Stappen in 1897. On the same side of the museum, seek out the **Greek and Roman sections** – among various statuary, pottery and other artefacts you'll find a fabulous mosaic depicting hunting scenes dating from the fifth century AD, which you can view from a balcony above. There's also a bronze of an emperor and a wonderful scale model of ancient Rome, again viewable from above. Next door, a lovely gallery displays artefacts from the **Islamic world**, with Persian and Ottoman ceramics, carpets, manuscripts and all sorts of beautiful objects. The same wing of the museum has a ton of **Mayan**, **Incan** and **Aztec artefacts** from southern and central America, including a Peruvian mummy that was Hergé's inspiration for two Tintin tales – *The Broken Ear* and *The Seven Crystal Balls*. Further non-European galleries hold a good collection of sculptures and other pieces from the **Far East**, including a couple of wooden sculptures from China dating back to 1200 or so.

Autoworld

South wing of Le Cinquantenaire • April–Sept daily 10am–6pm; Oct–March Mon–Fri 10am–5pm, Sat & Sun 10am–6pm • €9 • ⓦ autoworld.be

Housed in a vast hangar-like building, **Autoworld** is a chronological stroll through the short history of the automobile, with a huge display of **vintage vehicles** that begins with turn-of-the-twentieth-century motorized cycles and Model T Fords. European varieties predominate, with Peugeot, Renault and Benz well represented, and there are home-grown vehicles too, including a Minerva from 1925 that once

1

belonged to the Belgian monarch. American cars include early Cadillacs, a Lincoln from 1965 that was also owned by the Belgian royals, and some gangster-style Oldsmobiles. Among the British brands, there's a mint-condition Rolls-Royce Silver Ghost from 1921, one of the first Austins and, from the modern era, the short-lived De Lorean sports car. Upstairs you'll find a mishmash of assorted vehicles that don't fit into the main exhibition: early Porsches and Volvos, classic 1960s Jaguars and even a tuk-tuk from Thailand.

Musée Royal de l'Armée et d'Histoire Militaire

North wing of Le Cinquantenaire • Tues–Fri 9am–5pm, Sat & Sun 10am–6pm • Free • ⓦ www.klm-mra.be

The **Musée Royal de l'Armée et d'Histoire Militaire** traces the history of the "Belgian" army from the late eighteenth century to the present day by means of a vast hoard of weapons, armaments and uniforms. The **first part** of the collection is enjoyably old-fashioned, with a long series of glass cases holding a small army of life-sized model soldiers, with assorted rifles, swords and muskets nailed to the walls above. Of particular interest here are the sections dealing with "Belgian" regiments in the Austrian and Napoleonic armies, and the volunteers who formed the nucleus of the 1830 revolution. Elsewhere, there's an excellent **World War I** display, with uniforms and kit from every nationality involved in the conflict, together with a fearsome array of field guns, artillery pieces and very primitive early tanks. A second, larger hall covers **World War II**, including the Belgian experience of collaboration and resistance, all illustrated by a superb selection of blown-up period photographs. The **courtyard** outside has a large collection of World War II tanks, armoured cars and artillery pieces – British, American and German – and there's a third large **hall** dedicated to aviation, with a large array of aircraft, some of which you can clamber aboard.

The outer neighbourhoods

Central Brussels is full of interest beyond the petit ring, with the **outer neighbourhoods** of this multicultural city home to some of its most interesting attractions and finest restaurants. To the southeast, cobwebbed by tiny squares and narrow streets, the **St-Gilles** and **Ixelles** areas make a great escape from the razzmatazz of the city centre. St-Gilles, the smaller of the two *communes*, has patches of inner-city decay but is nicer the further east you go, its run-down streets giving way to attractive avenues and some of the city's best **Art Nouveau buildings**, including Victor Horta's own house and studio, now the glorious **Musée Victor Horta**. Ixelles, meanwhile, is one of the capital's most interesting and exciting neighbourhoods, with a diverse street life and arty, Bohemian vibe that has long drawn artists, writers and intellectuals – Karl Marx, Auguste Rodin and Alexandre Dumas all lived here. Ixelles is split in two by **avenue Louise**, a prosperous corridor that was laid out by Léopold II in the 1840s, and named after his eldest daughter. Some of Brussels' premier hotels, shops and boutiques flank the northern reaches of the avenue; further along it lies the enjoyable **Musée Constantin Meunier**, sited in the sculptor's old house. Northwest of the Gare du Midi, flanking the southwestern edge of the city centre, **Anderlecht** is best known for its football team, and remains a working-class neighbourhood at heart, with one very popular, very Brussels attraction in the **Cantillon Brewery**. Northwest of the petit ring, **Jette** is a well-heeled suburb that wouldn't merit a second glance if it weren't for the former home of René Magritte, now turned into the engaging **Musée René Magritte**, which pays detailed tribute to the artist, his family and friends. Just east of Jette and immediately north of the city centre, leafy **Laeken** is where the Belgian royal family hunker down. A short distance northwest of here lies **Heysel** with its trademark **Atomium** – a hand-me-down from the 1958 World's Fair. Finally, if you've an insatiable appetite for the monuments of the Belgian royal family, then you should venture out

HORTA'S PROGRESS

The son of a shoemaker, **Victor Horta** (1861–1947) was born in Ghent, where he failed in his first career, being expelled from the city's music conservatory for indiscipline. He promptly moved to Paris to study **architecture**, returning to Belgium in 1880 to complete his internship in Brussels with Alphonse Balat, architect to King Léopold II. Balat was a traditionalist, partly responsible for the classical facades of the Palais Royal – among many other prestigious projects – and Horta looked elsewhere for inspiration. He found it in the work of William Morris, the leading figure of the English Arts and Crafts movement, whose designs were key to the development of **Art Nouveau**. Taking its name from the Maison de l'Art Nouveau, a Parisian shop which sold items of modern design, Art Nouveau rejected the imitative architectures which were popular at the time – Neoclassical and neo-Gothic – in favour of an innovative style characterized by **sinuous, flowing lines**. In England, Morris and his colleagues had focused on book illustrations and furnishings, but in Belgium Horta extrapolated the new style into architecture, experimenting with new building materials such as steel and concrete, as well as traditional stone, glass and wood.

In 1893, Horta completed the curvaceous **Hôtel Tassel** (just off Avenue Louise), Brussels' first Art Nouveau building ("hôtel" meaning town house). Inevitably, there were howls of protest from the traditionalists, but no matter what his opponents said, Horta never lacked work again. The following years – roughly 1893 to 1905 – were Horta's most inventive and prolific. He designed over forty buildings, including the **Hôtel Solvay** (see p.71), the **Hôtel Max Hallet**, and his own beautifully decorated house and studio, now the **Musée Victor Horta** (see p.73). The delight Horta took in his work is obvious, especially when employed on private houses, and his enthusiasm was all-encompassing – he almost always designed everything from the blueprints to the wallpaper and carpets. He never kept a straight line or sharp angle where he could deploy a curve, and his **use of light** was revolutionary, often filtering through from above, with skylights and as many windows as possible. Horta felt that the architect was as much an artist as the painter or sculptor, and so he insisted on complete stylistic freedom. Curiously, he also believed that originality was born of frustration, so he deliberately created architectural difficulties, pushing himself to find harmonious solutions. His value system allied him with the **political Left** – as he wrote, "My friends and I were reds, without however having thought about Marx or his theories". Completed in 1906, the **Grand Magasin Waucquez** (see p.55) department store was a transitional building signalling the end of Horta's Art Nouveau period. His later works were more **Modernist** constructions, whose understated lines were a far cry from the ornateness of his earlier work. In Brussels, the best example is the **Palais des Beaux Arts (BOZAR)** of 1928 (see p.59 & p.92).

east of the city to **Tervuren**, where the king built the massive **Musée Royal de l'Afrique Centrale** on the edge of the woods of the Forêt de Soignes.

Musée Victor Horta

rue Americaine 25 • Tues–Sun 2–5.30pm • €8 • ⓦ hortamuseum.be • Tram #92 from place Louise or métro to Horta

The principal sight in the **St-Gilles** neighbourhood is the delightful **Musée Victor Horta**, which occupies the two houses Horta designed as his home and studio at the end of the nineteenth century, and was where he lived until 1919. The **exterior** sets the tone, a striking reworking of what was originally a modest terraced structure, the design fluidly incorporating knotted and twisted ironwork. Yet it is for his interiors that Horta is particularly famous, and **inside** is a sunny, sensuous dwelling exhibiting all the architect's favourite flourishes – wrought iron, stained glass, ornate furniture and panelling made from several different types of timber. The main unifying feature is the **staircase**, a dainty spiralling affair, which runs through the centre of the house illuminated by a large skylight. Decorated with painted motifs and surrounded by mirrors, it remains one of Horta's most magnificent and ingenious creations, giving access to a sequence of wide, bright rooms. Also of interest is the modest but enjoyable selection of **paintings**, many of which were given to Horta by friends and colleagues, including works by Félicien Rops and Joseph Heymans.

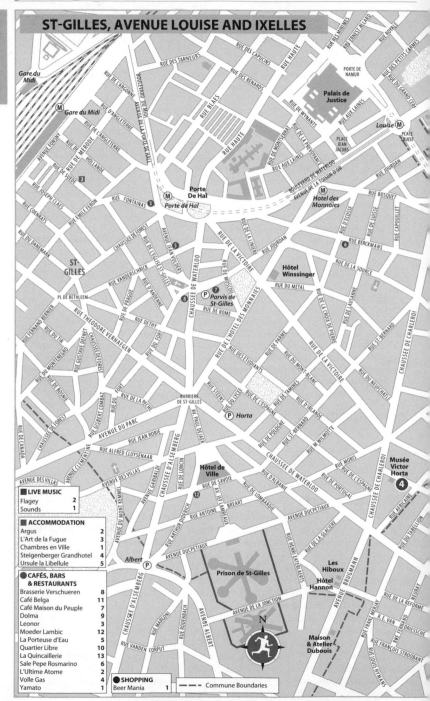

ST-GILLES, AVENUE LOUISE AND IXELLES

■ LIVE MUSIC

Flagey	2
Sounds	1

■ ACCOMMODATION

Argus	2
L'Art de la Fugue	3
Chambres en Ville	1
Steigenberger Grandhotel	4
Ursule la Libellule	5

● CAFÉS, BARS & RESTAURANTS

Brasserie Verschueren	8
Café Belga	11
Café Maison du Peuple	7
Dolma	9
Leonor	3
Moeder Lambic	12
La Porteuse d'Eau	5
Quartier Libre	10
La Quincaillerie	13
Sale Pepe Rosmarino	6
L'Ultime Atome	2
Volle Gas	4
Yamato	1

● SHOPPING

Beer Mania	1

– – – Commune Boundaries

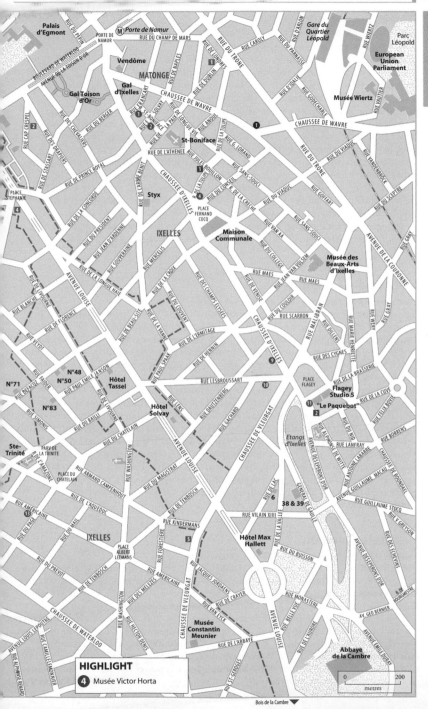

HIGHLIGHT

4 Musée Victor Horta

0 — 200
metres

Bois de la Cambre ▼

1

Musée Constantin Meunier

rue de l'Abbaye 59 • Tues–Fri 10am–noon & 1–5pm • Free • ⓘ 02 648 44 49, ⓦ fine-arts-museum.be/en/museums/musee-meunier-museum • Tram #94 from place Louise, rue de la Régence or rue Royale

The **Musée Constantin Meunier** is housed on the ground floor of the former home and studio of Brussels-born artist **Constantin Meunier** (1831–1905), who lived here for the last six years of his life. The museum has a substantial collection of his dark and brooding **bronzes**, with the largest and most important pieces in the old studio at the back, where a series of life-size depictions of muscular men – *Le Faucheur* (The Reaper), *Un Semeur* (A Sower) and *Le Marteleur* (The Metalworker), among others – strike heroic poses while going about their work. There are also a couple of large **paintings**, notably the gloomy dockside of *The Port*, one of Meunier's most forceful works. Meunier is best known as a chronicler of Belgium's rapid industrialization during the nineteenth century, and his anger over the dreadful living conditions of Belgium's working class – particularly (like Van Gogh before him) the harsh life of the coal miners of the Borinage – was poured into his art, with miners and other workers depicted in unflinching detail in the paintings and drawings displayed here. According to historian Eric Hobsbawm's *Age of Empire*, "Meunier invented the international stereotype of the sculptured proletarian".

Abbaye de la Cambre

Church open daily 9am–noon & 2–5pm • Free • Tram #94 from place Louise

The postcard-pretty **Abbaye de la Cambre** nestles in a lovely little wooded dell just to the east of avenue Louise and not far from the Meunier Museum. Of medieval foundation, the French Revolutionary army suppressed the abbey at the beginning of the nineteenth century, but its eighteenth-century brick buildings survived pretty much untouched and, after many toings and froings, have ended up as **government offices**. An extensive complex, the main courtyard is especially attractive and it serves as the main entrance to the charming **Notre-Dame de l'Abbaye church**, whose nave, with its barrel vaulting and rough stone walls, is an exercise in simplicity. The church is an amalgamation of styles, but Gothic predominates except in the furnishings of the nave, where carefully carved Art Deco wooden panelling frames a set of religious paintings of the Stations of the Cross. The church also holds Albert Bouts' tiny *Mocking of Christ*, a marvellous, early sixteenth-century **painting** in the left aisle that depicts a mournful, blood-spattered Jesus. There's a small **cloister** attached to the church and around the abbey's buildings are walled and terraced **gardens** plus the old abbatial pond, altogether an oasis of peace away from the hubbub of avenue Louise.

Brasserie Cantillon

rue Gheude 56 • Mon–Fri 9am–5pm, Sat 10am–5pm • Tours €7 • ⓦ cantillon.be

A short walk northwest of the Gare du Midi, in the heart of the working-class district of Anderlecht, the **Brasserie Cantillon** is one of the city's most popular attractions, and the only place in Brussels that still makes the local brew – otherwise known as lambic beer or gueuze (see box, p.77) – according to traditional methods. The beer, a sour, almost cidery concoction made only with water, barley and hops, is allowed to ferment naturally, reacting with the natural yeasts present in the Brussels air, and is bottled two years before it is ready to drink. You can do a quick **tour** of the mustily atmospheric brewery (best outside summer months when they are actually making the beer), and have a taste afterwards in the comfy bar area. Plus, of course, you can buy bottles to take home, and there is perhaps no better souvenir of Brussels than a bottle of Cantillon gueuze.

LAMBIC BEERS

One of the world's oldest styles of beer manufacture, Brussels' **lambic** beers are tart brews made with at least thirty percent raw wheat as well as the more usual malted barley. Their key feature, however, is the use of **wild yeast** in their production, a process of spontaneous fermentation in which the yeasts – which are specific to the air of the Brussels area – gravitate down into open wooden casks over a period of between two and three years. Draught lambic is extremely rare, but the bottled varieties are more commonplace; **Cantillon Lambic** is perhaps the most authentic, an excellent drink with a lemony zip. **Gueuze** is a blend of old and new lambics in a bottle, a little sweeter and fuller bodied than straight lambic, with an almost cider-like aftertaste; again, Cantillon's is the best you'll find (5%), although you may have to settle for Belle Vue Gueuze (5.2%), Timmermans Gueuze (5.5%) or Lindemans Gueuze (5.2%).

Musée René Magritte

rue Esseghem 135, Jette • Wed–Sun 10am–6pm • €7.50 • ⓦ magrittemuseum.be • Métro to Belgica and then tram #51

Northwest of the city centre, in the suburb of Jette, the enthralling **Musée René Magritte** holds a plethora of the Surrealist's paraphernalia as well as a limited collection of his early **paintings** and **sketches**. Magritte lived with his wife Georgette on the ground floor of this modest house for 24 years from 1930, an odd location for what was effectively the **headquarters** of the Surrealist movement in Belgium, most of whose leading lights met here every Saturday to concoct a battery of subversive books, magazines and images.

The ground floor

The **ground floor** has been faithfully restored to re-create the artist's studio and living quarters, using mostly original ornaments and furniture, with the remainder carefully replicated from photographs; the famous **bowler hat** which crops up in several of Magritte's paintings is hung near the indoor studio. Many features of the house itself also appear in a number of his works: the sash window, for instance, framed the painting entitled *The Human Condition*, while the glass doors to the sitting room and bedroom appeared in *The Invisible World*. Magritte built himself a studio – which he named **Dongo** – in the garden, and it was here that he produced his bread-and-butter work, such as graphics and posters, though he was usually unhappy when working on such mundane projects, and his real passions were painted in the **dining-room studio**, where he displayed just one work by another artist – a photo by Man Ray – which is there again today.

The first and second floors

You have to don shoe covers to visit the **first and second floors** of the house, which were separate apartments when the Magrittes lived here, but are now taken up by letters, photos, telegrams, lithographs, posters and sketches pertaining to the artist, all displayed in chronological order. There are two fine posters announcing the international film and fine arts festivals which took place in Brussels in 1947 and 1949, as well as Magritte's first painting, a naive landscape which he produced at the tender age of 12, the blue rug he had made for the bedroom and work by other Surrealists. Finally, there are a number of personal objects displayed in the **attic** (which he rented), including the easel he used at the end of his life. Overall, it's a fascinating glimpse into the life of one of the most important artists of the twentieth century.

Laeken

Mid-April to early May Tues–Thurs 9.30am–4pm, Fri 1–4pm, Sat & Sun 9.30am–4pm & 8–10pm • €2.50 • ⓦ www.monarchie.be

To the north of Brussels' city centre, **Laeken** is home to the Belgian royal family at the **Château Royal**. Built in 1790, its most famous occupant was Napoleon, who

1

stayed on a number of occasions and signed the declaration of war on Russia here in 1812. You can't visit the palace itself, but for three weeks every year they open up the **royal greenhouses** for public visits – worth doing not just for the plants but for the magnificent structures themselves. Be warned, though, that the queues can be long at weekends. Opposite the front of the royal palace, a wide footpath leads up to the fanciful neo-Gothic **monument** erected in honour of Léopold I, the focal point of the pretty **Parc de Laeken**. The park's glorious woods and grassy meadows, lawns and wooded thickets extend northwest for a couple of kilometres towards Heysel and are well worth a stroll and a picnic, particularly if you're en route to the Atomium.

The Atomium

Daily 10am–6pm • €11 • ⓦ atomium.be • Tram #23 or #51, or métro to Heysel

Most visitors come to the north part of Brussels to see the **Atomium**, a curious model of a molecule expanded 165 billion times. Built for the 1958 World's Fair in Brussels, it has never quite become the symbol of the city it was intended to be, but after restoration a few years ago it is looking better than it has for some time. **Visits** are in two parts: the lift whizzes you up to the top sphere for the views, after which you descend and then come back up again to take in the other three spheres, reached by a mixture of escalators and stairs. It's all pleasingly retro – the Atomium was quite a feat of technology in its day (its elevator was the world's fastest, the escalator connecting the spheres the world's longest), and its construction is remembered by apposite photos. There's not actually all that much to see – the spheres are mainly given over to **temporary exhibitions** and a **café**, and trudging up and down the stairs and escalators can turn into a bit of a slog – but it's an undeniably impressive sight overall and the views from the top are as spectacular as you would expect (enhanced by computer screens pointing out what you're looking at). One of the spheres also houses a rather nice **restaurant** with views.

Musée Royal de l'Afrique Centrale

Leuvensesteenweg 13 • Closed for renovation until 2017 • ⓦ africamuseum.be • Tram #44 from Métro Montgomery; the museum is a 2min walk from the tram terminus

Closed for renovation until 2017, the grandiose **Musée Royal de l'Afrique Centrale**, in the suburb of Tervuren, on the edge of the vast and beautiful expanse of the **Forêt de Soignies**, is the biggest monument there is to Belgium's murky colonial past. Personally presented with the vast **Congo River basin** by a conference of the European Powers in 1885, **King Léopold II** of Belgium became one of the world's richest men through exploiting the region's people and natural resources. In part aided and abetted by the explorer, **Henry Stanley**, who went to the Congo on a five-year fact-finding mission in 1879 (just a few years after he had famously found the missionary David Livingstone), Léopold's regime was chaotic and extraordinarily cruel even by the standards of the colonial powers. The Belgian **government** was finally shamed into taking over the territory in 1908 and installed a marginally more efficient state bureaucracy. But when the Belgian Congo gained independence as the **Republic of Congo** in 1960, it was poorly prepared and its subsequent history (as both Zaire and the Republic of Congo) has been one of the most bloodstained in Africa.

For the moment the museum's **grounds** are well worth a stroll, with formal gardens set around a series of geometric lakes flanked by woods, but the likelihood is that the museum will be completely changed when it reopens, with a more contemporary view of Belgium's colonial past.

ARRIVAL AND DEPARTURE
BRUSSELS

Brussels has Belgium's busiest **international airport** and is on the main routes heading inland from the Channel ports via Flanders. **Eurostar trains** arrive here direct from London and the city is also a convenient stop on the fast train line between France and Holland. The city has an excellent **public transport** system which puts all the main points of arrival – its airport, train and bus stations – within easy reach of the city centre.

BY PLANE

BRUSSELS AIRPORT

Most flights to Brussels land at the city's international airport – known as Brussels National – in the satellite suburb of Zaventem, 14km northeast of the city centre. For flight information call ☎ 0900 70 000 or go to ⓦ brusselsairport.be. There are around four trains an hour (5.30am–midnight) from Brussels National to the city's three main stations; the journey to Bruxelles-Centrale takes 17min and costs €8.50 each way (more if bought on board). There are also direct buses into the city centre from the airport's bus station, one floor below the arrivals hall, most usefully the hourly #12 (Mon–Fri until 8pm) which runs to place de Luxembourg in the EU quarter, stopping off at Schuman and other métro stops along the way, though note that on Saturdays and Sundays and during the week after 8pm, this becomes the slower bus #21. Outside of these times, you'll need to take a taxi to get to the city centre, a 20min journey for which you'll pay €40–45, though less if you ordered one in advance – more like €35–40 (see p.82).

BRUSSELS SOUTH (CHARLEROI) AIRPORT

Some airlines – principally Ryanair – fly to Brussels (Charleroi) airport, which is also sometimes called Brussels South, though it is in fact some 50km south of central Brussels. This secondary airport is rapidly expanding and has a reasonable range of facilities. For flight details call ☎ 0902 02 490 or go to ⓦ www .charleroi-airport.com. From the airport, there is a shuttle-bus service to the city centre (every 30min 7.50am–11.59pm; 1hr; €14 one-way), departing outside the terminal building and dropping off at the bus stop on the west side of Bruxelles-Midi train station at the junction of rue de France and rue de l'Instruction. Alternatively, you can take a local bus (every 30min;

20min) from the airport to Charleroi Sud train station, from where there are regular services to all three of Brussels' main stations (every 30min, hourly on Sat & Sun; 50min; €9.40 one-way). A taxi into Brussels city centre will cost €60–70, though less if booked in advance.

BY TRAIN

Stations Brussels has three main stations – Bruxelles-Nord, Bruxelles-Centrale and Bruxelles-Midi (see box, below). Most domestic trains stop at all three, but many international services only stop at Bruxelles-Midi, including Eurostar trains from London and Thalys express trains from Amsterdam, Paris, Cologne and Aachen. Bruxelles-Centrale is, as its name suggests, the most central of the stations, a 5min walk from the Grand-Place; Bruxelles-Nord lies among the bristling tower blocks of the business area just north of the main ring road; and Bruxelles-Midi is located in a slightly depressed area on the southern edge of the city centre.

Transfers If you need to transfer from one of the three main train stations to another, simply jump on the next available mainline train: there are services between them every 10min or so, the journey only takes minutes and all you'll have to do (at most) is swap platforms. You can find lots of information in English on the Belgian Railways (SNCB/NMBS) website ⓦ www.belgianrail.be or by calling ☎ 02 528 28 28 (daily 7am–9.30pm); for international services call ☎ 070 79 79 79.

Destinations Amsterdam Centraal Station (hourly; 2hr 30min); Antwerp (every 20–30min; 40min); Bruges (every 30min; 1hr); Charleroi (every 30min; 50min); Ghent (every 30min; 30min); Leuven (every 30 min; 25min); Liège (hourly; 1hr 20min); Luxembourg (hourly; 3hr); Mons (1–2 hourly; 50min); Namur (hourly; 1hr); Ostend (every 30min; 1hr 10min).

TRAIN STATION NAMES

When you first arrive, the city's bilingual signage can be confusing, especially with regard to the names of the **three main train stations**: Bruxelles-Nord (in Flemish Brussel-Noord), Bruxelles-Centrale (Brussel-Centraal) and, most bewildering of the lot, Bruxelles-Midi (Brussel-Zuid). To add to the puzzle, each of the three adjoins a **métro station** – respectively the Gare du Nord (Noordstation), Gare Centrale (Centraal Station) and Gare du Midi (Zuidstation). And in an extra twist of unhelpfulness, note that on **bus timetables** and on **maps of the city transit system** (including the one in this book), Bruxelles-Nord usually appears as "Gare du Nord", Bruxelles-Centrale as "Gare Centrale" and Bruxelles-Midi as "Gare du Midi", taking the names of their respective métro stops.

1

BY BUS

Most international bus services to Brussels, including Eurolines from Britain, use the Bruxelles-Nord station complex as their terminus. Belgium's comprehensive rail network means that it's unlikely that you'll arrive in the city by long-distance domestic bus, but if you do then Bruxelles-Nord is the main terminal for these services too.

GETTING AROUND

Operated by STIB (ⓦ stib.be; information line ☎ 070 23 2000), the **public transport** system comprises an integrated mixture of **bus**, **tram**, **underground tram** and **métro** lines that covers the city comprehensively. It's a user-friendly network, with every métro station carrying métro system diagrams, **route maps** available free from the tourist office and from most major métro stations, and **timetables** posted or signed at most bus and tram stops.

Tickets Valid on any part of the STIB system, tickets (€2.10 for a single) are available from métro kiosks, automatic machines at métro stations and from newsagents displaying the STIB sign; note that tram and bus drivers will only issue €2.50 single-journey tickets. At the beginning of each journey, you're trusted to stamp tickets yourself, using one of the machines on every métro station concourse or inside every tram and bus. After that, the ticket is valid for an hour, during which you can get on and off as many trams, métros and buses as you like.

Fares and travel cards The most convenient way to travel if you're around for more than a day or so is to invest in a MOBIB card, a credit card-style pass that you can purchase at any métro station for €5 plus as much credit as you want. You can then add credit to it using the machines and, at the end of your visit, either keep the card or return it and get your €5 back (MOBIB also gives discounts on the city bike scheme – see below). A single journey using MOBIB costs €2, and you can buy 10 journeys for €12.50. If you don't want to bother with MOBIB you can buy a five-journey ticket for €8 and a ten-journey ticket for €14. You can also buy a go-as-you-please 24hr pass for €7, which allows citywide travel on all of the system, €13 for 48hr or €17 for 72hr.

BY MÉTRO, PRÉMÉTRO OR TRAM

The métro system consists of four underground lines (Lines #1, #2, #5 and #6), though to a considerable extent they overlap (see map, p.81). The city also has a substantial tram system serving the centre and its suburbs. These trams are at their speediest when they go underground to form what is sometimes called the prémétro, which runs as lines #3 & #4 right beneath the heart of the city from Bruxelles-Nord, through De Brouckère and Bourse, to Bruxelles-Midi, Porte de Hal and on into St-Gilles. Times of operation and frequency vary considerably, but key parts of the system operate from 6am until midnight.

BY BUS

Trams and the métro are supplemented by a network of buses, in particular a limited night bus service on major routes – again timetable info is available in real time on the STIB website. In addition, De Lijn (☎ 070 22 02 00, ⓦ delijn.be) runs buses from the city to the Flemish-speaking communities that surround the capital, while TEC (☎ 010 230 53 53, ⓦ infotec.be) operates services to the French-speaking areas. Most of these buses run from – or at least call in at – the Gare du Nord complex.

BY LOCAL TRAIN

Supplementing the STIB network are local trains, run by Belgian Railways, which shuttle in and out of the city's seven train stations, connecting different parts of the inner city and the outskirts, but unless you're living and

---

GUIDED TOURS

Both **Brussels tourist offices** (see p.82) have the details of, and take bookings for, about twenty operators. Generally, the standard tours can be booked on the day, while the more exotic need to be booked **in advance**, either direct with the company concerned or with the tourist office, who normally require at least two weeks' notice.

ARAU (Atelier de Recherche et d'Action Urbaines) blvd Adolphe Max 55 ☎ 02 219 33 45, ⓦ arau.org. A heritage action group which provides tours exploring the city's architectural history – with particular emphasis on Art Nouveau – from April through to December. Prices vary with the length of the tour and the itinerary, but average about €10 per person for walking tours, €17 if there's transport involved.

City Sightseeing Brussels ⓦ www.city-sightseeing .com/tours/belgium/brussels.htm. Operates two hop-on-hop-off services year-round (daily every 15–30min; 1hr 15min), each of which makes over twenty stops, with 24hr tickets costing €22, 48hr tickets €30.

BRUSSELS MÉTRO AND PRÉMÉTRO

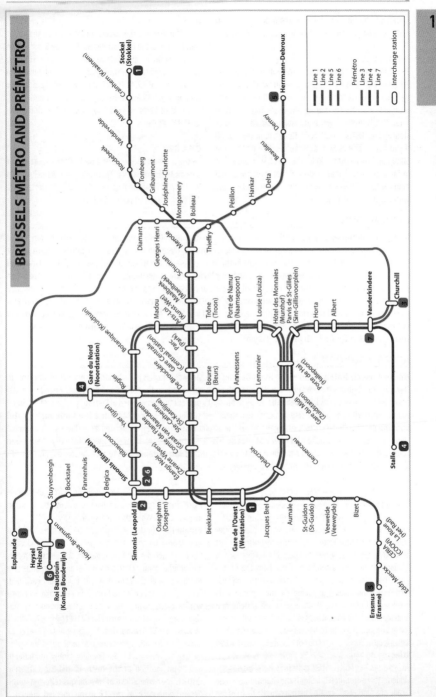

Line 1
Line 2
Line 5
Line 6

Prémétro
Line 3
Line 4
Line 7

O Interchange station

1

working in the city, you're unlikely to need to use them – ⓦ www.belgianrail.be or by calling ☎ 02 528 28 28.

BY BICYCLE

The city council operates an excellent public bicycle scheme (☎ 078 05 11 10, ⓦ villo.be) in which bikes can be taken from stands dotted across the city centre, and returned after use to another. There are 180 stands in total and rates are very reasonable: you pay a basic sign-up fee of €7.65/week or €1.60/day, or nothing at all if you have a MOBIB card; the bikes are free for the first 30min and then cost €0.50 for the next half-hour, rising in increments to a maximum of €2 for two and a half hours or more. There's a pay machine at every bike stand with multilingual instructions.

BY TAXI

Taxis don't cruise the streets, but can be picked up at stands around the city, notably on Place de Brouckère in the Lower Town and outside the main train stations. There is a fixed tariff consisting of two main elements – a fixed charge of €2.40 (€4.40 at night) and the price per kilometre (€1.35 inside the city). If you can't find a taxi, phone Taxis Verts on ☎ 02 349 49 49 or Taxi Orange on ☎ 02 349 43 43.

BY CAR

All the main companies have a desk at the airport and at Gare du Midi train station. Those at the airport include Avis (☎ 02 720 09 44); Europcar (☎ 02 721 05 92); Hertz (☎ 02 720 60 44); and Sixt (☎ 02 753 25 60).

INFORMATION

At the **international airport** you'll find a tourist information desk (daily 6am–9pm) in the arrivals hall, with a reasonable range of blurb on the city, including free maps. In the city, there's an office opposite the **Eurostar terminal** at Bruxelles-Midi (daily 9am–6pm), and two offices in the city centre – in the **Hôtel de Ville** on the Grand-Place (daily 9am–6pm; ☎ 02 513 89 40, ⓦ visitbrussels.be), and on **place Royale** at rue Royale 2 (Mon–Fri 9am–6pm, Sat & Sun 10am–6pm; same phone & website). Both issue free city and transport **maps**, have details of forthcoming events and concerts, make reservations on **guided tours** (see box, p.80) and sell the **Brussels Card** (see box, p.46). They can also make last-minute **hotel reservations**. If you're heading off into Flemish-speaking Belgium you can pick up oodles of information at **Tourism Flanders**, metres from the Grand-Place at rue du Marché aux Herbes 61 (Mon–Sat daily 10am–5pm; ☎ 02 504 03 90, ⓦ visitflanders.com).

ACCOMMODATION

With over seventy **hotels** dotted within its central ring of boulevards, Brussels has no shortage of convenient places to stay. Even so, finding accommodation can still prove difficult, particularly in the **spring** and **autumn**, when the capital enjoys what amounts to its **high seasons**. At peak times, it's prudent to reserve a bed at least for your first night, but if you do arrive with nowhere to stay, the city's two main tourist offices (see above) operate a free **same-night hotel booking service**. Hotel prices vary hugely, but as the accommodation scene is dominated by business you can almost always expect rates to be quite a lot **lower at weekends** than during the week: indeed, many of the city's higher-end hotels can sometimes as much as halve their rates at weekends. In **high summer**, they're a lot cheaper during the week too, when the EU especially pretty much shuts up shop.

THE LOWER AND UPPER TOWN

★**Amigo** rue de l'Amigo 1–3 ☎ 02 547 47 47, ⓦ roccofortehotels.com/hotels-and-resorts/hotel-amigo; Métro Gare Centrale or Bourse; map p.47. This lavish five-star Rocco Forte hotel must be Brussels' most desirable place to stay, with impeccable service and a fabulous location just around the corner from the Grand-Place. The building dates from the sixteenth century and has seen several incarnations, including the town prison, only becoming a hotel in the 1950s. Rooms are tasteful and contemporary in all-natural hues enhanced with splashes of colour. The superb *Bocconi* restaurant serves some of the best Italian food in Brussels. Rates do not include breakfast. **€250**
Atlas rue du Vieux Marché-aux-Grains 30 ☎ 02 502 60 06, ⓦ atlas.be; Métro Ste-Catherine; map pp.52–53. Modern three-star hotel behind the handsome stone facade of a nineteenth-century mansion in the heart of the

Ste-Catherine district, a 5min walk or so from the Grand-Place. The 88 rooms are a (slight) cut above those of the average chain. Wheelchair accessible. **€150**
Bloom rue Royale 250 ☎ 02 220 66 11, ⓦ hotelbloom .be; Métro Botanique; map pp.52–53. A good-value business hotel with a self-consciously cool vibe. Its 300 rooms are furnished with a clean modern feel and incorporate nice touches such as the hand-drawn mural behind each bed. They do a great buffet breakfast (you can make your own waffles if you're so inclined) and the restaurant does a good-value three-course lunch menu for €21. **€149**
★**Brussels Welcome Hotel** quai au Bois à Brûler 23 ☎ 02 219 95 46, ⓦ hotelwelcome.com; Métro Ste-Catherine; map pp.52–53. Friendly, family-run hotel in a brilliant location at the heart of the Ste-Catherine district. The owners' love of travelling is reflected in the design, with each of the 17 rooms themed around a

different country, from Bali to Japan, Morocco to Tibet. The Silk Road suite is a particularly sumptuous affair, and the Thai room at the top of the building is pretty good too. There's also an attractive wood-panelled breakfast room. **€95**

Le Dixseptième rue de la Madeleine 25 ☎02 517 17 17, ⓦledixseptieme.be; Métro Gare Centrale; map p.47. This place tries hard to be central Brussels' most elegant boutique hotel, with just 24 deluxe rooms and suites, and more or less pulls it off. Half are in the tastefully renovated seventeenth-century mansion at the front, the remainder in the new extension behind. There's a lovely downstairs sitting room and bar with comfy sofas to sink into, and the rooms themselves have a grand yet homely feel – all very soothing, and a real antidote to the mayhem outside. **€200**

★**The Dominican** rue Léopold 9 ☎02 203 08 08, ⓦthedominican.be; Métro De Brouckère or Bourse; map pp.52–53. This deluxe four-star boasts a prime location close to the Grand-Place, and a claim to fame as the place where the painter Jacques-Louis David (see p.63) drew his last breath in 1825 – hence the plaque on the facade. The spacious foyer sets the funky, stylish tone, as do the generous banquettes in the courtyard-style breakfast/restaurant area behind. Beyond, all 150 rooms are well appointed and stylishly kitted out with wooden floors and earthy tones. Prices fluctuate enormously, but weekend deals abound. **€170**

L'Esperance rue du Finistere 1 ☎02 219 10 28, ⓦwww.hotel-esperance.be; Métro De Brouckere; map pp.52–53. This pleasant Art Deco bar has 17 en-suite rooms upstairs, all very nicely furnished in a fresh style, with flatscreen TVs, wi-fi and lovely big bathrooms with walk-in power showers. They also do a decent buffet breakfast. Extremely good value. **€100**

La Légende rue du Lombard 35 ☎02 512 82 90, ⓦhotellalegende.com; Métro Bourse; map p.47. This old mansion set around a small courtyard is very centrally located but enjoys a pleasant, tucked-away feel. All of the 26 rooms have en-suite facilities and TV, and the decor – while a bit bland – is crisp and modern. **€70**

Métropole place de Brouckère 31 ☎02 217 23 00, ⓦmetropolehotel.com; Métro De Brouckère; map pp.52–53. Dating from 1895, this grand five-star is one of Brussels' finest hotels and boasts exquisite Art Nouveau decor in its public areas. Although some of the rooms beyond are comparatively routine, albeit very spacious, others retain their original fittings. **€160**

NH Grand Place Arenberg, rue d'Assaut 15 ☎02 250 16 16, ⓦwww.nh-hotels.com; Métro Gare Centrale; map pp.52–53. Opposite the cathedral, this 150-room hotel couldn't really be more central, with rooms finished in a simple contemporary style. The lobby has a self-service café and overall the feel is functional rather than posh, but it's very comfortable. **€125**

NH Grand Sablon, rue Brodenboek 2–4 ☎02 518 11 00, ⓦwww.nh-hotels.com; Métro Gare Centrale or Porte de Namur; map pp.52–53. A great location, and a bigger hotel than you might think from the outside, with nearly 200 rooms. It's comfy and welcoming, with a mixture of renovated, more modern rooms and some in classic style that are maybe due a renovation but still quite good enough. Bathrooms are a good size, and there's free wi-fi throughout. **€180**

Noga rue du Béguinage 38 ☎02 218 67 63, ⓦnogahotel.com; Métro Ste-Catherine; map pp.52–53. Not the grandest of the city's hotels, but this pleasant two-star offers 19 comfortable en-suite guest rooms, decorated in an old-fashioned country house-cum-cruise liner style. There's a library for guests' use, and a good breakfast buffet. **€95**

Royal Windsor rue Duquesnoy 5 ☎02 505 55 55, ⓦroyalwindsorbrussels.com; Métro Gare Centrale; map p.47. This long-established, five-star stalwart of the Brussels hotel scene has 200-odd deluxe rooms decorated in plush style – all heavy drapes and deep carpeting. If you want something a bit different you can opt for one of their "fashion rooms", each conceived by a top Belgian designer. **€169**

★**St-Gery** place Saint-Gery 29–32 ☎02 204 06 20, ⓦhotelstgery.com; Métro Bourse; map pp.52–53. Situated right on place St-Gery, so arguably enjoying one of the coolest locations in Brussels, this tall townhouse has 24 rooms, each done out with edgy, arty decor. They vary quite a lot in size and shape, and the ones at the front can inevitably be a bit noisy at weekends, but all are well furnished and sleek, and most have baths (sometimes in the room itself). Free wi-fi throughout. Breakfast is normally extra and not a buffet so fairly basic. **€165**

Saint-Michel Grand-Place 15 ☎02 511 09 56, ⓦhotel-saint-michel.be; Métro Bourse; map p.47. The only hotel to look out over the Grand-Place, this small, friendly establishment occupies an old guildhouse on the east side of the square. The handsome facade belies a rather humble interior, with 14 distinctly spartan en-suite rooms. Breakfast is taken downstairs at the 't Kelderke café or at café La Brouette across the square. If you're not a light sleeper (the revellers on the Grand-Place can make a real racket), treat yourself to one of the slightly more expensive rooms at the front. **€120**

La Vieille Lanterne rue des Grands Carmes 29 ☎02 512 74 94, ⓦlavieillelanterne.be; Métro Bourse; map p.47. This tiny, family-run one-star pension, tucked away above a souvenir shop overlooking the Manneken Pis, is perhaps the cheapest place to stay in the centre. It's certainly nothing special, but its six boxy rooms are perfectly adequate, simply furnished and each comes with shower and TV. There's free wi-fi

1

throughout, and breakfast – included in the price – is brought up to your room. **€95**

OUTSIDE THE PETIT RING

Argus rue Capitaine Crespel 6 ☎02 514 07 70, ⓦargus-hotel-brussels.com; Métro Louise; map pp.74–75. Although it's not in the city centre, this hotel enjoys a good location nonetheless, just to the south of the boulevards of the petit ring. The 42 modest rooms can be a bit on the small side, but they're cosy enough and the service is impeccable. A nice alternative to the gargantuan, expensive hotels that pepper this district. **€120**

L'Art de la Fugue rue de Suède 38 ☎0478 69 59 44, ⓦlartdelafugue.com; Métro Gare du Midi; map pp.74–75. At just a 2min walk from the Eurostar terminal, it's a shame this fabulous B&B doesn't have more rooms. Each of the three has its theme – "Laurence of Arabia" with an African flavour, "Indochina" with a collection of antique Buddhas, etc – and there's plenty of space to relax and enjoy the books and art of the owners, as well as an excellent continental breakfast. Book ahead as it quickly fills up. **€96**

Chambres en Ville rue de Londres 19 ☎02 512 92 90, ⓦchambresenville.be; Métro Trône; map pp.74–75. The four large and airy en-suite rooms in this distinguished, nineteenth-century Ixelles town house just off rue du Trône are decorated in a clever amalgam of traditional and modern styles. Each room is different, with boutique-style touches such as freestanding baths and original art on the walls, and rates include breakfast. **€110**

Du Congrès rue du Congrès 42 ☎02 217 18 90, ⓦhotelducongres.be; Métro Madou; map pp.52–53. Pleasant mid-range hotel occupying a set of attractive late nineteenth-century town houses in an appealing corner of the Upper Town. Each of the seventy-odd en-suite rooms is spacious and decorated in unfussy style. Published rates are high but there are always discounts. **€120**

Leopold rue du Luxembourg 35 ☎02 511 18 28, ⓦhotel-leopold.be; Métro Trône; map p.68. If you're staying in the EU quarter, it's easy to get stuck beside a thundering boulevard, but this fairly smart, four-star hotel has a first-rate location on a quiet(ish) side street, a brief walk from place du Luxembourg. There are over 100 guest rooms, all kitted out in no-nonsense, modern style. **€150**

Monty blvd Brand Whitlock 101 ☎02 734 56 36, ⓦmonty-hotel.be Métro Montogomery; map p.68. This pocket-sized place bills itself as a design hotel, and its eighteen guest rooms are housed in a handsome 1930s

mansion in which every fixture and fitting has been carefully chosen. **€100**

★**Steigenberger Grandhotel** ave Louise 71 ☎02 542 42 42, ⓦwww.steigenberger.com/Brussels; Métro Louise; map pp.74–75. Formerly the *Conrad*, this remains one of the capital's top hotels and former US President Clinton's top choice when in town. Housed in an immaculate tower block, with all sorts of retro flourishes, it boasts over 200 large and lavish rooms, comprehensive facilities and impeccable service. **€250**

Ursule la Libellule chaussée de Vleurgat 165 ☎0475 715 705, ⓦursule.be; tram #94 from Métro Louise; map pp.74–75. Two cosy en-suite rooms, decorated in pretty, country-cottage style, set in the garden of an old Ixelles town house. Guests are invited to help themselves to breakfast (included) from the fridge in the breakfast room, or there are plenty of cafés nearby. Discounts for stays of more than one night. **€110**

HOSTELS

Bruegel rue du Saint-Esprit 2 ☎02 511 04 36, ⓦwww.hihostels.com/hostels/brussels-brugel; Métro Gare Centrale; map pp.52–53. This official HI hostel, which occupies a functional modern building in a good location by the church of Notre-Dame de la Chapelle, has 135 beds in one- to four-berth rooms. A basic breakfast is included in the overnight fee. Note that there's a curfew. Dorm **€25**

Le Centre Vincent Van Gogh – CHAB rue Traversière 8 ☎02 217 01 58, ⓦchab.be; Métro Botanique; map pp.52–53. A rambling and spacious hostel with friendly staff, though things can seem a bit chaotic. Sinks in all rooms, but showers and toilets are shared, as is the launderette. Dorm **€21**, twin room **€57**

Jacques Brel rue de la Sablonnière 30 ☎02 218 01 87, ⓦwww.hihostels.com/hostels/brussels-jacques-brel-youth-hostel; Métro Madou or Botanique; map pp.52–53. This official HI hostel is maybe the best in the city, is modern and comfortable, and has a hotel-like atmosphere. All the one- to six-berth rooms have showers and breakfast is included in the price. There's no curfew and inexpensive meals can be bought at the café. Reservations advised. Dorm **€30**

Sleep Well rue du Damier 23 ☎02 218 50 50, ⓦsleepwell.be; Métro Rogier; map pp.52–53. Bright and breezy hostel close to the city centre and only a 5min walk from place Rogier. Hotel-style facilities plus a kitchen, bike rental and internet access. Sinks in every room, and shared showers. Dorm **€23**, twin **€63**

EATING AND DRINKING

Brussels can lay a decent claim to being one of Europe's best dining destinations, whatever your taste, price range or preferred cuisine. It's worth seeking out typically **Bruxellois** dishes, canny amalgamations of Walloon and Flemish ingredients and cooking styles, whether rabbit cooked in beer (usually Gueuze), *poulet à la Bruxelles*, fish or chicken *waterzooi*, or just plain *saucisses à la stoemp*. As for **where** to eat, as in the rest of Belgium the distinction between the city's cafés, café-bars and restaurants is fairly elastic: there are particular concentrations of bars and restaurants on and around place Ste-Catherine and Place St-Géry in the **Lower Town**, but really there are decent places to eat everywhere. **Drinking** in Brussels, as in the rest of the country, is a joy. The city boasts an enormous variety of **bars**: sumptuous Art Nouveau establishments, traditional joints with ceilings stained brown by a century's smoke, speciality beer bars with literally hundreds of different varieties of ale and, of course, more modern hangouts. Many of the more distinctive bars are handily located within a few minutes' walk of the **Grand-Place** and also in **Ixelles**, but really you'll be spoiled for choice.

RESTAURANTS

THE LOWER TOWN

Arcadi rue d'Arenberg 1B ☎ 02 511 3343; Métro Gare Centrale; map pp.52–53. At the north end of the Galeries St-Hubert, this busy café's long opening hours make it a perfect spot for breakfast, lunch, afternoon tea or a bite before the cinema. The menu offers lots of choices, but the salads, quiches and fruit tarts are particularly delicious and cost just a few euros each. Can get a little too crowded for comfort at lunch times. Daily 7.30am–11pm.

Au Bon Bol rue Paul Devaux 9 ☎ 02 513 16 88; Métro Bourse; map pp.52–53. You could walk right past this Chinese place and not notice it, but the vegetables are as fresh as they come and the noodles made on the premises. It's cheap too – huge bowls of noodle soup with beef, duck or seafood will set you back around €10. Not the place for a big night out though – your food is brought quickly and you're not encouraged to linger. Mon–Fri noon–3pm & 6–11pm, Sat & Sun noon–11pm.

Bar Bik quai aux Pierres de Taille 3 ☎ 02 219 75 00; Métro Rogier; map pp.52–53. This trendy Flemish restaurant, situated next to the Flemish-language theatre, is a bit of a culinary oasis in what is not a great neighbourhood, serving food that is rooted in Belgian styles and ingredients but with lots of international and contemporary twists. The menu changes regularly, and there are always lots of daily specials and veggie options, with starters going for around €10 and main courses for €20 or so. Mon–Sat noon–2pm & 6–9.30pm.

★ **Bij den Boer** quai aux Briques 60 ☎ 02 512 61 22, ⓦ bijdenboer.com; Métro Ste-Catherine; map pp.52–53. This atmospheric, bistro-style place with tiled floors and old posters on the walls is the best of the fish and seafood restaurants that line the Quais. Main courses average €25–35, but their four-course menus are excellent value at €29.50. Mon–Sat noon–2.30pm & 6–10.30pm.

Brasserie de la Roue d'Or rue des Chapeliers 26 ☎ 02 514 25 54; Métro Gare Centrale; map p.47. Just south of the Grand-Place, this is an eminently appealing old brasserie, with wood panelling, stained glass and brass fittings. It serves generous portions of Belgian regional specialities, with main courses hovering around €20–25. Daily noon–midnight, but closed for one month in summer, usually July.

La Cantina rue du Jardin des Olives 13–15 ☎ 02 513 42 76; Métro Anneessens; map pp.52–53. Brazilian warmth and exuberance at this colourful restaurant just west of the Grand-Place. The menu is short but awash with exotic ingredients, and naturally there are one or two cocktails to wash everything down. Buffet available at lunch times when you pay by weight, otherwise main courses around €15. Mon–Fri noon–3pm & 7–11pm, Sat 7–11pm.

Henri rue de Flandre 113–115 ☎ 02 218 00 08, ⓦ restohenri.be; Métro Ste-Catherine; map pp.52–53. Belgo-French fusion with everything made on site, right down to the stock cubes. The menu changes regularly, dishes are always seasonal and the ingredients top-notch. There's a lunch menu for €13, while the evening is à la carte – or rather from the blackboard – with mains (fish, steaks, croquettes, salads, mussels) for €12–18. Reservations recommended at all times. Tues–Fri noon–2.30pm & 6–10pm, Sat 6–10pm.

Houtsiplou place Rouppe 9 ☎ 02 511 38 16, ⓦ caat.be/houtsiplou; Métro Anneessens; map pp.52–53. This ode to Belgium features walls covered in cartoons depicting the country's history in true Surrealist style. An equally colourful menu offers home-made burgers with a plant pot of chips, a few Belgian classics and generous, delicious salads, plus a kids' menu. Pasta dishes around €12; most main courses around €14. Mon–Fri noon–2pm & 6–10.30pm, Sat noon–3pm & 6–10.30pm.

La Mirante Plattesteen 13 ☎ 02 511 15 80; Métro Bourse; map p.47. This small Italian serves the best pizza in the city, cooked in its wood-fired oven, along with all sorts of good and authentic Italian regional specialities. Always a few daily specials on offer. Pizzas from €8.50, pasta dishes from €10. Mon–Sat noon–2.30pm & 6–11.30pm. Closed Aug.

★ **Nuetnigenough** rue de Lombard 25 ☎ 02 513 78 84, ⓦ www.nuetnigenough.be; Métro Bourse; map p.47. You can't book at this small, unpretentious restaurant, but it's certainly worth a short wait – the Belgian food and beer are excellent and reasonably priced, and they tend to turn tables round quickly anyway. Lots of dishes are cooked in beer – including rabbit *à la Kriek* – and all come served with generous helpings of *stoemp* or fries and a salad for €13–17. Good beer list, too. Mon–Fri 5–11pm, Sat & Sun noon–11pm.

L'Ogenblik galerie des Princes 1 ☎ 02 511 61 51, ⓦ ogenblik.be; Métro Gare Centrale; map p.47. In the Galeries St-Hubert, this outstanding Franco-Belgian restaurant is kitted out in antique bistro style, right down to the ancient cash till, and serves a well-judged, wide-ranging menu that includes the basics – steak and chips with wild mushrooms, for instance – but also aims higher.

1

Starters from around €17; main courses €25–35. They also have an array of good-value three-course menus for €48–60. Mon–Sat noon–2.30pm & 7–11.30pm.

Orphyse Chaussette rue Charles Hanssens 5 ☎02 502 75 81; map pp.52–53. Chef and owner Philippe Renoux prides himself on original dishes with quality ingredients, and this cosy restaurant doesn't disappoint. There's always a non-meat dish available on the short, predominantly French menu too. The setting is candlelit and intimate, and the staff are willing to help you navigate your way around the extensive wine menu. Main dishes €15–25. Tues–Sat noon–2.30pm & 7–10pm.

Ploegmans rue Haute 148 ☎02 503 21 24, ⓦwww .ploegmans.be; Métro Gare Centrale; map pp.52–53. Situated right in the heart of the Marolles, this is one of Brussels' most authentic old brasseries, with lots of traditional grub, including meatballs or *carbonnades* with fries, steaks and *rognons de veau* (veal kidneys) for €14–17, and lots of hearty starters too for €12 upwards. Mon–Thurs noon–2.30pm & 6.30–9.30pm, Fri noon–2.30pm & 6.30–10.30pm, Sun noon–3pm.

★**Le Pré Salé** rue de Flandre 20 ☎02 513 65 45; Métro Ste-Catherine; map pp.52–53. Agreeable, typically Bruxellois neighbourhood restaurant, just off place Ste-Catherine, providing an appealing alternative to the swankier places nearby. The plain-cream tiled interior dates from the days it used to be a chip shop, but now the menu offers great mussels, fish dishes such as *anguilles au vert* (eels in a herb sauce) and other Belgian specialities; most mains go for around €20. Always crowded, not a place for a quiet dinner. Wed–Sun noon–2.30pm & 6.30–10.30pm.

★**Soul** rue de la Samaritaine 20 ☎02 513 52 13, ⓦsoulresto.com; Métro Gare Centrale; map pp.52–53. An evening at *Soul*, on the edge of the Marolles, is both a gastronomic delight and an education. The underpinning philosophy is that we are what we eat – but there's nothing ascetic about the mainly organic food. You can order à la carte – mains are €16–20, including lots of nice fish – or choose between the various themed menu options (Detox, Energy, etc), at €25–31 for two courses. Wed–Sat 7–10pm, Sun 7–9pm.

BEST OF BRUSSELS EATING

Bar food Monk see p.88
Belgian cuisine Nuetnigenough see p.85
Fish Mer du Nord/Noordzee see p.87
Health food Soul see p.86
Lunch Kwint see p.87
Moules-frites Le Pré Salé see p.86
Pizza La Mirante see p.85
Tapas Leonor see p.87

Vincent rue des Dominicains 8–10 ☎02 511 26 07, ⓦwww.restaurantvincent.com; Métro Bourse; map pp.52–53. This long-standing restaurant was a favourite with Jacques Brel and his cronies, who used to drink at the bar next door when it was called *Chez Stans*. The food is still good and you still have to walk through the kitchen to get to your table, which gives you a good view of the action. Belgo-French cuisine, with meat and seafood dishes that are a cut above what you'll find on nearby rue des Bouchers; main dishes €12–25. Daily noon–3pm & 6.30–11pm. Closed first two weeks in Aug.

Viva M'Boma rue de Flandre 17 ☎02 512 15 93; Métro Ste-Catherine; map pp.52–53. The name means "long live grandma" in the Brussels dialect, and this – a former tripe shop with minimalist decor – is one of the best stops in the city for tasting local cuisine prepared in the traditional manner. The food is great, and as refined or as rustic as you like, with lots of traditional Belgian dishes for €18–20. Always a handful of specials too. Mon, Tues & Thurs–Sat noon–2.30pm & 6.30–10.30pm.

UPPER TOWN AND THE EU QUARTER

Au Stekerlapatte rue des Prêtres 4 ☎02 512 86 81; Métro Hôtel des Monnaies; map pp.52–53. This long-established brasserie, on a side street tucked away behind the Palais de Justice, serves Franco-Belgian cuisine in a bustling atmosphere – great *carbonnades*, *stoemp*, steaks and other classics. Note that it gets pretty crowded. Tues–Thurs 7–11.30pm, Fri & Sat 7pm–1am.

Le Bier Circus rue de l'Enseignement 57 ☎02 218 00 34, ⓦbier-circus.be; Métro Parc; map pp.52–53. One of a number of restaurants on this popular Upper Town street, this place naturally has a great choice of beers but also lots of dishes cooked in them, including spaghetti bolognaise made with Chimay. Belgian classics too: meatballs in tomato sauce, *carbonnades flamandes*, fish *waterzooi*, etc. Bank on €14–17 for a main course. Tues–Fri 11.30am–2.30pm, & 6pm–midnight, Sat & Sun 6pm–midnight.

Café Bota rue Royale 236 ☎02 219 20 65, ⓦcafebota .be; Métro Botanique; map pp.52–53. Part of the Botanique arts centre (see p.91), this is perfect for a bite to eat before a concert, particularly if you sit out on the terrace – overlooking the city's skyscrapers, it's a very atmospheric spot at sunset. The food is basic, tasty, excellent-value Italian – the heaped antipasti plate is a winner, and there are good veggie options. Pasta dishes €11–12; *saltimbocca alla Romana* or escalope Milanese around €14. Daily 11am–11pm.

Et qui va promener le chien? rue de Rollebeek 2 ☎02 503 23 04, ⓦetquivaramenerlechien.be; Métro Gare Centrale; map pp.52–53. Situated on the pedestrianized street at the base of the Sablon, this curiously named restaurant – "And who is going to walk the dog?" – offers Belgian classics with a contemporary twist. All the old favourites are on offer: *waterzooi, carbonnade, boulettes* (meatballs) and at lunch they do a menu of starter, main course and coffee for just €15. Outside terrace too. Tues–Sun noon–2.30pm & 6–10.30pm.

L'Herbaudière place de la Liberté 9 ☎ 02 218 77 13; Métro Madou; map pp.52–53. Well-established Breton creperie in a lovely little square up near the Cirque Royale (see p.92). Long list of tasty sweet or savoury fillings (from €7.50) for the pancakes, which are prepared on the restaurant counter. Omelettes and salads too. The prim-and-proper decor is a good fit for this low-key, family-run café. Mon–Fri 11am–7pm.

Kwint Mont des Arts 1 ☎ 02 505 95 95, ⓦ kwintbrussels .com; Métro Gare; map pp.52–53. This smart, airy restaurant at the top of the Mont des Arts steps has nice views over the Lower Town and a real buzz about it, particularly at lunch times when they do an excellent-value three-course lunch for €19 (plus sandwiches and salads for upwards of €12). In the evening it feels like a special place to eat, without being the least bit pretentious. Food is Belgian with a few contemporary and international twists, with steaks, fish, risottos and pasta dishes for €16–20. Mon–Fri noon–2.30pm & 6–11.30pm, Sat 6–11pm, Sun 12.30–3pm & 6–11pm.

★ Mer du Nord/Noordzee rue de Luxembourg 62–64 ☎ 02 280 05 00, ⓦ vlshandelnoordzee.be; Métro Trone; map p.68. Just off Place du Luxembourg, spitting distance from the EU Parliament, this "fishbar" is the EU Quarter love child of the legendary stand-up seafood joint in Ste-Catherine. You still have to stand (at piles of fish crates) but the selection is slightly larger and there's a bit more space – you can eat out on the street and also upstairs. There are salads, sandwiches and all manner of fish and seafood goodies: succulent pieces of haddock, tuna, herring and tiny prawns, as sweet as you like. All come served with a big bowl of bread and salad, for just €5–8. Beer and wine too, if you want it. Mon–Wed 8am–8pm, Thurs 8am–10pm, Fri 8am–6pm.

THE OUTER NEIGHBOURHOODS

Dolma chaussée d'Ixelles 329 ☎ 02 649 89 81, ⓦ dolma.be; Métro Flagey; map pp.74–75. This new-agey, veggie joint is popular with the locals for the all-you-can-eat buffet lunch (€18) and dinner (€24.50). It offers a different set of menus each day and, although it's not the most refined vegetarian cuisine, it's good, tasty and excellent value. Tues–Sat noon–2pm & 7–9.30pm.

Leonor ave de la Porte de Hal 19 ☎ 02 537 51 56; Métro Porte de Hal; map pp.74–75. A real Brussels institution, this popular tapas bar and restaurant has been going strong for over thirty years. The ground floor doubles up as a bar, while upstairs the wooden tables and dimmer lighting make for more intimate dining. Most dishes go for between €14 and €20. No credit cards. Mon, Tues & Thurs–Sat noon–3pm & 6.30–10pm, Sun noon–3pm.

Quartier Libre rue Lesbroussart 16 ☎ 02 644 94 00; Métro Flagey; map pp.74–75. This bright and quirky restaurant offers a choice of four small dishes served together on your personalized tray. Each table has paper and pencils: you make your choice from the list on the blackboards, put your name on the top and hey presto! €17 for the four dishes, €11 for three at lunch. Mon noon–2pm, Tues–Fri noon–2pm & 7–10.30pm, Sat 7–10.30pm.

La Quincaillerie rue du Page 45 ☎ 02 533 98 33, ⓦ quincaillerie.be; map pp.74–75. Mouthwatering Franco-Belgian cuisine in this delightful restaurant, one of the longest-established in the ultra-cool Châtelain area. Set in an imaginatively converted old hardware shop with splendid Art Nouveau flourishes, it serves great fish and seafood (particularly oysters) and fabulous steaks, duck and chicken. Their "business lunch" menu is good value at €13.80, and there's a three-course evening menu for €29; à la carte mains run €17–25. Reservations advised, especially on Wednesday when the local market is on. Mon–Sat noon–2.30pm & 7pm–midnight, Sun 7pm–midnight.

Sale Pepe & Rosmarino rue Berckmans 98 ☎ 02 538 90 63; Métro Hôtel des Monnaies; map pp.74–75. Authentic, delicious Italian cuisine, where even the excellent pizzas are outdone by the frequently superb pastas and meat dishes, which change regularly according to the creative influence of owners Aurelio and Antonio. Main dishes around €12. Reservations essential. Mon–Fri noon–3pm & 7–11pm, Sat 7–11pm.

Volle Gas place Fernand Cocq 21 ☎ 02 502 89 17, ⓦ restaurant-volle-gas-bruxelles.be; Métro Port de Namur; map pp.74–75. This traditional, wood-panelled bar-brasserie serves classic Belgian cuisine in a friendly, family atmosphere. The Brussels specialities on offer include the delicious *carbonnades de boeuf à la Gueuze*, *waterzooi* and *lapin à la Kriek*, but there are also pastas and salads. Main dishes €12–20. Mon–Sat 11am–midnight.

Yamato rue Francart 11 ☎ 02 502 28 93; Métro Porte de Namur; map pp.74–75. Authentic Japanese food at this tiny, very modern place just round the corner from place St-Boniface. Affordable prices, though it's not the place for a leisurely lunch: it's eat and go Tokyo-style. Tues–Sat noon–2pm & 7–10pm, closed Thurs lunch time.

BARS AND CAFÉS

Belgians make little – or no – distinction between their bars and cafés: both serve alcohol, many stay open late (until 1am or even 2am) and most sell food as well. What you won't find (thank goodness) are lots of the coffee house chains that beleaguer so many big cities.

THE LOWER TOWN

À La Bécasse rue de Tabora 11 ⓦ alabecasse.com; Métro Bourse; map p.47. Just northwest of the Grand-Place, this old-fashioned, wood-panelled bar has long wooden benches

1

and ancient blue-and-white wall tiles. Authentic Lambic and Gueuze beer is served in earthenware jugs for just €5. Lots of snacks to go with your drink too. Mon–Thurs & Sun 11am–midnight, Fri & Sat 11am–1am.

Au Bon Vieux Temps rue du Marché aux Herbes 12; Métro Bourse; map p.47. Ancient little place tucked away down an alley near the Grand-Place. The building has all sorts of ancient bric-a-brac, including a stained-glass window which was originally in the local parish church. Popular with British servicemen just after the end of World War II, the bar still has old-fashioned signs advertising Mackenzie's port and Bass pale ale. Mon–Fri 11am–midnight, Sat & Sun 11am–2am.

Café Central rue Borgval 14 ✆0486 72 26 24, ⓦlecafecentral.com; Métro Bourse; map pp.52–53. Cool bar just off place St-Géry, with DJs, concerts and film screenings packing the agenda (see the website for details). You sometime have to battle at the bar for a drink, but there's a great atmosphere and clientele. Daily 5pm–1am.

Chaff place du Jeu de Balle 21, Marolles ✆02 502 58 48; Métro Gare du Midi; map pp.52–53. There's no better place to take in the hustle and bustle of the city's biggest and best flea market than at this amenable café-bar. There are some real bargains at lunch time from the blackboard menu, and it's also open in the evening for drinks only. Daily 8.30am–midnight.

Dolle Mol rue des Éperonniers 52; Métro Gare Centrale; map p.47. In the 1960s *Dolle Mol* was home to a band of anarcho-artistic regulars. Then it was closed down and the building abandoned until Jan Bucquoy – artist and political activist – came along and squatted in the building, eventually convincing the Flemish community to buy it as part of the local heritage. Now reopened, the beer is cheap and there is occasional entertainment. Wed–Sun 4pm–midnight.

★**La Fleur en Papier Doré** rue des Alexiens 53; Métro Gare Centrale; map pp.52–53. Cosy bar recently reopened by a group of enthusiasts keen to preserve this slice of Brussels heritage, *La Fleur* was one of the preferred watering holes of René Magritte, while novelist Hugo Claus apparently held his wedding reception here. Idiosyncratic antique decor and a good choice of beers, excellent house wine and classic Belgian food. Tues–Sat 11am–midnight, Sun 11am–7pm.

Café Le Fontainas rue Marché au Charbon 91; Métro Anneessens; map pp.52–53. Popular bar with a retro feel and a low-key gay affiliation. It's one of the nicest on this busy stretch, with Vedett on draught and lots of tables outside – but don't sit around waiting for a waiter as service is at the bar, which makes English folk feel very at home. Daily 11am–1am.

Le Greenwich rue des Chartreux 7; Métro Bourse; map pp.52–53. A short walk west of the Bourse, this is the city's

traditional chess café, with a lovely old wood-panelled, mirrored Interior and, in the men's, a fabulous antique ceramic urinal. Lots of hearty, reasonably priced Belgian food too. Daily 11am–midnight.

À l'Imaige de Notre-Dame impasse des Cadeaux, rue du Marché aux Herbes 6; Métro Bourse; map p.47. A welcoming, very quirky little bar, decorated like an old Dutch kitchen and situated at the end of a long, narrow alley. Good range of speciality beers – including seven on tap. Mon–Fri noon–midnight, Sat 3pm–2am, Sun 4pm–midnight.

De Markten rue de Vieux-Marché-aux-Grains 5 ⓦwww.demarkten.be; Métro Ste-Catherine; map pp.52–53. With a buzzy terrace and spacious interior, this Flemish bar is the pick of the places on place Marche-aux-Grains in Ste-Catherine, serving drinks and reasonable if unadventurous food – sandwiches, salads and omelettes from €4–6, and a few specials. Not the greatest service, but sitting outside on a summer's evening is a true Brussels experience. Mon–Sat 8.30am–midnight, Sun 10am–6pm.

Moeder Lambic Fontainas place Fontainas 8 ⓦwww.moederlambic.com; Métro Anneessens; map pp.52–53. Beer enthusiasts Jean Hummler and Nassim Dessicy have given a new lease of life to this small square off blvd Anspach, opening a sister-bar to the original behind the St Gilles town hall. Forty beers on tap and trained staff to give guidance and recommendations are enough temptation – particularly as these are not your run-of-the-mill beers, with small Belgian brewers such as Dupont, Val-Dieu and Cantillon from across the way in Anderlecht all on offer. Mon–Thurs & Sun 11am–1am, Fri & Sat 11am–2am.

★**Monk** rue Ste-Catherine 42 ⓦwww.monk.be; Métro Ste-Catherine; map pp.52–53. Named after the jazz musician Thelonious Monk, this big Ste-Catherine bar is probably the nicest place to drink in the area, with a few tables outside, and a large airy interior that attracts a young and largely Flemish-speaking crowd. Service is at the bar, and they serve lots of nice, thoroughly Belgian snacks – cheese, sausage, meatballs – as well as spaghetti dishes in the dining room at the back. Regular dancing and live music too. Mon–Thurs 11am–1am, Fri & Sat 11am–3am, Sun 1pm–1am.

À la Mort Subite rue Montagne aux Herbes Potagères 7 ⓦwww.alamortsubite.com; Métro Gare Centrale; map pp.52–53. Notorious 1920s bar that loaned its name to a popular bottled beer, occupying a long, narrow room with nicotine-stained walls, long tables and lots of mirrors. On a good night it's inhabited by a dissolute arty clientele, but on others by large groups of teenage tourists. Snacks are served, or just order a plate of cheese cubes to accompany your beer. Mon–Sat 11am–1am, Sun noon–midnight.

1

Café Novo place de la Vieille Halle aux Blés 37 ⓦ cafenovo.be; Métro Anneessens; map pp.52–53. Bright, quirky café with lots of original touches, from the menus in old books to the colourful selection of chairs both on the square out front and in the secluded back garden. Food – both Belgian and international – is available at lunch time and in the evening, and there's a wide selection of newspapers and books – *Novo* is part of a "book travelling" scheme. Mon–Sat noon–11.30pm, Sun noon–10.30pm.

Au Soleil rue Marché au Charbon 86; Métro Anneessens; map p.47. A short walk west from the Grand-Place, this popular bar, formerly a men's clothing shop, quenches the thirst of a young and arty Brussels clientele. Inexpensive bar snacks are on offer and there's a pavement terrace where you can while away the day over a coffee or something stronger. Generally laidback, but it's often difficult to get a seat come nightfall. Mon–Thurs & Sun 10am–1am, Fri & Sat 10am–2am.

Toone impasse Schuddeveld 6 ⓦ www.toone.be; map p.47. The bar of the famous Toone puppet theatre (see p.92), squeezed down a tight alley that most people walk straight by, and the perfect city-centre venue to enjoy a quiet beer and some good chat with a cat curled up next to you, overlooked by the puppets on the wall. Tues–Sun noon–midnight.

UPPER TOWN AND EU QUARTER

The Beer Factory place du Luxembourg 6, www.brasserie-beer-factory.be; Métro Trône; map p.68. A recent addition to the bevy of bars on this appealing square, metres from the European Parliament, and the chosen haunt of Eurocrats for after-work hobnobbing. Impressive building, with the centrepiece bar made out of an old beer vat and, as the name suggests, there's a good range of beers alongside some pretty decent food – *stoemp-saucisses*, *carbonades*, burgers and the like for €12, and specials for €9.95. Mon–Fri 10am–10.45pm.

Le Perroquet rue Watteeu 31; Métro Gare Central; map pp.52–53. Busy, semicircular café-bar occupying attractive Art Nouveau premises on a pleasant street corner. Imaginative range of stuffed pittas, salads and other tasty snacks – though you'll find it difficult to get a seat on Friday or Saturday night. Excellent beer menu. Daily noon–midnight.

Piola Libri rue Franklin 66–68 ⓦ www.piolalibri.be; Métro Trône; map p.68. Popular with EU workers, in particular the Italians, this Italian bookshop and bar is perfect for an *aperitivo*, with a selection of the tasty

antipasti on the counter to go with your glass of wine or prosecco. Mon noon–8pm, Sat noon–6pm.

THE OUTER NEIGHBOURHOODS

Café Belga place Flagey 18; Métro Flagey; map pp.74–75. This is a bar for any time of day: coffee and croissants on the terrace after the market, buffet lunches or an evening nibble before a film or concert at the cultural centre next door, and boozing into the early hours with the mixed crowd who flock here from all over the city. Daily 8am–2am.

Brasserie Verschueren parvis de St-Gilles 11–13; Métro Parvis de St-Gilles; map pp.74–75. Art Deco neighbourhood bar with a laidback atmosphere and football league results on the wall – essential in the days before television. A good range of Belgian beers, and food too (meatballs, spaghetti, *croques*, etc). Daily 11am–2am.

★**Café Maison du Peuple** parvis de St-Gilles 39 ⓦ cafemdp.be; Métro Parvis de St-Gilles; map pp.74–75. Built in 1907 for the education and entertainment of the workers, the "People's House" of St-Gilles is nowadays a spacious café hosting DJs and concerts, exhibiting local artists and providing a perfect spot for breakfast or lunch while visiting the market. Worth checking the website for what's on. Mon–Thurs & Sun 8.30am–1am, Fri & Sat 8.30am–3am.

Moeder Lambic rue de Savoie 68 ⓦ www .moederlambic.com; Métro Albert; map pp.74–75. This small and very popular bar, just behind the Hôtel de Ville in St-Gilles, has over a thousand beers available, including 500 or so Belgian varieties, mostly bottled. For a wider selection on draught, check out its sister bar in the Lower Town (see p.88). Mon–Thurs & Sun 11am–1am, Fri & Sat 11am–2am.

La Porteuse d'Eau ave Jean Volders 48a ⓦ www .laporteusedeau.be; Métro Porte de Hal; map pp.74–75. Refurbished Art Nouveau café on the corner of rue Vanderschrick, near the Porte de Hal. The food isn't up to much, but the beer menu is excellent and the ornate interior is well worth the price of a glass. Daily 11am–11pm.

L'Ultime Atome rue St-Boniface 14 ⓦ www .ultimeatome.be; Métro Porte de Namur; map pp.74–75. The large selection of beers and wines, simple but tasty food and late opening hours make this hip café-bar a hit with the fashionable Ixelles crowd on weekdays and weekends alike. Its location, on the appealing place St-Boniface, also makes it a great place to sit outside with a newspaper in the summer. Daily 8am–12.30am.

NIGHTLIFE AND ENTERTAINMENT

The city has a decent nightlife scene, including a number of established **clubs**, but most of the action revolves around nights with moveable locations – pick up flyers in bars and clubs for the latest and best events, or go to

ⓦbrussels.n1ght.com. Brussels is also a good place to catch **live music**, with a couple of central, well-established venues (see below) and festivals (see box below), plus a strong jazz scene. As for **classical music**, the Orchestre National de Belgique enjoys an international reputation (see p.92), while **opera** lovers should make a beeline for La Monnaie (see p.92). The free, trilingual *Agenda*, published every Thursday, has the most comprehensive **listings** of concerts and events, and can be picked up in most métro stations, bars and cafés. **Tickets** for most concerts are available at Fnac in the City 2 shopping complex on rue Neuve, or from the venue websites listed below; **last-minute tickets** are available at reduced prices at Arsène50, in the VisitBrussels office at rue Royale 2–4, or from ⓦarsene50.be.

CLUBS

Le Bazaar rue des Capucins 63, Marolles ☎02 511 26 00, ⓦbazaarbrussels.com; Métro Gare Centrale; map pp.52–53. Formerly a restaurant with music, this is now primarily a club, with two spaces for live music, DJs and dancing. Free. Tues–Thurs & Sun 7.30pm–midnight, Fri & Sat 7.30pm–4am.

The Fuse rue Blaes 208, Marolles ⓦfuse.be; Métro Gare du Midi; map pp.52–53. Widely recognized as the finest techno club in Belgium, this pulsating venue has played host to some of Europe's top DJs. Three floors of techno, house and occasional hip-hop, as well as the usual chill-out rooms and visuals. Tickets normally €8 before midnight, €12 after – more if there's a big-name DJ. Sat 11pm–7am.

Havana rue de l'Epée 4, Marolles ⓦhavana-brussels .com; Métro Gare Centrale; map pp.52–53. Off rue Haute, in the Marolles, just by the public lift, this Cuban-themed club is popular with a thirty-something expat crowd, who dance till dawn to the Latino tunes. Quite full on and not always friendly. Free. Thurs 7pm–2am, Fri 7pm–5am, Sat 7pm–7am.

★**Madame Moustache** quai aux Bruler 5–7 ⓦmadamemoustache.be; Métro Ste-Catherine; map pp.52–53. Centrally located bar and club that hosts live bands early on – indie, grunge, garage, that sort of thing – and has regularly themed evenings, from rock'n'roll to ska. Entry €5, €7 after midnight. Tues–Sat 7pm–4am.

You rue du Duquesnoy 18 ⓦleyou.be; Métro Gare Centrale; map p.47. A short walk southeast of the Grand-Place, *You* is one of the city's most notorious

clubs, with an interior designed by Miguel Câncio Martins (the man behind the *Buddha Bar* in Paris) and famously choosy doormen. Set over two levels, with comfy couches in the bar-lounge, DJs play everything from funk and disco to electro and house. There are gay tea dances on Sundays, too. Admission €10, including two drinks. Thurs–Sun 11.30pm–late.

LIVE MUSIC

AB (Ancienne Belgique) blvd Anspach 110 ☎02 548 24 24, ⓦabconcerts.be; Métro Bourse; map p.47. The capital's leading rock venue; artists perform either in the main auditorium or the smaller space on the first floor. Usually around four gigs a week. Usually closed from early July until the last week of Aug.

★**L'Archiduc** rue Antoine Dansaert 6 ☎02 512 06 52, ⓦarchiduc.net; Métro Bourse; map pp.52–53. Art Deco jazz bar with live sets on Mondays and at the weekend, including a free concert every Sat and Sun afternoon (from 5pm). Great cocktails, too. Daily 4pm–5am.

Beursschouwburg rue Auguste Orts 20–28 ⓦbeursschouwburg.be; Métro Bourse; map pp.52–53. Occupying a handsomely restored building from 1885, this is a fine venue that makes the most of its different spaces, from the cellar to the stairs, the theatre to the café. Features DJs of all genres, plus an eclectic live music programme catering for a wide range of tastes. Thurs–Sat 7pm–late.

Botanique rue Royale 236 ☎02 218 37 32, ⓦbotanique.be; Métro Botanique; map pp.52–53. The Francophone cultural centre hosts exhibitions and regular live music– look out especially for Les Nuits Botanique in

FESTIVALS IN BRUSSELS

Like most European capitals, there's always something going on in Brussels, and the city hosts a number of cultural and arts events throughout the year. The city's **Gay Pride** festival (ⓦthepride.be) takes place in May and has attracted more than 100,000 people in recent years. The *Rainbow House* (see p.93) plays a big part in organizing proceedings. The **Vendôme** cinema (see p.93) hosts the city's annual gay and lesbian film festival in February. Other **film festivals** include the Flagey Cinema's Brussels Festival of European Film in the first two weeks of June (ⓦfffb.be) and the utterly fantastical Brussels Festival of Fantasy Film, Science Fiction and Thrillers (ⓦbifff.net) in April. **Music festivals** include the internationally acclaimed Jazz Marathon held every May (ⓦbrusselsjazzmarathon.be); the Ars Musica festival of contemporary classical music held in March (ⓦarsmusica.be); and May's prestigious Concours Musical Reine Elisabeth competition (ⓦconcours-reine-elisabeth.be).

1

May to hear lots of new bands in a festival atmosphere. Usually closed for concerts during July & Aug.

BOZAR rue Ravenstein 23 ☎ 02 507 82 00, ⓦ bozar .be; Métro Gare Centrale; map pp.52–53. August venue that presents an innovative programme of events including theatre, world music and themed cultural nights in its 2000-seater Art Deco concert hall, as well as several smaller auditoria. Hosts the Orchestre National de Belgique (ⓦ nob.be) and the Rideau de Bruxelles theatre company.

Cirque Royal rue de l'Enseignement 81 ☎ 02 218 20 15, ⓦ cirque-royal.org; Métro Madou; map pp.52–53. Formerly an indoor circus, the Upper Town's Cirque Royal works with the Botanique down below. The larger venue of the two, it is a regular on the roster of big-name rock, pop and jazz tours.

Flagey place Sainte-Croix, Ixelles ☎ 02 641 10 20, ⓦ flagey.be; Métro Flagey map pp.74–75. Place Flagey's wonderful Art Deco cultural centre hosts a regular roster of eclectic live music from world to orchestral to jazz. Always something interesting.

Forest National ave du Globe 36 ☎ 0900 00 991, ⓦ forestnational.be; tram #32 from the city centre, #82 from Gare du Midi or #97 from Louise; get off at stop Zaman. This large arena is Brussels' main venue for big-name international concerts, with space for around 11,000 people.

Magazin 4 ave du Port 51 ☎ 02 223 34 74, ⓦ magasin4 .be; Métro Yser; map pp.52–53. In an old warehouse off blvd d'Anvers, this is a favourite venue for up-and-coming Belgian indie bands, as well as a smattering of punk, rap and hip-hop. Entrance is around €10. Only open for gigs, but usually 8pm–5am.

Sounds rue de la Tulipe 28, Ixelles ☎ 02 512 92 50, ⓦ soundsjazzclub.be; Métro Porte de Namur; map pp.74–75. Off place Fernand Cocq, this atmospheric café has showcased both local and internationally acclaimed jazz acts for over twenty years. Live music most nights (from around 10pm), but the biggies usually appear Sat. Mon–Sat 8pm–4am.

THEATRE AND OPERA

La Monnaie place de la Monnaie ☎ 02 229 12 11, ⓦ lamonnaie.be; Métro De Brouckère. Belgium's premier opera house consistently earns glowing reviews and is much

lauded for its adventurous repertoire. It nurtures promising singers rather than casting the more established stars, Is home to Brussels' main dance venue, hosts classical concerts and chamber music recitals, and overall has a reputation for contemporary interpretations of classic operas and an eclectic repertoire (Maurice Béjart's old company regularly performs here). Book well in advance.

Théâtre Royal de Toone Impasse Schuddeveld 6 ☎ 02 511 71 37, ⓦ www.toone.be; Métro Bourse or Gare Centrale. Puppet theatre with a long and distinguished pedigree offering one performance every evening, two on Saturdays, mostly in French but sometimes in the traditional Bruxellois dialect known as Brusselse Sproek or Marollien, a colourful, ribald brand of Flemish which is in danger of dying out. Entry €10 (no cards).

The Warehouse rue Waelham 69A ☎ 02 203 53 03, ⓦ atcbrussels.com; tram #92 from Louise or #55 from place Rogier. Home of the American Theatre Company, English Comedy Club and the Irish Theatre Group, who perform here in English as well as at other locations around the city.

CINEMA

In Brussels, the vast majority of films are shown in the original language and subtitled in French and/or Flemish (coded "VO", version originale). The main exception is in a few of the multi-screen cinemas, where some films, especially kids' movies, are likely to be dubbed into French (look out for "VF", version française). Brussels has an excellent range of small cinemas and these consistently undercut prices at the multi-screens, though you are expected to tip the usher who checks your ticket – 50 cents will do. The city's annual film festivals are highly recommended (see box, p.91). Cinemas usually change their programmes on Wednesday.

Actors' Studio rue de la Fourche 17–19 ☎ 02 512 16 96, ⓦ actorsstudio.cinenews.be; Métro Bourse or Gare Centrale. This small cinema is a good place to catch art-house or independent films. It's cheaper than its more commercial rivals and has the added advantage that you can buy a beer or a coffee from outside and take it in with you.

Flagey Cinema place Sainte-Croix, Ixelles ☎ 02 641 10 20, ⓦ flagey.be; Métro Flagey. Part of place Flagey's Art Deco cultural centre, this studio cinema showcases an

---

FOOTBALL IN BRUSSELS

Brussels has several soccer teams, of which **Royal Sporting Club (RSC) Anderlecht** (☎ 02 529 40 67, ⓦ rsca.be) is by far the best known. They play in the Jupiler Pro League and their stadium is the **Stade Constant Vanden Stock**, at ave Théo Verbeeck 2, within comfortable walking distance of Métro St-Guidon. It has a capacity of 21,000 and tickets for home games cost a very reasonable €25–35, if you can get one – games are frequently sold out. Your best bet is to try at the stadium box office (Mon–Fri 9am–5.30pm, Sat 10am–noon) – you'll need your passport – or various online sites such as ⓦ viagogo.com.

impressive range of films, usually focusing on a particular genre or director, and is main host to the Brussels Festival of European Film (see box, p.91).

Vendôme chaussée de Wavre 18, Ixelles ☎02 502 37 00, ⓦwww.cinema-vendome.be; Métro Porte de Namur. Five-screen cinema that's well known for its wide selection of art films as well as more mainstream flicks. Also hosts a number of film festivals dedicated to short films, plus Brazilian, Arab and gay and lesbian film (see box, p.91). They offer a multiple ticket – six films for €30.30 – which is pretty good value.

GAY AND LESBIAN

The focus of the city's scene is the Rainbow House at rue Marché au Charbon 42 (☎02 503 59 90, ⓦrainbowhouse .be; Mon–Fri 10am–6pm), in the heart of Brussels' gay area, where you can pick up all sorts of up-to-date information. They also help to organize the city's Gay Pride festival (see box, p.91).

Le Belgica rue Marché au Charbon 32 ⓦlebelgica.be; Métro Bourse; map p.47. Arguably the capital's most popular gay bar and pick-up joint. It's a tad run-down, with Formica tables and dilapidated chairs that have seen better days, but if you're out for a lively, friendly atmosphere, you could do a lot worse. Come at the weekend when the place is heaving – all are welcome, whether male, female, gay or straight – and be sure to slam back a few of the house speciality lemon-vodka "Belgica" shots. Thurs–Sat 10pm–3am.

Chez Maman rue des Grands Carmes 7 ⓦchezmaman .be; Métro Anneessens; map pp.52–53. Not a lesbian place per se, but this tiny bar has achieved cult-like status for the transvestite cabaret of the proprietor, Maman, with crowds flocking in from all corners of Brussels to see him and his protégés strut up and down. Jam-packed every weekend. Occasional lesbian nights Thurs, otherwise Fri & Sat midnight until dawn.

La Démence at The Fuse rue Blaes 208, Marolles ☎02 538 99 31, ⓦlademence.com; Métro Gare du Midi; map pp.52–53. The city's most popular gay party night, held monthly on two floors in The Fuse (see p.91) and playing cutting-edge techno. Bus-loads of guys from Amsterdam, Cologne and Paris muster here, making the crowd a bit difficult to pigeonhole – expect to find a hybrid mix of muscle men, transsexuals and out-and-out ravers. Check website for dates. Usually last Fri of the month 11pm–7am.

Le Duquesnoy rue Duquesnoy 12 ☎02 502 38 83, ⓦduquesnoy.com; Métro Gare Centrale; map p.47. Simply "Le Duq" to its regulars, this gay bar/club is open every night and is fairly hardcore, with a leather/rubber/ latex/uniform dress code – no suits or ties. Mon–Thurs & Sun 9pm–3am, Fri & Sat 9pm–4am.

Homo Erectus rue des Pierres 57, ⓦlhomoerectus .com; Métro Bourse; map p.47. Another long-standing stalwart of the Brussels gay scene, situated in the heart of the gay village and attracting a mixed crowd for drinks, shows, drag nights and more. Daily 4pm–2am.

SHOPPING

Brussels has a supreme selection of small, **independent shops**, a good range of **open-air markets** and a number of **charming galleries**: covered shopping "streets" dating back to the nineteenth century. The main downtown shopping street, **rue Neuve**, is dominated by chain stores; the **Galeries St-Hubert**, near the Grand-Place, are much more distinctive, accommodating a smattering of upmarket shops and stores, while the nearby **Galerie Agora** peddles bargain-basement leather jackets, incense, jewellery and ethnic goods. Behind the Bourse, rue Antoine Dansaert caters for the young and fashionable, housing the stores of **upcoming designers** as well as big Belgian names like Strelli, and nearby streets like rue des Riches Claires and rue du Marché au Charbon are good for **streetwear**. Avenue Louise and around is home to the big **international designers**. More than anything else, however, Brussels is famous for three things: **comic strips**, **chocolate** and **beer**, and there are shops all over the city centre selling all three – place du Grand Sablon alone has at least half a dozen chocolate shops.

BOOKS AND COMICS

La Boutique Tintin rue de la Colline 13 ☎02 514 51 52, ⓦtintinboutique.com; Métro Gare Centrale; map p.47. Tintinarama, from comics to all sorts of branded goods – postcards, stationery, figurines, T-shirts and sweaters. Geared up for the tourist trade, it's located just off the Grand-Place. Mon–Sat 10am–6pm, Sun 11am–5pm.

★**Brüsel** blvd Anspach 100 ☎02 511 08 09, ⓦbrusel .com; Métro Bourse; map p.47. This vital comic shop stocks more than eight thousand new issues and specializes in French underground editions – *Association, Amok* and *Bill*, to

name but three. You'll also find the complete works of Belgian comic-book artist Schuiten, most popularly known for his controversial comic *Brüsel*, which depicts the architectural destruction of a city (guess which one) in the 1960s. Mega Tintin collection and small English section too. Mon–Sat 10.30am–6.30pm, Sun noon–6.30pm.

Passa Porta rue Antoine Dansaert 46 ☎02 502 94 60, ⓦpassaporta.be; Métro Ste-Catherine; map pp.52–53. The manager of this book-lover's haven practises his theory that you wouldn't buy clothes without first trying them on – and the same goes for books – hence the readings and regular events in all languages here, with guest authors

1

and an increasingly popular literary festival in March. About ten percent of the total stock is in English. Mon–Sat 11am–7pm, Sun noon–6pm.

Slumberland rue des Sables 20 ☎ 02 219 19 80, ⓦ slumberlandbd.com; Métro Botanique; map pp.52–53. Based in the Centre Belge de la Bande Dessinée (see p.55), and worth a visit whether or not you're visiting the museum, with one of the city's best selections of comics and graphic novels. Tues–Sun 10am–6pm.

Sterling Books rue du Fossé aux Loups 38 ☎ 02 223 78 35, ⓦ www.sterlingbooks.be; Métro De Brouckère; map pp.52–53. The largest independent English-language bookshop in Belgium, with more than 40,000 UK and US titles, including a decent selection of magazines. There's a children's corner with a small play area too. Mon–Sat 10am–6pm.

CHOCOLATES

★ **Frederic Blondeel Chocolatier** quai aux Briques 24 ☎ 02 502 21 31, ⓦ frederic-blondeel.com; Métro Ste-Catherine; map pp.52–53. This café-cum-shop from the renowned Flanders chocolatier is simply paradise for chocolate connoisseurs. All the chocolate is made on site, beautifully displayed and reasonably priced, while the café's Madagascan chocolate and Tahitian vanilla ice cream in a chocolate-filled cone is heaven on earth. Mon–Fri 10.30am–6.30pm, Sat 10.30am–10.30pm, Sun 1–6.30pm.

Galler rue au Beurre 44 ☎ 02 502 02 66, ⓦ galler.com; Métro Bourse; map p.47. Galler is the chocolatier to the king – and therefore the holder of the Royal Warrant – but is still less well known than many of its rivals, and rarely seen outside Belgium, so a good choice for a special present. Excellent dark chocolate – 250g will set you back €13.90. Daily 10am–10pm.

Pierre Marcolini rue des Minimes 1 ☎ 02 514 12 06, ⓦ marcolini.be; Métro Louise; map pp.52–53. Grand Sablon flagship store of the chocolatier considered by many to be the best in the world. Pierre Marcolini is a true master of his art – try his spice- and tea-filled chocolates to get the point. Classy service, beautiful packaging and a mouthwatering choice of chocolate cakes. On a winter weekend you can have a glass of wonderful hot chocolate at the shop's small bar. Mon–Thurs 10am–7pm, Fri & Sat 10am–8pm, Sun 11am–6pm.

Wittamer place du Grand Sablon 6 ☎ 02 512 37 42, ⓦ wittamer.com; Métro Louise; map pp.52–53. Brussels' most famous patisserie and chocolate shop, established in 1910 and still run by the Wittamer family, who sell gorgeous (if expensive) light pastries, cakes, mousses and chocolates. They also serve speciality teas and coffees in their tearoom along the street at no. 12. Mon 8am–6pm, Tues–Sat 7am–7pm, Sun 7am–6pm.

FOOD AND DRINK

Beer Mania chaussée de Wavre 174–176, Ixelles ☎ 02 512 17 88, ⓦ www.beermania.be; Métro Trone; map pp.74–75. A drinker's heaven, this shop stocks more than 400 different types of beer, and you can even buy the correct glass to match your favourite. It's one of the few places where you can get hold of the elusive Trappist beer from Westvleteren (€12 per bottle), usually only for sale at the abbey gates, and there's a small bar, where you can taste before you buy. The owner's own brew, Mea Culpa, includes ten different herbs and is served in an impressive Bohemian glass. Mon–Sat 11am–9pm.

Dandoy rue au Beurre 31 ☎ 02 511 03 26, ⓦ maisondandoy.com; Métro Bourse; map p.47. Biscuits have been made at this famous shop just off the Grand-Place since 1829, so it's no surprise they have it down to a fine art. The main speciality is known locally as "speculoos", a kind of hard gingerbread which comes in every size and shape imaginable – the largest are the size of a small child and cost as much as €50. Daily 10am–7pm.

★ **Délices et Caprices** rue des Bouchers 68 ☎ 02 512 14 51, ⓦ the-belgian-beer-tasting-shop.be; Métro Gare Centrale; map p.47. Probably the city centre's best beer store, not just because owner Pierre sources some truly unusual and special brews, but also for their tasting sessions with food. Mon & Thurs–Sun noon–8pm.

La Maison du Miel rue du Midi 121 ☎ 02 512 32 50, ⓦ lamaisondumiel.be; Métro Bourse; map p.47. As the name suggests, this tiny, family-run shop is stacked high with jar upon jar of honey and its multifarious by-products, from soap to candles, plus a number of curious honeypots and receptacles. Mon–Sat 9.30am–6pm.

La Maison du Thé Plattesteen 11 ☎ 02 512 32 26; Métro Bourse; map p.47. A shop dedicated to the good old cuppa, but a far cry from the average English brew. Floor-to-ceiling tins harbour a vast range of teas to smell, taste and buy. Lots of tea-related paraphernalia too. Tues–Sat 9am–7pm.

MARKETS

Ateliers des Tanneurs rue de Tanneurs 58–62, Marolles; Métro Gare du Midi; map pp.52–53. Indoor organic food market in a good-looking Art Nouveau building on the west side of the Marolles quarter. Good prices for high-quality products, mostly from local producers, plus a café that serves an excellent brunch buffet at weekends. Fri–Sun 10am–3pm.

Gare du Midi Métro Gare du Midi; map pp.52–53. One of Brussels' largest and most colourful food markets is held here outside the main station every Sunday, with traders crammed under the railway bridge and spilling out into the surrounding streets. Among the vegetables and cheap clothes, numerous stands sell pitta, olives, North African raï music cassettes, spices and herbs. There's a first-rate flower and plant section too. Sun 6am–1.30pm.

Place du Grand Sablon Métro Louise; map pp.52–53. The swankiest antiques and collectables market in town, and plenty of pricey antique shops in the surrounding streets too. Sat 9am–6pm, Sun 9am–2pm.

Place du Jeu de Balle Marolles; Métro Gare du Midi; map pp.52–53. This sprawling flea market opens up every morning, but it's at its biggest and best on the weekend, when an eccentric muddle of colonial spoils, quirky odds and ends, and domestic and ecclesiastical bric-a-brac give an impression of a century's fads and fashions. Daily 7am–2pm.

DIRECTORY

Banks and exchange There are ATMs dotted right across the city centre, including one at Grand-Place 7 and another at rue Marché-aux-Herbes 6. There are also bureaux de change with extended opening hours at Gare du Midi (Mon–Sat 7am–8.30pm, Sun 9am–5pm) and Gare du Nord (Mon–Fri 8am–6pm, Sat 9am–3pm).

Dentist Standby municipal dentist ☎ 02 426 10 26.

Doctor Standby municipal doctor ☎ 02 479 18 18.

Embassies Australia, ave des Arts 56 ☎ 02 286 05 00; Canada, ave de Tervuren 2 ☎ 02 741 06 11; Ireland, chaussée d'Etterbeek 180 ☎ 02 282 34 00; New Zealand, ave des Nerviens 9–31 ☎ 02 512 10 40; UK, ave d'Auderghem 10 ☎ 02 287 62 11; US, blvd du Régent 27 ☎ 02 811 40 00.

Emergencies Phone ☎ 112.

Left luggage There are coin-operated lockers at all three main train stations.

Lost property For the métro, buses and trams, the lost property office is at ave de la Toison d'Or 15 (Mon, Wed & Fri noon–5.30pm, Wed & Thurs noon–7pm; ☎ 02 515 23 94).

Post The main post office is at Gare du Midi, exit rue Fonsny (Mon–Fri 8am–7.30pm & Sat 10.30am–4.30pm). Post office counters are located in many supermarkets.

Pharmacies Multipharma, near the Grand-Place at rue du Marché aux Poulets 37 (☎ 02 511 35 90). Details of 24hr pharmacies are available on ☎ 070 66 01 60 or ⓦ servicedegarde.be, and details of duty pharmacies are usually posted on the front door of every pharmacy.

Police Brussels Central Police Station, rue du Marché au Charbon 30 ☎ 02 279 79 79.

Flanders

GHENT

Flanders

The Flemish-speaking provinces of West Vlaanderen and Oost Vlaanderen (West Flanders and East Flanders) roll east from the North Sea coast, stretching out towards Brussels and Antwerp. With the exception of the range of low hills around Oudenaarde and the sea dunes along the coast, Flanders is pretty much pancake-flat, a wide-skied landscape seen at its best in its quieter recesses, where poplar trees and whitewashed farmhouses decorate sluggish canals. There are also many reminders of Flanders' medieval greatness, beginning with the ancient and fascinating cloth cities of Bruges and Ghent, both of which hold marvellous collections of early Flemish art.

Less familiar is the region's clutch of intriguing smaller towns, most memorably **Oudenaarde**, which has a delightful town hall and is famed for its tapestries; **Kortrijk**, with its classic small-town charms; and **Veurne**, whose main square is framed by a beguiling medley of fine old buildings. There is also, of course, the legacy of **World War I**. By 1915, the trenches extended from the North Sea coast to Switzerland, cutting across West Flanders via Diksmuide and Ieper, and many of the key engagements of the war were fought here. Every year hundreds of visitors head for **Ieper** (formerly Ypres) to see the numerous cemeteries and monuments around the town – sad reminders of what proved to be a desperately pointless conflict. Not far from the battlefields, the Belgian coast is **beach** territory, an almost continuous stretch of golden sand that is crowded with tourists every summer. An excellent **tram** service connects all the major seaside resorts, and although a lot of the development has been crass, cosy **De Haan** has kept much of its late nineteenth-century charm. The largest town on the coast is **Ostend**, a lively seaside resort sprinkled with popular bars and restaurants, the pick of which sell a wonderful range of seafood.

Brief history

As early as the thirteenth century, Flanders was one of the most prosperous parts of Europe, with an advanced, integrated economy dependent on the **cloth trade** with England. The boom times lasted a couple of centuries, but by the sixteenth century, with trade slipping north towards the Netherlands and England's cloth manufacturers beginning to undermine Flanders' economic base, the region was in decline. The speed of the collapse was accelerated by **religious wars**, for though the great Flemish towns were by inclination Protestant, their kings and queens were Catholic. Flanders sank into poverty

OSTEND BEACH

Highlights

❶ Bruges By any measure, Bruges is one of western Europe's most beautiful cities, its jangle of ancient houses overlooking a cobweb of picturesque canals. **See pp.101–125**

❷ Ostend beach The Belgian coast boasts a first-rate sandy beach for almost its entire length, and Ostend has an especially fine slice. **See p.127**

❸ Ieper Flanders witnessed some of the worst of the slaughter of World War I, and Ieper is dotted with the sad and mournful reminders. **See pp.138–143**

❹ Flemish tapestries Small-town Oudenaarde was once famous for its tapestries, and a superb selection is on display today. **pp.151–152**

❺ Ghent's Adoration of the Mystic Lamb This wonderful Jan van Eyck painting is absolutely unmissable. **pp.155–160**

HIGHLIGHTS ARE MARKED ON THE MAP ON P.100

and decay, a static, priest-ridden and traditional society where nearly every aspect of life was controlled by decree, and only three percent of the population could read or write.

With precious little say in the matter, the Flemish peasantry of the seventeenth and eighteenth centuries saw their lands crossed and re-crossed by the armies of the Great Powers, for it was here that the relative fortunes of dynasties and nations were decided. Only with **Belgian independence** did the situation begin to change: the towns started to industrialize, tariffs protected the cloth industry, Zeebrugge was built and Ostend was modernized, all in a flurry of activity that shook Flanders from its centuries-old torpor. This steady progress was severely interrupted by the German occupations of both world wars, but Flanders has emerged prosperous, its citizens maintaining a distinctive cultural and linguistic identity, often in sharp opposition to their Walloon (French-speaking) neighbours.

Bruges

Passing through **BRUGES** in 1820, William Wordsworth declared that this was where he discovered "a deeper peace than in deserts found". Crowds tend to overwhelm the place nowadays – its reputation as a perfectly preserved medieval city has made it the most popular tourist destination in Belgium – but you'd be mad to come to Flanders and miss it: Bruges' museums hold some of the country's finest collections of Flemish art, and its intimate, winding streets, woven around a skein of narrow canals and lined with gorgeous ancient buildings, live up to even the most inflated tourist hype.

Wordsworth was neither the first nor the last Victorian to fall in love with Bruges; by the 1840s there was a substantial **British colony** here, its members enraptured by the city's medieval architecture and air of lost splendour. Neither were the expatriates slow to exercise their economic muscle, applying an architectural **Gothic Revival** brush to parts of the city that weren't "medieval" enough. Time and again, they intervened in municipal planning decisions, allying themselves to like-minded Flemings in a movement that changed, or at least modified, the face of the city. Thus, Bruges is not the perfectly preserved medieval city of much tourist literature, but rather a clever, frequently seamless combination of medieval original and nineteenth- and sometimes twentieth-century additions.

The obvious start to an exploration of the city is the two principal squares: the **Markt**, overlooked by the mighty **belfry**, and the **Burg**, flanked by the city's most impressive architectural ensemble. Almost within shouting distance are the three main museums, among which the **Groeninge** offers a wonderful sample of early Flemish art. Another short hop brings you to **St-Janshospitaal** and the important paintings of the fifteenth-century artist **Hans Memling**, as well as Bruges' most impressive churches, the **Onze Lieve Vrouwekerk** and **St-Salvatorskathedraal**. Further afield, the gentle canals and maze-like cobbled streets of eastern Bruges – stretching out from **Jan van Eyckplein** – are extraordinarily pretty. The most characteristic architectural feature is the crow-step gable, popular from the fourteenth to the eighteenth century and revived by the restorers of the 1880s, but there are also expansive Georgian-style mansions and humble, homely cottages. Time and again the eye is surprised by the sober and subtle variety of the cityscape, featuring everything from intimate arched doorways and bendy tiled roofs to wonky chimneys and a bevy of discreet shrines and miniature statues.

Brief history

Bruges started out as a ninth-century fortress built by the warlike first count of Flanders, **Baldwin Iron Arm**, who was intent on defending the Flemish coast from Viking attack. The settlement prospered, and by the fourteenth century it shared effective control of the **cloth trade** with its two great rivals, Ghent and Ypres (now Ieper), turning high-quality English wool into clothing that was exported all over the known world. An immensely profitable business, it made the city a focus of international trade, and at its peak the town was a key member of – and showcase for the products of – the **Hanseatic League**, the most powerful economic alliance in medieval Europe. Through the harbours and docks of Bruges, Flemish cloth and Hansa goods were exchanged for hogs from Denmark, spices from Venice, hides from Ireland, wax from Russia, gold and silver from Poland and furs from Bulgaria. The business of these foreign traders was protected by no fewer than 21 consulates, and the city developed a wide range of support services, including banking, money-changing and maritime insurance.

Trouble and strife

Despite (or perhaps because of) this lucrative state of affairs, Bruges was dogged by **war**. Its weavers and merchants were dependent on the goodwill of the **kings of England** for the proper functioning of the wool trade, but their feudal overlords, the counts of Flanders, and their successors, the dukes of Burgundy (from 1384), were vassals of the rival **king of France**. Although some of the dukes and counts were strong enough to defy their king, most felt obliged to obey his orders and thus take his side against the English when the two countries were at war. This conflict of interests was compounded by the designs the French monarchy had on the independence of Bruges itself. Time and again, the French sought to assert control over the cities of West Flanders, but more often than not they encountered armed rebellion. In Bruges, **Philip the Fair** precipitated the most famous insurrection at the beginning of the fourteenth century. Philip and his wife, Joanna of Navarre, had held a grand reception in Bruges, but it had only served to feed their envy. In the face of the city's splendour, Joanna moaned, "I thought that I alone was Queen, but here in this place I have six hundred rivals". The opportunity to flex royal muscles came shortly afterwards when the city's guildsmen flatly refused to pay a new round of taxes. Enraged, Philip dispatched an army to restore order and garrison the town, but at dawn on Friday May 18, 1302, a rebellious force of Flemings crept into the city and massacred Philip's sleepy army – an occasion later known as the **Bruges Matins**: anyone who couldn't correctly pronounce the Flemish shibboleth *schild en vriend* ("shield and friend") was put to the sword. There is a statue celebrating the leaders of the insurrection – Jan Breydel and Pieter de Coninck – in the Markt (see below).

Decline and revival

The **Habsburgs**, who inherited Flanders – as well as the rest of present-day Belgium and the Netherlands, in 1482 – chipped away at the power of the Flemish cities, no-one more so than **Emperor Charles V**. As part of his policy, Charles favoured Antwerp at the expense of Flanders and, to make matters worse, the Flemish cloth industry began its long decline in the 1480s. Bruges was especially badly hit and, as a sign of its decline, failed to dredge the silted-up **River Zwin**, the town's trading lifeline to the North Sea. By the 1510s, the stretch of water between Sluis and Damme was only navigable by smaller ships, and by the 1530s the city's sea trade had collapsed completely. Bruges simply withered away, its houses deserted, its canals empty and its money spirited north with the merchants. Some four centuries later, **Georges Rodenbach**'s novel *Bruges-la-Morte* alerted well-heeled Europeans to the town's aged, quiet charms, and Bruges – frozen in time – escaped damage in both world wars to emerge as the perfect tourist attraction.

The Markt

At the heart of Bruges is the **Markt**, an airy open space edged on three sides by rows of gabled buildings and with horse-drawn buggies clattering over the cobbles. The burghers of nineteenth-century Bruges were keen to put something suitably civic in the middle of the square and the result was the conspicuous **monument** to the leaders of the Bruges Matins (see p.102), Pieter de Coninck, of the guild of weavers, and Jan Breydel, dean of the guild of butchers. Standing close together, they clutch the hilt of the same sword, their faces turned to the south in slightly absurd poses of heroic determination.

The biscuit-tin buildings flanking most of the Markt form a charming architectural chorus, their mellow ruddy-brown brick shaped into a long string of pointed gables, each slightly different from its neighbour. Most are late nineteenth- or even twentieth-century re-creations – or re-inventions – of older buildings, though the old **post office**, which hogs the east side of the square, is a thunderous neo-Gothic edifice from 1878 that refuses to camouflage its modern construction – witness the squat and square windows.

Belfort

Markt • Daily 9.30am–5pm • €8 • ☎ 050 44 87 43, ⓦ visitbruges.be • Entry via the Hallen (see below)

Filling out the south side of the Markt, the mighty **Belfort** was long a potent symbol of civic pride and municipal independence, its distinctive octagonal lantern visible for many kilometres across the surrounding polders. The Belfort was begun in the thirteenth century, when the town was at its richest and most extravagant, but has had a blighted history. The original wooden version was struck by lightning and burned to the ground in 1280. Its brick replacement received its octagonal stone lantern and a second wooden spire in the 1480s, but the new spire was lost to a thunderstorm a few years later. Undeterred, the Flemings promptly added a third spire, though when this went up in smoke in 1741 the locals gave up, settling for the present structure, with the addition of a stone parapet in 1822. Few would say the Belfort is good-looking – it's large and really rather clumsy – but it does have a certain ungainly charm, though this was lost on G.K. Chesterton, who described it as "an unnaturally long-necked animal, like a giraffe".

The **belfry staircase** begins innocuously enough, but it gets steeper and much narrower as it nears the top. On the way up, it passes several mildly interesting chambers, beginning with the **Treasury Room**, where the town charters and money chest were locked for safe keeping. Here also is an iron trumpet with which a watchman could warn the town of a fire outbreak – though given the size of the instrument, it's hard to believe this was very effective. Further up is the **Carillon Chamber**, where you can observe the slow turning of the large spiked drum that controls the 47 bells of the municipal carillon (see p.206). The city still employs a full-time bell ringer – you're likely to see him fiddling around in the Carillon Chamber – who puts on regular **carillon concerts** (mid-June to mid-Sept Mon, Wed & Sat at 9pm, plus Sun at 2pm; mid-Sept to mid-June Wed at 11am, Sat & Sun at 2pm; free). A few stairs up from here and you emerge onto the belfry **roof**, which offers fabulous views, especially in the late afternoon when the warm colours of the city are at their deepest.

Hallen

Open access

Now used for temporary exhibitions, the **Hallen** is another much-restored thirteenth-century edifice, its style and structure modelled on the Lakenhalle in Ieper (see p.139). In the middle, overlooked by a long line of galleries, is a rectangular courtyard, which

---

BRUGES CITYCARD AND PASSES

Tourist information and the major museums sell a variety of **passes**, with the most economic being the **Brugge CityCard**, a two- or three-day pass (€40/45) covering all the major sights; included is a canal boat trip plus discounts at certain shops and concerts. The main competition is the **Museum Pass**, which is valid for three days, covers entry to all the main museums and costs €20 (12–25-year-olds €15).

2

Damme

BRUGES

N

KLOOSTERLUIK
H. SWIN ST
KARMELIETENSTR
DELAPLAETSESTR
Kruispoort
EBESTRAAT
KLOOSTERSTRAAT
SPORTSTRAAT
POOLSTRK
DAMPOORTSTR
DAMPOORTSTR
PARADIJSSTR
ZUIDERSTRAAT
ZUIDERSTRAAT
St-Janshuis-molen
KRUISVEST
G. Gezelle Museum
KRUISVEST
VERLISSTR
LANGEWAPPER
STIJN STREUVELS
BALSEMBOOMSTRAAT
ROOS
Engels Klooster
BONINS
VERRISSTR
PEPERSTRAAT
ANGEVERSTR
Kantmuseum
Kantcentrum
PETERSELLESTRAAT
Potteriemuseum
OLIEBAAN
Volkskundemuseum
BALSTRAAT
Jeruzalemkerk
KWEKERIJ
ROODESTRAAT
SPEELMANSREI
BOUTESTR
VERBRAND NIEUWLAND
MOLENMEERS
VERBRAND
LANGEREI
POTTERIEREI
SASPLEIN
S. GRAVENSTRAAT
KOMVEST
DUINENABDIJSTR
ROPEERDSTR
RIJKEPIJNDERSSTR
E. ZORGHESTR
SNAGGAARDSTR
CARMERSSTRAAT
JERUZALEMSTR
ST-ANNAREI
ST-ANNAREI
BLEKERSSTR
KVERVERSDIJK
HANDPOORTSTR
ST-ANNAKERKSTR
BOOMGAARDSTR
RIDDERSTR
ST-JANSSTRAAT
Handelskom
FORT LAPIN
J. EN M. SABBESTRAAT
LANGEREI
CALVARIEBERGSTRAAT
C. MANSIONSTR
BALIESTRAAT
ANNUNTIATENSTRAAT
LANGE RA AMSTRAAT
GOUDEN-HANDSTR
GOUDEN HANDREI
GENTHOF
GOEZEPUTSTR
KONINGSTR
ENGELSE STR
WALWEINSTRAAT
Vlotkom
KOMVEST
ST-CLARADORPE
ST-CLARASTRAAT
BIDDERSTR
W. GISTELHOF
HOEDENMAKERSR
AUGUSTIJNENREI
SPANJAARDSTR
SPAANSELOSKAAI
KUIPERSSTRAAT
VLAMINGSTRAAT
ST-PIETERSKAAI
KONWEST
JAN MIRAELSTR
JAN MIRAELSTR
ST-JORISSTRAAT
GRAUWWERKERSSTR
NAALDENSTRAAT
ST-JAKOBS-STRAAT
IJZERSTRAAT
ST-CLARADORPE
VLAMINGDAM
VLAMINGDAM
ST-JORISSTRAAT
LAKSE POTERIJSTRAAT
St-Jakobskerk
DIKSMUIDESTRAAT
GOMBERTSTRAAT
WERF PLEIN
WERFSTRAAT
KONINGIN ELISABETHLAAN
EZELSTRAAT
RAAMSTRAAT
ROZENDAL
BEENHOUWERSTR
OUDE ZAK
ST-PIETERSKAAI
LEOPOLD II-LAAN
KARL MERCIERSTRAAT
SCHERSDAELLAAN
Ezelpoort
FILIPS DE GOEDELAAN
GULDEN-VLIESLAAN
Graaf Visart park
BEVRIJDINGSLAAN
KOLENKAAI
STEENKAAI
SPEELMANSREI OOSTENDESE STEENWEG N9
LEOPOLD I-LAAN
GOUDEN-BOOMSTR
LEIZER KAREL STRAAT
KEIZER KARELSTRAAT
KAREL DE STOUTELAAN
LAUWERSTRAAT
MARIA VAN BOURGONDIELAAN
N351
N351
DAMPOORT
BUITEN KRUISVEST R30

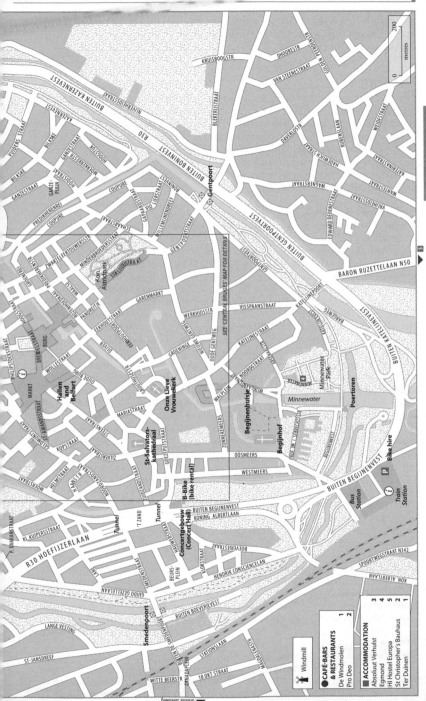

originally served as the city's principal market, its cobblestones once crammed with merchants and their wares. On the north side of the courtyard, up a flight of steps, is the entrance to the belfry.

The Burg

From the east side of the Markt, Breidelstraat leads through to the city's other main square, the **Burg**, named after the fortress built here by the first count of Flanders, Baldwin Iron Arm, in the ninth century. The fortress disappeared centuries ago, but the Burg long remained the centre of political and ecclesiastical power with the **Stadhuis** (which has survived) on one side and **St-Donaaskathedraal** (which hasn't) on the other. The French army destroyed the cathedral in 1799 and, although the foundations were laid bare in the 1950s, they were promptly re-interred – they lie in front of and underneath the *Crowne Plaza Hotel*.

Heilig Bloed Basiliek

Burg • April–Oct daily 9.30am–noon & 2–5pm; Nov–March daily except Wed 9.30am–noon & 2–5pm • Free, but treasury €2 • ⓦ holyblood.com

The southern half of the Burg is fringed by the city's finest group of buildings, beginning on the right with the **Heilig Bloed Basiliek** (Basilica of the Holy Blood), named after the holy relic that found its way here in the Middle Ages. The church divides into two parts. Tucked away in the corner, the **lower chapel** is a shadowy, crypt-like affair, originally built at the beginning of the twelfth century to shelter another relic, that of St Basil, one of the great figures of the early Greek Church. The chapel's heavy and simple Romanesque lines are decorated with just one relief, carved above an interior doorway and showing the baptism of Basil in which a strange giant bird, representing the Holy Spirit, plunges into a pool of water. Next door, approached up a wide, low-vaulted, curving staircase, the **upper chapel** was built a few years later, but has been renovated so frequently that it's impossible to make out the original structure; it also suffers from excessively rich nineteenth-century decoration.

That said, it does house a magnificent silver **tabernacle** that holds the rock-crystal **phial of the Holy Blood**, the gift of Albert and Isabella of Spain in 1611. One of the holiest relics in medieval Europe, the phial purports to contain a few drops of blood and water washed from the body of Christ by Joseph of Arimathea. Local legend asserts that it was the gift of Diederik d'Alsace, a Flemish knight who distinguished himself by his bravery during the Second Crusade and was given the phial by a grateful patriarch of Jerusalem in 1150. It is, however, rather more likely that the relic was acquired during the **sacking of Constantinople** in 1204, when the Crusaders simply ignored their collective job description and robbed and slaughtered the Byzantines instead – hence the historical invention. Whatever the truth, after several weeks in Bruges, the relic was found to be dry, but thereafter it proceeded to liquefy every Friday at 6pm until 1325, a miracle attested to by all sorts of church dignitaries, including Pope Clement V.

The phial of the Holy Blood is still venerated and, despite modern scepticism, reverence for it remains strong. It's sometimes available for visitors to touch under the supervision of a priest inside the chapel, and on Ascension Day (mid-May) it's carried through the town centre in a colourful but solemn procession, the **Heilig-Bloedprocessie**, a popular event for which grandstand tickets are sold at the main tourist information office (see p.118).

Treasury

The **shrine** that holds the phial of the Holy Blood during the Heilig-Bloedprocessie is displayed in the tiny **Schatkamer** (treasury), next to the upper chapel. Dating to 1617, it's a superb piece of work, the gold and silver superstructure encrusted with jewels and decorated with tiny religious figures. The treasury also contains an

2

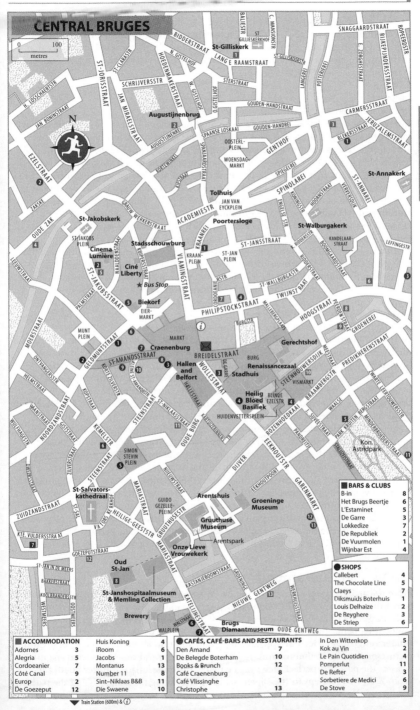

CENTRAL BRUGES

0 — 100 metres

ACCOMMODATION			
Adornes	3	Huis Koning	4
Alegria	5	iRoom	6
Cordoeanier	7	Jacobs	1
Côté Canal	9	Montanus	13
Europ	2	Number 11	8
De Goezeput	12	Sint-Niklaas B&B	11
		Die Swaene	10

CAFÉS, CAFÉ-BARS AND RESTAURANTS			
Den Amand	7	In Den Wittenkop	5
De Belegde Boterham	10	Kok au Vin	2
Books & Brunch	12	Le Pain Quotidien	4
Café Craenenburg	8	Pomperlut	11
Café Vlissinghe	1	De Refter	3
Christophe	13	Sorbetiere de Medici	6
		De Stove	9

BARS & CLUBS	
B-in	8
Het Brugs Beertje	6
L'Estaminet	5
De Garre	3
Lokkedize	7
De Republiek	2
De Vuurmolen	1
Wijnbar Est	4

SHOPS	
Callebert	4
The Chocolate Line	5
Claeys	7
Diksmuids Boterhuis	1
Louis Delhaize	2
De Reyghere	3
De Striep	6

Train Station (600m) & (i)

incidental collection of ecclesiastical bric-a-brac plus a handful of old paintings. Look out also for the faded strands of a locally woven **seventeenth-century tapestry** depicting St Augustine's funeral, the sea of helmeted heads, torches and pikes that surround the monks and abbots very much a Catholic view of a muscular State supporting a holy Church.

Stadhuis

Burg • Daily 9.30am–5pm • €4 including the Renaissancezaal (see below) • ⓦ visitbruges.be

Immediately to the left of the basilica, the **Stadhuis** has a beautiful fourteenth-century sandstone facade, though its statues, mostly of the counts and countesses of Flanders, are modern replacements for those destroyed by the occupying French army in 1792. Inside, a flight of stairs climbs up to the magnificent **Gothic Hall**, dating from 1400 and the setting for the first meeting of the States General (parliamentary assembly) in 1464. The ceiling – dripping pendant arches like decorated stalactites – has been restored in a vibrant mixture of maroon, dark brown, black and gold. The ribs of the arches converge in twelve circular **vault-keys**, picturing scenes from the New Testament. These are hard to see without binoculars, but down below – and much easier to view – are the sixteen gilded **corbels** that support them, representing the months and the four elements. The **frescoes** around the walls were commissioned in 1895 to illustrate the history of the town – or rather history as the council wanted to recall it, with the largest scene commemorating the victory over the French at the Battle of the Golden Spurs in 1302 (look out for the dog with a mismatched body and head).

Renaissancezaal 't Brugse Vrije

Burg • Daily 9.30am–12.30pm & 1.30–5pm • €4 including Stadhuis • ⓦ visitbruges.be

Next door but one to the Stadhuis, pop into the **Paleis van het Brugse Vrije** (Mansion of the Liberty of Bruges), a comparatively demure building, where just one room has survived from the original fifteenth-century structure. This, the Schepenkamer (Aldermen's Room), now known as the **Renaissancezaal 't Brugse Vrije** (Renaissance Hall of the Liberty of Bruges), is dominated by an enormous marble and oak **chimneypiece**, a superb example of Renaissance carving completed in 1531 to celebrate the defeat of the French at Pavia six years earlier and the advantageous Treaty of Cambrai that followed. A paean of praise to the Habsburgs, the work features the Emperor Charles V and his Austrian and Spanish relatives, though it's the trio of bulbous **codpieces** that really catches the eye. The **alabaster frieze** running below the carvings was a caution for the Liberty's magistrates, who held their courts here. In four panels, it relates the then-familiar biblical story of **Susanna**, in which – in the first panel – two old men surprise her bathing in her garden and threaten to accuse her of adultery if she resists their advances. Susanna does just that, and the second panel shows her in court. In the third panel, Susanna is about to be put to death, but the magistrate, Daniel, interrogates the two men and uncovers their perjury. Susanna is acquitted and, in the final scene, the two men are stoned to death.

The Vismarkt and around

From the arch beside the Stadhuis, **Blinde Ezelstraat** (Blind Donkey Street) leads south across the canal to the sombre eighteenth-century Doric colonnades of the **Vismarkt** (fish market), which is still in use by a handful of traders today. The fish sellers have done rather better than the tanners and dyers who used to work in neighbouring **Huidenvettersplein**. Both disappeared long ago and nowadays tourists converge on this picturesque square in their droves, holing up in its bars and restaurants and snapping away at the postcard-perfect views of the belfry from the adjacent **Rozenhoedkaai**. From here, it's footsteps to the **Dijver**, which tracks along the canal passing the path to the first of the city's main museums, the **Groeninge**.

Groeninge Museum

Dijver 12 • Tues–Sun 9.30am–5pm • €8 including Arentshuis (see p.111) • ☏ 050 44 87 11, ⓦ visitbruges.be

The **Groeninge Museum** possesses one of the world's finest samples of early Flemish paintings, from Jan van Eyck through to Jan Provoost. The description below details some of the most important works: most if not all should be on display, though note that the collection is regularly rotated. Be sure to pick up a floor plan at reception.

Jan van Eyck

Arguably the greatest of the early Flemish masters, **Jan van Eyck** (1385–1441) lived and worked in Bruges from 1430 until his death eleven years later. He was a key figure in the development of oil painting, modulating its tones to create paintings of extraordinary clarity and realism. The Groeninge has two gorgeous examples of his work, beginning with the miniature portrait of his wife, *Margareta van Eyck*, painted in 1439 and bearing his motto, "als ich can" (the best I can do). The painting is very much a private picture and one that had no commercial value, marking a small step away from the sponsored art – and religious preoccupations – of previous Flemish artists. The second Eyck painting is the remarkable *Madonna and Child with Canon George van der Paele*, a glowing and richly symbolic work with three figures surrounding the Madonna: the kneeling canon, St George (his patron saint) and St Donatian. St George doffs his helmet to salute the infant Christ and speaks by means of the Hebrew word "*Adonai*" (Lord) inscribed on his chin strap, while Jesus replies through the green parrot he holds: folklore asserted that this type of parrot was fond of saying "*ave*", the Latin for "welcome" or "hail". The canon's face is exquisitely executed, down to the sagging jowls and the bulging blood vessels at his temple, while the glasses and book in his hand add to his air of deep contemplation. Audaciously, van Eyck has broken with tradition by painting the canon among the saints rather than as a lesser figure – a distinct nod to the humanism that was gathering pace in contemporary Bruges.

Rogier van der Weyden

The Groeninge possesses two fine and roughly contemporaneous copies of paintings by **Rogier van der Weyden** (1399–1464), one-time official city painter to Brussels. The first is a tiny *Portrait of Philip the Good*, in which the pallor of the duke's aquiline features, along with the brightness of his hatpin and chain of office, is skilfully balanced by the sombre cloak and hat. The second and much larger painting, *St Luke painting the Portrait of Our Lady*, is a rendering of a popular if highly improbable legend that Luke painted Mary – thereby becoming the patron saint of painters. The painting is notable for the detail of its Flemish background and the cheeky smile of the baby Christ.

Hugo van der Goes

One of the most gifted of the early Flemish artists, **Hugo van der Goes** (d.1482) is a shadowy figure, though it is known that he became master of the painters' guild in Ghent in 1467. Eight years later, he entered a Ghent priory as a lay brother, perhaps on account of the prolonged bouts of depression that afflicted him. Few of his paintings have survived, but these exhibit a superb compositional balance and a keen observational eye – as in his last work, the luminescent *Death of Our Lady*. Sticking to religious legend, the Apostles have been miraculously transported to Mary's deathbed, where, in a state of agitation, they surround the prostrate woman. Mary is dressed in blue, but there are no signs of luxury, reflecting both der Goes's asceticism and his polemic – the artist may well have been appalled by the church's love of glitter and gold.

Hans Memling

Hans Memling (1430–94) is represented by a pair of *Annunciation* panels from a triptych – gentle, romantic representations of an angel and Mary in contrasting shades of grey. Here also is Memling's *Moreel Triptych*, in which the formality of the design is offset by the warm colours and the gentleness of the detail – St Giles strokes the fawn and the knight's hand lies on the donor's shoulder. The side panels show the donors and their sixteen children; there are more Memling paintings in Bruges at St-Janshospitaal (see p.113).

Gerard David

Born near Gouda in the Netherlands, **Gerard David** (c.1460–1523) moved to Bruges in his early twenties. Soon admitted into the local painters' guild, he quickly rose through the ranks, becoming the city's leading artistic light after the death of Memling. Official commissions rained in on David, mostly for religious paintings, which he approached in a formal manner but with a fine eye for detail. The Groeninge holds two excellent examples of his work, starting with the *Baptism of Christ Triptych*, in which a boyish, lightly bearded Christ is depicted as part of the Holy Trinity in the central panel. There's also one of David's few secular ventures, the intriguing *Judgement of Cambyses*, painted on two oak panels. Based on a Persian legend related by Herodotus, the first panel's background shows the corrupt judge Sisamnes accepting a bribe, with his subsequent arrest by grim-faced aldermen filling the rest of the panel. The aldermen crowd in on Sisamnes with a palpable sense of menace and, as the king sentences him to be flayed alive, a sweaty look of fear sweeps over the judge's face. In the gruesome second panel the king's servants carry out the judgement, applying themselves to the task with clinical detachment. Behind, in the top right corner, the fable is completed with the judge's son dispensing justice from his father's old chair, which is now draped with the flayed skin. Completed in 1498, the painting was hung in the council chamber by the city burghers to encourage honesty among its magistrates.

Hieronymus Bosch

The Groeninge also holds **Hieronymus Bosch**'s (1450–1516) *Last Judgement*, a trio of oak panels crammed with mysterious beasts, microscopic mutants and scenes of awful cruelty – men boiled in a pit or cut in half by a giant knife. It looks like unbridled fantasy, but in fact the scenes were read as symbols, a sort of strip cartoon of legend, proverb and tradition. Indeed, Bosch's religious orthodoxy is confirmed by the appeal his work had for that most Catholic of Spanish kings, Philip II.

Jan Provoost

There's more grim symbolism in **Jan Provoost**'s (1465–1529) crowded and melodramatic *Last Judgement*, painted for the Stadhuis in 1525, and his striking *The Miser and Death*, which portrays the merchant with his money in one panel, trying desperately to pass a promissory note to the grinning skeleton in the next. Provoost's career was typical of many of the Flemish artists of the early sixteenth century. Initially he worked in the Flemish manner, his style greatly influenced by Gerard David, but from about 1521 his work was reinvigorated by contact with the German painter and engraver Albrecht Dürer, who had himself been inspired by the artists of the early Italian Renaissance. Provoost moved around too, working in Valenciennes and Antwerp, before settling in Bruges in 1494.

Pieter Pourbus

The Groeninge's collection of late sixteenth- and seventeenth-century paintings isn't especially strong, but there's enough to discern the period's watering down of religious themes in favour of more secular preoccupations. **Pieter Pourbus** (1523–84) is well represented by a series of austere and often surprisingly unflattering portraits of the movers and shakers of his day. There's also his *Last Judgement*, a much larger but atypical work, crammed with muscular men and fleshy women; completed in 1551, its inspiration came from Michelangelo's Sistine Chapel. Born in Gouda, Pourbus moved to Bruges in his early twenties, becoming the leading local portraitist of his day as well as squeezing in work as a civil engineer and cartographer.

The Symbolists

There is a substantial collection of nineteenth- and early twentieth-century Belgian art at the Groeninge. One obvious highlight is the work of the Symbolist **Fernand Khnopff** (1858–1921), who is represented by *Secret Reflections*, not perhaps one of his better paintings, but interesting in so far as its lower panel – showing St Janshospitaal reflected in a canal – confirms one of the movement's favourite conceits: "Bruges the dead city". This was inspired by Georges Rodenbach's novel *Bruges-la-Morte*, a highly stylized muse on love and obsession first published in 1892. The book started the craze for visiting Bruges, the so-called "dead city" where the action unfolds. The upper panel of Khnopff's painting is a play on appearance and desire, but it's pretty feeble, unlike his later attempts, in which he painted his sister, Marguerite, again and again, using her refined, almost plastic beauty to stir a vague sense of passion – for him she was desirable and unobtainable in equal measure.

The Expressionists

The museum has a healthy sample of the work of the talented **Constant Permeke** (1886–1952). Wounded in World War I, Permeke's grim wartime experiences helped him develop a distinctive **Expressionist** style in which his subjects – usually agricultural workers, fishermen and so forth – were monumental in form, but invested with sombre, sometimes threatening, emotion. His charcoal drawing the *Angelus* is a typically dark and earthy representation of Belgian peasant life dated to 1934. In a similar vein is the enormous *Last Supper* by **Gustave van de Woestijne** (1881–1947), another excellent example of Belgian Expressionism, with Jesus and the disciples, all elliptical eyes and restrained movement, trapped within prison-like walls.

The Surrealists

The Groeninge also owns a clutch of works by the inventive **Marcel Broodthaers** (1924–76), most notably his tongue-in-cheek (and very Belgian) *Les Animaux de la Ferme*. **Magritte** (1898–1967; see p.64) appears too, in his characteristically unnerving *The Assault*, while **Paul Delvaux** (1897–1994) is well represented by the spookily stark Surrealism of his *Serenity*. Delvaux has a museum all to himself in St-Idesbald (see p.133).

Arentshuis

Dijver 16 • Tues–Sun 9.30am–5pm • €4, but free with Groeninge ticket • ⓦ visitbruges.be

The **Arentshuis** occupies an attractive eighteenth-century mansion with a stately portico-framed entrance. Now a museum, the interior is divided into two separate sections: the ground floor is given over to temporary exhibitions, usually of fine art or lace, while the **Brangwyn Museum** upstairs displays the moody sketches, etchings, lithographs, studies and paintings of the much-travelled artist Sir Frank Brangwyn (1867–1956). Born in Bruges of Welsh parents, Brangwyn flitted between Britain and Belgium, donating this sample of his work to his native town in 1936. Apprenticed to William Morris in the early 1880s and an official UK war artist in World War I, Brangwyn was nothing if not versatile, turning his hand to several different media, though his forceful drawings and sketches are much more appealing than his paintings, which often slide into sentimentality.

Arentspark

The Arentshuis stands in the north corner of the pocket-sized **Arentspark**, whose pair of forlorn stone columns are all that remains of the Waterhalle, a large trading hall which once straddled the most central of the city's canals but was demolished in 1787 after the canal was covered over. Also in the Arentspark is the tiniest of humpbacked bridges – **St Bonifaciusbrug** – whose stonework is framed against a tumble of antique brick houses. One of Bruges' most picturesque (and photographed) spots, the bridge looks like the epitome of everything medieval, but in fact it was built in 1910.

Gruuthuse Museum

Dijver 17 • Tues–Sun 9.30am–5pm • €8, but closed for refurbishment until 2016 • Ⓦ visitbruges.be

The **Gruuthuse Museum** is located inside a rambling mansion that dates to the fifteenth century. The building is a fine example of civil Gothic architecture and it takes its name from the house owners' historical right to tax the *gruit*, the dried herb and flower mixture once added to barley during the beer-brewing process to improve the flavour. The last lord of the *gruit* died in 1492 and, after many twists and turns, the mansion was turned into a museum to hold a hotchpotch of Flemish fine, applied and decorative arts, mostly from the medieval and early modern periods. The museum's most famous artefact is a polychromatic terracotta **bust** of a youthful Emperor Charles V and its most unusual feature is the oak-panelled **oratory** that juts out from the first floor to overlook the altar of the Onze Lieve Vrouwekerk next door. A curiously intimate room, the oratory allowed the lords of the *gruit* to worship without leaving home – a real social coup.

Onze Lieve Vrouwekerk

Mariastraat • Mon–Sat 9.30am–5pm, Sun 1.30–5pm • Free, but chancel €6 • Ⓦ visitbruges.be

The **Onze Lieve Vrouwekerk** (Church of Our Lady) is a rambling shambles of a building, a clamour of different dates and styles whose brick spire is – at 122m – one of the tallest in Belgium. Entered from the south, the **nave** was three hundred years in the making, an architecturally discordant affair, whose thirteenth-century grey-stone central aisle is the oldest part of the church. The central aisle blends in with the south aisle but the later, fourteenth-century north aisle doesn't mesh at all – even the columns aren't aligned. This was the result of changing fashions, not slapdash work: the High Gothic north aisle was intended to be the start of a complete remodelling of the church, but the money ran out before the project was finished. In the south aisle is the church's most acclaimed objet d'art, a delicate marble *Madonna and Child* by **Michelangelo**. Purchased by a Bruges merchant, this was the only one of Michelangelo's works to leave Italy during the artist's lifetime and it had a significant influence on the painters then working in Bruges, though its present setting – beneath gloomy stone walls and set within a gaudy Baroque altar – is hardly prepossessing.

The chancel

Michelangelo apart, the most interesting part of the church is the **chancel**, beyond the black and white marble rood screen. Here you'll find the **mausoleums** of Charles the Bold and his daughter Mary of Burgundy (see box p.113), two exquisite examples of Renaissance carving, their side panels decorated with coats of arms connected by the most intricate of floral designs. The royal figures are enhanced in the detail, from the helmet and gauntlets placed gracefully by Charles' side to the pair of watchful dogs nestled at Mary's feet. Oddly enough, the **hole** dug by archeologists beneath the mausoleums during the 1970s to discover who was actually buried here was never filled in, so you can see Mary's coffin, the urn containing the heart of her son and the burial vaults of several unknown medieval dignitaries, three of which have now been moved across to the Lanchals Chapel.

Lanchals Chapel

Just across the ambulatory from the mausoleums is the **Lanchals Chapel**, which holds the imposing Baroque gravestone of Pieter Lanchals, a one-time Habsburg official who had his head lopped off by the citizens of Bruges for corruption in 1488. In front of the Lanchals gravestone are three relocated **medieval burial vaults**, each plastered with lime mortar. The inside walls of the vaults sport brightly coloured **grave frescoes**, a type of art which flourished hereabouts from the late thirteenth to the middle of the fifteenth century. The iconography is fairly consistent, with the long sides mostly bearing one, sometimes two, angels apiece, and most of the angels are shown swinging thuribles (the vessels in which incense is burnt during religious ceremonies). Typically, the short sides show the Crucifixion and a Virgin and Child. The background decoration is more varied, with crosses, stars and dots all making appearances as well as two main sorts of flower – roses and bluebells. The frescoes were painted freehand and executed at great speed – Flemings were then buried on the day they died – hence the delightful immediacy of the work.

St-Janshospitaal

Mariastraat

Opposite the entrance to the Onze Lieve Vrouwekerk is **St-Janshospitaal**, a sprawling complex that sheltered the sick of mind and body until well into the nineteenth century. The oldest part – at the front on Mariastraat, behind two church-like gable ends – has been turned into the excellent **St-Janshospitaalmuseum**, while the nineteenth-century annexe, reached along a narrow passageway on the north side of the museum, has been converted into a really rather tatty exhibition-cum-shopping centre called – rather confusingly – **Oud St-Jan**.

St-Janshospitaalmuseum

Mariastraat • Tues–Sun 9.30am–5pm • €8 • Ⓦ visitbruges.be

St-Janshospitaalmuseum divides into two, with one large section (in the former hospital ward) exploring the historical background to the hospital through documents, paintings and religious objets d'art. Highlights include a pair of sedan chairs used to carry the

---

THE EARTHLY REMAINS OF MARY OF BURGUNDY AND CHARLES THE BOLD

The last independent rulers of Flanders were **Charles the Bold**, the Duke of Burgundy, and his daughter **Mary of Burgundy**, both of whom died in unfortunate circumstances: Charles during the siege of the French city of Nancy in 1477; Mary after a riding accident in 1482. Mary was married to **Maximilian**, a Habsburg prince and future Holy Roman Emperor, who inherited her territories on her death – thus, at a dynastic stroke, Flanders was incorporated into the Habsburg empire.

In the sixteenth century, the Habsburgs relocated to Spain, but they were keen to emphasize their connections with, and historical authority over, Flanders. Nothing did this quite as well as the ceremonial burial – or reburial – of bits of royal body. Mary was safely ensconced in Bruges's Onze Lieve Vrouwekerk (see p.112), but the body of Charles was in a makeshift grave in **Nancy**. Emperor Charles V, the great grandson of Charles the Bold, had this body exhumed and carried to Bruges, where it was reinterred next to Mary. Or at least he thought he had: there were persistent rumours that the French – the traditional enemies of the Habsburgs – had deliberately handed over a dud skeleton. In the 1970s, **archeologists** had a bash at solving the mystery by digging beneath Charles and Mary's mausoleums in the Onze Lieve Vrouwekerk. But among the assorted tombs, they failed to authoritatively identify either the body or even the tomb of Charles. Things ran more smoothly in Mary's case, however, with her skeleton confirming the known details of her hunting accident. Moreover, buried alongside her was the **urn** which contained the heart of her son, Philip the Fair, placed here in 1506. More archeological harrumphing over the remains of poor old Charles is likely during the current refurbishment of the chancel.

infirm to the hospital in emergencies, and Jan Beerblock's *The Wards of St Janshospitaal*, a minutely detailed painting of the hospital ward as it was in the late eighteenth century, the patients tucked away in row upon row of tiny, cupboard-like beds. Other noteworthy paintings include an exquisite *Deposition of Christ*, a late fifteenth-century version of an original by Rogier van der Weyden, and a stylish, intimately observed diptych by Jan Provoost that includes images of Christ, the donor (a friar) and a skull.

The Memling collection

The Hospitaalmuseum also possesses six wonderful works by **Hans Memling** (1433–94). Born near Frankfurt, Memling spent most of his working life in Bruges, where Rogier van der Weyden (see p.109) instructed him. He adopted much of his tutor's style and stuck to the detailed symbolism of his contemporaries, but his painterly manner was distinctly restrained and often pious and grave. Graceful and warmly coloured, his figures also had a velvet-like quality that greatly appealed to the city's burghers, whose enthusiasm made Memling a rich man – in 1480 he was listed among the town's major moneylenders.

Reliquary of St Ursula

Of the six Memling works on display, the most unusual is the **Reliquary of St Ursula**, comprising a miniature wooden Gothic church painted with the story of St Ursula. Memling condensed the legend into six panels with Ursula and her ten companions landing at Cologne and Basle before reaching Rome at the end of their pilgrimage. Things go badly wrong on the way back: they leave Basle in good order, but are then – in the last two panels – massacred by Huns as they pass through Germany. Memling had a religious point to make, but today it's the mass of incidental detail that makes the reliquary so enchanting, providing an intriguing evocation of the late medieval world.

Mystical Marriage of St Catherine

Equally delightful is the **Mystical Marriage of St Catherine**, the middle panel of a large triptych depicting St Catherine, who represents contemplation, receiving a ring from the baby Jesus to seal their spiritual union. The complementary side panels depict the beheading of St John the Baptist and a visionary St John writing the Book of Revelation on the bare and rocky island of Patmos. Again, it's the detail that impresses: between the inner and outer rainbows above St John, for instance, the prophets play music on tiny instruments – look closely and you'll spy a lute, a flute, a harp and a hurdy-gurdy.

Portrait of a Young Woman

Memling's skill as a portraitist is demonstrated to exquisite effect in his **Portrait of a Young Woman**, where the richly dressed subject stares dreamily into the middle distance, her hands – in a superb optical illusion – seeming to clasp the picture frame. The lighting is subtle and sensuous, with the woman set against a dark background, her gauze veil dappling the side of her face. A high forehead was then considered a sign of great womanly beauty, so her hair is pulled right back and was probably plucked – as are her eyebrows. There's no knowing who the woman was, but in the seventeenth century her fancy headgear convinced observers that she was one of the legendary Persian sibyls who predicted Christ's birth; so convinced were they that they added the cartouche in the top left-hand corner, describing her as *Sibylla Sambetha* – and the painting is often referred to by this name.

Two Memling triptychs and a diptych

Two further Memling triptychs are on display, a *Lamentation* and an *Adoration of the Magi*, in which there's a gentle nervousness in the approach of the Magi, here shown as the kings of Spain, Arabia and Ethiopia. The sixth and final painting, the **Virgin and Martin van Nieuwenhove** diptych, depicts the eponymous merchant in the full flush of youth and with a hint of arrogance: his lips pout, his hair cascades down to his shoulders and he is dressed in the most fashionable of doublets – by the middle of the 1480s, when the portrait was commissioned, no Bruges merchant wanted to appear too pious. Opposite, the Virgin gets the full stereotypical treatment from the oval face and the almond-shaped eyes through to full cheeks, thin nose and bunched lower lip.

St-Salvatorskathedraal

Steenstraat • Mon–Sat 10am–1pm & 2–5.30pm, Sun 11.30am–noon & 2–5pm • ☎ 050 33 68 41, ⓦ visitbruges.be

The high and mighty **St-Salvatorskathedraal** (Holy Saviour Cathedral) is a bulky Gothic edifice that mostly dates from the late thirteenth century, though the ambulatory was added some two centuries later. A parish church for most of its history, it was only made a cathedral in 1834 following the destruction of St Donatian's (see p.106) by the French. This change of status prompted lots of ecclesiastical rumblings – nearby Onze Lieve Vrouwekerk (see p.112) was bigger and its spire higher – and when part of St Salvator's went up in smoke in 1839, the opportunity was taken to make its tower higher and grander in a romantic rendition of the Romanesque style.

The nave

Slowly emerging from a seemingly interminable restoration, the cathedral's **nave** remains a cheerless, cavernous affair despite lashings of new paint. The star turn is the **set of eight paintings** by Jan van Orley displayed in the transepts. Commissioned in the 1730s, the paintings were used for the manufacture of a matching set of **tapestries** from a Brussels workshop and, remarkably enough, these have survived too and hang in sequence in the choir and nave. Each of the eight scenes is a fluent, dramatic composition featuring a familiar episode from the life of Christ – from the Nativity to the Resurrection – complete with a handful of animals, including a remarkably determined Palm Sunday donkey. The tapestries are actually mirror images of the paintings as the weavers worked with the rear of the tapestries uppermost on their looms; the weavers also had sight of the tapestry paintings – or rather cartoon copies, as the originals were too valuable to be kept beside the looms. Adjoining the nave, in the floor of the porch behind the old main doors, look out also for the six recently excavated tombs, whose interior walls are decorated with **grave frescoes** that follow the same design as those in the Lanchals Chapel (see p.112).

The Treasury

Daily except Sat, 2–5pm • Free

The cathedral **Treasury** (Schatkamer) occupies the adjoining neo-Gothic chapterhouse, whose cloistered rooms are packed with ecclesiastical bits and pieces, from religious paintings and statues through to an assortment of reliquaries, vestments and croziers. The labelling is poor, however, so it's a good idea to pick up the English-language mini-guide at the entrance. **Room B** holds the treasury's finest painting, a gruesome, oak-panel triptych, *The Martyrdom of St Hippolytus*, by **Dieric Bouts** (1410–75) and **Hugo van der Goes** (d. 1482). The right panel depicts the Roman Emperor Decius, a notorious persecutor of Christians, trying to persuade the priest Hippolytus to abjure his faith. He fails, and in the central panel Hippolytus is pulled to pieces by four horses.

The Begijnhof

Begijnhof • Daily 6.30am–6.30pm • Free • ⓦ visitbruges.be

The tourist throng zones in on the **Begijnhof**, where a rough circle of old and infinitely pretty whitewashed houses surrounds a central green, which looks a treat in spring, when a carpet of daffodils pushes up between the wispy elms. There were once *begijnhofs* all over Belgium, and this is one of the few to have survived in good nick. They date back to the twelfth century, when a Liège priest – a certain Lambert le Bègue – encouraged widows and unmarried women to live in communities, the better to do pious acts, especially caring for the sick. These communities were different from convents in so far as the inhabitants – the **Beguines** (*begijns*) – did not have to take conventual vows and had the right to return to the secular world if they wished. Margaret, Countess of Flanders, founded Bruges' *begijnhof* in 1245, and although most of the houses now standing date from the eighteenth century, the medieval layout has survived intact, preserving the impression of the *begijnhof* as a self-contained village, with access controlled through two large gates. Almost all of the houses are still in private hands but, with the Beguines long gone, they're now occupied by a mixture of single, elderly women and Benedictine nuns, whom you'll see flitting around in their habits, mostly on their way to and from the **Begijnhofkerk**, a surprisingly large church with a set of gaudy altarpieces.

Begijnenhuisje

Begijnhof • Mon–Sat 10am–5pm, Sun 2–5pm • €2

Only one house is open to the public – the **Begijnenhuisje**, a small-scale celebration of the simple life of the Beguines comprising a couple of living rooms and a mini-cloister. The prime exhibit is the *schapraai*, a traditional Beguine's cupboard, which was a frugal combination of dining table, cutlery cabinet and larder.

Minnewater

Facing the more southerly of the *begijnhof*'s two gates is the **Minnewater**, often hyped as the city's "Lake of Love". The tag certainly gets the canoodlers going, but in fact the lake – more a large pond – started life as a city harbour. The distinctive stone **lock house** at the head of the Minnewater recalls its earlier function, though it's actually a very fanciful nineteenth-century reconstruction of the medieval original. The **Poertoren**, on the west bank at the far end of the lake, is more authentic, its brown brickwork dating from 1398 and once forming part of the city wall. This is where the city kept its gunpowder – hence the name, "powder tower". Beside the Poertoren, a footbridge spans the southern end of the Minnewater to reach the leafy expanse of **Minnewaterpark**.

Jan van Eyckplein and around

Jan van Eyckplein, a five-minute walk north of the Markt, is one of the prettiest squares in Bruges, its cobbles backdropped by the easy sweep of the Spiegelrei canal. The centrepiece of the square is an earnest **statue of Jan van Eyck**, erected in 1878, while on the north side is the **Tolhuis**, whose fancy Renaissance entrance is decorated with the coat of arms of the dukes of Luxembourg, who long levied tolls here. The Tolhuis dates from the late fifteenth century, but was extensively remodelled in medieval style in the 1870s, as was the **Poortersloge** (Merchants' Lodge; no public entry), whose slender tower pokes up above the rooftops on the west side of the square. Theoretically, any city merchant was entitled to be a member of the Poortersloge, but in fact membership was restricted to the richest and the most powerful. An informal alternative to the Town Hall, it was here that key political and economic decisions were taken – and this was also where local bigwigs could drink and gamble discreetly.

Spiegelrei canal

Running east from Jan van Eyckplein, the **Spiegelrei canal** was once the heart of the foreign merchants' quarter, its frenetic quays overlooked by the trade missions of many of the city's trading partners. The medieval buildings were demolished long ago but they have been replaced by an exquisite medley of architectural styles, from expansive Georgian mansions to pirouetting crow-step gables.

The Spanish merchants' quarter and Augustijnenbrug

At the far end of Spiegelrei, a left turn brings you onto one of the city's prettiest streets, **Gouden-Handrei**, which – along with its continuation, Spaanse Loskaai – was once the focus of the **Spanish merchants' quarter**. The west end of Spaanse Loskaai is marked by the **Augustijnenbrug**, the city's oldest surviving bridge, a sturdy three-arched structure dating from 1391. The bridge was built to help the monks of a nearby (and long demolished) Augustinian monastery get into the city centre speedily; the benches set into the parapet were cut to allow itinerant tradesmen to display their goods here.

Spanjaardstraat

Running south from Augustijnenbrug is **Spanjaardstraat**, another part of the Spanish enclave. It was here, at no. 9, in a house formerly known as **De Pijnappel** (The Fir Cone), that the founder of the Jesuits, Ignatius Loyola (1491–1556), spent his holidays while he was a student in Paris – unfortunately the town's liberality failed to dent Loyola's nascent fanaticism.

Jeruzalemkerk

Peperstraat 1 • Mon–Sat 10am–4.45pm • €3 • ☎ 050 33 00 72

Beyond the east end of the Spiegelrei canal is an old working-class district, whose low brick cottages surround a substantial complex of buildings that originally belonged to the wealthy Adornes family, who migrated here from Genoa in the thirteenth century. The complex is dominated by one of the city's real oddities, the **Jeruzalemkerk** (Jerusalem Church), which was built by the family in the fifteenth century as an approximate copy of the Church of the Holy Sepulchre in Jerusalem after one of their number, Pieter, had returned from a pilgrimage to the Holy Land. The interior is on **two levels**: the lower one is dominated by a large and ghoulish altarpiece, decorated with skulls and ladders, in front of which is the black marble tomb of Anselm Adornes, the son of the church's founder, and his wife Margaretha. There's more grisliness at the back of the church, where a vaulted chapel holds a **replica of Christ's tomb** with an imitation body – it's down a narrow tunnel behind the iron grating. To either side of the main altar, steps ascend to the choir, which is situated right below the eccentric, onion-domed lantern tower.

Kantcentrum

For many years, the huddle of cottages that shares the Adornes complex with the Jeruzalemkerk has held both the **Kantcentrum** (Lace Centre) and the **Kantmuseum** (Lace Museum). The Kantmuseum is set to move into new premises (see below), but the Kantcentrum may well stay here, offering informal demonstrations of traditional lacemaking in the afternoon (no set times). They sell the stuff too, but it isn't cheap.

Kantmuseum

Balstraat 16 • Tues–Sun 9.30am–5pm • €4

The **Kantmuseum** (Lace Museum) traces the history of the industry here in Bruges and displays a large sample of antique, handmade lace, the most elaborate of which – Chantilly lace especially – dates from the late nineteenth century. Renowned for the fineness of its thread and beautiful motifs, Belgian lace – or **Flanders lace** as it was formerly known – was once worn in the courts of Brussels, Paris, Madrid and London, with Bruges the centre of its production. Handmade lace reached the peak of its popularity in the early nineteenth century, when hundreds of Bruges women and girls worked as home-based lacemakers. The industry was, however, transformed by the arrival of **machine-made lace** in the 1840s and, by the end of the century, handmade lace had been largely supplanted, with the lacemakers obliged to work in factories. This highly mechanized industry collapsed after World War I when lace, a symbol of an old and discredited order, suddenly had no place in the wardrobe of most women. Most **lace shops in Bruges** (see p.124) sell lace manufactured in the Far East, especially China.

Volkskundemuseum

Balstraat 43 • Tues–Sun 9.30am–5pm • €4 • ☎ 050 44 87 11

The **Volkskundemuseum** (Folklore Museum) occupies a long line of low-ceilinged almshouses set beside a trim courtyard. It's a varied collection, comprising a string of period rooms and workshops with the emphasis on the nineteenth and early twentieth centuries, but the labelling is patchy so it's best to pick up an English guidebook at reception.

The windmills

St-Janshuismolen May–Aug Tues–Sun 9.30am–12.30pm & 1.30–5pm • €3 • ☎ 050 44 87 43

East of the Volkskundemuseum, a quartet of **windmills** perches atop the long and wide **earthen bank** that marks the route of the old town walls. Two are clearly visible close by and another two lie just out of sight, about 300m and 500m to the north. You'd have to be something of a windmill fanatic to want to visit them all, but the nearest two are mildly diverting – and the closest, **St-Janshuismolen**, is in good working order.

ARRIVAL AND DEPARTURE   BRUGES

By train or bus The train and adjacent bus station are about 2km southwest of the town centre. Local buses depart for the centre from outside the train station every few minutes; most services stop on the Markt, the main square, others in the surrounding side streets. A taxi from the train station to the Markt costs about €10.

Destinations by train Brussels (every 30min; 1hr); Ghent (every 20min; 20min); Knokke (every 30min; 20min); Ostend (every 30min; 15min); Zeebrugge (hourly; 15min).

Destinations by bus Damme (Mon–Fri 1 or 2 daily; 20min).

By car The E40, running west from Brussels to Ostend, skirts Bruges. Bruges is clearly signed from the E40 and its oval-shaped centre is encircled by the R30 ring road. Parking in the centre can be a real tribulation; easily the best and most economical option is to use the 24/7 car park by the train station, particularly as the price – €3.50 per day – includes the cost of the bus ride to and from the centre.

GETTING AROUND

By bus Local buses are operated by De Lijn (☎ 070 22 02 00, ⊚ delijn.be). A standard one-way fare costs €1.30 in advance from a ticket machine, €2 from the driver. There are ticket machines at the train station and at major bus stops. De Lijn also has an information kiosk outside the train station (Mon–Fri 10.30am–5.45pm, Sat 10am–5.15pm). They will supply bus timetables – as will tourist information (see below).

By bike Flat as a pancake, Bruges and its environs are a great place to cycle (see box, p.124), especially as there are cycle lanes on many of the roads and cycle racks dotted across the centre. There are about a dozen bike rental places

in town – tourist information has the full list. One of the larger outlets is Fietspunt Station, beside the train station (Mon–Fri 7am–7pm; April to mid-Nov also Sat & Sun 9am–9pm; ☎ 050 39 68 26). Another good choice is B-Bike Concertgebouw on 't Zand (April to mid-Oct daily 10am–noon & 1–7pm; mid-Oct to March Fri & Sat 10am–noon & 1–7pm; ☎ 0479 97 12 80), just across from the main tourist information on the side of the Concertgebouw. Both charge €12 per day for a basic model.

By taxi There are taxi ranks on the Markt and outside the train station. Fares are metered – and the most common journey, from the train station to the centre, costs about €12.

INFORMATION

Tourist information There are three tourist information points: a small one at the train station (Mon–Fri 10am–5pm, Sat & Sun 10am–2pm); the main one in the Concertgebouw (Concert Hall) complex, on the west side of the city centre on 't Zand (Mon–Sat 10am–5pm, Sun 10am–2pm); and a third at Markt 1 (daily 10am–5pm), in the same building as the

ghastly Historium where, allegedly, you can "Experience the magic of the medieval period". They have a common phone line and website (☎ 050 44 46 46, ⊚ visitbruges.be). All three issue bus and train timetables, sell tickets for many events and performances, and operate a last-minute/same-night accommodation service.

CLOCKWISE FROM TOP ST-JANSHOSPITAALMUSEUM (P.113); CANAL NEAR ST BONIFACIUSBRUG (P.112); DAMME (P.124) >

2

GUIDED TOURS AND BOAT TRIPS IN AND AROUND BRUGES

Guided tours are big business in Bruges. Tourist information (see p.118) has comprehensive details, but among the many options one long-standing favourite is a **horse-drawn carriage ride**. Carriages hold a maximum of five, and line up on the Markt (daily 10am–10pm; 30min; €40 per carriage) to offer a short canter around town; demand can outstrip supply, so expect to queue at the weekend. Half-hour **boat trips** of the city's central canals leave from a number of jetties south of the Burg (March–Nov daily 10am–6pm; €7.60). Boats depart every few minutes, but long queues still build up during high season, with few visitors seemingly concerned by the canned commentary. In winter (Dec–Feb), there's a spasmodic service at weekends only.

Quasimodo Tours ☎ 050 37 04 70, ⊛ quasimodo.be. Bruges has a small army of tour operators but this is one of the best, running a first-rate programme of excursions both in and around Bruges and out into Flanders. Highly recommended is their "Flanders Fields" minibus tour of the World War I battlefields near Ieper (see pp.143–146). Tours cost €65 (under 26 €55), including picnic lunch, and last about eight hours. Reservations required; hotel or train station pick-up can be arranged.
Quasimundo ☎ 050 33 07 75, ⊛ quasimundo.be.

Quasimodo's sister organization runs several bike tours, starting from the Burg. Their "Bruges by Bike" excursion (daily March–Oct; 2.5hr; €28) zips round the main sights and then explores less-visited parts of the city, while their "Border by Bike" tour (daily March–Oct; 4hr; €28) is a 25km ride out along the poplar-lined canals to the north of Bruges, visiting Damme and Oostkerke with stops and stories along the way. Both are good fun and the price includes mountain-bike and rain-jacket hire; reservations are required.

ACCOMMODATION

Bruges has over a hundred hotels, dozens of B&Bs and several youth hostels, but still can't accommodate all its visitors at busy times, especially in the high season (roughly late June to early September) and Christmas. Indeed, at any time of the year you'd be well advised to **book ahead** – though tourist information (see p.118) does operate a last-minute/same-night accommodation booking service. Most of the city's hotels are **small** – twenty rooms, often fewer – and few are chains. Standards are generally high among the hotels and B&Bs, less so with the city's hostels.

HOTELS

★**Adornes** St Annarei 26 ☎ 050 34 13 36, ⊛ adornes .be; map p.107. Medium-sized three-star in a tastefully converted old Flemish town house. Both the public areas and the comfortable bedrooms are decorated in attractive pastel shades which emphasize the antique charm of the place. The location's great – at the junction of two canals near the east end of Spiegelrei – and the breakfasts delicious. Also very child-friendly. **€130**

★**Alegria** St-Jakobsstraat 34 ☎ 050 33 09 37, ⊛ alegria-hotel.com; map p.107. Formerly a B&B, this appealing, family-run three-star has a dozen or so large and well-appointed rooms, each decorated in attractive shades of brown, cream and white. The rooms at the back, overlooking the garden, are quieter than those at the front. The owner is a mine of information about where and what to eat, and the hotel is in a central location, near the Markt. **€110**

Cordoeanier Cordoeaniersstraat 18 ☎ 050 33 90 51, ⊛ cordoeanier.be; map p.107. Medium-sized, family-run two-star hotel handily located in a narrow side street a couple of minutes' walk north of the Burg. Mosquitoes can be a problem here, but the 22 rooms are neat, trim and modern. **€95**

Egmond Minnewater 15 ☎ 050 34 14 45, ⊛ egmond .be; map pp.104–105. Set in a neo-Gothic manor house, this rambling three-star stands in a quiet location with its own gardens, just metres from the Minnewater. The public rooms are a tad dishevelled, but they do have wooden beamed ceilings and fine eighteenth-century chimneypieces, while the eight guest rooms are comfortable-traditional and surprisingly affordable. Parking too – something of a rarity in Bruges. **€140**

Europ Augustijnenrei 18 ☎ 050 33 79 75, ⊛ hoteleurop .com; map p.107. Two-star hotel in a late nineteenth-century town house overlooking a canal about a 5min walk north of the Burg. The public areas are somewhat frumpy and the modern bedrooms distinctly spartan, but the prices are very competitive. **€90**

De Goezeput Goezeputstraat 29 ☎ 050 34 26 94, ⊛ hotelgoezeput.be; map p.107. In a charming location near the cathedral, this enjoyable two-star hotel occupies a thoroughly refurbished eighteenth-century convent. The guest rooms, which vary considerably in size, have been done out in contemporary style in shades of brown and cream, though the old wooden beams have been left in place. **€90**

Jacobs Baliestraat 1 ☎ 050 33 98 31, ⊛ hoteljacobs .com; map p.107. A good budget option, this three-star hotel in a quiet, central location occupies a modernized old brick building complete with a precipitous crow-step gable. The twenty-odd rooms are decorated in a crisp, modern style, though some are a little small. €95

★**Montanus** Nieuwe Gentweg 78 ☎050 33 11 76, ⓦmontanus.be; map p.107. This four-star hotel occupies a big old house that has been sympathetically modernized with few of the decorative over-elaboration of many of its rivals. The twelve rooms here are large, comfortable and modern – and there are twelve more at the back, in chalet-like accommodation at the far end of the large garden. There's also an especially appealing room in what amounts to a (cosy and luxurious) garden shed. The garden also accommodates *Den Heerd* (see p.107), an up-market restaurant. €100

Die Swaene Steenhouwersdijk 1 ☎050 34 27 98, ⓦdieswaene.com; map p.107. In a perfect location, beside a particularly pretty and peaceful section of canal close to the Burg, this long-established, slightly faded four-star has thirty guest rooms decorated in an individual and rather sumptuous antique style. There's also a heated pool and sauna. €150

★**Ter Duinen** Langerei 52 ☎050 33 04 37, ⓦhotelterduinen.eu; map pp.104–105. Charming three-star hotel in a lovely part of the city, beside the Langerei canal fifteen minutes' walk from the Markt. Occupies a beautifully maintained eighteenth-century villa, with period public areas and modern rooms. Superb breakfasts, too. €130

BED & BREAKFASTS

Absoluut Verhulst Verbrand Nieuwland 1 ☎050 33 45 15, ⓦb-bverhulst.com; map pp.104–105. Immaculate B&B with a handful of en-suite rooms in a tastefully modernized seventeenth-century house with its own walled garden. The Loft Suite is larger (and slightly more expensive) than the other rooms. €95

Côté Canal Hertsbergestraat 8–10 ☎0475 45 77 07, ⓦbruges-bedandbreakfast.be; map p.107. Deluxe affair in a pair of handsome – and handsomely restored – eighteenth-century houses, with four large guest rooms/suites kitted out in grand period style down to the huge, flowing drapes. Central location; the garden backs onto a canal. €160

Huis Koning Oude Zak 25 ☎0476 25 08 12, ⓦhuiskoning.be; map p.107. A plushly renovated B&B in a seventeenth-century, step-gable terrace house with a pleasant canalside garden. The three en-suite guest rooms are decorated in a fresh-feeling modern style and two have canal views. €110

iRoom Verversdijk 1 ☎050 33 73 53, ⓦiroom.be; map p.107. Three well-equipped and well-appointed modern rooms, all en suite, in a sympathetically updated nineteenth-century house within easy walking distance of the centre. Competitively priced. €100

Number 11 Peerdenstraat 11 ☎050 33 06 75, ⓦnumber11.be; map p.107. In the heart of old Bruges, on a traffic-free side street, this first-rate B&B in an ancient terrace house has just three lavish guest rooms: all wooden floors, beamed ceilings and expensive wallpaper. Every comfort is laid on – and smashing breakfasts too. €150

Sint-Niklaas B&B St-Niklaasstraat 18 ☎050 61 03 08, ⓦsintnik.be; map p.107. In a good-looking, three-storey, eighteenth-century townhouse on a side street near the Markt, this well-kept B&B has three modern, en-suite guest rooms. One has a lovely view of the Belfort. €120

HOSTELS

HI Hostel Europa Baron Ruzettelaan 143 ☎050 35 26 79, ⓦjeugdherbergen.be/en; map pp.104–105. Big and somewhat institutional-looking hostel in its own grounds, a (dreary) 2km south of the centre in the suburb of Assebroek. There are over 200 beds in a mixture of rooms from singles through to six-bed dorms, most en suite. Breakfast is included in the price and there are security lockers, wi-fi, free parking, a bar and a lounge. City bus #2 from the train station goes within 150m – ask the driver to let you off at the Wantestraat bus stop. Dorm €20, double €52

St Christopher's Bauhaus Langestraat 135 ☎050 34 10 93, ⓦbauhaus.be; map pp.104–105. This lively, laid-back hostel a 15mins walk east of the Burg has a bit of a boho air and offers a mishmash of rooms accommodating between two and ten bunks each. Bike rental, lockers, a bar and café also available. Dorm €21, double €68

EATING

There are scores of cafés, café-bars and restaurants in Bruges, and thankfully precious few are owned by chains. Many are aimed at the **day-trippers**, with variable results, but there's also a slew of **first-rate places**, from the expensive to the affordable. Most waiters speak at least a modicum of **English** – many are fluent – and multilingual menus are the norm.

CAFÉS AND CAFÉ-BARS

★**De Belegde Boterham** Kleine St-Amandsstraat 5 ☎050 34 91 31, ⓦdebelegdeboterham.be; map p.107. Most of the cafés in and around the Markt are firmly tourist-orientated, but this bright and breezy little place, in attractively renovated old premises down a narrow lane, has a strong local following on account of its wonderfully

fresh sandwiches (€9–11) and substantial, absolutely delicious salads (€14). Mon–Sat 11.30am–4pm.

Books & Brunch Garenmarkt 30 ☎050 70 90 79, ⓦbooksandbrunch.be; map p.107. There's a cosy, family vibe at this cheerful little café, where they do tasty, healthy lunches and light meals prepared from organic sources. Cakes too – try the cupcakes – and a tasty cup of coffee. Mon–Fri

9am–5pm, but closed during some school holidays.

Café Craenenburg Markt 16 ☎050 33 34 02, ⓦcraenenburg.be; map p.107. Unlike the Markt's other tourist-dominated café-restaurants, this old-fashioned place still attracts a loyal local clientele. With its leather and wood panelling, wooden benches and mullion windows, the *Craenenburg* has the flavour of old Flanders, and although the daytime-only food is routine (mains from €18), it has a good range of beers, including a locally produced, tangy brown ale called Brugse Tripel. No cards. Daily 10am until late.

★**Café Vlissinghe** Blekersstraat 2 ☎050 34 37 37, ⓦcafevlissinghe.be; map p.107. With its wood panelling, antique paintings and long wooden tables, this is one of the oldest and most distinctive bars in Bruges, thought to date from 1515. The atmosphere is relaxed and easy-going, with the emphasis on quiet conversation – there are certainly no jukeboxes here – and the café-style food is very Flemish. There's a pleasant garden terrace too. Wed & Thurs 11am–10pm, Fri & Sat 11am–midnight, Sun 11am–7pm.

In Den Wittenkop St-Jakobsstraat 14 ☎050 33 20 59, ⓦindenwittenkop.be; map p.107. This cosy, split-level restaurant with its hotchpotch decor specializes in traditional Flemish dishes – try, for example, the rabbit in prunes or the local speciality of pork and beef stewed in Trappist beer. There's smooth jazz as background music too. Mains average €22. Tues–Sat 6–10.30pm.

Le Pain Quotidien Philipstockstraat 21 ☎050 33 60 50, ⓦlepainquotidien.com; map p.107. This first-rate bread shop, part of a chain, doubles as a wholefood café, with one long wooden sharing table – which can be good fun – and a few smaller side tables too. The home-made soup and bread makes a meal in itself, or you can chomp away on a range of snacks and cakes. Mon–Sat 7am–6.30pm, Sun 8am–5.30pm.

Sorbetiere de Medici Geldmuntstraat 9 ☎050 33 93 41, ⓦdemedici.be; map p.107. This two-floor café, with its huge mirror and spindly curving staircase, serves great coffee plus tasty pastas and salads. But these are as nothing compared to the hot dessert pies – the almond with red berry juice will have you weeping with delight. Mon–Sat 9am–6pm.

De Windmolen Carmersstraat 135 ☎050 33 97 39; map p.107. This amiable neighbourhood café-bar in an old brick house at the east end of Carmersstraat is a pick for its setting – away from the crowds and next to the grassy bank that marks the course of the old city wall. Has a competent beer menu and dishes up a decent line in inexpensive snacks – keep to the simpler offerings. Has a pleasant outside terrace and an interior dotted with folksy knick-knacks. Mon–Thurs 10am–10pm, Fri & Sun 10am–3pm.

RESTAURANTS

Den Amand St-Amandstraat 4 ☎050 34 01 22, ⓦdenamand.be; map p.107. This informal, family-run restaurant offers an inventive range of dishes combining Flemish, Italian and even Chinese cuisines. Mains from the limited but well-chosen menu – for instance, brill in coconut milk – average a very reasonable €20. It's a small place, so best to book a few hours in advance. Daily except Wed & Sun noon–2.15pm & 6–9.15pm.

Christophe Garenmarkt 34 ☎050 34 48 92, ⓦchristophe-brugge.be; map p.107. Rural chic furnishings and fittings make for a relaxing atmosphere at this little bistro, where a Franco-Flemish menu is especially strong on meat. One exception is the excellent bouillabaisse. Mains average €24. Mon & Thurs–Sun 7–11pm.

Kok au Vin Ezelstraat 19 ☎050 33 95 21, ⓦkok-au-vin.be; map p.107. Chic restaurant in tastefully modernized old premises on the north side of the city centre. An ambitious menu covers all the Franco-Belgian bases and then some, with mains averaging around €27, though lunch is half that. Try the signature dish – coq au vin. Reservations essential. Daily except Sun & Mon noon–2pm & 6.30–10pm.

★**Pomperlut** Minderbroedersstraat 26 ☎050 70 86 26, ⓦpomperlut.be; map p.107. This outstanding restaurant has got just about everything right – from the ersatz medievalism of the decor (the house is old, but the wood beams and large chimneypiece were inserted during the refurbishment) through to the Franco-Flemish cuisine: there is no menu as such but a daily selection written on a blackboard. Mains average €26. Reservations essential. Tues–Sat noon–2.30pm & 6–10pm.

Pro Deo Langestraat 161 ☎050 33 73 55, ⓦbistroprodeo.be; map pp.104–105. This informal bistro-style restaurant is a local favourite, its enterprising menu emphasizing traditional Flemish cuisine: try, for example, the *stoofvlees* (Flemish beef stew) for just €17. The decor is very folksy and there's a jazz meets soul soundtrack. Tues–Sat noon–2pm & 6–10pm.

De Refter Molenmeers 2 ☎050 44 49 00, ⓦbistrorefter.com; map p.107. Fashionable bistro-restaurant with über-cool decor where the emphasis is on classic Flemish dishes using local, seasonal ingredients – try the meatballs in a tarragon sauce. Competitively priced too, with a two-course set meal costing just €25. Outside terrace for summertime dining; one criticism: the tables are too close together. Tues–Sat noon–2pm & 6.30–10pm.

De Stove Kleine St-Amandsstraat 4 ☎050 33 78 35, ⓦrestaurantdestove.be; map p.107. Small Franco-Belgian restaurant that's recommended by just about everyone. The menu is carefully constructed, with both fish and meat dishes given equal prominence. A la carte mains around €30, but the big deal is the three-course set menu for €50 (€65 with wine). Reservations essential. Mon, Tues and Fri–Sun 7–10pm, plus Sat & Sun noon–2pm.

DRINKING AND NIGHTLIFE

Few would say Bruges' bars are cutting-edge, but neither are they staid and dull. Indeed, **drinking** in the city can be a real pleasure and one of the potential highlights of any visit. As for the **club scene**, Bruges struggles to make a real fist of it, though a couple of places are enjoyable enough.

B-in Mariastraat 38 ☎050 31 13 00, ⓦb-in.be; map p.107. The coolest place in town, this slick bar, club and restaurant is kitted out in attractive modern style with low sofa-seats and an eye-grabbing mix of coloured fluorescent tubes and soft ceiling lights. Guest DJs play funky, uplifting house and the drinks and cocktails are reasonably priced. The club side of things gets going about 11pm. Free entry. Tues–Sat 11am–3am, sometimes later.

Het Brugs Beertje Kemelstraat 5 ☎050 33 96 16, ⓦbrugsbeertje.be; map p.107. This small and friendly speciality beer bar claims a stock of three hundred brews (plus guest beers on draught), which aficionados reckon is one of the best selections in Belgium. There are tasty snacks too, such as cheeses and salad, but note that the place is very much on the (backpacker) tourist trail. Mon & Thurs–Sun 4pm–1am.

★**L'Estaminet** Park 5 ☎050 33 09 16; map p.107. Groovy café-bar with a relaxed neighbourhood feel and (for Bruges) a diverse and cosmopolitan clientele. Drink either in the dimly lit interior or outside on the large sheltered terrace. Has a well-chosen beer menu, which skilfully picks its way through Belgium's vast offering. Daily 11.30am–1am or later, Thurs from 4pm.

★**De Garre** De Garre 1 ☎050 34 10 29, ⓦdegarre.be; map p.107. Down a narrow alley off Breidelstraat, in between the Markt and the Burg, this cramped but charming tavern has an outstanding range of Belgian beers and tasty snacks, while classical music adds to the relaxing

air. Mon–Fri & Sun noon–midnight, Sat 11am–1am.
Lokkedize Korte Vuldersstraat 33 ☎050 33 44 50, ⓦlokkedize.be; map p.107. This popular café-bar is an atmospheric sort of place, all subdued lighting and soft sounds. There is regular live music too, everything from jazz and *chanson* through to R&B. Wed–Sun 6pm to midnight.
★**De Republiek** St-Jacobsstraat 36 ☎050 34 02 29; map p.107. One of the most fashionable and popular spots in town, this large and darkly lit café-bar attracts an arty, mostly youthful clientele. Very reasonably priced snacks, including vegetarian and pasta dishes, plus the occasional gig. Terrace at the back for summertime drinking. Daily from 11am until 3/4am.
De Vuurmolen Kraanplein 5 ☎050 33 00 79, ⓦfacebook.com/Vuurmolen; map p.107. This crowded, student-meets-local bar has a reasonably wide range of beers, a large front terrace and some of the best DJs in town playing a mix of music – techno through to house and beyond. Daily 11am–3am.
Wijnbar Est Braambergstraat 7 ☎050 33 38 39, ⓦwww.wijnbarest.be; map p.107. The best wine bar in town, with a friendly and relaxed atmosphere, an extensive cellar and over twenty wines available by the glass every day. It's especially strong on New World vintages. There's live (and free) jazz, blues and folk music every Sunday from 8pm and the premises are smallish, so expect a crush. Mon & Thurs–Sun 4pm–1am.

SHOPPING

Callebert Wollestraat 25 ☎050 33 50 61, ⓦcallebert.be; map p.107. Bruges' top contemporary homeware, ceramics and furniture shop, featuring leading brands such as Alessi and Bodum, as well as less familiar names. They also stock everything from bags, watches and jewellery to household utensils, textiles and tableware, and the art gallery presents the best of contemporary design, primarily in glass and ceramics.

Mon 2–6pm, Tues–Sat 10am–noon & 2–6pm, Sun 3–6pm.
The Chocolate Line Simon Stevinplein 19 ☎050 34 10 90, ⓦthechocolateline.be; map p.107. The best chocolate shop in town – and there's some serious competition – with everything handmade on the premises using natural ingredients. Truffles and figurines are a speciality. Boxes of mixed chocolates are sold in various

---

FESTIVALS AND EVENTS IN BRUGES

Leading **festivals** in Bruges' crowded calendar include the **Musica Antiqua** festival of medieval music at the beginning of August (ⓦmusica-antiqua.be), though this is but one small part of the more generalized **Festival van Vlaanderen** (Flanders Festival; March–Oct; ⓦfestival.be), which comprises over 500 classical concerts distributed among the big Flemish-speaking cities, including Bruges. Bruges also hosts two big-deal music festivals: the **Cactusfestival** (ⓦcactusmusic.be) of rock, reggae, rap and roots, spread over three days on the second weekend of July; and **Moods** (ⓦmoodsbrugge.be), two and a half weeks (usually from the last weekend of July) devoted to just about every type of music you can think of, with bands and artists drawn from every corner of the globe.

2

sizes: a 250g box costs €14. Tues–Sat 9.30am–6.30pm, Mon & Sun 10.30am–6.30pm.

Claeys Katelijnestraat 54 ☎050 33 98 19, ⓦclaeysantique.com; map p.107. Diane Claeys studied lace history and design in various parts of Europe before opening this shop in 1980. She now sells handmade antique-style lace, from handkerchiefs to edging and tablecloths, plus handmade jewellery. Daily 9am–6pm.

Diksmuids Boterhuis Geldmuntstraat 23 ☎050 33 32 43, ⓦdiksmuidsboterhuis.be; map p.107. One of the few traditional food shops to have survived in central Bruges, this Aladdin's cave of a place specializes in cooked meats, breads, butters and Belgian cheeses. Mon–Sat 9.30am–12.30pm & 2–6.30pm.

Louis Delhaize Noordzandstraat 7; map p.107. Ordinary shops have all but disappeared from central Bruges, but there are a couple of smallish supermarkets – and this is probably the best. Mon–Sat 9am–7pm.

De Reyghere Markt 12 ☎050 33 34 03, ⓦwww .dereyghere.be; map p.107. Founded over a 100 years ago, De Reyghere is a local institution and a meeting place for every book-lover in town. The shop stocks a wide range of domestic and foreign literature, art and reference books, and is also good for international newspapers, magazines and periodicals. Its sister shop, the adjacent Reisboekhandel, specializes in travel. Mon–Sat 8.30am–6.15pm.

De Striep Katelijnestraat 42 ☎050 33 71 12, ⓦstriepclub .be; map p.107. Comics are a Belgian speciality (remember Tintin), yet this is the only comic-strip specialist in Bruges, stocking everything from run-of-the-mill cheapies to collector items in Flemish, French and even English. Mon 1.30–7pm, Tues–Sat 10am–12.30pm & 1.30–7pm.

ENTERTAINMENT

Bruges puts on a varied programme of **performing arts**, mostly as part of its annual schedule of festivals and special events (see box, p.123). As for **film**, Bruges has two excellent art-house cinemas; films are normally shown in the original language, with Dutch subtitles as required. For details of **upcoming events**, either consult the tourist information website (ⓦvisitbruges.be/calendar) or pick up their free, monthly events calendar, "events @brugge".

MAJOR VENUES

Concertgebouw 't Zand ☎050 47 69 99, ticket line ☎070 22 33 02, ⓦconcertgebouw.be. Built to celebrate Bruges' year as a European Capital of Culture in 2002 and now hosting all the performing arts, from opera and classical music through to big-name bands.

Stadsschouwburg Vlamingstraat 29 ☎050 44 30 40, ⓦccbrugge.be. Occupying a big neo-Renaissance building from 1869, and with a wide-ranging programme, including theatre, dance, musicals, concerts and opera.

CYCLING AROUND BRUGES

Some 2km from the centre on the site of what was once a city gate, Bruges' **Dampoort** marks the edge of a pretty parcel of land that extends as far as the E34/N49 motorway, about 14km further to the northeast. This rural backwater is ideal **cycling country**, its green fields crisscrossed by drowsy canals and causeways, each of which is shadowed by poplar trees which quiver and rustle in the prevailing westerly winds. If you want to explore the myriad routes in this area, you should buy the detailed **Fietsnetwerk Brugse Ommeland Noord** (cycling map; 1:50,000) from any major bookshop or Bruges tourist information before you pedal off.

One especially delightful itinerary is a 28km round trip that begins by leaving Dampoort to the northeast along the **Brugge-Sluis canal**, which you follow as far as the quaint village of **DAMME**, 7km northeast of Bruges and in medieval times the town's main seaport via the River Zwin. At its height, Damme boasted a population of ten thousand, but the river silted up in the fifteenth century and Damme slipped into a long decline until the second-homers arrived to create the genteel village of today. Damme's main street, **Kerkstraat**, lies at right angles to the canal and is worth a quick gander, its proudest building being the fifteenth-century **Stadhuis** (no public access), whose elegant, symmetrical facade was funded by a special tax on barrels of herrings.

Returning to the Brugge-Sluis canal, carry on east as far as the tiny hamlet of **Hoeke**, cycling over the wider **Leopoldkanaal** on the way. At Hoeke, just over the bridge, turn hard left for the narrow causeway – the **Krinkeldijk** – that wanders straight back in the direction of Bruges, running to the north of the Brugge-Sluis canal. Just over 3km long, the Krinkeldijk drifts across a beguiling landscape of whitewashed farmhouses and deep-green grassy fields before reaching an intersection where you turn left to regain the Brugge-Sluis waterway.

CINEMAS

Ciné Liberty Kuipersstraat 23 ☎050 33 20 11, ⓦcinema-liberty.be. Right in the centre of town, this cinema offers a choice selection of English and American mainstream and cult films.

Cinema Lumière Sint Jacobstraat 36 ☎050 34 34 65, ⓦcinenews.be. Bruges' premier venue for alternative, cult, foreign and art-house movies, with three screens.

DIRECTORY

ATMs ATMs in central Bruges include: Europabank at Vlamingstraat 13 and ING at St-Amandstraat 13, just off the Markt. There are also ATMs at the train station.

Doctors and emergencies For night-time doctors (7pm–8am), call ☎078 15 15 90; for medical emergencies call ☎112.

Pharmacies Liberally distributed across the city centre, with late-night duty rotas usually displayed in the window; for late-night and weekend pharmacies, you can also call ☎0900 10 500.

Post office Markt 5 (Mon–Fri 9am–6pm, Sat 9am–3pm).

Ostend and the coast

The *Baedeker* of 1900 distinguished **OSTEND** as "one of the most fashionable and cosmopolitan watering places in Europe". The gloss may be gone today, and the aristocratic visitors have certainly moved on to more exotic climes, but Ostend remains a likeable, liveable seaport with a clutch of first-rate seafood restaurants, a string of earthy bars, an enjoyable art museum and – easily the most popular of the lot – a long slice of sandy **beach**.

Ostend also marks the midway point of the Belgian **coast**, which stretches for some 70km from Knokke-Heist in the east to De Panne in the west. A superb sandy **beach** extends along almost all of the coast, but the dunes that once backed onto it have largely disappeared beneath an ugly covering of apartment blocks and bungalow settlements, a veritable carpet of concrete that obscures the landscape and depresses the soul. There are, however, one or two breaks in the aesthetic gloom, principally **De Haan**, a charming little seaside resort with easy access to a slender slice of pristine coastline; the substantial remains of the **Atlantikwall** built by the Germans to repel the Allies in World War II; and the enjoyable Paul Delvaux Museum in **St-Idesbald**. Exploring the coast by public transport could not be easier: a fast and frequent **tram** – the **Kusttram** – runs from one end to the other (see box, p.130).

Brief history

The old fishing village of **Ostend** was given a town charter in the thirteenth century, in recognition of its growing importance as a port for trade across the Channel. Flanked by an empty expanse of sand dune, it remained the only important coastal settlement hereabouts until the construction of Zeebrugge six centuries later – the dunes were always an inadequate protection against the sea and precious few people chose to live along the coast until a chain of massive **sea walls** was completed in the nineteenth century. Like so many other towns in the Spanish Netherlands, Ostend was attacked and besieged time and again, winning the admiration of Protestant Europe in resisting the Spaniards during a desperate **siege** that lasted from 1601 to 1604. Later, convinced of the wholesome qualities of sea air and determined to impress other European rulers with their sophistication, Belgium's first kings, Léopold I and II, turned Ostend into a chichi **resort**, demolishing the town walls and dotting the outskirts with prestigious buildings and parks. Several of these have survived, but others were destroyed during **World War II**, when the town's docks made it a prime bombing target. One of the escapees at this time was the young **Ralph Miliband**, the father of the Labour politicians Ed and David. Subsequently, Ostend resumed its role as a major **cross-Channel port** until the completion of the Channel Tunnel in 1994 undermined its position. Since then, Ostend has had to reinvent itself, emphasizing its charms as a seaside resort and centre of culture. There's some way to go – but Ostend is on the up.

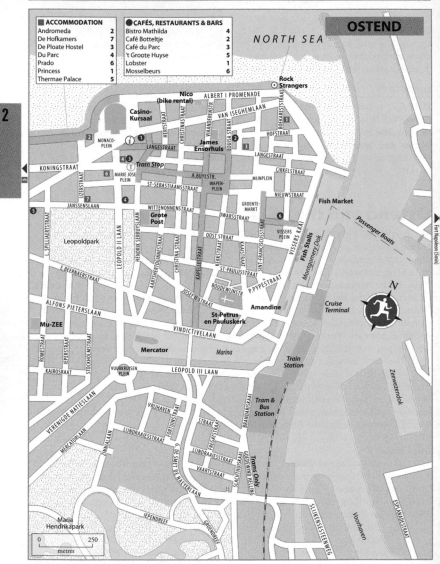

■ ACCOMMODATION		● CAFÉS, RESTAURANTS & BARS	
Andromeda	2	Bistro Mathilda	4
De Hofkamers	7	Café Botteltje	2
De Ploate Hostel	3	Café du Parc	3
Du Parc	4	't Groote Huyse	5
Prado	6	Lobster	1
Princess	1	Mosselbeurs	6
Thermae Palace	5		

OSTEND

NORTH SEA

St-Petrus-en-Pauluskerk

St-Paulussstraat • Daily 9am–4pm • Free

Ostend's town centre is a largely modern affair, with narrow, straight streets lined by a battery of apartment blocks. The whopping **St-Petrus-en-Pauluskerk** appears to buck this trend, but the church does in fact date from the early twentieth century. At the back is the last remnant of its predecessor, a massive sixteenth-century brick **tower** with a canopied, distinctly morbid shrine of the Crucifixion at its base.

> ### MARVIN GAYE'S OSTEND
>
> One of the greatest soul singers of all time, **Marvin Gaye** arrived in Ostend on February 14 1981 and stayed here until the following year, when family and musical ties pulled him back to the US. Just two years later, he was killed by his father in bizarre circumstances in Los Angeles. Tourist information have prepared a "Marvin Gaye Midnight Love Tour" audio tour (€5), which guides you round every place with a Gaye connection in Ostend – and good fun it is too.

Wapenplein

At the northern end of pedestrianized **Kapellestraat**, the principal shopping street, is the **Wapenplein**, a pleasant open space that zeros in on an old-fashioned bandstand. Typical of so much of Ostend, the square was once in the doldrums, but canny planning and sympathetic redevelopment have turned it into a very sociable spot. The south side of the square is dominated by the former **Feest-en Kultuurpaleis** (Festival and Culture Hall), an imposing 1950s building that is now a shopping centre.

James Ensorhuis

Vlaanderenstraat 27 · Daily except Tues 10am–noon & 2–5pm · €2 · ☎ 059 50 81 18

The **James Ensorhuis** is of some specialist interest as the artist's home for the last thirty years of his life. It was from here that his aunt and uncle sold shells and souvenirs – hence the assorted knick-knacks in the window – but the shop is long gone and the ground floor now exhibits a few Ensor-related incidentals, masks and so forth. Upstairs you'll find the painter's living room-cum-studio – the **Blue Room** – which has been returned to something like its appearance at the time of his death, a cluttered and somehow rather repressed room decorated with his intense paintings, though these aren't originals.

Visserskaai

Fish stalls Tues–Sun from 7am; fish market daily from 8am

With a string of restaurants on one side and fish stalls on the other, **Visserskaai** cuts a jaunty path up along the side of the **Montgomery Dok**, named after the British commander and formerly the main car-ferry dock. The **fish stalls** offer an astounding range of fresh, cooked and dried fish partly supplied by Ostend's own fishing fleet. Here also is the fish market, the **Vistrap**, and the jetty for the passenger ferry (see p.128) that shuttles across the harbour to Fort Napoleon (see p.128). The north end of Visserskaai sports a large and somehow rather engaging piece of contemporary sculpture, the orange-red figures of *Rock Strangers* by Belgium's own Arne Quinze (b. 1971).

The seafront and beach

Casino Gaming daily 9am–5am · Ⓦ casinooostende.be · Kursaal Ⓦ kursaaloostende.be

Ostend **casino**, housed in an expansive structure dating from 1953, is attached to the glassy, modern **Kursaal** exhibition and concert centre. The two abut Ostend's main attraction, its **sandy beach**, which extends as far as the eye can see. On summer days, thousands drive into town to soak up the sun, swim and amble along the seafront **promenade**, which runs along the top of the sea wall. Part sea defence and part royal ostentation, the promenade was built to link the town centre with the Wellington racecourse, 2km to the west. It was – and remains – an intentionally grand walkway that pandered to the grandiose tastes of King Léopold II. To hammer home the royal point, the king's **statue**, with fawning Belgians and Congolese at its base, still stands in the middle of a long line of columns towards the promenade's west end. These columns now adjoin the **Thermae Palace Hotel**, which was the epitome of luxury when it was added in the 1930s.

Léopold II-laan

Mercator daily 10am–5pm • €4 • ⓦ zeilschipmercator.be

The dead-straight boulevard of **Léopold II-laan** cuts past the little lakes, bandstand and mini-bridges of the **Léopoldpark**, a delightful and especially verdant park laid out in the 1860s. Across the boulevard, unmissable on Hendrik Serruyslaan, is the former post office, the **Grote Post**, a forceful 1950s building with a mighty statue of a messenger standing on a parapet to a design by Belgium's Gaston Eysselinck. Further down the boulevard you reach the sailing ship **Mercator**, the old training vessel of the Belgian merchant navy, which has been converted into a marine museum holding a hotchpotch of items accumulated during her voyages.

Mu.ZEE

Romestraat 11 • Tues–Sun 10am–6pm • €5, though exhibitions cost extra • ☏ 059 50 81 18, ⓦ muzee.be

Mu.ZEE (Kunstmuseum aan Zee), Ostend's capacious fine art museum, displays a wide selection of modern Belgian paintings drawn from its permanent collection alongside temporary exhibitions, mostly of contemporary works. The paintings are regularly rotated (and the museum's lay-out can be puzzling) but highlights of the permanent collection include the harsh Surrealism of *The Ijzer Time* by **Paul Delvaux** (1897–1994) and several piercing canvases by **Leon Spilliaert** (1881–1946). A native of Ostend, Spilliaert was smitten by the land and seascapes of his home town, using them in his work time and again – as in *De Windstoot* (*Gust of Wind*), with its dark, forbidding colours and screaming woman, and the comparable *Melancholie*. There's also an excellent sample of the work of **James Ensor** (1860–1949), who was born in Ostend, the son of an English father and Flemish mother. Barely noticed until the 1920s, Ensor spent nearly all his 89 years working in his home town, and is nowadays considered a pioneer of Expressionism. His first paintings were rather sombre portraits and landscapes, but in the early 1880s he switched to brilliantly contrasting colours, most familiarly in his *Self-portrait with Flowered Hat*, a deliberate variation on Rubens' famous self-portraits. Less well known is *The Artist's Mother in Death*, a fine, penetrating example of his preoccupation with the grim and macabre.

Fort Napoleon

Vuurtorenweg • April–June & Sept–Oct Wed–Sun 10am–5pm; July–Aug daily 10am–5pm; Nov–March Wed 1–5pm, Sat & Sun 10am–5pm • €6 • ☏ 059 32 00 48, ⓦ fortnapoleon.be • Take coastal tram to "Duin en Zee" stop, from where it's a 5–10min walk; or catch passenger ferry (April–Sept daily every 30min–1hr 6.30am–9pm; Oct–March daily, hourly 8am–6pm; free) across the harbour from Montgomery Dok to Maritiemplein, a 10min walk from the fort

Completed in 1812, **Fort Napoleon** is one of the best-preserved Napoleonic fortresses in Europe, an impressive star-shaped structure whose concentric brick walls are planted on the dunes immediately behind the seashore on the eastern side of Ostend's harbour. The careful design meant that potential attackers could be fired on from almost every angle and so confident were the French of the fort's impregnability that the garrison never exceeded 260 men (and 46 cannon). It takes about twenty minutes to wander the fort's long, echoing galleries, but in truth there's nothing much to see apart from the actual structure.

ARRIVAL AND GETTING AROUND   OSTEND

By train Ostend train station is on the east edge of the town centre, a 10min stroll from the tourist information office.

Destinations Bruges (every 30min; 15min); Brussels (hourly; 1hr 20min); Ghent (every 30min; 40min).
By coastal tram The station for the coastal tram

(see box, p.130) is next door to the train station. The Kusstram has two stops in central Ostend – it also stops on Marie Joséplein.

Destinations De Panne (every 15min in summer, every 30min in winter; 1hr 10min); Knokke (same frequency; 1hr).

By bike One of the most reliable bike rental places is Nico, at Albert 1-Promenade 44A (☎059 23 34 81, ⓦnicokarts.be).

By ferry There are currently no car ferries from the UK to Ostend and the nearest you'll get is Zeebrugge, a few kilometres east along the coast, which has a ferry link with Hull (see p.22). There's also a passenger ferry across Ostend harbour from the Montgomery Dok for visitors heading to Fort Napoleon (see p.128).

By car Try Europcar at Zandvoordeschorredijkstraat 48 (☎059 50 12 18); tourist information has a complete list of local car rental places.

INFORMATION AND PASSES

Tourist information Opposite the casino at Monacoplein 2 (April to mid-Nov daily 10am–6pm; mid-Nov to March daily 10am–5.30pm; ☎059 70 11 99, ⓦvisitoostende.be).

City pass Sold at the tourist information office, the Ostend City Pass is valid for all attractions – including the "Marvin Gaye Midnight Love Tour" audio tour (see box, p.127) – and costs €12 (24hr), €15 (48hr) or €20 (72hr).

ACCOMMODATION

The best option is a **beachside** hotel, but these are few and far between (most of the seashore is given over to apartment blocks) so you might plump instead for the area round **Léopoldpark** on the west side of the centre, a pleasant district with a relaxed and easy air. Tourist information can help you find **last-minute** accommodation in one of Ostend's many hotels and guesthouses at no charge. There's also a good HI hostel in town.

HOTELS

Andromeda Kursaal Westhelling 5 ☎059 80 66 11, ⓦandromedahotel.be. Smart, modern four-star high-rise next door to the casino, and overlooking the town's beach. Many rooms have balconies and sea views (for a surcharge of around €50), plus there are fitness facilities and an indoor pool. **€150**

★**De Hofkamers** Ijzerstraat 5 ☎059 70 63 49, ⓦdehofkamers.be. A family-run three-star hotel whose somewhat dour exterior belies its cosy public areas, kitted out with all sorts of local bygones, and the comfortable bedrooms beyond. The nicest room, on the top (sixth) floor, has its own mini-balcony with a view (albeit a somewhat distant one) of the sea. Excellent breakfasts too. **€150**

Du Parc Marie Joséplein 3 ☎059 70 16 80, ⓦhotelduparc.be. Located in a fetching Art Deco block a short stroll from the beach, this medium-sized three-star hotel offers attractively furnished modern rooms at competitive prices. The ground-floor café (see p.130), with its Tiffany glass trimmings, is a favourite with older locals. **€90**

★**Prado** Léopold II-laan 22 ☎059 70 53 06, ⓦhotelprado.be. Very likeable three-star hotel with neatly furnished modern rooms, attentive staff, especially tasty breakfasts, and views over a mini-park-cum-square, Marie Joséplein. Ask for a room at the front, overlooking the square – and a few floors up from the traffic. **€130**

Princess Boekareststraat 7 ☎059 70 68 88, ⓦhotelprincess.be. Family-owned 35-room hotel in a modern block on a narrow side street a couple of minutes' walk from the beach. The rooms are modestly decorated and the better ones have mini-balconies. **€85**

Thermae Palace Koningin Astridlaan 7 ☎059 80 66 44, ⓦthermaepalace.be. Four-star hotel a 10min walk west of the centre that long enjoyed the reputation of being Ostend's best. The building is certainly striking – think Art Deco extravagance, expansive public rooms and spacious bedrooms offering sea views – yet the place can't help but seem a little sorry for itself: there's just so much here to keep in good working order. **€120**

HOSTEL

De Ploate Hostel Langestraat 72 ☎059 80 52 97, ⓦjeugdherbergen.be/en. Well maintained and recently moved into bright new premises, this HI hostel sits right in the centre of town and offers 49 en-suite rooms of varying sizes. There's a decent café serving inexpensive meals, wi-fi, a bar and self-catering facilities. The overnight fee includes breakfast. Reservations are strongly advised in summer. Dorm **€23**, double **€52**

EATING AND DRINKING

Ostend has scores of cafés, café-bars and restaurants, with the big gastronomic deal being seafood – as also evidenced by the **seafood stalls** set up along Visserskaai. The tourist board has led a campaign to encourage the use of less familiar fish, and the results are visible on many a menu. The city centre's **bars** are, on the other hand, rather harder to warm to, with the majority pretty rough and ready, or at least dark and gloomy.

2

★**Bistro Mathilda** Léopold II–laan 1 ☎ 059 51 06 70, ⓦ bistromathilda.be. Smooth, slick and stylish restaurant in modern premises with attentive service and a wonderfully creative menu that's especially strong on seafood. Mains average €26. Wed–Sun noon–2.30pm & 6–10pm.

Café Botteltje Louisastraat 19 ☎ 059 70 09 28. Ersatz brown café with a bit more character than most of the bars in downtown Ostend – plus a formidable selection of bottled and draught beers. Mon 4.30pm–1am, Tues–Sun 11.30am–1am.

Café du Parc Marie Joséplein 3 ☎ 059 51 13 05, ⓦ brasserieduparc.be. Old-fashioned café, part of the *Hotel du Parc* (see p.129), whose main claim to fame is its Art Deco furnishings and fittings – from the Tiffany glass down to the wooden chairs and leather benches. Avoid the food. Daily 8am–10pm, but closed on Mon in winter.

't Groote Huyse Karel Janssenlaan 10 ☎ 059 70 10 67, ⓦ tgroothuys.be. Set in a cleverly reconfigured nineteenth-century mansion, this delightful café-restaurant offers an inventive menu which is particularly strong on salads and pasta dishes, which average about €13. Pancakes too (from €3). Has a lovely, leafy terrace at the back. Tues–Thurs 10.30am–6.30pm, Fri & Sat 11am–9pm.

Lobster Van Iseghemlaan 64 ☎ 059 50 02 82, ⓦ lobster.be. No prizes for guessing the house speciality at this long-established restaurant, which deserves its good reputation. Don't be put off by the rather dismal entrance, as the dining area itself is fine. A two-course "Menu of the Month" costs €38. Mon noon–2pm, Wed–Sun noon–2pm & 6.30–9.30pm.

Mosselbeurs Dwarsstraat 10 ☎ 059 80 73 10, ⓦ demosselbeurs.be. One of the liveliest restaurants in town, with cheerfully naff nautical fittings and top-notch fishy dishes, especially eels and mussels. Reasonable prices, too, with mains from €22. No cards. Wed–Sun noon–2pm & 6–10pm.

The coast east of Ostend

Heading east along the coast from Ostend, the undoubted highlight is **De Haan**, the prettiest and the most appealing seaside resort of them all. Beyond lie kiss-me-quick **Blankenberge**, the heavily industrialized port of **Zeebrugge** and sprawling **Knokke-Heist**. The latter is not an immediately appealing place, but you might be drawn here by one of its many **festivals**, most notably the International Cartoon Festival (ⓦ knokke-heist.info), which runs from the middle of July to the middle of September.

De Haan

Flanked by empty sand dunes, **DE HAAN** is a popular family resort with an excellent **beach** and a pleasant seafront promenade. It was established at the end of the nineteenth century, conceived as an exclusive seaside village in a rustic Gothic Revival style known as *Style Normand*. The building plots were irregularly dispersed between the tram station and the sea, with the whole caboodle set around a pattern of winding streets reminiscent of – and influenced by – contemporary English suburbs. The only formality was provided by a central circus with a casino plonked in the middle, though this was demolished in 1929. Casino apart, De Haan has survived pretty much intact – a welcome relief from the surrounding apartment-block development.

THE KUSTTRAM – THE COASTAL TRAM

Fast and efficient, the **Kusttram** (ⓦ delijn.be/dekusttram) travels the length of the Belgian coast from Knokke-Heist train station in the east to De Panne train station in the west, putting all the Belgian resorts within easy striking distance of each other. Services are **regular**: in both directions, trams depart every ten or fifteen minutes in summer and every half-hour in winter. There are **multilingual ticket machines** at most tram stops and there's a De Lijn **ticket office** at Ostend tram station. Tickets can also be bought from the driver, but in this case you pay a small premium. **Fares** are relatively inexpensive – Ostend to either Knokke-Heist or De Panne, for instance, costs €2 (€3 from the driver). You can also buy tickets for unlimited tram travel, valid for either one day (*dagpas*; €5, €7 from the driver) or three days (*driedagenpas*; €10, €12).

ARRIVAL AND GETTING AROUND

By tram De Haan aan Zee coastal tram stop is a 5–10min walk from the beach.

By bike Cycle rental, is available at André Fietsen, Leopoldlaan 9 (☎ 059 23 37 89, ⓦ fietsenandre.be).

INFORMATION

Tourist information Next to De Haan tram stop (April–Oct daily 9.30am–noon & 1.30–5pm; Nov–March Sat & Sun 10am–noon & 2–5pm; ☎ 059 24 21 35, ⓦ www.dehaan.be). They issue a useful English-language leaflet describing local cycling routes.

ACCOMMODATION

Auberge des Rois Beach Hotel Zeedijk 1 ☎ 059 23 30 18, ⓦ beachhotel.be. This smart, modern, medium-sized hotel has a splendid location, overlooking the beach and just a few metres from an undeveloped tract of sand dune. The guest rooms are spick and span and the best have wide sea views (attracting a €30 premium). **€140**

Manoir Carpe Diem Prins Karellaan 12 ☎ 059 23 32 20, ⓦ manoircarpediem.com. Chichi, four-star hotel in a handsome *Style Normand* villa, which perches on a grassy knoll about 400m from the beach. It's all very period – from

2

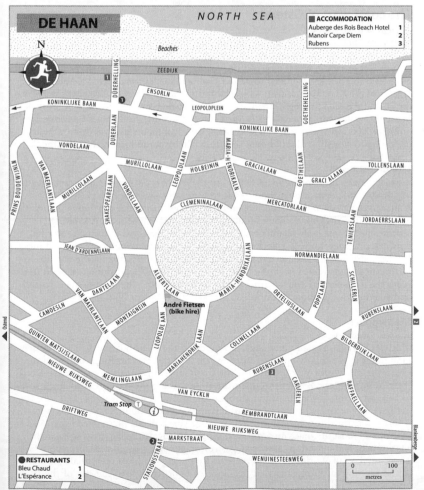

DE HAAN

NORTH SEA

Beaches

■ ACCOMMODATION
Auberge des Rois Beach Hotel 1
Manoir Carpe Diem 2
Rubens 3

ZEEDIJK
DÜRERHELLING
ENSORLN
KONINKLIJKE BAAN
LEOPOLDPLEIN
GOETHEHELLING
VONDELAAN
DURERLAAN
KONINKLIJKE BAAN
MURILLOLAAN
LEOPOLDLAAN
HOLBEINLN
GRACIALAAN
GOETHELAAN
TOLLENSLAAN
MARIA-HENDRIKALN
PRINS BOUDEWIJNLN
VAN MAERLANTLAAN
MURILLOLAAN
SHAKESPEARELAAN
VONDELLAAN
GRACI ALAAN
MERCATORLAAN
CLEMENINALAAN
TENIERSLAAN
JORDAERRSLAAN
JEAN D'ARDENNELAAN
NORMANDIELAAN
ALBERTLAAN
MARIA-HENDRIKALAAN
SCHILLERLN
DANTELAAN
André Fietsen (bike hire)
ORTELIUSLAAN
POPPLAAN
VAN MAERLANTLAAN
MONTAIGNELN
CAMOESLN
LEOPOLDLAAN
RUBENSLAAN
QUINTEN MATSIJSLAAN
MARIAHENDRIK LAAN
COLINELLAAN
BILDERDIJKLAAN
NIEUWE RIJKSWEG
MEMLINGLAAN
RUBENSLAAN
CARVERLN
RAFFAELLAAN
VAN EYCKLN
DRIFTWEG
Tram Stop
REMBRANDTLAAN
NIEUWE RIJKSWEG
STATIONSSTRAAT
MARKSTRAAT
WENUINESTEENWEG

Ostend
Blankenberge

● RESTAURANTS
Bleu Chaud 1
L'Espérance 2

0   100
metres

the Dutch gables, open fires and heavy drapes through to the fifteen guest rooms, which are decorated in an attractive version of country-house style. There's an immaculate garden and an outside pool too. **€180**

Hotel Rubens Rubenslaan 3 ☏059 24 22 00,

ⓦhotel-rubens.be. In a tastefully decorated, cottage-like house, the guest rooms at this three-star hotel are spotless and cosy in equal measure. The hotel prides itself on its banquet breakfasts, which can be taken outside in the garden when the weather is good. There's also an outside pool. **€100**

EATING AND DRINKING

Bleu Chaud Koninklijk Baan 15 ☏059 32 38 35, ⓦbleuchaud.be. Bright and pleasantly decorated modern restaurant where the grilled meats are the speciality, cooked on an open range. Delicious beef stews too. Mains average €20. April–Oct Wed–Fri 6–9.30pm, Sat & Sun noon–2.30pm & 6–9.30pm; Nov–March Fri 6–9.30pm, Sat & Sun noon–2.30pm & 6–9.30pm.

L'Espérance Driftweg 1 ☏059 32 69 00. De Haan is chock-a-block with cafés and restaurants and this is one of the classiest, a small, smart and intimate place with an open kitchen preparing French dishes. A three-course set meal costs about €40. Reservations advised. Mon & Thurs–Sun noon–2.30pm & 6–10pm.

The coast west of Ostend

Travelling west from Ostend, the Kusttram (coastal tram) skirts the sand dunes of a long and almost entirely undeveloped stretch of coast dotted with the substantial military remains of the **Atlantikwall** (Atlantic Wall), built during the German occupation of World War II to guard the coast from Allied invasion. Beyond, the tram ploughs through a series of medium-sized resorts before cutting inland to round the estuary of the River Ijzer. It then scuttles through the small town of **Nieuwpoort**, scene of some of the bloodiest fighting in World War I, before proceeding onto **St-Idesbald**, home to the intriguing **Paul Delvaux Museum**. After St-Idesbald comes **De Panne**, an uninspiring resort at the west end of the Belgian coast that is partly redeemed by its proximity to a pristine slice of beach and dune, **Staatsnatuurreservaat De Westhoek**.

The Atlantikwall

Nieuwpoortsesteenweg · Late March to mid-Nov daily 10.30am–5pm · €6.50 · ☏059 70 22 85 · From the Domein Raversijde tram stop (not the Raversijde stop), take the conspicuous wooden stairway over the dunes and then follow the signs – a 5–10min walk

A slice of coast just to the west of Ostend has managed to dodge development and it's here you'll find the **Domein Raversijde**, a protected area whose most interesting attraction is the open-air **Atlantikwall**, a series of well-preserved gun emplacements, bunkers, pillboxes, tunnels, trenches and artillery pieces that line up along the dunes just behind the beach and the coastal tram line. The Germans had these elaborate fortifications constructed in World War II to forestall an Allied invasion, though in the event the Allies landed much further to the west in France. The remains are extensive and take well over an hour to explore.

Nieuwpoort

Nieuwpoort Stad tram stop

NIEUWPOORT hasn't had much luck. Founded in the twelfth century, it was besieged nine times in the following six hundred years, but this was nothing compared to its misfortune in World War I. In 1914, the first German campaign reached the River Ijzer, prompting the Belgians to open the sluices along the Noordvaart Canal, just to the east of the town. The water stopped the invaders in their tracks and permanently separated the armies, but it also put Nieuwpoort on the front line, where it remained for the rest of the war. Four years of shelling reduced the town to a ruin, and most of what you see today, especially the attractive main square, the Marktplein, is the result of a meticulous restoration that lasted well into the 1920s. The grim days of World War I are recalled by the assorted **war memorials** placed round the ring of sluice gates that lies beside the bridge just to the east of the Nieuwpoort Stad tram stop. The largest monument consists of a sombre Art Deco rotunda with an equestrian King Albert I at the centre. A new visitor centre is currently under construction beside the rotunda.

St-Idesbald: the Paul Delvaux Museum

Paul Delvauxlaan 42, off Pannelaan • April–Sept Tues–Sun 10.30am–5.30pm; Oct–Dec Thurs–Sun 10.30am–5.30pm • €8 •
☎ 058 52 12 29, ⓦ www.delvauxmuseum.com • From the Koksijde St-Idesbald tram stop, walk 100m west towards De Panne, turn left (away from the coast) down the resort's main street, Strandlaan, and keep going until you reach Albert Nazylaan, where you go right, following the signs to the museum – allow 15min

ST-IDESBALD, one hour by tram from Ostend, is a well-heeled seaside town and resort that would be of no particular interest were it not for the artist **Paul Delvaux** (1897– 1994), who stumbled across what was then an empty stretch of coast at the end of World War II and stayed here – despite the development that went on all around him – for the rest of his life. Delvaux's old home and studio have been turned into the **Paul Delvaux Museum**, which holds a comprehensive collection of his work, following his development from early Expressionist days through to the Surrealism that defined his oeuvre from the 1930s onwards. Two of his pet motifs were train stations, in one guise or another, and nude or semi-nude women set against some sort of classical backdrop. His intention was to usher the viewer into the unconscious with dreamlike images where every perspective is exact, but, despite the impeccable craftsmanship, there's something very cold about his vision. At their best, his paintings achieve an almost palpable sense of foreboding, good examples being *The Garden* of 1971 and *The Procession* dated to 1963, while *The Station in the Forest* of 1960 has the most wonderful trees.

De Panne

From St-Idesbald, it only takes the tram a couple of minutes to slide into **DE PANNE**, sitting close to the French border and now one of the largest settlements on the Belgian coast – a mishmash of apartment blocks and second homes shunting up against the beach. As late as the 1880s, De Panne was a tiny fishing village of low white cottages, nestling in the wooded hollow (*panne*) from which it takes its name. The town achieved ephemeral fame in World War I, when it was part of the tiny triangle of Belgian territory that the German army failed to occupy, becoming the temporary home of King Albert's government.

Staatsnatuurreservaat De Westhoek

The main access point is about 2km west of the town centre on Schuilhavenlaan • Open access • Free • From the De Panne Esplanade tram stop, proceed along Dynastielaan, which ends at a T-junction, where you turn left onto Schuilhavenlaan

On the western edge of De Panne – and the main reason to come this far – lies a chunk of coast protected in the **Staatsnatuurreservaat De Westhoek**, whose dunes, grasslands and scrub are fringed by a long sandy beach. It feels surprisingly wild here, and you can explore the reserve along a network of marked footpaths. In 1940, the retreating British army managed to reach these same sand dunes between De Panne and Dunkirk, 15km to the west, just in time for their miraculous evacuation back to England – in eight days, an armada of vessels of all sizes and shapes rescued over three hundred thousand Allied soldiers.

Veurne and around

Rural Flanders at its prettiest, **VEURNE** is a charming market town, whose clutch of ancient buildings, relaxed atmosphere and pavement cafés make for an enjoyable overnight stay. The town was founded in the ninth century as one of a chain of **fortresses** built to defend the region from the raids of the Vikings, yet without much success: Veurne failed to flourish and, two centuries later, remained a small, poor and insignificant place. All that changed, though, when Robert II of Flanders returned from the Crusades in 1099 with a piece of the True Cross. His ship was caught in a gale and, in desperation, he vowed to offer the relic to the first church he saw if he survived. He did, and the lucky beneficiary was Veurne's **St-Walburgakerk**, which became an important centre of medieval pilgrimage for some two hundred years, a real fillip to the local economy. These days, Veurne's main attraction is its **Grote Markt**, one of the best preserved town squares in Belgium, but it's also a useful base for exploring, preferably by bike, the **Veurne-Ambacht**, a flat agricultural region of quiet villages and narrow country lanes that stretches south of the town, encircled by the French border and the canalized River Ijzer. Of all the villages hereabouts, **Lo** is the most delightful, but the district also holds a sprinkling of World War I sights that lie dotted along the line of the **River Ijzer**, which formed the front line for most of the war; the most interesting of these are in the vicinity of the small town of **Diksmuide**.

Grote Markt: the Stadhuis and around

Grote Markt 27 • Guided tours: Mon 8am–noon & 4–6pm; Tues–Fri 8am–noon • €3

All of Veurne's leading sights are on or around the **Grote Markt**, beginning in the northwest corner with the **Stadhuis**, an engaging mix of Gothic and Renaissance styles built between 1596 and 1612 and equipped with a fine blue-and-gold decorated stone loggia projecting from the original brick facade. The interior displays items of unexceptional interest, the pick of which is a set of leather wall coverings made in Córdoba.

The Stadhuis connects with the more austere classicism of the **Gerechtshof** (Law Courts), whose symmetrical columns and long, rectangular windows now hold tourist information, but once sheltered the Inquisition as it set about the Flemish peasantry with gusto. The attached tiered and balconied **Belfort** (belfry; no public access) was completed in 1628, its Gothic lines culminating in a dainty Baroque tower, from where carillon concerts ring out over the town throughout the summer.

St-Walburgakerk

St-Walburgastraat • April–Sept daily 9am–6pm • Free

Just off the Grote Markt stands **St-Walburgakerk**, a replacement for the original

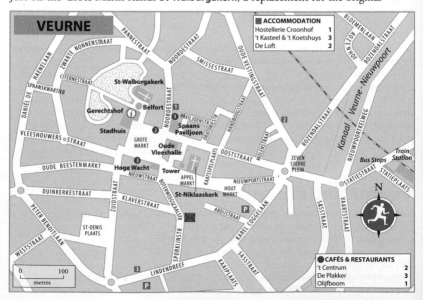

2

VEURNE'S BOETEPROCESSIE (PENITENTS' PROCESSION)

In 1650 a young soldier by the name of Mannaert was on garrison duty in Veurne when he was persuaded by his best friend to commit a **mortal sin**. After receiving the consecrated wafer during Communion, he took it out of his mouth, wrapped it in a cloth, and returned to his lodgings where he charred it over a fire, under the delusion that by reducing it to powder he would make himself invulnerable to injury. The news got out, and he was later arrested, tried and executed, his friend suffering the same fate a few weeks later. Fearful of the consequences of this sacrilege in their town, the people of Veurne resolved that something must be done, deciding on a procession to commemorate the Passion of Christ. This survives as the **Boeteprocessie** (Penitents' Procession; ⓦ boeteprocessie.be), held on the last Sunday in July, whose leading figures dress up in the brown cowls of the Capuchins to carry wooden crosses that weigh anything up to 50kg through the streets. Until very recently, the procession was a serious-minded, macabre affair, but nowadays lots of locals clamber into all manner of vaguely "biblical" gear to join in, which makes it all rather odd.

---

church that Robert II of Flanders caught sight of, which was burnt to a cinder in 1353. The new church was begun in style with a mighty, heavily buttressed choir, but the money ran out during construction and the nave – a truncated affair if ever there was one – was only finished off in 1904. The interior has three highlights: the ornately carved Flemish Renaissance choir stalls; a handsome set of stained-glass windows, some Gothic, some neo-Gothic; and the superb stonework of the tubular, composite columns at the central crossing.

Spaans Paviljoen

Northeast corner of the Grote Markt

The **Spaans Paviljoen** (Spanish Pavilion) was built as the town hall in the middle of the fifteenth century, but takes its name from its later adaptation as the officers' quarters of the Habsburg garrison. It's a self-confident structure, the initial square brick tower, with its castellated parapet, extended by a facade of long, slender windows and flowing stone tracery in the true Gothic manner – an obvious contrast to the Flemish shutters and gables of the **Oude Vleeshalle** (Old Meat Hall) standing directly opposite.

Hoge Wacht and St-Niklaaskerk

Southeast corner of the Grote Markt

Originally home to the town watch, the **Hoge Wacht** displays a fetching amalgam of styles, its brick gable decorated with a small arcaded gallery. The east side of this building edges the Appelmarkt, home to the low-slung medieval brickwork of **St-Niklaaskerk**, whose detached bell tower has refused to accept the several spires that have been added to it at one time or another.

ARRIVAL AND GETTING AROUND — VEURNE

By train or bus Veurne's train and adjacent bus station are a 5min stroll from the Grote Markt.
Destinations by train De Panne (hourly; 10min); Diksmuide (hourly; 10min); Ghent (hourly; 1hr).
Destinations by bus Ieper (Sept–June Mon–Fri 7 daily, Sat 4 daily & Sun 2 daily; July–Aug daily, hourly; 1hr); Lo (Sept–June Mon–Fri 7 daily; 35min; July & Aug limited call-bus service: contact tourist information or De Lijn buses, ⓦ delijn.be).

By bike The most central bicycle rental outlet is at the *De Loft* hotel (see p.136); cycling maps are on sale at Veurne tourist information.

INFORMATION

Tourist information Grote Markt 29 (April to early Nov Mon–Fri 9am–5pm, Sat & Sun 10am–5pm; early Nov to March Mon–Fri 9am–5pm, Sat & Sun 1–5pm; ☎ 058 33 55 31, ⓦ veurne.be).

ACCOMMODATION

Hostellerie Croonhof Noordstraat 9 ☎058 31 31 28, ⓦcroonhof.be. This smart and well-cared-for three-star hotel, in an attractively converted old house just off the Grote Markt, has fourteen spotless rooms of modern demeanour. Advance reservations are advised in the summer. **€100**

★**'t Kasteel & 't Koetshuys** Lindendreef 5 ☎058 31 53 72, ⓦkasteelenkoetshuys.be. Family-run hotel in a sympathetically renovated Edwardian mansion that now holds eight large and well-appointed guest rooms, each of

which is decorated in relaxing pastel shades with high ceilings and marble fireplaces. A sauna and hot tub complete the appealing picture. **€110**

De Loft Oude Vestingstraat 36 ☎058 31 59 49, ⓦdeloft.be. In a cleverly recycled industrial building, this eight-room hotel is an inventive affair, with a café, a kids' play area and a small art gallery. The guest rooms are kitted out in the full flush of modern style with lots of greys, creams and blues. Cycle rental available too. **€185**

EATING AND DRINKING

't Centrum Grote Markt 33 ☎058 31 13 37. Popular café-bar, with a large pavement terrace, offering reasonably priced snacks and meals from a straightforward Flemish menu. Mains average €18. Tues–Sun 8am–11pm.

De Plakker Grote Markt 14 ☎058 31 51 20, ⓦdeplakker.be. Bistro-style restaurant with a wide-ranging menu from pastas to mussels and chips, home-made shrimp croquettes and beef stew, though its

hallmark dish is South American steak. Kitchen: daily 11.30am–2.30pm & 5.30–10pm; bar: daily 10.30am–11pm.

Olijfboom Noordstraat 3 ☎058 31 70 77, ⓦwww.olijfboom.be. Arguably the best restaurant in town, this chic and modern place has a well-considered French menu where the lobster (*kreeft*) and bouillabaisse are hard to beat. Mains average €25. Tues–Sat noon–2pm & 7–9.30pm.

Lo

The agreeable little hamlet of **LO**, off the N8 some 15km southeast of Veurne, has one claim to fame: it was here that Julius Caesar tethered his horse to a yew on his way across Gaul, an event recalled by a plaque and a battered old tree beside what is now the **Westpoort**, whose twin turrets and gateway are all that remains of Lo's medieval ramparts. Less apocryphally, the village once prospered under the patronage of its Augustinian **abbey**, founded in the twelfth century and suppressed by the French Revolutionary army. Today, it's the peace and quiet that appeals, with the village's old stone houses fanning out from the most pleasant of main squares.

ARRIVAL AND DEPARTURE   LO

By bus Buses pull in on the Eiermart, a 3min walk west of Lo's main square, the Markt.
Destinations Ieper (Jan–June & Sept–Dec Mon–Fri 7 daily; 35min); Veurne (Sept–June Mon–Fri 7 daily; 25min).

In July and August there's a limited "call-bus" service: contact the nearest tourist information or De Lijn buses (☎070 220 200, ⓦdelijn.be).

ACCOMMODATION AND EATING

Hotel Stadhuis Markt 1 ☎058 28 80 16, ⓦstadhuis-lo.be. Right in the centre of the village, the old town hall – a much-modified sixteenth-century structure with a slender tower – has been converted into a small hotel. Its five

bedrooms are neat, trim and comfortable, and the smart ground-floor restaurant (closed Tues & Wed) serves good-quality Flemish food in pleasant surroundings. Mains cost around €20. **€70**

Diksmuide

DIKSMUIDE, a modest little town halfway between Ieper and Ostend, sits on the east bank of the River Ijzer – which turned out to be a particularly unfortunate location in World War I. In 1914, the German offensive across Belgium came to a grinding halt when it reached the river, which then formed the front line for the next four years. As a result, Diksmuide was literally shelled to pieces, so much so that by 1918 its location could only be identified from a map. Painstakingly rebuilt in the 1920s, the reconstruction works best in the **Grote Markt**, a pleasant, spacious square flanked by an attractive set of brick gables in traditional Flemish style. Presiding over the square is a statue of an heroic-looking **Colonel Jacques** (1858–1928), a Belgian commander who did a great deal to delay the German advance in 1914. The Grote Markt is also within easy striking distance of two World War I sites, the **Ijzertoren**, a ten-minute walk away, and the **Dodengang**, 2km or so outside of town.

The Ijzertoren

Ijzerdijk • April–Sept Mon–Fri 9am–6pm, Sat & Sun 10am–6pm; Oct–March Mon–Fri 9am–5pm, Sat & Sun 10am–5pm • €8 • ☎ 051 50 02 86, ⓦ ijzertoren.org • On the west bank of the River Ijzer, a 10min walk from the Grote Markt via General Baron Jacquesstraat and Ijzerlaan

The domineering, 84m-high **Ijzertoren** is a massive war memorial and museum that rises high above the River Ijzer. The present structure, a brooding affair dating from the 1950s, bears the letters **AVV-VVK** – Alles voor Vlaanderen ("All for Flanders") and Vlaanderen voor Kristus ("Flanders for Christ") – in a heady mix of religion and nationalism. The tower is actually the second version: the original, erected in 1930, was blown up in mysterious circumstances in 1946. Belgium's French-speakers usually blame Flemish Fascists disappointed at the defeat of Hitler for its destruction, while the Flemings accuse French-speaking leftists, who allegedly took offence at the avowedly Flemish character of the memorial. In front of the Ijzertoren are a few incidental memorials, principally the **Pax gateway** of 1950, built of rubble from the original tower, a **crypt** holding the gravestones of a number of Belgian soldiers, and a new and rather incongruous 20m-long segment of replica World War I **trench**.

Museum aan de Ijzer

Inside the Ijzertoren, lifts whisk visitors up to the top, from where there are grand views out across West Flanders, and this is also where you start a visit to the **Museum aan de Ijzer**, one of the province's best war museums spread over a number of floors, each getting larger as you descend the tapering tower. The museum begins with a good section on the build-up to World War I and thereafter traces the course of the war with particular reference to the Belgian army. Included are a couple of re-created **trenches** – and very convincing they are too – as well as a number of mini-sections on the likes of gas and gas masks, trench communications and subterranean warfare. There's also an excellent section on the atrocities committed by the Germans during the invasion of 1914 and another on the unequal treatment dished out to the Flemings by the Belgian army's Francophone officer class. A later section explains how the original Ijzertoren became a focus of **Flemish nationalism** in the 1930s and even during World War II, when many members of the Flemish Nationalist Movement collaborated with the Germans; several of its leaders, most notably August Borms, were shot for their treachery after the war's end.

The Dodengang

Ijzerdijk 65, 1.5km north of Ijzertoren • April to mid-Nov daily 10am–5pm; mid-Nov to March Tues & Fri 9.30am–4pm • Free • ☎ 051 50 02 86, ⓦ ijzertoren.org

There's a second reminder of World War I to the north of the Ijzertoren along the west bank of the river. The **Dodengang** ("Trench of Death") was an especially dangerous slice of trench that was held by the Belgians throughout the war. Around 400m of trench are viewable, and although the original sandbags have, of necessity, been replaced by concrete imitations, it's all very well done – and the attached museum fills in the military background.

ARRIVAL AND INFORMATION   **DIKSMUIDE**

By train or bus Diksmuide's train and adjacent bus station are a 5min walk from the Grote Markt along

L-shaped Stationsstraat.
Destinations by train De Panne (hourly; 20min); Ghent

(hourly; 50min); Veurne (hourly; 10min).
Destinations by bus Ieper (Mon–Fri 6 daily, Sat 4 daily; 50min).

Tourist information Grote Markt 28 (Easter to mid-Nov daily 10am–noon & 2–5pm; mid-Nov to Easter Sat & Sun 10am–noon & 2–5pm; ☎ 051 79 30 50, ⓦ diksmuide.be).

ACCOMMODATION AND EATING

Fijnbakkerij Vandooren Grote Markt 17 ☎ 051 50 01 84, ⓦ fijnbakkerijvandooren.be. Cheerful modern café where the coffee is good and the cakes are better – especially the mousses. Mon & Sun 7am–4pm, Wed–Sat 7am–6.30pm.

De Groote Waere Vladslostraat 21 ☎ 0477 24 19 38, ⓦ degrootewaere.be. Easily the best accommodation hereabouts, this top-notch B&B is located on a farm about 4.5km from Diksmuide. Breakfast is served in the attractively modernized farmhouse, and the barnlike annexe behind holds several comfortable, modern rooms

with all mod cons. To get there, drive east from Diksmuide on the N35, take the Vladslo turning and it's beside the road on the left. **€75**

Polderbloem Grote Markt 8 ☎ 051 50 29 05, ⓦ polderbloem.be. This combined café, restaurant and bar is a convivial place with trim, modern decor and a pavement terrace that fills up fast at weekends. The menu is creative, with the emphasis on local, seasonal ingredients. Main courses average about €20. Daily except Tues 8am–11pm.

Ieper and around

At heart, **IEPER**, about 30km southeast of Veurne, is a pleasant, middling sort of place, a typical Flemish small town with a bright and breezy main square overlooked by the haughty reminders of its medieval heyday as a centre of the cloth trade. Initial appearances are, however, deceptive, for all the old buildings of the town centre were built from scratch after World War I, when Ieper – or **Ypres** as it was then known – was shelled to smithereens, the reconstruction a tribute to the determination of the town's citizens. Today, with its clutch of good-quality restaurants and hotels, Ieper is an enjoyable place to spend a night or two, especially if you're after exploring the assorted **World War I** cemeteries, monuments and memorials that speckle both the town and its environs, the most famous of which are the **In Flanders Fields Museum**, the **Menin Gate** and **Tyne Cot**.

Brief history

Ieper's long and troubled history dates back to the tenth century when it was founded at the point where the Bruges–Paris trade route crossed the River Ieperlee. Success came quickly and the town became a major player in the **cloth trade**, its thirteenth-century population of some 200,000 sharing economic control of the region with rivals Ghent and Bruges. The most precariously sited of the great Flemish cities, Ypres was too near the French frontier for comfort, and too strategically important to be ignored by any of the armies whose campaigns crisscrossed the town's surroundings with depressing frequency. The city governors kept disaster at bay by reinforcing their defences and **switching allegiances** whenever necessary, fighting against the French at the Battle of the Golden Spurs in 1302 (see p.148), and with them forty years later at Roosebeke. The first major misjudgement came in 1383 when Ypres allied itself with France against Bruges, Ghent and an English army. Ypres was besieged and, although a French army finally appeared to save the day, the damage was done. Ypres never recovered and, unable to challenge its two main competitors again, many of its weavers upped sticks and migrated. The process of **depopulation** proved irreversible, and by the sixteenth century the town had shrunk to a mere five thousand inhabitants.

Disaster: Ieper and World War I

In **World War I**, the first German thrust of 1914 left a bulge in the Allied line to the immediate east of Ypres. This **Salient** (see pp.143–146) preoccupied the generals of both sides and during the next four years a series of bloody and particularly futile offensives attempted to break the stalemate – with disastrous consequences for Ypres, which served as the Allied communications centre. Comfortably within range of the German artillery, Ypres was rapidly **reduced to rubble** and its inhabitants had to be evacuated in 1915. After the war, the returning population decided to rebuild their town, a twenty-year project in which the most prominent medieval buildings – the old **cloth hall** (the Lakenhalle) and the **cathedral** – were meticulously reconstructed. The end result must once have seemed strangely antiseptic – old-style edifices with no signs of decay or erosion – but now, after ninety-odd years, the brickwork has mellowed and the centre looks authentically antique and really rather handsome.

Lakenhalle

On the Grote Markt

A monument to the power and wealth of the medieval guilds, the **Lakenhalle** is a copy of the thirteenth-century original that once stood beside the River Ieperlee, which now flows underground. A singularly impressive structure, the Lakenhalle was built with practical considerations uppermost: no fewer than 48 doors once gave access from the

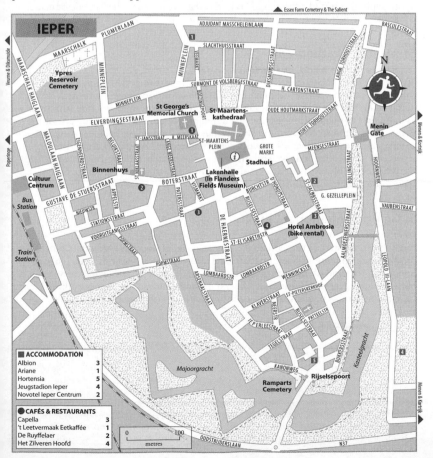

street to the old selling halls, while boats sailed in and out of the jetty on the west wing, under the watchful eyes of the mighty turreted belfry. At its eastern end, the Lakenhalle remains attached to the dinky little **Stadhuis**, whose fancy Renaissance facade rises above an elegant arcaded gallery.

In Flanders Fields Museum

Lakenhalle, Grote Markt • April to mid-Nov daily 10am–6pm; mid-Nov to March Tues–Sun 10am–5pm • €9 • ☎ 057 23 92 75, ⓦ inflandersfields.be

Inside the Lakenhalle, the outstanding **In Flanders Fields Museum** focuses on the experiences of those caught up in the war rather than the ebb and flow of the military campaigns, though these are sketched in too. At the start, there is an excellent introduction to the origins of the war, followed by a detailed section on the German invasion of Belgium in 1914, describing the damage the invaders inflicted and the atrocities they committed. Thereafter, the museum outlines the creation of the **Ypres Salient** and the gruesome nature of trench warfare with discrete subsections on, for example, the evolution of mortars, the use of gas, and tunnelling. Taken as a whole, the exhibits are wide-ranging and thoughtful, and the multilingual quotations well chosen, but above all it's the photographs that steal the show: soldiers grimly digging trenches; the pathetic casualties of a gas attack; flyblown corpses in the mud; and panoramas of a blasted landscape.

St-Maartenskathedraal

St-Maartensplein • Daily 9am–noon & 2–6pm except during services • Free

To the rear of the Lakenhalle rises **St-Maartenskathedraal**, a 1930 copy of the thirteenth-century Gothic original. The church's cavernous nave is a formal, rather bland affair, but the rose window above the south transept door is a fine tribute to **King Albert I** of Belgium, its yellow, green, red and blue stained glass the gift of the British armed forces. Some of the British may have envied the Belgians their commander: realizing that offensives always resulted in heavy casualties, Albert repeatedly refused requests to lend his men to the French and the British when they were launching attacks and, as a result, Belgian losses were by percentage far fewer than those of her main allies.

St George's Memorial Church

Elverdingsestraat 1 • Daily 9am–7pm • Free

Just to the northwest of the cathedral is the Anglican **St George's Memorial Church**, a modest brick building finished in 1929. The interior is crowded with brass plaques honouring the dead of many British regiments, and almost all the chairs carry individual and regimental tributes. It's hard not to be moved, for there's nothing vainglorious in this public space, so consumed as it is with private grief.

FELINE TERRORS

During winter, wool was stored on the upper floor of the Lakenhalle and **cats** were brought in to keep the mice down. The cats may have had a good time in winter, but they couldn't have relished the prospect of spring, when they were thrown out of the windows to a hostile crowd below as part of the **Kattenstoet** or Cats' Festival, the slaughter intended to symbolize the killing of evil spirits. The festival ran right up until 1817 and was revived in 1938, when the cats were (mercifully) replaced by cloth imitations. Since then it's developed into Ieper's principal shindig, held every three years on the second Sunday in May – the next one is in 2015. The main event is the **parade** – a large-scale celebration of all things catty, complete with dancers and bands and some of the biggest models and puppets imaginable.

Ypres Reservoir Cemetery

From St George's, it's a brief walk to the silent graves of the **Ypres Reservoir Cemetery**, laid out to a pre-ordained plan (see p.143) and one of two British Commonwealth graveyards in the town centre. In use from 1915 onwards, just over 2500 men are buried here, though only half were identified. Many were brought in from the Salient to die of their wounds in field hospitals, but others were killed in the town itself. Among this number were sixteen men of the Duke of Cornwall's Light Infantry, who were billeted in the vaults of the Cathedral when they were interred by a giant, long-range German shell: they were not the only ones to be killed by what the soldiers grimly called the "Ypres Express". Here also are three graves of men **shot at dawn** by British firing squad – Ernest Lawrence, Charles Frederick McColl and Thomas Moles.

The Binnenhuys and Vismarkt

Boterstraat

The **Binnenhuys** is an elegant eighteenth-century mansion in the French style that was, remarkably enough, the only Ieper building to survive World War I intact. Close by, also on Boterstraat, watch out for the fancy Baroque portal that leads through to the old **Vismarkt** (fish market), another 1920s reconstruction, complete with canopied stone stalls and a dinky little tollhouse.

Menin Gate

East of the Grote Markt, the massive **Menin Gate** war memorial was built on the site of the old Menenpoort, which served as the main route for British soldiers heading for the front. It's a simple, brooding monument, towering over the edge of the town, its walls covered with the names of those fifty thousand British and Commonwealth troops who died in the Ypres Salient but have no grave. The simple inscription above the lists of the dead has none of the arrogance of the victor, but rather a sense of great loss. The self-justifying formality of the memorial did, however, offend many veterans and prompted a bitter verse from Siegfried Sassoon:

Was ever an immolation so belied
As these intolerably nameless names?
Well might the Dead who struggled in slime
Rise and deride this sepulchre of crime.

Volunteers from the local fire brigade sound the **Last Post** beneath the gate each and every evening at 8pm. Sometimes it's an extremely moving ceremony, especially when the fire brigade is joined by other bands, but at other times it's noisy and really rather crass with scores of school children milling around.

The ramparts

Curiously, the seventeenth-century brick and earthen **ramparts** on either side of the Menin Gate were strong enough to survive World War I in good condition – the vaults even served as some of the safest bunkers on the front. These massive ramparts and their protective moat still extend right round the east and south of the town centre, and a pleasant **footpath** runs along the top amid scores of mature horse-chestnut trees to a second British Commonwealth graveyard, the small and very quiet **Ramparts Cemetery**, which slopes down towards the old moat.

ARRIVAL AND GETTING AROUND

IEPER

By train or bus Ieper's train and adjacent bus station stand on the western edge of the centre, a 10min walk from the Grote Markt.

Destinations by train Kortrijk (hourly; 30min).

Destinations by bus Diksmuide (Mon–Fri 6 daily, Sat 4 daily; 50min); Lo (Sept–June Mon–Fri 7 daily; 35min); Veurne (Sept–June Mon–Fri 7 daily, Sat 4 daily & Sun 2 daily; July–Aug daily, hourly; 1hr).

By bike There are three bike rental outlets in Ieper, including the *Hotel Ambrosia* in the centre at D'Hondtstraat

54 (daily 7.30am–7.30pm; ☎057 36 63 66). They charge €12 per day for a standard-issue bike.

By car There are no major car rental companies, but tourist information has details of local suppliers. One of them is Garage Duran at Albert Dehemlaan 3 (☎057 20 78 83), around 1.5km north of the Grote Markt. Reckon on €50 a day for a basic vehicle.

By taxi There are several taxi firms; try Taxi Leo (☎057 20 04 13).

INFORMATION

Tourist information In the Lakenhalle on the Grote Markt (April to mid-Nov Mon–Fri 9am–6pm, Sat & Sun 10am–6pm; mid-Nov to March Mon–Fri 9am–5pm, Sat & Sun 10am–6pm; ☎057 23 92 20,

Ⓦwww.toerisme-ieper.be). The attached shop has booklets and leaflets describing car and cycle routes around the Salient and also sells a first-rate range of books on World War I.

ACCOMMODATION

Tourist information's website (Ⓦwww.toerisme-ieper.be) has comprehensive accommodation listings. There are around twenty B&Bs, though the majority are out in the sticks, whereas most of Ieper's hotels are in the centre; there's a handily located campsite too. During the centenary commemorations for World War I (2014–2018), you can expect prices to increase.

★**Albion Hotel** St-Jacobsstraat 28 ☎057 20 02 20, Ⓦalbionhotel.be. Very appealing three-star hotel with eighteen large and well-appointed en-suite guest rooms decorated in a spick-and-span, unfussy modern style. The public areas are commodious, the breakfasts are good, and it's in a handy location, a brief stroll from the Grote Markt. **€130**

Ariane Slachthuisstraat 58 ☎057 21 82 18, Ⓦariane.be. A prim and proper garden with a water fountain flanks this ultramodern four-star hotel, which occupies a secluded location, a 5min walk north of the Grote Markt. The fifty en-suite rooms are large, well appointed and very comfortable. **€150**

Hortensia Rijselstraat 196 ☎0473 84 84 07, Ⓦbbhortensia.be. A stone's throw from one of the old town gates, this 1920s terrace house has been pleasantly re-equipped to accommodate a six-bedroom B&B. The rooms are all en suite and decorated in a fetching

manner with wooden floors and neat furnishings. **€80**

Novotel Ieper Centrum St-Jacobsstraat 15 ☎057 42 96 00, Ⓦnovotel.com. The building itself might be a bit of a modern bruiser, but the hundred-odd rooms are all comfortably modern in true *Novotel* style, and there are fitness facilities and a sauna. **€100**

CAMPING

Jeugstadion Ieper Bolwerkstraat 1, off Karel Steverlijncklaan ☎057 21 72 82, Ⓦjeugdstadion.be. Pocket-sized campsite in a leafy location across the canal from the southeast tip of town. You can walk there via Léopold III-laan – it takes about 25min from the train station – but drivers have to use the ring road, the N37. There are tent pitches as well as car and tent pitches, bike rental and three hikers' huts. Open March to mid-Nov. Pitch, tent, car and two adults **€18**, hikers' hut **€37**

EATING AND DRINKING

★**Capella** Kiekenmarkt 7 ☎057 36 61 32, Ⓦrestaurantcapella.be. This attractive restaurant, one of Ieper's best, has a charmingly idiosyncratic appearance, from the gold-sprayed posts to the dinky chandeliers. The menu is not overly extensive, but it does cover all the Flemish classics and then some – try, for example, the brill in white wine sauce (€26). Outside terrace too. Wed–Fri & Sun noon–2.30pm & 6–9pm, Sat 6–10pm.

'**t Leetvermaak Eetkaffée** Korte Meersstraat 2 ☎057 21 63 85, Ⓦleetvermaak.be. Excellent café-restaurant with a cosy interior and a smooth, jazzy soundtrack. The cuisine is largely Flemish, with a

sprinkling of Italian and Spanish/Portuguese dishes adding interest. Mains hover around €20. Cultural events are staged here too. Tues–Thurs & Sat 5–11pm, Fri & Sun 11am–2pm & 5–11pm.

★**De Ruyffelaer** Gustave de Stuersstraat 11 ☎057 36 60 06, Ⓦderuyffelaer.be. This homely, weekends-only restaurant is kitted out with all sorts of local trinkets and offers delicious home-made food, with Flemish dishes uppermost – the stews are outstanding. Mains average €16. Wash it down with Hommel, the tangy local ale from the neighbouring town of Poperinge. Fri & Sat 5.30–9pm, Sun 11.30am–2 & 5.30–9pm.

Het Zilveren Hoofd Rijselsestraat 49 ☎057 36 03 67, ⓦhetzilverenhoofd.be. Laidback café-restaurant in tidy modern premises serving from a standard menu, including salads and pastas and a regular turnaround of three vegetarian dishes; the steaks are especially good (€20). Tues–Sat 11am–2pm & 6.30–10pm.

The Ypres Salient

Immediately to the east of Ieper, the **Ypres Salient** occupies a basin-shaped parcel of land about 25km long, and never more than 15km deep. For the generals of World War I, the area's key feature was the long and low sequence of ridges that sweeps south from the hamlet of Langemark to the French border. These gave the occupants a clear view of Ieper and its surroundings, and consequently the British and Germans spent the war trying to capture and keep them. The dips and sloping ridges that were then so vitally important are still much in evidence today, but the tranquillity of the landscape makes it difficult to imagine what the war was actually like.

The most resonant reminders of the blood-letting are the 160 or so **British Commonwealth War Cemeteries** that dot the landscape, each immaculately maintained by the Commonwealth War Graves Commission. Every cemetery, including the most famous, **Tyne Cot**, has a **Cross of Sacrifice** in white Portland stone, and the larger ones also have a sarcophagus-like **Stone of Remembrance** bearing the legend "Their Name Liveth For Ever More", a quotation selected by

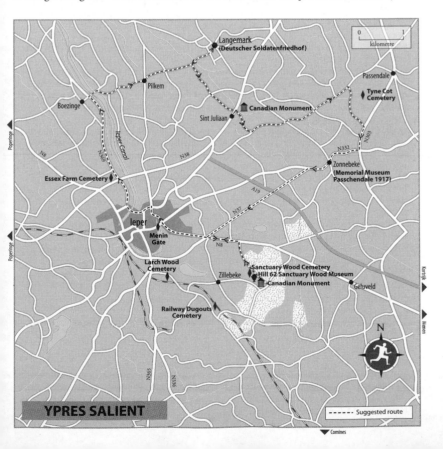

2

Rudyard Kipling from Ecclesiasticus. The **graves** line up at precisely spaced intervals and, wherever possible, headstones bear the individual's name, rank, serial number, age and date of death, plus the badge of the relevant military unit or a national emblem, an appropriate religious symbol and, at the base, an inscription chosen by relatives. All the graves are numbered and at each cemetery a **registry book** is kept in an alcove at the entrance recording alphabetically who is buried where – if, of course, the remains have been identified: thousands of gravestones do not carry any or all of these tags as the bodies were buried without anyone knowing who they were. If you are looking for the grave of someone in particular, consult the **Commonwealth War Graves Commission**'s excellent website (Ⓦ cwgc.org).

GETTING AROUND, INFORMATION AND TOURS   YPRES SALIENT

Getting around There's no way you can explore the Ypres Salient by public transport. Short of taking a guided tour, the sites we have described below can be combined into a short driving or cycling tour, which can be completed comfortably in half a day, or a day if you really take your time.

BLOODY STALEMATE: THE YPRES SALIENT

The creation of the **Ypres Salient** was entirely accidental. When the German army invaded Belgium and so launched the war in the west, they were following earlier military principles – as laid down by a previous chief of the German General Staff, Alfred von Schlieffen – to avoid fighting a war on two fronts. The plan was for the German army to advance through Belgium, outflank the French and **capture Paris** well before the Russians could assemble on the eastern frontier. But the initial German offensive ground to a halt, and so two lines of opposing **trenches** were dug on the Franco-German frontier, which soon stretched from the North Sea down to Switzerland.

Attention then focused on the two main **bulges** – or salients – in the line, one at Ieper, the other at Verdun. To the Allied generals, the bulge at Ieper – the **Ypres Salient** – was a good place to puncture the German lines; to the Germans it represented an ideal opportunity to break the deadlock by attacking enemy positions from several sides at the same time. Contemporary **military doctrine** on both sides held that the way to win a war was to destroy the enemy's strongest forces first – a theory based on cavalry tactics, where a charge that broke the enemy's key formations brought victory. However, **technological changes** had shifted the balance of war in favour of defence: machine guns had become more efficient, barbed wire more effective and the railways could shift defensive reserves faster than an advancing army could march. Another issue was **supply**. These vast armies couldn't live off the land, and once they advanced much beyond the reach of the railways, the supply problems were enormous. As the historian A.J.P. Taylor put it, "Defence was mechanized; attack was not".

The generals had no answer to the stalemate save for an amazing profligacy with people's lives. Their tactical innovations were limited, and two of the new techniques – gas attack and a heavy preliminary bombardment – made matters worse. The **shells** forewarned the enemy of an offensive and churned the trenches into a muddy maelstrom where men, horses and machinery were simply engulfed; the gas was as dangerous to the advancing soldiers as it was to the retreating enemy. **Tanks** could have broken the impasse, but their development was never prioritized.

For four years war raged in and around the Ypres Salient, the scene of **four major battles**. The first, in October and November of 1914, settled the lines of the bulge as both armies tried to outflank each other; and the second was a German attack the following spring that moved the trenches a couple of kilometres west. The third, launched by British Empire soldiers in July 1917, was even more pointless, with thousands of men dying for an advance of only a few kilometres. It's frequently called the **Battle of Passchendaele**, but Lloyd George more accurately referred to it as the "battle of the mud", a disaster that cost 250,000 British lives. The fourth and final battle, in April 1918, was another German attack inspired by General Ludendorff's desire to break the British army. Instead it broke his own, leading to the **November 11 Armistice**.

Information and maps If you're undertaking a detailed exploration then the best place to start is Major & Mrs Holt's *Pocket Battlefield Guide to the Ypres Salient*, a thoroughly researched book that details all its nooks and crannies. It's on sale at Ieper tourist information (see p.142), but note that the maps in the book are insufficient – you're best off supplementing them with the detailed Westhoek Zuid map, also available at tourist information.

Guided tours Guided tours of the Salient beginning in Ieper are provided by both Flanders Battlefield Tours (☎ 057 36 04 60, ⓦ ypres-fbt.com), which offers 4hr and 2.5hr trips for €38 and €30 respectively, and Salient Tours (☎ 057 21 46 57, ⓦ salienttours.be), with a similar programme at similar prices. For those staying in Bruges, Quasimodo operates excellent all-inclusive battlefield tours from Bruges to Ieper and back (see p.120).

Essex Farm Cemetery

Diksmuidseweg • Open access • Free • 3km north of Ieper along the N369 (to Diksmuide), just beyond the flyover

Essex Farm Cemetery is where the dead were brought from the neighbouring battlefield. In the bank behind and to the left of the cemetery's Cross of Sacrifice are the remains of several British bunkers, part of a combined forward position and first-aid post dug into the west side of the canal. It was here that the Canadian **John McCrae** wrote the war's best-known poem, *In Flanders Fields*:

... We are the Dead. Short days ago
We lived, felt dawn, saw sunsets glow,
Loved and were loved, and now we lie
In Flanders fields ...

Deutscher Soldatenfriedhof

Klerkenstraat, Langemark • Open access • Free

On the northern edge of the hamlet of **LANGEMARK** is the Salient's only German war cemetery, the **Deutscher Soldatenfriedhof**. Nearly 45,000 German soldiers are buried here, mostly in communal graves, but others are interred in groups of eight with stone plaques above each tomb carrying the names of the dead (where known). The entrance gate is a squat neo-Romanesque structure, whose style is continued by the basalt crosses dotting the rest of the site, and overlooking it all is a sad and moving **bronze** of four mourning soldiers by the Munich sculptor Emil Krieger.

Tyne Cot

Vijfwegestraat, Passendale • Open access; visitor centre daily 10am–6pm • Free

Tyne Cot is the largest British Commonwealth war cemetery in the world, containing no fewer than 11,956 graves as well as the so-called **Memorial to the Missing**, a semicircular wall inscribed with the names of a further 35,000 men whose bodies were never recovered. The soldiers of a Northumbrian division gave the place its name, observing, as they tried to fight their way up the ridge, that the Flemish house on the horizon looked like a Tyneside cottage. The house disappeared during the war, but the largest of the concrete **pillboxes** the Germans built to defend the ridge has survived, incorporated within the mound beneath the **Cross of Sacrifice** at the suggestion of George V – you can still see a piece of it where a slab of stone has been deliberately omitted. Strangely, the Memorial to the Missing at the back of the cemetery wasn't part of the original design: the intention was that these names be recorded on the Menin Gate, but there was not enough room. Beside the car park, the **visitor centre** gives further background information and displays a selection of World War I photos.

Passendale

Tyne Cot cemetery overlooks the shallow valley that gently shelves up to the hamlet of **PASSENDALE**, known then as **Passchendaele**. This village was the British objective in the **Third Battle of Ypres**, but torrential rain and intensive shelling turned the valley into a giant quagmire. The whole affair came to symbolize the futility of the war and the incompetence of its generals: when Field-Marshal Haig's Chief of Staff ventured out of his HQ to inspect progress, he allegedly said, "Good God, did we really send men to fight in that?"

Memorial Museum Passchendaele 1917

Pilstraat, Zonnebeke • Daily 9am–5pm • €7.50 • ☎ 051 77 04 41, ⓦ passchendaele.be

Beside the main road in the middle of **Zonnebeke**, and occupying a nineteenth-century château and its grounds, is the **Memorial Museum Passchendaele 1917**, with the region's largest collection of World War I artefacts. Displays are focused on the Third Battle of Ypres (see box, p.144), illustrating this desperately futile conflict with photos, military hardware and reconstructions of a trench and a dugout.

Hill 62 Sanctuary Wood Museum

Canadalaan/Hill 62, a turning off the N8 • Daily 10am–6pm or dusk • €10

Heading up Canadalaan, you soon reach the **Sanctuary Wood Cemetery**, holding two thousand British and Commonwealth dead, and then the privately owned **Hill 62 Sanctuary Wood Museum**, which holds a ragbag of shells, rifles, bayonets, billycans and other incidental artefacts. Outside, things have been left pretty much as they were the day the war ended, a zigzag of (mostly reconstructed) **sandbagged trenches** with accompanying shell craters that combine to convey the flavour of the fighting. The woods beside the museum and on the adjacent Hill 62 were bitterly contested. From the museum, it's about 5km back to Ieper.

Kortrijk

KORTRIJK (Courtrai in French), just 8km from the French border, is the largest town in this part of West Flanders, a lively, busy sort of place with a couple of excellent hotels, several good places to eat and a smattering of distinguished medieval buildings. The town traces its origins back to a **Roman settlement** called Cortoriacum, but its salad days were in the Middle Ages when its burghers made a fortune producing linen and flax. The problem was its location: Kortrijk was just too close to France for comfort and time and again the town was embroiled in the wars that swept across Flanders, right up to the two German occupations of the last century.

The Grote Markt

Heavily bombed during World War II, Kortrijk's **Grote Markt** is a comely but architecturally incoherent mixture of bits of the old and a lot of the new, surrounding the forlorn, turreted **Belfort** – all that remains of what was once a splendid medieval cloth hall. At the northwest corner of the Grote Markt stands the **Stadhuis**, a sedate edifice with modern statues of the counts of Flanders on the facade. Inside, through the side entrance on the left, things pick up in the **Historisch Stadhuis** (July & Aug Tues, Thurs, Sat & Sun 3–5pm; free) with two fine sixteenth-century **chimneypieces**. The first is in the old **Schepenzaal** (Aldermen's Room) on the ground floor, a proud, intricate work decorated with municipal coats of arms and carvings of bishops, saints and the Archdukes Albert and Isabella of Spain; the other, upstairs in the **Raadzaal** (Council Chamber), is a more didactic affair, ornamented by three rows of precise statuettes representing, from top to bottom, the virtues, the vices (to either side of the Emperor Charles V), and the torments of hell.

St-Maartenskerk

St-Maartenskerkstraat • Mon–Fri 9am–5pm, Sat & Sun 10am–5pm, but closed to visitors during services • Free

Just off the Grote Markt rises the heavyweight tower of **St-Maartenskerk**, whose

CLOCKWISE FROM TOP HILL 62 (P.146); ST-BAAFSKATHEDRAAL, GHENT (P.155); DESIGN MUSEUM, GHENT (P.162) >

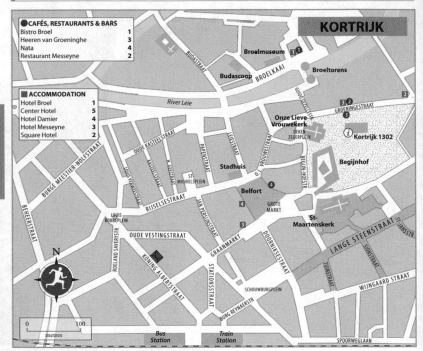

CAFÉS, RESTAURANTS & BARS
Bistro Broel	1
Heeren van Groeninghe	3
Nata	4
Restaurant Messeyne	2

ACCOMMODATION
Hotel Broel	1
Center Hotel	5
Hotel Damier	4
Hotel Messeyne	3
Square Hotel	2

gleaming white-stone exterior, dating from the fifteenth century, is distinguished by its slender spire. The outside of the church may be handsome, but the cavernous interior is a yawn with the exception of the intricately carved, 6.5m-high tabernacle tucked away among the columns of the nave near the high altar and dated to the sixteenth century.

Begijnhof

Begijnhofstraat • Daily 7am–8pm, 9pm in summer • Free

Founded in 1238 by the Countess of Flanders, Joanna of Constantinople, the **Begijnhof** (see box, p.327) is an especially pretty corner of Kortrijk, its huddle of ancient whitewashed cottages flanking a network of narrow cobbled lanes. A small visitor centre is planned and you can pop into the **chapel**, where the organ is one of the oldest in the country, dating from 1678.

Onze Lieve Vrouwekerk

Deken Zegerplein • Mon–Fri 8am–6pm, Sat 9am–6pm & Sun 11am–6pm • Free

The **Onze Lieve Vrouwekerk** (Church of Our Lady) is a hulking grey structure that formerly doubled as part of the city's fortifications. In July 1302, the nave of the church was crammed with hundreds of spurs, ripped off the feet of dead and dying French knights at the **Battle of the Golden Spurs**, one of the most important military engagements of the period. These plundered spurs were all that remained of the army Philip the Fair had sent to avenge the slaughter of the Bruges Matins earlier that year (see p.102). The two armies, Philip's heavily armoured cavalry and the lightly armed Flemish weavers, had met outside Kortrijk on marshy ground.

Despising their lowly born adversaries, the French knights made no reconnaissance and ended up milling around in the mud like cumbersome dinosaurs. They were massacred, the first time an amateur civilian army had defeated professional mail-clad knights.

The interior

The spurs disappeared long ago and today the church's **interior** is a medley of styles, from the Gothic and the Baroque to the Neoclassical. The gloomy and truncated north transept holds one splendid painting, **Anthony van Dyck**'s *Raising of the Cross*, a muscular, sweeping work with a pale, deathly Christ, completed just before the artist went to England. Across the church, the **Counts' Chapel** has an unusual series of somewhat crude nineteenth-century portraits painted into the wall niches, but the highlight is a sensuous medieval alabaster **statue of St Catherine**, her left hand clutching a representation of the spiked wheel on which her enemies tried to break her (hence the "Catherine wheel" firework).

The Broelmuseum

Broelkaai 6 • Tues–Fri 2–6pm, Sat & Sun 11am–6pm • €3 • ☎ 056 277 780, ⓦ kortrijk.be/broelmuseum

Over the bridge and beyond the **Broeltorens** – a pair of enormously strong and conical towers that are all that remains of the old town walls – lies the town's best museum, the **Broelmuseum**. Pride of place here goes to the paintings of Kortrijk's own **Roelandt Savery** (1576–1639) who trained in Amsterdam and worked for the Habsburgs in Prague and Vienna before returning to the Low Countries. To suit the tastes of his German patrons, he infused many of his landscapes with the romantic classicism that they preferred – Orpheus and the Garden of Eden were two favourite subjects – but the finely observed detail of his paintings was always in the true Flemish tradition. Among the works on display is the striking *Plundering of a Village*, where there's a palpable sense of outrage in contrast to *The Drinking-Place*, depicting a romanticized, arboreal idyll. The museum also possesses a passable collection of nineteenth-century land- and seascapes plus local scenes by another native artist, **Emmanuel Viérin** (1869–1954).

Kortrijk 1302

Above tourist information in the Begijnhofpark • June–Aug Tues–Fri 10am–6pm, Sat & Sun 10am–5pm; Sept–May Tues–Sun 10am–5pm • €6 • ☎ 056 277 850, ⓦ kortrijk.be/1302

Hammering home the importance of the Battle of the Golden Spurs, **Kortrijk 1302** provides a detailed account of the engagement and its historical context, culminating in a short feature film. Also on display are a number of original artefacts, most memorably the metal tips of the long pikes carried by the Flemings. This weapon was crucial to the success of the guildsmen who, with true gallows humour, named it the *Goedendag* (Good Day) because the French knights had to nod their heads when the pike was aimed at one of their weak spots – the gap between their helmet and breastplate. A later section explores the way in which the battle served as propaganda: Flemish nationalists trumpeted the success of their forebears and the French tried to gainsay their defeat by alleging that the Flemings disguised the marshy ground with brushwood – almost certainly untrue.

ARRIVAL AND INFORMATION   KORTRIJK

By train Kortrijk train and bus stations are a 5min walk from the Grote Markt.
Destinations by train Brussels (every 30min to hourly; 1hr 10min); Ghent (every 30min; 20min); Ieper (hourly; 30min); Lille, France (hourly; 30min); Oudenaarde (hourly; 15min).

Tourist information In a clunky modern building in the Begijnhofpark (June–Sept Mon–Fri 10am–6pm, Sat & Sun 10am–5pm; Oct–May daily 10am–5pm; ☎ 056 27 78 40, ⓦ tourismkortrijk.be). Shares its premises with Kortrijk 1302 (see above).

2

ACCOMMODATION

★ **Hotel Broel** Broelkaai 8 ☎ 056 21 83 51, ⓦ sandton .eu/nl/kortrijk. The plain exterior of this four-star hotel on the north bank of the River Leie is deceptive, for the interior of this one-time tobacco factory has a mock-monastic theme, with tunnels and stone-trimmed arches that are entirely bogus but great fun. Each of the seventy spacious, en-suite rooms is decorated in a tasteful, country-house style. **€100**

Center Hotel Graanmarkt 6 ☎ 056 21 97 21, ⓦ centerhotel.be. Medium-sized three-star hotel in a handy location near the Grote Markt. There's nothing fancy about the rooms, but they're comfortable and each is kitted out in a sharp, minimalist manner. **€80**

Hotel Damier Grote Markt 41 ☎ 056 22 15 47, ⓦ hoteldamier.be. The approach to this hotel – down through the old carriage archway that forms part of the handsome Neoclassical facade – is impressive and it leads to a wood-panelled foyer decorated in English country-house style. The problem is that the rooms beyond are a tad stuffy and staid, though perfectly adequate. **€125**

★ **Hotel Messeyne** Groeningestraat 17 ☎ 056 21 21 66, ⓦ hotelmesseyne.be. Excellent four-star in a creatively modernized eighteenth-century mansion. There's a sauna and a health centre, and 28 large, well-appointed rooms, most of which are decorated in fetching creams and browns, some with timber-beam ceilings. **€140**

Square Hotel Groeningestraat 39 ☎ 056 28 89 50, ⓦ hotelmesseyne.be. Owned by the *Hotel Messeyne*, this is their three-star venture, featuring 26 trim, modern rooms designed with visiting business folk in mind. **€110**

EATING AND DRINKING

★ **Bistro Broel** Broelkaai 8 ☎ 056 21 83 51, ⓦ sandton .eu/nl/kortrijk. Smart and charming, stone-flagged restaurant on the ground floor of the *Hotel Broel* (see above). The emphasis is very much on Flemish cuisine (mains average €26), with a French twist or two – try, for example, the river eel in spinach sauce (*rivierpaling in 't groen*) and don't miss out on the earth-shattering shrimp soup with a hint of Calvados. Mon–Fri & Sun 11am–10pm, Sat 3–10pm.

Heeren van Groeninghe Groeningestraat 36 ☎ 056 25 40 25, ⓦ deheerenvangroeninghe.be. Set in a cleverly revamped eighteenth-century mansion, this popular bistro-style bar and restaurant does a fine line in Flemish and Italian dishes and is also strong on salads.

Eat inside or outside on the terrace. Mains from a very reasonable €18. June–Sept Mon & Thurs–Sun 10am–10pm; Oct–May Thurs–Sun 10am–10pm.

Nata Grote Markt 4 ☎ 056 20 12 20, ⓦ natakortrijk.be. Of all the café-bars that line up along the Grote Markt, this is perhaps the best, serving a good selection of Franco-Flemish dishes in bright, modern surroundings. Mains average €19. Daily 8am–10pm.

Restaurant Messeyne Groeningestraat 17 ☎ 056 21 21 66, ⓦ hotelmesseyne.be. Small and deluxe-meets-bijou restaurant in the *Hotel Messeyne* (see above). The menu is extremely well chosen and the cuisine French – the *jus* are particularly delicious. Mains hover around €28. Mon–Fri noon–2pm & 7–9.30pm, Sat 7–9.30pm.

Oudenaarde

Hugging the banks of the River Scheldt about 30km to the east of Kortrijk, **OUDENAARDE**, literally "old landing place", is a beguiling sort of place, an easy-paced little town with a clutch of fascinating old buildings, a sprinkling of enjoyable bars and restaurants and a museum that features Oudenaarde's main claim to fame, its **tapestries** (see box, p.152). The town has a long and chequered history. Granted a charter in 1193, it concentrated on cloth manufacture until the early fifteenth century, when its weavers switched to tapestry-making, an industry that made its burghers rich and the town famous, with the best tapestries becoming the prized possessions of the kings of France and Spain. So far so good, but Oudenaarde became a key **military objective** during the religious and dynastic wars of the sixteenth to the eighteenth centuries. Attacked and besieged time and again, Oudenaarde found it impossible to sustain any growth, and the demise of the tapestry industry pauperized the town, rendering it an insignificant backwater in one of the poorest parts of Flanders – until recently, when the canny use of regional development funds has put the spring back in the municipal step.

Tacambaroplein war memorial

On the way into town from the train station, the only surprise is the romantic **war memorial** occupying the middle of **Tacambaroplein**. For once it's nothing to do with either world war, but instead commemorates those who were daft or unscrupulous enough to volunteer to go to Mexico and fight for **Maximilian**, the Habsburg son-in-law of the Belgian king, Léopold I. Unwanted and unloved, Maximilian was imposed on the Mexicans by a French army provided by Napoleon III, who wanted to create his own western empire while the eyes of the US were averted by the American Civil War. It was, however, all too fanciful and the occupation rapidly turned into a fiasco. Maximilian paid for the adventure with his life in 1867, and few of his soldiers made the return trip. The reasons for this calamity seem to have been entirely lost on Maximilian, who declared, in front of the firing squad that was about to polish him off, "Men of my class and lineage are created by God to be the happiness of nations or their martyrs…Long live Mexico, long live independence".

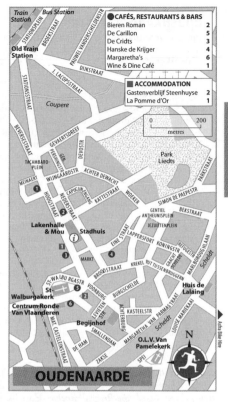

CAFÉS, RESTAURANTS & BARS

Bieren Roman	2
De Carillon	5
De Cridts	3
Hanske de Krijger	4
Margaretha's	6
Wine & Dine Café	1

ACCOMMODATION

Gastenverblijf Steenhuyse	2
La Pomme d'Or	1

OUDENAARDE

Stadhuis

Markt • Occasional guided tours; details from tourist information (see p.153)

The airy and expansive **Markt** at the heart of Oudenaarde is overlooked by the **Stadhuis**, one of the finest examples of Flamboyant Gothic in the country. Built around 1525, its elegantly symmetrical facade spreads out on either side of a slender central tower, whose extravagant tiers, balconies and parapets are topped by the gilded figure of a knight, *Hanske de Krijger* ("Little John the Warrior"). Underneath the knight, the cupola is in the shape of a crown, a theme reinforced by the two groups of cherubs on the dormer windows below, who lovingly clutch the royal insignia. Inside, a magnificent oak **doorway** forms the entrance to the old Schepenzaal (Aldermen's Hall). A stylistically influential piece of 1531, the doorway consists of an intricate sequence of carvings, surmounted by miniature cherubs who frolic above three coats of arms and a 28-panel door.

MOU

Markt • March–Sept Tues–Sun 10am–5.30pm; Oct–Feb Tues–Fri 10am–5pm, Sat & Sun 2–5pm • €6 • ☎ 055 31 72 51, ⓦ mou-oudenaarde.be

Attached to the back of the Stadhuis, the thirteenth-century **Lakenhalle** now holds **MOU**, the town's principal museum. Spread over several floors, the museum begins with a modest history of Oudenaarde and follows up with a large quantity of silverware, but the main event is a magnificent collection of **tapestries**, exhibited to fine effect in a capacious, high-ceilinged hall. Among the fifteen tapestries on display, look out for a

2

OUDENAARDE TAPESTRIES

Tapestry manufacture in Oudenaarde began in the middle of the fifteenth century, an embryonic industry that soon came to be based on a dual system of **workshop** and **outworker**, the one with paid employees, the other with workers paid on a piecework basis. From the beginning, the town authorities took a keen interest in the business, ensuring its success by a rigorous system of quality control, which soon gave Oudenaarde an international reputation for consistently well-made tapestries.

The first great period of the town's tapestry-making lasted until the middle of the sixteenth century, when **religious conflict** overwhelmed the town and many of its Protestant-inclined weavers, who had come into direct conflict with their Catholic masters, migrated north. In 1582 Oudenaarde was finally incorporated into the Spanish Netherlands, precipitating a revival of tapestry production fostered by the king and queen of Spain, who were keen to support the industry and passed draconian laws banning the movement of weavers. Later, however, French occupation and the shrinking of the Spanish market led to diminishing production, with the industry finally fizzling out in the late eighteenth century.

There were two significant types of tapestry: **decorative** – principally *verdures*, showing scenes of foliage in an almost abstract way (the Oudenaarde speciality) – and **pictorial**, which were usually variations on the same basic themes, particularly rural life, knights, hunting parties and religious scenes. Over the centuries, changes in style were strictly limited, though the early part of the seventeenth century saw an increased use of elaborate woven borders and an appreciation of perspective.

Standard-size Oudenaarde tapestries took **six months** to make and were produced exclusively for the very wealthy. The tapestries were normally in yellow, brown, pale blue and shades of green, with an occasional splash of red, though the most important clients would, on occasion, insist on the use of gold and silver thread. Some also insisted on the employment of the most famous **artists** of the day for the preparatory painting – Pieter Paul Rubens and Jacob Jordaens both completed tapestry commissions.

---

trio of wonderful, late sixteenth-century, classical pieces celebrating Alexander the Great – *Alexander is offered the Crown*; *Alexander before the high priest Iaddo*; and *The Army Camp beside the River Granikos*. Equally delightful is *Scipio and Hannibal*, in which the border is decorated with medallions depicting the Seven Wonders of the World – though the Hanging Gardens of Babylon appear twice to create the symmetry. Romanticized pastoral scenes were perennially popular too: the seventeenth-century *Landscape with Two Pheasants* frames a distant castle with an intricate design of trees and plants, while *La Main Chaude* (or *Pat-a-Cake* as it's labelled here) depicts a game of blind man's buff.

St-Walburgakerk

Markt • April, May & Oct Tues, Thurs & Sat 2.30–5pm, plus Thurs 10–11am; June–Aug Tues–Sun 2.30–5pm • Free • ☎ 055 31 72 51

Soaring high above the town, **St-Walburgakerk** is a hulking, rambling mass of Gothic masonry that took a real hammering from the Protestants, who trashed almost all the original furnishings and fittings. Nowadays, gaudy Baroque altarpieces dot the cavernous interior, but the church does possess several fine tapestries, most memorably an exquisite *Calvary* in which two symbols of Christ's suffering – a spear and a stick with a sponge – are nailed to the Cross instead of the Christ himself.

Centrum Ronde van Vlaanderen

Markt 43 • Tues–Sun 10am–6pm • €8 • ☎ 055 33 99 33, ⓦ crvv.be

Oudenaarde is home to a noteworthy special interest museum, the **Centrum Ronda Van Vlaanderen**, with everything you could ever want to know about Belgium's premier professional cycling competition, the **Tour of Flanders**, including a film and cycling simulators. Enthusiasts can also drop by the shop, where they sell cycling maps, books and equipment – including retro-style jerseys.

ARRIVAL AND GETTING AROUND OUDENAARDE

By train or bus Oudenaarde train station is a 10min walk from the town centre; the bus station is adjacent. Incidentally, the present train station has usurped its neo-Gothic predecessor, which stands lonely and forlorn next door.
Destinations by train Brussels (every 30min to hourly; 50min); Ghent (Mon–Fri hourly, Sat & Sun every 2hr; 25min); Kortrijk (hourly; 15min).

By bike Bike rental is available from Asfra, a short walk southeast of the centre at Bergstraat 75 (☎ 055 31 57 40, ⓦ asfra.be). Tourist information sells cycling maps of the Vlaamse Ardennen (Flemish Ardennes), the ridge of low, wooded hills that rises from the Flanders plain a few kilometres to the south of town.

INFORMATION

Tourist information occupies the same premises as the MOU museum, in the Lakenhalle at the back of the Stadhuis (March–Sept Tues–Sun 9.30am–5.30pm; Oct–Feb

Tues–Fri 9.30am–5pm, Sat & Sun 2–5pm; ☎ 055 31 72 51, ⓦ www.oudenaarde.be).

ACCOMMODATION

★ **Gastenverblijf Steenhuyse** Markt 37 ☎ 055 23 23 73, ⓦ steenhuyse.info. This charming four-star hotel occupies a tastefully modernized eighteenth-century mansion, whose handsome stone facade faces onto the Markt. The large and well-appointed rooms come with all mod cons (wi-fi, rainshower etc). **€120**

La Pomme d'Or Markt 62 ☎ 055 31 19 00, ⓦ pommedor.be. In a large and good-looking old building on the main square, this ten-room, three-star hotel offers plain but perfectly adequate, modern rooms. Be sure to try one of their splendid, advocaat-laced cappuccinos in the bar. **€100**

EATING AND DRINKING

Oudenaarde may only have a population of 30,000, but it punches above its weight in terms of cafés and bars, the pick of which are either on or lie close to the Markt.

Bieren Roman Hoogstraat 21. The local Roman brewery rules the Oudenaarde roost, and this traditional neighbourhood bar is devoted to its products – try, for example, the Tripel Ename, a strong blond beer, or the Roman Dobbelen Bruinen, a snappy filtered stout. Daily 11am–11pm.

De Carillon Markt 49 ☎ 055 31 14 09, ⓦ decarillon.be. Old-fashioned café-bar that occupies an ancient brick-gabled building in the shadow of St-Walburgakerk. It's at its best in the summertime, when the large pavement terrace heaves with drinkers (rather than eaters). Tues–Sun 9am till late.

De Cridts Markt 58 ☎ 055 31 17 78, ⓦ brasseriedecridts .be. Friendly, traditional and family-owned café-restaurant serving standard-issue but tasty Flemish dishes at very reasonable prices – main courses average €19. Daily except Wed 9am–11pm.

Hanske de Krijger Einestraat 3 ☎ 0472 56 16 00. Youthful

bar-cum-café painted in deep, dark shades and with a good selection of ales. Gets jam-packed with Oudenaarde's finest (drinkers) on the weekend. Opening times vary.

Margaretha's Markt 40 ☎ 055 21 01 01, ⓦ www .margarethas.be. Oudenaarde tends to be low-key, so it's something of a surprise to find this extraordinarily lavish restaurant here, right bang in the centre of town. The place has the appearance of a stately home and the cuisine is very French with due prominence given to local, seasonal ingredients. Set meals are the order of the day for €72, €92 with wine, but less at lunch. Wed–Sun noon–2pm & 7–9pm.

Wine & Dine Café Hoogstraat 34 ☎ 055 23 96 97, ⓦ wine-dine.be. Nattily decorated café-restaurant offering a choice selection of Franco-Flemish food served with style and panache. Fish and meat dishes here cost around €22, salads €18. Tues–Sat 11.30am–2.30pm & 6–10.30pm.

Ghent

Of all the cities in Belgium, it's hard to trump **GHENT**, a vital, vibrant metropolis whose booming restaurant and bar scene wends its way across a charming cityscape, a network of narrow canals overseen by dozens of antique red-brick houses. If Bruges is a tourist industry with a town attached, Ghent is the reverse – a proudly Flemish city which, with a population of around 250,000, is now Belgium's third-largest conurbation. Evidence of Ghent's medieval pomp is to be found in a string of superb Gothic buildings including **St-Baafskathedraal**, whose principal treasure is Jan van Eyck's remarkable *Adoration of the Mystic Lamb*, one of the world's most important paintings. Supporting the cathedral are the likes of **St-Niklaaskerk**, with its soaring arches and pencil-thin turrets; the forbidding castle of the counts of Flanders, **Het Gravensteen**; and the delightful medieval guildhouses of the Graslei. These central attractions are supplemented by a trio of outlying museums within comfortable strolling distance of the Korenmarkt: **S.M.A.K**, an enterprising Museum of Contemporary Art; **STAM**, the city's brand-new historical museum; and the fine art of the excellent **Museum voor Schone Kunsten**.

Brief history

The principal seat of the counts of Flanders and one of the largest towns in western Europe during the thirteenth and fourteenth centuries, **Ghent** was once at the heart of the **Flemish cloth trade**. By 1350, the city boasted a population of fifty thousand, of whom no fewer than five thousand were directly involved in the industry, a prodigious concentration of labour in a predominantly rural Europe. Like Bruges, Ghent prospered throughout the Middle Ages, but it also suffered from endemic disputes between the count and his nobles (who supported France) and the cloth-reliant citizens (to whom friendship with England was vital). In the early sixteenth century, the relative decline of the cloth trade and the move into export-import did little to ease the underlying tension, as the people of Ghent were still resentful of their ruling class, from whom they were now separated by **language** – French against Flemish – and **religion** – Catholic against Protestant. The catalyst for conflict was usually **taxation**: long before the Revolt of the Netherlands (see p.330), Ghent's merchants and artisans found it hard to stomach the financial dictates of their rulers – the Habsburgs after 1482 – and time and again they rose in revolt, only to be crushed and punished. In 1540, for example, the Holy Roman Emperor **Charles V** lost patience and stormed the town, abolishing its privileges, filling in the moat and building a new castle at the city's expense.

Incorporation within the Spanish Netherlands

In 1584, with the Netherlands well on the way to independence from Habsburg Spain, Philip II's armies captured Ghent. It was a crucial engagement: thereafter Ghent proved to be too far south to be included in the United Provinces and was reluctantly pressed into the **Spanish Netherlands**. Many of its citizens fled north, and those who didn't may well have regretted their decision when the Inquisition arrived and the Dutch forced the Habsburgs to close the River Scheldt, Ghent's economic lifeline, as the price of peace in 1648.

Nineteenth century till today

In the centuries that followed, Ghent slipped into a slow decline from which it only emerged during the **industrial boom** of the nineteenth century, when it filled up with factories, whose belching chimneys encrusted the old city with soot and grime, a disagreeable measure of the city's economic revival. Indeed, its entrepreneurial mayor, Emille Braun, even managed to get the **Great Exhibition**, showing the best in contemporary design and goods, staged here in 1913.

Ghent remains an industrial city, but in the last twenty years it has benefited from an extraordinarily ambitious programme of **restoration and refurbishment**, thanks to which the string of fine Gothic buildings that dot the ancient centre have been returned to their original glory. Nevertheless, the street plan of the city centre still reflects Ghent's ancient class and linguistic divide. The streets to the south of the

> **CITYCARD GHENT**
>
> A bargain if you're set on seeing most of the sights, a **CityCard Ghent** covers all of the key attractions, provides free and unlimited use of the city's buses and trams and includes a boat trip; it costs €30 for 48hr, €35 for 72hr. It's on sale at any of the participants as well as from tourist information.

Korenmarkt (Corn Market), the traditional focus of the city, tend to be straight and wide, lined with elegant old mansions, the former habitations of the wealthier, French-speaking classes, while, to the north, Flemish Ghent is all narrow alleys and low brick houses.

St-Baafskathedraal

St-Baafsplein • April–Oct Mon–Sat 8.30am–6pm & Sun 1–6pm; Nov–March Mon–Sat 8.30am–5pm & Sun 1–5pm • Free • ☎ 09 225 1626, ⓦ sintbaafskathedraal.be

The best place to start an exploration of the city is the mainly Gothic **St-Baafskathedraal** (St Bavo's Cathedral), squeezed into the eastern corner of St-Baafsplein. The third church on this site, and 250 years in the making, the cathedral is a tad lop-sided, but there's no gainsaying the imposing beauty of the **west tower**, with its long, elegant windows and perky corner turrets. Some 82m high, the tower was the last major part of the church to be completed, topped off in 1554 – just before the outbreak of the religious wars that were to wrack the country for the next hundred years.

The nave, transepts and crypt

The chapel displaying the *Adoration of the Mystic Lamb* (see pp.155–160) is at the beginning of the cathedral's mighty, fifteenth-century **nave**, whose tall, slender columns give the whole interior a cheerful sense of lightness, though the Baroque marble screen spoils the effect by darkening the choir. In the nave, the principal item of interest is the Rococo **pulpit**, a whopping oak and marble affair, where the main timber represents the Tree of Life with an allegorical representation of Time and Truth at its base. Nearby, the **north transept** holds a characteristically energetic painting by **Rubens** (1577–1640) entitled *St Baaf entering the Abbey of Ghent*. Dating to 1624, it includes a self-portrait – he's the bearded head. St Baaf (aka St Bavo) turns up again above the **high altar**, a marble extravaganza featuring the saint ascending to heaven on an untidy heap of clouds. Also in the north transept is the entrance to the dank and capacious vaulted **crypt**, a survivor from the earlier Romanesque church. The crypt is stuffed with religious bric-a-brac of only limited interest with the exception of a superb triptych, *The Crucifixion of Christ*, by **Justus van Gent** (1410–80). The painting depicts the crucified Christ flanked, on the left, by Moses purifying the waters of Mara with wood, and to the right by Moses and the bronze serpent which cured poisoned Israelites on sight.

The Adoration of the Mystic Lamb

April–Oct Mon–Sat 9.30am–5pm, Sun 1–5pm; Nov–March Mon–Sat 10.30am–4pm, Sun 1–4pm • €4, including audio • ☎ 09 225 1626, ⓦ sintbaafskathedraal.be

In a small **chapel** to the left of the entrance resides Ghent's greatest treasure, a **winged altarpiece** known as *The Adoration of the Mystic Lamb* (*De Aanbidding van het Lam Gods*), a seminal work of the early 1430s, though of dubious provenance. Since the discovery of a Latin verse on its frame in the nineteenth century, academics have been arguing about who actually painted it. The inscription reads that **Hubert van Eyck** "than whom none was greater" began, and **Jan van Eyck**, "second in art", completed the work, but as nothing else is known of Hubert, some art historians doubt his existence. They argue that Jan, who lived and worked in several cities (including Ghent), was entirely

CAFÉS, BARS & CLUBS

Decadence	4
Greenway	2
Hotsy Totsy	1
Vooruit	3

ACCOMMODATION

Best Western Chamade	5
Camping Blaarmeersen	4
Hostel 47	1
Monasterium Poortackere	3
Sandton Grand Hotel Reylof	2

0 — 200 metres

2

GHENT'S MYSTIC LAMB: SCARES AND ALARUMS

Despite appearances, the **Just Judges panel** is not authentic. It was added during the 1950s to replace the original, which was stolen in 1934 and never recovered. The lost panel features in **Albert Camus**'s novel *The Fall*, whose protagonist keeps it in a cupboard, declining to return it for a complex of reasons, one of which is "because those judges are on their way to meet the Lamb …[but]…there is no lamb or innocence any longer". Naturally enough, there has been endless speculation as to who stole the panel and why, with suspicion ultimately resting on a certain **Arsène Goedertier**, a stockbroker and conservative politician from just outside of Ghent, who made a deathbed confession in 1934. Whether he was acting alone or as an agent for others is still hotly contested – some argue that the Knights Templar orchestrated the theft, others accuse the Nazis, but no one really knows.

The theft was just one of many **dramatic events** to befall the painting – indeed, it's remarkable that the altarpiece has survived at all. The Calvinists wanted to destroy it; Philip II of Spain tried to acquire it; the Emperor Joseph II disapproved of the painting so violently that he replaced the nude Adam and Eve with a clothed version of 1784 (exhibited today on a column at the start of the nave just inside the church entrance); and, near the end of World War II, the Germans hid it in an Austrian salt mine, where it remained until American soldiers rescued it in 1945.

responsible for the painting and that only later, after Jan had firmly rooted himself in the rival city of Bruges, did the citizens of Ghent invent "Hubert" to counter his fame. No one knows the altarpiece's authorship for sure, but what is certain is that in his manipulation of the technique of **oil painting** the artist – or artists – was able to capture a needle-sharp, luminous realism that must have stunned his contemporaries.

Note that the altar piece is undergoing a long-term **restoration**, which will last until 2018; during this period, one or other of the panels may not be displayed.

The cover screens

The altarpiece is now displayed with its panels open, though originally these were kept closed and the painting only revealed on high days and holidays. Consequently, it's actually best to begin round the back with the **cover screens**, which hold a beautiful Annunciation scene with the Archangel Gabriel's wings reaching up to the timbered ceiling of a Flemish house, the streets of a town visible through the windows. In a brilliant coup of **lighting**, the shadows of the angel dapple the room, emphasizing the reality of the apparition – a technique repeated on the opposite cover panel around the figure of Mary. Below, the donor and his wife, a certain Joos Vydt and Isabella Borluut, kneel piously alongside statues of the saints.

The upper level

By design, the restrained exterior was but a foretaste of what lies within – a striking, visionary work of art whose brilliant colours and precise draughtsmanship still take the breath away. On the **upper level** sit God the Father (some say Christ Triumphant), the Virgin and John the Baptist in gleaming clarity; to the right are musician-angels and a nude, pregnant Eve; and on the left is Adam plus a group of singing angels, who strain to read their music. The celebrated sixteenth-century Flemish art critic Karel van Mander argued that the singers were so artfully painted that he could discern the different pitches of their voices: it is undoubtedly the **detail** that impresses, especially the richly embroidered trimmings on the cloaks.

The lower central panel

In the **lower central panel**, the Lamb, the symbol of Christ's sacrifice, is depicted in a heavenly paradise – "the first evolved landscape in European painting", suggested Kenneth Clark – seen as a sort of idealized Low Countries. The Lamb stands on an altar whose rim is minutely inscribed with a quotation from the Gospel of St John, "Behold the Lamb of God, which taketh away the sins of the world". Four groups

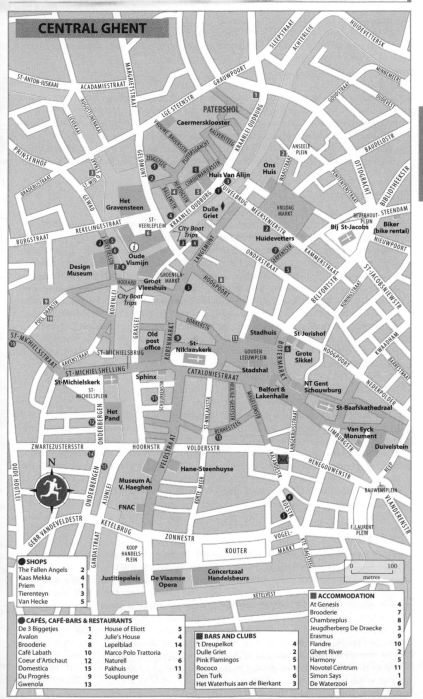

CENTRAL GHENT

2

SHOPS

The Fallen Angels	2
Kaas Mekka	4
Priem	1
Tierenteyn	3
Van Hecke	5

CAFÉS, CAFÉ-BARS & RESTAURANTS

De 3 Biggetjes	1	House of Eliott	5
Avalon	2	Julie's House	4
Brooderie	8	Lepelblad	14
Café Labath	10	Marco Polo Trattoria	7
Coeur d'Artichaut	12	Naturell	6
Domestica	15	Pakhuis	11
Du Progrès	9	Souplounge	3
Gwenola	13		

BARS AND CLUBS

't Dreupelkot	4
Dulle Griet	2
Pink Flamingos	5
Rococo	1
Den Turk	6
Het Waterhuis aan de Bierkant	3

ACCOMMODATION

At Genesis	4
Brooderie	7
Chambreplus	8
Jeugdherberg De Draecke	3
Erasmus	9
Flandre	10
Ghent River	2
Harmony	5
Novotel Centrum	11
Simon Says	1
De Waterzooi	6

converge on the Lamb from the corners of the central panel. In the bottom right is a group of male saints and up above them are their female equivalents; the bottom left shows the patriarchs of the Old Testament and above them is an assortment of bishops, dressed in blue vestments and carrying palm branches.

The side panels
On the **side panels**, approaching the Lamb across symbolically rough and stony ground, are more saintly figures. On the right-hand side are two groups, the first being St Anthony and his hermits, the second St Christopher, shown here as a giant with a band of pilgrims. On the left-hand side panel come the horsemen, the inner group symbolizing the Warriors of Christ (including St George bearing a shield with a red cross) and the outer group showing the Just Judges, each of whom is dressed in fancy Flemish attire.

The Lakenhalle

Botermarkt • No public access except to visit the attached Belfort (see below)

Across from the cathedral, on the west side of St Baafsplein, stands the **Lakenhalle** (Cloth Hall), a sombre hunk of a building with an unhappy history. Work began on the hall in the early fifteenth century, but the cloth trade slumped before it was finished and it was only grudgingly completed in 1903. Since then, no one has ever worked out what to do with the building and today it's little more than an empty shell, though its basement did once serve as the town prison. The entrance to the prison was round on the west side of the Lakenhalle through the **Mammelokker** (The Suckling), a grandiose Louis XIV-style portal of 1741 that stands propped up against the main body of the building. Part gateway, part warder's lodging, the Mammelokker is adorned with a bas-relief sculpture illustrating the classical legend of Cimon, whom the Romans condemned to death by starvation. Pero, his daughter, saved him by turning up daily to feed him from her breasts – hence the name.

The Belfort

Botermarkt • Daily 10am–6pm • €6 • Ⓦ belfortgent.be

The first-floor entrance on the south side of the Lakenhalle is the only way to reach the adjoining **Belfort** (Belfry), a much-amended medieval edifice whose soaring spire is topped by a comically corpulent gilded copper dragon. Once a watchtower and storehouse for civic documents, the interior is now little more than an empty shell displaying a few old bells, a carillon drum or two and incidental statues alongside the rusting remains of an antique dragon, which formerly perched on top of the spire. The belfry is equipped with a **glass-sided lift** that climbs up to the roof, where consolation is provided in the form of excellent views over the city centre.

The Stadhuis

Botermarkt • Guided tours only May–Sept Mon–Fri as the first 45min of the 2hr walking tour organized by the Guides' Association (see p.167) • Full 2hr tour €8, Stadhuis only €5 • For further details, contact tourist information (see p.167).

Stretching along the west side of the Botermarkt is the **Stadhuis** (City Hall), whose discordant facade comprises two distinct sections. Dating from the 1580s, the later section, which frames the central stairway, is a fine example of Italian Renaissance architecture, its crisp symmetries faced by a multitude of black-painted columns. In stark contrast are the wild, curling patterns of the section to the immediate north, carved in Flamboyant Gothic style at the beginning of the sixteenth century to a design by one of the era's most celebrated architects, **Rombout Keldermans** (1460–1531). The whole of the Stadhuis was originally to have been built by Keldermans, but the money ran out when the wool trade collapsed and the city couldn't afford to finish it off until much later – hence today's mixture of styles.

2

Guided tours of the Stadhuis amble round a series of halls and chambers, the most interesting being the old Court of Justice or **Pacificatiezaal** (Pacification Hall), where the Pacification of Ghent was signed in 1576. A plaque commemorates this treaty, which momentarily bound the rebel armies of the Low Countries (today's Belgium and the Netherlands) together against their rulers, the Spanish Habsburgs. The hall's charcoal-and-cream **tiled floor** is designed in the form of a maze. No one's quite certain why, but it's thought that more privileged felons (or sinners) had to struggle round the maze on their knees as a substitute punishment for a pilgrimage to Jerusalem – a good deal if ever there was one.

St-Niklaaskerk

Cataloniestraat • Mon 2–5pm, Tues–Sun 10am–5pm • Free • Ⓦ cultuurinkerken.be

Just along the street from the Lakenhalle is **St-Niklaaskerk**, an architectural hybrid dating from the thirteenth century that was once the favourite church of the city's principal merchants. It's the shape and structure that pleases most, especially the arching buttresses and pencil-thin turrets which, in a classic example of the early Scheldt Gothic style, elegantly attenuate the lines of the nave. Inside, many of the original Baroque furnishings and fittings have been removed and the windows un-bricked, thus returning the church to its early appearance. One feature you can't miss is the giant-sized Baroque **high altar** with its mammoth representation of God the Father glowering down its back, blowing the hot wind of the Last Judgement from his mouth and surrounded by a flock of cherubs. The church is sometimes used for temporary **art exhibitions**.

The Korenmarkt

St-Niklaaskerk marks the southern end of the **Korenmarkt** (Corn Market), a long and wide cobbled area where the grain which once kept the city fed was traded after it was unloaded from the boats that anchored on the Graslei dock nearby (see below). The one noteworthy building here is the former **post office**, whose combination of Gothic Revival and neo-Renaissance styles illustrates the eclecticism popular in Belgium at the beginning of the twentieth century. The carved heads encircling the building represent the great and the good who came to the city in numbers for the Great Exhibition of 1913 – among them was Florence Nightingale.

St-Michielsbrug

Behind the old post office, **St-Michielsbrug** (St Michael's bridge) offers fine views back over the towers and turrets that pierce the Ghent skyline. This is no accident: the bridge was built in 1913 to provide visitors to the Great Exhibition with a vantage point from which to admire the city centre. The bridge also overlooks the city's oldest harbour, the **Tussen Bruggen** (Between the Bridges), from whose quays – the **Korenlei** and the **Graslei** – boats leave for trips around the city's canals (see box, p.166).

The guildhouses of the Graslei

Ghent's boatmen and grain-weighers were crucial to the functioning of the medieval city, and they built a row of splendid **guildhouses** along the **Graslei**, each gable decorated with an appropriate sign or symbol. Working your way north from St Michielsbrug, the first building of distinction is the **Gildehuis van de Vrije Schippers** (Guildhouse of the Free Boatmen), at no. 14, where the badly weathered sandstone is decorated with scenes of boatmen weighing anchor plus a delicate carving of a caravel – the type of Mediterranean sailing ship used by Columbus – located above the door. Medieval Ghent had **two boatmen guilds**: the Free, who could discharge their cargoes within the city, and the

Unfree, who could not. The Unfree Boatmen were obliged to unload their goods into the vessels of the Free Boatmen at the edge of Ghent – an inefficient arrangement by any standard, though typical of the complex regulations governing the guilds.

Next door, the seventeenth-century **Cooremetershuys** (Corn Measurers' House), at Graslei 12–13, was where city officials weighed and graded corn behind a facade graced by cartouches and garlands of fruit. Next to this, at no. 11, stands the quaint **Tolhuisje**, another delightful example of Flemish Renaissance architecture, built to house the customs officers in 1698, while the adjacent limestone **Spijker** (Staple House), at no. 10, boasts a surly Romanesque facade dating from around 1200. It was here that the city stored its grain supply for over five hundred years until a fire gutted the interior.

Finally, three doors down at no. 8, the splendid **Den Enghel** takes its name from the banner-bearing angel that decorates the facade; the building was originally the stonemasons' guildhouse, as evidenced by the effigies of the four Roman martyrs who were the guild's patron saints, though they are depicted in medieval attire rather than togas and sandals.

The Groentenmarkt and Groot Vleeshuis

The jumble of old buildings at the **Groentenmarkt** (Vegetable Market) makes for one of the city's prettiest squares. The west side of the square is flanked by a long line of stone gables which were once the retaining walls of the **Groot Vleeshuis** (Great Butchers' Hall), a covered market in which meat was sold under the careful control of the city council. The gables date from the fifteenth century but are in poor condition and the interior is only of interest for its intricate wooden roof.

The Korenlei

Across the **Grasbrug** bridge lies the **Korenlei**, where a series of expansive, Neoclassical merchants' houses, mostly dating from the eighteenth century, overlooks the western side of the old city harbour. It's the general ensemble that appeals rather than any particular building, but the **Gildehuis van de Onvrije Schippers** (Guildhouse of the Unfree Boatmen), at no. 7, does boast a fetching eighteenth-century facade decorated with whimsical dolphins and bewigged lions, all bulging eyes and rows of teeth.

St-Michielskerk

St-Michielsplein • April–Sept Mon–Sat 2–5pm • Free

At the south end of Korenlei, beside St Michielsbrug, rises the bulky mass of **St-Michielskerk**, a heavy-duty Gothic edifice begun in the 1440s. The city's Protestants seem to have taken a particularly strong dislike to the place, ransacking it twice – once in 1566 and again in 1579 – and the repairs were never quite finished, as witnessed by the forlorn and clumsily truncated tower. The interior is much more enticing, the broad sweep of the five-aisled nave punctuated by tall and slender columns that shoot up to the arching vaults of the roof. Here also, in the north transept, is a splendidly impassioned *Crucifixion* by **Anthony van Dyck** (1599–1641). Trained in Antwerp, where he worked in Rubens' workshop, van Dyck made extended visits to England and Italy in the 1620s, before returning to Antwerp in 1628. He stayed there for four years – during which time he painted this *Crucifixion* – before migrating to England to become portrait painter to Charles I and his court.

Design Museum

Jan Breydelstraat 5 • Tues–Sun 10am–6pm • €8 • ☎ 09 267 99 99, ⓦ designmuseumgent.be

The enjoyable **Design Museum** focuses on Belgian decorative and applied arts, with the collection divided into two distinct sections. At the front, squeezed into what was once an eighteenth-century patrician's mansion, is an attractive sequence of **period rooms**, mostly illustrating the Baroque and the Rococo. The original dining room is especially fine, from its fancy painted ceiling, ornate chandelier and Chinese porcelain through to its intricately carved elm panelling. The second section, at the back of the mansion, comprises a **modern display** area used both for temporary exhibitions and to showcase the museum's eclectic collection of applied arts, dating from 1880 to the present day. Here, the Art Nouveau material is perhaps the most visually arresting, especially the finely crafted furnishings of the Belgian **Henry van der Velde** (1863–1957).

Het Gravensteen

St-Veerleplein • Daily: April–Oct 10am–6pm; Nov–March 9am–5pm • €10 • ⓦ gravensteengent.be

The cold, dark walls and unyielding turrets of **Het Gravensteen**, the castle of the counts of Flanders, look sinister enough to have been lifted from a Bosch painting. They were first raised in 1180 as much to intimidate the town's unruly citizens as to protect them, and, considering the castle has been used for all sorts of purposes since then (even a cotton mill), it has survived in remarkably good nick. The imposing **gateway** comprises a deep-arched, heavily fortified tunnel leading to a large **courtyard**, which is framed by protective battlements complete with ancient arrow slits and apertures for boiling oil and water.

Overlooking the courtyard are the castle's two main buildings: the **count's residence** on the left and the **keep** on the right, the latter riddled with narrow, interconnected staircases set within the thickness of the walls. A **self-guided tour** takes you through this labyrinth, the first highlight being a room full of medieval military hardware, from suits of armour, pikes, swords, daggers and early pistols through to a pair of exquisitely crafted sixteenth-century crossbows. Beyond is a gruesome collection of instruments of torture; a particularly dank, underground dungeon (or *oubliette*); and the counts' vaulted session room – or council chamber. It's also possible to walk along most of the castle's encircling wall, from where there are pleasing views over the city centre.

St-Veerleplein and the Oude Vismijn

Public punishments ordered by the counts and countesses of Flanders were carried out in front of the castle on **St-Veerleplein**, now an attractive cobbled square, but with an ersatz punishment post plonked here in 1913 and topped off by a lion carrying the banner of Flanders. At the back of the square, beside the junction of the city's two main canals, is the grandiloquent Baroque facade of the **Oude Vismijn** (Old Fish Market), in which Neptune stands on a chariot drawn by sea horses. To either side are allegorical figures representing the River Leie (Venus) and the River Scheldt (Hercules), the two rivers that spawned the city. After years of neglect, the Oude Vismijn has been redeveloped and is now home to **tourist information** (see p.167).

Huis van Alijn Museum

Kraanlei 65 • Tues–Sat 11am–5.30pm, Sun 10am–5.30pm • €6 • ☎ 09 269 2350, ⓦ huisvanalijn.be

The **Huis van Alijn** folklore museum occupies a series of pretty little almshouses set around a central courtyard. Dating from the fourteenth century, the almshouses were built following a major scandal reminiscent of *Romeo and Juliet*. In 1354, two members of the Rijms family murdered three of the rival Alijns when they were at Mass in St-Baafskathedraal. The immediate cause of the affray was jealousy – one man from each clan was after the same woman – but the dispute went deeper, reflecting the commercial animosity of two guilds, the weavers and the fullers. The murderers fled for their lives and were condemned to death in absentia, but were eventually – eight years later – pardoned on condition that they paid for the construction of a set of almshouses, which was to be named after the victims. The result was the Huis van Alijn, which became a hospice for elderly women and then a workers' tenement until the city council snapped it up in the 1940s.

The **museum** consists of two sets of rooms, either side of the courtyard, depicting local life and work in the nineteenth and twentieth centuries. There are reconstructions of a variety of shops and workshops – a dispensary, a barber's and so forth – plus small thematic displays illustrating particular aspects of traditional Flemish society such as popular entertainment, funerals and death, but the labelling is very skimpy. One particular highlight, in one of the rooms on the museum's right-hand side, is a bank of miniature TV screens showing short, locally made **amateur films** in a continuous cycle. Some of these date back to the 1920s and they are regularly rotated, but most are postwar, including a snippet featuring a local 1970s soccer team dressed in terrifyingly tight shorts.

The Patershol

Provinciaal Cultuurcentrum Caermersklooster: Tues–Sun 10am–5pm • Free • ☎ 09 269 29 10, ⓦ caermersklooster.be

Behind the Kraanlei are the lanes and alleys of the **Patershol**, a tight web of brick terraced houses dating from the seventeenth century. Once the heart of the Flemish working-class city, this thriving residential quarter had, by the 1970s, become a slum threatened with demolition. After much debate, the area was saved from the developers and a process of gentrification begun, the result being today's gaggle of good bars and restaurants. The only specific attraction is the grand old Carmelite Monastery on Vrouwebroersstraat, now the **Provinciaal Cultuurcentrum Caermersklooster**, which showcases occasional exhibitions of contemporary art, photography, design and fashion.

Dulle Griet

From the Kraanlei, an antiquated little bridge leads over to **Dulle Griet** (Mad Meg), a lugubrious fifteenth-century **cannon** whose failure to fire provoked a bitter row between Ghent and the nearby Flemish town of Oudenaarde, where it was cast. In the 1570s, fearful of a Habsburg attack, Ghent purchased the cannon from Oudenaarde. As the region's most powerful siege gun, able to propel a 340kg cannonball several hundred metres, it seemed a good buy, but when Ghent's gunners tried it out, the barrel cracked on first firing. The useless lump was then rolled to the edge of the Vrijdagmarkt, where it has stayed ever since – and much to the chagrin of Ghent city council, Oudenaarde simply refused to offer a refund.

Vrijdagmarkt and Bij St-Jacobs

From Dulle Griet, it's just a few metres to the **Vrijdagmarkt**, a wide and open square that was long the political centre of Ghent, the site of both public meetings and executions – sometimes at the same time. In the middle of the square stands a nineteenth-century statue of the guild leader **Jacob van Artevelde** (see box, p.165), portrayed addressing the people in heroic style. Of the buildings flanking the Vrijdagmarkt, the most appealing is the old headquarters of the trade unions, the whopping **Ons Huis** (Our House), a sterling edifice built in eclectic style at the beginning of the twentieth century.

Adjoining Vrijdagmarkt is **Bij St-Jacobs**, a sprawling square set around a glum medieval church. The square hosts the city's biggest and best **flea market** (*prondelmarkt*) on Fridays, Saturdays and Sundays from 8am to 1pm.

STAM

Bijlokesite, Godshuizenlaan • Tues–Sun 10am–6pm • €8 • ☎ 09 267 14 00, ⓦ stamgent.be

The old Cistercian **Bijlokeabdij** (Bijloke Abbey), just to the west of the River Leie, was

2

JACOB VAN ARTEVELDE COMES TO A STICKY END

One of the shrewdest of Ghent's medieval leaders, **Jacob van Artevelde** (1290–1345) was elected captain of all the guilds in 1337. Initially, he steered a delicate course during the interminable wars between France and England, keeping the city neutral – and the textile industry going – despite the machinations of both **warring countries**. Ultimately, however, he was forced to take sides, plumping for England. This proved his undoing: in a burst of Anglomania, Artevelde rashly suggested that a son of Edward III of England become the new count of Flanders, an unpopular notion that prompted a mob to storm his house and hack him to death. Artevelde's demise fuelled further outbreaks of communal **violence** and, a few weeks later, the Vrijdagmarkt witnessed a riot between the fullers and the weavers that left five hundred dead. This rumbling vendetta – one of several that plagued the city – was the backdrop to the creation of the Huis van Alijn (see p.163).

---

founded in the thirteenth century. Much of the medieval complex survived and, with subsequent additions, now occupies a sprawling multi-use site. At its core is **STAM**, a new museum which explores the city's history via paintings and a battery of original artefacts. Visits begin in a bright, new **cube-like structure** and continue in the former **abbey church** and **cloisters**, with a particular highlight being the dramatic medieval wall paintings in the former refectory.

Citadelpark

A large chunk of greenery, **Citadelpark** takes its name from the fortress that stood here until the 1870s, when the land was cleared and prettified with the addition of grottoes and ponds, statues and fountains, a waterfall and a bandstand. These nineteenth-century niceties survive today and, as an added bonus, the park seems refreshingly hilly after the flatness of the rest of Ghent. In the 1940s, a large brick complex was built on the east side of the park and, after various incarnations, it now divides into two – one part fenced off waiting redevelopment, the other holding the **S.M.A.K. art gallery**.

S.M.A.K.

Citadelpark • Tues–Sun 10am–6pm • €8 • ☎ 09 221 1703, ⓦ smak.be

S.M.A.K, the Stedelijk Museum voor Actuele Kunst (Municipal Museum of Contemporary Art), is one of Belgium's most adventurous contemporary art galleries and one that is largely devoted to temporary displays of international standing. These exhibitions are supplemented by a regularly rotated selection of sculptures, paintings and installations drawn from the museum's **permanent collection**. S.M.A.K possesses examples of all the major artistic movements since World War II – everything from Surrealism, the CoBrA group and Pop Art through to Minimalism and conceptual art – as well as their forerunners. Perennial favourites include the installations of the influential German **Joseph Beuys** (1921–86), who played a leading role in the European avant-garde art movement of the 1970s, and Panamarenko's eccentric polyester zeppelin entitled *Aeromodeller*.

Museum voor Schone Kunsten

Fernand Scribedreef • Tues–Sun 10am–6pm • €8 • ☎ 09 240 07 00, ⓦ mskgent.be

Opposite S.M.A.K., the **Museum voor Schone Kunsten** (Fine Art Museum) holds the city's principal art collection and runs an ambitious programme of temporary exhibitions. It occupies an imposing Neoclassical edifice, though the interior can be a tad confusing – be sure to pick up a floor plan at reception.

2

Early Flemish paintings

In Room 2, one highlight of the museum's small but eclectic collection of early Flemish paintings is **Rogier van der Weyden**'s (1399–1464) *Madonna with Carnation*, a charming work where the proffered flower, in all its exquisite detail, serves as a symbol of Christ's passion. Also in Room 2 are two superb works by **Hieronymus Bosch** (1450–1516), his *Bearing of the Cross* showing Christ mocked by some of the most grotesque and deformed characters he ever painted. Among the grotesques, you'll spy a singularly wan penitent thief confessing to a monstrously ugly monk and St Veronica, whose cloak carries the imprint of Christ's face. This struggle between good and evil is also the subject of Bosch's *St Jerome at Prayer*, in the foreground of which the saint prays, surrounded by a brooding, menacing landscape.

Rubens and his contemporaries

Room 5 features a powerful *St Francis* by **Rubens** (1577–1640), in which a very sick-looking saint bears the marks of the stigmata, while **Jacob Jordaens** (1593–1678), who was greatly influenced by Rubens, is well represented in Room 7 by the whimsical romanticism of his *Allegory of Fertility*. Jordaens was, however, capable of much greater subtlety and his *Studies of the Head of Abraham Grapheus*, also in Room 7, is an example of the high-quality preparatory paintings he completed, most of which were later recycled within larger compositions. In the same room, **Anthony van Dyck**'s (1599–1641) *Jupiter and Antiope* wins the bad taste award for its portrayal of the lecherous god with his tongue hanging out in anticipation of sex with Antiope.

The eighteenth century onwards

The museum's eighteenth- and nineteenth-century collection includes a handful of romantic historical canvases, plus – and this is a real surprise – a superbly executed portrait of a certain *Alexander Edgar* by the Scot **Henry Raeburn** (1756–1823). Also on display are several key paintings by Ostend's **James Ensor** (1860–1949), notably the ghoulish *Skeleton looking at Chinoiserie* and *Pierrot and Skeleton in Yellow Robe*, though you have to take pot luck with the museum's most famous Ensor, his much-lauded *Self-Portrait with Flower Hat*, as this is often out on loan. Other high points include several characteristically unsettling works by both **Paul Delvaux** (1897–1994) and **René Magritte** (1898–1967). A case in point is Magritte's *Perspective II. Manet's Balcony*, in which wooden coffins have replaced the figures from Manet's painting.

ARRIVAL AND DEPARTURE   **GHENT**

By train Ghent has three train stations, but the one you're almost certain to arrive at is Gent St-Pieters (🕸 belgianrail.be), about 2km south of the city centre.

From the station, tram #1 (destination Evergem, NOT Flanders Expo) runs up to the Korenmarkt at the heart of the city every few minutes.

GUIDED TOURS AND BOAT TRIPS IN GHENT

Guided walking tours are popular in Ghent and there are several different types to choose from, but the standard tour, organized by the Guides' Association, is a two-hour jaunt around the city centre (May–Sept daily at 2.30pm; €8), including a visit to either the Stadhuis (Mon–Fri) or the Cathedral (Sat & Sun). Tickets are on sale at tourist information (see p.167) and advance booking – at least a few hours ahead of time – is strongly recommended. Alternatively, **horse-drawn carriages** line up outside the Lakenhalle, on St Baafsplein, offering a thirty-minute canter round town for €30 (Easter to Oct daily 10am–6pm & most winter weekends). Throughout the season, **boat trips** explore Ghent's inner waterways, departing from the Korenlei quay, just near the Korenmarkt, as well as from the Vleeshuisbrug, beside the Kraanlei (March–Oct daily 10am–6pm; Nov–Feb daily 11am–4pm; €6.50). Trips last forty minutes and leave every fifteen minutes or so, though the wait can be longer as boats often delay their departure until they are reasonably full.

Destinations by train Antwerp Centraal (every 30min; 50min); Bruges (every 20min; 20min); De Panne (hourly; 1hr 15min); Diksmuide (hourly; 50min); Kortrijk (every 30min; 20min); Mechelen (hourly; 50min); Ostend (every 30min; 40min); Oudenaarde (Mon–Fri hourly, Sat & Sun every 2hr; 25min); Veurne (hourly; 1hr 10min).

By car The E40, the Brussels-Ostend motorway, clips the southern edge of the city. There are lots of city-centre car parks with one of the most convenient being the 24-hour one beneath the Vrijdagmarkt.

GETTING AROUND

By tram and bus Trams and buses are operated by De Lijn (☎ 070 22 02 00, ☒ delijn.be). A standard one-way fare costs €1.30 in advance, €2 from the driver, but note that at peak times some tram and bus drivers don't take money or issue tickets. There are ticket machines at the train station and at major tram and bus stops. A 24-hour city transport pass, the Dagpas, costs €5 (€7 from the driver). Note also that a Ghent city pass (see p.155) includes public transport. Tourist information issues free maps of the transport system.

By bike Ghent is good for cycling: the terrain is flat and there are cycle lanes on many of the roads and cycle racks dotted across the centre. Bike rental is available from Biker, on the northeast side of the city centre at Steendam 16 (Tues–Sat 9am–12.30pm & 1.30–6pm; ☎ 09 224 29 03, ☒ bikerfietsen .be); for a standard bike they charge €9 per day.

By taxi Try V-Tax on ☎ 09 222 22 22.

INFORMATION

Tourist information is in the Oude Vismijn, opposite the castle on St-Veerleplein (daily: mid-March to mid-Oct 9.30am–6.30pm; mid-Oct to mid-March 9.30am–4.30pm; ☎ 09 266 56 60, ☒ visitgent.be). It supplies a wide range of free city information, including good-quality maps, and operates a last-minute/same-night accommodation booking service.

Books and maps A reasonably good selection of English paperbacks and Belgian walking maps is available at FNAC, Veldstraat 88 (Mon–Sat 10am–6.30pm; ☎ 09 223 40 80, ☒ www.nl.fnac.be).

ACCOMMODATION

Ghent has around forty **hotels** and a small army of **B&Bs** with several of the most stylish and enjoyable places located in the centre, which is where you want to be. The city also has a good supply of bargain-basement accommodation, notably a couple of bright and cheerful **hostels** and a large suburban **campsite**. Tourist information will make last-minute/same-night accommodation reservations on your behalf and their website has comprehensive listings (☒ visitgent.be).

HOTELS

Best Western Chamade Koningin Elisabethlaan 3 ☎ 09 220 15 15, ☒ chamade.be; map pp.156–157. Standard, three-star accommodation in bright, modern bedrooms at this family-run hotel, which occupies a distinctive, six-storey modern block, a 5min walk north of the train station. €130

★ **Erasmus** Poel 25 ☎ 09 224 21 95, ☒ erasmushotel .be; map p.159. Friendly, family-run two-star located in a commodious old town house a few metres away from the Korenlei. Each room is thoughtfully decorated and furnished in traditional style with lots of antiques. The breakfast is excellent and reservations are strongly advised in summer. €99

Flandre Poel 1 ☎ 09 266 06 00, ☒ hoteldeflandre.be; map p.159. Four-star hotel in an imaginatively refashioned nineteenth-century mansion with a modern annexe at the back. The spacious public areas are kitted out in sharp style, with original floorings and low sofa seats, and the 62 bedrooms beyond are neat and trim, though they do vary considerably in size. The rooms towards the rear are quieter than those on the Poel. Competitively priced. €110

Ghent River Waaistraat 5 ☎ 09 266 10 10, ☒ ghent-river-hotel.be; map p.159. Four-star hotel whose austere modern facade doesn't do it any favours, but persevere: the interior is much more appealing and most of the guest rooms occupy that part of the building which was once a cotton mill – hence the bare-brick walls and industrial trappings. €125

Harmony Kraanlei 37 ☎ 09 324 26 80, ☒ hotel-harmony.be; map p.159. In an immaculately renovated old mansion, this deluxe four-star hotel has just twenty-odd guest rooms decorated in an attractive modern style: all wooden floors and shades of brown and cream. The best rooms are on the top floor and come complete with their own mini-terrace, affording grand views over the city. €155

Monasterium Poortackere Oude Houtlei 56 ☎ 09 269 22 10, ☒ monasterium.be; map pp.156–157. This unusual hotel-cum-guesthouse occupies a rambling and somewhat spartan former nunnery and orphanage, whose ageing brickwork dates from the nineteenth century. There's a choice between unassuming, en-suite rooms in the hotel section (one-star) or the more authentic nunnery-cell experience in the guesthouse, where some rooms have shared facilities. Breakfast is taken in the old chapterhouse. A 5min walk west of Veldstraat. Hotel room €95, guesthouse €75

Novotel Centrum Goudenleeuwplein 5 ☎ 09 293 90 02, ☒ novotel.com; map p.159. The guest rooms at this brisk, three-star chain hotel are pretty routine, but the location – just near the Cathedral – is hard to beat, the price is very competitive, and there's an outdoor swimming pool – a rarity in central Ghent and great if the sun is out. €90

★**Sandton Grand Hotel Reylof** Hoogstraat 36 ⓣ09 235 40 70, ⓦsandton.eu/en/gent; map pp.156–157. This superb chain hotel occupies a spacious nineteenth-century mansion, whose elegant, high-ceilinged foyer sets the perfect tone. Beyond, the 158 rooms vary in size and facilities, but most are immaculate and spacious and decorated in an appealing rendition of country-house style. The former coach house is now a spa and there is a patio terrace. The least expensive deals exclude breakfast. €120

2

B&BS

At Genesis Hertogstraat 15 ⓣ09 224 21 08, ⓦstayatgenesis.com; map p.159. In the heart of the Patershol, in a sympathetically modernized old terrace house, this B&B offers two second-floor guest rooms – one for a maximum of three guests, the other six – located above an artist's studio. Both come with a kitchenette and have lots of nice decorative touches plus beamed ceilings. One guest €78, two guests €96

Brooderie Jan Breydelstraat 8 ⓣ09 225 06 23, ⓦwww.brooderie.be; map p.159. The owners of this appealing little café (see below) rent out three neat and trim if modest little rooms immediately above it. Breakfast is excellent, but if you're a light sleeper go elsewhere – it gets noisy outside. Metres from the Korenmarkt. €55

★**Chambreplus** Hoogpoort 31 ⓣ09 225 37 75, ⓦchambreplus.be; map p.159. Charming B&B with three extremely cosy guest rooms: one is decorated in the manner of a sultan's room, another the Congo, with the third occupying a self-contained mini-house – complete with hot tub – at the back of the garden, though this is €50 extra. The garden, with its dinky little pond, is a delightful place to sit and read and breakfasts are delicious, as are the home-made chocolates (one of the owners is a chocolatier). Smashing central location, too. €135

Simon Says Sluizeken 8 ⓣ09 233 03 43, ⓦsimon-says.be; map p.159. On the edge of the Patershol, in a good-looking building with an Art Nouveau facade, this combined coffee bar and B&B has just two guest rooms, both fairly small and straightforward modern, en-suite affairs. Smashing breakfasts – be sure to try the croissants – and reasonably priced. €130

De Waterzooi St-Veerleplein 2 ⓣ0475 43 61 11, ⓦdewaterzooi.be; map p.159. Superbly renovated eighteenth-century mansion with a handful of handsome rooms that manage to make the most of their antique setting but are extraordinarily comfortable at the same time – the split-level attic room is the most ambitious. Wonderful views of the castle, and if the weather is good you can take breakfast outside in the garden-patio. €180

HOSTELS AND CAMPING

Camping Blaarmeersen Zuiderlaan 5 ⓣ09 266 81 60, ⓦgent.be/blaarmeersen; map pp.156–157. Among the woods beside a watersports centre to the west of town, this large campsite is equipped with laundry, shop, cafeteria and various sports facilities. March–Oct. Bus #38 from the Korenmarkt (25min). Tent pitch, car and two adults €28

Hostel 47 Blekerijstraat 47 ⓣ0478 71 28 27, ⓦhostel47.com; map pp.156–157. Well-kept hostel with spacious and clean two- to six-bed dormitories in an old house about a 15min walk from the city centre. There's a small garden, internet access and shared bathrooms. A basic breakfast is included in the price. Dorm €30, double €66

Jeugdherberg De Draecke St-Widostraat 11 ⓣ09 233 70 50, ⓦjeugdherbergen.be/en; map p.159. Well-equipped, HI-affiliated hostel that's just a five-minute walk north of the Korenmarkt. Has 27 en-suite rooms of varying size, wi-fi, lockers, a library, bar and lounge. Advance reservations are advised, especially in summer. Currently being expanded. Breakfast is included. Dorm €22, double €52

EATING

Ghent's multitude of **cafés**, **café-bars** and **restaurants** offers the very best of Flemish and French food alongside an international cast of other cuisines. The city has a battalion of prestige restaurants, where the food is great and prices high, but there are lots of reasonably priced places too. Ghent is particularly good for **vegetarians**: tourist information has a free brochure detailing all the places where they serve vegetarian food. Many restaurants close on **Sundays**.

CAFÉS

★**Avalon** Geldmunt 32 ⓣ09 224 37 24, ⓦrestaurantavalon.be; map p.159. This long-established vegetarian restaurant offers a wide range of well-prepared dishes – be sure to look out for the daily specials, which cost about €12. Choose from one of the many different rooms or the terrace at the back in the summer. Tues–Sat 11.30am–2.30pm.

Brooderie Jan Breydelstraat 8 ⓣ09 225 06 23, ⓦwww.brooderie.be; map p.159. Pleasant and informal café with a health-food slant, offering wholesome breakfasts, lunches, sandwiches and salads (from around €9), plus cakes and coffee. Also offers B&B accommodation (see above). Tues–Sun noon–4pm.

Café Labath Oude Houtlei 1 ⓣ09 225 28 25, ⓦcafelabath.be; map p.159. Specialist coffee house in neat, modern premises that makes much of the quality of its beans – with good reason. Snacks, soups and teas too.

Attracts a boho bunch. Mon–Fri 8am–7pm, Sat 9am–5pm, Sun 10am–6pm.

Greenway Nederkouter 42 ❶09 269 07 69, ⓦgreenway.be; map pp.156–157. Straightforward café-cum-takeaway decorated in sharp modern style, selling a wide range of eco-friendly foods, from organic burgers to pastas, noodles and baguettes, all for just a few euros each. Mon–Sat 11am–10pm.

Gwenola Voldersstraat 66 ❶09 223 17 39, ⓦgwenola .be; map p.159. This long-established pancake house may be a bit over the hill decoratively, but who cares when the pancakes are so good – and inexpensive, from €2.50 and up. Note that the sugar looks as if it has been added with a trowel. Mon–Sat 11am–7pm.

★**Julie's House** Kraanlei 13 ❶09 233 33 90, ⓦjulieshouse.be; map p.159. "Baked with love and served with joy" is the boast here – it's a little OTT, but *Julie's* home-made cakes and patisseries are truly delicious. They also serve tasty breakfasts (till 2pm) and pancakes. The premises are appealing too, with the café squeezed into an ancient terrace house. Wed–Sun 9am–6.30pm.

Souplounge Zuivelbrugstraat 6 ❶09 223 62 03, ⓦwww.souplounge.be; map p.159. Bright and cheerful self-service café, where the big bowls of freshly made soup are the main event – from €6. Sandwiches and salads too. Daily 10am–7pm.

RESTAURANTS

★**Coeur d'Artichaut** Onderbergen 6 ❶09 225 33 18, ⓦartichaut.be; map p.159. Set in a handsome eighteenth-century mansion with a lovely courtyard at the back, this smooth and polished restaurant specializes in salads – and they really are quite superb – plus innovative French, Thai and Italian dishes. Salads, as a main course, start at €16. Tues–Sat noon–2.30pm & 6–10pm.

Domestica Onderbergen 27 ❶09 223 53 00, ⓦdomestica.be; map p.159. Smart and chic brasserie-restaurant serving up an excellent range of Belgian dishes – both French and Flemish – in nouvelle cuisine style. Has a garden terrace for good-weather eating. Main courses from €25. Mon & Sat 6.30–10pm, Tues–Fri noon–2pm & 6.30–10pm.

Du Progrès Korenmarkt 10 ❶09 225 17 16, ⓦduprogres.be; map p.159. Few would say this busy place is their favourite café-restaurant in Ghent, but it does have a few things in its favour: a central location; rapid-fire service; great steaks (€20–25); competitive prices; and Sunday opening. Kitchen: Mon & Thurs–Sun 11.30am–10pm; café-bar: daily 11am–11.30pm.

★**House of Eliott** Jan Breydelstraat 36 ❶09 225 21 28, ⓦthehouseofeliott.be; map p.159. Idiosyncratic split-level restaurant that's liberally sprinkled with Edwardian bric-a-brac – you'll even spot some vintage models' dummies. The menu offers a limited but well-chosen selection of freshly prepared meat and fish dishes (mains average €25) – try, for example, the wood pigeon risotto. The window tables overlook a canal and, if the weather holds, you can eat out on the pontoon at the back. Reservations strongly advised. Mon & Fri–Sun noon–2pm & 6–10pm, Thurs 6–10pm.

Lepelblad Onderbergen 40 ❶09 324 02 44, ⓦlepelblad.be; map p.159. Very popular restaurant, with a heaving pavement terrace, where the ever-changing menu is inventive and creative with pasta dishes and salads to the fore (mains around €14): try, for example, the mushroom linguini in gorgonzola sauce. The arty decor is good fun too. Wed–Sun 11.30am–11pm.

Marco Polo Trattoria Serpentstraat 11 ❶09 225 04 20; map p.159. This rustic restaurant is part of the Italian "slow food" movement in which the emphasis is on organic, seasonal ingredients prepared in a traditional manner. All the dishes are freshly prepared and delicious. Mains from €18, pizzas €10. Tues–Fri noon–2.30pm & 6–10pm, Sat 6–10pm.

Naturell Jan Breydelstraat 10 ❶09 279 07 08, ⓦnaturell-gent.be; map p.159. The brightly coloured furnishings and fittings may be informal but they take their food very seriously here, with the emphasis on local, seasonal ingredients used in gastronomic set meals. A five-courser will set you back €75, four-courses €65. Reservations advised. Wed–Sat noon–3pm & 7.30–10pm & Sun noon–3pm.

Pakhuis Schuurkenstraat 4 ❶09 223 55 55, ⓦpakhuis .be; map p.159. Set in a creatively remodelled old warehouse with acres of glass and metal plus a large outside area, this lively bistro-brasserie is one of Ghent's more fashionable options. The extensive menu features Flemish and French dishes, with mains averaging €24, but the simpler dishes are what they do best. Down a narrow alley near St-Michielsbrug. Mon–Sat noon–2.30pm & 6.30–11pm.

De 3 Biggetjes Zeugsteeg 7 ❶09 224 46 48, ⓦde3biggetjes.com; map p.159. This small and intimate restaurant occupies an old terrace house in the heart of the Patershol. The menu features the freshest of ingredients prepared with creative gusto – hake and leeks in a brown-beer sauce, for example. Main courses €25; set lunch €19. Mon–Wed & Fri 7–10pm, Sat noon–2pm & 7–10pm.

DRINKING AND NIGHTLIFE

Ghent's **bars** are a real delight, and some of the most noteworthy – with a beer list long enough to strain any liver – are within easy strolling distance of the Korenmarkt. The **club** and **live music** scene is also first-rate, with Ghent's students taking the lead, congregating at the string of bars and clubs that line Overpoortstraat, just south of St-Pietersplein.

Decadance Overpoortstraat 76 ☎09 329 0054, ⓦdecadance.be; map pp.156–157. Long a standard-bearer for the city's nightlife, this club near the university (hence the abundance of students) offers one of the city's best nights out, with either live music – most of Belgium's bands have played here at one time or another – or DJs. Mon–Sat 10pm until 9am or later.

't Dreupelkot Groentenmarkt 12 ☎09 224 2120, ⓦdreupelkot.be; map p.159. Cosy bar specializing in jenever (Belgian gin), of which it stocks more than 200 brands, all kept at icy temperatures – the vanilla flavour is particularly delicious. It's down a little alley leading off the Groentenmarkt, and next door to *Het Waterhuis* (see below). Daily 4pm until late.

Dulle Griet Vrijdagmarkt 50 ☎09 224 2455, ⓦdullegriet.be; map p.159. Long, dark and atmospheric bar with all manner of incidental objets d'art and an especially wide range of beers. Mon 4.30pm–1am, Tues–Sat noon–1am & Sun noon–7.30pm.

★**Hotsy Totsy** Hoogstraat 1 ☎09 224 2012; map pp.156–157. Long the gathering place of the city's intelligentsia – though less so today – this ornately decorated bar, with its Art Nouveau flourishes, has ranks of drinkers lining up along its long wooden bar. Regular live jazz and blues sessions too. Mon–Fri from 6pm till late, Sat & Sun from 8pm.

★**Pink Flamingos** Onderstraat 55 ☎09 233 4718, ⓦpinkflamingos.be; map p.159. Weird and wonderful place – the interior is the height of kitsch, with plastic statues of film stars, tacky religious icons and Barbie dolls – a great place for an aperitif or cocktails. Mon–Wed

noon–midnight, Thurs & Fri noon–3am, Sat 2pm–3am, Sun 2pm–midnight.

Rococo Corduwaniersstraat 57; map p.159. This intimate café-cum-bar attracts a cool clientele and is a perfect place to be on a cold winter evening, with candles flickering and the fire roaring. Stocks a good range of wines and beers, and also has home-made cakes. Tues–Sun 9pm–midnight.

Den Turk Botermarkt 3 ☎09 233 0197, ⓦcafedenturk .be; map p.159. Thought to be the oldest bar in the city, this tiny rabbit warren of a place offers a good range of beers and whiskies, though the decor lacks vitality. Frequent live music, mainly jazz. Daily 11am until late.

★**Vooruit** St-Pietersnieuwstraat 23 ☎09 267 28 28, ⓦvooruit.be; map pp.156–157. The Vooruit performing arts centre (see p.171) has good claim to be the cultural centre of the city (at least for the under-40s), offering a wide-ranging programme of rock and pop through to dance. It also occupies a splendid building, a twin-towered and turreted former festival hall that was built for Ghent's socialists in an eclectic rendition of Art Nouveau in 1914. The café-bar is a large barn-like affair that stays jam-packed until early in the morning. Café-bar: Mon–Sat 10am–1am, Sun noon–1am.

★**Het Waterhuis aan de Bierkant** Groentenmarkt 9 ☎09 225 0680, ⓦwaterhuisaandebierkant.be; map p.159. More than a hundred types of beer are available in this engaging canal-side bar, which is popular with tourists and locals alike. Be sure to try Stropken (literally "noose"), a delicious local brew named after the time, in 1540, when Charles V compelled the rebellious city burghers to parade outside the town gate with ropes around their necks. Daily 11am–2am.

SHOPPING

There's a large and popular **flea market** (*prondelmarkt*) on Bij St-Jacobs and adjoining Beverhoutplein (Fri, Sat & Sun 8am–1pm); a daily **flower market** on the Kouter, just off Veldstraat, though this is at its best and busiest on Sundays (7am–1pm); **organic foodstuffs** on the Groentenmarkt (Fri 7.30am–1pm); and a **bird market** (not for the squeamish) on the Vrijdagmarkt on Sundays (7am–1pm).

The Fallen Angels Jan Breydelstraat 29–31 ☎09 223 94 15, ⓦthe-fallen-angels.com. Mother and daughter run these two adjacent shops, selling all manner of antique bric-a-brac, from postcards and posters through to teddy

bears and toys. Intriguing at best, twee at worst, but a useful source of unusual gifts. Thurs–Sat 1.30–5.30pm.

Kaas Mekka Koestraat 9 ☎09 225 83 66, ⓦhetmekkavandekaas.be. Literally the "Cheese Mecca",

---

GHENT FESTIVALS

Ghent boasts a hatful of festivals, some an excuse for a(n alcoholic) knees-up, others more demure (read cultural). To begin with, there's the prestigious **Festival van Vlaanderen** (Flanders Festival; ⓦfestival.be), a classical music event which runs from March to October with concerts in all of the major cities of Flanders, including Ghent. There's also the **Gentse Feesten** (ⓦgentsefeesten.be): ten days of partying, including all sorts of gigs, held in mid- to late July and always including July 21; and last but not least the **Ghent Film Festival** (ⓦfilmfestival.be), held over twelve days in October and one of Europe's foremost cinematic events, showcasing around two hundred feature films from all over the world and screening Belgian films well before they hit the circuit.

this small specialist shop offers a remarkable range of traditional and exotic cheeses – try some of the delicious Ghent goat's cheese (*geitenkaas*). Sells a good range of wine, too. Tues–Fri 9am–1pm & 1.30–6.30pm, Sat 9am–6.30pm.

Priem Zuivelbrugstraat 1 ☎ 09 223 25 37. One of the oddest shops in Ghent, Priem has an extraordinary range of vintage wallpaper dating from the 1950s. Zuivelbrugstraat is the location of the main shop, but there are three other neighbouring premises on the Kraanlei. Mon 2–5.30pm, Tues–Fri 9.30am–12.30pm & 2–6pm, Sat 9.30am–12.30pm & 2–5.30pm.

Tierenteyn Groetenmarkt 3 ☎ 09 225 83 36, ⓦ tierenteyn-verlent.be. This traditional shop, one of the city's most delightful, makes its own mustards – wonderful, tongue-tickling stuff displayed in shelf upon shelf of ceramic and glass jars. A small jar will set you back about €4. Mon 10am–6pm, Tues–Fri 9am–6pm, Sat 9.30am–6pm.

Van Hecke Koestraat 42 ☎ 09 225 43 57, ⓦ chocolaterievanhecke.be. Many locals swear that this independent, family-run chocolatier sells the best chocolates and cakes in town. Mouthwatering stuff. Mon, Tues & Thurs–Sat 9am–6pm, Wed 10am–5pm.

ENTERTAINMENT

Ghent prides itself on its **performing arts** scene, with five first-rate venues, two very good art-house cinemas, a premier opera company (that it shares with Antwerp) and half a dozen theatre troupes. For upcoming **events**, consult the tourist information website (ⓦ visitgent.be). Tickets are available from venues direct or from **Uitbureau Gent**, at the back of the Museum Arnold Vander Haeghen, Veldstraat 82 (Mon–Sat 10.30am–5.30pm; ☎ 09 233 77 88, ⓦ uitbureau.be).

MAJOR VENUES

De Bijloke Jozef Kluyskensstraat 2 ☎ 09 269 92 92, ⓦ debijloke.be. The old Bijloke abbey complex now holds the STAM historical museum (see p.164) and a Muziekcentrum, which includes a smart new Concert Hall.

Concertzaal Handelsbeurs Kouter 29 ☎ 09 265 91 60, ⓦ handelsbeurs.be. The city's primary concert hall with two auditoria and hosting a wide and diverse programme.

NT Gent Schouwburg Sint Baafsplein ☎ 09 225 01 01, ⓦ ntgent.be. Right in the centre of the city, the municipal theatre accommodates the Nederlands Toneel Gent, the regional repertory company. Almost all of their performances are in Flemish, though they do play occasional host to touring English-language theatre companies.

Vlaamse Opera Gent Schouwburgstraat 3 ☎ 09 268 10 11, ⓦ vlaamseopera.be. Handsomely restored nineteenth-century opera house, where the city's opera company performs when not on tour.

Vooruit St-Pietersnieuwstraat 23 ☎ 09 267 28 28, ⓦ vooruit.be. One of Ghent's leading venues for rock, pop and jazz concerts, with an excellent on-site café-bar (see p.170).

ART-HOUSE CINEMAS

Sphinx Sint-Michielshelling 3 ☎ 09 225 60 86, ⓦ sphinx-cinema.be. Sphinx focuses on foreign-language and art-house films (with original soundtrack).

Studio Skoop Sint Annaplein 63 ☎ 09 225 08 45, ⓦ studioskoop.be. The cosiest of the city's cinemas, but still with five screens.

DIRECTORY

ATMs ATMs are liberally distributed across the city centre. ING has ATMs at most of its branches, including Belfortstraat 18, and Europabank has one on the Groetenmarkt.

Pharmacies Two central pharmacies are at St Michielsstraat 15 and Nederkouter 123. Duty rotas, detailing late-night opening pharmacies, should be displayed in every pharmacy window.

Post office The main post office is at Lange Kruisstraat 55 (Mon–Fri 9am–6pm, Sat 9am–3pm).

Antwerp and the northeast

SCHELDT RIVER, ANTWERP

Antwerp and the northeast

Stretching up to the border with the Netherlands, the provinces of Antwerp and Limburg, together with a chunk of Brabant, constitute the Flemish-speaking northeast rim of Belgium. The main attraction here is the sprawling, intriguing city of Antwerp, which retains many reminders of its sixteenth-century golden age – expect splendid medieval churches and as fine a set of museums as you'll find anywhere in Belgium, with the stirring legacy of Rubens adding artistic élan. Antwerp also has a much-vaunted fashion scene built on the success of its home-grown designers, incorporates one of Europe's biggest ports and is the international centre of the diamond trade. But these roles by no means define its character: for one thing its centre has a range of bars and restaurants to rival almost any city in northern Europe.

The city is also within easy striking distance of a string of old Flemish towns that make for ideal day-trips. In the **province of Antwerp**, the obvious targets are **Lier**, whose centre is particularly quaint and diverting, and **Mechelen**, the ecclesiastical capital of Belgium, which weighs in with its handsome Gothic churches, most memorably a magnificent cathedral. Southeast from here, over in **Vlams-Brabant** (Flemish Brabant) – and just beyond the reaches of Brussels' sprawling suburbs – the magnet is the lively university town of **Leuven**, which boasts its own cluster of fine medieval buildings and a vibrant atmosphere. Further to the east, the **province of Limburg** is, unlike Antwerp, seldom visited by tourists, its low-key mixture of small towns and rolling farmland rarely given due attention. It's true that **Hasselt**, the capital, is really rather unremarkable, but pint-sized **Tongeren**, which claims to be the oldest town in Belgium, is the most relaxing of places and one that makes a good hand of its Roman history. With Tongeren as a base, you can cycle off into the surrounding countryside, where the village of **Zoutleeuw** is distinguished by its medieval church – the only one in Belgium that managed to avoid the depredations of Protestants, iconoclasts and invading armies.

Antwerp

Some 50km north of Brussels, **ANTWERP**, Belgium's second city, lays claim to being the de facto capital of Flemish Belgium, boosting its credentials with an animated cultural scene, a burgeoning fashion industry, a batch of beautiful old buildings and more top-ranking cafés and restaurants than you could possibly sample – quite enough to keep anyone busy for a few days, if not more. The city fans out carelessly from the east bank of the Scheldt, its nucleus a rough polygon formed and framed by its enclosing boulevards and the river. The **centre** is a hectic and immediately likeable place, with a dense concentration of things to see, not least the magnificent Gothic

RUBENSHUIS

Highlights

❶ **Antwerp cathedral** This supreme example of the Gothic is both magnificent and stunningly beautiful. **See p.182**

❷ **Rubens** Don't leave Antwerp without viewing at least some of Rubens' paintings, most stirringly inside the Cathedral and at the Rubenshuis, the great man's former home and studio. **See p.182 & p.185**

❸ **Antwerp's MoMu** Antwerp's first-class fashion museum has an international

reputation for the quality of its temporary exhibitions. **See p.186**

❹ **Antwerp at night** The city boasts a mouthwatering selection of restaurants and bars, more than enough for the pickiest of gourmands and the strongest of livers. **See pp.195–198**

❺ **Tongeren** An amiable, traditional kind of place, well off the beaten track, which makes for a gentle day-trip. **See p.215**

HIGHLIGHTS ARE MARKED ON THE MAP ON P.176

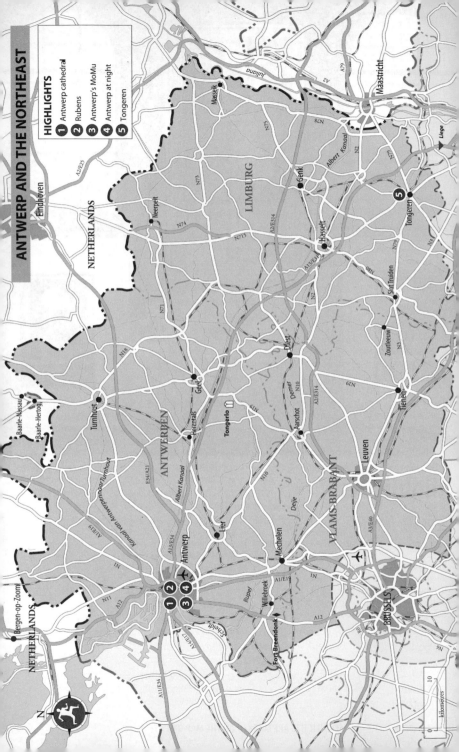

ANTWERP AND THE NORTHEAST

HIGHLIGHTS

1. Antwerp cathedral
2. Rubens
3. Antwerp's MoMu
4. Antwerp at night
5. Tongeren

Onze Lieve Vrouwekathedraal, home to a quartet of paintings by Rubens. There's also the fascinating old printing house of Christopher Plantin, now the **Museum Plantin-Moretus**, the sinuous Baroque of **St-Pauluskerk**, a pair of small but superb collections of paintings at the **Rockoxhuis** and the **Museum Mayer van den Bergh**, and **ModeNatie**, a large-scale celebration of the city's fashion industry, incorporating a brilliant museum, **MoMu**.

To the **east of the centre**, the star turns are the **Rubenshuis**, one-time home and studio of Rubens, and the cathedral-like **Centraal Station**, which itself abuts the **diamond district**. The area to the **south of the centre**, **Het Zuid**, is of interest too, a long-neglected but now resurgent residential district whose wide boulevards, with their long vistas and geometrical roundabouts, were laid out at the end of the nineteenth century. The obvious targets here are **M HKA** (the Museum of Contemporary Art) and the **Koninklijk Museum voor Schone Kunsten** (Fine Art Museum), though this is currently closed for a thoroughgoing revamp which will stretch until 2017, maybe longer. Finally, **north of the centre** lies **Het Eilandje** (the Little Isle), where the city's old docks and wharves have been rejuvenated and deluxe apartments shoehorned into former warehouses, the whole caboodle overseen by the soaring modernism of the **MAS (Museum Aan de Stroom)**.

Brief history

In the beginning **Antwerp** wasn't much desired: it may have occupied a prime river site, but it was too far east to be important in the cloth trade and too far west to be on the major trade routes connecting Germany and Holland. However, in the **late fifteenth century** it benefited from both a general movement of commerce to the west and the decline of the Anglo-Flemish cloth trade. Within the space of just 25 years, many of the great trading families of western Europe had relocated here, and the tiny old fortified settlement of yesteryear was transformed by a deluge of splendid new mansions and churches, docks and harbours. In addition, the new masters of the region, the **Habsburgs**, had become frustrated with the turbulent burghers of Flanders, and both the emperor Maximilian and his successor **Charles V** patronized the city at the expense of its Flemish rivals, underwriting its success as the leading port of their expanding empire.

Religious turmoil

Antwerp's golden age lasted for less than a hundred years, prematurely stifled by Charles V's son **Philip II**, who inherited Spain and the Low Countries in 1555. Fanatically Catholic, Philip viewed the reformist stirrings of the Low Countries with horror, and his sustained attempt to bring his Protestant subjects to heel brought war and pestilence to the region for decades – with Protestantism having taken root in Antwerp early on, the city seethed with discontent as Philip's intentions became all too clear. The spark was the **Ommegang** of August 18, 1566, when priests carting the image of the Virgin through the city's streets insisted that all should bend the knee as it passed. The parade itself was peaceful enough, but afterwards the city's Protestant guildsmen and their apprentices smashed the inside of the cathedral to pieces – the most extreme example of the "**iconoclastic fury**" that then swept the whole region.

Catholic reaction

Philip responded by sending in an army of occupation, which sought to intimidate the local citizenry from a brand-new citadel built on the south side of town. Nine years later, it was this same garrison that sat unpaid and underfed in its fortress, surrounded by the wealth of what the soldiers regarded as a "heretical" city. Philip's mercenaries **mutinied**, and at dawn on November 4, 1576, they stormed Antwerp, running riot for three long days, plundering public buildings and private mansions, and slaughtering some eight thousand of its inhabitants in the "**Spanish fury**", a catastrophe that finished

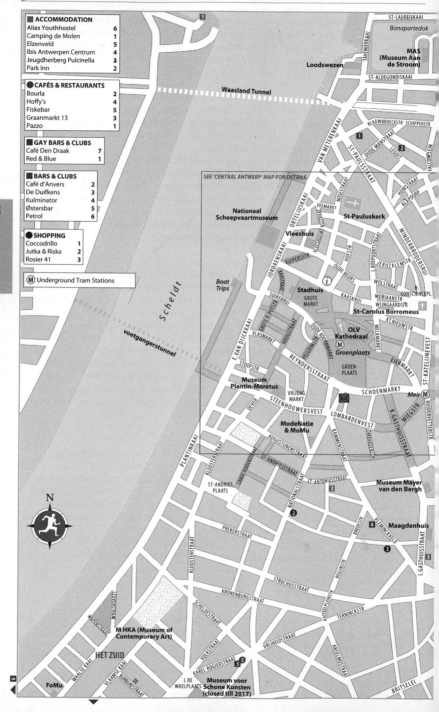

ACCOMMODATION
Alias Youthhostel	6
Camping de Molen	1
Elzenveld	5
Ibis Antwerpen Centrum	4
Jeugdherberg Pulcinella	3
Park Inn	2

CAFÉS & RESTAURANTS
Bourla	2
Hoffy's	4
Fiskebar	5
Graanmarkt 13	3
Pazzo	1

GAY BARS & CLUBS
Café Den Draak	7
Red & Blue	1

BARS & CLUBS
Café d'Anvers	2
De Duifkens	3
Kulminator	4
Østersbar	5
Petrol	6

SHOPPING
Coccodrillo	1
Jutka & Riska	2
Rosier 41	3

Ⓜ Underground Tram Stations

3

SEE 'CENTRAL ANTWERP' MAP FOR DETAILS

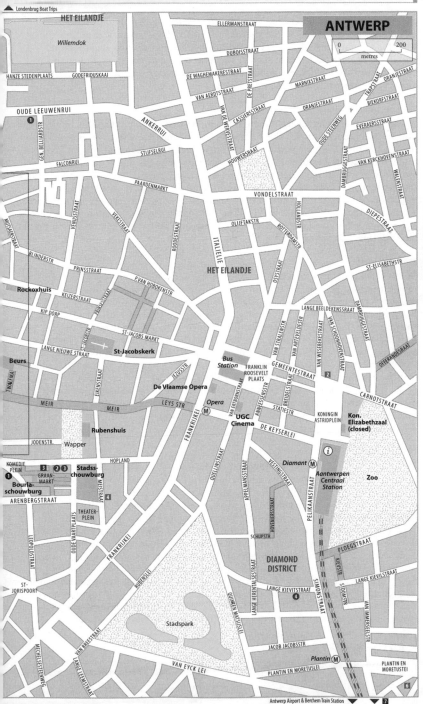

Londenbrug Boat Trips

HET EILANDJE

Willemdok

ANTWERP

0 ———————— 200
metres

ELLERMANSTRAAT

DUBOISSTRAAT

DE WAGHEMAKERESTRAAT
DE PRETSTRAAT

MARNIXSTRAAT

TRAPSTRAAT
ORANJESTRAAT

HANZE STEDENPLAATS   GODEFRIDUSKAAI

VAN AERDTSTRAAT

ORANJESTRAAT

BIEKORFSTRAAT

OUDE LEEUWENRUI ❶

CASSIERSSTRAAT
VAN DE WERVESTRAAT

OUDE STEENWEG

EVERAERSSTRAAT

GEN. BELLIARDSTR

ANKERRUI

HOUWERSTRAAT

DAMBRUGGESTRAAT

VAN KERCKHOVENSTRAAT

FALCONRUI

STUFSELRUI

WALKESTRAAT

PAARDENMARKT

VONDELSTRAAT

DIEPESTRAAT

MUIZAESTRAAT

VENUSSTRAAT

VEKESTRAAT

ROODESTRAAT

ITALIELEI

OLIJFTAKSTR

HOLLANDSTR

ROTTERDAMSTR

BLINDERSTR

PRINSSTRAAT

HET EILANDJE

OSSYSTRAAT

ST-ELISABETHSTR

Rockoxhuis

KEIZERSTRAAT

P. VAN HOBOKENSTR

LANGE BEELDEKENSSTRAAT

DAMBRUGGESTRAAT

KIP DORP

PRINSESSTRAAT

VAN SCHOONHOVENSTRAAT

ST-JACOBS MARKT

LANGE NIEUWE STRAAT

St-Jacobskerk

VAN STRAALENSTR

VAN ARTEVELDESTR

VAN WESENBEESTRAAT

OFFERANDESTRAAT

Beurs

EIKENSTRAAT

MEERBURGSTRAAT

GEMEENTESTRAAT

Bus Station

FRANKLIN ROOSEVELT PLAATS

TWAALFMA

MEIR   MEIR

LEYS STR

De Vlaamse Opera

Opera Ⓜ

BREDESTRAAT

ANNEESSENSTRAAT

STATIESTR

❷

CARNOTSTRAAT

Rubenshuis

FRANKRIJKEI

UGC Cinema

DE KEYSERLEI

KONINGIN ASTRIDPLEIN

Kon. Elizabethzaal (closed)

JODENSTR. **Wapper**

HOPLAND

Diamant Ⓜ

Aantwerpen Centraal Station

ⓘ

Zoo

KOMEDIE PLEIN ❶

❸ ❷❸

GRAAN-MARKT

Stadss-chouwburg

MEISTRAAT

APPELMANSSTRAAT

QUELLINSTRAAT

VESTINGSTRAAT

PELIKAANSTRAAT

Bourla-schouwburg

ARENBERGSTRAAT

❹

THEATER-PLEIN

OUDE VAARTPLAITS

HOVENIERSSTRAAT

SCHUPSTR

PLOEGSTRAAT

LEOPOLDSTRAAT

FRANKRIJKEI

RUBENSLEI

SCHUPSTR.

DIAMOND DISTRICT

LANGE HERENTALSESTRAAT

SIMONSSTRAAT

KEYSTR

STOOMSTR

LANGE KIEVITSTRAAT

ST-JORISPOORT

LANGE KIEVITSTRAAT ❹

QUINTEN MATSIJSLEI

VAN IMMERSEELSTR

MECHELSESTEENWEG

VAN BREESTRAAT

LANGE LEEMSTRAAT

Stadspark

VAN EYCK LEI

JACOB JACOBSSTR

Plantin Ⓜ

PLANTIN EN MORETUSTEI

PLANTIN EN MORETUSLEI

❻

3

the city's commercial supremacy. More disasters were to follow. Philip's soldiers were driven out after the massacre, but they were back in 1585, laying siege outside the city walls for seven months, their success leading to Antwerp's ultimate incorporation within the **Spanish Netherlands**. Under the terms of the capitulation, Protestants had two years to leave town, and a flood of skilled workers poured north to the relative safety of Holland, further weakening the city's economy.

Decline and resurgence

In the early seventeenth century there was a modest recovery, but the Dutch, who were now free of Spain, controlled the waterways of the **Scheldt** and were determined that no neighbouring Catholic port would threaten their trade. Consequently, in 1648, under the **Peace of Westphalia**, which finally wrapped up the Thirty Years' War, they forced the closure of the Scheldt to all non-Dutch shipping. This ruined Antwerp, and the city remained firmly in the doldrums until the French army arrived in 1797, **Napoleon** declaring it to be "little better than a heap of ruins...scarcely like a European city at all". The French rebuilt the docks and reopened the Scheldt to shipping, and the city revived to become independent Belgium's **largest port**, a role that made it a prime target during both world wars.

Modern times

In 1914, the invading German army overran Antwerp's outer defences with surprising ease, forcing the Belgian government – which had moved here from Brussels a few weeks before – into a second hasty evacuation along with Winston Churchill and the Royal Marines, who had only just arrived. During **World War II**, both sides bombed Antwerp, but the worst damage was inflicted after the Liberation, when the city was hit by hundreds of Hitler's V1 and V2 rockets. After the war, Antwerp quickly picked up the pieces, becoming one of Europe's major **seaports** and, more recently, acting as a cultural and political focus for those Flemish-speakers looking for greater independence within (or without) a federal Belgium. It has also consolidated its position at the heart of the worldwide **diamond** trade and developed an international reputation for its innovative **fashion** designers, from the so-called "Antwerp Six" to talent such as Tim Vansteenbergen, A.F. Vandevorst and Stephan Schneider.

Grote Markt

The centre of Antwerp is the **Grote Markt**, at the heart of which stands the 1887 **Brabo Fountain**, a haphazard pile of roughly sculpted rocks surmounted by a bronze of legendary Roman soldier Silvius Brabo, depicted flinging the hand of the prostrate giant Antigonus into the Scheldt. Legend asserts that Antigonus extracted tolls from all passing ships, cutting off the hands of those who refused to pay. He was eventually beaten by the valiant Brabo, who tore off his hand and threw it into the river, giving the city its name, which literally means "hand-throw". There are more likely explanations of the city's name, but this is the most colourful, and it certainly reflects Antwerp's early success at freeing the river from the innumerable taxes levied on shipping by local landowners. The north side of the Grote Markt is lined with daintily restored **guildhouses**, their sixteenth-century facades decorated with appropriate reliefs and topped by finely cast gilded figures basking in the afterglow of the city's Renaissance lustre. No. 7, the **House of the Crossbowmen**, with its figures of St George

---

ANTWERP CITY CARD

The **Antwerp City Card** gives free access to almost all the major sites plus a variety of supplementary discounts. It costs €19 for 24hr, €25 for 48hr and €29 for 72hr; it's on sale at tourist information (see p.194).

and the dragon, is the tallest and most distinctive; it stands next to the **Coopers' House**, with its barrel motifs and statue of St Matthew.

Stadhuis

Grote Markt

Presiding over the square, the **Stadhuis** was completed in 1566 to an innovative design by Cornelis Floris de Vriendt, though there have been several modifications. The building's pagoda-like roof gives it a faintly oriental appearance, but apart from the central gable it's quite plain, with a long pilastered facade of short and shallow Doric and Ionic **columns**. These, along with the windows, lend it a simple elegance, in contrast to the purely decorative **gable** (there's no roof behind it). Here, the niches at the top contribute to the self-congratulatory aspect of the building, with a statue of the Virgin Mary set above representations of *Justice* and *Wisdom*, virtues the city burghers reckoned they had in plenty.

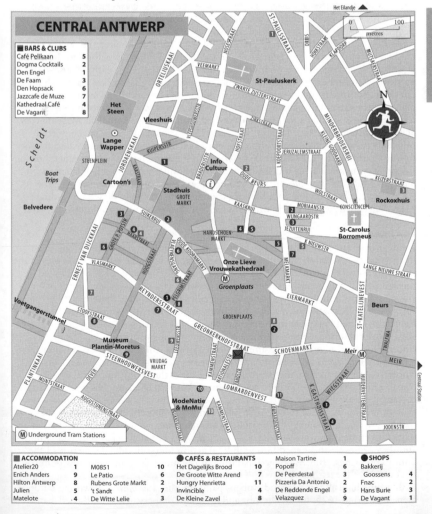

ACCOMMODATION				CAFÉS & RESTAURANTS		Maison Tartine	1	SHOPS	
Atelier20	1	M0851	10	Het Dagelijks Brood	10	Popoff	6	Bakkerij	
Enich Anders	9	Le Patio	6	De Groote Witte Arend	7	De Peerdestal	3	Goossens	4
Hilton Antwerp	8	Rubens Grote Markt	2	Hungry Henrietta	11	Pizzeria Da Antonio	2	Fnac	2
Julien	5	't Sandt	7	Invincible	4	De Reddende Engel	5	Hans Burie	3
Matelote	4	De Witte Lelie	3	De Kleine Zavel	8	Velazquez	9	De Vagant	1

Handschoenmarkt

Leaving the Grote Markt by its southeast corner, you'll soon come to the triangular **Handschoenmarkt** (the former Glove Market), an appealing little square with the cathedral on one side and an attractive ensemble of antique gables on the other two. The conspicuous **stone well** in the corner of the Handschoenmarkt is adorned with a graceful iron canopy and bears the legend "It was love connubial taught the smith to paint" – a reference to the fifteenth-century painter **Quinten Matsys**, who learned his craft so he could woo the daughter of a local artist: at the time, marriage between families of different guilds was strongly discouraged. The Handschoenmarkt is the most westerly of a somewhat confusing cobweb of pedestrianized streets and **tiny squares** that laps round the edge of the cathedral.

Onze Lieve Vrouwekathedraal

Handschoenmarkt • Mon–Fri 10am–5pm, Sat 10am–3pm, Sun 1–4pm • €6 • ☎ 03 213 99 51, ⓦ www.dekathedraal.be

One of the finest Gothic churches in Belgium, the **Onze Lieve Vrouwekathedraal** (Cathedral of Our Lady) is a forceful, self-confident structure that mostly dates from the middle of the fifteenth century. Its graceful, intricate **spire** dominated the skyline of the medieval city and was long a favourite with travellers – William Beckford, for instance, fresh from spending millions on his own house in Wiltshire in the early 1800s, was particularly impressed, writing that he "longed to ascend it that instant, to stretch myself out upon its summit and calculate, from so sublime an elevation, the influence of the planets". The cathedral's **paintings** are an additional draw, not least since it took temporary possession of a number of key works from the city's **Koninklijk Museum voor Schone Kunsten** (Fine Art Museum; see box p.192), specifically those which were originally commissioned for the church. Pride of place among the loaned paintings goes to a 1618 triptych by Rubens entitled *Christ on the Straw*, after its central panel showing Joseph of Arimathea laying out the body of Jesus. Similarly memorable is **Quinten Matsys**' (1465–1530) *Lamentation*, a profound and moving triptych portraying the Christ, his forehead flecked with blood, surrounded by grieving followers including Mary Magdalene, who tenderly wipes his feet with her hair as tears roll down her face.

The interior

Inside, the seven-aisled **nave** is breathtaking, if only because of its sense of space, an impression that's reinforced by the bright, light stonework. The religious troubles of the sixteenth century – primarily the Iconoclastic Fury of 1566 (see p.177) – polished off the cathedral's early furnishings and fittings, so what you see today are largely Baroque embellishments, most notably four early paintings by **Pieter Paul Rubens** (1577–1640). Of these, the *Descent from the Cross*, a triptych painted after the artist's return from Italy in 1612 and hung just to the right of the central crossing, is without doubt the most beautiful, displaying an uncharacteristically moving realism derived from Caravaggio. Christ languishes in the centre in glowing white, surrounded by mourners tenderly struggling to lower him. As was normal practice at the time, students in Rubens' studio worked on the painting, among them the young **van Dyck**, who completed the face of the Virgin and the arm of Mary Magdalene. His work was so masterful that Rubens is supposed to have declared it an improvement on his own, though this story appears to originate from van Dyck himself. Oddly enough, the painting was commissioned by the **guild of arquebusiers**, who asked for a picture of St Christopher, their patron saint; Rubens' painting was not at all what they had in mind, and they promptly threatened him with legal action unless he added a picture of the saint to the wings. Rubens obliged, painting in the muscular giant who now dominates the outside of the left panel.

Above the **high altar** is a second Rubens painting, the *Assumption*, a swirling Baroque scene painted in 1625, full of cherubs and luxuriant drapery, while on the left-hand side of the central crossing, the same artist's *The Raising of the Cross* is a grandiloquent canvas full of straining, muscular soldiers and saints; this triptych was painted in 1610, which makes it the earliest of the four. On the right-hand side of the ambulatory in the second **chapel** along, there's the cathedral's fourth and final Rubens, the *Resurrection*, painted in 1612 for the tomb of his friend, the printer Jan Moretus, showing a strident, militaristic Christ carrying a red, furled banner.

Groenplaats

Flanked by some of the busiest cafés in town, **Groenplaats**, the expansive open square behind the cathedral, actually started out as the municipal graveyard, though presumably the bodies were moved before the construction of today's underground car park. In the middle of the square stands a really rather uninspiring **statue** of Rubens, the work of the prolific Willem Geefs (1806–60), one of King Léopold II's favourite sculptors.

Museum Plantin-Moretus

Vrijdagmarkt 22 • Tues–Sun 10am–5.30pm • €8 • ☎ 03 221 14 50, ⓦ museumplantinmoretus.be

The intriguing **Museum Plantin-Moretus** occupies the old mansion of the printer Christopher Plantin, who rose to fame and fortune in the second half of the sixteenth century. Born in Tours in 1520, Plantin moved to Antwerp when he was 34 to set up a small bookbinding business, but in 1555 he was forced to give up all heavy work when, in a case of mistaken identity, he was wounded by revellers returning from carnival. Paid to keep quiet about his injuries, Plantin used the money to start a printing business. He was phenomenally successful, his fortune assured when King Philip II granted him the monopoly of printing missals and breviaries for the whole of the **Spanish Empire**. On Plantin's death, the business passed to his son-in-law, Jan Moerentorf, who Latinized his name, in accordance with the fashion of the day, to Moretus, as did his son, Balthasar, who was a close friend of Rubens. The family sold their mansion to the city in 1876.

The collection

From the **entrance**, a clearly signed route takes visitors through most of the rooms of the house, which is set around a pretty central courtyard. The mansion is worth seeing in itself, its warren of small, dark rooms equipped with mullioned windows and lockable wooden window shutters, plus a brace of handsome libraries and oodles of **leather wallpaper** in the Spanish style (from Room 10 onwards). As for the exhibits, they provide a marvellous insight into how Plantin and his descendants conducted their business with the tools of their trade – printing presses, typesets, woodcuts, copper-plate engravings, etc – and all exhibited beside the books they created. Particular **highlights** include a seventeenth-century bookshop in Room 4, where you'll also spot a list of prohibited books – the Habsburgs' Librorum Prohibitorum; several fine tapestries in Room 6; and, in Room 14B, a copy of the famous 36-line Bible printed by **Johannes Gutenberg** (1398–1468), the inventor of moveable type printing.

From the Vrijdagmarkt to the waterfront

Across Vrijdagmarkt from the museum is **Leeuwenstraat**, a narrow little street flanked by some very old terraced houses. At the end, turn left and then first right for **Pelgrimstraat**, which provides one of the best views of the cathedral, with a sliver of sloping, uneven roofs set against the majestic lines of the spire behind. By no. 6, an ancient alley called **Vlaeykensgang** (Pie Lane) is a surviving fragment of the honeycomb of narrow lanes that made up medieval Antwerp. Today, it twists a quaint route through to **Oude Koornmarkt**, which soon leads west into **Suikerrui**, a wide street connecting the Grote Markt with the east bank of the Scheldt, clearly separated from the town since Napoleon razed the riverside slums and constructed proper wharves in the early 1800s. Jutting out into the river at the end of Suikerrui is an overblown **belvedere**, where the Belgian middle classes once took the air, looking out over the water, before taking the ferry from the jetty next door. The latter is long gone – several roads and a pedestrian tunnel now run under the Scheldt – and there's precious little to gaze at now except the belvedere itself, which can't help but seem a little eccentric. This is also the departure point for summertime **river trips** (see box, p.194).

Vleeshuis Museum

Vleeshouwersstraat 38 • Thurs–Sun 10am–5pm • €5 • ☎ 03 292 61 00

Conspicuous amid the narrow side streets just north of the Grote Markt are the tall, turreted gables of the **Vleeshuis** (Meat Hall), a strikingly attractive building of 1503, whose alternating layers of red brick and cream stone resemble rashers of bacon – appropriately enough, as this was where the Guild of Butchers (see box below) had their headquarters. Inside, the vaulted brick hall that comprises the ground floor now holds the **Klank van de Stad** (Sound of the City), an ambitious if not entirely successful exhibition on **music** and **dance** in the city over the last six hundred years. Software handed out at reception enables visitors to listen to a wide range of historic instruments, but somehow it's all too fiddly and a bit tedious. The museum does hold an excellent range of sixteenth- and seventeenth-century musical instruments, most memorably a platoon of primly decorated **clavichords** and **harpischords**, some of which were produced locally in the Ruckers workshop.

Veemarkt

The streets around the Vleeshuis and the **Veemarkt** were badly damaged by wartime bombing, leaving a string of bare, open spaces edged by some of the city's worst slums. In the last decade or two, however, the area has largely been rebuilt and revamped, the prostitutes who once congregated here moved north to Verversrui (see p.192), near the Willemdok, and the crumbling terraces were replaced by cosy modern houses, whose pinkish brick facades imitate the style of what went before – **urban renewal** at its best.

St-Pauluskerk

Veemarkt • April–Oct daily 2–5pm • Free • ☎ 03 232 32 67

Entered via an extravagant Baroque portal on the Veemarkt, **St-Pauluskerk** is one of the city's most delightful churches, an airy, dignified, late Gothic structure built for the Dominicans in the early sixteenth century. The monks were expelled when the Calvinists looted the church in 1578 but, less than a decade later, after the Spanish

---

THE BUTCHERS' BLUNDER

The **Vleeshuis** was built as the grand headquarters of the **Guild of Butchers**, one of the most powerful of Antwerp's medieval guilds. It was here in 1585, with the Spanish army approaching, that the butchers made a fateful decision: they opposed the opening of the dykes along the River Scheldt as advised by the Protestant commander, **William the Silent**, who realized that the best way to defend the city was by flooding its immediate surroundings. The butchers were, however, more worried about the safety of their sheep, which grazed the threatened meadows, and so they sent a deputation to the city magistrates to object. The magistrates yielded, and the consequences were disastrous – the Spaniards were able to close the Scheldt and eventually force the town to **surrender**, a defeat that placed Antwerp firmly within the Spanish Netherlands. Protestant butchers hightailed it north to the Netherlands.

recaptured the city, they were restored to their property and proceeded to refashion St-Pauluskerk in a Baroque style that was designed to glorify the Catholic Church, thereby grinding salt into the wounds of the defeated Protestants. To hammer home the ecclesiastical point, the Dominicans commissioned a series of **paintings** to line the wall of the **nave's north aisle**. Dating from 1617, this series, which depicts the "Fifteen Mysteries of the Rosary", has survived intact, a remarkable snapshot of Antwerp's artistic talent with works by the likes of Cornelis de Vos (1584–1651) – *Nativity* and *Presentation at the Temple*; David Teniers the Elder (1582–1649) – *Gethsemane*; van Dyck (1599–1641) – *The Bearing of the Cross*; and Jordaens (1593–1678) – *The Crucifixion*. But it is **Rubens'** contribution – the *Scourging at the Pillar* – which stands out, a brilliant, brutal canvas showing Jesus clad in a blood-spattered loincloth. There's more Rubens close by – at the far end of the *Mysteries* series – in the *Adoration of the Shepherds*, an early work of 1609 which has a jaunty secular air, with a smartly dressed Mary imperiously lifting the Christ's bedsheet to the wonder of the shepherds.

Our Lady of the Rosary

Stuck to a pillar next to the nave's north aisle is **Our Lady of the Rosary**, an early sixteenth-century polychromed wood statuette. It's a charming effigy, with the Virgin robed in the Spanish manner – it was the Spaniards who first introduced dressed figurines to Flemish churches – and to either side are two folksy **bas-relief medallions**. They relate a Faustian story of a rich woman who is fooled by the devil, shown here as a sort of lion with an extremely long tail. The first panel sees the woman entrapped by the devil's letter, the second shows the good old Dominicans coming to the rescue and the devil being carted off by an angel.

The rest of the church

The **south transept** exhibits Rubens' *Disputation on the Nature of the Holy Sacrament*, again completed in 1609, but this time forming part of a grand marble altarpiece sprinkled with observant cherubs. The marble was crafted by **Pieter Verbruggen the Elder**, who was also responsible for the extraordinary woodcarving of the **confessionals** and stalls on either side of the nave, flashy work of arabesque intricacy decorated with flowers, fruit, a herd of cherubs and pious saints. Verbruggen must take some responsibility for the huge and ugly **high altar** too: he didn't fashion the black and white marble – that was the work of a certain Frans Sterbeeck – but he erected it.

Calvarieberg

Finally, glued to the exterior buttresses of the south transept, just off the passageway linking the Baroque portal and the church, is the **Calvarieberg**, a curious **mound of rock and slag** decorated with statues of angels, prophets and saints beneath a crucified Christ. It was built in the early eighteenth century at the behest of the Pilgrims of Jerusalem, a society keen to encourage the devout to visit the Holy Land. Writing in the nineteenth century, the traveller Charles Tennant got things about right when he described it as being "a more striking instance of religious fanaticism than good taste".

Rockoxhuis

Keizerstraat 10 • Tues–Sun 10am–5pm • €6 • ☏ 03 201 92 50, ⓦ rockoxhuis.be

The **Rockoxhuis** holds a small but highly prized collection of fine art in what was once the town house of Nicolaas Rockox, friend and patron of Rubens, though not that much remains of the original furnishings and fittings. Other than pieces by **Pieter Bruegel the Younger** and **Rubens**, highlights of the collection include a gentle *Holy Virgin and Child* by **Quinten Matsys** (1465–1530) and *St Christopher Bearing the Christ Child*, a typical work by Matsys' collaborator **Joachim Patenier** (1485–1524). There are also two contrasting paintings by Antwerp's own **Joachim Beuckelaer** (1533–73), a flashy and fleshy genre painting entitled *Woman Vegetable Seller*; and the much more restrained *Flight into Egypt*, revealing a bustling riverbank where – in true Mannerist style – the Holy Family are hard to spot. Finally, while the Koninklijk Museum voor Schone Kunsten (Royal Fine Art Museum; see box, p.192) is undergoing its renovations, the Rockoxhuis has temporarily taken in a batch of paintings, most memorably two tiny and especially delicate works by **Jan van Eyck** (1390–1441), a *Madonna at the Fountain* and a *St Barbara*.

Pieter Bruegel the Younger
Pieter Bruegel the Younger's (1564–1638) *Proverbs* is an intriguingly folksy work, a frenetic mixture of the observed and imagined set in a Flemish village – one of several paintings he did on this subject in direct imitation of his father. The meaning of many of the pictured **proverbs** has been the subject of long debate; unfortunately, the museum doesn't provide a caption, but there's little doubt about the significance of the central image depicting an old man dressed in the blue, hooded cape of the cuckold. Other signifiers are the cakes on the roof representing prosperity; the man banging his head against the wall – stupidity; the pig shearer as a symbol of foolishness; and the monk giving Jesus a false beard – blasphemy.

Rubens
The Rockoxhuis owns two pictures by **Rubens** (1577–1640): the small and romantic *Virgin in Adoration Before the Sleeping Christ Child*, which depicts the Virgin with the features of Rubens' first wife and models Jesus on the artist's son; and *Christ on the Cross*, a fascinating oil sketch made in preparation for an altarpiece he never had time to paint.

St-Carolus Borromeus
Hendrik Conscienceplein • Mon–Sat 10am–12.30pm & 2–5pm • Free • ☎ 03 231 37 51

One of the most agreeable piazzas in central Antwerp, tiny **Hendrik Conscienceplein** takes its name from a local nineteenth-century novelist who wrote prolifically on all things Flemish. Presiding over the square is the church of **St-Carolus Borromeus**, whose finely contrived facade may well have been based on designs by Rubens. Much of the barrel-vaulted interior was destroyed by fire at the beginning of the eighteenth century, but inside, on the right-hand side of the nave, the ornate **Onze Lieve Vrouwekapel** (Chapel of Our Lady) has survived, its ornate giltwork and luxurious mix of marbles a fancy illustration of the High Baroque. Streaky, coloured marble was a key feature of the original design and here it serves as the background for a series of tiny pictures placed to either side of the **high altar**.

ModeNatie
Nationalestraat 28 • ☎ 03 226 14 47, Ⓦ modenatie.com

Spread over several floors, **ModeNatie** is a lavish and extraordinarily ambitious fashion complex, which incorporates both the fashion department of the Royal Academy of Fine Arts and the Flanders Fashion Institute. As such, it reflects the international success of local designers, beginning in the 1980s with the so-called "**Antwerp Six**" – including Dries van Noten, Dirk Bikkembergs, Marina Yee and Martin Margiela – and continuing with younger designers like A.F. Vandevorst, Stephan Schneider and Tim Vansteenbergen; all are graduates of the academy.

MoMu
Tues–Sun 10am–6pm • €8 • ☎ 03 470 27 70, Ⓦ momu.be

Part of the Modenatie building has been converted into a fashion museum, **MoMu** (Mode Museum), whose adventurous, brilliantly presented and thought-provoking

FASHION SHOPPING IN ANTWERP

The international success of Antwerp's **fashion designers** has spawned dozens of excellent designer shops (see p.198). To help visitors get a grip on it all, the tourist board has produced two **mini-brochures**: one called "The Antwerp Selection", the other "The Deluxe Selection". Each carries about fifty potted descriptions of the most innovative **shops** and both have city **maps** marked with their locations, with a particular concentration around the ModeNatie complex. There's also an associated website and **app**: ◍ fashioninantwerp.be.

temporary displays cover a lot of ground – everything from the walking stick as fashion statement through to the evolution of the trench coat and the use of plumes and feathers in fashion from the 1920s to the present day. Each **temporary exhibition** generally lasts for around five months, and many of the exhibits are drawn from MoMu's huge stock of fashion-related items.

Museum Mayer van den Bergh

Lange Gasthuisstraat 19 • Tues–Sun 10am–5pm • €8 • ☎ 03 338 81 88, ◍ museummayervandenbergh.be

The appealing **Museum Mayer van den Bergh** comprises the art collection of Fritz Mayer van den Bergh, a member of a wealthy merchant family who gave his artistic hoard to the city in 1920. Very much a connoisseur's collection, it offers a superb sample of **Netherlandish paintings** as well as examples of many branches of the **applied arts**, from tapestries to ceramics, silver, illuminated manuscripts and furniture, all crowded into the house that the family had built in the style of a sixteenth-century mansion in 1904.

Rooms 2, 3 and 4

Room 2 holds a number of charming children's portraits, including a delightful portrait of a young brother and sister by the Dutchman Cornelis Ketel (1548–1616). Next door, in **Room 3**, is the earliest panel painting ever to be found in Belgium, a thirteenth-century Italian work entitled the *Virgin and Child Enthroned* by Simeone and Machilone of Spoleto. Pride of place in **Room 4** goes to a *Crucifixion* triptych by **Quinten Matsys** (1465–1530), with the unidentified donors painted on the wings. Intriguingly, the female donor is pictured alongside one of the family's patron saints, Mary of Egypt, a repentant prostitute who spent her final years in the desert miraculously sustained by three little loaves.

Room 5 – the Bruegels

Room 5 is almost entirely devoted to the **Bruegels** and it's here you'll find the museum's most celebrated painting, **Pieter the Elder**'s (1525–69) *Dulle Griet* or "Mad Meg", one of his most Bosch-like works. Experts have written volumes on the painting's iconography, but in broad terms there's no disputing it's a misogynistic allegory in which a woman, weighed down with possessions, stalks the gates of hell in a surrealistic landscape of monsters and pervasive horror. The title refers to the archetypal shrewish woman who, according to Flemish proverb, "could plunder in front of hell and remain unscathed". Hanging next to it is the same artist's *Twelve Proverbs*, a more relaxed vision of the world, in which a sequence of **miniatures** illustrates popular Flemish aphorisms, including an old favourite – the man in a blue, hooded cape, the symbol of the cuckold.

Rooms 6 to 10

Room 6 is devoted to an exquisite collection of small-scale **medieval sculptures** and **Room 10** features two tiny panels from a fifteenth-century **polyptych** that once adorned a travelling altar. The twin panels are beautifully decorated with informal

3

scenes – St Christopher, the patron saint of travellers, crosses a stream full of fish, and Joseph cuts up his socks to use as swaddling clothes for the infant Jesus.

The Bourlaschouwburg and Stadsschouwburg

Fringed with pleasant pedestrianized streets and squares, the **Bourlaschouwburg** (Bourla Theatre; see p.198) – now the Toneelhuis – is an elegant nineteenth-century rotunda with a handsomely restored interior. Just beyond, at the end of the Graanmarkt, lurks its modern concrete and steel equivalent, the huge and really rather brutal **Stadsschouwburg** (municipal theatre; see p.198), which is now attached to a large glass and metal roof that shelters **market** traders on Saturdays and Sundays (see p.198).

Maagdenhuis

Lange Gasthuisstraat 33 • Mon & Wed–Fri 10am–5pm, Sat & Sun 1–5pm • €7 • ☎ 03 338 26 20, ⓦ maagdenhuismuseum.be

Formerly a hospital and orphanage for children of the poor, the **Maagdenhuis** (Maidens' House) is now jointly occupied by the city's social security offices and a small **museum**. Created in the middle of the sixteenth century, the orphanage was strictly run, its complex rules enforced by draconian punishments. On the other hand, those children who were left here were fed and taught a skill, and desperate parents felt that they could at least retrieve their children if their circumstances improved. To make sure their offspring could be identified (in an illiterate age) they were given **tokens**, usually irregularly cut playing cards or images of saints – one part was left with the child, the other kept by the parent. If the city fathers didn't actually encourage this practice, they certainly accepted it, and several municipal buildings even had specially carved **alcoves** on their facades where foundlings could be left under shelter, certain to be discovered in the morning.

Inside the **museum**, particular highlights in the chapel to the right of the entrance include a cabinet of foundling tokens, a petite *Adoration of the Shepherds* triptych by Jan van Scorel (1495–1562), and fifty-odd colourful, late medieval porridge bowls – the largest collection of its sort in Belgium. In the five rooms across from the chapel, three **paintings** are worth seeking out: at the end of the corridor is *Orphan Girl at Work* by Cornelis de Vos (1584–1651), a touching composition showing the young woman cheered by the offer of a red carnation, a symbol of fidelity; and in the end room on the right are both **van Dyck**'s (1599–1641) mournful *St Jerome* and **Jordaens**' (1593–1678) profound study of Christ in his *Descent from the Cross*.

East of the centre

Meir, Antwerp's pedestrianized main shopping street, connects the city centre with Centraal Station, some fifteen minutes' walk away to the **east**. Taken as a whole, this part of the city lacks any particular character – being an indeterminate medley of the old and the new – but there's no disputing the principal sight: the **Rubenshuis**, the cleverly restored former home and studio of Rubens. Rubens was buried nearby in **St-Jacobskerk**, a good-looking Gothic church that well deserves a visit, but the architectural highlight hereabouts is the neo-Baroque **Centraal Station**, a sterling edifice dating from 1905. The station presides over Koningin Astridplein, a large and very busy square that adjoins the city's excellent **zoo**.

Rubenshuis

Wapper 9 • Tues–Sun 10am–5pm • €8 • ☎ 03 201 15 55, ⓦ rubenshuis.be

Not so much a house as a mansion, the **Rubenshuis** was where the great man lived for most of his adult life, but it was only acquired by the city in 1937, by which time it was little more than a shell. Skilfully restored, it opened as a **museum** in 1946, and the reconstruction is both delightful and very convincing with the gabled Flemish house where he lived on the left and his classical studio to the right. Rubens had an enviably successful career, spending the first years of the seventeenth century studying the Renaissance masters in Italy, before settling here in 1608. Soon after, he painted two wonderful canvases for the cathedral (see p.182) and his fame spread, both as a painter and diplomat, working for Charles I in England and receiving commissions from all over Europe.

The interior

A clearly arrowed **tour** begins by twisting its way through the neatly panelled and attractively furnished domestic interiors of the **Flemish house** where Rubens lived. Beyond, at the back – and in contrast to the cramped living quarters – is the elegant **art gallery**, an Italianate chamber where Rubens displayed his favourite pieces to a chosen few in a scene comparable to that portrayed in Willem van Haecht's *The Gallery of Cornelis van der Geest*, which is displayed here. The arrows then direct you on into the **great studio**, which is overlooked by a narrow gallery and equipped with a special high door to allow the largest canvases to be brought in and out with ease. Several of Rubens' **paintings** are displayed here, including a playful *Adam and Eve*, an early work in which the couple flirt while the serpent slithers back up the tree, and a more characteristic piece, the *Annunciation*, where you can sense the drama of the angel Gabriel's appearance to Mary, who is shown in her living room complete with wicker basket and a sleeping cat. There's also a remarkable, visionary *Crucifixion* in which Rubens dispensed with the customary supporting cast – there are no crucified thieves or figures at the foot of the Cross – to concentrate on the dying Christ, his broken body set against a dark, louring sky.

St-Jacobskerk

Lange Nieuwstraat • April–Oct daily 2–5pm • €2 • ☎ 03 232 10 32

Rubens died in 1640 and was buried in **St-Jacobskerk**, a short walk from the Rubenshuis. Very much the church of the Antwerp nobility, who were interred in its multiple vaults and chapels, this is a mighty Gothic structure whose construction ground on from 1491 to 1659. This delay means that much of its Gothic splendour is hidden by an over-decorous **Baroque interior**, the soaring heights of the nave flattened by heavy marble altars and a huge marble rood screen.

The Rubens chapel

Nine chapels radiate out from the ambulatory, including the **Rubens chapel** directly behind the high altar, where the artist and his immediate family are buried beneath the tombstones in the floor, with a lengthy Latin inscription giving details of Rubens' life and honours. The chapel's **altar** was the gift of Helena Fourment, Rubens' second wife, and shows one of his last works, *Our Lady and the Christ Child Surrounded by Saints* (1634), in which he painted himself as St George, his wives as Martha and Mary, and his father as St Jerome. It's as if he painted this knowing it would be his epitaph: Rubens is said to have asked for his burial chamber to be adorned with nothing more than a painting of the Virgin Mary with Jesus in her arms, encircled by various saints – and that is pretty much what he got.

Two more chapels

The **chapel** next to, and north of, the tomb of Rubens is also worth a peek for its clumsily titled *St Charles Borromeo Pleading with the Virgin on Behalf of those Stricken by the Plague*, completed by Jacob Jordaens in 1655. A dark, gaudy canvas, it's not without its ironies: Borromeo, the Archbishop of Milan, was an ardent leader of the Counter-Reformation, while the artist was a committed Protestant. Look out also for the

> ## BUYING DIAMONDS IN ANTWERP
>
> Scared of being cheated or conned, tourists are often reluctant to **buy diamonds** in Antwerp, and to combat this reticence several bodies – both private and public – have combined to launch a quality-control label called **Antwerp's Most Brilliant** (🌐 antwerpsmostbrilliant.be). To be accepted onto the label, diamond sellers must pass a rigorous inspection scheme.

flamboyant *St George and the Dragon* in the chapel at the far end of the **south aisle**: the baroness who gave the church the picture in the nineteenth century said it was a van Dyck – but it isn't.

Centraal Station

Heading east from the Rubenshuis, De Keyserlei offers a fine view of **Centraal Station**, a magnificent neo-Baroque structure whose medley of spires and balconies, glass domes and classical pillars was completed in 1905 to a design by **Louis Delacenserie**, who had made his reputation as a restorer of Gothic buildings in Bruges. By any standard, the station is an extraordinary edifice, a well-considered blend of earlier architectural styles and fashions – particularly the Gothic lines of the main body of the building and the **ticket hall**, which has all the darkened mystery of a medieval church – yet displays all the self-confidence of the new age of industrial progress. The station also proved to be large enough to adapt to modern use with the Belgians digging away until they created the extra **subterranean platforms** that exist today.

The diamond district

The anonymous streets just to the southwest of Centraal Station, along and around **Lange Kievitstraat** and pedestrianized **Schupstraat/Hoveniersstraat**, are home to the largest **diamond market** in the world. Behind these indifferent facades precious stones pour in from every continent to be cut or re-cut, polished and sold. There's precious little indication that all this is going on – no show of wealth, no grand bazaar and no tax collector could ever keep track of the myriad deals which make the business hum – the only exception being the string of **diamond shops** that fill up the outer precincts of Centraal Station beside **Pelikaanstraat**. Playing a leading role in Antwerp's diamond trade are **Orthodox Jews**, whose ancestors arrived here from Eastern Europe towards the end of the nineteenth century, and whose presence is often the only outward indication that the business exists at all. They act as middlemen in a chain that starts in the producer countries, especially South Africa, with no less than **eighty-five percent** of the world's rough diamonds, and half the total supply of cut diamonds, traded here in Antwerp.

Antwerp ZOO

Koningin Astridplein • Daily: Jan & Feb, Nov & Dec 10am–4.45pm; March–April & Oct 10am–5.30pm; May–June & Sept 10am–6pm; July & Aug 10am–7pm • €22.50, children 3 to 17 years €17.50 • ☎ 03 224 89 10, 🌐 zooantwerpen.be

Metres from Centraal Station, **Antwerp ZOO** is one of the oldest zoos in the world, dating back to 1843. In recent decades, it has done its best to keep ahead of the animal-welfare curve, enlarging and improving its assorted **compounds**. There are around thirty separate areas today, including a bird building, a "nocturama" for nocturnal animals, a reptile house, an aquarium and areas for hippos, lions and penguins.

South of the centre: Het Zuid

Fanning out from Léopold de Waelplaats, the wide avenues and symmetrical squares of **Het Zuid** (The South), a couple of kilometres south of the centre, and reachable by tram

CLOCKWISE FROM TOP LEFT CAFÉ PELIKAAN (P.196); MOMU (P.186); ZIMMERTOREN (P.201); POPOFF (P.195) >

> ## THE KONINKLIJK MUSEUM VOOR SCHONE KUNSTEN
>
> Occupying an immense Neoclassical edifice dating from the 1880s, Antwerp's prestigious **Koninklijk Museum voor Schone Kunsten** (KMSKA; Royal Fine Art Museum; Ⓦ kmska.be), on Léopold de Waelplaats, possesses a first-rate collection of Belgian art from the fifteenth century onwards, but it's closed for a long-term refurbishment until at least **2017**. In the meantime, **key paintings** have been put on display in other locations, principally at the cathedral (see p.182) and the Rockoxhuis (see p.185).

from Groenplaats, were laid out at the end of the nineteenth century on the site of the old **Spanish citadel**, of which nothing now remains. The district hit the skids in the 1960s, with many of its grand French-style mansions left to decay, but it's bounced back to become one of Antwerp's most **fashionable** residential quarters. Setting aside the district's cafés and bars, the obvious targets here are **M HKA**, the enterprising Museum of Contemporary Art; **FoMu**, which is well known for its photography exhibitions; and the **Koninklijk Museum voor Schone Kunsten**, home to an extensive collection of Belgian art, but closed until at least 2017.

M HKA
Leuvenstraat 32 • Tues–Sun 11am–6pm, Thurs till 9pm • €8 • ☎ 03 260 99 99, Ⓦ muhka.be

Het Zuid once had its own **dock**, in between Vlaamse Kaai and Waalsekaai, but this was filled in years ago, becoming the wide and open square of today. There are two museums on the west side of the square, the more northerly being **M HKA** (Museum of Contemporary Art), which occupies a cumbersome functionalist building that backs up towards the River Scheldt. M HKA specializes in large-scale, **avant-garde exhibitions** – a delight for some, obscurantism gone mad for others.

FoMu
Waalsekaai 47 • Tues–Sun 10am–6pm • €8 • ☎ 03 242 93 00, Ⓦ fotomuseum.be

Housed in a big old warehouse down near the River Scheldt, FoMu owns a huge collection of **photographic images** relating to the evolution of Antwerp in particular and Belgium in general. A regularly rotated selection of these images is on display here, but the museum is better known for its temporary photographic exhibitions from international figures such as William Klein and Anton Corbijn.

North of the centre: Het Eilandje

Antwerp has always been reliant on its sea trade and the assorted docks and wharves of **Het Eilandje** (The Little Isle), just to the north of the city centre, abutting the River Scheldt, were the city's economic hub for many decades. Work on these maritime facilities began in the sixteenth century, but the economic collapse following the **Spanish Fury** (see p.331) stopped the digging in its tracks, and it was only much later, in the 1860s, that work resumed in earnest. Thereafter, the docks of this district were crowded with vessels from every corner of the globe, and its quays lined with warehouses, sheds, offices and factories. But the boom times were short-lived. The docks were unable to accommodate the **larger vessels** that were built after World War II and Het Eilandje went into free fall in the late 1950s, becoming a neglected, decaying corner of the city – until forty years later when, in the manner of dockside developments right across western Europe, plans were laid to rejuvenate the whole district. It's very much a work in progress, but a stroll round the area is a pleasant way to while away a couple of hours, with the obvious target being **MAS (Museum aan de Stroom)**, though you can also explore much more of the docks on a boat trip (see p.193). Less palatably, the district is also home to **Verversrui**, the pedestrianized centre of Antwerp's **red-light district**, which is seedy and dispiriting in equal measure.

Bonapartedok and Willemdok

Approaching from the south, via **Falconplein**, where seamen once hung out in numbers, you soon reach the **Bonapartedok** and the **Willemdok**, the first of a chain of docks that extends north for many kilometres. Dating from the nineteenth century, these two docks were the first to be protected from the tides of the River Scheldt by means of locks. Both are now **marinas** – albeit in a low-key sort of way – and the warehouses that overlook them have been turned into apartments. Apart from the Museum aan de Stroom, plonked on the jetty between the docks, the one notable old building is the sooty **Loodswezen**, a grand neo-Gothic edifice of 1885 that once housed the city's river pilots and tugboat crews.

MAS (Museum aan de Stroom)

Hanzestedenplaats • April–Oct Tues–Fri 10am–5pm, Sat & Sun 10am–6pm; Nov–March Tues–Fri 10am–5pm, Sat & Sun 10am–5pm • €5, but extra for temporary exhibitions • ☎ 03 338 44 00, ⓦ mas.be

The striking, distinctly Cubist building that rises high above the Willemdok and the Bonapartedok is a flashy home for the **MAS (Museum aan de Stroom)**, whose several floors tackle historical themes – from "Life and Death" to "Displays of Power". Some artefacts relate back to Antwerp, others do not, but there are also sections more relevant to Antwerp, specifically its sea-trade and its seafaring traditions. It's an ambitious museum – and certainly the exhibits are well presented – but how well the mixture works is a matter of debate, though at least the **views** over the city from the top of the building are smashing.

ARRIVAL AND DEPARTURE ANTWERP

BY TRAIN

Antwerp has two main train stations, Berchem and Antwerpen Centraal. A few domestic and international trains pauśe at Berchem, 4km southeast of downtown, before bypassing Centraal, but the majority call at both. Centraal Station, which lies about 2km east of the city centre, is much more convenient for most of the major sights and the Grote Markt, the main square. If you do have to change, connections between the two stations are frequent and fast (10 hourly; 5min). For train timetables, consult ⓦ www.belgianrail.be.

Getting to the centre from Centraal Station Trams from Centraal Station to the city centre depart from the adjacent underground tram station (#9 or #15, direction Linkeroever). Get off at Groenplaats.

Destinations from Antwerp Centraal Station Amsterdam (every 30min; 2hr); Bruges (hourly; 1hr 30min); Brussels (every 20min; 45min); Ghent (every 30min; 1hr); Hasselt (hourly; 1hr 10min); Lier (every 15min; 15min); Leuven (hourly; 50min); Mechelen (every 15min; 25min); Tongeren (hourly; 1hr 30min).

BY BUS

Most long-distance buses arrive at the bus station on Franklin Rooseveltplaats, a 5min walk from Centraal Station; Eurolines international buses pull in at the edge of the bus station on Van Stralenstraat. The bus station's information kiosk deals with domestic bus services.

BY PLANE

Antwerp's tiny airport (ⓦ antwerp-airport.be) is located about 6km southeast of the city centre in the suburb of Deurne. There are regular buses from the airport into the city centre.

GETTING AROUND

By bus and tram Operated by De Lijn (☎ 070 220 200, ⓦ delijn.be), a first-rate tram and bus system serves the city and its suburbs from two main hubs, Groenplaats and Centraal Station. A standard single fare within the city centre costs €1.30 in advance (€2 from the driver); a 24-hour unlimited day pass, called a *dagpas*, costs €5 (€7 from the driver), or €10 (€12) for three days. Advance tickets are sold all over the place, but most conveniently at every underground tram station, where there are multilingual ticket machines.

By bike The city operates a bike rental scheme, Velo Antwerpen (ⓦ www.velo-antwerpen.be), with racks liberally distributed across the centre. There's a registration fee (€3.60/day, €8/week) and then an hourly charge (€0.50 for the first hour, €1 for up to 90min, €5 per hour thereafter). After registration, you receive a user code and select a self-chosen pass code. Payment can be made by credit card, and bikes returned to any rack.

By car Among many car rental companies, Europcar has a branch in the bowels of Centraal Station at Pelikaanstraat 3 (☎ 03 226 74 44), while Sixt are at the airport (☎ 070 22 58 00).

By taxi There is a taxi rank outside Centraal Station. Antwerp Taxi is on ☎ 03 238 38 38.

BOAT TRIPS IN ANTWERP

From the west end of Suikerrui, **Flandria** (☎03 231 31 00, ✆flandria.nu) operates **River Scheldt cruises** that last a little under an hour (July & Aug 3 daily Tues–Sun; Sept Sat & Sun 3 daily; €8). The same company also runs **tours of the port**, both a short version (1hr 30min; May–Sept 1 Tues–Sun; €11) and a longer edition (2hr 30min; same frequency; €15). These depart from beside the Londenbrug bridge, on Lodenstraat, about 250m north of the Willemdok (see p.193) in the Het Eilandje district. Advance reservations – at least a couple of hours ahead of time – are advised.

INFORMATION

Tourist information The main tourist office is bang in the city centre at Grote Markt 13 (Mon–Sat 9am–5.45pm, Sun 9am–4.45pm; ☎03 232 01 03, ✆visitantwerpen.be). Info Cultuur (see p.198), which sells tickets for concerts and events, is next door but one at Wisselstraat 12. There's a second tourist information inside Centraal Station (same details).

ACCOMMODATION

Antwerp has the range of **hotels** you'd expect of Belgium's second city, a healthy supply of **B&Bs** and several **hostels**. Consequently, finding accommodation is rarely difficult, although there are surprisingly few places in the centre, which is by far the best spot to soak up the city's atmosphere. Tourist information issues a free and comprehensive **booklet** that details the options (excluding the seedier establishments), and you can also make bookings on their website (✆visitantwerpen.be).

HOTELS

Elzenveld Lange Gasthuisstraat 45 ☎03 202 77 11, ✆elzenveld.be; map pp.178–179. More of a conference centre than a hotel, the *Elzenveld* occupies a sympathetically modernized former monastery and its gardens. There are 34 spick-and-span modern rooms, but the main pleasure is the quiet, almost secluded setting rather than the decor. Breakfast included. **€110**

Hilton Antwerp Groenplaats 32 ☎03 204 12 12, ✆antwerp.hilton.com; map p.181. Good points: central location, the handsome, nineteenth-century facade, the fitness centre and the rooftop terrace. Bad points: decoratively predictable modern rooms, and part of an international chain. **€150**

Ibis Antwerpen Centrum Meistraat 39 ☎03 231 88 30, ✆ibishotel.com; map pp.178–179. An *Ibis* is an *Ibis* – or so you might think. But this one has especially friendly staff, an excellent buffet breakfast and a handy location, close to the Rubenshuis. The building's concrete exterior is ghastly, however. **€60**

Julien Korte Nieuwstraat 24 ☎03 229 06 00, ✆hotel-julien.com; map p.181. Deluxe boutique hotel with just 22 rooms and lots of stylish flourishes, from rainshowers and flat-screen TVs to oodles of greys, creams and browns. Handy central location too. **€180**

Matelote Haarstraat 11A ☎03 201 88 00, ✆hotel-matelote.be; map p.181. Decorated in crisp, modernist style, this small and really rather handsome hotel occupies intelligently revamped and remodelled old premises on a narrow street a (long) stone's throw from the Grote Markt. The rooms are large and well appointed. **€100**

Park Inn Koningin Astridplain 14 ☎03 202 31 70, ✆parkinn.com/hotel-antwerpen; map pp.178–179. In a conspicuous tower block facing Centraal Station, this bright and breezy chain hotel has 59 well-appointed modern rooms at very competitive rates. **€80**

★ **Rubens Grote Markt** Oude Beurs 29 ☎03 222 48 48, ✆hotelrubensantwerp.be; map p.181. Arguably the most agreeable hotel in town, this four-star establishment has just 36 large guest rooms in a real mix of styles, though the default button is set to modern. It occupies a smashing downtown location, on a quiet side street a couple of minutes' walk from the Grote Markt, and has a dinky little courtyard overseen by a very old brick tower, evidence that the building started out as a medieval mansion. **€140**

★ **'t Sandt** Zand 13 ☎03 232 93 90, ✆hotel-sandt .be; map p.181. In a tastefully converted, centrally located, seventeenth-century mansion, this four-star hotel has 29 stylish rooms and suites decorated in an appealing mixture of modern-meets-country-house style. Tasty breakfasts plus a pleasant garden patio out the back. **€140**

De Witte Lelie Keizerstraat 16 ☎03 226 19 66, ✆dewittelelie.be; map p.181. Immaculate four-star – the city's ritziest – with just ten charming rooms in a handsomely renovated seventeenth-century merchant's house, a 5min walk from the Grote Markt. With prices like these, you'd expect each room to be different – and they are, from duplexes with wood-beam ceilings through to the country-house-style "Room Fourteen". **€250**

B&BS

Atelier20 St-Paulusstraat 20 ☎0479 74 14 55, ⓦatelier20.be; map p.181. In an immaculately maintained and creatively furnished old house that was once within the walls of St-Paulus monastery, this appealing B&B offers just two guest suites, both en suite and one each on the second and third floors. **€142**

Enich Anders Leeuwenstraat 12 ☎0476 99 86 01, ⓦenich-anders.be; map p.181. Six compact and simply furnished studios with bathroom and kitchenette sharing premises with a sculptor's workshop on a narrow street just off the Vrijdagmark; the breakfast part of the arrangement (an extra €5 each) comes to your room in a basket. **€75**

★**M0851** Nationalestraat 19 ☎0496 21 32 64, ⓦm0851.be; map pp.178–179. Two, modern, self-contained guest rooms above the M0851 shop, each kitted out in slick modernist style – painted floorboards and lots of blacks and whites. Both have internet access and kitchenettes; breakfast is by coupon at a nearby café. **€75**

Le Patio Pelgrimstraat 8 ☎03 232 76 61, ⓦlepatio.be; map p.181. In a handy location on a side street near the cathedral, this agreeable B&B has three cosy modern rooms squeezed into an old terrace house. Has a pleasant little patio area too. **€105**

HOSTELS AND CAMPSITE

Alias Youthhostel Provinciestraat 256 ☎03 230 05 22, ⓦaliasyouthhostel.com; map pp.178–179. Basic, medium-sized hostel offering bargain-basement singles, doubles and dorm beds, some en suite. Breakfast is included. No cards. A 10min walk south of Centraal Station. Dorm **€21**, double **€50**

Camping de Molen Jachthavenweg 6 ☎03 219 81 79, ⓦcamping-de-molen.be; map pp.178–179. This straightforward camping and caravan site occupies what amounts to a field on the left-hand side of the River Scheldt – it's roughly opposite the Bonapartedok, and a short stroll from the slab of shingly sand that passes for the city beach. To get there from the centre on foot or by bike, use the Voetgangerstunnel under the Scheldt from St-Jansvliet. Advance reservations recommended; open mid-March to mid-Oct. Tent pitch **€16**, 4-berth cabin **€50**

Jeugdherberg Pulcinella Bogaardeplein 1 ☎03 234 03 14, ⓦjeugdherbergen.be; map pp.178–179. New and well-equipped HI-affiliated hostel in a bright modern block just to the south of the city centre. Has 160 beds in two- four- and six-bed en-suite rooms. There's a bar and restaurant serving lunch and dinner, free wi-fi and a bicycle shed. Breakfast included in the rate. Dorm **€24**, double **€62**

EATING

Antwerp's busy, bustling centre is liberally sprinkled with cafés, café-bars and restaurants and standards are generally high. The default option is **Flemish cuisine** but, as you would expect of a big city, there are lots of alternatives, with Italian and French restaurants, leading the way. There's an appealing **informality** about eating in Antwerp too, with smart (read stuffy) places thin on the ground.

CAFÉS AND CAFÉ-BARS

Het Dagelijks Brood Steenhouwersvest 48 ☎03 226 76 13, ⓦlepainquotidien.be; map p.181. Though part of a chain, this distinctive café has relaxing, vaguely New Age decor. The variety of breads is the main event, served with wholesome soups and light meals at one long wooden table. Mon–Sat 7am–7pm.

★**De Groote Witte Arend** Reyndersstraat 18 ☎03 233 50 33, ⓦdegrootewittearend.be; map p.181. Eminently appealing café-bar occupying one wing and the courtyard of an old mansion. Great range of beers – including authentic *gueuze* and *kriek* – plus superb salads and delicious Flemish dishes, such as *stoemp* (mashed potato with veg) and *stoofvlees* (beef cooked in beer). The classical music soundtrack fits the bill perfectly. Mains average €15. Daily 11.30am–11.30pm.

Hoffy's Lange Kievitstraat 52 ☎03 234 35 35, ⓦhoffys .be; map pp.178–179. Reliable, simply decorated traditional Jewish/Yiddish kosher restaurant and takeaway near Centraal Station. Very reasonable prices. Try the *gefillte fisch*. Mon–Thurs & Sun 10am–10pm, Fri 10am–3.30pm.

Maison Tartine Minderbroedersrui 60 ☎0483 49 04 10; map p.181. Friendly little café where they offer tasty breakfasts, lunches and snacks from neat and modern premises. Lots of the goodies are home-made, from cakes and cookies through to lemonade. Tues–Fri 8am–5pm, Sat 9am–6pm, Sun 9am–4pm.

★**Popoff** Oude Koornmarkt 18 ☎03 232 00 38, ⓦpopoff.be; map p.181. You can pretend to come here for the salads and the quiches (which are very nice), but let's be honest – it's really the mouthwatering, earth-shattering desserts, tarts and gateaux that are the main draw at this modern little café with its pavement terrace. Wed–Sun noon–10pm.

RESTAURANTS

★**Bourla** Graanmarkt 7 ☎031 232 1632, ⓦbourla .be; map pp.178–179. A mixed bag of a place with an extensive outside terrace and an antique interior – think leather banquettes, big old mirrors, chandeliers and lots of Art Nouveau flourishes. The menu concentrates on Flemish dishes, with the beef stew nigh-on perfect, and when the kitchen closes it morphs into a bar. Main courses average €18. Mon–Sat 11am–11.30pm; kitchen Mon–Fri noon–2.30pm & 6–10pm, Sat noon–10pm.

Fiskebar Marnixplaats 11, Het Zuid ☎ 03 257 13 57, ⓦ fiskebar.be; map pp.178–179. This fashionable place, with its tiled interior and simple furnishings, has dispensed with unnecessary fripperies to concentrate on the seafood – and it's generally reckoned to be one of the best fish restaurants in Antwerp. Try, for example, the lobster with lemon-basil butter, tomatoes and lobster ravioli. A full (set) meal will rush you around €78, but there's à la carte too. Reservations advised. Mon 6–9.30pm, Tues–Fri noon–2pm & 6–9.30pm, Sat noon–10pm, Sun noon–9pm.

Graanmarkt 13 Graanmarkt 13 ☎ 03 337 79 91, ⓦ graanmarkt13.be; map p.181. Sleek modern restaurant occupying spilt-level premises on a pleasant square. Prides itself on its use of locally sourced ingredients and the creativity of its menu – from quail to monkfish. A set meal, three courses, costs €39 at night, €29 at lunch times. Tues–Sat noon–2.30pm & 6.30–10pm.

Hungry Henrietta Lombardenvest 19 ☎ 03 232 29 28, ⓦ hungryhenrietta.be; map p.181. Something of a city institution, this family-owned restaurant is decorated to a modern spec and touches base with all the Flemish classics. Locals swear by the steaks. Mains average €24, but daily specials cost half that. Mon–Fri noon–2pm & 6–9pm.

Invincible Haarstraat 9 ☎ 03 231 32 07, ⓦ invincible .be; map pp.178–179. Flashy little restaurant near the Grote Markt, where you're best off perched on a bar stool in full view of the chef. The menu is short but extremely well considered, giving due prominence to seasonal ingredients – for example, spring chicken in tarragon. Three-course set menu for €35. Reservations advised. Mon–Fri noon–2pm & 6.30–10pm.

★ **De Kleine Zavel** Stoofstraat 2 ☎ 03 231 96 91, ⓦ kleinezavel.be; map p.181. Bistro-style restaurant with wooden floors, old-style furniture and Franco-Belgian cuisine at its tastiest – the *jus* are simply wonderful and there's a particularly strong line in seafood. It's set on a narrow side street in between the Grote Markt and the river. Mains from €25. Reservations recommended. Wed–Fri & Sun noon–2pm & 6–10pm, Sat 6–10pm.

Pazzo Oude Leeuwenrui 12, Het Eilandje ☎ 03 232 86 82, ⓦ pazzo.be; map pp.178–179. Well-regarded restaurant attracting a wealthy clientele and featuring inventive cooking – roast fillet of lamb with goat's cheese, peppers, aubergine and olive crumble gives the idea. A great selection of wines and a jazz soundtrack are further pros. Mains average €25. The only fly in the ointment is the setting – it's on a main road in a fairly careworn part of Het Eilandje. Has a separate wine bar on the first floor. Mon–Fri noon–3pm & 6–11pm.

De Peerdestal Wijngaardstraat 8 ☎ 03 231 95 03, ⓦ depeerdestal.be; map p.181. A few metres from Hendrik Conscienceplein, this popular, long-established restaurant, with its slightly rusticated decor, is *the* place to try a traditional Belgian speciality – horsemeat (*paardenvlees*). Mains start at €25. Daily 11am–3pm & 5–10pm.

Pizzeria Da Antonio Grote Markt 6 ☎ 03 232 17 07; map p.181. Central Antwerp heaves with Italian restaurants and this is one of the better ones, serving tasty pasta and pizza from as little as €10. Very popular. Daily noon–10pm.

De Reddende Engel Torfburg 3 ☎ 03 233 66 30, ⓦ www .de-reddende-engel.be; map p.181. In the shadow of the cathedral, this long-established restaurant attracts an older clientele, drawn here by the antique decor and tasty Flemish cuisine. Particularly strong on seafood – hence the lobster tank. For a three-course meal, reckon on €30. Mon, Thurs, Fri & Sun noon–2pm & 6–10pm, Sat 6–10pm.

★ **Velazquez** Steenhouwersvest 29 ☎ 03 234 97 00, ⓦ velazquez.be; map p.181. Decoratively neat and trim, this outstanding restaurant offers a short but select menu with Flemish cuisine at its heart. Try, for example, the wolf fish with baby octopus, samphire and new potatoes. It's on a narrow side street footsteps from the Vrijdagmarkt and there's a shaded pavement terrace too. The restaurant is named after its decorative centrepiece, a strange modern painting done in the manner of Velazquez. Mains average €28. Wed–Sun noon–2.30pm & 6–9.30pm.

DRINKING AND NIGHTLIFE

Antwerp is a great place to **drink**. There are lots of bars in the city centre, mostly dark and tiny affairs exuding a cheerful vitality, a few featuring live music. The favourite local tipple is De Koninck, a light ale drunk in a *bolleke*, or small, stemmed glass. The **club scene** is in rude health, with a handful of boisterous places dotted round the peripheries of the city centre, both gay and straight. They get going around midnight and admission fees are typically modest except for when big-name DJs are in. There's a competent **jazz** scene too.

BARS

Café Pelikaan Melkmarkt 14; map p.181. There's nothing smart and touristy about the *Pelikaan*, a packed and somewhat battered-looking bar metres from the cathedral where (an occasionally confused and raucous set of) locals get down to some serious drinking. Daily from 9am till late.

Dogma Cocktails Wijngaardstraat 5 ☎ 0496 95 33 77,

ⓦ dogmacocktails.be; map p.181. If you're tired of swimming in a sea of Belgian beer, then drop by this lively cocktail bar, which occupies pleasantly refurbished premises near Hendrik Conscienceplein. Wed–Sun 5pm–2am.

De Duifkens Graanmarkt 5 ☎ 03 225 10 39; map pp.178–179. This old-style Antwerp café-bar with its wood-panelled interior has long been a favourite haunt of the city's actors, who hunker down here after appearing at one of the nearby theatres. The range of beers is a little limited (by Belgian standards), but it's a convivial spot, and when the weather is good customers spill out onto the lovely terrace. Daily from noon till late.

★**Den Engel** Grote Markt 3 ☎03 233 12 52, ⓦcafedenengel.be; map p.181. Traditional bar with an easy-going, occasionally anarchic atmosphere. Occupies the ground floor of a guildhouse on the northwest corner of the main square and attracts a bubbly mix of business-people and locals from the residential enclave round the Vleeshuis. Late-night dancing (of no particular merit) too. Daily from 10am till late.

De Faam Grote Pieter Potstraat 12 ☎03 234 05 78, ⓦdefaam.be; map p.181. Cool bar in small, sparingly lit premises near the Grote Markt. An eclectic soundtrack – from *chanson* to jazz. Attracts a thirty-something crowd. Daily from 4pm till late.

Den Hopsack Grote Pieter Potstraat 24 ☎03 233 44 40, ⓦdenhopsack.be; map p.181. Postmodern bar – all wood and spartan fittings – with highbrow conversation and an amenable, low-key atmosphere. All sorts of special events too – from live music through to poetry readings. Daily except Tues from 8pm.

Kathedraalcafé Torfbrug 10 ☎03 289 34 66; map p.181. Hard by the cathedral, this old bar has become something of a tourist trap, but it's still worth visiting for the kitsch, nineteenth-century religious statues that cram the interior. Don't bother with the food, though. Daily from 10am till late.

Kulminator Vleminckveld 32 ☎03 232 45 38; map pp.178–179. No one could accuse the *Kulminator* of bending the knee to gentrification – but this dark, cave-like place literally heaves with beers, packed in here, there and just about everywhere and totalling several hundred different brews. Fortunately, there's a helpful beer menu to steer you on your alcoholic path. Mon 8pm–midnight, Tues–Sat 4pm–midnight.

Østersbar Marnixplaats 11, Het Zuid ☎03 257 13 57, ⓦfiskebar.be; map pp.178–179. Sharing the same premises as the Fiskebar restaurant (see p.196), the big deal at this oyster bar is the tasty mollusc – washed down, as custom seems to dictate, with champagne of some sort or another. Wed–Sun 6–10pm.

De Vagant Reyndersstraat 25 ☎03 233 15 38, ⓦdevagant.be; map p.181. Something of a rarity, this small and homely bar specializes in Belgian and Dutch jenever, served ice cold and a popular drink with Flemish workers from time immemorial. A baffling range to choose from – ask and all will be revealed. Small pavement terrace too. Mon–Sat from 11am till late, Sun from noon.

CLUBS AND LIVE MUSIC

Café d'Anvers Verversrui 15, Het Eilandje ☎03 226 38 70, ⓦwww.cafe-d-anvers.com; map pp.178–179. Youthful, fashionable, energetic club, billed as a "temple to house music", but perhaps a little too well established to be cutting edge. North of the centre in the red-light district. Thurs–Sat from 11pm, plus additional nights as per website.

Jazzcafe de Muze Melkmarkt 15 ☎03 226 01 26, ⓦjazzmuze.be; map p.181. With its bare-brick walls and retro film posters, this funky, popular café-bar is the best jazz joint in town, with live bands most nights (usually at 10pm). Daily from 1pm.

Petrol d'Herbouvillekaai 25 at General Armstrongweg, Het Zuid ☎03 226 49 63, ⓦpetrolclub.be; map pp.178–179. One of the hottest clubs in town for both DJs and live concerts. Way south out of the city centre, housed in a former waste disposal centre in an old industrial area beside the River Scheldt – take a taxi. Admission €15; advance tickets available from Fnac bookshop (see p.198). Always open Fri and Sat night; check website for weekday programme.

GAY BARS AND CLUBS

Café Den Draak Draakplaats 1 ☎03 290 53 04, ⓦdendraak.be; map pp.178–179. If there is a centre to Antwerp's gay and lesbian scene it's this busy café-bar, which is part of a larger gay and lesbian project, Het Roze Huis (☎03 288 00 84, ⓦhetrozehuis.be). Draakplaats is a 15min walk south from Centraal Station: take Pelikaanstraat and its continuation Simonsstraat/Mercatorstraat, turn left down Grote Hondstraat, and it's at the end of the street. Daily noon till late.

Red & Blue Lange Schipperskapelstraat 13, Het Eilandje ☎03 213 05 55, ⓦredandblue.be; map pp.178–179. Other nights have other incarnations, but Saturday here is gay night (men only), with house and techno, and a throbbing dancefloor. Busy from around 1am. €12 entry. Sat 11pm–6/7am.

ENTERTAINMENT

Antwerp has a vibrant **cultural scene** with regular performances by Flemish ballet, theatre and opera companies as well as by the internationally acclaimed **Royal Flemish Philharmonic Orchestra** (ⓦdefilharmonie.be), who are using several venues – including deSingel (see p.198) – while their usual home, the Koningin Elisabethzaal, on Koningin Astridplein, is being redeveloped. The city also possesses a first-rate **art-house cinema**, where – as per usual in Flemish Belgium – English-language films are subtitled (as opposed to dubbed). For **upcoming events**, ask at tourist information or check their website (ⓦvisitantwerpen.be)

3

Tickets Tickets for concerts and events are on sale either direct from the venue concerned or from Info Cultuur (Tues–Sat 11am–5.45pm; ☎03 338 95 85, ⊛infocultuur.be), just off the Grote Markt at Wisselstraat 12. A comparable service is provided at the Fnac store (see below), on the Groenplaats.

THEATRES AND CONCERT HALLS

deSingel Desguinlei 25 ☎03 248 28 28, ⊛desingel.be. Major arts centre and performance venue on the southern edge of the city. Occasional home to the Royal Flemish Philharmonic Orchestra.

Stadsschouwburg Theaterplein 1 ☎03 202 83 60, ⊛stadsschouwburgantwerpen.be. A big bruiser of a modern building not far from the Rubenshuis that mostly hosts musical concerts, musicals and theatrical performances.

Toneelhuis Komedieplaats 18 ☎03 224 88 44, ⊛toneelhuis.be. This handsomely restored nineteenth-

century theatre – the Bourlaschouwburg – is the city's premier venue for theatre as performed by the Toneelhuis repertory company.

De Vlaamse Opera Frankrijklei 1 ☎070 22 02 02, ⊛vlaamseopera.be. The excellent Vlaamse Opera (Flemish Opera) mostly performs here at this grand, early twentieth-century building on the ring road, about halfway between the Grote Markt and Centraal Station. The Koninklijk Ballet Vlaanderen (Royal Ballet of Flanders; ⊛koninklijkballetvanvlaanderen.be) mostly performs here too.

CINEMA

Cartoon's Kaasstraat 4, off Suikerrui ☎03 232 96 32, ⊛cinemacartoons.be. The most distinctive downtown cinema, showing both mainstream and art-house films in several auditoria.

SHOPPING

Antwerp loves its **open-air markets**. There are lots to choose from, but three of the best are the **antique and jumble** market near the cathedral on Lijnwaadmarkt (Easter–Oct Sat 9am–5pm); the Bio Market, an **organic foods** market on the Falconplein (Sun 8am–4pm); and the large, **general market** on Theaterplein and its surroundings (Sun 8am–1pm). The city is also a hub of the **diamond** trade (see box, p.190).

Bakkerij Goossens Korte Gasthuisstraat 31 ☎03 226 07 91; map p.181. Join the queue at the best bakery in town, selling a superb range of breads as well as cakes and tarts. Tues–Sat 7am–7pm.

Coccodrillo Schuttershofstraat 9 ☎03 233 20 93, ⊛coccodrillo.be; map p.181. Top-of-the-range men's and women's shoe shop selling from a well-chosen selection of leading designers. Not as expensive as you might think at first glance. Mon–Sat 10am–6pm.

Fnac Groenplaats 31 ☎03 213 56 11, ⊛www.nl.fnac .be; map p.181. This sprawling store has, among much else, a wide range of Belgian road and hiking maps and a reasonably good selection of English novels. It's inside the Grand Bazar shopping mall. Daily 10am–6.30pm.

Hans Burie Korte Gasthuisstraat 3 ☎03 232 36 88, ⊛burie-chocoladepralines-antwerpen.be; map p.181. Belgians love their chocolates and, although it's a matter of

hot debate, many reckon this to be the best chocolatier in town – three cheers for Hans. Mon–Sat 9.30am–4.30pm.

Jutka & Riska Nationalestraat 87 ☎03 203 04 97, ⊛jutkaenriska.nl; map p.181. Comfortably the best vintage clothes shop for women in Antwerp – browse its serried ranks of dresses, skirts and shoes plus much, much else. Mon–Sat 10am–6.30pm.

Rosier 41 Rosier 41 ☎03 225 53 03, ⊛rosier41.be; map p.181. Large store selling a raft of Belgian designers, from established names to the up-and-coming. Also gets discounted clothes straight from designers' showrooms. Mon–Sat 10.30am–6pm.

De Vagant Reyndersstraat 21 ☎03 233 15 38, ⊛devagant.be; map p.181. Opposite the bar of the same name (see p.197), this specialist off-licence sells every type of jenever known to Belgium – and a mind-boggling range there is too. Mon & Thurs–Sat 11am–6pm.

DIRECTORY

Pharmacy Apotheek Rubens (☎03 232 20 32) is at Groenplaats 6. Details of 24hr pharmacies are available from the tourist office; duty rotas should also be displayed

on all pharmacists' windows or doors.
Post office The main post office is at Groenplaats 43 (Mon–Fri 9am–6pm, Sat 9am–3pm).

Lier

An ideal day-trip, likeable **LIER**, just 17km southeast of Antwerp, has an amenable, small-town air, its pocket-sized centre boasting a particularly pretty **Grote Markt** and a cluster of handsome medieval buildings, especially **St-Gummaruskerk**. Lier was founded in the eighth century, but despite its ancient provenance the town has never managed to dodge the shadow of its much larger neighbour, Antwerp – even when **Felix Timmermans**, one of Belgium's best-known writers, lived here. All the same, Timmermans did add a certain local sparkle – and it may have been needed: other Belgians once referred to Lier's citizens as "sheepheads" (*schapenkoppen*), a reference to their reputation for stubbornness and stupidity.

Grote Markt

Spreading out from the expansive **Grote Markt**, Central Lier's ancient streets and alleys are encircled and bisected by the waterways that mark the course of its old harbours and moat. At the centre of the Grote Markt is the turreted fourteenth-century **Belfort**, an attractively spikey affair incongruously attached to the classically elegant **Stadhuis**, which was built to replace the medieval cloth hall in 1740. Otherwise, the square is an attractive medley of "neos", with neo-Gothic, neoclassical and even neo-Romanesque buildings, mostly dating from the 1920s, jostling for space and attention.

3

St-Gummaruskerk

Kardinaal Mercierplein • Easter to Oct Mon & Sun 2–5pm, Tues–Fri 10am–noon & 2–5pm, Sat 2–4.30pm • Free, but chancel & treasury €1.50 • ☎ 0472 45 36 66, ⓦ sintgummaruskerktelier.be

Lier's ecclesiastical highlight is **St-Gummaruskerk**, which takes its name from a courtier of the king of France who, repenting of his sinful ways, settled in Lier as a hermit in the middle of the eighth century. Dating from 1425, the church is a fine illustration of the Flamboyant (or Late) Gothic style, its sturdy buttresses surmounted by a tiered and parapeted tower. Inside, chunky pillars rise up to support a vaulted roof, whose simplicity contrasts with the extraordinary intricacy of the conspicuous stone **rood screen** down below.

Chancel

Beyond the rood screen, the **chancel**'s stained-glass windows are reckoned to be some of the finest in Belgium, especially the five stately, elongated ones usually seen above the high altar. These were presented to the town by the Emperor Maximilian in 1516, though currently these are being repaired and no one is quite sure when they will be reinstalled. Beside the first side-chapel on the left is displayed the church's most interesting **painting**, a triptych whose side panels are the work of Rubens, one a representation of St Francis, the other of St Clara carrying a monstrance, after the time she popped out of her convent (with said monstrance in hand), to ward off hostile soldiers; the central panel of St Francis and the Virgin was also by Rubens, but this is a copy – Napoleon's soldiers stole the original Rubens, and the French never gave it back.

BAARLE-HERTOG: A LEG IN EACH COUNTRY

Filling out the northeast corner of Belgium, just beyond Antwerp, are the flat, sandy moorlands of the **Kempen**. Once a barren wasteland dotted with the poorest of agricultural communities – and punctuated by tracts of acid heath, bog and deciduous woodland – the Kempen's more hospitable parts were first cultivated and planted with pine by pioneering **Cistercian monks** in the twelfth century. The monks helped develop and sustain a strong regional identity and dialect, which survives in good order today, though the area's towns and villages are in themselves uniformly drab. The Kempen was also the subject of endless territorial bickering during the creation of an independent Belgium in the 1830s, a particular point of dispute being the little town of **Baarle-Hertog**, about 35km northeast of Antwerp. The final compromise verged on the ridiculous: Baarle-Hertog was designated as being part of Belgium, but it was surrounded by Dutch territory and the international border between it and the adjoining (Dutch) town of **Baarle-Nassau** actually cut through houses, never mind dividing streets. If you're eager to have one leg in the Netherlands, another in Belgium, then here's the spot.

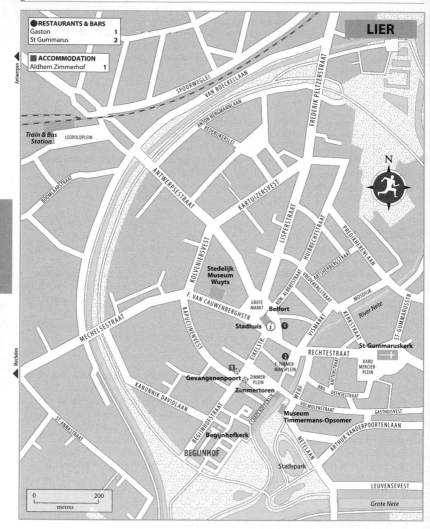

Treasury

A passageway leads off the nave into the **treasury** (*Schatkamer*), a tiny affair with one remarkable exhibit: an extremely rare and very early copy of the **Turin Shroud** from 1516, the old linen cloth that supposedly bears the image of the crucified Christ, at one tenth the size of the original.

Museum Timmermans-Opsomer

Netelaan 4 • Tues–Sun 10am–noon & 1–5pm • €2 • ☎ 03 800 03 94

The riverside **Museum Timmermans-Opsomer** celebrates the town's two most famous inhabitants, the writer Felix Timmermans (1886–1947) and the painter Isidore Opsomer (1878–1967). The two were good friends and thought of themselves as leading custodians of Flemish culture, the one writing of traditional village life, most memorably in the earthy humour of his *Pallieter*; the other proud of his sea- and townscapes, and of his influence on contemporary Belgian painters. The interior displays a comprehensive selection of Opsomer's work, including a batch of seriously bourgeois portraits and a large (and laughable), pseudo-religious painting entitled *Christ Preaches in Lier*. There's also an extensive display on Timmermans' life and times supported by **old photographs** and several first editions of his writings, but there's not much on the controversy surrounding his behaviour in World War II, which resulted in accusations of collaboration. Throughout, the labelling is in Flemish only.

Zimmertoren

Zimmerplein • Tues–Sun 10am–noon & 1–5pm • €4 • ☎ 03 800 03 95, ⓦ zimmertoren.be

The **Zimmertoren**, an old tower on Zimmerplein, was formerly part of the city ramparts before being equipped with the colourful **Jubelklok** (Centenary Clock), whose many dials show the phases of the moon, the zodiac, the tides of Lier and just about everything else you can think of. The clock was the work of one **Lodewijk Zimmer** (1888–1970), a wealthy city merchant who constructed it in 1931 in an effort to dispel local superstition and show his fellow townspeople how the cosmos worked. Inside the tower you can see the bevy of rotating dials which makes the clock tick, along with Zimmer's astronomical studio, while in the adjoining pavilion is Zimmer's no-less-detailed **Wonderklok** (Wonder Clock), which was exhibited at the World's Fairs of Brussels and New York in the 1930s. A **guide** explaining the internal works of the clocks and the meaning of all the dials is available in English.

Begijnhof and Gevangenpoort

Begijnhof Daily 7am–10pm • Free • Begijnhofkerk Easter to mid-Oct Sun 2–5pm

From the Zimmertoren, Schapekoppenstraat leads southwest past a wry modern **sculpture** of a shepherd and his metal sheep to a side-gate into the **Begijnhof**, whose lovely seventeenth-century cottages are mixed up with the slightly grander terraced houses that were inserted later. It's one of the region's best-preserved *begijnhofs* (see p.327), its narrow cobbled lanes stretching as far as the earthen bank that marks the line of the old city wall, and you can also pop into the appealingly ornate **Begijnhofkerk**. On the far side of the Begijnhof, Begijnhofstraat leads back to the Zimmerplein through the arches of the **Gevangenpoort**, a strongly fortified medieval gate which served as the town's prison for many a year.

Stedelijk Museum Wuyts-Van Campen & Baron Caroly

Florent van Cauwenberghstraat 14 • Tues–Sun 10am–noon & 1–5pm • €4 • ☎ 03 800 03 96

The enjoyable **Stedelijk Museum Wuyts-Van Campen & Baron Caroly**, which spreads over just three rooms, boasts two paintings by **Pieter Bruegel the Younger** (1564–1638), namely *St John the Baptist Preaching to a Crowd*, who are dressed in an idiosyncratic mix of rural Flemish and imaginary Middle Eastern attire; and his *Flemish Proverbs* (*Vlaamse Spreekworden*), illustrating over eighty proverbs satirizing every vice and foolery imaginable. The latter is one of several almost identical proverbs' paintings completed by Bruegel. The museum also possesses a small but well-chosen selection of nineteenth-century Belgian and Dutch **landscapes**, a pious preparatory sketch of *St Theresa* by Rubens (1577–1640), and a cruelly drawn *Brawling Peasants* by Jan Steen (1626–79). Look out also for several works by **David Teniers the Younger** (1610–90), who made a small fortune by churning out earthy peasant scenes such as his *Jealous Wife* and *The Backgammon Players*.

By train and bus From Lier's train and adjoining bus station, it's a 10min walk southeast to the Grote Markt. Destinations by train Antwerp (every 15min; 15min); Hasselt (hourly; 55min); Leuven (hourly; 45min); Mechelen (every 30min; 30min; change at Antwerp Berchem).

Tourist information In the basement of the Stadhuis, on the Grote Markt (April–Oct Mon–Fri 9am–noon & 1.30–4.30pm, Sat & Sun 9am–12.30pm & 1–4pm; Nov–March Mon–Fri 9am–noon & 1.30–4.30pm; ☎ 03 800 05 55, ⓦ toerismelier.be).

ACCOMMODATION, EATING AND DRINKING

Aldhem Zimmerhof Begijnhofstraat 2 ☎ 03 490 03 90, ⓦ zimmerhof.be. Lier is too small (and too near Antwerp) to have much in the way of accommodation, but this appealing hotel, with its 23 smart, modern rooms, occupies a sympathetically updated nineteenth-century courtyard complex next to the Gevangenpoort. A refreshing and enjoyable place to stay. **€110**

Gaston Grote Markt 61 ☎ 03 298 88 94, ⓦ gaston.be. A battery of café-restaurants lines up along Zimmerplein and the Grote Markt, but the swankiest spot in town is this

first-rate seafood restaurant with its immaculate, modern fittings and pavement terrace. A great place to try that old Flemish favourite, eel braised in spinach (*paling in 't groen*). Mains average €26. Wed–Fri & Sun noon–2pm & 6–9pm, Sat 6–9pm.

St Gummarus Felix Timmermansplein 2 ☎ 03 290 56 63. Traditional small-town pub down by the river with a cosy interior and a pleasant pavement terrace. Good range of bottled beers too. Mon, Thurs & Fri noon–midnight, Wed 5pm–midnight, Sat 10am–1.30am, Sun noon–10pm.

Mechelen and around

Midway between Antwerp and Brussels, **MECHELEN**, the home of the Primate of Belgium and the country's ecclesiastical capital, is an ancient and intriguing city of just 80,000 inhabitants. In recent years, a well-conceived municipal plan to freshen up the centre has worked wonders, resulting in the pleasant and appealing town of today. The key sights – primarily a cache of **medieval churches**, including a splendid **cathedral** – are easily seen on a day-trip from either of its neighbours, but spend the night here and you'll give the place the attention it deserves. One scar on Mechelen's history was its use by the Germans as a transit camp for Jews in World War II: the **Kazerne Dossin** museum recalls these terrible times and a short train ride or drive away is **Fort Breendonk**, a one-time Gestapo interrogation centre.

Brief history

Mechelen's Christian heritage dates back to **St Rombout**, an Irish evangelist who converted the locals in the seventh century. Little is known about Rombout, but legend asserts he was the son of a powerful chieftain, who gave up his worldly possessions to preach to the heathens – not that it did him much good: he crossed a Mechelen stonemason, who proceeded to chop him up. In the way of such things, Rombout's remains were retrieved and showed no signs of decay, easily enough justification for the construction of a **shrine** in his honour. Rombout proved a popular saint and pilgrims flocked here, ensuring Mechelen a steady revenue. By the **thirteenth century**, Mechelen had become one of the more powerful cities of medieval Flanders and it entered a brief golden age after 1473, when the Burgundian prince, **Charles the Bold**, decided to base major parts of his administration here. Charles died four years later and his redoubtable widow, **Margaret of York**, moved to Mechelen, where she formed one of the most famous courts of the day in conjunction with her stepdaughter, **Mary of Burgundy**. Mary died in 1482 and Margaret followed in 1503, but Mary's daughter – and Margaret's great-stepdaughter – **Margaret of Austria** returned to Mechelen in 1507 to become Habsburg governor of the Low Countries and guardian of the future emperor, Charles V. It was during the governorship of Margaret of Austria that Mechelen peaked, with artists and scholars drawn here from all over Flanders, attracted by the Renaissance pomp and ceremony, with enormous feasts in fancy clothes in fancy buildings. For the men, two particular peccadilloes were **pointed shoes** (whose length – up to about 60cm – reflected social status) and bright, two-colour hoses. This glamorous facade camouflaged serious political intent: surrounded by wealthy, independent merchants and powerful, well-organized guilds, Margaret – as well as Mary and Margaret of York before her – realized they had to impress and overawe as a condition of their survival. Margaret of Austria died in 1530, the capital moved to Brussels and Mechelen was never quite the same, though many of its older buildings did survive the **industrial boom** of the nineteenth century to emerge intact today.

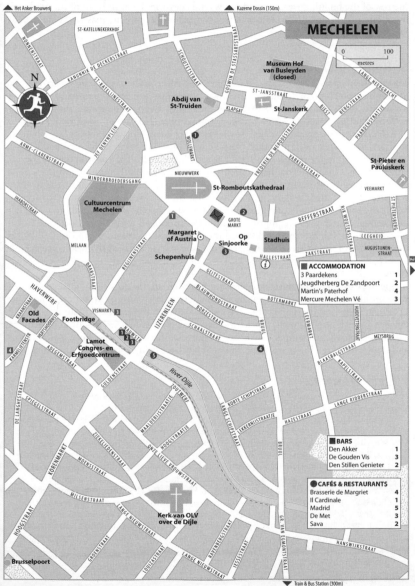

MECHELEN

0   100
metres

ACCOMMODATION
3 Paardekens	1
Jeugdherberg De Zandpoort	2
Martin's Paterhof	4
Mercure Mechelen Vé	3

BARS
Den Akker	1
De Gouden Vis	3
Den Stillen Genieter	2

CAFÉS & RESTAURANTS
Brasserie de Margriet	4
Il Cardinale	1
Madrid	5
De Met	3
Sava	2

Grote Markt

The centre of town is, as ever, the **Grote Markt**, an especially handsome and expansive affair offering a superb view of the cathedral. It's flanked on its eastern side by the **Stadhuis**, whose bizarre and incoherent appearance does it no favours: the left-hand side of the building, comprising an ornate arcaded loggia fronting a fluted, angular edifice, was commissioned by Margaret of Austria and designed by Rombout Keldermans. The plan was to extend the Stadhuis further along the Grote Markt, but the money ran out after Margaret's death and the **plain stonework** and simple gables of the rest of the building were only added several centuries later. In front of the Stadhuis is a modern sculpture of **Op Sinjoorke** (see box below), the town's mascot, being tossed in a blanket.

St-Romboutskathedraal

Grote Markt • April–Oct Mon–Sat 8.30am–5.30pm, Sun 2–5.30pm; Nov–March Mon–Sat 8.30am–4.30pm, Sun 2–5.30pm • Free

St-Romboutskathedraal dominates the town centre just as it was supposed to. It's the cathedral's mighty square **tower** that takes the breath away, a wonderful, almost imperial Gothic structure with soaring, canopied pinnacles and extraordinarily long and slender apertures. It's matched down below by heavy-duty buttressing, which supports a sequence of high-arched pointed windows that encircle the nave and the choir, rising up to the delicate fluting of a stone balustrade. The **construction** of the church has not been without its problems. Work began with the draining of the marshes on which it was to be built in 1217, but the money ran out before the tower was erected, and the initial design had to be put on hold until the fifteenth century. In 1451, the pope obligingly provided the extra funds when he put St Rombout's on a list of specified churches where pilgrims could seek absolution for their sins without visiting Rome. The money rolled in and the tower was completed by 1546 – just before the outbreak of the religious wars that would surely have stymied the whole project.

Nave

Inside the cathedral, the thirteenth-century **nave** has all the cloistered elegance of the Brabantine Gothic style, although the original lines are spoiled by an unfortunate series of seventeenth-century statues of the Apostles. Between the arches lurks an extraordinary Baroque **pulpit**, a playful mass of twisted and curled oak dotted with carefully camouflaged animal carvings – a squirrel, a frog and a snail here, a salamander and a pelican there. The main scene shows **St Norbert** being thrown from his horse, a

---

MECHELEN MEN

Once a generalized symbol of male irresponsibility, the effigy of **Op Sinjoorke** and its forebears enjoyed a variety of names – *vuilen bras* (unfaithful drunkard), *sotscop* (fool) and *vuilen bruidegom* (disloyal husband) – until the events of 1775 redefined its identity. Every year it was customary for the dummy to be paraded through Mechelen and tossed up and down in a sheet. In 1775, however, a young man from Antwerp allegedly attempted to steal it and was badly beaten for his pains: the people of Mechelen were convinced he was part of an Antwerp plot to rob them of their cherished mascot. The two cities were already fierce **commercial rivals**, and the incident soured relations even further. Indeed, when news of the beating reached Antwerp, there was sporadic **rioting** and calls for the city burghers to take some sort of revenge. Refusing to be intimidated, the people of Mechelen derisively renamed the doll after their old nickname for the people of Antwerp – "Op Sinjoorke", from "Signor", a reference to that city's favoured status under earlier Spanish kings. It was sweet **revenge** for an incident of 1687 that had made Mechelen a laughing stock: staggering home, a drunk had roused the town when he thought he saw a fire in the cathedral. In fact, the "fire" was moonlight, earning the Mechelaars the soubriquet "**Maneblussers**" (Moondousers).

narrow escape that convinced this twelfth-century German prince to give his possessions to the poor and dedicate his life to the church. At the far end of the nave, take a look at the elaborate doors of the **high altar**, which hide the gilt casket containing the remains of St Rombout (see p.202). They are only opened on major religious festivals, principally during the **Hanswijkprocessie**, held in May, when the reliquary is paraded through the town centre.

The nave's other curiosity, in the side-chapel next to the north transept, is the **tomb** of Mechelen's **Cardinal Mercier** (1851–1926), plus a plaque, presented by the Church of England, commemorating his part in coordinating the **Mechelen Conversations**. These investigated the possibility of reuniting the two churches of England and Rome and ran from 1921 up to the time of Mercier's death, but with little result. In Belgium, Mercier is more often remembered for his staunch opposition to the German occupation of World War I. His pastoral letters, notably "Patriotism and Endurance", proclaimed loyalty to the Belgian king, paid tribute to the soldiers at the front and condemned the invasion as illegal and un-Christian.

South transept

The **south transept** displays the cathedral's most distinguished painting, **Anthony van Dyck**'s dramatic *Crucifixion*, which portrays the writhing, muscular bodies of the two thieves in the shadows to either side of Christ, who is bathed in a white light of wonderful clarity. The painting now forms part of a heavy, marble Baroque **altarpiece** carved for the Guild of Masons, but it was only installed here after the French revolutionary army razed the church where the painting was originally displayed.

Ambulatory

Exhibited in the **ambulatory** are 25 **panel paintings** relating the legend of St Rombout. Such devotional series were comparatively commonplace in medieval Flanders, but this is one of the very few to have survived, painted by several unknown artists between 1480 and 1510. As individual works of art, the panel paintings are not perhaps of the highest order, but the cumulative attention to detail – in the true Flemish tradition – is quite remarkable, with all manner of **folksy minutiae** illuminating what would otherwise be a predictable tale of sacrifice and sanctity. The panels are exhibited (and numbered) in chronological order, beginning with Rombout's appointment as bishop of Dublin (Panel 1) and continuing, via assorted miracles, to Rombout's arrival in Mechelen (Panel 7) and finally the Brotherhood of St Rombout honouring its patron saint (Panel 25). Two of the most interesting scenes are those where Rombout publicly admonishes a local stonemason for adultery (Panel 12) and the saint's **martyrdom** at the hands of the same man (see p.202), while his workmate picks Rombout's pockets (Panel 13).

Tower

Mon, Tues & Thurs–Sun 1–6pm • €7; tickets from tourist information (see p.209)

The energetic can now clamber up **St-Romboutstoren**, an exhausting 500-step climb that leads past assorted bell and carillon chambers (see box, p.206) to the observation platform right at the top. As you might expect, there are panoramic views from the platform and on a clear day you can spy the Brussels Atomium (see p.78), but mostly you'll realize just how flat this part of Belgium actually is.

St-Janskerk

St-Janstraat • April–Oct Mon, Tues & Thurs–Sun 1–5pm, Nov–March Mon, Tues & Thurs–Sun 1–4pm • Free • ☎ 015 29 40 30

With its imposing tower and handsome high-pointed windows, **St-Janskerk** is a fine illustration of the Gothic style, mostly dating from the fifteenth century. Inside, almost everything is on the grand scale, from the massive pulpit and the whopping **organ**

3

THE BELLS, THE BELLS

It was during the fourteenth century that **bells** were first used in Flemish cities as a means of regulating the working day, reflecting the development of a **wage economy** – employers were keen to keep tabs on their employees. Bells also served as a sort of **public-address system**: pealing bells, for example, announced good news; tolling summoned the citizens to the main square; and a rapid sequence of bells warned of danger. By the early fifteenth century, a short peal marked the hour, and from this developed the **carillon** (*beiaard*), in which the ringing of a set of bells is triggered by the rotation of a large drum with metal pegs; the pegs pull wires attached to the clappers in the bells, just like a giant music box. Later, the mechanics were developed so that the carillon could be played by means of a keyboard, giving the player (*beiaardier*) the chance to improvise.

Carillon playing almost died out in the nineteenth century, when it was dismissed as being too folksy for words, but now it's on the rebound, and several Flemish cities – including Bruges (see p.103) and Mechelen – have their own municipal carillon player. Mechelen's **cathedral** tower (see p.204) has Belgium's finest carillon, a fifteenth-century affair of 49 bells, and the city is also home to the renowned **Koninklijke Beiaardschool** (Royal Carillon School), which attracts students from right around the world. Mechelen's carillon resounds over town on high days and holidays and there are also regular, hour-long **performances** on Saturdays (11.30am), Sundays (3pm), and from June through to mid-September on Monday evenings (8.30pm).

---

through to two large and unusual canons' pews. But it's the Baroque high altarpiece that really grabs the attention, a suitably flashy setting for a flashy but wonderful painting – **Rubens**' *Adoration of the Magi*. Painted in 1619, the central panel, after which the triptych is named, is an exquisite example of the artist's use of variegated lighting – and also features his first wife portrayed as the Virgin. The side panels are rotated, so on the left-hand side you'll either see Jesus baptized by John the Baptist, or John the Baptist's head on a platter; to the right, it's St John on Patmos or the same saint being dipped in boiling oil.

Museum Hof van Busleyden

Frederik de Merodestraat 65 · Closed until 2017 · ☎ 015 29 40 30, ⓦ stedelijkemuseamechelen.be

Mechelen's principal museum, the **Museum Hof van Busleyden**, occupies a large and particularly attractive Renaissance complex built for the wealthy Busleyden family in the early seventeenth century. For many years, this palatial complex was home to the Berg van Barmhartigheid (Mountain of Charity), which provided interest-free loans to Mechelen's poor, but the building was badly damaged in World War I and subsequently passed to the city; the museum is currently closed and the date of its reopening has yet to be fixed.

Kazerne Dossin

Goswin de Stassartstraat 153 · Mon, Tues & Thurs–Sun 10am–5pm, but closed Jewish holidays · €10 · ☎ 015 29 06 60, ⓦ www.kazernedossin.eu

During the German occupation, Nazi officials chose Mechelen as a staging point for Belgian and refugee Jews destined for the concentration camps of eastern Europe. Their reasoning was quite straightforward: most of Belgium's Jews were in either Antwerp or Brussels and Mechelen was halfway between the two. These desperate times are recalled at the **Kazerne Dossin**, whose several floors are divided thematically in an attempt to tie in what happened to the Jews with wider issues of human rights, racism and oppression. **Floor 1** sets the scene and looks at Jewish life in Belgium in the 1930s; **Floor 2** investigates the sliding scale of cooperation, collaboration and resistance as

applicable to Belgium; and **Floor 3**, titled "Death", details the fate of most of the Jews temporarily interred here: between 1942 and 1944 over 25,000 Jews passed through the city; most ended up in Auschwitz and only 1200 survived. The personal testimonies and accompanying photos and films can't help but be harrowing, and some bring a deep chill to the soul, none more so than the pleading postcard thrown from a deportation train. The museum's location is no accident – across the street are the **old barracks** that were used as the internment centre. Most of the barracks has been turned into flats, but one wing has been left as a memorial to the dead with four bleak, bare and sombre rooms.

South of the Grote Markt

The innocuous **statue of Margaret of Austria** on the south side of the Grote Markt dates from 1849, but it was only moved here from the centre of the square a couple of years ago. Behind the statue stands the **Schepenhuis** (Aldermen's House), a fetching Gothic structure of 1374 that marks the start of the **Ijzerenleen**, the focus of one of the region's best Saturday **food markets** (8am–1pm). At the far end of Ijzerenleen, turn right down Nauwstraat for the cluster of bars at the heart of Mechelen's drinking scene (see p.209). Here also a footbridge spans the river, leading over to **Haverwerf** (Oats Wharf), where the old Lamot brewery has been turned into the architecturally predictable, very modern **Lamot Congres- en Erfgoedcentrum** (Lamot Conference & Heritage Centre; ⓦlamot-mechelen.be), where they host conferences and put on special events.

Haverwerf facades

Three old and contrasting **facades** overlook **Haverwerf**. On the right is **Het Paradijske** (The Little Paradise), a slender structure with fancy tracery and mullioned windows that takes its name from the Garden of Eden reliefs above the first-floor windows. Next door, the all-timber **De Duiveltjes** (The Little Devils), a rare survivor from the sixteenth century, is also named after its decoration, this time for the carved satyrs above the entrance. Finally, on the left and dating to 1669, is **St-Jozef**, a graceful example of the Baroque merchant's house, where the fluent scrollwork swirls over the top of the gable and camouflages the utilitarian, upper-storey door: trade goods were once pulled up the front of the house by pulley and shoved in here for safekeeping. A **pontoon walkway** extends southeast along the river from Haverwerf, making a pleasant stroll en route to the Kerk van Onze Lieve Vrouw over de Dijle.

Kerk van Onze Lieve Vrouw over de Dijle

Onze-Lieve-Vrouwestraat • April–Oct Mon, Tues & Thurs–Sun 1–5pm, Nov–March Mon, Tues & Thurs–Sun 1–4pm • Free

The **Kerk van Onze Lieve Vrouw over de Dijle** (Church of Our Lady across the River Dijle) is a massive pinnacled and turreted affair that was begun in the fifteenth century and finally completed two hundred years later – hence the mix of late Gothic and Baroque features. Apart from its sheer size, the interior is really rather mundane, its mediocrity only redeemed by **Rubens**' *Miraculous Draught of Fishes*, an exquisite triptych painted for the Fishmongers' Guild in 1618 and displayed in the south transept. The central panel has all the usual hallmarks of Rubens in his pomp – note the thick, muscular arms of the fishermen – but it's the glistening and wriggling fish that inspire.

ARRIVAL AND INFORMATION   MECHELEN

By train and bus Mechelen's train and bus stations are a 15min walk from the town centre, straight ahead down Hendrik Consciencestraat and its continuation Graaf van Egmontstraat and Bruul. Do not take Leopoldstraat, the more obvious road leading from the stations.

Destinations by train Antwerp (every 15min; 25min);

Brussels (every 15min; 25min); Ghent (hourly; 45min); Leuven (2 hourly; 40min); Lier (every 30min; 30min; change at Antwerp Berchem).

Tourist information On the Grote Markt, across from the Stadhuis at Hallestraat 2 (April–Oct Mon–Fri 10am–5pm, Sat 10am–4pm, Sun 12.30–4pm; Nov–March Mon–Sat 10am–4pm, Sun 12.30–4pm; ☎070 22 00 08, ⓦvisitmechelen.be).

ACCOMMODATION

3 Paardekens Begijnenstraat 3 ☎015 34 27 13, ⓦ3paardekens.be. Down a narrow side street within shouting distance of the cathedral, this medium-sized, three-star hotel has 33 pleasantly modern rooms with bare faux-wood floors and big beds. The roof-top breakfast room has smashing views of the cathedral. **€90**

Jeugdherberg De Zandpoort Zandpoortvest 70 ☎015 27 85 39, ⓦjeugdherbergen.be. HI-affiliated hostel in an attractively designed modern tower block, with 112 beds in one-, two-, three- and four-berth rooms. All rooms are en suite, breakfast is included in the price and there's wi-fi, a dining room and bar. The hostel is a dull 10min walk northeast of the train station via Stationsstraat. Dorm **€25**, double **€58**

★**Martin's Paterhof** Karmelietenstraat 4 ☎015 46 46 46, ⓦmartinshotels.com. One of a small chain, this deluxe four-star hotel occupies an immaculately and imaginatively renovated nineteenth-century church complete with the original stained-glass windows and neo-Gothic arches. The seventy or so rooms – both in the church and in a side building – are divided into five categories, from the "Cosy" to the "Exceptional"; in terms of decor, all are über-modern. Breakfasts, which are very good, are served in the former choir. **€120**

Mercure Mechelen Vé Vismarkt 14 ☎015 20 07 55, ⓦhotelve.com. Enjoyable and distinctive four-star hotel which occupies two intelligently recycled former 1920s factories – an old fish smokery at the front and a cigar-making factory at the back. Some thought has gone into the decor, with pride of place going to a large tubular sculpture, and the clean, modern rooms are well appointed. The only fly in the ointment is the night-time noise from the square in front – request a room at the back. There's also an on-site spa and fitness centre. **€90**

EATING AND DRINKING

Mechelen has a clutch of good-to-excellent **cafés** and **restaurants** plus a band of busy bars down on the **Vismarkt**, the focus of the night-time action. While you are here, be sure to try one particular local beer, **Gouden Carolus** (Golden Charles), a delicious dark-brown or blond barley beer once tippled by (so they say) the Emperor Charles V – it's still brewed in town at **Brouwerij Het Anker**, Guldo Gezellelaan 49 (ⓦhetanker.be).

CAFÉS AND RESTAURANTS

Brasserie de Margriet Bruul 52 ☎015 21 00 17. Popular brasserie in one wing of a former seminary, though this part of the building has been rehashed with standard-issue modern furnishings, so only the odd flourish – such as the mullioned windows – gives a hint as to what went before. The menu covers all the usual Flemish standards with a few surprises, notably local delicacy *Mechelse Koekoek* (Mechelen cuckoo), a particularly succulent variety of chicken. The cuckoo costs €21, other mains about the same, but daily specials are as little as €14. Courtyard eating in the summertime. Mon–Thurs 10am–8pm, Fri & Sat 10am–9.30pm.

★**Il Cardinale** Wollemarkt 22 ☎0468 21 00 91, ⓦilcardinale.be. Bright and breezy café, with an especially pleasant pavement terrace, where they specialize in burgers from €9.50 – try the house version with grilled vegetables, watercress and spinach pesto. Tues–Sat noon–2pm & 5–10pm, Sun 5–10pm.

Madrid Lange Schipstraat 4 ☎015 29 03 95, ⓦmadridmadrid.be. Long-established Spanish restaurant from whose cosy (meets small) premises are served good, tangy tapas – try, for example, the roasted Iberian sirloin with lentils and chorizo. Three tapas for €39. Mon, Thurs, Fri & Sun noon–2pm & 6–10pm, Sat 6–10pm.

De Met Grote Markt 29 ☎015 20 68 81, ⓦdemetmechelen.be. One of the best of the Grote Markt's plentiful restaurants, this bright, modern place offers a good range of Flemish dishes geared to the seasons and using, as often as not, local produce. The daily specials are especially delicious. Mains average €24. Mon–Sat 10am–11pm (kitchen noon–10pm).

Sava Grote Markt 13 ☎015 64 70 90, ⓦsavamechelen .be. Bright and attractive café with a stylish (very wooden) interior and a pavement terrace. Offers a good range of wines and local beers to wash down a small but tasty range of authentic tapas – try the meatballs. Tapas cost €4–6. Daily 9am–midnight.

BARS

Den Akker Nauwstraat 11 ☎015 33 10 78. Laidback, vaguely New Age bar with an outside terrace overlooking the river. Hot and steaming in the summer; cool and cuddlesome in winter. Mon–Sat from 11.30am, Sun from 3pm.

De Gouden Vis Nauwstraat 7 ☎015 20 72 06. As for *Den Akker*, but a couple of doors along and with ancient chandeliers and a slightly hipper clientele. Mon–Fri from noon, Sat from 10am, Sun from 3pm.

3

Den Stillen Genieter Nauwstraat 9 ☎ 015 21 95 04. This curious bar, "The Silent Hedonist", is rather like a dusty, ramshackle cave, where the host presides over several hundred types of beer. No gentrification allowed. Tues–Sat from 8pm till late.

Fort Breendonk

Brandstraat 57, Willebroek, 12km west of Mechelen • Daily 9.30am–5.30pm, last admission 4.30pm • €8 • ☎ 03 860 75 25, ⓦ breendonk.be • Take the train from Mechelen to Willebroek (hourly; 10min) and the fort is on the edge of town, a 2.5km walk from the station; by car, the fort is a stone's throw from the A12 linking Antwerp and Brussels, and well signposted

Built as part of the circle of fortifications that ringed early twentieth-century Antwerp, **Fort Breendonk** became notorious as a Gestapo interrogation centre during World War II. The fort's surly concrete buildings were originally encased in a thick layer of sand, but the Germans had this carted away by their prisoners in 1940. After the war, Breendonk was preserved as a **national memorial** in honour of the four thousand men and women who suffered or perished in its dark, dank tunnels and cells. As you might expect, it's a powerful, disturbing place to visit, with a clearly marked tour taking you through the SS tribunal room, poignantly graffitied cells, the prisoners' barrack room and the bunker that was used as a torture chamber. There's also a **museum** dealing with the German occupation of Belgium, prison life and the postwar trial of Breendonk SS criminals and their collaborators. Other displays explore the origins of fascism and the development of the concentration camps.

Leuven

Half an hour by train from both Mechelen and Brussels, **LEUVEN** offers an easy and enjoyable day-trip from either. The town is the seat of Belgium's oldest **university** (see box below), whose students give the place a lively, informal air – and sustain an army of inexpensive bars and cafés. There are also a couple of notable medieval buildings, the splendid **Stadhuis** and the imposing **St-Pieterskerk**, which is home to three wonderful early Flemish paintings, and in the **Oude Markt** Leuven possesses one of the region's most personable squares. Otherwise, the centre is not much more than an undistinguished tangle of streets with a lot of the new and few remnants of the old. Then again, it's something of a miracle that any of Leuven's ancient buildings have survived at all, since the town suffered badly in both world wars: in 1914 much of Leuven was razed during the first German offensive; thirty years later the town was heavily bombed.

LEUVEN: ACADEMIC TEARS AND TRAVAILS

The history of the **university** isn't a particularly happy one, though everything began rosily enough. Founded in 1425, it soon became one of Europe's most prestigious educational establishments: the cartographer Mercator (see p.349) was a student here, and it was here that the religious reformer **Erasmus** (1466–1536) founded the Collegium Trilingue for the study of Hebrew, Latin and Greek, as the basis of a liberal (rather than Catholic) education. However, in response to the rise of Lutheranism, the authorities changed tack, insisting on strict Catholic orthodoxy and driving the university into educational retreat. In 1797 the French suppressed the university, and then, when Belgium fell under Dutch rule, William I replaced it with a **Philosophical College** – one of many blatantly anti-Catholic measures which fuelled the Belgian revolution. Re-established after independence as a bilingual Catholic institution, the university became a hotbed of **Flemish Catholicism**, and French and Flemish speakers were long locked in a bitter nationalist dispute. In 1970 a separate, French-speaking university was founded at Louvain-la-Neuve, just south of Brussels – a decision that propelled Leuven into its present role as a bastion of **Flemish thinking**, wielding considerable influence over the region's political and economic elite.

The Stadhuis

Grote Markt

Overlooking the **Grote Markt** is Leuven's magnificent **Stadhuis**, an extraordinarily light and lacy confection, crowned by soaring pinnacles and a dainty, high-pitched roof studded with dormer windows. It's a beautiful building, though it is slightly spoiled by the clumsiness of its nineteenth-century **statues**, representing everything from

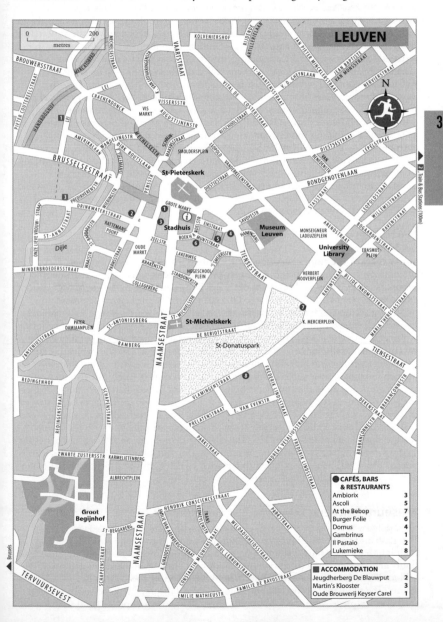

3

CAFÉS, BARS
& RESTAURANTS

Ambiorix	3
Ascoli	5
At the Bebop	7
Burger Folie	6
Domus	4
Gambrinus	1
Il Pastaio	2
Lukemieke	8

ACCOMMODATION

Jeugdherberg De Blauwput	2
Martin's Klooster	3
Oude Brouwerij Keyser Carel	1

important citizens to virtues and vices. In contrast, the niche bases supporting the statues are exuberantly medieval, depicting biblical subjects in a free, colloquial style and adorned by a panoply of grotesques.

St-Pieterskerk

Grote Markt • Mon, Tues & Thurs–Sat 10am–4.30pm, Sun 11am–4.30pm • Free, but chancel €3 • ☎ 016 29 51 33

Across the square from the Staduis, **St-Pieterskerk** is a rambling, heavily buttressed late Gothic pile whose western facade defeated its architects – hence its stumpy appearance. Work began on the present church in the 1420s and continued until the start of the sixteenth century when the Romanesque towers of the western facade, the last remaining part of an earlier church, were pulled down to make way for a grand replacement. It didn't work out – the foundations proved too weak – and finally, another hundred years on, the unfinished second-attempt towers were capped, creating the truncated, asymmetrical versions that rise above the west entrance today.

Inside, the church is distinguished by its soaring nave whose enormous composite pillars frame a fabulous **rood screen**, an intricately carved piece of stonework surmounted by a wooden Christ. The nave's Baroque **pulpit** is also striking, a weighty wooden extravagance which shows St Norbert being thrown off his horse by lightning, a dramatic scene set beneath spiky palm trees. It was this brush with death that persuaded Norbert, a twelfth-century German noble, to abandon his worldly ways and dedicate himself to the Church, on whose behalf he founded a devout religious order, the Premonstratensian Canons, in 1120.

The chancel

Same times as church • €3

In the **chancel**, the ambulatory holds three important paintings dating from the fifteenth century. There's a copy of **Rogier van der Weyden**'s marvellous triptych, the *Descent from the Cross*, and two of the few surviving paintings by Weyden's apprentice **Dieric Bouts** (c.1415–75), who worked for most of his life in Leuven, ultimately becoming the city's official painter. Bouts' carefully contrived paintings are inhabited by stiff and slender figures in religious scenes that are almost totally devoid of action – a frozen narrative designed to stir contemplation rather than strong emotion. Of the two **triptychs** on display here, the gruesome *Martyrdom of St Erasmus*, which has the executioners extracting the saint's entrails with a winch, is less interesting than the *Last Supper*, showing Christ and his disciples in a Flemish dining room; the two men standing up, as well as the couple peeping through the service hatch, are the rectors of the fraternity who commissioned the work. It was customary for Judas to be portrayed in a yellow robe, the colour of hate and cowardice, but Bouts broke with tradition and made Judas almost indistinguishable from the others – he's the one with his face in shadow and his hand on his left hip. The change of emphasis, away from the betrayal to the mystery of the Eucharist, is continued on the **side panels**: to the left Abraham is offered bread and wine above a Jewish Passover; to the right the Israelites gather manna and, below, the prophet Elijah receives angelic succour.

Museum Leuven

Leopold Vanderkelenstraat 28 • Daily except Wed 11am–6pm, Thurs till 10pm • €12 • ☎ 016 27 29 29, 🖥 mleuven.be

Big, flash and really rather groovy, the **Museum Leuven** occupies a striking modern building that's been squeezed into the grounds of an old mansion. There are three main floors here, two devoted to temporary exhibitions, often of modern art, and one – Floor 0 – to the permanent collection, and the museum also hosts gigs and special events. The **permanent collection** includes piecemeal displays devoted to the likes of medieval sculpture, vestments, porcelain, silver and glassware, plus a good showing for

Belgian nineteenth-century sculptors and painters, especially **Constantin Meunier** (see p.76). There's also a room full of medieval paintings, most memorably two works by **Rogier van der Weyden**, an exquisite *Seven Sacraments* and a *Holy Trinity*, though this has, at some point, been altered: if you look closely at Christ's shoulder, you'll spot a pair of bird's feet. Originally, these were the feet of the dove that represented the Holy Spirit, but somewhere along the line someone decided that God the Father and the Son would suffice.

The Oude Markt and Groot Begijnhof

The **Oude Markt**, a large cobblestoned square just to the south of the Grote Markt, is the boisterous core of Leuven's nightlife, its assorted bars and cafés occupying a handsome set of tall gabled houses that mostly date from the nineteenth century. To the immediate east of Oude Markt, Naamsestraat leads south towards the **Groot Begijnhof**, a labyrinthine enclave of tall and rather austere red-brick houses tucked away beside the River Dijle. Once home to around three hundred *begijns* – women living as nuns without taking vows – the Begijnhof was bought by the university in 1962, since when its mostly seventeenth-century buildings have been painstakingly restored as **student residences**, and very nice they are too.

ARRIVAL AND INFORMATION · LEUVEN

By train and bus From the train and adjacent bus station, it's an easy 10min walk west along Bondgenotenlaan to the Grote Markt.

Destinations by train Antwerp (hourly; 50min); Brussels (every 30min; 30min); Hasselt (every 30min; 50min); Hasselt (every 30min; 50min); Lier (hourly; 45min); Mechelen (every 30min; 40min); Tongeren (hourly; 1hr 10min).

Tourist information Round the side of the Stadhuis at Naamsestraat 3 (Mon–Sat 10am–5pm; March–Oct also Sun 10am–5pm; ☎016 20 30 20, ⊛leuven.be).

ACCOMMODATION

Jeugdherberg De Blauwput Martelarenlaan 11A ☎016 63 90 62, ⊛jeugdherbergen.be. A fair old hoof from the city centre – it's just on the far side of the train station – this popular HI hostel offers bunks in two- to six-bed en-suite rooms. There's a bar, café, wi-fi and a garden. Dorm €25, double €58

★**Martin's Klooster** Onze-Lieve-Vrouwstraat 18 ☎016 21 31 41, ⊛martins-hotels.com. The town's most distinctive hotel by a long chalk, this smooth and polished place occupies an immaculately renovated former monastery complete with mullioned windows and handsome brick gables. The 100-odd rooms are tastefully decorated, with beiges and creams predominant, and the location is central, too. Part of a medium-sized chain. €110

Oude Brouwerij Keyser Carel Lei 15 ☎016 22 14 81, ⊛keysercarel.be. Chichi B&B in a rambling old mansion, parts of which date back to the seventeenth century. Has three neat and trim modern guest rooms, all en suite, plus a mini-gym and lovely gardens. €120

EATING AND DRINKING

With all those students to feed and water, the centre of Leuven heaves with **fast-food joints** and frayed-at-the-edges **bars** with a particular concentration along and around Oude Markt. There's a gaggle of more up-market **restaurants** too – and indeed Leuven has its own "restaurant street", **Muntstraat**.

Ambiorix Oude Markt 3 ☎016 22 26 64. Student bar par excellence – though quite why the place is kitted out in a sort of ersatz medievalism is hard to fathom: perhaps it provides historical context? Daily from noon.

Ascoli Muntstraat 17 ☎016 23 93 64, ⊛www.ascoli .be. Well-established Italian restaurant offering all the classics and then some from its modern premises at the heart of Leuven's restaurant quarter. Mains around €20, pizzas from €8. Mon–Wed & Fri–Sun noon–10.30pm.

At the Bebop Tiensestraat 82 ☎016 20 86 04, ⊛atthebebop.be. Mixed bag of a place with a café, restaurant and a dancefloor. Frequent live gigs, mostly jazz and indie. One of the liveliest spots in town. Tues–Sat 4pm till late.

Burger Folie Muntstraat 4 ☎016 88 66 08, ⊛burgerfolie.be. Crisp, modern place with a pavement terrace where they specialize in burgers – gourmet burgers, to be precise. Good-quality meat, a wide range and competitive prices. Tues–Sat noon–2pm & 6–10pm.

3

Domus Tiensestraat 8 ☎ 016 20 14 49, 🖰 domusleuven
.be. If not the best bar in town, then certainly the most
distinctive, spread over two large floors with ancient
beamed ceilings, old bygones on the walls and a small
brewery out the back. Offers an excellent range of ales as
well as a (competent) bar menu. Daily except Mon
9am–1am.

Gambrinus Grote Markt 13 ☎ 016 20 12 38. The food
may be uninspiring, but this handsome old café, with its
1890s leather banquettes, chandeliers and murals, beats
all its rivals for decor. Has a pleasant pavement terrace too.

Mon–Sat from 10am.

Il Pastaio Parijsstraat 33 ☎ 016 23 09 02, 🖰 ilpastaio
.be. Small, informal café-restaurant serving authentic
Italian cuisine at very affordable prices – ravioli from €18,
lasagne €16. Downstairs is a *traiteur* for takeaway. Tues–
Sat 10am–10pm.

Lukemieke Vlamingenstraat 55 ☎ 016 22 97 05,
🖰 lukemieke.be. Long-established vegetarian café
housed in attractive premises and with a good line in daily
specials at around €9. Verdant garden terrace for outside
eating, too. Mon–Fri noon–2pm & 6–8.30pm.

Hasselt

HASSELT, the capital of the province of **Limburg**, is a busy, modern town that acts as
the administrative centre for the surrounding region. A pleasant but unremarkable
place, the roughly circular city centre fans out from a series of small **interlocking
squares**, with surprisingly few old buildings as evidence of its medieval foundation. To
compensate for this lack of obvious appeal, the local authority has spent millions of
euros on lavish and imaginative prestige projects, from an excellent range of indoor and
outdoor sports facilities to a **cultural complex** that aims to attract some of the world's
finest performers. Hasselt also holds a full complement of museums, among which the
Nationaal Jenevermuseum is the pick.

Nationaal Jenevermuseum

Witte Nonnenstraat 19, about 500m north of the Grote Markt • April–Oct Tues–Sun 10am–5pm; Nov–March Sat & Sun10am–5pm • €6 •
☎ 011 23 98 50, 🖰 jenevermuseum.be

The **Nationaal Jenevermuseum** occupies an attractively restored nineteenth-century
distillery and its assorted displays explore the history of Belgium's favourite liquor,
jenever, which is a type of gin. The museum is stuffed with jenever-related artefacts
– from stone jars and shot glasses through to advertising posters and brand labels – and
provides lots of interesting details: how in good times it was made from corn, in bad
times from molasses, and how the government was periodically concerned with the
effect it had on the efficiency of the average Belgian worker.

ARRIVAL AND INFORMATION   HASSELT

By train and bus Hasselt's train and adjoining bus station
are a 10min walk from the Grote Markt: turn right out of
the train station and proceed down Stationsplein/
Bampslaan to the inner ring road; here, cross the road, veer
to the right and follow Ridder Portmansstraat and its
continuation, Havermarkt.
Destinations by train Antwerp (hourly; 1hr 10min);

Leuven (every 30min; 50min); Liège (hourly; 50min); Lier
(hourly; 1hr); St-Truiden (hourly; 15min); Tongeren (hourly;
20min).
Tourist information To the east of the Grote Markt at
Maastrichterstraat 59 (April–Oct Mon–Fri 9am–6pm, Sat
10am–6pm, Sun 10am–6pm; Nov–March same hours
except Sun 10am–4pm; ☎ 011 23 95 40, 🖰 hasselt.eu).

ACCOMMODATION AND EATING

De Kwizien Jeneverplein ☎ 011 24 23 44,
🖰 dekwizien.be. Smart and lively, bistro-style
restaurant with an imaginative menu – try the hare or
rabbit. Set menus are the order of the day with two
courses at €64 in the evening, half that at lunch times.
Located a few metres from the Nationaal Jenevermuseum
(see p.214). Mon, Thurs, Fri & Sun noon–2pm & 6.30–

9.30pm, Sat 6.30–9.30pm.
Radisson Blu Torenplein 8 ☎ 011 77 00 00,
🖰 radissonblu.com. Among Hasselt's several hotels, this is
perhaps the most comfortable, its spick-and-span modern
rooms occupying a large and conspicuous tower block a
short walk southeast of the Grote Markt. Has spa facilities
too. **€95**

Tongeren

Engaging **TONGEREN**, about 20km southeast of Hasselt, is a small and amiable market town on the border of Belgium's language divide. It's also – and this is its main claim to fame – the oldest town in Belgium, built on the site of a **Roman camp** that guarded the road to Cologne. Its early history was plagued by misfortune – it was destroyed by the Franks and razed by the Vikings – but it did prosper during the Middle Ages in a modest sort of way as a dependency of the bishops of Liège. Nowadays, it's hard to imagine a more relaxing town, quiet for most of the week except on Sunday mornings (from 7am), when the area around Leopoldwal and the Veemarkt is taken over by the stalls of a vast **flea and antiques market**, one of the country's largest.

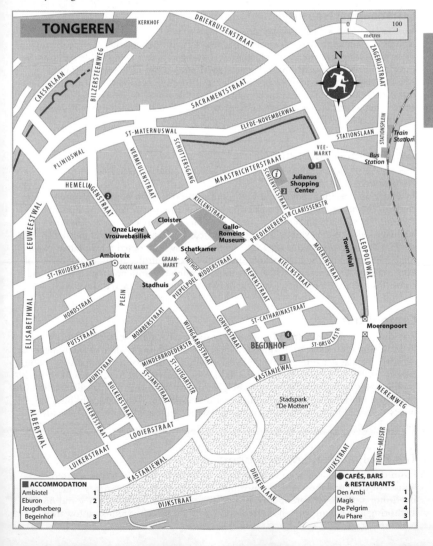

3

■ ACCOMMODATION	
Ambiotel	1
Eburon	2
Jeugdherberg	
Begeinhof	3

● CAFÉS, BARS & RESTAURANTS	
Den Ambi	1
Magis	2
De Pelgrim	4
Au Phare	3

Onze Lieve Vrouwebasiliek

Grote Markt • Daily 9am–5pm • Free

Shadowing the Grote Markt, the mostly Gothic **Onze Lieve Vrouwebasiliek** (Basilica of Our Lady) towers over the town with an impressive symmetrical elegance, its assorted gargoyles, elaborate pinnacles and intricate tracery belying its piecemeal construction: it's the eleventh- to sixteenth-century outcome of an original fourth-century foundation, which was the first church north of the Alps to be dedicated to the Virgin. Still very much in use, the yawning interior, with its high, vaulted nave, has preserved an element of Catholic mystery, its holiest object a bedecked, medieval, walnut statue of Our Lady of Tongeren – "**Mariabeeld**" – which stands in the transept surrounded by candles and overhung by a gaudy canopy.

Schatkamer (Treasury)

Graanmarkt • April–Sept Mon 1.30–5pm, Tues–Sun 10am–noon & 1.30–5pm • €4

Round the side of the church on the Graanmarkt is the **Schatkamer**, one of the region's most interesting, crowded with reliquaries, monstrances and reliquary shrines from as early as the tenth century. Three artefacts stand out – a beautiful sixth-century Merovingian buckle; a pious, haunting eleventh-century *Head of Christ*; and an intricate, bejewelled, thirteenth-century *Reliquary Shrine of the Martyrs of Trier*, celebrating a large group of German Christians killed at the hands of the Romans in the third century AD.

Gallo-Romeins Museum

Kielenstraat • Tues–Fri 9am–5pm, Sat & Sun 10am–6pm • €7, extra for temporary exhibitions • ☎ 012 67 03 30, ⓦ gallo-romeinsmuseum.be

In a large and beetling modern building, the ambitious **Gallo-Romeins Museum** tracks through the history of Tongeren from prehistoric times to the fall of the Roman Empire. The displays are almost exclusively in Flemish, but a scholarly, English-language guide to the exhibits is available for free at reception. Perhaps inevitably, some sections are light on original artefacts – and here they have opted for dioramas (with mixed results) – but the best section, dealing with the culture, attitudes and beliefs of **Roman Tongeren**, is supported by all manner of remains, from pottery, glassware and coins through to tombstones, a mosaic or two and chunks of carved stonework.

Grote Markt

Presiding over the **Grote Markt** is a haughty statue of Ambiorix, with his tumbling locks, bushy moustache and winged helmet. Erected in the middle of the nineteenth century, the statue commemorates a local chieftain who gave the Romans a drubbing here in 54 BC – but whatever he looked like, he surely didn't look much like this, his "noble savage" visage owing more to Belgian nationalism than historical accuracy. On the Grote Markt also is the eighteenth-century **Stadhuis**, whose graceful lines are nicely balanced by an external staircase, the whole caboodle imitative of the town hall in Liège.

The Begijnhof and Moerenpoort

From the Grote Markt, it's a five-minute stroll to the pretty cottages and terraced houses of the **Begijnhof**, which was founded in the thirteenth century. The Begijnhof abuts the **Moerenpoort**, one of Tongeren's six medieval gates and now anchoring a surviving stretch of medieval city wall, which extends up towards Clarissenstraat.

ARRIVAL, GETTING AROUND AND INFORMATION TONGEREN

By train and bus Tongeren's train and adjoining bus station are a 5–10min walk from the Grote Markt.

Destinations by train Antwerp (hourly; 1hr 30min); Hasselt (hourly; 20min); Liège (hourly; 30min); Leuven (hourly; 1hr 10min); St-Truiden (hourly; 55min).

By bike Tourist information rents out bikes (€5 a day, plus €10 deposit) and Vespa scooters (€59/€250). They also sell cycling maps (see box below).

Tourist information is in the Julianus Shoppingcenter, off Maastrichterstraat (April–June & Sept Mon–Fri 8.30am–noon & 1–5pm, Sat & Sun 9.30am–5pm; July & Aug Mon–Fri 8.30am–5pm, Sat & Sun 9.30am–5pm; Oct–March Mon–Fri 8.30am–noon & 1–5pm, Sat & Sun 10am–4pm; ☎012 80 00 70, ⊛tongeren.be).

ACCOMMODATION

★**Ambiotel** Veemarkt 2 ☎012 26 29 50, ⊛ambiotel .be. Modern, three-star hotel with 22 spacious rooms that somehow manages to be quite beguiling – it's not the decor, which is routine, but the small-town flavour of the place. **€120**

Eburon De Schiervelstraat 10 ☎012 23 01 99, ⊛eburonhotel.be. Slightly self-conscious boutique hotel with lots of bells and whistles, from flatscreen TVs to rainforest showers. The design is firmly modernist, with acres of white and grey intercepted by streaks of red and

brown, all shoehorned into a grand eighteenth-century building that started out as a convent. **€120**

Jeugdherberg Begeinhof St-Ursulastraat 1 ☎012 39 13 70, ⊛jeugdherbergen.be. Designed with groups in mind, this HI hostel has over seventy beds in four- to twelve-berth rooms, plus a communal lounge, a bar and internet access. Occupies a creatively modernized older building in the Begijnhof. Breakfast is included in the overnight rate. Dorm **€18**

EATING AND DRINKING

★**Den Ambi** Veemarkt 2 ☎012 26 29 50. Modern café-restaurant, where the home-style cooking is really very tasty and the seafood an absolute treat. Reckon on €21 for a main course. Part of the *Ambiotel* (see above). Daily 9am–11pm, kitchen till 9pm.

Magis Hemelingenstraat 23 ☎012 74 34 64, ⊛restaurantmagis.be. Smart and well-regarded restaurant in a sympathetically modernized nineteenth-century mansion with a garden terrace out the back. The menu is international, the tendency nouvelle. Particularly strong on local produce, with main courses averaging €30. Mon, Thurs, Fri & Sun noon–2pm & 7–9.30pm, Sat 7–9.30pm.

De Pelgrim Brouwersstraat 9 ☎012 23 83 22. This infinitely cosy bar-cum-café occupies antique, wood-beamed premises in the Begijnhof. Offers a good range of bottled beers. Mon 6–11pm & Thurs–Sun 11am–11pm.

Au Phare Grote Markt 21 ☎0497 99 83 38. Nothing much seems to have changed here for decades – as of yore, there are ornamental plates on the pelmet and rugs on the tables. The beer menu is wide-ranging and, if you're really lucky, you'll get Jim Reeves on the sound system rather than Engelbert Humperdinck. Who knows how much longer the place will survive in its present format, so enjoy it while you can. Daily from 10am till late.

CYCLING THE HASPENGOUW

Filling out the southern part of the **province of Limburg**, in between Tongeren and St-Truiden, is the **Haspengouw**, an expanse of gently undulating land, whose fertile soils are especially suited to fruit growing. The area is at its prettiest during **cherry-blossom** time, but at any time of the year its quiet lanes, cycle routes and tiny villages make for a pleasant detour, with **Tongeren** the obvious base, especially as bicycles can be rented from that town's tourist information (see above). As for particular targets, the cream of the crop is **Zoutleeuw**, some 30km from Tongeren and 7km west of St-Truiden. This tiny hamlet on the peripheries of the Haspengouw boasts splendid, pre-Reformation **St-Leonarduskerk** (April–Sept Tues–Sun 2–5pm; Oct Sat & Sun 2–5pm; €2.50), which somehow managed to avoid the attentions of both the Protestants and the Napoleonic army. The church is crammed with the accumulated treasures of several hundred years, from reliquaries and religious paintings through to **medieval carvings**, including a statue of St Catherine of Alexandria, shown merrily stomping on the Roman Emperor Maxentius, who had her put to death.

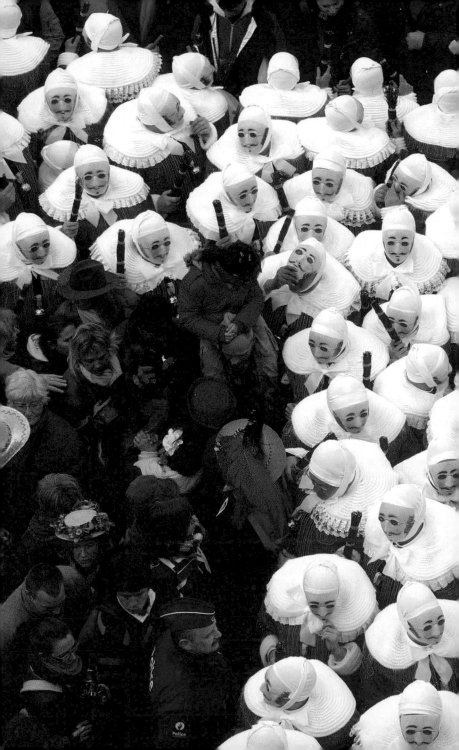

Hainaut and Wallonian Brabant

BINCHE CARNIVAL

Hainaut and Wallonian Brabant

South of Brussels, the western reaches of Wallonia comprise the province of Hainaut and the French-speaking portion of Brabant, Brabant Walloon. The area has its beauty spots, with plenty of rolling farmland and wooded hills dotted across the entire region, but industry sets the general tone, especially between Mons and Charleroi, although even here the landscape is green and pleasant, and puckered with grassed-over spoil tips from the region's coal-mining heyday. In the western part of the province, close to the French border, Tournai is something of a highlight – once part of France, it is now a vibrant, unpretentious town with a number of decent museums, some good restaurants and a magnificent cathedral.

East of Tournai, the town of **Mons** is perhaps Hainaut's nicest base, with a vibrant street life and beautiful main square, and is perfectly placed to see some of the region's more scattered attractions, including the zoo at **Pairi Daiza**. East again, **Binche** is a humdrum place best known for its explosive February carnival, and its carnival museum. To the north of here, in Wallonian Brabant, the various battlefield sights at **Waterloo** are the main draw, though there's also the fabulous **Hergé Museum** in the otherwise undistinguished town of **Louvain-la-Neuve**; the Romanesque abbey of Ste-Gertrude in **Nivelles**; and the elegiac ruins of the **Abbaye de Villers**, in a wooded valley on the edge of the town of **Villers-la-Ville**. To the south, the industrial and engineering centre of **Charleroi** is easily the biggest city in Hainaut. Few would call it pretty, but it is gallantly attempting to reinvent itself, and there are a couple of worthwhile attractions on its southern outskirts: namely, an excellent museum of photography and the mining museum of **Bois du Cazier**. South of Charleroi, the rural **Botte du Hainaut** is actually an extension of the Ardennes and is named for its shape, as it juts boot-like into France; most of the "boot" is part of Hainaut, but it also incorporates a narrow slice of Namur province. Largely bypassed by the Industrial Revolution, the area is a quiet corner of the country, its undulating farmland and forests dotted with the smallest of country towns. Among them, **Chimay**, with its castle and pretty old centre, is the most diverting, and is well endowed with facilities for holidaymakers, since hundreds of vacationing Belgians hunker down in cottages in the surrounding countryside.

Tournai

TOURNAI is one of Wallonia's most interesting and enjoyable towns, its ancient centre latticed by narrow cobbled streets and straddling the sluggish, canalized River Escaut (Scheldt in Dutch). Its pride and joy is its magnificent medieval **cathedral**, a seminal

ABBAYE DE VILLERS

Highlights

❶ Cathédrale Notre-Dame, Tournai One of the most stunning cathedrals in the whole of Belgium. **See p.224**

❷ Pairi Daiza Voted the best zoo and theme park in Belgium in recent years – and justifiably so. Not just for kids. **See p.233**

❸ Binche Carnival Probably the liveliest, most colourful carnival in the country. **See p.235**

❹ Abbaye de Villers The ruins of this Cistercian abbey comprise one of the region's most evocative sights. **See p.238**

❺ Bois du Cazier Perhaps the best insight into the region's industrial heritage. **See p.244**

❻ Chimay A charming country town with a picture-postcard Grand-Place. **See p.247**

HIGHLIGHTS ARE MARKED ON THE MAP ON PP.222–223

HAINAUT AND WALLONIAN BRABANT

HIGHLIGHTS

1. Cathédrale Notre-Dame, Tournai
2. Pairi Daiza
3. Binche Carnival
4. Abbaye de Villers
5. Bois du Cazier
6. Chimay

N

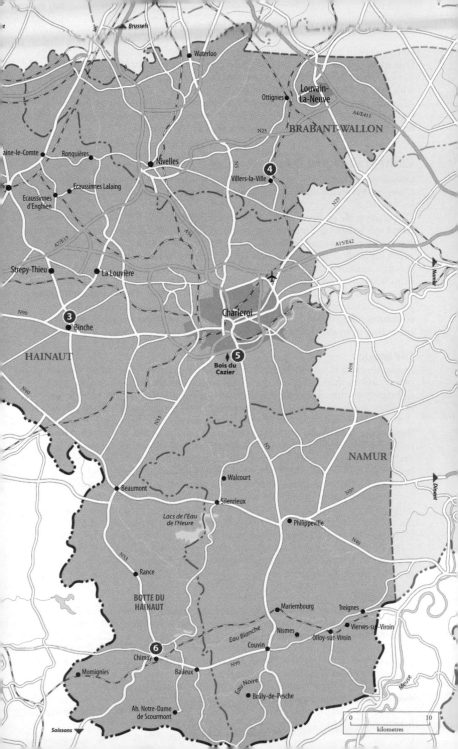

construction whose stirring amalgamation of Romanesque and early Gothic styles influenced the design of other churches far and wide. But the town centre also holds lots of handsome eighteenth-century **mansions** in the French style – stately structures with double doors, stone lower and brick upper storeys, and, often as not, fancy balconies and a central courtyard. Add to this a handful of **museums** and several decent **restaurants**, and you've reason enough to stay a night or two, especially as tourism here remains distinctly low-key, with barely a tour bus in sight.

Cathédrale Notre-Dame

Cathedral place de l'Evêché 1 • April–Oct Mon–Fri 9am–6pm, Sat & Sun 9am–noon & 1–6pm; Nov–March 9.15am–noon & 2–5pm • Free • **Treasury** April–Oct Mon–Fri 10am–6pm, Sat & Sun 1–6pm; Nov–March Mon–Fri 9.30am–noon & 2–5pm, Sat & Sun 2–5pm • €2.50

Dominating the skyline with its distinctive five towers, Tournai's **Cathédrale Notre-Dame** was built with the wealth of the flourishing wool and stone trades – a seminal construction whose stirring amalgamation of Romanesque and early Gothic styles was much imitated all along the Escaut valley. The present cathedral is the **third church** on this site, most of it completed in the latter half of the twelfth century, although the choir was reconstructed in the middle of the thirteenth. The cathedral is under restoration at the moment, and is likely to be so for some time, but in the meantime you should inspect the **west facade**, on place de l'Evêché, with its three tiers of **sculptures** filling out the back of the medieval portico, before entering the church either here or by the **main entrance** on the south side.

The interior

Inside, the **nave** is part of the original structure, erected in 1171, as are the intricately carved capitals that distinguish the lowest set of columns, but the vaulted roof is eighteenth century. The **choir** was the first manifestation of the Gothic style in Belgium, and its too-slender pillars later had to be reinforced at the base: the whole choir still leans slightly to one side due to the unstable soil beneath. In front, the Renaissance **rood screen** is a flamboyant marble extravaganza by Cornelis Floris, embellished by biblical events such as Jonah being swallowed by the whale. The majestic late twelfth-century **transepts** are the cathedral's most impressive – and most beautiful – feature, imparting a lovely diffuse light through their many windows, some of which (in the south transept) hold superb sixteenth-century **stained glass** depicting semi-mythical scenes from far back in Tournai's history. Opposite, in the north transept, is an intriguing twelfth-century mural, a pockmarked cartoon strip relating the story of St Margaret, a shepherdess martyred on the orders of the Emperor Diocletian. Its characters are set against an exquisite blue background reminiscent of – and clearly influenced by – Byzantine church paintings. Take a look, too, at **Rubens'** characteristically bold *The Deliverance of Souls from Purgatory*, which hangs, newly restored, beside the adjacent chapel.

The treasury

Be sure also to see the **treasury**, whose three rooms kick off with a splendid wood-panelled, eighteenth-century meeting room and a chapel hung with a rare example of a medieval **Arras tapestry**, made up of fourteen panels depicting the lives of St Piat and of St Eleuthère, the first bishop of Tournai. Next door, have a look at the silver and gilded copper *chasse de Notre-Dame*, completed in 1205 by Nicolas de Verdun and festooned with relief figures clothed in fluidly carved robes, and a wonderful early sixteenth-century *Ecce Homo* by Quentin Matsys, showing Christ surrounded by monstrous faces. The treasury also once hosted a gem-studded Byzantine Cross, which was stolen in a high-profile armed raid a couple of years ago – hence the current heightened security.

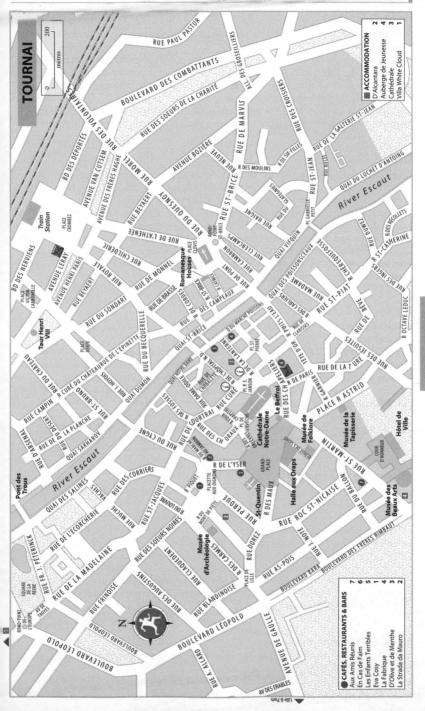

TOURNAI

0 — 200 metres

ACCOMMODATION
D'Alcantara	2
Auberge de Jeunesse	4
Cathédrale	3
Villa White Cloud	1

CAFÉS, RESTAURANTS & BARS
Aux Amis Réunis	7
En Cas de Faim	6
Les Enfants Terribles	5
Eva Cosy	1
La Fabrique	4
D'Olive et de Menthe	3
La Strada da Mauro	2

Lille & Paris

4

Beffroi (Belfry)

rue Vieux Marché-aux-Poteries 14 • April–Oct Tues–Sun 10am–5.30pm & 2–6.30pm; Nov–March Tues–Sat 10am–noon & 2–5pm, Sun 2–5pm • €2.10 • ☎ 069 22 20 45

A short stroll from the cathedral, virtually on the corner of the Grand-Place, **Le Beffroi** or Belfry is the oldest such structure in Belgium, its lower portion dating from 1200. The bottom level once held a prison cell, and the minuscule **balcony** immediately above was where public proclamations were announced. Climb the 257 steps to the top, where the **carillon tower** has been subjected to all sorts of architectural tinkering from the sixteenth through to the nineteenth century – hence its ungainly appearance.

Grand-Place

A few steps west of the belfry, the **Grand-Place** is an open and airy piazza, the middle of which is occupied by a **statue** of Christine de Lalaing, in heroic "to the ramparts" pose, clad in armour and holding a hatchet. A local aristocrat, Lalaing led the locals in a last-ditch stand against the Spanish Habsburg army in 1581, but to no avail. The south side of the Grand-Place holds the seventeenth-century **Halle aux Draps** (Cloth Hall), a crisply symmetrical edifice whose facade is graced by slender Renaissance pilasters and a row of miniature lions on the balustrade. The hall's far, western end is anchored by the impressive bulk of the church of **St-Quentin**, an impressive, bare stone, Romanesque creation from the twelfth century.

Musée de Folklore

réduit des Sions 36 • Mon & Wed–Sun 9.30am–12.30pm & 2–5.30pm; Nov–March Mon & Wed–Sat 10am–noon & 2–5pm, Sun 10am–noon • €2.60 • ☎ 069 22 40 69

Just off the Grande-Place, the amiably old-fashioned **Musée de Folklore** is one of the city centre's best museums, housed in an antique high-gabled brick mansion known as the Maison Tournaisienne and crammed with a treasure-trove of objects. There are reconstructions of various workshops and domestic rooms, a mock-up of a **tavern** with its old-fashioned *jeu de fer* game (a sort of cross between billiards and boules), and exhibits of Tournai's blue and white pottery. Look also at the replica **cloister** on the first floor, where one of the cells exhibits the pathetic tokens left by those impoverished parents forced to leave their children with the nuns; and a **scale model** of Tournai in 1701 on the top floor.

Musée de la Tapisserie

place Reine Astrid 9 • April–Oct Mon & Wed–Sun 9.30am–12.30pm & 2–5.30pm; Nov–March Mon & Wed–Sat 10am–noon & 2–5pm, Sun 10am–noon • €2.60 • ⓦ www.tamat.be

Just southeast of the Grand-Place, the **Musée de la Tapisserie** features a small selection of old tapestries alongside modern work, temporary exhibitions and a **restoration workshop**. Tournai was among the most important pictorial tapestry centres in Belgium in the fifteenth and sixteenth centuries, producing characteristically huge works juxtaposing many characters and several episodes of history. The pick here are three tapestries recounting Homer's tale of Hercules and his dealings with Laomedon, the shifty king of Troy – they're still richly coloured, and crammed with detail and wry observation.

Musée des Beaux Arts

enclos St Martin • April–Oct Mon & Wed–Sun 9.30am–12.30pm & 2–5.30pm; Nov–March Mon & Wed–Sat 10am–noon & 2–5pm, Sun 10am–noon • €2.60 • ☎ 069 33 24 31

On the southern edge of the town centre, behind the eighteenth-century Hôtel de Ville, the **Musée des Beaux Arts** occupies an elegant Art Nouveau edifice designed by

> ## PONT DES TROUS AND MONT ST-AUBERT
>
> A ten-minute walk north of the town centre, the **Pont des Trous** still spans the River Escaut, and is the only surviving part of Tournai's medieval ramparts. It's the starting point for a walk out into the surrounding countryside to **Mont St-Aubert**, 6km or so north of town. There are smashing views from the top of this 149m hill, which was long the focus of all sorts of pagan shenanigans until the Catholic Church adopted it, naming it after St Aubert, an eighth-century French saint who founded France's hilltop Mont St-Michel. Free walking **maps** are available from Tournai tourist office (see below), and the whole excursion takes about three hours.

Victor Horta, and its central hall and radiating rooms provide a suitably attractive setting for a small but enjoyable collection of mainly Belgian painting, from the Flemish primitives to the twentieth century. The works here are regularly rotated, and its but the first room on the left is usually devoted to the nineteenth-century medievalist **Louis Gallait** (whose statue is in the gardens outside), two of whose vast and graphic historical canvases – the *Plague of 1092* and the *Abdication of Charles V* – cover virtually a whole wall each. Other works you may see include an exquisite *Virgin and Child* by Rogier van der Weyden, *St Donatius* by Jan Gossaert, a winter scene by **Pieter Bruegel the Younger** and a variety of French and Belgian nineteenth-century paintings: works by Manet and Monet; gritty working-class scenes by Constantin Meunier; and paintings and drawings by **James Ensor**.

Musée d'Archéologie

rue des Carmes 8 • April–Oct Mon & Wed–Sun 9.30am–12.30pm & 2–5.30pm; Nov–March Mon & Wed–Sat 10am–noon & 2–5pm, Sun 10am–noon • €2.10

Inhabiting a rambling old brick building, the **Musée d'Archéologie** displays a hotchpotch of local archeological finds, including a heavy-duty Gallo-Roman lead sarcophagus downstairs and, upstairs, the skeleton of a horse and a smattering of rare Merovingian artefacts, from weapons to brooches and **bee-shaped jewellery**. The latter is thought to have come from the tomb of the Merovingian king Childeric, which was accidentally unearthed in 1653 on place Clovis, just north of the river. Interestingly, Napoleon adopted the Merovingian bee as his symbol in preference to the **fleur-de-lys**.

ARRIVAL AND INFORMATION　　　　　　　　　　　TOURNAI

By train Tournai's train and bus stations are located on the northern edge of town, about a 10min walk from the centre.
Destinations by train Ath (every 30min; 20min); Brussels (every 30min; 1hr); Mons (every 30min; 30–45min).

Tourist information The tourist office is opposite the cathedral at place Paul-Emile Janson 1 (April–Oct daily 9.30am–6pm; Nov–March daily 9.30am–12.30pm & 1.15–5pm; ☎ 069 22 20 45, ⍟ visittournai.be).

ACCOMMODATION

D'Alcantara rue des Bouchers St-Jacques 2 ☎ 069 21 26 48, ⍟ hotelalcantara.be. Friendly, family-run hotel located in an ingeniously converted Spanish mansion, with 25 modern rooms behind its eighteenth-century brick and stone facade, a pleasant courtyard garden and terrace, and some parking. The most welcoming option in town, so book in advance. **€99**

Auberge de Jeunesse rue St-Martin 64 ☎ 069 21 61 36, ⍟ laj.be. Occupying an attractive old mansion, a couple of minutes' walk south of the Grand-Place, this is a well-cared-for, friendly hostel. It has around one hundred beds, the majority in dormitories of five or six,

though there are also a handful of two- and four-bunk rooms. The restaurant serves breakfast, lunch and dinner. Disabled access. Closed Jan. Dorm €17.50, private **€43**

Cathédrale place St-Pierre 2 ☎ 069 25 00 00, ⍟ hotel-cathedrale.be. Right in the centre of town, close to the cathedral, this modern, medium-sized hotel offers over fifty comfortable rooms with all conveniences, including free wi-fi, and a decent breakfast. **€80**

Villa White Cloud rue de la Station 145, Néchin ☎ 0479 93 76 45, ⍟ villawhitecloud.com. Just outside Tournai in the village of Néchin, this place describes itself as

4

a prestigious bed and breakfast, and that it certainly is. But what it's most famous for is being part of French actor Gérard Depardieu's burgeoning business empire in the Tournai area. Whether you get to see Gérard or not, it's a lovely place to stay, with four large and beautifully furnished double rooms and one suite. **€135**

EATING AND DRINKING

Aux Amis Réunis rue St-Martin 89. Dating back to 1911, this traditional Belgian bar has a good range of domestic beers, and its wood-panelled walls and antique feel make it one of the town's most agreeable watering holes. It also has a table for *jeu de fer* (a cross between billiards and boules). Mon–Sat 10am–1am.

En Cas de Faim rue des Chapeliers 50 ☎ 069 56 04 84. A Belgian restaurant with a Norwegian chef who specializes in Mediterranean cuisine. All the food is seasonal and freshly prepared, though the service can be somewhat haphazard. Starters around €9, main courses €15–18. Mon, Tues & Thurs noon–2.30pm, Fri & Sat noon–2.30pm & 7–9.30pm.

Les Enfants Terribles rue de l'Yser 35 ☎ 069 84 48 22, ⓦ enfants-terribles.be. Just off the Grand-Place, with brasserie-style food – steaks, brochettes and salads – in a contemporary, minimalist setting. You can watch the chef at work on the television screen behind the bar. Starters €8–14, main course €13–20. Mon–Sat noon–3pm & 7–11pm.

★**Eva Cosy** rue Piquet 6 ☎ 069 77 22 59. Cosy café-tearoom that's perfect for breakfast, lunch or afternoon tea, with lots of different teas and coffee, home-made cakes, a salad buffet (€12.50–14.50), soup (€5, with bread) and sandwiches (€10.50, with salad). Mon–Fri 8.30am–6pm, Sat 9am–6pm, Sun 3–6pm.

La Fabrique quai du Marché aux Poissons 13b ☎ 069 21 66 72. This busy, boisterous bar is one of the town centre's best places for a drink, with a terrace where you can sip a beer by the river. Daily 10am–1am.

D'Olive et de Menthe quai du Marché aux Poissons 5 ☎ 069 77 69 00. The people who run this riverfront North African restaurant used to have a place down the quai, but this is their latest, more refined venture, with excellent, authentic tagines and couscous for €16–27 served in a lovely serene environment. Daily noon–3pm & 7–10pm.

La Strada da Mauro rue de l'Yser 2 ☎ 069 23 51 69, ⓦ lastradadamauro.be. Brash, busy southern Italian that serves good pizzas cooked in a stone oven (from €7) and giant bowls of pasta (from €9). Mon & Thurs–Sun 11.45am–3pm & 7–11pm, Tues noon–3pm.

Mons and around

Perhaps the most attractive of Hainaut's historic towns – particularly since a thorough sprucing-up for its 2015 stint as **European Capital of Culture** – MONS, spread over the hill that gave it its name, is most familiar to many people for its military associations: it was the site of battles that for Britain marked the beginning and end of **World War I**, and in 1944 the location of the first big American victory on Belgian soil in the **liberation campaign**. It has also been a key **military base** since 1967, when NATO, including SHAPE (Supreme Headquarters Allied Powers in Europe), was expelled from Paris by Charles de Gaulle. SHAPE subsequently moved to **Maisières**, just outside Mons, and both continue to provide employment for hundreds of Americans and other NATO nationals locally, their presence giving the place a bustling feel that belies its size. With a few decent places to stay, it also makes a good **base** for much of the region: railways and roads radiate out from Mons in all directions, putting central Hainaut's key attractions within easy reach and making for several enjoyable day-trips.

PLUG STREET

Thirteen kilometres south of Ieper (see p.138–143), though a part of Hainaut province, "Plug Street" was the tommies' name for **Ploegsteert**, a village in a tiny, almost stranded French-speaking enclave on the Belgium-France border. It was on the front line for the majority of World War I but remained in British hands throughout (apart from one brief interval), and is perhaps best known as the site of the **Christmas Day 1914 truce**, when troops on both sides laid down their weapons and convened for a game of football in no-man's land. There are several **British war cemeteries** in the woods to the north of the village, and you can stop at the circular Ploegsteert Memorial, opposite the Royal Berkshire regiment cemetery on the Messines road, where the **Last Post** is still sounded on the first Friday of every month at 7pm.

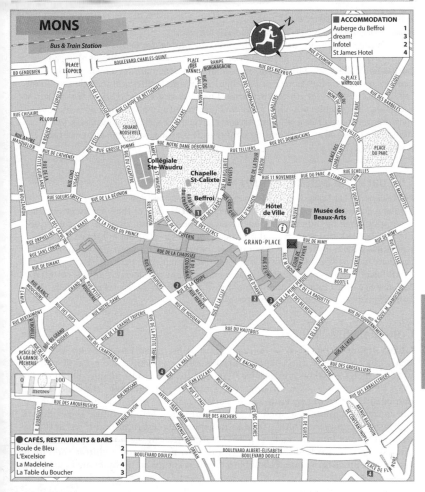

Grand-Place

Mons zeroes in on its **Grand-Place**, a long, elegant square flanked by terrace cafés and framed by a medley of substantial stone merchants' houses and narrower brick buildings, both old and new. The fifteenth-century **Hôtel de Ville** dominates the square, a considerably altered building whose tiny cast-iron **monkey** on the front wall is reputed to bring at least a year of happiness to all who stroke him with their left hand – hence his bald, polished crown. Inside, some of the rooms are open for guided tours in July and August, though the odd fancy fireplace, tapestry and painting are hardly essential viewing. The porch of the double-doored gateway on the front of the Hôtel de Ville carries several commemorative **plaques**. One is for the food sent to the town by the Americans at the end of World War II, another recalls the Canadian brigade who liberated Mons in 1918, and yet another – the most finely executed – honours the bravery of the Irish Lancers, who defended the town in 1914. The tunnel on the far side of the courtyard brings you out to a small enclosed **garden** that's not only a peaceful retreat from the buzz of the square outside: the flanking buildings are also soon to be home to a museum detailing the town's colourful annual event, the **Doudou** (see box, p.231).

Musée des Beaux-Arts

rue Neuve 8 • Tues–Sun 10am–6pm • €9 • ☎ 065 40 53 12, ⓦ www.bam.mons.be

Around the corner from the Hôtel de Ville, the **Musée des Beaux-Arts** occupies an impressive modern building and puts on regular **contemporary shows** alongside its **permanent collection**, which comprises mainly Belgian paintings from the sixteenth century onwards. High points of this regularly rotated collection include a striking *Ecce Homo* by the fifteenth-century artist Dieric Bouts, a *Virgin and Child* by Jan Gossaert, the mischievous *Soup Eater* by Frans Hals, and a selection of works by the local Expressionists Pierre Paulus, Arsene Detry and Fernand Gommaerts, who depicted Mons and its surrounding countryside and industrial landscapes in the 1920s and 1930s.

The park and beffroi (belfry)

Park May to mid-Sept Tues–Sun 10am–6pm • Free • **Chapelle St-Calixte** Tues–Sun noon–6pm

To the southwest of the Grand-Place, **rue des Clercs** is one of the prettiest streets in town, shadowed by old mansions as it weaves around the hill that was once occupied by the medieval castle. At the end of a steep lane, the top of the hill now holds a miniature **park** and the town's Baroque **beffroi** or belfry (no admission), from where there are fine views over the town and its surroundings. The park also incorporates a small tower that is pretty much all that remains of the medieval castle and the **Chapelle St-Calixte**, whose crypt was used as a bomb shelter in World War II and which has a handful of artefacts and some fresco fragments.

Collégiale Ste-Waudru

Collégiale Ste-Waudru rue du Chapitre 1 • Daily 9am–6pm, till 5pm on Sun • Free • **Treasury** Tues–Sun noon–6pm • €1.50

Below the belfry park, the **Collégiale Ste-Waudru** is a massive and majestic church which displays a striking uniformity in its architecture, most memorably in the long, sweeping lines of the windows and its soaring **Gothic nave**. The church is named after a virtuous seventh-century aristocrat, who dedicated much of her life to the church and founded a small religious community here in Mons. The elaborate, eighteenth-century "**Car d'Or**", used to transport her casket around town in the annual Doudou festival (see box, p.231), can be seen in the north aisle. More interesting is the work of the local sixteenth-century sculptor, architect and builder **Jacques du Broeucq**, whose alabaster rood loft was broken up by French

---

THE ANGELS OF MONS

Mons has figured prominently in both world wars. During **World War I**, in the latter part of August 1914, the British forces here found themselves outnumbered by the advancing Germans to the tune of about twenty to one. The subsequent **Battle of Mons** began on August 26, and the British – in spite of great heroics (the first two Victoria Crosses of the war were awarded here) – were inevitably forced to retreat. The casualties might have been greater, had the troops not been hard-bitten veterans. Meanwhile, back in England, the horror-story writer Arthur Machen wrote an avowedly fictional tale for the *Evening News* in which the retreating troops were assisted by a host of bowmen, the ghosts of Agincourt. Within weeks, rumour had transmogrified Machen's bowmen into the **Angels of Mons**, which had supposedly hovered overhead just at the point when the Germans were about to launch their final attack, causing them to fall back in fear and amazement. Machen himself was amazed at this turn of events, but the angel story was unstoppable, taking on the status of legend, and those soldiers lucky enough to return home obligingly reported similar tales of supernatural happenings on the battlefield. There's a **painting** of the angelic event, by one Marcel Gillis, in the Mons Hôtel de Ville.

THE DOUDOU

Every year, in late May or early June on the weekend before Trinity Sunday, Mons hosts the festival of the Ducasse de Mons, or **Doudou**, which kicks off with a solemn ceremony on the Saturday, when the casket holding the remains of St Waudru is given to the city's mayor. On Sunday morning the casket is processed around the town in a golden carriage – the **Car d'Or** – accompanied by a thousand-odd costumed participants, with everyone joining in to push the carriage back up the hill to the church with one huge shove: failure to get it there in one go brings bad luck. After the relics are safely back in the church, chaos erupts on the Grand-Place, with a battle – known here as "Lumeçon" – between **St George and the Dragon**. St George and his 38 helpers slug it out with the dragon and his entourage – it's considered good luck to grab a hair or ribbon from the dragon's tail, which the crowd tries to do as it whips through the air just above their heads. Inevitably, George and crew always emerge victorious. You can see costumes and find out more about the history of the event in the proposed **Doudou Museum** (⊛ www.museedudoudou.mons.be) behind the town hall, though its opening date is not confirmed.

Revolutionary soldiers in 1797 and is now spread around different parts of the church. These high-relief carvings are wonderful, designed to explain the story of Christ to a largely illiterate congregation: the **north transept** holds the reliefs of the *Resurrection*, the *Ascension* and the *Descent of the Holy Ghost*; the **south transept** has the *Flagellation of Christ* and the *Bearing of the Cross*, as well as Broeucq's memorial plaque; while chapels in the **ambulatory** display other fragments, including *The Last Supper*. Further work is incorporated in the main **altar**, which shows scenes from the Passion of Christ, including another *Last Supper*. The church **treasury** is also of some interest, with the usual reliquaries and statuettes alongside the original shroud of Saint Waudru and the leather bag used to carry her body, along with a later shroud from the twelfth century.

ARRIVAL AND INFORMATION   MONS

By train Mons' new, smart train station and adjacent bus station are on the western edge of the town centre, fronting onto place Léopold. From here, there's a free bus shuttle to the Grand-Place, or it's a 10min walk up the hill to the Grand-Place.
Destinations Ath (hourly; 30min); Brussels (every 30min;

45min); Charleroi-Sud (every 30min; 30min); La Louvière-Sud (hourly; 15min); Tournai (every 30min; 30–45min).
Tourist information The tourist office is in the ground floor of the Hôtel de Ville at Grand-Place 22 (Mon–Sat 10am–6pm, Sun 11am–5pm; ☎ 065 33 55 80, ⊛ visitmons.be).

ACCOMMODATION

Auberge du Beffroi rampe du Château 2 ☎ 065 87 55 70, ⊛ laj.be. Well-equipped, modern HI hostel in a great location, metres from the Grand-Place, at the foot of the belfry. There are self-catering facilities, a bar, car parking and free wi-fi, and 115 beds in 29 one- to four-berth rooms. Dorm **€19.50**, double **€47**
★ **dream!** rue de la Grande Triperie 17 ☎ 065 32 97 20, ⊛ www.dream-mons.be. An ingenious church conversion – to the extent that, apart from the Gothic window tracery and giant columns, you might not realize you're in a church at all – this is Mons' designer hotel, with 48 spacious rooms kitted out in black, white and grey with flatscreen TVs, walk-in showers and bespoke carpets with signature graffiti and doodles. There's a bar serving cocktails, a brasserie and a more upscale restaurant downstairs. Comfy and convenient. **€90**

Infotel rue d'Havré 32 ☎ 065 40 18 30, ⊛ hotelinfotel .be. Set in a refurbished eighteenth-century house with a modern extension, this oddly named but very friendly hotel has nineteen pleasantly appointed rooms, all with free wi-fi. Great location too, just 100m from the Grand-Place, and free parking. **€80**
St James Hotel place de Flandre 8 ☎ 065 72 48 24, ⊛ hotelstjames.be. This small hotel in a solid stone-and-brick nineteenth-century house, a 10min walk east of the Grand-Place, is the closest Mons gets to "boutique", with very comfortable rooms in modernist style, either in the main building or an equally well-appointed garden annexe. Free parking, and wi-fi in the main building. They also rent a number of self-catering apartments nearby. **€90**

EATING AND DRINKING

Boule de Bleu rue de la Coupe 46 ☎ 065 84 58 19, ⓦ bouledebleu.be. Good organic soups, huge salads and filled focaccia alongside a wide selection of teas and organic wines and beers. Coffee desserts served in glasses with ice cream and plenty of cream are especially popular. The interior is rustic and inviting, and there's a covered courtyard in the back, as well as tables on the street. Mon–Thurs 11am–3pm, Fri & Sat 11am–11pm.

L'Excelsior Grand-Place 29 ☎ 065 36 47 15. There is no shortage of bars on the main square, but the leather benches and wooden panelling of this one give it a warm and welcoming feel. Decent food and, like the rest, plenty of tables outside. Daily 8am–1am.

La Madeleine rue de la Halle 42 ☎ 065 35 13 70, ⓦ restolamadeleine.be. Excellent and quite posh fish and seafood restaurant with cool maritime decor and a good wine cellar. Main courses start at a reasonable €22 but rise to around €38, for which they do an excellent bouillabaisse, while *moules marinières* is €25; they also offer fabulous platters of shellfish (six oysters or langoustine from €20, lobster €42). Tues–Sun noon–3pm & 7–11pm.

★ **La Table du Boucher** rue d'Havré 49 ☎ 065 31 68 38, ⓦ www.latableduboucher.be. There's nothing much for veggies, but this is a great little restaurant, serving perfectly cooked steaks, lamb and veal dishes from a blackboard menu. Prices are moderate to high: €10–20 for most starters and averaging around €30 for main courses. Good service, though, and a cosy interior with banquette seats and lots of bottles and wine cases. Daily noon–3pm & 6–11pm, Fri & Sat till midnight.

Around Mons

Mons is a great base for seeing some of the best of Hainaut, with a central position in the province and good transport connections. The region around the town is known as the **Borinage**, a poor, densely populated working-class area that, in the latter half of the nineteenth century, was one of Belgium's three main **coalfields**, an ugly jigsaw of mining villages and spoil tips, though the latter now form not entirely unattractive wooded hillocks that dot the otherwise flattish landscape. A couple of attractions may tempt you out into this post-industrial sprawl, specifically a house that **Vincent van Gogh** once lived in, and the **Grand-Hornu**, a very real remnant of the region's industrial past. East towards Charleroi, the otherwise unremarkable small town of **Binche** is home to Belgium's best-known and most serious **carnival** – and has a museum dedicated to the event – while in the opposite direction, towards Ath (see box, p.234), it's worth a special trip to visit the excellent zoo-cum-theme park of **Pairi Daiza**, beyond which there are the chateaux of **Beloeil** and **Attre** – though on the whole these last two are best visited with your own transport. Finally, to the northeast, there's the **Canal du Centre** and its amazing boat lifts, a UNESCO World Heritage Site that is perhaps the most tangible working manifestation of the region's industrial past.

Vincent van Gogh house

rue du Pavillon 3 · Tues–Sat 10.30am–noon & 1.30–6pm, Sun 10.30am–noon & 2–6pm · ☎ 065 35 56 11 · €2.50 · Bus #1 from outside Mons train station, direction St-Ghislain (every 30min; 10min); the bus stop (ask driver) is 200m from the house

On the southern outskirts of Mons, the suburb of **Cuesmes** was home to Vincent van Gogh from 1879 until the following year, and the tidily restored two-storey brick **house** where he lodged is open to the public. Van Gogh was sent to the Borinage as a missionary, living in acute poverty and helping the villagers in their fight for social justice, and it was here that he first started **drawing** seriously, taking his inspiration from the hard life of the miners – "I dearly love this sad countryside of the Borinage and it will always live with me," he said. Sadly, despite this, there's actually very little to recall his time here – merely a couple of **period rooms** and no original artwork.

Grand-Hornu

rue Saint-Louis 82, Hornu · Tues–Sun 10am–6pm · €8, including Musée des Arts Contemporains · Grand-Hornu ⓦ grand-hornu.eu; Museum ⓦ mac-s.be · Bus #7 or #9 from Mons train station (every 15min; 20min); get off at place Verte, from where it's a 5min walk

Between 1810 and 1830, in the village of Hornu, the French industrialist Henri De Gorge set about building the large complex of offices, stables, workshops, foundries and furnaces that comprises **Grand-Hornu**. De Gorge owned several collieries in the area, so the project made economic sense, but still he opted to build in an elegant version of Neoclassical style and constructed more-than-adequate **workers' houses** just outside, which survive to this day. This progressiveness did not necessarily win the affection of the workers – in 1830 they came close to lynching him during an industrial dispute over wages – but De Gorge's mines, as well as Grand-Hornu, remained in operation until 1954. Thereafter the complex fell into disrepair, but it was revived in the 1990s and, with its large elliptical **courtyard** and derelict **workshops**, it's a compelling slice of nineteenth-century industrial history. The old office buildings on one side now hold the **Musée des Arts Contemporains** (same hours), which has established a reputation for the quality of its temporary exhibitions of contemporary art. There's a bookshop and café, and a nice restaurant too, the latter overlooking the courtyard.

Pairi Daiza

Domaine de Cambron, Brugelette • April–Oct daily 10am–6pm, till 7pm during July & Aug • €27, children €22 • ☎ 068 25 08 50, ⓦ pairidaiza.eu • Pairi Daiza is just off the N56 between Mons and Ath (parking costs €7); by train, Cambron-Casteau station on the Mons-Ath line is a 10min walk away

A large private zoo founded among the ruins of a Cistercian monastery, **Pairi Daiza** is undeniably and justifiably popular. The name means "walled garden" or "paradise" in ancient Persian, and features a lake, beautiful **gardens** and a series of deftly created **habitats** – you could happily spend a whole day and not see anything twice. One zone is dotted with oriental temples and streams crossed by bridges, and has a rope walkway that gives views over the entire park; it's also home to the park's star pair of **pandas**, Hao Hao and Xing Hiu. There's an African habitat, with elephants, rhinos, lions, cheetahs, and giraffes you can pet while they're feeding, and an "Indian Kingdom of Ganesh", where **Indian elephants** are treated to the most sumptuous of enclosures, plus their own swimming pool. There's also a **reptile house** fashioned out of a beached container ship, which you can reach via a fabulous "African village" on stilts. Predictably, places to eat and shop abound, but overall Paira Daiza is what it sets out to be – a *jardin des mondes* that feels quite apart from the world outside and is worth a day of anyone's time, with kids or without.

Beloeil

rue du Chateau 11, Beloeil • April, May, June & Sept Sat & Sun 1–6pm; July & Aug daily 1–6pm • €9, gardens only €4 • ☎ 069 68 94 26, ⓦ chateaudebeloeil.com • Best visited by car, though you can take a train from Mons to Blaton (20min) and a bus from there

Roughly halfway between Mons and Tournai, the château of **Beloeil** broods over the village that bears its name, its long brick and stone facades redolent of the enormous wealth and power of the Ligne family, regional bigwigs since the fourteenth century. This aristocratic clan began by strengthening the medieval fortress built here by their predecessors, subsequently turning it into a commodious **moated castle** that was later remodelled and refined on several occasions. The wings of the present structure date from the late seventeenth century, while the main body, though broadly compatible, was in fact rebuilt after a fire in 1900. Without question a stately building, it has a gloomy air, and the lavish **interior** is stuffed with tapestries, paintings and furniture – the collected indulgences (and endless portraits) of various generations of Lignes. Despite all this grandeur, only one member of the family – **Charles Joseph** (1735–1814) – cuts much historical ice. A diplomat, author and field marshal in the Austrian army, Joseph's pithy comments were much admired by his fellow aristocrats. Several of Beloeil's rooms contain paintings of Charles' life and times, and there's also a small selection of his personal effects, including the **malachite clock** given to him by the Tsar of Russia. Otherwise, the best parts are the **library**, which contains twenty thousand volumes, many ancient and beautifully bound, and the eighteenth-century formal **gardens**, the largest in the country, whose lakes and flower beds stretch away from the house to a symmetrical design by Parisian architect and decorator Jean-Michel Chevotet.

> ### ATH'S DUCASSE
> Just along the rail line from Attre, **Ath** is a run-of-the-mill town that boasts a major claim to fame in its festival, the **Ducasse**, held on the fourth weekend in August and featuring the **"Parade of the Giants"**, in which massive models, representing both folkloric and biblical figures, waggle their way round the town. If you're in the area around this time, don't miss it.

Château d'Attre

avenue du Château 8, Attre • April–June, Sept & Oct Sun 2–6pm; July & Aug Sat & Sun 1–6pm • Park and castle €6.50; park only €3.50 • ☎ 068 45 44 60 • Best visited by car; nearest station is Brugelette, some 3km east of the château, on the Mons-Ath line

Completed in 1752, the elegant, Neoclassical **Château d'Attre**, just to the northeast of Beloeil, was built on the site of a distinctly less comfortable **medieval fortress** on the orders of the count of Gomegnies, chamberlain to Emperor Joseph II. It soon became a favourite haunt of the ruling Habsburg elite – especially the archduchess Marie-Christine of Austria, the governor of the Southern Netherlands.

The château

The original, carefully selected furnishings and decoration have survived pretty much intact, providing an insight into the tastes of the time – from the **sphinxes** framing the doorway and the silk wrappings of the Chinese room through to the extravagant parquet floors, the ornate moulded plasterwork and the archducal room hung with the first **hand-painted wallpaper** ever to be imported into the country, in about 1760. There are also excellent silver, ivory and porcelain pieces, as well as **paintings** by Frans Snyders, a friend of Rubens, and the Frenchman Jean-Antoine Watteau, whose romantic, idealized canvases epitomized early eighteenth-century aristocratic predilections. Neither is the castle simply a display case: it's well cared for and has a lived-in, human feel, in part created by the arrangements of freshly picked flowers chosen to enhance the character of each room.

The park

The surrounding **park** straddles the River Dendre and holds several curiosities, notably a 24m-high **artificial rock** with subterranean corridors and a chalet-cum-hunting lodge on top – all to tickle the fancy of the archduchess. The ruins of a **tenth-century tower**, also in the park, must have pleased her risqué sensibilities too; it was reputed to have been the hideaway of a local villain, a certain Vignon who, disguised as a monk, robbed and ravished passing travellers.

Binche

There's not much to bring you to **BINCHE**, a sleepy little town halfway between Mons and Charleroi, at the southern end of Hainaut's most decayed industrial region. However, it comes to life every year when it hosts perhaps the best and most renowned **carnival** (see box, p.235) in the country, and it's this that provides the main reason for a visit – not just when the carnival's on, but also to take in the **museum** dedicated to this event and to carnivals in general. The museum is at the far end of Binche's **Grand-Place**, a spacious square edged by the onion-domed **Hôtel de Ville**, built in 1555 by Jacques du Broeucq to replace a version destroyed by the French the previous year. Close by, a small **park** marks the site of the town's medieval **ramparts**, which date from the twelfth to the fourteenth centuries and curve impressively around most of the town centre, complete with 27 towers.

Musée International du Carnaval et du Masque

rue de Saint-Moustier 10 • Tues–Fri 9.30am–5pm, Sat & Sun 10.30am–5pm • €6 • ☎ 064 33 57 41, ⊛ www.museedumasque.be

Housed in a former school, the fascinating **Musée International du Carnaval et du Masque** is signalled by a statue of a Gille – one of the figures that dance through the city

---

CARNIVAL IN BINCHE

Carnival has been celebrated in Binche since the fourteenth century. The festivities last for several weeks, getting started in earnest on the Sunday before Shrove Tuesday, when thousands turn out in costume. During the main events on **Shrove Tuesday** itself, the traditional **Gilles** – males born and raised in Binche – appear in clogs and embroidered costumes from dawn onwards, banging drums and stamping on the ground. In the morning they wear "green-eyed" **masks**, dancing in the Grand-Place carrying bunches of sticks to ward off bad spirits. In the afternoon they don their **plumes** – a mammoth piece of headgear made of ostrich feathers – and throw oranges to the crowd as they pass through town in procession. The rituals of the carnival date back to pagan times, but the Gilles were probably inspired by the fancy dress worn by Mary of Hungary's court at a banquet held in honour of Charles V in 1549: Peru had recently been added to the Habsburg Empire, and the courtiers celebrated the conquest by dressing up in (their version of) **Inca gear**.

---

streets during carnival. Naturally the emphasis is on the Binche festivities, and they do a good job of explaining the event with the help of a free **audio guide**, wall-mounted screens and photos that really get across how central carnival is to the town and its people. Costumes and various objects complete the picture and are complemented by an assortment of **masks** and fancy dress from other carnivals around the world – in fact, they claim to have the largest assortment of carnival artefacts in the world.

ARRIVAL AND INFORMATION BINCHE

By train To get to Binche from Mons, take the hourly Charleroi train and change at La Louvière-Sud – allow 40–50min for the whole journey.
Destinations La Louvière-Sud (hourly; 15min).
Tourist information Binche tourist office is located in the Hôtel de Ville on the Grand-Place (Mon–Fri 10am–noon & 1–5pm, Sat & Sun 2–6pm; ☎ 064 33 67 27, ⓦ binche.be), a 10min walk from the train station: take rue Gilles Binchois from the square in front of the station building and keep straight until you reach the end of rue de la Gaieté, where you turn left.

Canal du Centre

To the east of Mons lies one of the quietest corners of Hainaut, a pocket-sized district where drowsy little villages and whitewashed farmhouses dot a bumpy landscape patterned by a maze of narrow country lanes. It's perhaps best known for the **Canal du Centre**, which has flowed through this region since its inception in 1888 to connect the rivers Meuse and Scheldt – a distance of around 20km. Classified as a **UNESCO World Heritage Site**, the canal climbs over 20m overall by means of six locks, and includes a final section that, too steep for locks, can only be climbed by means of four boat lifts, which were built in the late nineteenth and early twentieth centuries and are still in working order and accessible to visitors; you can also visit one of the canal's huge locks at Ronquières.

Strépy-Thieu

rue Raymond Cordier 50, Strépy-Thieu • ☎ 078 05 90 59, ⓦ voiesdeau.hainaut.be • **Boat trips** April–Oct daily 10am & 2pm • 2hr boat trips €14.25; 4hr boat trips €19.25; day-trips taking in Strépy-Thieu and several other lifts €22–24

You can visit the only remaining working boat lift at **Strépy-Thieu**, where you can watch a film showing how the lift was built. During summer, it's possible to scale the lift in a boat, and also to hop on one of the all-day tourist boats that run between here and Ronquières.

Ronquières

route Bacara 1, Ronquières • ☎ 078 05 90 59, ⓦ voiesdeau.hainaut.be • **Tower** April–Oct daily 10am–7pm • €7.50 • **Boat trips** April–June Sat noon, 2pm & 4.30pm; July & Aug Tues, Thurs & Fri noon, 2pm & 4.30pm • €4.50, combined ticket with tower €10

The so-called sloping lock of **Ronquières**, just off the N6 about 15km east of Soignies, is one of the most impressive of the canal's locks – a massive **transporter** lock that, when it was completed in 1968, cut the journey time between Charleroi and Brussels by around seven hours. It's a gargantuan contraption, consisting of two huge water tanks – each 91m long – and a ramp, which together shift barges up or down 68m over a distance of 1.5km. The main **tower** at the top, 125m high, houses the winch room, where you can watch a video describing how the whole thing works and life aboard the barges, as well as getting a bird's-eye view of proceedings. There are also hour-long **boat trips** downstream to Ittre, though the tower should be quite sufficient for all but the most enthusiastic.

Brabant Walloon

To the northeast of Mons you cross the border into **Brabant**, whose southern, French-speaking districts, known as **Brabant Walloon**, form a band of countryside that rolls up to and around **Waterloo**, now pretty much a suburb of Brussels. **Nivelles** is the obvious distraction en route, an amiable, workaday town worth a visit for its interesting church as well as its proximity to the beguiling ruins of the Cistercian abbey at **Villers-la-Ville**, a short car ride away (train travellers have to make the trip via Charleroi). The **Hergé museum**, meanwhile, is the highlight of the otherwise entirely missable new town of Louvain-la-Neuve.

Nivelles

NIVELLES grew up around its **abbey**, which was founded in the seventh century and became one of the most powerful religious houses in Brabant until its suppression by the French Revolutionary Army in 1798. Nowadays, the abbey is recalled by the town's one and only significant sight, the giant bulk of the **Collégiale Ste-Gertrude**.

Collégiale Ste-Gertrude
place Lambert Schiffelers 1 • April–Oct daily 9am–6pm; Nov–March daily 9am–5pm • Free • ⓦ collegiale.be

The **Collégiale Ste-Gertrude**, a vast edifice that utterly dominates the Grande-Place at the heart of the town, was erected as the abbey church in the tenth century. Little is known of Gertrude, but her cult was very popular on account of her supposed gentleness – her symbol is a pastoral staff with a mouse running along it. Built in the **Ottonian style** (the forerunner of Romanesque), with a transept and chancel at each end of the nave, the church itself is a beautiful and unusual construction, in better shape now than it has been for years following a long restoration. The west chancel represents imperial authority, the east papal – an architectural illustration of the tension between the pope and the emperor that defined much of Otto's reign. The simple **interior** is long and lofty, with a nave supported by sturdy pillars, between which sits a flashy oak and marble **pulpit** by the eighteenth-century Belgian artist Laurent Delvaux, who also executed the statues at the western end of the nave and in the apse. The heavily restored, fifteenth-century **wooden wagon** kept nearby is used to carry the coffin of Ste Gertrude in procession through the fields once a year. Unfortunately, the original thirteenth-century casket was destroyed in 1940, but a modern replacement has been made and is kept in the chapel to the right of the eastern choir, and the traditional autumn procession has recently been revived.

> ## VLAAMS BRABANT
> The Flemings claim the lion's share of the Brabant province, and **Vlaams Brabant** (Flemish Brabant) actually encircles the capital, with a narrow corridor of Flemish-speaking communities running round the southern edge of **Brussels** too. The highlights of Vlaams Brabant are covered in Chapter 3 (see pp.210–214).

CLOCKWISE FROM TOP LEFT BOIS DU CAZIER (P.244); HERGÉ MUSEUM (P.239); CHÂTEAU D'ATTRE (P.234); PAIRI DAIZA (P.233) >

By train It's a 10min walk west down from Nivelles' train station along rue de Namur to the U-shaped Grand-Place.

Destinations Brussels (every 30min; 25–40min); Charleroi (every 10min; 20–30min); Ottignies (every 30min; 50min);

Waterloo (every 30min; 15min).

Tourist information The tourist office is a 5min walk up the hill from the Grand-Place at rue des Saintes 48 (daily 8.30am–5pm; ☎ 067 84 08 64, ⓦ tourisme-nivelles.be).

EATING AND DRINKING

Dis Moi Où rue Ste-Anne 5 ☎ 067 64 64 64, ⓦ www .dis-moiou.be. Just off Nivelles' main square this inviting French restaurant isn't cheap but serves excellent food, with lunch menus for €32 and mains for €16–22. Tues–Fri noon–3pm & 7–10pm, Sat 7–10pm.

P'tit Gabriel square Gabrielle 11 ☎ 067 44 36 16, ⓦ leptitgabriel.be. Just off the corner of the main square, this fab little place serves excellent traditional Burgundian fondues from €19.50 a head – accompanied by chips, salads and various sauces. Mon–Sat 6–11pm, Sun noon–10pm.

Abbaye de Villers

rue de l'Abbaye 55, just off the N93, 16km east of Nivelles • April–Oct daily 10am–6pm; Nov–March Mon & Wed–Sun 10am–5pm • €6 • ☎ 071 88 09 80, ⓦ villers.be • Hourly trains run to Villers-la-Ville from Charleroi to the south and Ottignies to the north; the abbey is 1.6km from Villers-la-Ville station: follow the sign to Monticelli, head up and over a little slope until, after about 100m, you reach a T-junction; turn right and follow the road round until you see the ruins ahead

The ruined Cistercian **Abbaye de Villers** nestles in a lovely wooded dell on the edge of **VILLERS-LA-VILLE**, and is altogether one of the most haunting and evocative sights in the whole of Belgium. The first monastic community settled here in 1146, consisting of just one abbot and twelve monks. Subsequently the abbey became a wealthy local landowner, managing a domain of several thousand acres, with numbers rising to about a hundred monks and three hundred lay brothers. A healthy annual income funded the construction of an extensive **monastic complex**, most of which was erected in the thirteenth century, though the less austere structures, such as the **Abbot's Palace**, went up in a second spurt of activity some four hundred years later. In 1794 French Revolutionaries ransacked the monastery, and later a railway was ploughed through the grounds, but more than enough survives – albeit in various states of decay – to pick out Romanesque, Gothic and Renaissance features and to make some kind of mental reconstruction of abbey life possible.

From the entrance, a path crosses the courtyard in front of the Abbot's Palace to reach the **warming room** (*chauffoir*), the only place in the monastery where a fire would have been kept going all winter, and which still has its original chimney. The fire provided a little heat to the adjacent rooms: on one side the monks' **workroom** (*salle des moines*), used for reading and studying; on the other the large Romanesque-Gothic **refectory** (*réfectoire*), lit by ribbed twin windows topped with chunky rose windows. Next door is the **kitchen** (*cuisine*), which contains a few remnants of the drainage system which once piped waste to the river, and of a central hearth, whose chimney helped air the room. Just behind this lies the **pantry** (*salle des convers*), where a segment of the original vaulting has survived, supported by a single column; beyond, on the northwestern edge of the complex, is the **guesthouse** (*brasserie*), one of the abbey's biggest and oldest buildings. The most spectacular building, however, is the **church** (*église*), which fills out the north corner of the complex. With pure lines and elegant proportions, it displays the change from Romanesque to Gothic – the transept and choir are the first known examples of **Brabantine Gothic**. The building has the dimensions of a cathedral, 90m long and 40m wide, with a majestic nave whose roof was supported on strong cylindrical columns. An unusual feature is the series of bull's-eye windows which light the transepts. Of the original twelfth-century **cloister** (*cloître*) adjoining the church, a pair of twin windows is pretty much all that remains, flanked by a two-storey section of the old monks' quarters.

TINTIN

Tintin was the creation of Brussels-born **Georges Remi**, aka **Hergé** (1907–83). Remi's first efforts (pre-Tintin) were sponsored by a right-wing Catholic journal, *Le XXième Siècle*, and in 1929, when this same paper produced a kids' supplement – *Le Petit Vingtième* – Remi was given his first major break. He was asked to produce a two-page comic strip and the result was **Tintin in the Land of the Soviets**, a didactic tale about the evils of Bolshevism. Tintin's Soviet adventure lasted until May 1930, and to round it all off the director of *Le XXième Siècle* decided to stage a PR-stunt reception to celebrate Tintin's return from the USSR. Remi – along with a Tintin lookalike – hopped on a train just east of Brussels and when they pulled into the capital they were mobbed by scores of excited children. Remi and Tintin never looked back. Remi decided on the famous **quiff** straight away, but other features – the mouth and expressive eyebrows – only came later. His popularity was – and remains – quite phenomenal: *Tintin* has been translated into sixty languages and over **twenty million copies** of the comic *Le Journal de Tintin*, Remi's own independent creation first published in 1946, have been sold – and that's not mentioning all the *Tintin* TV cartoon series.

Musée Hergé

rue du Labrador 26 • Tues–Fri 10.30am–5.30pm, Sat & Sun 10am–6pm • €9.50, includes audio guide in English • ☎ 010 48 84 21, ⓦ www.museeherge.com • Trains run from Brussels to Ottignies (every 30min; 30min); from there, bus #20 runs to Louvain-la-Neuve (hourly; 10min)

Established in the 1960s as a French-speaking rival to the ancient Flemish university town of Leuven, **LOUVAIN-LA-NEUVE** is like any new town: a mixture of roundabouts and underpasses, with the university supplemented by a couple of shopping centres and arts complexes. But its most recent addition, the **Musée Hergé**, is perhaps Louvain's greatest achievement, and since it honours perhaps the most famous Belgian of them all, the creator of **Tintin** (see box above), it's likely to feature on anyone's itinerary. The brainchild of Hergé's second wife, **Fanny Rodwell**, the museum concentrates on his life and work, but his most celebrated creation inevitably figures extremely prominently. A couple of rooms take you through Hergé's "dreary but happy" childhood, his early cartoon creations and work in advertising and design, while later ones examine the inception of the Tintin stories in detail, with displays on each of the principal characters as well as Hergé's influences in creating them – foreign travel, science and cinema among them. It's all made accessible and entertaining by **audio guides**, which provide excellent commentary and background, though whether Hergé was quite the towering creative genius the museum makes him out to be is debatable. Nonetheless, it's all brilliantly done, and enjoyable whether you're a fan of the man and his bequiffed reporter or not.

Waterloo

WATERLOO is easily the most popular attraction in Brabant Walloon, a run-of-the-mill suburb of Brussels that most people see on a day-trip from the capital. Unsurprisingly, the town has a resonance far beyond its size. On June 18, 1815, at this small crossroads town on what was once the main route to Brussels from France, **Wellington** masterminded the battle (see box, p.240) that put an end to the imperial ambitions of **Napoleon**. The battle turned out to have far more significance than even its generals realized, for not only was this the last throw of the dice for the formidable army born of the French Revolution, but it also marked the end of France's prolonged attempts to dominate Europe militarily.

Nevertheless, the historic importance of Waterloo has not saved the **battlefield** from interference – a motorway cuts right across it – and if you do visit you'll need a lively imagination to picture what happened and where – unless, that is, you're around to see the large-scale re-enactment which takes place every five years in June; the next are scheduled for 2015 and 2020. Scattered round the battlefield are several monuments and memorials, the most satisfying of which is the **Butte de Lion**, a huge earth mound that's part viewpoint and part commemoration. The battlefield is 3km south of the centre of Waterloo, where the **Musée Wellington** is easily the pick of several museums dedicated to the battle.

Musée Wellington

chaussée de Bruxelles 147 • Daily: April–Sept 9.30am–6.30pm; Oct–March 10am–5pm • €6.50, or included in Pass 1815 (see p.242) • Ⓦ museewellington.be

The **Musée Wellington** occupies the old inn where Wellington slept the nights before and after the battle. It's an enjoyable affair, whose displays detail the build-up to – and the course of – the battle via plans and models, alongside an engaging hotchpotch of personal effects. **Room 4** holds the bed where Alexander Gordon, Wellington's principal aide-de-camp, was brought to die, and here also is the artificial leg of Lord Uxbridge, another British commander: "I say, I've lost my leg," Uxbridge is reported to have said during the battle, to which Wellington replied, "By God, sir, so you have!" After the battle, Uxbridge's leg was buried here in Waterloo, but it was returned to London when

---

THE BATTLE OF WATERLOO

Having escaped from imprisonment on the Italian island of Elba on February 26, 1815, **Napoleon** landed in Cannes three days later and moved swiftly north, entering Paris on March 20 just as his unpopular replacement – the slothful **King Louis XVIII** – high-tailed it to Ghent (see pp.153–171). Thousands of Frenchmen rallied to Napoleon's colours and with little delay Napoleon marched northeast to fight the two armies that threatened his future. Both were in Belgium: one, an assortment of British, Dutch and German soldiers, was commanded by the **Duke of Wellington**; the other was a Prussian army led by **Marshal Blücher**. At the start of the campaign, Napoleon's army was about 130,000 strong, larger than each of the opposing armies but not big enough to fight them both at the same time. Napoleon's strategy was to stop Wellington and Blücher from joining together – and to this end he crossed the Belgian frontier near Charleroi to launch a quick attack. On June 16, the French hit the Prussians hard, forcing them to retreat and giving Napoleon the opportunity he was looking for. Napoleon detached a force of 30,000 soldiers to harry the retreating Prussians, while he concentrated his main army against Wellington, hoping to deliver a knockout blow. Meanwhile, Wellington had assembled his troops at **Waterloo**, on the main road to Brussels.

At **dawn on Sunday June 18**, the two armies faced each other. Wellington had some 68,000 men, about one third of whom were British, and Napoleon around five thousand more. The armies were deployed just 1500m apart, with Wellington on the ridge north of – and uphill from – the enemy. It had rained heavily during the night, so Napoleon delayed his first attack to give the ground a chance to dry. At **11.30am**, the battle began when the French assaulted the fortified farm of Hougoumont, which was crucial for the defence of Wellington's right. The assault failed, and at approximately **1pm** there was more bad news for Napoleon when he heard that the Prussians had eluded their pursuers and were closing fast. To gain time he sent 14,000 troops off to impede their progress and at **2pm** he tried to regain the initiative by launching a large-scale infantry attack against Wellington's left. This second French attack also proved inconclusive, and so at **4pm** Napoleon's cavalry charged Wellington's centre, where the British infantry formed into squares and just managed to keep the French at bay – a desperate engagement that cost hundreds of lives. By **5.30pm**, the Prussians had begun to reach the battlefield in numbers to the right of the French lines and, at **7.30pm**, with the odds getting longer and longer, Napoleon made a final bid to break Wellington's centre, sending in his Imperial Guard. These were the best soldiers Napoleon had, but, slowed down by the mud churned up by their own cavalry, the veterans proved easy targets for the British infantry, and they were beaten back with great loss of life. At **8.15pm**, Wellington, who knew victory was within his grasp, rode down the ranks to encourage his soldiers before ordering the large-scale counterattack that proved decisive.

he died to join the rest of his body. Such insouciance was not uncommon among the British ruling class and neither were the bodies of the dead soldiers considered sacrosanct: **tooth dealers** roamed the battlefields of the Napoleonic Wars pulling out teeth, which were then stuck on two pieces of board with a spring at the back – primitive dentures known in England as "Waterloos".

In Wellington's bedroom, **Room 6**, there are copies of the messages Wellington sent to his commanders during the course of the battle, curiously formal epistles laced with phrases such as "Could you be so kind as to . . .". Finally, an **extension** at the back of the museum reprises what has gone before, albeit on a slightly larger scale, with more models, plans and military paraphernalia plus a lucid outline of the immediate historical background.

Church of Saint Joseph

chaussée de Bruxelles, • Daily 8am–7pm • Free • W sjoseph.be

Across the street from the Musée Wellington, the **church of Saint Joseph** is a curious affair, its domed, circular **portico** of 1689 built as part of a larger chapel on the orders of a Habsburg governor in the hope that it would encourage God to grant King Charles II of Spain an heir. It didn't, but the plea to God survives in the Latin inscription on the pediment. The portico holds a bust of Wellington and a monument to all those British soldiers who died at Waterloo, and there's an assortment of British **memorial plaques** at the back of the chapel beyond. They are, however, a rather jumbled bunch as they were plonked here unceremoniously when the original chapel was demolished in the nineteenth century to be replaced by the substantial building of today. Most of the plaques were paid for by voluntary contributions from the soldiers who survived – in the days when the British state rarely coughed up for any but the most aristocratic of its veterans.

The Battlefield: the Hameau du Lion

route du Lion 252–254 • T 02 385 19 12, W waterloo1815.be • All four sites open daily: April–Sept 9.30am–6.30pm; Oct–March 10am–5pm • Three entry options: €7 pass, includes Butte de Lion and the Panorama only; Hameau du Lion Pass €9 (includes Butte du Lion, Panorama & two films); Pass 1815 €13.50, includes Hameau de Lion Pass, plus Musée Wellington and Wellington's last HQ).

Some 4km south of town, the Waterloo **battlefield** is a landscape of rolling farmland, interrupted by a couple of main roads and more pleasingly punctuated by the odd copse and farmstead. The ridge where Wellington once marshalled his army now holds a motley assortment of attractions collectively known as **Le Hameau du Lion** (Lion's Hamlet). This comprises four separate sites all within a few metres of each other, with the added offering of a 45-minute battlefield tour in a four-wheel-drive. Of the four sites, the **Centre du Visiteur**, with its dire audio-visual display on the battle, and the **Musée de Cires**, a dusty wax museum, are entirely missable.

Butte de Lion

The best site is the 100m-high **Butte de Lion**, built by local women with soil from the battlefield. The Butte marks the spot where Holland's Prince William of Orange – one of Wellington's commanders and later King William II of the Netherlands – was wounded. It was only a nick, so goodness knows how high it would have been if William had been seriously injured, but even so the mound is a commanding monument, surmounted by a regal **28-tonne lion** atop a stout column. From the **viewing platform**, there's a panoramic view over the battlefield, and a plan identifies which army was where.

Panorama de la Bataille

Also enjoyable is the **Panorama de la Bataille**, where a circular, naturalistic painting of the battle, on a canvas no less than 110m in circumference, is displayed in a purpose-built, rotunda-like gallery – to a thundering soundtrack of bugles, snorting horses and cannon fire. Panorama painting is extremely difficult – controlling perspective is always a real problem – but it was very much in vogue when the Parisian artist **Louis Dumoulin** began this effort in 1912. Precious few panoramas of this kind have survived, and this one is a bit past its best, but it does at least give a sense of the battle. You can also venture out onto the battlefield under your own steam by following the old **track** that cuts south across the fields from beside the Panorama.

ARRIVAL AND DEPARTURE WATERLOO

By train and bus There are direct trains to Waterloo from Brussels' three main stations to the north (25min) and also from Braine l'Alleud (4min) and Nivelles to the south. From Waterloo's train station, it's an easy 15min walk to the Waterloo tourist office and Musée Wellington in the centre of the town – turn right outside the station building and then first left along rue de la Station. After you've finished at the museum, you can take bus #W (every 30–40min) from across the street – the chaussée de Bruxelles – to the battlefield and the Butte de Lion. The bus stops beside the Esso gas station about 500m from the Butte de Lion. After visiting the

Butte, you can then return to the same bus stop and catch bus #W on to Braine-l'Alleud train station or back to Waterloo.
By bus Bus #365 runs twice an hour from Brussels (Gare du Midi) to Waterloo (get off at "Église"), and the advantage over the train is that it drops you right in the centre (though it takes 40min in all); after that you can take bus #W to the battlefield (see p.241). The other plus to taking the bus is that you can get a day ticket for €8, which is valid for all your bus journeys.
By car Take the Brussels Ring east, and come off at junction 26.

INFORMATION

Tourist office Waterloo tourist office is handily located in the centre of town, opposite the Musée Wellington at chaussée de Bruxelles 218 (daily: June–Sept 9.30am–6pm; Oct–May 10am–5pm; ☎ 02 352 09 10, ⓦ waterloo-tourisme.com). They issue free town maps

and sell a combined ticket, the Pass 1815 (€13.50), for all the battle-related attractions, which makes things easier but doesn't work out as a saving unless you want to see everything.

ACCOMMODATION AND EATING

Most people visit Waterloo as a **day-trip**, but the tourist office does have the details of several local hotels.

Hotel Le 1815 route du Lion 367–369 ☎ 02 387 01 60, ⓦ le1815.com. This comfortable three-star has rooms turned out in an attractive modern style and couldn't be more convenient for the battlefield, right opposite the Butte de Lion. **€100**

La Brioche chaussée de Bruxelles 161 ☎ 02 353 02 22. A pleasant, modern café serving up a good line in sandwiches, pancakes and pastries; it's located just up and across the street from the Waterloo tourist office. Daily 7am–6.30pm.

Charleroi

Once the epicentre of one of Belgium's main industrial areas, home to glassworks, coal mines and iron foundries, the twentieth century wasn't kind to **CHARLEROI** and its outskirts. It's best known these days for being the home of Brussels' second **airport**, and with that impetus it's busily trying to re-invent itself, sprucing up its main attractions and large parts of the city centre – for example, an area across the river from the station is being massively redeveloped for the forthcoming "Rive Gauche" shopping centre. Although there's a long way yet to go, it's not a bad place to **break your journey** if you're travelling either to the Botte du Hainaut (see p.245–249) or east to the Ardennes (see pp.252–293).

The Lower Town

Charleroi's **lower town** lies down by the River Sambre, recently cleaned up and spanned by the **Pont Roi Baudouin**, which sports two **statues** of workers by that champion of the working class, Constantin Meunier. Before the railways, the Sambre was crucial to the industrialization of the region, its dark waters crowded with coal and iron-ore barges.

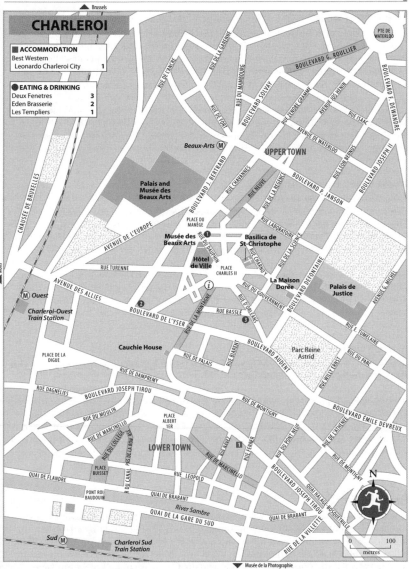

CHARLEROI

ACCOMMODATION

Best Western	
Leonardo Charleroi City	1

EATING & DRINKING

Deux Fenetres	3
Eden Brasserie	2
Les Templiers	1

Musée de la Photographie

On the far side of the bridge lies Charleroi Sud train station; on the other the riverside quai de Brabant and rue du Canal lead to the heart of the lower town, and to the **Passage de la Bourse** – an attractive covered arcade whose late nineteenth-century, wooden-framed shops have survived in fine fettle. Beyond here, **place Albert 1er** is home to a daily morning market, beyond which busy **boulevard Tirou** leads to the cobbled shopping street of **rue de la Montagne**, which clambers toward the Upper Town. On the way, look out for the *sgraffiti* decorating the facade of rue de la Montagne 38, the work of one of Belgium's most talented Art Nouveau painters and architects, **Paul Cauchie** (1875–1952).

The Upper Town

Rue de la Montagne emerges into circular **place Charles II**, the centre of the **upper town** and formerly the site of a substantial fortress, built on the top of the hill in the 1660s. Nothing remains of the fortress today, but the area's gridiron street plan recalls its presence. Two fine Art Deco buildings flank place Charles II: one, the **Basilica de Saint Christophe** (daily 8am–7pm), has a stunning 200m-square gold-leaf apse mosaic illustrating the Book of Revelation, completed in 1957 to a design by local artist Jean Ransy; the other, the **Hôtel de Ville**, has a handsome period lobby and staircase and, around the back, a display on the life and times of one Jules Destrée (1863–1936), a local poet, lawyer and socialist politician who campaigned hard for improvements in working conditions in Wallonia during the early years of the twentieth century.

Musée des Beaux Arts

place du Manege 1 • Tues–Sat 10am–6pm • Free

Behind the Hôtel de Ville, busy **place du Manège** is overlooked by the striking Art Deco lines of the **Palais des Beaux Arts**, which is home to the **Musée des Beaux Arts**, accessed by way of the glass extension on the right. The museum has a fine collection of Hainaut artists, supplemented by the work of other Belgian painters who lived or worked here. **Highlights** include the romantic Neoclassical paintings of Charleroi artist François Joseph Navez as well as the contrasting naturalism of Constantin Meunier, whose grim vision of industrial life was balanced by the heroism he saw in the working class. There are also a number of canvases by the talented Pierre Paulus, whose oeuvre takes up where Meunier's leaves off, and a handful by Magritte, Felicien Rops and James Ensor.

Musée de la Photographie

ave Paul Pastur 11 • Tues–Sun 10am–6pm • €6, free 1st Sun of the month • ☎ 071 43 58 10, ⓦ www.museephoto.be • Buses #70, #71 or #170 from Charleroi-Sud to place de Mont-sur-Marchienne

Charleroi's best museum is outside the city centre, the inventive **Musée de la Photographie**, housed in the imaginatively renovated neo-Gothic Carmelite monastery of Mont-sur-Marchienne. Around 5km southwest but easily reachable by bus, the museum holds a thought-provoking collection of nearly sixty thousand **creative** and **documentary-style photographs**, which are displayed in rotation, and a well-organized and reasonably interesting permanent exhibition which takes you through the history of photography to the present day. Temporary exhibitions are held regularly, too.

Bois du Cazier

rue du Cazier 80 • Tues–Fri 9am–5pm, Sat & Sun 10am–6pm • €7; audio guides in English free • ⓦ www.leboisducazier.be

As compelling as the photography museum, Charleroi's other outlying attraction, the **Bois du Cazier**, is a former coal mine which gained a tragic notoriety in August 1956 when over two hundred miners died in a fire here. Most of the **mine buildings** remain intact, and are both a memorial to those who died (more than half of whom were Italian immigrants) and a memorable piece of industrial heritage. There is lots of information in English, including a short film about the 1956 catastrophe, and the outbuildings hold a host of related objects and exhibitions, most interestingly a **museum of industry** full of heavy machinery from times gone by, although the most intriguing exhibits are those original to the mine: the showers where the miners ended their shift, or the punch clocks where they would begin.

ARRIVAL AND DEPARTURE   CHARLEROI

By train Charleroi has two train stations, Charleroi-Sud by the River Sambre, where you're likely to arrive, and the less important Charleroi-Ouest, a short walk west of the upper town.

Destinations from Charleroi-Sud Brussels (every 30–50min; 45min); Couvin (hourly; 1hr); La Louvière-Sud (every 30min; 30min); Mariembourg (hourly; 1hr); Mons (every 30min; 35min); Namur (every 30min; 40min); Nivelles (every 30min; 20min); Ottignies (hourly; 40min–1hr); Villers-la-Ville (every 30min; 20min); Walcourt (hourly; 20min).

By plane The city's airport – rather cheekily called Brussels South Charleroi – is 6km north of town; Ryanair flies here from the UK and Ireland (see p.21).

GETTING AROUND AND INFORMATION

By bus or métro Charleroi-Sud station also acts as the hub for local buses, most usefully a shuttle service to the upper town's place du Manège – a route that is followed by Charleroi's pocket-sized métro.

Tourist office The city's main tourist office is at place Charles II 20 (Mon–Sat 9am–6pm, Sun 9am–3pm; ☎071 86 14 14, ⍟paysdecharleroi.be).

ACCOMMODATION, EATING AND DRINKING

Best Western Leonardo Charleroi City blvd Tirou 96 ☎071 31 98 11, ⍟leonardo-hotels.com. Charleroi's most comfortable and central hotel, occupying a modern block just 5min from the station, with around fifty pleasantly appointed modern rooms. **€50**

★**Deux Fenetres** rue Basslé 27 ☎071 63 43 03, ⍟2fenetres.be. An excellent and authentic Italian restaurant in a converted garage, serving great food and wine in an appealing and fun environment. Four-course menus €50, otherwise pasta dishes around €15 and mains €18–23; good main-course salads, too. Tues–Fri noon–3pm & 6.30–9.30pm.

Eden Brasserie blvd Jacques Bertrand 1 ☎071 31 12 12, ⍟eden-charleroi.be. This bar-cum-cultural centre is open for lunch and dinner, after which it moves back the tables to make way for live music and other events. Good food from an interesting and varied menu: pasta, salads, a kids' menu, and always a plat du jour for €10. Tables outside in summer. Mon–Fri noon–2.30pm, and in the evening for 1hr before each event.

Les Templiers place du Manège 7 ☎071 32 18 36. A great little bar-cum-restaurant on the corner of place du Manège – always busy, with a few tables outside, and a good choice of beers on tap and food at lunch time from a blackboard menu. Lots of good traditional Belgian stuff, from meatballs to sole *meunière* for €13–20, as well as sandwiches and bar snacks. Daily 10am–10pm, food served noon–3pm and Fri eve too during mussel season.

Botte de Hainaut

A tongue of land jutting south into France, the **Botte de Hainaut** (Boot of Hainaut) is a natural extension of the Ardennes range further east, if a little flatter and less wooded. It's mostly visited for its gentle scenery and country towns, among which **Walcourt** and **Chimay** are the most appealing – the former graced by a handsome basilica, the latter by a charming château and one of the prettiest main squares in the whole of Wallonia. The Boot's one and only **train line** runs south from Charleroi to Walcourt, Philippeville and ultimately to Couvin; **local buses** fill in most of the gap, with a good service between Charleroi, Couvin and Chimay, but really the best way to get around is with your own car. The other complication is that, apart from campsites, **accommodation** (see p.248) is thin on the ground.

Walcourt: the Basilique Ste-Materne

Summer daily 8.30am–5pm • From Walcourt train station, it's a steep 1200m walk to the church: turn right outside the station building, hang a left down the short access road, turn right at the T-junction and then follow the road as it curves upwards

The straggling hillside settlement of **WALCOURT**, about 20km – and half an hour by train – from Charleroi, is a pleasant old town whose pride and joy is the medieval, artichoke-domed **Basilique Ste-Materne**, which dominates the town from its hilltop location at the top of the Grand-Place. The church is an imperious building from the outside, very dark and spiritual within, distinguished by a marvellous **Gothic rood screen**, adorned by a flurry of Renaissance decoration, that was presented to the church by the emperor Charles V on the occasion of a pilgrimage he made to the **Virgin of Walcourt**, a silver-plated wooden statue that now stands in the north transept. An object of considerable veneration even today, the statue is believed to have been crafted in the tenth century, making it one of the oldest such figures in Belgium. Equally fascinating are the late medieval **choir stalls**, which sport a wealth of naturalistic detail, with centaurs and griffins, rams locking horns and acrobats alongside biblical scenes.

The Lacs de l'Eau de l'Heure

route de la Plate Taille 99 • Visitor centre April–June & Sept daily 10am–6pm; July & Aug daily 10am–7pm • ☎ 071 50 92 92, ⓦ www.lacsdeleaudheure.be • **Guided tours of dam** Daily at 11.30am, 1.30pm, 3.30pm & 5.30pm • €7.50 • **Crocodile Rouge Boat trips** April–June & Sept Wed, Sat & Sun 1–6pm; July & Aug daily 1–6pm • €15

A short way south of Walcourt, the main road bisects the **Lacs de l'Eau de l'Heure**, a series of lakes formed by the damming of the river here and which are now home to all kinds of leisure activities. There's a **visitor centre** just off the main road, before the bridge over the lakes, where you can rent bikes and canoes, and which also gives access to the **dam** itself, which is accessible via regular guided tours; the visitor centre is also a pick-up point for the so-called **Crocodile Rouge**, a sort of bus-cum-boat which makes circuits of the main lake. There's also an indoor leisure pool, tennis courts and gardens.

Philippeville

It's a short hop southeast from Walcourt by train to unexciting **PHILIPPEVILLE**, whose gridiron street plan reflects its origins as a **fortress town**. Built to the latest star-shaped design by Charles V in 1555, the fortress has disappeared save for a couple of subterranean artillery galleries, the *souterrains*. Charles didn't actually intend to build the fort at all but, irritatingly, the French had captured the emperor's neighbouring stronghold of Mariembourg, just 12km to the south, and Charles was obliged to respond.

Couvin

COUVIN, 5km south of Mariembourg, was one of the first settlements in Hainaut to be industrialized, its narrow streets choked by forges and smelting works as early as the eighteenth century. As it turned out, Couvin was soon marginalized by the big cities further north, but it has battled gainfully on as a pint-sized **manufacturing centre**. Tourism has also had an impact, as the town lies at the heart of a popular holiday area, a quiet rural district whose forests and farmland are liberally sprinkled

---

THE TROIS VALLÉES STEAM TRAIN

Ten kilometres south of Phillipeville, **MARIEMBOURG** is the base of the **Chemin de fer à vapeur des Trois Vallées**, a refurbished steam engine that takes two hours to puff its way east across the surrounding countryside, from its terminus 800m south of Mariembourg train station to Treignes, near the French border (July & Aug daily 11.30am–6.30pm; rest of year Sat & Sun 11.30am–6.30pm; ☎ 060 31 24 40; €12, including museum). There's also a small **museum** of locomotives and other bits and pieces at the station (March–June & Sept–Nov Tues–Fri 10am–5pm, Sat & Sun 10am–6pm; July & Aug daily 10am–6pm; €5). You can combine a one-way train trip with a **bike ride**; cycles can be rented in Mariembourg from P. Caussin, at rue de la Gare 57 (☎ 060 31 11 36), and you can take off along **RAVeL 2**, the disused railway line turned cycle path, which begins behind the train station, in the direction of **Hermeton-sur-Meuse**. Turn off towards Treignes at Matagne-la-Petite and you can jump on the steam train for the trip back to Mariembourg – bikes travel for free.

with country cottages and second homes. Long and slim, and bisected by the River Eau Noire, Couvin is short on specific sights, but it does possess a good-looking if small **old quarter**, set on top of a rocky hill high above the river and main road, where you'll find the boringly modern main square, **place du Général Piron**.

Grottes de Neptune

rue de l'Adujoir 24 • Tours (45min–1hr) April & May daily 11am–4pm; July & Aug daily 11am–5.30pm; June & Sept daily 1–3.15pm; Oct & Feb–March Sat & Sun 1–3.15pm • €8, €12 including Brûly-de-Pesche • ☎ 060 31 19, ⓦ grottesdeneptune.be

Some 3km north of the small town of Couvin, in a lovely spot that's difficult to reach without your own transport, the **Grottes de Neptune** are a big local attraction, a small network of **caverns** that you can see in part by boat on an underground river – a journey that's enhanced by some dramatic and accomplished music and light shows at the end.

Brûly-de-Pesche

place St Meen • Easter–Sept daily 10.30am–5pm • €6, €12 including Grottes de Neptune • ☎ 060 34 01 40

South of Couvin on the N5, it's a couple of kilometres to the 5km-long turn-off that weaves its way up into the wooded hills to the small village of **BRÛLY-DE-PESCHE**, where Hitler had his advance headquarters during the invasion of 1940. The Nazis commandeered the entire village, drawing up the terms of the French surrender in the church, and Hitler himself took refuge in the so-called **Abri d'Hitler**, which lies in a wooded park nearby. There are a couple of **rebuilt huts** here showing a film on the 1940 campaign, and there's a display on the Resistance and a couple of decrepit concrete bunkers – the only survivors from the war.

Chimay

It's best known for the beer brewed by local Trappists, but the small and ancient town of **CHIMAY**, 14km west of Couvin, is a charming old place in its own right, governed for several centuries by the de Croy family, a clan of local bigwigs. Many of the de Croy family were buried in the **Collégiale des Saints Pierre et Paul** (Mon–Fri 9am–noon & 2–4.30pm, Sat 9am–5pm, Sun 11am–5pm), a mostly sixteenth-century limestone pile with a high and austere vaulted nave that squeezes into the town's slender **Grand-Place**, an eminently bourgeois and exceedingly pretty little square surrounding the dinky **Monument des Princes**, a water fountain erected in 1852 in honour of the de Croys. Incidentally, one of Chimay's most delicious specialities is **Bernadins de Chimay** biscuits, made with almonds, honey and brown sugar; you can buy at the Pâtisserie Hubert, Grand-Place 32, and they make a perfect souvenir of the town if you don't like beer.

Château des Princes de Chimay

rue du Château • End of March to mid-Nov Tues, Wed & Sun guided tours at 2.30pm & 3.45pm, Thurs–Sat at 11am, 3pm & 3.45pm • €9 • ☎ 060 21 45 31, ⓦ chateaudechimay.be

The town's main sight is the **Château des Princes de Chimay**, just off the main square in the centre of town. A considerably altered structure, it was originally built in the fifteenth century, but was reconstructed in the seventeenth, then badly damaged by fire and partly rebuilt to earlier plans in the 1930s. Today the main body of the building is fronted by a long series of rectangular windows, edged by a squat **turreted tower**. Tours are sometimes led by the elderly Princess Elizabeth de Croy herself, who is an engaging and personable guide and speaks excellent English. She'll show you the old chapel in one of the turrets, lots of family portraits (right up to the present day), a hotchpotch of

CHIMAY'S TRAPPISTS

The **Trappist** monks of the Cistercian Order of the Strict Observance live outside Chimay in the **Abbaye Notre-Dame de Scourmont**, an architecturally dull complex dating from the 1850s near the French border, about 10km out of town (no public transport). The monastery itself is out of bounds, but you can wander round the grounds and visit the church, though frankly this is not exactly riveting stuff. The Trappists no longer brew **beer** at the abbey – the modern brewery is some way away and is also closed to the public – but you can sample their beers and cheeses at the nearby *l'Auberge de Poteaupré* (☎060 21 14 33, ⓦchimay.com), a restaurant-brasserie and shop in a converted school about 500m from the abbey on the main road. They offer accommodation too (see below). Shops and restaurant open Jan Sat & Sun only 10am–10pm; Feb–April & mid-Oct to mid-Dec Tues–Thurs 10am–6pm, Fri–Sun 10am–10pm; May to mid-June & mid-Sept to mid-Oct Mon–Thurs 10am–6pm, Fri–Sun 10am–10pm; Easter holidays & mid-June to mid-Sept daily 10am–10pm.

period furniture and – the highlight – the carefully restored **private theatre**, modelled on the Louis XV theatre at Fontainebleau, where you can watch a short film on the family and the property.

ARRIVAL AND INFORMATION
BOTTE DE HAINAUT

By bus and train The Botte's train line runs south from Charleroi to Walcourt, Philippeville and ultimately to Couvin. Chimay is best accessed by bus from Couvin.
Destinations from Chimay Charleroi (every 2hr; 1hr 30min); Couvin (hourly; 1hr); Mariembourg (hourly; 45min).
Destinations from Couvin Charleroi (hourly; 50min);

Chimay (hourly; 1hr); Namur (hourly; 1hr 30min); Walcourt (hourly; 30–40min).
Tourist office Chimay's tourist office is a few paces east of the Grand-Place at rue de Noailles (July & Aug daily 8.30am–6pm; rest of year Mon–Fri 8.30am–5pm, Sat & Sun 10am–5pm; ☎060 21 98 84, ⓦbotteduhainaut .com).

ACCOMMODATION

Chimay is your best bet, but consider making **advance reservations** in all cases, either direct or via the main regional **websites**: ⓦbotteduhainaut.com and the more comprehensive ⓦpaysdesvallees.be.

L'Auberge de Poteaupré rue de Poteaupré 5 ☎060 21 14 33, ⓦchimay.com. Simple modern rooms in the Chimay Trappist complex (see above), decorated in the red and blues of the Chimay monks and equipped with en-suite bathrooms, TV and wi-fi. Closed weekdays during Jan and Feb. **€70**
Hostellerie Dispa rue du Jardinet 7, Walcourt ☎071 61 14 23, ⓦhostelleriedispa.be. Down a narrow side street near the station , this tidy, well-cared-for place in a pretty old house with crisp, modern furnishings. It also has the best restaurant in town (see p.249) Closed late Feb &

early March. **€80**
Hostellerie du Gahy rue de Gahy 2, Momignies ☎060 51 10 93. About 12km west of Chimay, this restaurant has six stylish rooms in an imaginatively converted farmhouse. **€80**
★**Le Petit Chapitre** place du Chapitre 5, Chimay ☎060 21 10 42, ⓦwww.lepetitchapitre.be. A delightful B&B comprising a handful of period rooms in attractive old premises, metres from the Grand-Place. All with en-suite baths, TVs and wi-fi. Price includes breakfast. **€85**

EATING AND DRINKING

Les Armes de Philippeville place d'Armes 3, Philippeville ☎071 66 62 41. Philippeville's main square is home to this deservedly popular restaurant, which serves excellent Belgian food at moderate prices in its restaurant and lighter fare in the bar. Mon & Thurs–Sun noon–3pm & 6pm–midnight.
★**L'Auberge de Poteaupré** rue de Poteaupré 5 ☎060 21 14 33, ⓦchimay.com. Cosy, busy restaurant

near Abbaye N-D de sourmont serving some of the best food in the region, and with a bit of something for everyone: a tasting menu of goodies to have with Chimay's various cheeses and beers; sandwiches and a short menu of Belgian "tapas"; and a full menu of classic Belgian mains, with meatballs, rabbit in kriek, steaks, local trout meunière and a fabulous fondue – most for €12–17. Jan Sat & Sun only 10am–10pm; Feb–April & mid-Oct to mid-Dec

Tues–Thurs 10am–6pm, Fri–Sun 10am–10pm; May to mid-June & mid-Sept to Oct Mon–Thurs 10am–6pm, Fri–Sun 10am–10pm; Easter holidays & mid-June to mid-Sept daily 10am–10pm.

★**Brasserie des Fagnes** route de Nismes Couvin ☎ 060 31 15 70, ⓦ www.brasseriedesfagnes.com. Just outside Couvin on the way to Mariembourg, this is one of the best places to eat hereabouts: a fabled and very popular brewery restaurant which does delicious, crispy pizza-breads topped with cheeses and ham, and serves them with its own beer, Super des Fagnes – there are no fewer than five hundred varieties, from the usual brown, blond and cherry brews to daily specials such as a coriander and orange-flavoured ale. Tues–Fri 11.30am–8pm, Sat & Sun 10am–10pm.

La Chimassiette Grand Place 16, Chimay ☎ 060 21 90 42. One of the best places to eat in Chimay is this small modern restaurant serving excellent home-cooked food including escavèche, a mix of either eel or trout with onions, white wine and vinegar that's a speciality of the Botte. Fixed-price menus from €23. Wed–Sun 11.45am–3pm & 6–10pm.

Hostellerie Dispa rue du Jardinet 7, Walcourt ☎ 071 61 14 23, ⓦ hostelleriedispa.be. Not far from the station, this hotel-restaurant is Walcourt's best place to eat by some way, serving delicious seafood at reasonable prices – two-course lunch menus €24 and three-course menus from €35. Mon noon–3pm & 6–11pm, Tues noon–3pm, Thurs–Sun noon–3pm & 6–11pm.

Queen Mary Grand-Place 22, Chimay ☎ 060 21 23 81. Chimay's nicest option just for a drink is this cosy and popular bar decked out to look like an English pub. Chimay Tripel on tap. Daily 3pm–1am.

Destinations from Couvin by bus Charleroi (hourly; 50min); Chimay (hourly; 1hr); Namur (hourly; 1hr 30min); Walcourt (hourly; 30–40min)

4

The Ardennes

THE HAUTES FAGNES

5

The Ardennes

Belgium's southernmost region – known as the Ardennes – is a striking contrast to the crowded, industrial cities of the north, the flat polders morphing into rugged landscapes of rolling hills and forests. The Ardennes actually begin in France and stretch east across Luxembourg and Belgium before continuing on into Germany, covering three Belgian provinces en route – Namur in the west, Luxembourg in the south and Liège in the east. The highest part, lying in the German-speaking east of the country, is the Hautes Fagnes (the High Fens), an expanse of windswept heathland that extends from Eupen to Malmédy.

The region's major towns – **Namur** and the capital **Liège** – have quaint charm, with the latter boasting a scruffy yet culturally rich district in Outremeuse, and the former's atmospheric Old Town lying under the watchful eye of an impressive citadel. But the Ardennes' most attractive and popular areas are to be found further south, around **Dinant**, **La Roche-en-Ardenne** and **Bouillon**. Characterized by river valleys and high green peaks, this is ideal kayaking territory, and there are good caving opportunities too around the **Meuse**, **Ourthe** and **Lesse** valleys, whose underground rivers have cut through and dissolved the limestone hills, leaving stalagmites and stalactites in their wake. Generally, travelling about the Ardennes feels less frenetic than in Flanders – instead of ticking off UNESCO-listed sites and ogling one gilded Grand-Place after another, the Ardennes region is more about meandering through ancient hilltop villages, enjoying French-style food and savouring the distinctly laidback mood. Finally, make a literary pilgrimage to bookish **Redu** or take a dip in **Spa**'s thermal waters for Ardennes relaxation of a slightly different order.

Namur and around

Just 60km southeast of Brussels, **NAMUR** is a logical gateway to the Ardennes, and is refreshingly clear of the industrial belts of Hainaut and Brabant. Strategically sited at the confluence of the Sambre and Meuse **rivers**, it was the quintessential military town from the sixteenth century right up until 1978, when the Belgian army finally moved out. Namur's pride and joy is its massive, mostly nineteenth-century hilltop citadel – once one of the mightiest fortresses in Europe – but its quaint **Old Town**, down below, also musters a handful of decent museums – particularly the Trésor d'Oignies – plus some lovely restaurants and, for the Ardennes, a fairly lively **bar scene**. Visit at the end of May, and you join in the four-day Namur en Mai (ⓦnamurenmai.be) celebrations, when jugglers, stilt-walkers and all sorts of spectaculars pack the streets.

Highlights

❶ Trésor d'Oignies, Namur A unique collection of exquisitely crafted, jewel-encrusted metalwork from the thirteenth century. **See p.258**

❷ Stavelot Carnival One of Belgium's most flamboyant festivals – watch out for the Blancs Moussis, with their white robes and long red noses. **See p.272**

❸ Hautes Fagnes Belgium's highest terrain, with genuinely wild walking through windy moorland and forest. **See p.275**

❹ Kayaking and rafting Take your pick from the rivers Ourthe or Lesse. **See p.279 & p.285**

❺ Redu Quaint hamlet that serves as the world's second official book town. **See p.284**

❻ Bouillon Château The best-preserved medieval castle in the country. **See p.287**

HIGHLIGHTS ARE MARKED ON THE MAP ON PP.254–255

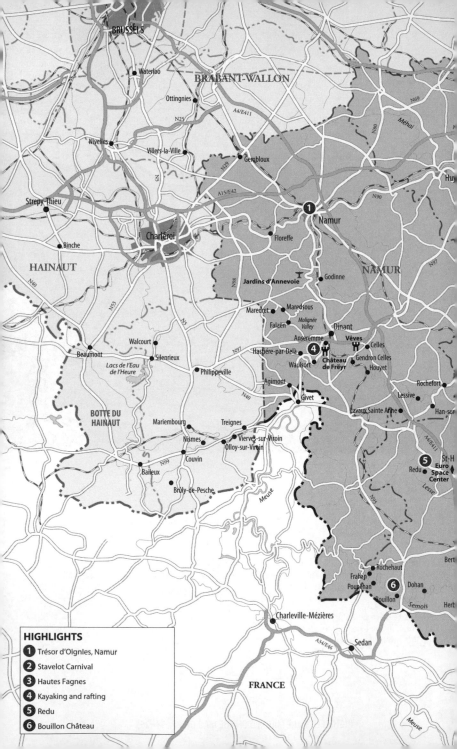

HIGHLIGHTS

1 Trésor d'Olgnles, Namur

2 Stavelot Carnival

3 Hautes Fagnes

4 Kayaking and rafting

5 Redu

6 Bouillon Château

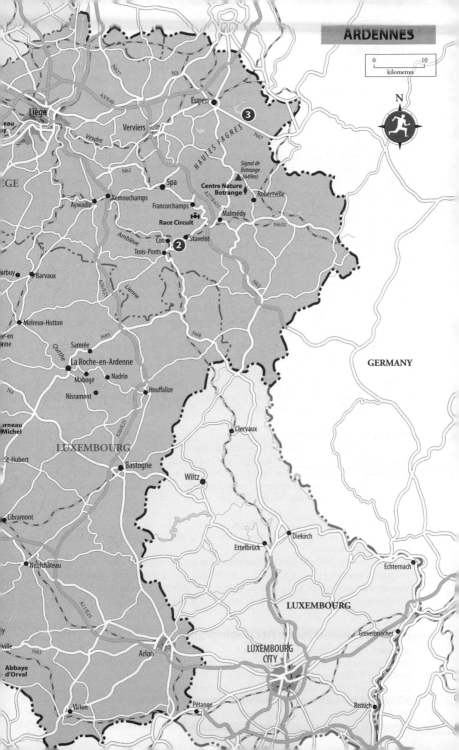

5

The citadel

Citadel route Merveilleuse • Open daily; Terra Nova Information desk open April–Sept daily 8am–6pm; Oct–March Wed, Sat & Sun 10am–5pm; school holidays daily; closed Dec 21–Jan 5 • Free; charges imposed April–Sept for additional attractions, which are cheaper with the Citadelle Pass (€9/adult; €6/child) bought at information desk • ☎ 081 65 45 00, ⓦ citadelle.namur.be • **La Médiévale tour** April–Sept daily 10.30am & 2.30pm • €5/adult, €4/child • **Tourist train** April–Sept, hourly departures 10.30am–5.30pm • €5/adult, €4/child

The result of centuries of military endeavour, Namur's **citadel** is an immense complex which crawls all over the steep and craggy hill that rises high above the confluence of the rivers Sambre and Meuse. It's a curious mixture of styles and periods: during the medieval period, a succession of local counts made elaborate additions to each other's fortifications, which were gradually abandoned when the section near the top of the hill – now loosely known as the **Château des Comtes** – was incorporated into a partly subterranean fortress, the **Médiane**, whose ramifications occupy the eastern portion of the present citadel. This part of the fortress was always the most vulnerable to attack, and for the next two hundred years successive generations of military engineers, including Vauban and the Dutchman Von Coehoorn, tried to work out the best way to protect it. The surviving structure reflects this preoccupation, with the lines of defence becoming more complex and extensive the further up you go. To further strengthen the defences, the Spanish completed the **Terra Nova** bastion at the west end of the citadel in the 1640s, separating the two with a wide **moat**; this made Namur one of the strongest fortresses in Europe, but didn't stop Louis XIV besieging the town in 1692. The Dutch rebuilt the citadel between 1816 and 1825, and much of today's remains date to this period.

The **views** from the citadel, over the town and the surrounding countryside, are fantastic, and the information office can provide details of **walking trails** of varying lengths. During the warmer months activities are laid on: one excellent **tour** (entitled La Médiévale) takes in the medieval parts of the complex and evokes what life was like during the Middle Ages, while a tourist train also runs during this period, taking in a handful of pretty town panoramas.

Underground casemates

April–Sept tours at 10.30am, noon, 2pm, 3.30pm & 5pm • €5/adult, €4/child

Dubbed "The Termite Nest of Europe" by Napoleon, these 7km of **underground casemates** stretch under Terra Nova and Médiane and are the largest such network in Europe. One-hour guided tours tell you about the labyrinth's 500-year-old history and how they were used during World War II.

Atelier de Parfumerie Guy Delforge

route Merveilleuse 60 • April–Oct Mon–Sat 10am–6pm; Nov–Mar Mon–Sat 10am–5.30pm • Free; guided tour Sat 3.30pm €3.50 • ☎ 081 22 17 92, ⓦ delforge.com

At the **Atelier de Parfumerie Guy Delforge**, the award-winning scent maker crafts his unique creations in the cellars of the citadel and sells them in the smart shop. A fifty-minute guided, or audio guide, **tour** – available on Saturdays only – gives a glimpse into the alchemy behind the creation of the perfumes.

Halle Al' Chair (Musée Archéologique)

rue du Pont 21 • Tues–Sun 10am–5pm • €3 • ☎ 081 23 16 31

Right on the river by the Pont du Musée, the red-brick **Halle Al' Chair** is one of the stand-out buildings of Namur's Old Town. Built by the Spanish in the sixteenth century, and originally a meat market, it now houses a branch of the tourist office (see p.259) and Namur's small **archeological museum**, with mosaics and other finds from the Roman era. Its most interesting exhibit is a scale model of Namur in the eighteenth century, a copy of the original in the Les Invalides museum in Paris.

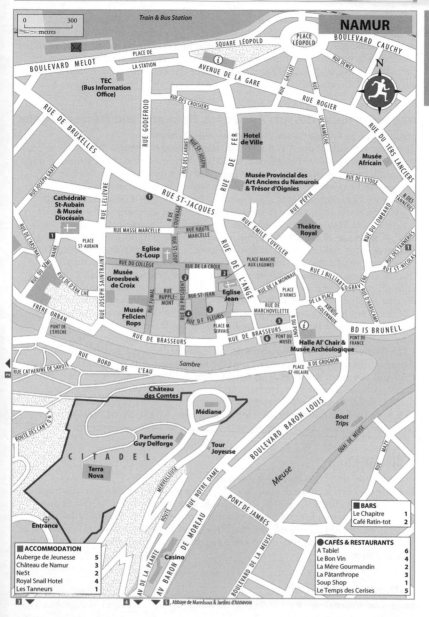

Musée Félicien Rops

rue Fumal 12 • Jan–June & Sept–Dec Tues–Sun 10am–6pm; July & Aug daily 10am–6pm • €3 (audio guide €2) • ☎ 081 77 67 55,
Ⓦ www.museerops.be

Housed in his in-laws' former townhouse, the **Musée Félicien Rops** is devoted to the life and work of painter, graphic artist and illustrator Félicien Rops (1833–98), a native of Namur who settled in Paris in the 1870s and illustrated the works of the likes of

5

Baudelaire. He had a reputation for a debauched lifestyle – including fathering a child by his sister – but was also an accomplished artist, best known for his erotic and macabre **drawings**, of which there is a good selection on display here – skeletons, nuns and priests depicted in oddly compromising poses, or old men serviced by young, partially clad women. Some are just perverse, but the wit in his work is hard to deny: check out his famous *Pornocrates*, on the second floor.

Musée Provincial des Arts Anciens du Namurois et Trésor d'Oignies

rue de Fer 24 • Tues–Sun 10am–6pm • €3 • ☎ 081 77 67 54, ⓦ www.museedesartsanciens.be

The **Musée Provincial des Arts Anciens du Namurois and Trésor d'Oignies** – the collections of which were combined in 2010 – is housed in one of Namur's finest eighteenth-century mansions and set back from the street behind a formal gateway and courtyard. The Oignies Priory treasury is a unique hoard of the exquisitely beautiful gold and silver work of **Brother Hugo d'Oignies**, one of the region's most gifted medieval metalworkers. From the eleventh to the thirteenth centuries, the Meuse valley was famous for the skill of its craftsmen, and Hugo was an innovator in the art of **filigree**, raising the decoration from the background so that the tiny human figures and animals seem to be suspended in space. The pieces here are elaborately studded with precious and semiprecious stones and display an exquisite balance between ornament and function, depicting, for example, minute hunting scenes, with animals leaping convincingly through delicate foliage. In particular, look out for the dazzling **reliquary cover** for St Peter's rib, the charming songbird and goblet of St Marie of Oignies, and a magnificent cover for a Book of the Gospels. The free audio guide in English helps to make sense of it all.

The **Provincial Museum of Ancient Arts**, meanwhile, displays a variety of artworks dating from the Middle Ages through to the Renaissance. The collection begins with an enjoyable sample of devotional **metal work** from the Mosan, most memorably the dinky geometrics of the brass enamels, and moves on to medieval sculptures and painted wooden panels. Of the many **paintings**, the most distinguished are by Henri Blès, an early sixteenth-century Antwerp-based artist who favoured panoramic landscapes populated by tiny figures.

Église St-Loup

rue du Collège • Free • ☎ 081 22 80 85, ⓦ www.eglisesaintloup.be

Perhaps the best of Namur's churches, the **Église St-Loup** is a Baroque extravagance built for the Jesuits between 1621 and 1645, with a fluently carved facade and a sumptuous interior of marble walls and sandstone vaulting. The **high altar** is actually wood painted to look like marble – the ship carrying the last instalment of Italian marble sank and the Jesuits ended up having to finish the church off with this imitation.

Cathédrale St-Aubain

Cathedral place du Chapitre 4 • Free • ☎ 081 24 12 74, ⓦ cana.be • **Musée Diocésain** place du Chapitre 1 • By appointment only • €3 • ☎ 081 44 42 85

The elaborate Neoclassical **Cathédrale St-Aubain** is decorated with acres of creamy white paint and its choir is decorated with melodramatic **paintings** by Jacques Nicolai, one of Rubens' less talented pupils. Attached is the the **Musée Diocésain**, containing sculptures, paintings, silver pieces, textiles and manuscripts gathered from churches across Namur province.

> **NAMUR WALKING AND BOAT TOURS**
>
> Guided tours of Namur's pedestrianized Old Town (July & Aug Mon–Wed & Fri–Sun 2.30pm; May, June & Sept Mon 2.30pm; €3) can be booked at, and set off from, the tourist office (see below).
>
> **La Compagnie des Bateaux** ☎082 22 23 15, ⓦbateaux-meuse.be. Runs 50min return boat trips along the rivers (mid-April to June 1.30pm, 3pm & 5pm; July to mid-Sept 11am, 1.30pm & 5pm; €7.50/adult, €5.50/child). Excursions to Wepion – the strawberry capital – are also offered (July & Aug Mon, Tues & Thurs–Sun 3pm; 1hr 45min; €13/adult, €11/child). All boats depart from Le Grognon (see map, p.257).

Musée de Groesbeeck de Croix

rue Joseph Saintraint 3 • Tues–Sun 10am–12.30pm & 1.15–5pm • €3 • ☎ 081 24 87 20

A large and rambling eighteenth-century mansion, the **Musée de Groesbeeck de Croix** gives a fine impression of the lifestyle of a patrician family during the Enlightenment. It's an appealing mixture of the grand and the homely, with the dining table laid out for tea, a fabulously authentic **eighteenth-century kitchen** and a delightful French-style **garden** out the back. There's not much in the way of standout exhibits, but the feel of the place, as if the owners had just left the building, is satisfyingly authentic.

Musée Africain

rue du 1er Lanciers 1 • Tues, Thurs & Sun 2–5pm • €3 • ☎ 081 23 13 83, ⓦ museeafricainnamur.be

The guardroom of the old army barracks contains the ten-room **Musée Africain**, which is the only one in Wallonia to make reference to King Léopold II's occupation of the Congo. The **atrocities** are somewhat glossed over, but the mishmash of photographs, pottery, African art, basketry and handicrafts is interesting enough.

ARRIVAL AND INFORMATION

NAMUR

By train Namur's train station is 500m north of the town centre, on place de la Station.

Destinations Arlon (hourly; 1hr 35min); Brussels (every 30min; 1hr); Charleroi (hourly; 30–40min); Dinant (hourly; 30min); Liège (hourly; 45min); Luxembourg City (hourly; 1hr 40min).

By bus The square is also the terminus for local and regional buses, which stop outside the Maison du TEC at place de la Station 25 (Mon–Fri 7am–6pm, Sat 8.30am–5pm; ☎ 081 25 35 55, ⓦ infotec.be), which has lots of information about bus services across the whole of French-speaking Belgium.

Tourist information The main tourist office is on square Léopold (daily 9.30am–6pm; ☎ 081 24 64 49, ⓦ namurtourisme.be). Staff can help with accommodation, issue free town maps and brochures, give details of guided tours and provide information on what's on in the town and its environs. There's another tourist office by the river, in the Halle Al' Chair (April–Sept daily 9.30am–6pm; Jan–March & Oct–Dec Tues–Sun 10am–5pm; ☎ 081 24 64 48), which offers the same services as the main office and sells tickets for river cruises.

GETTING AROUND

By bike Li Bia Velo (☎ 078 05 11 12, ⓦ en.libiavelo.be) is a rental scheme with stations dotted around town. The charge is an initial €1/day or €3/week paid by bank card; the first 30min are then free, charged at 50 cents/hr thereafter.

By shuttle train The Citad'In shuttle train uphill to the citadel departs (July to mid-Sept daily; March–June & mid-Sept to early Nov Sat & Sun) from opposite the tourist information office (see above). Round-trip costs €2 (€3 with commentary).

By river taxi Les Namourettes (July & Aug daily; June & Sept Sat & Sun; €1 one-way; ☎ 081 24 65 96) are river taxis that ferry passengers across the Sambre and Meuse rivers, and to the town of Jambes.

ACCOMMODATION

Surprisingly, Namur has relatively few hotels, so be sure to **book ahead** if visiting during July and August.

Auberge de Jeunesse ave Félicien Rops 8 ☎ 081 22 36 88, ⓦ aubergesdejeunesse.be. Offers twins and three-, four- and five-bed dorms. There's a bar with a terrace overlooking the river, a communal kitchen and another

5

serving breakfast and evening meals (mains €5), TV room, free wi-fi and laundry. It's 3km from the train station: walk along the river or take bus #3 or #4 from the centre (€1.75). Sheets and breakfast included. €3 extra for non-HI members. Rates cheaper in low season. Dorm €25, double €62

Château de Namur ave de l'Ermitage 1 ☎ 081 72 99 00, ⓦ chateaudenamur.com. This hotel has 29 well-appointed rooms and occupies a large French château in the wooded park at the top of the citadel. The restaurant trains students from the Namur Hotel School – you can be sure of an innovative menu (around €24 for two courses) and friendly service. €150

Ne5t allée de Menton 26 ☎ 081 58 88 88, ⓦ ne5t.com. Luxurious renovated farmhouse with six spacious, top-of-the-range studios. Guests have discounted access to the on-site spa, which offers a range of facials and massages. €260

★ **Royal Snail Hotel** ave de la Plante 23 ☎ 081 57 00 23, ⓦ theroyalsnail.com. Namur's first boutique hotel sits in the shadow of the impressive citadel and boats clean, white rooms with pops of colour, a gastronomic restaurant (mains €30–40), a slim-line pool and wellness centre offering massages. €135

Les Tanneurs rue des Tanneries 13 ☎ 081 24 00 24, ⓦ tanneurs.com. Right in the town centre, this hotel occupies a lavishly and imaginatively renovated seventeenth-century building, with fifteen rooms in the old building and 32 modern rooms in an extension – opt for the former if budget allows, though all are well equipped and comfortable. There's (limited) parking, wi-fi and two good restaurants, and the more expensive rooms are sometimes discounted during the off season and at weekends. Modern €100, traditional €185

EATING AND DRINKING

Namur has a first-rate selection of **cafés** and **restaurants** as well as a good supply of **bars**, many of them clustered on and around the quaint, pedestrianized squares just west of rue de l'Ange.

CAFÉS AND RESTAURANTS

A Table! rue des Brasseurs 21 ☎ 081 26 16 26, ⓦ atablenamur.be. A rustic café serving organic light bites and super salads for around €14. Wander through to the back for tables with views of the Sambre and the citadel. Tues & Wed 11.30am–2.30pm, Thurs–Sat 11.30am–2.30pm and 6.30–9pm.

Le Bon Vin rue du Président 43 ☎ 081 22 28 08, ⓦ lebonvinnamur.be. A popular organic café with freshly prepared and seasonal food and, as the name suggests, a good selection of wine. Three courses and a *quart* of wine will set you back about €32. Bookings advised. Wed–Sun lunch time, and Thurs, Fri & Sat also eve.

La Mère Gourmandin rue du Président 13 ☎ 081 22 72 08. Candle-lit option famous for its delicious savoury crêpes (€11.80) and tumblers of home-made cider (€2.80). There's a small outdoor terrace out the back. Mon–Thurs noon–2pm, Fri & Sat noon–2pm & 6.30–9.30pm.

Le Pâtanthrope place Chanoine Descamps 15 ☎ 081 22 80 43, ⓦ lepatanthrope.be. An intimate dining room in the heart of the Old Town with exposed brick walls and Botticelli-esque paintings. Dishes are elegant and made with regional ingredients. The three-course evening menu

costs around €36 without wine. Tues–Sun noon–2.30pm & 6.30–10.30pm.

Soup Shop rue de Bruxelles 35 ☎ 081 84 93 51. For a hearty and healthy lunch, this is the place to come. As you would expect from the name, soup is the main event, but the salads, quiches and desserts are delicious too – and great value, all at less than €10. Mon–Sat noon–6pm.

Le Temps des Cerises rue des Brasseurs 22 ☎ 081 22 53 26, ⓦ cerises.be. Intimate, cherry-coloured and cherry-themed restaurant offering a quality menu of French and Basque dishes. Main courses average around €18. Tues–Fri noon–2.30pm & 6.30–10pm, Sat 6.30–10pm.

BARS

Café Ratin-tot place Marché-aux-Légumes 1. With attractive antique decor, including an old French cockerel or two, this is Namur's oldest bar, open since 1616. Mon–Sat 10am–8pm, Sun 11am–8pm (2pm in winter).

Le Chapitre rue du Séminaire 4. Unassuming bar with an extensive beer list. Popular with students and a very busy and convivial place for a drink late evening. Daily 2pm–late.

Les Jardins d'Annevoie

rue des Jardins d'Annevoie 37A, Annevoie-Rouillon; 18km south of Namur · April–June, Sept & Oct daily 9.30am–5.30pm; July & Aug daily 9.30am–6.30pm · €7.80 · ☎ 082 67 97 97, ⓦ annevoie.be · Hourly Namur-Dinant trains stop at Godinne, 2km east of the gardens; bus #21 Namur-Maredsous (4 daily; 30min) stops just outside the gardens; the Namur-Dinant bus #34 (Mon–Fri 1 daily; 30min) stops on the main road, a 10min walk away

A highly recommended stop on the road between Namur and Dinant (see p.276), **Les Jardins d'Annevoie** are reckoned to be among Belgium's finest gardens. The estate

5

THE MOLIGNÉE VALLEY BY RAILBIKE

Down below Maredsous, the beautiful **Molignée valley** winds it way towards the Meuse. With a good map you can explore on foot, but you might instead want to opt for a journey by **railbike** – adapted "bikes" which can carry up to four people along the disused railway tracks between **Falaën**, 4km south of Maredsous, and **Warnant**, about 10km to the northeast. Railbikes are available at the Railbike premises in Falaën at rue de la Gare 82 (daily 11am, 1pm, 3pm & 5pm; single person from €18 and groups of 2–4 people from €16 per person; ☎ 082 69 90 79, ⓦ molignee.be). TEC bus #35 departs from Maredsous station, stopping in Falaën and Warnant (3 daily; 10–15min).

– both manor house and gardens – has been in the hands of the Montpelliers since 1675, and one of the clan, a certain Charles Alexis, turned his hand (or rather those of his gardeners) to garden design in the 1770s. Charles was inspired by his travels in France, Italy and England, picking up tips which he then rolled into one homogeneous creation. From the French came **formal borders**, from the Italians the romance of mossy banks and arbours, while the English influence is most obvious in the **grotto of Neptune**. They are architectural rather than flower gardens, and the common denominator is water – everywhere you look there are **fountains**, jets and **mini-waterfalls**, all worked by natural pressure from the tree-lined **Grand Canal**, immediately above the gardens. If you visit in July, you can also pick raspberries at the end of the walking circuit, and there's a pleasant café, the *Orangerie*, above the shop offering views over the garden and the local Maredsous beer on tap.

Abbaye de Maredsous

rue de Maredsous 11, Denée; 12km west of Annevoie • St Joseph's Visitor Centre March–Oct Mon–Sat 9am–6pm, Sun 9am–8pm; Nov–Feb Mon–Sat 10am–6pm • ☎ 082 69 82 84, ⓦ tourisme.maredsous.be • Bus #21 from Namur bus station (2–4 daily; 50min) or bus #35 from Dinant train station (2–3 daily; 35min); both stop at or near the Abbaye de Maredsous; alternatively, take the railbike (see above)

Founded in the 1870s, the neo-Gothic **Abbaye de Maredsous** in Denée is renowned for its beers – yet they haven't been brewed here since 1963, when the licence and recipes were bought by Duvel Moortgat. You're free to wander round the **monastery** and abbey **gardens**, but since guided tours (arranged at the visitor centre) are only available in French or Dutch, most people head instead to the **St-Joseph visitor centre**, a complex containing a café, bookshop and shop. The latter does a roaring trade in Maredsous produce, selling bread, butter, cheese, pâté and, of course, the abbey's various beers – they produce a blond, a bruin and a strong tripel.

Huy and around

Midway between Namur and Liège, and easily accessible by train from either, the bustling town of **HUY** spreads across both sides of the River Meuse. One of the oldest settlements in Belgium and for a long time a flourishing market town, the place was badly damaged by Louis XIV in the late seventeenth century and mauled by several passing armies thereafter. Consequently, little remains of the old town, but Huy is certainly worth a brief stop, mainly for its splendid **church** and dramatic **citadel**.

The Grand-Place and around

The central **Grand-Place** features an ornate bronze fountain of 1406 decorated with a representation of the town walls interspersed with tiny statues of the same saints commemorated in the church; the wrought-iron and stone vats were added later, in the eighteenth century. The square is flanked by the **Hôtel de Ville**, a self-confident,

5

château-style edifice dating from the 1760s, behind which is tiny **place Verte**, overlooked by an attractive Gothic church and lying at the start of a pretty maze of narrow lanes and alleys that stretch north to rue Vankeerberghen.

Collégiale Notre-Dame et Saint-Domitien

Church Tues–Sun 9am–noon & 2–5pm (6pm in July & Aug) • Free • **Treasury** April–June Sat & Sun 2–4.45pm; July & Aug Tues–Sun 2–4.45pm • €3

Down by the river, the imposing Gothic bulk of the **Collégiale Notre-Dame et Saint-Domitien** dominates the town, towering over the banks of the River Meuse with the high cliffs and walls of the citadel behind. Built between 1311 and 1536, the church's interior is decked out with fine stained glass, especially the magnificent **rose window**. On the right side of the nave as you enter, stairs lead down to a Romanesque **crypt** and **trésor** (treasury), where the relics of Huy's patron saint, St Domitian, were once venerated, and whose original twelfth-century shrine is on display, along with three other large shrines crafted by the Mosan gold- and silversmiths for which Huy was once famous. They're somewhat faded, but the beauty and skill of their execution shines through. Outside, on the side of the church facing the town centre, look out for the **Porte de Bethléem**, topped by a mid-fourteenth-century arch decorated with scenes of the Nativity.

Fort de Huy

chaussée Napoléon • April–June & Sept Mon–Fri 9.30am–5pm, Sat & Sun 10am–6pm; July & Aug daily 10am–6pm • €4, free first Sun of month • Accessible from quai de Namur by taking the path up to the left just beyond tourist office; or take the *téléphérique* cable car (June & Sept Sat & Sun 11am–12.15pm & 1–6.30pm; July & Aug daily 11am–12.15pm & 1–6.30pm; single €3.50, €4.50 return) from ave De Batta on the far side of the river: cross over Pont Roi Baudouin and turn left • ☎ 085 21 78 21

There's been a fortress here since the ninth century, though the medieval castle that once occupied the site was demolished in 1717; the present **Fort de Huy**, partly hewn out of solid rock, was erected by the Dutch in the early nineteenth century. The fort is a massive complex, and although much of it can be visited, the most compelling and coherent section is the dozen or so rooms used by the Germans as a **prison** during World War II, when no fewer than seven thousand prisoners passed through this bleak place. The cells, dormitories and interrogation chambers are grim enough, but the mountain of press cuttings, photos and personal effects pertaining to the Resistance and, in particular, to **concentration camps** are simply harrowing; it's a relief to emerge into the daylight of the central courtyard, from where you can climb up onto the top for what are, predictably, stunning **views** over Huy and the countryside around.

ARRIVAL AND INFORMATION   HUY

By train Huy's train station is on the opposite (west) side of the river from the town centre, a 15min walk: head straight out of the station down to the river, turn right and cross the Pont Roi Baudouin to reach the Collégiale Notre-Dame. Several trains depart hourly (25–30min) from both Namur and Liège.

Tourist information The tourist office is right by the river and church at quai de Namur 1 (April–Sept Mon–Fri 8.30am–6pm, Sat & Sun 10am–6pm; Oct–March Mon–Fri 9am–4pm, Sat & Sun 10am–4pm; ☎ 085 21 29 15, ✆ pays-de-huy.be).

ACCOMMODATION AND EATING

Arômes et Volup'thés rue Vierset Godin 3 ☎ 085 24 04 33, ✆ aromesetvolupthes.be. Swish yet affordable café serving a huge array of speciality teas and coffees, with sweet treats to accompany them. Tues–Sat 10am–6pm.
Hôtel du Fort chaussée Napoleon 5–6 ☎ 085 21 24 03, ✆ hoteldufort.be. Five minutes' walk along the river, past

the tourist office, this place has 28 en-suite rooms, some with baths. Breakfast costs €7.50 extra per person and wi-fi is charged at €1/30min. **€75**
Pane e Vino Grand Place 3 ☎ 085 51 44 54. Far from your bog-standard pizzeria, this place has a large terrace and serves flavourful lamb, risotto and excellent pastas for

5

€20, as well as money-saving menus. Mon–Sat 11.30am–2.30pm & 6–11.30pm.
Sur Cour rue Grianne 14 ☎085 31 16 30, ⓦrestaurantsurcour-1660.be. This restaurant's ancient

greying exterior conceals a modern dining room and sunny courtyard terrace. The €19 French-cuisine lunch menu is recommended. Tues, Wed, Fri & Sun noon–2pm & 7–9pm, Sat 7–9pm.

Château de Jehay

rue du Parc 1 • Mon–Fri 2–6pm, Sat & Sun 11am–6pm • €5 • ☎ 085 82 44 00, ⓦ www.chateaujehay.be • Either drive along the E42 towards Namur, then take exit 5 towards Amay, or jump on TEC bus #85 from Huy

Flecked with white stones, the pretty, moat-surrounded **Château de Jehay** has belonged to the Counts of van den Steen since the seventeenth century, and the latest count still calls it home. Most of what you see today dates from the beginning of the sixteenth century; only the keep remains medieval. The newer, nineteenth-century sections – in Gothic Revival style – are the work of architect **Alphonse Balat**, who was also behind Brussels' Royal Greenhouses of Laeken (see p.78). Inside, the lavish **interior** is filled with antique furniture, tapestries and art. Lovely formal **gardens** are found out the back too.

Liège

The capital of the Ardennes, and of its own province, **LIÈGE**, straddling the River Meuse, is an underdog among Belgian towns. It has struggled to shake off its reputation as a large, grimy, **industrial city**, but these assessments are somewhat outdated and unfair. The city is steeped in folkloric romance – locals know it as La Cité Ardente ("The Passionate City") – and it has a strong culinary identity with a growing band of **excellent restaurants** and hotels, attributes that more than make up for the city's lack of notable sights, and which warrant at least a day's exploration. Winter is a good time to visit: the wooden chalets of the **Christmas markets** line the squares throughout December and, at the end of January, the biennial **Festival de Liège** (ⓦfestivaldeliege.be) puts on a lively programme of contemporary theatre, music and dance.

The bulk of the city centre lies on the west bank of the river and congregates around three main **squares**: place du Marché, place St-Lambert and place de la République Française. What's known as the **old town** runs east from place du Marché, with Féronstrée as its spine, and is home to the city's best museums and a smattering of historic buildings. The livelier **new town**, the city's commercial centre and home to most of its shops, bars, restaurants and nightlife, nudges south from place St-Lambert and place de la République Française. To the east of the river, on what is in effect an island in the Meuse, the district of **Outremeuse** is the traditional home of the true Liégeois, and harbours a cluster of bars and restaurants and its own distinctive traditions and dialect.

Brief history

For most of its history, Liège was an independent principality; from the tenth century onwards it was the seat of a long line of **prince-bishops**, who ruled until 1794, when the French Revolutionary army expelled the last, torching his cathedral to hammer home the point. Later, Liège was incorporated into the Belgian state, rising to prominence as an industrial city. The **coal** and **steel** industries hereabouts date back to the twelfth century, but it was only in the nineteenth century that real development of

---

LIÈGE CITY PASS

The **Liège City Pass** grants free entry to all the main museums, a free Simenon walking-tour audio guide (see p.268), and allows you to buy a full-day bus pass for the bargain price of €3. It costs €16, is valid for 48 hours and can be bought from tourist information (see p.269).

5

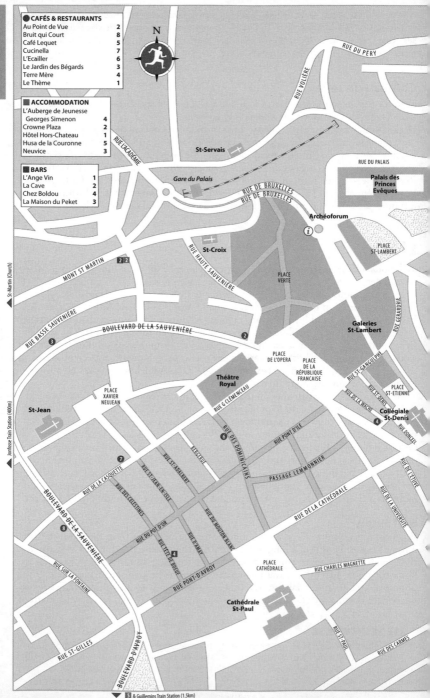

● CAFÉS & RESTAURANTS
Au Point de Vue	2
Bruit qui Court	8
Café Lequet	5
Cucinella	7
L'Ecailler	6
Le Jardin des Bégards	3
Terre Mère	4
Le Thème	1

■ ACCOMMODATION
L'Auberge de Jeunesse Georges Simenon	4
Crowne Plaza	2
Hôtel Hors-Chateau	1
Husa de la Couronne	5
Neuvice	3

■ BARS
L'Ange Vin	1
La Cave	2
Chez Boldou	4
La Maison du Peket	3

RUE DU PERY
RUE VOLLÈRE
RUE L'ACADÉMIE
St-Servais
Gare du Palais
RUE DE BRUXELLES
RUE DE BRUXELLES
RUE DU PALAIS
Palais des Princes Evêques
Archéoforum
PLACE ST-LAMBERT
St-Martin (Church)
MONT ST MARTIN
RUE HAUTE SAUVENIÈRE
St-Croix
PLACE VERTE
RUE BASSE SAUVENIÈRE
BOULEVARD DE LA SAUVENIÈRE
Galeries St-Lambert
RUE GÉRARDRIE
PLACE DE L'OPERA
PLACE DE LA RÉPUBLIQUE FRANCAISE
RUE ST-GANGULPHE
Théâtre Royal
RUE G CLEMENCEAU
PLACE XAVIER NEUJEAN
St-Jean
Jonfosse Train Station (400m)
RUE ST-DENIS
RUE DE LA WACHE
PLACE ST-ETIENNE
Collégiale St-Denis
RUE DONCEEL
RUE DES DOMINICAINS
RUE PONT D'ILE
PASSAGE LEMMONNIER
RUE DE L'ETUVE
RUE DE LA CATHÉDRALE
RUE DE LA UNIVERSITÉ
BOUCHERIE
RUE ST-ADALBERT
RUE DE LA CASQUETTE
RUE DES CÉLESTINES
RUE ST-JEAN-EN-ISLE
RUE DU MOUTON BLANC
BOULEVARD DE LA SAUVENIÈRE
RUE DU POT D'OR
RUE D'AMAY
RUE ETIENNE BEBOUE
RUE PONT-D'AVROY
PLACE CATHÉDRALE
RUE CHARLES MAGNETTE
RUE SUR LA FONTAINE
Cathédrale St-Paul
RUE ST-PAUL
RUE DES CARMES
RUE ST-GILLES
BOULEVARD D'AVROY

5

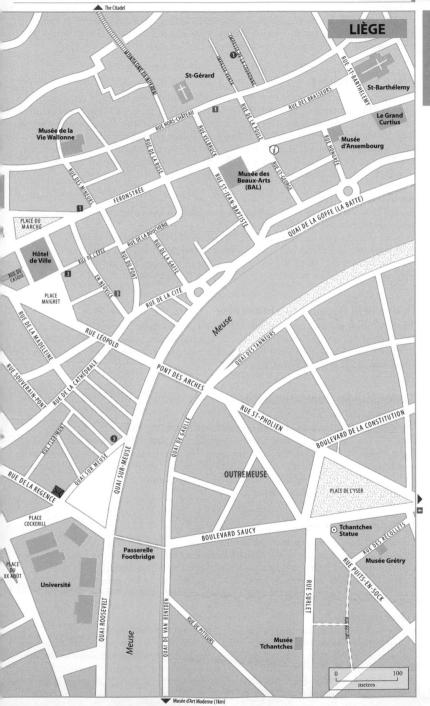

▲ The Citadel

LIÈGE

St-Gérard

IMPASSE DE LA COURONNE

IMPASSE VERTA

RUE DE LA POULE

RUE DES BRASSEURS

RUE ST-BARTHÉLEMY

St-Barthélemy

Le Grand Curtius

RUE HORS-CHÂTEAU

RUE VELBRUCK

Musée de la Vie Wallonne

RUE DE LA ROSE

Musée d'Ansembourg

RUE HONGRÉE

RUE DES MINEURS

FERONSTRÉE

RUE ST-GEORGE

RUE ST-JEAN-BAPTISTE

Musée des Beaux-Arts (BAL)

PLACE DU MARCHÉ

RUE DE LA BOUCHERIE

QUAI DE LA GOFFE (LA BATTE)

Hôtel de Ville

RUE DE L'ÉPÉE

RUE DE LA GRÈFE

RUE DU CASQUE

RUE DU PONT

EN NEUVICE

PLACE MAIGRET

RUE DE LA CITÉ

Meuse

RUE DE LA MADELEINE

RUE LÉOPOLD

QUAI DES TANNEURS

PONT DES ARCHES

RUE SOUVERAIN-PONT

RUE DE LA CATHÉDRALE

RUE ST-PHOLIEN

RUE FLORIMONT

BOULEVARD DE LA CONSTITUTION

QUAI DE GAULLE

OUTREMEUSE

RUE DE LA REGENCE

QUAI SUR MEUSE

QUAI-MEUSE

PLACE DE L'YSER

PLACE COCKERILL

Tchantches Statue

RUE DES RECOLLETS

Musée Grétry

RUE PUITS-EN-SOCK

BOULEVARD SAUCY

PLACE DU XX AOÛT

Passerelle Footbridge

Université

QUAI ROOSEVELT

QUAI DE VAN BENEDEN

RUE SURLET

RUE FOSSE

RUE DE PITEURS

Meuse

Musée Tchantches

0   100
metres

▼ Musée d'Art Moderne (1km)

5

the city's natural resources took place, principally under one **John Cockerill** (1790–1840), a British entrepreneur whose family name you still see around town – though unfortunately for Liège and its workers, its industries are now in steep decline.

Place St-Lambert

The true centre of Liège, the large, open **Place St-Lambert** was formerly the site of the great Gothic cathedral of St-Lambert, destroyed by the French in 1794; metal columns mark where the church once stood. The square's only real distinction is provided by the long frontage of the **Palais des Princes Evêques** (Palace of the Prince-Bishops), a neo-Gothic edifice mostly dating from the mid-nineteenth century. It's now used as a combination of law courts and provincial government offices, and you can usually wander into its two **courtyards** during office hours.

Archéoforum

place Saint-Lambert • Tues–Fri 10am–5pm, Sat 10am–5pm • €6, hourly guided tours or self-tour with iPad; €8 combi ticket with St Paul's treasury • ☎ 04 250 93 70, Ⓦ www.archeoforumdeliege.be

You can visit the excavated site of the city's former Gothic cathedral in the **Archéoforum**, underneath place St-Lambert. It was the fourth successor to a church that was built at the site of St Lambert's murder in the eighth century, and is mixed up with the remains of an extensive second-century **Roman villa**.

Place de la République Française

The city's third main square, **Place de la République Française**, sits to the west of place St-Lambert and is edged on one side by the shed-like Neoclassical **Théâtre Royale**, in front of which stands a statue of the Liège-born composer **André Grétry**, whose heart is contained in the urn just below.

Collégiale St-Denis de Liège

rue de la Cathédrale 64 • Mon–Sat 9.30am–5pm, Sun noon–5pm

The **Collégiale St-Denis** is worth a visit not for the building itself, which is gloomy and formless, but for a striking early sixteenth-century **wooden retable**, standing a good 5m high, which is displayed in the south transept. The top – and principal – section has six panels showing the Passion of Christ, full of drama and assertively carved. The bottom set of panels is later and gentler in style, with smaller figures telling the story of St Denis from baptism to decapitation.

Cathédrale St-Paul

place Cathédrale • Daily 8am–5pm • ☎ 04 232 61 31, Ⓦ cathedraledeliege.be

The imposing grey steeple of the **Cathédrale St-Paul** makes a useful city landmark. The church was promoted to cathedral status in 1794, after the destruction of the city's former cathedral by the French. Inside are some swirling **ceiling paintings** of 1570 and a late thirteenth-century polychrome *Madonna and Child* at the base of the choir.

Trésor de Liège

rue Bonne-Fortune 6 • Tues–Sun 2–5pm; guided tour daily 3pm • €5 • ☎ 04 232 61 32, Ⓦ tresordeliege.be

The cathedral's **Trésor de Liège** features a mammoth 90kg bust reliquary of St Lambert, the work of a goldsmith from Aachen, dating from 1512, which contains the skull of the saint and depicts scenes from his life – the miracles he performed as a boy, his burial in Maastricht and the relocation of his body from Maastricht to Liège by St Hubert, who succeeded him as bishop. There are also some lovely examples of **ivory**

5

work from the eleventh century, and a similarly dated missal, stained by the waters of a 1920s flood that inundated the church.

Place du Marché

The northern side of the tree-lined **Place du Marché** is flanked by a row of atmospheric bars and restaurants, behind which looms the curiously Russian-looking onion dome of the **Église Saint-André**. The south side of the square is occupied by the run-of-the-mill eighteenth-century **Hôtel de Ville**, while in the middle stands **Le Perron**, a grandiose symbol of civic independence, comprising a cumbersome water fountain of 1697 surmounted by a long and slender column.

The old town

From place du Marché, **rue Féronstrée** heads east to form the backbone of the **old town**, an historic, much quieter part of town – except on Sunday mornings, when the vigorous **La Batte market** takes over the nearby riverbank. For an impressive, panoramic view over the whole of Liège, make for **rue Hors-Château**, from where 400-odd steps ascend the very steep **Montagne de Bueren** up to the **citadel**, which is now little more than a set of ramparts enclosing a modern hospital. Well worth the genuinely lung-wrenching trek, the views are superlative, looking right out over the city and the rolling countryside beyond.

Musée de la Vie Wallonne

cours des Mineurs • Tues–Sun 9.30am–6pm • €5, free first Sun of month • ☎ 04 237 90 40, ⓦ www.provincedeliege.be/viewallonne • **Puppet shows** mid-Nov to April Wed 2.30pm & Sun 10.30am • €2

Devoted to Walloon culture, the **Musée de la Vie Wallonne** is housed in a beautifully restored former Franciscan friary. It's a nostalgic collection, with lots of assorted items from past eras, including **carnival masks** and puppets, children's toys and old brands of soap and cigarettes, all displayed with a contemporary and serious approach. A series of room tableaux illustrate the changing fashions and technologies of the past century, and there are also displays examining **Walloon militancy** and separatism, and the decline of local industry (particularly the mines). Pick up an audio guide in English from the front desk. Look out for the occasional puppet show featuring **Tchantchès** (see box, p.268).

Musée des Beaux-Arts (BAL)

rue Féronstrée 86 • Tues–Sun 10–6pm • €5 • ☎ 04 221 89 11, ⓦ beauxartsliege.be

Once known as the **Musée de l'Art Wallon**, this modern building, now called the **Musée des Beaux-Arts (BAL)**, also houses the artworks that once belonged to the Museum of Modern and Contemporary Art, which has closed and will reopen in the future as an International Centre of Art and Culture. The museum showcases an attractive selection of works by French-speaking Belgian artists, including sixteenth-century paintings by Henri Bles, plus a few canvases by Liège's greatest artist, **Lambert Lombard** (1505–66). The nineteenth- and early twentieth-century sections are particularly strong, ranging from Antoine Wiertz's immense and wonderfully overblown *Greeks and Trojans in Dispute over the Body of Patrocles* to the small group of works by **Delvaux** and **Magritte**, notably the former's wacky *L'Homme de la Rue*, showing a bowler-hatted businessman imperviously reading his newspaper amid a landscape of Classical ruins and cavorting nymphs.

Musée d'Ansembourg

rue Féronstrée 114 • Thurs–Sun 10am–6pm • €5 • ☎ 04 221 94 02, ⓦ lesmuseesdeliege.be/ansembourg

Occupying a grand eighteenth-century mansion, the **Musée d'Ansembourg**'s interior is distinguished by its sweeping wooden staircase, stucco ceilings and leather wallpaper. This provides a suitably lavish setting for a **sumptuous collection** of period furniture,

5

Delftware, a selection of clocks (including a unique six-faced specimen by Hubert Sarton from 1795), and portraits of various local bigwigs – including several of Liège's prince-bishops – in various stages of self-importance.

Grand Curtius

rue Féronstrée 136 • Mon & Wed–Sun 10am–6pm • €9 • ☎ 04 221 68 17, ⓦ grandcurtiusliege.be

Dedicated to decorative and applied arts, the collection at the **Grand Curtius** is a bit of a romp through history, studiously covering all ages from the medieval period to Art Nouveau, and it's all beautifully displayed, with some info in English. The Mosan metalwork is a standout, as are the **religious woodcarving** from the Middle Ages and the small collection of Flemish paintings. When you've had enough, check out the museum shop and ground-floor bistro, with its shady courtyard garden.

Église St-Barthélemy

place St-Barthélemy • Mon–Sat 10am–noon & 2–5pm, Sun 2–5pm • €2 • ☎ 04 250 23 72, ⓦ st-barthelemy.be

Originally a Romanesque edifice dating back to the twelfth century, the interior of the **Église St-Barthélemy** was entirely re-equipped six centuries later. Of most significance is the magnificent Romanesque bronze **baptismal font** of 1118. The work of a certain Renier de Huy, the font rests on ten oxen, who bend their heads and necks as if under the weight of the great bowl.

Outremeuse

Across the River Meuse, **Outremeuse** is a working-class quarter that's said to be the home of the true Liégeois. The district's inhabitants were long known for their forthright radicalism, rioting against their rulers on many occasions and refusing, during the German occupation of World War I, to keep the city's small-arms factories in production. Their appointed guardian was the folkloric figure known as **Tchantchès** (see box below), and the quarter is also the birthplace of acclaimed writer **Georges Simenon** (1903–89), creator of Inspector Maigret – the tourist office has a leaflet entitled "Following Simenon's Footsteps", with an accompanying **audio guide** that costs €4.50, though it's free with the City Pass (see box, p.263).

Musée Tchantchès

rue Surlet 56 • Tues & Thurs 2–6pm • €1 • ☎ 04 342 75 75, ⓦ tchantches.eu • **Puppet shows** Oct–April Wed 2.30pm & Sun 10.30am • €3

Also known as the Royal Theatre, the **Musée Tchantchès** is dedicated to Outremeuse's cheeky mascot and displays his various costumes and child-size marionettes sculpted by puppet-maker Denis Bisscheroux. From October to April, they host **puppet shows** on a beautiful old stage – great for kids.

Musée Grétry

rue dés Recollets 34 • Fri–Sun 10am–6pm • Free; temporary exhibitions €2.25

The **Musée Grétry** is named after André-Modeste Grétry, the inventor of comic opera, who was born in this house – which contains a hotchpotch collection of his belongings, instruments and sheet music – in February 1741.

TCHANTCHÈS

Tchantchès (Liège slang for "Francis"), the so-called "Prince of Outremeuse", is an earthy, independent-minded, brave but drunken fellow, who is said to have been born between two Outremeuse paving stones on August 25, 760. In later life, legend claims, he was instrumental in the campaigns of Charlemagne, thanks to the use of his enormous nose. Nowadays, Tchantchès can be seen in action in traditional Liège **puppet shows** (see p.267); he's also represented in a **statue** on place l'Yser, the traditional place of his death.

ARRIVAL AND DEPARTURE

5

By train Liège has three train stations: all trains stop at the revamped main terminal, Guillemins, about 2km south of the centre. Most services also call at Liège's other two stations: Jonfosse, not far from boulevard de la Sauvenière, just to the west of the centre; and Palais, near place St-Lambert in the city centre. Note, however, that express trains from Brussels and Luxembourg City only stop at Guillemins. To get to the centre of town from Guillemins station, either take the train to Palais or catch bus #1 or #4 to place St-Lambert; the taxi fare for the same journey is about €10.

Destinations from Liège-Guillemins Brussels (hourly; 1hr); Coo (every 2hr; 50min); Eupen (hourly; 40min); Huy (every 20min; 20–30mins); Jemelle (hourly; 1hr 30min); Luxembourg City (hourly; 2hr 30min); Melreux-Hotton (hourly; 1hr); Namur (hourly; 45min); Spa, via Verviers (hourly; 55min); Trois Ponts (every 2hr; 55min).

INFORMATION AND GETTING AROUND

Tourist information The main city tourist office is located to the east of place St-Lambert at rue Féronstrée 92 (May–Sept Mon–Fri 9am–5pm, Sat 10am–4pm, Sun 10am–3pm; Oct–April Mon–Fri 9am–5pm, Sat 10am–4pm, Sun 10am–3pm; ☎042 21 92 21, ⓦ www.liege.be/tourisme). They can book accommodation and tickets for the tourist train (see below) and provide a couple of local walking maps.

Tourist train One-hour tours of the city departing from place St-Lambert (April–Sept Tues–Sun noon, 1.30pm, 3pm & 4.30pm; Oct Sat & Sun same times; Nov–March only during holidays; €5/3.50 adult/child). Buy tickets from the tourist office.

ACCOMMODATION

L'Auberge de Jeunesse Georges Simenon rue Georges Simenon 2 ☎043 44 56 89, ⓦ lesaubergesdejeunesse .be. Modern, well-equipped hostel with 215 beds in a pleasant old building In the heart of Outremeuse, 1km or so east of place St-Lambert. Has self-catering facilities, a café, internet access and a laundry. Closed most of Jan; rates cheaper in low season. Dorm **€25**, double **€62**

Crowne Plaza Mont Saint Martin 9 ☎042 22 94 94, ⓦ crowneplazaliege.be. Occupies a pair of sixteenth-century townhouses that were painstakingly restored and now offer ultra-modern, luxurious five-star rooms, a stunning vaulted-ceiling bar, spa, brasserie with an impressive terrace, and a gastronomic restaurant. Doesn't feel like a chain at all. **€150**

★**Hôtel Hors Château** rue Hors Château 62 ☎042 50 60 68, ⓦ hors-chateau.be. Listed building right in the heart of Liège's old quarter with nine intimate, modern rooms decorated in shades of black and aubergine. Free wi-fi. **€95**

Husa de la Couronne place des Guillemins 11 ☎04 340 30 00, ⓦ www.hotelhusadelacouronne.be. Trendy, Italian-style three-star right opposite Guillemins station. Caters to businessmen, but the free wi-fi, 24-hour bar and epic breakfast buffet appeals to all. Online rates very reasonable. **€69**

★**Neuvice** En Neuvice 45 ☎04 375 97 40, ⓦ hotelneuvice.be. Crisp, modern boutique-style option spread through three historic buildings on the oldest street in town. Has ten spacious rooms, a library, and the breakfast (€15) is served in a restored fifteenth-century cellar. City tax €5 extra per person. **€150**

EATING

Liégeois cuisine is deliciously **hearty** rather than refined – in particular, look out for *boulets avec sirop de Liège* (meatballs drizzled in a sweet local syrup).

Au Point de Vue place Verte 10 ☎04 223 64 82, ⓦ brasserie-aupointdevue.be. This cosy pub with an outside terrace right in the city centre has been going for years, and is a good place to try traditional Liégeois food – meatballs, rabbit, veal kidneys and the like. Daily 8am–11pm.

Bruit qui Court blvd de la Sauvenière 142 ☎04 232 18 18, ⓦ bruitquicourt.be. Simple and reasonably priced meals – and vegetarian friendly to boot. There's also a lively bar in the old converted bank vault downstairs. Mains average about €12. Mon–Fri 11am–midnight, Sat 11am–2am, Sun evening only.

★**Café Lequet** quai sur-Meuse 17 ☎04 222 21 34. Authentic bygone-era restaurant that serves the best *boulet-frites* – meatballs doused in sweet *sirop de Liège* – in the city. Attracts people from far and wide, plus it's cheap and has a lovely buzz. Mon & Wed–Sun noon–2.30pm & 6–9pm.

Cucinella rue de la Casquette 26 ☎04 222 36 52. Top-quality Italian restaurant with a sleek black-and-white interior and a garden out the back for summer evenings. Pasta dishes €16, osso bucco and other mains €20. Mon, Tues & Thurs–Sat noon–2.30pm & 6.30–11pm, Wed noon–2.30pm.

L'Ecailler rue des Dominicains 26 ☎04 222 07 80, ⓦ lecailler.be. Behind the Théâtre Royale, this cosy old-fashioned joint is a long-term favourite and does great

5

oysters and seafood platters. Main courses around €20. Mon–Thurs & Sun 11.45am–2.15pm & 6.30–10pm, Fri & Sat 11.45am–2.15pm & 6.30–10.30pm.

Le Jardin des Bégards blvd de la Sauvenière 70B ☎ 04 222 92 34, ⓦ lejardindesbegards.be. Exquisite Italian food prepared by self-taught, award-winning chef François Piscitello at this stylish wood-and-leather-clad brasserie once voted the best Mediterranean restaurant in Belgium. Mains around €27. Tues–Fri noon–1.30pm & 7–9.30pm, Sat 7–9.30pm.

Terre Mère rue de la Régence 21 ☎ 04 221 38 05, ⓦ terremere.be. Rammed at lunch times and rightly so: their organic, veggie sandwiches and salads are inventive and tasty. Be sure to try the home-made rosemary, thyme, lemon and grape juice. Mon–Fri 10am–3.30pm, Sat 10am–4.30pm.

★ **Le Thème** Impasse de la Couronne 9 ☎ 04 222 02 02, ⓦ letheme.com. Tucked down a tiny alleyway in the old town, this is one of Liège's best restaurants with innovative, seasonal three-course (€32) and five-course (€38) menus and ever-changing decor. Reservations essential. Mon–Sat 7pm–late.

DRINKING AND NIGHTLIFE

The grid of streets in the new town running north from rue Pont d'Avroy to rue de la Casquette is the hub of the city's nightlife, with loads of good, largely **student-oriented bars** that can get very raucous later on. Rue Pont d'Avroy itself has lots of drinking haunts, but most of the best are found in the **tiny alleyways** of rue Tête de Boeuf and the parallel rue d'Amay. There's a clutch of more sedate venues on and around the **place du Marché**.

L'Ange Vin place du Marché 43 ☎ 04 221 29 21. A wine bar, as the name suggests, which gets pretty lively in the evenings and attracts a mixed gay and straight crowd. Mon–Fri & Sun 11am–midnight, Sat 3pm–midnight.

★ **La Cave** mont-Saint-Martin 9. Sip cocktails (€12.50) in this former artillery room with a sixteenth-century vaulted-brick ceiling inside the *Crowne Plaza Hotel*. Thurs–Sat 5pm–1am.

Chez Boldou rue Tête de Boeuf 15. Entertainingly decorated bar full of eclectic bric-a-brac. It's popular with students and there's live music at weekends (no cover charge), as well as a nightclub, *En Bas*, downstairs (free). Daily 7pm–5am; nightclub Fri & Sat 11pm–8am.

La Maison du Peket rue de l'Epée 4 ☎ 04 250 67 83, ⓦ maisondupeket.be. The place to taste the local drink *peket* – a type of gin – in 250 varieties from guava and mango in the fruit section, to the dusty old bottles of the vintage shelves. Daily 10am–late.

Spa

SPA, about 30km southeast of Liège, was the world's first health resort, established way back in the sixteenth century: Pliny the Elder knew of the healing properties of the waters here and Henry VIII was an early visitor, but it was **Peter the Great** who clinched the town's fame, heralding it as "the best place to take the waters". Since then, the town has given its name to thermal resorts worldwide, reaching a height of popularity in the eighteenth and nineteenth centuries, when it was known as the "Café of Europe", being graced by monarchs, statesmen, intellectuals and aristocrats from every corner of the continent. Later the town went into slow decline – when the poet Matthew Arnold visited in 1860, he claimed it "astonished us by its insignificance" – but Spa is regaining its chicness thanks to the modern thermal complex, **Les Thermes de Spa**, on the hill overlooking the town. It also makes a good base for excursions into the **Hautes Fagnes** (see p.275), a short drive to the south and southeast.

The **town centre** has a faded elegance thanks to a cluster of grand Neoclassical buildings, presided over by the three towering steeples of the church of **Notre-Dame et St-Remacle**. Chief among these are the former **thermal baths**, which are now closed and awaiting a new role. The neighbouring **casino**, the oldest in the world, was founded in 1763 under the improbable auspices of the prince-bishop of Liège, though the current building dates only from 1919. Curiously enough, it hosts the annual **Francofolies** festival, which plays tribute to the heady world of French *chanson* (ⓦ francofolies.be). The town also has a good **flea market** in the Léopold II Gallery just behind the tourist office on Sunday morning (8am–1pm).

Pouhon-Pierre-le-Grand and other springs

rue Royale • Daily: April–Sept 10am–6pm; Oct–March 10am–5pm • €1

At the town's central main mineral spring, **Pouhon-Pierre-le-Grand**, you can drink the cloudy waters, which are allegedly beneficial for lung and heart ailments as well as rheumatism. It's housed in a barnlike Neoclassical pavilion – also home to the relocated tourist office (see below) – and named after Peter the Great, who appreciated the therapeutic effects of its waters and visited often. Spa's **other springs** – notably Tonnelet, Barisart, Géronstère and Sauvenière – can be visited on a summer **mini-train** (see below). These are open all year round and free to enter.

Musée de la Ville d'Eaux

ave Reine Astrid 77 • Daily 2–6pm • €4, free first Sun of month • ☎ 087 77 44 86, ⊛ spavillaroyale.be

Five minutes' walk west of the town centre, situated in the former mansion of Queen Marie-Henriette, the **Musée de la Ville d'Eaux** displays posters and objects relating to the resort and its waters. The stables next door have been turned into the **Musée du Cheval**, exhibiting all things equine.

Les Thermes de Spa

Colline d'Annette et Lubin • Mon–Thurs & Sat 9.30am–9pm, Fri 9.30am–10pm, Sun 9.30am–8pm • €20/3hr, €31/day • ☎ 087 77 25 60, ⊛ thermesdespa.com • Take funicular from place Royale (€1 each way), or follow path through the woods just to the side

On the hill immediately above central Spa stands the town's leading attraction, **Les Thermes de Spa**, a thermal complex offering a multitude of treatments. On arrival you can sample three different types of Spa spring water – Reine, Clementine and the iron-rich Marie-Henriette – and beyond there is both an outdoor and indoor **pool** with water-massage jets and hot tubs galore. Upstairs is reserved for saunas, steam rooms and a relaxation area with chill-out music and a **panoramic view** of the valley below. For massage, mud wraps or water treatments in the famous retro copper baths, you need to book in advance.

ARRIVAL AND GETTING AROUND   SPA

By train Spa has two train stations, but the one you want for the town centre is Spa-Géronstère, a 5min walk south of the casino.

Destinations Liège (hourly; 50min); Namur (every 2hr; 1hr 40min).

By mini-train Throughout July and Aug a mini-train plies around the outskirts of town, departing from outside the main baths every hour (daily 11am–5pm; €5.50/2.80 adult/child).

By cable car A cable car running up and down the hillside connects the Thermes de Spa with the lower town; tickets costs €1 each way.

INFORMATION

Tourist office Situated inside the Neoclassical pavilion which houses the Pierre-Le- Grand spring fountain at rue du Marche 1A (April–Sept Mon–Fri 9am–6pm, Sat & Sun 10am–6pm; Oct–March Mon–Fri 9am–6pm, Sat & Sun 10am–5pm; ☎ 087 79 53 53, ⊛ spatourisme.be). There are twenty walking routes around the surrounding countryside and the office sells a map detailing them for €5.

ACCOMMODATION

Best Western Hotel Villa des Fleurs rue Albin Body 31 ☎ 087 79 50 50, ⊛ villadesfleurs.be. Right in the centre of town, this is Spa's most characterful and comfortable option, a handsome old town house dating from the 1880s with just twelve large guest rooms decorated in a modern version of period style – and with a nice private garden too. **€172**

Camping Spa d'Or Stockay 17, Sart-les-Spa ☎ 087 47 44 00, ⊛ campingspador.be. Situated 4km northeast of town, this four-star campsite sits beside the small Wayai River. As well as camping spots, travellers can rent mobile homes, tents or book a dorm bed. Also on site is a large open-air, heated swimming pool, a restaurant, bar, well-stocked shop and two computers

5

SPA-FRANCORCHAMPS

Spa-Francorchamps, 10km southeast of Spa, is renowned as one of the most scenic and historic venues in the motorsports world. The highlight by far is September's **Belgian Grand Prix**, but the circuit is busy almost every day between March and November, hosting all kinds of events, some of which are free. Anyone can visit, and most of the time there's free access to the paddock and pit lane, as well as the panoramic top-floor brasserie. It's also possible to see more of the circuit – the media centre and **race control room**, for example – by way of a **guided tour** (March 15–November 15, 2pm first & third Tues & second Wed of each month; 1hr 30min; €9.50; ☎087 29 37 00, ⓦspa-francorchamps.be).

with internet access. Children's entertainment activities are organized during summer. Camping: pitch, plus two people <u>€32.50</u>, dorm <u>€14.50</u>

★ **Radisson Blu** Palace place Royale 39 ☎087 27 97 00, ⓦradissonblu.com/palacehotel-spa. Seated at the base of the hill in the centre of town, this hotel's winning feature is its own private cable car to Les Thermes de Spa, so guests (who also receive discounts) can travel to and fro in their dressing gowns. <u>€275</u>

Le Relais place du Monument 22 ☎087 77 11 08, ⓦwww.hotelrelais-spa.be. This small, well-cared-for hotel has eleven guest rooms, each kitted out in functional style, at a variety of prices. Great central location, and good restaurant downstairs too. <u>€54</u>

EATING AND DRINKING

La Belle Époque place du Monument 15 ☎087 77 54 03. As the name suggests, this place has a beautiful interior. Serves excellent fish mains from around €17 and three-course menus for €25. Wed–Sun noon–2pm & 6.30–9.30pm.

Le Grand Maur rue Xhrouet 41 ☎087 77 36 16, ⓦlegrandmaur.com. Sophisticated townhouse restaurant famous for its seasonal menus, which at the time of writing featured lobster, lamb and rhubarb. Two courses with wine costs around €46 per person. Reservations essential. Tues–Sat 7–10pm.

★ **La Luna/La Brasserie des Thermes** place Royale 25 ☎087 77 45 25, ⓦbrasseriedesthermes.be. Split into two parts: *La Luna* is a romantic brasserie serving superb steak-frites (€20), while *Brasseries des Thermes* serves cheaper grub such as simple pasta dishes in less smart surroundings. Daily 10am–9pm.

Stavelot

The small and tranquil town of **STAVELOT** rambles up the hill from the River Amblève. It grew up around its **abbey**, which ran the area as an independent principality until the French Revolutionary army ended its privileges at the end of the eighteenth century. The town was also the scene of fierce fighting during the Ardennes campaign of the last world war, and some of the Nazis' worst atrocities in Belgium were committed here.

These days it's a pleasant old place, the pretty streets of its **tiny centre** flanked by a battery of half-timbered houses that mostly date from the eighteenth century. The best time to be here is for its renowned annual **carnival**, the **Laetare**, first celebrated here in 1502 and held on the third weekend before Easter, from Saturday to Monday evening; the main protagonists are the **Blancs Moussis** – white-robed, masked figures with obscenely long red noses – of which you'll see depictions adorning various Stavelot houses. There are also **festivals** of theatre and music in July and August respectively, with performances in the abbey buildings.

Abbaye de Stavelot

Cour de l'Abbaye 1 • Daily 10am–6pm • €8.50 for a combined ticket for all three museums • ☎080 88 08 78, ⓦabbayedestavelot.be

The **Abbaye de Stavelot's** sprawling complex of mainly eighteenth-century buildings sit in front of the stumpy foundational columns of the former abbey. Today, the abbey buildings house the **tourist office** (see p.273) and three modern **museums**.

Musée Historique de la Principauté de Stavelot-Malmédy

The multimedia layout here traces the **history of the principality** from the seventh century to the present day by means of religious artefacts, town crafts and folkloric exhibits. There's also interesting **3D creations** of what the original walled abbey would have looked like.

Musée du Circuit de Spa-Francorchamps

In the vaulted cellars of the abbey, this museum contains a collection of racing cars and motorcycles from the nearby **racetrack** (see box, p.272), home of the Belgium Formula 1 Grand Prix, including the 1974 Lotus of Belgian ace Jackie Ickx.

Musée du Poete Guillaume Apollinaire

The second-floor museum is dedicated to **Guillaume Apollinaire**, the influential French writer and poet who spent the summer of 1899 in Stavelot (he left without paying his bill, apparently) and wrote many poems about the town and the Ardennes prior to his early death in 1918.

Église St-Sebastien

place du Vinâve • Mon–Sat 10am–12.30pm & 2–5pm • Free

The **Église St-Sebastien** is home to the enormous thirteenth-century **shrine** of St Remacle, the seventh-century founder of Stavelot abbey, who is said to have built the abbey with the aid of a wolf he supposedly tamed for the purpose. The Romanesque shrine is made of gilt and enamelled copper with filigree and silver statuettes, though you can normally view it only from a distance.

ARRIVAL AND INFORMATION   STAVELOT

By train and bus Take the train as far as Trois-Ponts on the Liège-Luxembourg line and then catch bus #294 (every 2hr; 10min) from outside Trois-Ponts train station and alight at "Stavelot: Place E Grandprez".

Tourist information Stavelot's tourist office is in the glass-window corridor of Stavelot abbey (daily 10am–1pm & 1.30–5pm; ☎080 86 27 06, ⊛tourisme.stavelot.be). Sells the Pays de Stavelot walking map and is the meeting point for the free guided nature walks in summer (July–Sept Sat 2pm; 3hr).

ACCOMMODATION AND EATING

Figaro place du Vinâve 4 ☎080 86 42 86, ⊛restaurant-figaro.be. Rustic Italian serving traditional pizzas (€12) and pasta, but it's the home-made *osso bucco* (€20) that makes this place really worth a visit. April–Oct Mon–Fri noon–2pm & 5–10pm, Sat & Sun noon–2.30pm & 5–10.30pm; Nov–March Mon–Fri noon–2pm & 5–9.30pm, Sat & Sun noon–2.30pm & 5–10pm.

Hôtel-Restô ô Mal Aimé rue Neuve 12 ☎080 86 20 01, ⊛omalaime.be. Lively two-star with unforgettable character: its six spotless rooms are painted in bright, happy shades of blue, lime green and pink. The restaurant (closed July) and public areas are decorated with quirky art. __€95__

Le Loup Gourmand ave Ferdinand Nicolay 19 ☎080 86 29 95, ⊛le-loup-gourmand.be. Serves a good selection of Belgian staples – plus couscous and pasta if that doesn't suit – in a relaxed environment. The *plat du jour* is a bargain €9. Mon, Tues & Thurs–Sun noon–3pm & 6–10pm.

Le Val d'Amblève route de Malmédy 7 ☎080 28 14 40, ⊛levaldambleve.be. Family-run option just 200m from the centre, with 24 excellent rooms: four in the main building and the rest in a separate section nearby. Romantic restaurant with views of the garden, and small wellness centre too. Free wi-fi. Pets accepted. Closed mid-Dec to mid-Jan. __€150__

Coo and around

Just west of Stavelot, perched above the banks of the Amblève, **COO** is a nice enough village, but the real action is down by the river, where the modest **waterfalls** have given birth to a thriving resort area, made up of a cluster of hotels and restaurants in **Petit**

5

Coo and, in **Grand Coo** on the other side of the river, the unfortunately named **Plopsa Coo**, an adventure and theme park aimed at families.

Plopsa Coo

April–June 10.30am–5/5.30pm; July & Aug daily 10am–6pm; Sept & Oct Sat & Sun 11am–5pm; check website as hours and days vary • €25, children 85cm–1m €9.99, less than 85cm free • ⓦ plopsa.be • Parking costs €6, but it's possible to park in Petit Coo and walk across

For families, the **Plopsa Coo** theme park is an ideal day's distraction, particularly as you can wander around for free and only have to buy a ticket to try out any of the **rides**. These include the mildly terrifying "Mega Mindy Flyer", while the two-person chair lift up the mountain is an exhilarating experience, but not for those nervous of heights. You can also ride down a dry **bobsleigh**, go go-karting or try any number of other activities.

INFORMATION AND ACTIVITIES   COO

Tourist office Petit Coo has a small tourist office (March–June daily 11am–3pm; July & Aug daily 10am–4pm; Sept & Oct Sat & Sun 11am–3pm; ☎ 080 68 46 39).
Outdoor activities Coo Adventure at Petit Coo 4 (☎ 080

68 91 33, ⓦ coo-adventure.com) offers kayak (€16 for 9km paddle) and mountain-bike rental (from €15/4hr), as well as paintballing, rafting, karting, etc.

Grottes de Remouchamps

rue de Louveigné 3, Remouchamps • Feb–Nov daily 10am–5.30pm (last visit 4.15pm); Dec & Jan Sat & Sun 10am–4pm • €12, €27 combined ticket with Monde Sauvage • ☎ 04 36 09 70, ⓦ mondesauvage.be • **Zoo** Fange de Deigné 3, Aywaille • mid-March to mid-Nov daily from 10am • €19 adult/€15 for ages 3–11, €27 combined ticket with Grottes de Remouchamps

About 25km from Coo, the **Grottes de Remouchamps** are the country's second-largest caves after Han (see p.282) and have been open to visitors since 1828. **Tours** last over an hour and take you some 1200m through the heart of the cave system, which is 6km in length overall, before punting you back 700m to the entrance by **river** – a head-ducking and somewhat claustrophobic journey, but one not to be missed. Ticket grants access to the (missable) museum. Situated 5km north of the caves is the large safari park/zoo **Monde Sauvage**, but it's of dubious benefit to the animals since no conservation programmes seem to be in place and cages border on the small side – one to avoid.

Malmédy

About 8km northeast of Stavelot, the bustling resort of **MALMÉDY** is a popular tourist destination, its attractive streets flanked by lively restaurants, smart shops and cheap hotels. The town itself is thin on sights – most people come for the surrounding scenery – but it's a pleasant place to spend a night or two and makes a relatively inexpensive base for the Hautes Fagnes (see p.275). Malmédy is also home to the **Cwarmê**, one of Belgium's most famous festivals, held over the four days leading up to Shrove Tuesday. The main knees-up is on the Sunday, during which roving groups of masked figures in red robes and plumed hats – the so-called **Haguètes** – wander around town seizing people with long wooden pincers derived, it's thought, from the devices that were once used to give food to lepers.

Malmundarium

place du Châtelet 10 • Daily: April–Oct 10am–6pm; Nov–March 10am–5pm • €6 • ☎ 080 79 96 68, ⓦ www.malmundarium.be

Housed in the ancient Malmédy monastery – most of which dates from the early eighteenth century – the **Malmundarium** museum is the pride and joy of the town and displays items from the eighteenth-century **cathedral treasury**, as well as having rooms that explain the local **carnival folklore** and traditions of making paper and leather. Audio guides are available in English.

Baugnez 44

route de Luxembourg 10 • Wed–Sun 10am–6pm • €7.50 • ☎ 080 44 04 82, ⊛ baugnez44.be

The **Baugnez 44** museum focuses on the Battle of the Ardennes and the events that led up to the "Malmédy Massacre" at Baugnez, 4km southeast of Malmédy, when 84 American prisoners of war were murdered by their German captors in December 1944. The exhibits are explained via an individual 90-minute **audio-guide tour**, and there's a restaurant on site.

ARRIVAL AND INFORMATION   MALMÉDY

By bus Bus #745 (every 2hr; 25min) departs from outside Trois-Pont station on the Liège-Luxembourg line and drops you in front of Malmédy tourist office, stop "Malmedy: Place Albert 1er".

Tourist information The well-equipped tourist office, on place Albert 1er (low season: Wed–Sat 10am–6pm; high season: daily 10am–6pm; ☎080 33 02 50, ⊛malmedy.be), has truckloads of information on the town and its environs.

ACCOMMODATION AND EATING

Albert 1er place Albert 1er 40 ☎ 080 33 04 52, ⊛ hotel-albertpremier.be. These six rooms, situated above a good restaurant, might not be anything special, but they're well looked-after and right in the centre. **€95**

Auberge de Jeunesse Haute Fagnes route d'Eupen 36 ☎ 080 33 83 86, ⊛ lesaubergesdejeunesse.be. Rustic chalet-style youth hostel that can help arrange activities, rents mountain-bikes, has wi-fi and whose restaurant serves a bargain *plat du jour* for €8.50. Dorm **€21.50**, double **€56**

Au Coin de la Rue rue Derrière L'Eau 2 ☎ 0497 47 66 87, ⊛ aucoindelarue.be. Central B&B offering three stylish rooms: two on the ground floor and one above. In between is the breakfast room/lounge with an open fire and wi-fi. The owner doesn't speak much English, but the welcome is warm and breakfast hearty. **€105**

Au Petit Chef place de Rome 5–6 ☎ 080 33 07 49. Has a *friterie* tacked onto its right-hand side, but the brasserie/ restaurant serves toasties (€6), omelettes and hearty local meat dishes for around €13, plus mussels cooked a million ways. Mon, Tues & Thurs–Sun 11am–10pm (open Wed July & Aug).

The Hautes Fagnes

The high plateau that stretches north of Malmédy up as far as Eupen (see box below) is known as the **Hautes Fagnes** (in German, the Hohes Venn, or High Fens) and is now protected as a national park. This area marks the end of the Ardennes proper and has been twinned with the Eifel hills to form the sprawling **Deutsch-Belgischer Naturpark**. The Hautes Fagnes accommodates Belgium's highest peak, the **Signal de Botrange** (694m), but the rest of the area is boggy heath and woods, windswept and rather wild – excellent **hiking** country, though often fearsome in winter.

EUPEN

The pleasant but unexceptional little town of **Eupen** is the capital of the German-speaking region of Belgium, or **Deutschsprachige Gemeinschaft Belgiens**, a pint-sized area pushed tight against the German border that's home to around 75,000 people and enjoys the same federal status as the other two linguistic areas of the country. Once part of **Prussia**, the area was ceded to Belgium by the Treaty of Versailles at the end of World War I. It has a distinctive Rhineland feel, but that aside there's precious little reason to visit. Direct **trains** depart from Liège-Guillemins station (hourly; 40min). Travelling from either Coo or Spa takes considerably longer and requires a change of station.

5

> ## WALKING IN THE HAUTES FAGNES
>
> Large parts of the **Hautes Fagnes** are protected zones and are only open to walkers with a registered guide. Three- and six-hour walks in these areas are arranged by the **Centre Nature Botrange** (see below) on most weekends from March to November (€4–6). Each walk is organized around a feature of the local ecology, from medicinal plants to the endangered black grouse. In summer the walks can feel a bit crowded, and the guide's patter is normally in French or German, but they're a good way to see some genuinely **wild country** that would otherwise be off limits.
>
> To see some of the moorland on your own, ask staff at the centre for their free **map** (*Ronde de Botrange*) showing footpaths in the area. Many of them run along the edges of the protected areas, giving you a chance to see something of the *fagnes* even if you can't get on a guided walk.

Centre Nature Botrange

Centre Nature Botrange route de Botrange 131, 7km north of Robertville, on the road to Eupen • Daily 10am–6pm; café Tues–Sun 10am–6pm • ☎ 080 44 03 00, ⊕ botrange.be • Bus #394 (7 daily; 20min) runs to the centre from Eupen station (see box, p.275); otherwise you'll need your own car to get there • **Fania museum** Daily 10am–6pm, last entry 5pm • €6, including nature film • **Electric bike rental** March–Nov 10am–5pm • €21 with €100 deposit • **Ski rental** Wintertime • €9

The **Centre Nature Botrange** provides a focus for explorations of the national park. Its **Fania museum** describes the flora and fauna of the area and explains how the *fagnes* were created and how they have been exploited. The centre also rents out **electric bikes** and, in winter, **skis**; it also runs organized hikes (see box above). The rustic *Fagn'eteria* café serves hot meals and beers.

Signal de Botrange

Just a 3km walk up the main N676 road is the **Signal de Botrange**, Belgium's highest point at 694m, though the high-plateau nature of the Hautes Fagnes means it doesn't feel very high at all. A **tower** marks the summit, offering a good panorama over the *fagnes*, and there's a restaurant that's popular with coach parties and walkers alike.

Dinant and around

Some 30km south of Namur, picture-postcard **DINANT** is slung along the River Meuse beneath craggy green cliffs, its onion-domed **Notre-Dame church** looming over the barges and tourist cruise boats that ply the calm waters. It's a lovely town to wander around, but the scenery is not nearly as wild as you'll find deeper in the Ardennes. The sites associated with the city's most famous son, **Adolphe Sax** (see box, p.278) – inventor of the saxophone – make for an interesting little tour, while there are plentiful kayaking and hiking opportunities in the surrounding villages of **Anseremme**, **Gendron** and **Houyet**.

Brief history

The Romans were the first to put the place on the map, occupying the settlement and naming it after **Diana**, the goddess of the hunt, but the town's heyday came much later, in the fourteenth century, when it boomed from the profits of the **metalworking** industry, turning copper, brass and bronze into ornate jewellery known as *dinanderie*. Local counts slugged it out for possession of the town until, in 1466, Charles the Bold decided to settle his Dinant account by simply razing it to the ground. One result of all this medieval blood and thunder was the construction of an imposing **citadel** on the cliff immediately above Dinant. Although the town was sacked on several subsequent occasions and badly damaged in both world wars, the fortress has survived to become the town's principal attraction.

RIGHT DINANT AND THE RIVER MEUSE (PP.276–279) >

5

SAX APPEAL

Dinant's most famous native is **Adolphe Sax** (1814–94), the inventor of the saxophone. Saxophiles will want to have a look at the musician's old home, right in the centre at rue Adolphe Sax 35, marked by a commemorative **plaque** and a neat stained-glass mural of a man blowing his horn (sadly, the house is not open to the public), along with a statue of the king of cool reclining on a bench outside.

Collégiale Notre-Dame de Dinant

place Reine Astrid • Daily 9am–6pm, free guided visits July & Aug Sun 3pm • ☎ 082 22 62 84, ⓦ doyennededinant.com

Dinant's most distinctive landmark, the **Collégiale Notre-Dame de Dinant** church is topped with a distinctive bulbous spire that features on all the tourist brochures. Rebuilt on several occasions, and lastly in the 1820s, there's actually not much of interest to see inside except the stained-glass windows and an unfinished painting by one of Dinant's most famous sons, the nineteenth-century artist **Antoine Wiertz**. Situated on the right of the ambulatory, it's a mawkish affair dedicated to his parents and entitled *We'll Meet Again in Heaven*.

The citadel

place Reine Astrid 3–5 • April–Sept daily 10am–6pm; Oct to mid-Nov daily 10am–5.30pm; mid-Nov to Dec, Feb & March Mon–Thurs, Sat & Sun 10am–4.30pm; Jan Sat & Sun 10am–4.30pm • €8 • ☎ 082 22 36 70, ⓦ citadellededinant.be • Cable car open only weekends out of season

Next to Notre-Dame church lies the entrance to Dinant's **citadel**, which mostly dates from the Dutch occupation of the early nineteenth century, after the French destroyed the medieval castle in 1703. The citadel saw heavy **fighting** in both world wars: in 1914, having struggled to dislodge French soldiers from the stronghold, Germans troops took revenge on the locals, executing over six hundred and deporting several hundred more before torching the town; the Germans captured the citadel again in 1940, and it was the scene of even worse fighting when the Allies took Dinant in 1944. There's a memorial to those who gave their lives here, a **historical museum** with models re-creating particular battles and the Dutch occupation, plus a section with weapons from the Napoleonic era to the last world war. You can also see the wooden beams which supported the first **bridge** in Dinant, built nine hundred years ago by monks and found again by accident in 1952, as well as **dungeons** and the kitchen and bakery of the Dutch fortress. You can see the various rooms of the citadel by joining one of the one-hour **guided tours** that depart regularly in summer. To save yourself climbing the 400-odd steps up to the citadel, take the free *téléphérique* (cable car).

Grotte la Merveilleuse

route de Philippeville 142, on the far side of the river about 750m from the bridge; look for the signposts • Tours run April, Sept & Oct Tues–Sun 11am–4pm; May & June daily 11am–5pm; July & Aug daily 11am–5pm, Sat & Sun 10am–6pm: Nov–March Sat & Sun 11am, noon, 1pm, 2pm & 3pm • €9 • ☎ 082 22 22 10

One of Belgium's most beautiful grottoes, the **Grotte la Merveilleuse** cave system was discovered in 1904 during the construction of a railway. It's not the largest of the Ardennes cave complexes by any means, but the fifty-minute **tours** take you some 40m below ground, and give a good grounding in the science of stalagmites and stalactites, rock formations, and caves in general.

ARRIVAL AND INFORMATION   DINANT

By train Dinant's train station is 300m from the bridge that spans the Meuse over to Notre-Dame church.

Destinations Brussel-Zuid/Bruxelles-Midi (hourly; 1hr 40min); Liège (hourly; 1hr 40min); Namur (hourly; 30min).

ACTIVITIES AROUND DINANT

With access to two **rivers** – the wide and sluggish River Meuse and prettier River Lesse – and surrounded by steep, wooded cliffs, Dinant is the ideal base to try some sporting activities.

RIVER MEUSE CRUISES

A range of boat tours depart from **avenue Winston Churchill** – the main stretch of street next to Dinant's citadel – with prices and itineraries pretty consistent whichever company you choose.

La Compagnie des Bateaux rue Daoust 64, Dinant ☎082 22 23 15, ⊛www.bateaux-meuse.be. Two good options offered are the cruises to Anseremme (mid-April to Sept hourly; return trip 45min; €7.50), where you can hike off into the surrounding countryside; and to Freÿr (May to mid-Sept 2.30pm; return trip 2hr; €13). There are also boats north along the Meuse to

Namur (see p.252). Office open Mon–Fri 8am–5pm.
Dinant Evasion rue du Vélodrome 15, Dinant ☎082 22 43 97, ⊛dinant-evasion.be. Runs a similar set-up to La Compagnie des Bateaux, with cruises to Anseremme (mid-April to Sept 10.30am–6.30pm hourly; return trip 45min; €7.50); and to Freÿr (May–Sept 7 2.30pm; return trip 2hr; €13). Cash only.

HIKING AND BIKING

The Dinant tourist office sells the €7.50 *Carte Dinant*, which shows nineteen signposted **walks** in the Dinant area, as well as one 25km cycling circuit and two 21km and 23km **mountain-biking routes**. The 5km **Walk 5** takes in much of the locality's most pleasant scenery, weaving its way along and around the River Lesse between Anseremme and another hamlet, Pont à Lesse, while the 8km **Walk 8** allows you to visit a couple of places of interest: **Château de Vêves** (April–Oct daily 10am–5pm; €7.50; ⊛chateau-de-veves.be), an inordinately picturesque fifteenth-century château with spiky turrets and mostly eighteenth-century period rooms; and **Celles**, one of the prettier villages hereabouts and home to the Romanesque Église St-Hadelin (daily 9am–6pm; free).

Moss Bikes rue de Sûre 108, Dréhance ☎0479 91 49 78, ⊛mossbikes-dinant.be. Rents mountain-bikes for between four hours (€13) and five days (€70) with a

€20–50 deposit depending on length of rental. Helmets cost €1.50 to rent. Book in advance.

KAYAKING ALONG THE RIVER LESSE

Wilder and prettier than the River Meuse, the **River Lesse**, which spears off the Meuse in Anseremme, is open to kayakers from April to September. Visitors travelling by train can make for the villages of **Gendron** or **Houyet** and pick up a kayak at either – but remember to reserve them in advance. Both Gendron-Celles and Houyet train stations are metres from the river and the boats. Travellers who are driving can park their cars and buy tickets at Anseremme, and then take the train to either Gendron for the shorter 12km two-and-a-half-hour paddle back, or to Houyet for the longer 21km, five-hour paddle. Both routes cross two gentle, 50cm-deep **rapids**; the first has a stunning view of Walzin **castle**. The Lesse itself is wild and winding, with great scenery running past the rocky **Les Aiguilles de Chaleux** cliffs, though be warned that it sometimes gets so packed that there's a veritable canoe log jam. Consequently, it's a good idea to set out as early as possible to avoid some of the crush.

Dinant Evasion Lesse Kayaks place Baudouin 1er 2, Anseremme ☎082 22 43 97, ⊛dinant-evasion .be. Rents out one- and two-seater kayaks, and three-person canoes. Per person, reckon on paying €19 for a single kayak, €15–17 for a double, or around €15 for a three-person canoe. Train tickets to Houyet and

Gendron, plus ultra-light paddles, can be purchased as extras.
Kayaks Jaunes-Kayaks Libert quai de Meuse 1, Anseremme ☎082 22 61 86, ⊛kayaks-libert.com. Charges €20–23 for a single kayak, €30–38 for a double, or €44 for a three-person canoe.

Tourist information The tourist office is located at avenue Cadoux 8 (July & Aug Mon–Fri 9am–5.30pm, Sat 9.30am–6pm, Sun 10am–4pm; Nov–March Mon–Fri

9am–5.30pm, Sat 9.30am–4pm, Sun 10.30am–2pm; April–June daily 9am–5.30pm; ☎082 22 28 70, ⊛dinant-tourisme.be).

5

ACCOMMODATION

Camping Villatoile route de Walzin, Anseremme ☎ 082 22 22 85, ⓦ villatoile.be. A wooded setting beside the River Lesse in Anseremme, about 4km south of town. There's also a shop selling fresh bread, a bar and children's play area. March–Oct. Pitch €9, per person €5.50

Ibis Dinant Rempart d'Albeau 16 ☎ 082 21 15 00, ⓦ ibis.com. Chain hotel in a conspicuous brick block metres from the river, 1km or so south of the town bridge. No points for originality, but at least its neat and trim, modern rooms look out over the water. €115

Le Freÿr chaussée des Alpinistes 22, Anseremme

☎ 082 22 25 75, ⓦ lefreyr.be. Very comfortable hotel in Anseremme, with just six rooms and a first-rate restaurant. Set in a good-looking older building close to the Meuse about 4km south of Dinant. €85

★**La Merveilleuse** Charreau des Capucins 23 ☎ 082 22 91 91, ⓦ lamerveilleuse.be. Perched on a hill overlooking town, this neo-Gothic nineteenth-century nunnery was transformed into a hotel in 2008 with 16 rooms that range from fairly spartan to luxurious, plus there's an adjoining high-tech spa with pool and fine restaurant (see below). €120

EATING AND DRINKING

Catering for Dinant's passing tourist trade is big business, which means that **run-of-the-mill cafés** and **restaurants** are ten-a-penny. That said, there are still a couple of quality places worth mentioning.

A la Ville de Bruges rue Adolphe Sax 39 ☎ 082 22 41 55. Next door to the Adolphe Sax house, this is a friendly and unpretentious place, serving a safe but delicious menu of steaks and Belgian staples for lunch and dinner. Most mains €10–12. Daily 11.30am–9.30pm.

La Broche rue Grande 22 ☎ 082 22 82 81, ⓦ labroche .be. Smart and well-regarded French restaurant that does an excellent three-course menu for €30. Mon & Thurs–Sun noon–2.30pm & 6.30–9.30pm.

★**Coin à Tapas** Place St-Nicolas 6 ☎ 082 67 73 00. Snug and central low-key café serving tasty tapas for around €3.90 a plate. Closed mid-Dec to March. Thurs 6–9.30pm, Fri–Sun noon–9.30pm (occasionally closed 3–6pm at quiet times).

Le Couvent De Bethléem Charreau des Capucins 23

☎ 0479 54 91 78, ⓦ lamerveilleuse.be. Part of *La Merveilleuse* hotel (see above), this romantic restaurant sits beneath a vaulted glass roof and tables are scattered underneath olive trees. Their €25 "Discovery" menu available Wed and Thurs is superb. Closed mid-Sept to mid-Oct & last week of March. Wed–Sat noon–2.30pm & 7–9.30pm, Sun noon–2.30pm.

Patisserie Jacobs rue Grande 147 ☎ 082 22 21 39. Patisserie with a small café section at the back that, among other things, sells *couques de Dinant*, a honey-flour combination that's better admired than consumed unless you have the teeth of a horse. Daily 9am–6pm.

Le Sax place Reine Astrid 13. Unpretentious bar with a good beer selection; sit outside when the traffic has calmed down and peer up at the flood-lit citadel. Hours vary.

Château de Freÿr

Freÿr 12, Hastière, 6.5km south of Dinant • April–June & Sept to mid-Nov Sat & Sun 11am–5pm; July & Aug Tues–Sun 11am–5pm • €8, cash only • ☎ 082 22 22 00, ⓦ freyr.be

South of Dinant and a short walk from the village of Anseremme, the solitary **Château de Freÿr** is a crisply symmetrical, largely eighteenth-century brick mansion pushed up against the main road and the river. Once the summer home of the Dukes of Beaufort-Spontin, it's still privately owned and can be explored using an information folder picked up from reception or via a **guided tour** that must be prebooked with the Dinant tourist office (p.279). Inside, the opulent rooms are distinguished by their period furniture and thundering fireplaces. Running parallel to the river are the adjoining **gardens**, laid out in the formal French style, spreading over three terraces and including a **maze** and three-hundred-year-old **orange trees**. A pavilion at the highest point provides a lovely view over the château and river.

Rochefort and around

A scenic 33km southeast of Dinant lies one of the Ardennes' most beautiful regions, a thickly wooded terrain of plateaux, gentle hills and valleys, with quiet roads perfect for cycling. At its centre is the tourist resort of **Rochefort**, which, though short on specific sights, is the best base for rural wanderings thanks to its good range of accommodation – plus it has fewer crowds than the equally popular **Han-sur-Lesse**.

Castle of the Counts

rue Jacquet • Guided tours only July & Aug on selected dates (see website), departing from castle entrance at 2pm • €2 for tour • ☎ 084 21 44 09, ⓦ chateaurochefort.be

Once the largest fortress in the area, all that remains of Rochefort's medieval **Castle of the Counts** – perched atop a rocky outcrop off to the right of rue Jacquet – are the old walls, a couple of **wells** and, in the small **park** just below the entrance, the eighteenth-century arcades that were added to prop up the château's fashionable formal **gardens**. It does, however, afford super views of the town below.

ARRIVAL AND INFORMATION
ROCHEFORT

By train and bus Access by public transport is easiest from Namur; take the 40min train to Jemelle, from where it's about 3km west to Rochefort; the hourly bus #29 links Jemelle, Rochefort and Han-sur-Lesse. Buses #166A and #421 also ply between Jemelle and Rochefort. Buses pull in on Rochefort's main street, rue de Behogne.

Tourist information The well-organized tourist office is at rue de Behogne 5 (Easter–June & Sept Mon–Fri 8am–5pm, Sat & Sun 9.30am–5pm; July & Aug Mon–Fri 8am–6pm, Sat & Sun 9.30am–5pm; Oct–Easter Mon–Fri 8am–5pm, Sat 10am–5pm, Sun 10am–4pm; ☎ 084 34 51 72, ⓦ valdelesse.be) and has multilingual staff, free wi-fi and internet access (€0.30/15min), and sells walking maps.

ACCOMMODATION

Camping Les Roches rue du Hableau 26 ☎ 084 21 19 00, ⓦ les-roches.blogspot.be. A 10min walk east of the centre of town, this four-star campsite has every possible amenity, plus an open-air swimming pool, tennis courts, playground and internet at reception. Take route de Marche from the crossroads and the first left after the river along rue du Hableau. April–Oct. Tent, two people and car **€22**

★ **La Malle Poste** rue de Behogne 46 ☎ 084 21 09 86, ⓦ www.malleposte.be. A beautifully restored coaching

inn with large, handsomely finished rooms and public spaces. Its rates are high for Rochefort but there are loads of facilities – an indoor pool, fitness centre and a beautiful garden and restaurant (see below). **€110**

Le Vieux Logis rue Jacquet 71 ☎ 084 21 10 24, ⓦ levieuxlogis.be. A quaint three-star hotel, with just ten rooms, housed in a lovely old building with an immaculate, antique interior composed of wooden-beam ceilings and country-style floral wallpaper. Breakfast can be taken in the attractive gardens when the weather is fine. **€90**

EATING

La Calèche rue de Behogne 46 ☎ 084 21 09 86, ⓦ mallepost.be. Fancy French restaurant of the *La Malle Poste* hotel (see above), where the €35 menu is a bargain compared to the pricey à la carte mains for upwards of €26. Closed mid-June to mid-July and last two weeks of Aug. Mon, Tues & Fri–Sun noon–2.30pm & 7–9pm.

★ **La Gourmandise** rue de Behogne 24 ☎ 084 22 21 81, ⓦ la-gourmandise.be. Opposite the tourist office, this place has a big menu of local dishes such as *tomate-crevettes* from around €17 and does excellent crêpes too. Daily 9am–9.30pm.

Le Limbourg place Albert 1er 21 ☎ 084 21 10 36,

ACTIVITIES AROUND ROCHEFORT

Crisscrossed by rivers, the handsome countryside around Rochefort provides lots of opportunities for walking, canoeing and mountain biking. **Walkers** need the *Rochefort et ses villages* guide (on sale at the tourist offices in Rochefort and Han; €7.50), which lists 44 numbered walks, as well as six routes for **mountain-bikers** and four for **cyclists**.

Cyclesport rue de Behogne 59, Rochefort ☎ 084 21 32 55, ⓦ cyclesport.be. Rent mountain or trekking bikes from €10 for two hours, or electric bikes from €15

for two hours. Tues–Sat 9.30am–noon and 1.30–6.30pm, Sun 9.30am–noon.

5

ⓦ whotellimbourg.be. A modern brasserie that does a good line in local specialities for lunch or dinner, with main courses averaging about €15 and a good-value €25 three-course "Promenade" menu. Closed Wed & mid-Feb to mid-March. Mon & Thurs–Sun 11am–2pm & 6–10pm, Tues 11am–2pm.

Château de Lavaux-Sainte-Anne

rue du Château 8, Lavaux-Ste-Anne • April–Nov 11 Wed–Sun 10am–6pm • €8 • ☎ 084 38 83 62, ⓦ chateau-lavaux.com

Roughly 16km southwest of Rochefort, the pretty, moat-surrounded **Château de Lavaux-Sainte-Anne** contains three **museums**: the first depicts the everyday life of locals during the nineteenth and early twentieth centuries; the second shows how the lords of Lavaux lived in comparison; and the third is a nature museum. Nearby, a new **marshland** has been created to encourage nature back into the area – lovely for a walk. There's a brasserie on site too, in case tummies start to rumble.

Han-sur-Lesse

Just 6km southwest of Rochefort, **HAN-SUR-LESSE** – as the name suggests – sits on the banks of the River Lesse. It is a popular **summer resort** with a handful of attractions that also works well as a day-trip.

Grottes de Han and La Grotte de Lorette

Grottes de Han rue J Lamotte 2 • Daily: April–June, Sept & Oct 10am–4pm; July & Aug 10am–5.30pm; tours (around 1hr 45min) leave every 30min during summer and hourly in April, Sept & Oct • €16, combined ticket €26; tickets bought online €2 cheaper • ☎ 084 37 72 13, ⓦ grotte-de-han.be • There is a ticket office in the centre of the village, from where trams (no extra charge) transport visitors to the caves; after the tour, you make your own way back to the village on foot, which is a 5–10min walk • **La Grotte de Lorette** One-hour tours depart April–June & Sept Mon, Tues & Thurs–Sun 10.30am, noon, 2pm, 3.30pm; July–Aug daily every 45min between 10.30am and 4.15pm • €8.50, combi tickets with Han Caves available • ⓦ grotte-de-han.be

Discovered at the beginning of the nineteenth century, the **Grottes de Han** are a series of limestone galleries carved out of the hills by the River Lesse millions of years ago. **Tours** of the caves are well worth it, although you visit only a small portion of the 8km cave system, taking in the so-called Salle du Trophée, the site of the largest **stalagmite**; the Salle d'Armes, where the Lesse reappears after travelling underground for 1km; and the massive Salle du Dôme – 129m high – which contains a small **lake**. The ticket price automatically includes entry to **PrehistoHan**, with displays of prehistoric artefacts and a 3D film about excavations, while add-ons permit entry to **Han Yesteryear** – a rather dull series of tableaux depicting life in 1900 – or the superb, 2.5-square-kilometre **wildlife reserve**, that sits above the cave system and is home to European bison, Przewalski's horses, wolf and lynx. Here you can join a safari bus tour, or follow a 2km forest path. It's also possible to visit Han's smaller sister cave, **La Grotte de Lorette**, which reaches 60m below ground – at this point the guide usually releases a balloon so you can see just how large the chambers are.

ARRIVAL AND DEPARTURE
HAN-SUR-LESSE

By bus and train Take the train to Jemelle and catch the hourly #29 bus linking Jemelle, Rochefort and Hans.

Tourist information Han's tourist office is right on the central square, place Théo Lannoy 2 (daily 9.30/10am–4/5pm; ☎ 084 37 75 96, ⓦ valdelesse.be). Rents mountain-bikes for €10/2hr, €25/day. Free wi-fi.

ACCOMMODATION AND EATING

Camping le Pirot rue Charleville ☎ 084 37 72 90, ⓦ campingshansurlesse.be. Just 100m from the village's centre and seated by the river's edge, this site has washing and barbecue facilities. April–Sept. Pitch €6, per person €4

Chez PomPon rue des Chasseurs Ardennais 11

☎ 084 37 78 70. Hearty Belgian food – meatballs and chips, steaks and other classics – served to simple wooden tables and chairs in a restaurant beside the chip shop. Mains around €10. Mon & Tues 11.30am–2.30pm & 6–8.30pm, Fri–Sun 11.30am–2.30pm & 6–9.30pm.

Cocoon Hotel Grenier des Grottes rue des Chasseurs

Ardennais 1 ☏ 084 37 72 37, ⓦ hotelgrenierdesgrottes .nl. Reliable four star straight across from the entrance to the caves and wildlife reserve, this elegant hotel has 41 rooms decked out in calming cream, plus an old-fashioned restaurant and sauna, hot tub and hammam. **€86**

Naturotel rue des Grottes 2 ☏ 084 40 19 37, ⓦ naturotel.be. Just down the road from the cave entrance, this hotel has simple, old-fashioned rooms in a peaceful setting. Pay a few euros more and ask for a room overlooking the garden. Free wi-fi. **€90**

La Stradella rue d'Hamptay 59 ☏ 084 37 91 39, ⓦ hansurlesse.be. The food is much better than the plastic tables and pink paper tablecloths at this proficient Italian that serves woodfired pizzas and pastas from €9, as well as good mussels and game when they're in season. Mon & Wed–Sun noon–2pm & 7–9pm.

St-Hubert and around

ST-HUBERT, about 20km southeast of Rochefort, is another popular Ardennes resort, perched on a plateau and surrounded by **forest**. A small town with just under six thousand inhabitants, it's well worth paying a visit to the town's star **basilica**, and maybe hiking out into the surrounding woods. Travellers with children could take their budding scientists to the **Euro Space Center** on the outskirts of town, while would-be writers will be right at home in the official "book town" of **Redu**, a short journey west of St Hubert.

Basilique St-Hubert

place de l'Abbaye 1 · Daily: April–Oct 9am–6pm; Nov–March 9am–5pm · Free; audio guide €2 · ☏ 061 61 23 88, ⓦ basiliquesainthubert.be

The **Basilique St-Hubert** is easily the grandest religious edifice in the Ardennes and has been an important place of pilgrimage since the thigh bones of the eponymous saint were moved here in the ninth century. **St Hubert** (c.656–727 AD) was, according to legend, formerly Count Hubert, a Frankish noble whose love of hunting culminated in a vision of Christ between the antlers of a stag, after which he gave his money away and dedicated his life to the church, and was later canonized as the patron saint of hunters and trappers. The first **abbey** here predated the cult of St Hubert, but after the saint's relics arrived, the abbey – as well as the village that grew up in its shadow – was named in his honour. In medieval times, the abbey was one of the region's richest and a major landowner; it was suppressed by the French in the 1790s, but the abbey church – now the basilica – plus several of the old buildings survived, and flank the grand rectangular **piazza** that leads to the basilica's main entrance.

From the outside, the basilica's outstanding feature is the Baroque **west facade** of 1702, made of limestone and equipped with twin pepper-pot towers, a clock and a carving on the pediment depicting the miracle of St Hubert. Inside, the clear lines of the Gothic nave and aisles have taken an aesthetic hammering from both an extensive Baroque refurbishment and a heavy-handed neo-Gothic makeover in the 1840s. It's impressive more for its size rather than for any particular features, but do take a look at the **choir stalls**, typically Baroque and retelling the legend of St Hubert (on the right-hand side) and St Benedict (on the left), as well as the elaborate **tomb** of St Hubert, on the left at the beginning of the ambulatory, carved in the 1840s (King Léopold I, a keen huntsman, picked up the bill). Above the tomb is the only stained-glass **window** to have survived from the sixteenth century, a richly coloured, wonderfully executed work of art.

Musée Redouté

rue Redouté 11 · Daily July–Aug 1–5pm; Sept–June on request · €2.50 · ☏ 061 61 14 67, ⓦ www.musee-pierre-joseph-redoute.be

Only open during the summer months, but worth a visit if you're artistically inclined, the intimate **Musée Redouté** gallery showcases the work of Pierre-Joseph Redouté, a

5

St-Hubert native born in 1759 who was famous for his watercolours of **roses**. He was well known during his lifetime and gave lessons to a host of royalty, including Queen Marie-Antoinette.

ARRIVAL AND INFORMATION   ST-HUBERT

By train Direct trains from Namur to "Poix St Hubert" depart hourly (1hr 35min).

By taxi Taxi Jean-Claude (☏ 061 61 38 88) is based in Libramont.

Tourist information The tourist office is at rue St-Gilles 12 (daily 9am–5.30pm; ☏ 061 61 30 10, ⓦ saint-hubert-tourisme.be), just across the street from the basilica. They sell the local artisanal beers, La Saint-Hubert Cuvée du Borq and Le Semeur.

ACCOMMODATION AND EATING

Hôtel de l'Abbaye place du Marché 18 ☏ 061 61 10 23, ⓦ hoteldelabbaye.be. Bang opposite the basilica, Hemingway hunkered down here in 1944 as he advanced across Europe with the US army. That aside, though, its twenty rooms – of which fourteen are en suite – are pretty ordinary. Downstairs restaurant (daily) does good trout. **€80**

★ **L'Ancien Hôpital** rue de la Fontaine 23 ☏ 061 41 69 65, ⓦ ancienhopital.be. A seventeenth-century hospital once used as a hunting lodge by King Léopold I. Offers six plush rooms above a respected restaurant. A two-night minimum booking applies Sept 1–Dec 22. Its excellent restaurant (Mon, Thurs–Sun noon–2pm and 6.30–9.30pm) serves French and Belgian classics with tables set around an open wood fire in winter and in the garden come summer. **€105**

Aux Caves de Marie place du Marché 13c ☏ 061 51 14 02. Flouts convention by pairing its old, arched stone ceiling with brightly coloured cushions and red walls with traditional rabbit dishes and regional beers. Mains around €10, snacks €5. Wed–Sun 11am–9.30pm.

Fourneau St-Michel

8km north of St-Hubert • March–June & Sept–Nov Tues–Sun 9.30am–5pm; July & Aug daily 9.30am–5.30pm • €5 • ☏ 084 21 08 90, ⓦ fourneausaintmichel.be

One of the walks recommended by the St-Hubert tourist office is the two-to three-hour trek up to **Fourneau St-Michel**, an outdoor **museum** of rural life in Wallonia spread across two hundred acres of beautiful green valley. Its most important and interesting part is made up of old buildings brought from all over the county – bakeries, farmhouses, forges, chapels, schools – reassembled here according to region and linked by paths that give the impression of strolling from one village to another. There are a couple of **cafés** but really it's a lovely place for a picnic.

Euro Space Center

12km west of St-Hubert, right by the E411 (Exit 24) • April–June & Sept–Oct Tues–Sun 10am–4pm; July & Aug daily 10am–5pm • €11/8 adult/6–12; Moonwalk simulator or Planetarium €4 extra or €6 for both • ☏ 061 65 01 35, ⓦ eurospacecenter.be

The **Euro Space Center** is a hugely popular attraction, easily identified by the space rocket parked outside. Its hangar-like premises house a hi-tech **museum** about space travel and the applications of space and satellite technology, with lots of buttons for kids to press in the interactive displays, as well as **full-scale models** of the space shuttles and of the Mir space station.

Redu

18km west of St-Hubert • ⓦ redu-villagedulivre.be • Take TEC bus #51 from St-Hubert to Libramont Gare (3 daily; 30min), then pick up bus #61 to Redu (4 daily; 45min)

REDU is the world's second official book town after the UK's Hay-on-Wye. The hamlet features a quaint cluster of seventeen **bookshops**, and travellers can watch book-binding and paper-making demonstrations, as well as illustrators showing off their talents at the annual **Fête du Livres** (30 March–1 April). Bring money: there's no ATM or bank in the village and many of the bookshops only accept cash.

Most of the books are in French or Flemish, but several have a reasonable selection of **English titles**: try De Eglantier (rue Transinne 34) and De Griffel (rue Transinne 34a). The region is also renowned for its **raspberries** and you can buy locally made jams, vinegars and spirits at café-cum-shop La Framboiseraie (rue de Daverdisse 66).

ARRIVAL AND INFORMATION
REDU

By train and bus or taxi Catch the train as far as Libramont-Chevigny, then take TEC bus #61 to "Redu Eglise". There's no service on Sunday. Alternatively, you can catch a taxi outside Chevigny train station; a single fare usually costs €45. From St-Hubert you'll have to arrange a taxi.

Tourist information The tourist office is located at place de l'Esro 60 (Daily: March–Oct 9am–6pm, Nov–Feb 9.30am–4.30pm; ☎061 65 66 99, ⓦhaute-lesse -tourisme.be).

ACCOMMODATION AND EATING

Le Fournil place de l'Esro 58, ☎061 65 56 32, ⓦle-fournil.be. Seated in the heart of the village, this B&B has six 3-star en-suite rooms above its respected restaurant. Book a "comfort" double if you can (€110): they're larger, have a bath and sitting room, as well as a Senseo coffee machine. **€95**

La Gourmandine rue de St-Hubert 16 ☎016 65 63 90. A cosy wooden-beam café (also with a few rooms upstairs) whose walls are decorated with watercolour paintings by local artist Jamotte Maguy. A classic Belgian steak costs around €17, and try their *crêpe aux framboises de Redu* in season. Mon, Tues & Fri–Sun 11am–7pm.

La Roche-en-Ardenne and around

About 25km northeast of St-Hubert, **LA ROCHE-EN-ARDENNE** is amazingly picturesque, hidden by hills and some of the wildest scenery in the Ardennes until you're right on top of it, and crowned by romantic **castle ruins**. The secret of its beauty has spread, though, and come summer high season the town is teeming with people. Most come for the superb **outdoor activities**: from kayaking and rafting along the **River Ourthe**, to hiking, biking, horse riding and caving.

The château

rue du Purnalet • April–June, Sept & Oct daily 11am–5pm; July & Aug daily 10am–6pm; Nov–March Mon–Fri 1–4pm, Sat & Sun 11am–4.30pm • €5 • ☎084 41 13 42, ⓦchateaudelaroche.be • To get to the castle, take the steps that lead up from place du Marché, at the south end of the high street

The ninth-century **château** was destroyed in the late eighteenth century on the orders of the Habsburgs to stop it falling into the hands of the French, and today its ruins still command sweeping views over the valley and of the surviving fragments of the curtain wall that once enclosed the town. During the summer, medieval activities and **falconry shows** are organized.

LA ROCHE-EN-ARDENNE ACTIVITIES

The wild terrain surrounding La Roche-en-Ardenne is an outdoor enthusiast's dream come true: a wide range of sports is on offer here, from kayaking to caving.

Ardennes Aventures rue de l'Eglise 35 ☎084 41 19 00, ⓦardenne-aventures.be. Offers long (€21; 5hr) and short (€16; 1hr 30min) kayak trips year-round, leaving hourly in high season; mountain-biking (€25; 4hr); horse riding (€45; 2hr); rafting (Jan–April, Nov & Dec; €19; 1hr 30min). You can get good rates if you combine two activities on one day.

Brandsport Auberge La Laiterie, Mierchamps 15, 10km south of La Roche on the N89 ☎084 41 10 84, ⓦbrandsport.be. Arranges orienteering (€16.50/half-day); kayaking (€13.50/half-day); caving (€46.50/half-day); archery (€26.50/half-day), as well as horse riding, abseiling and caving.

5

Musée Bataille des Ardennes

rue Chamont 5 • July & Aug daily 10am–6pm; April–June & Sept–Dec Wed–Sun 10am–6pm • €6.40 • ☏ 084 41 17 25, ⓦ batarden.be

One of the best of the Ardennes battle museums, the **Musée Bataille des Ardennes** offers a homespun but effective collection foraged from the surrounding hills, including anti-tank guns and light weaponry, medical supplies and ancient unopened cigarette packs, all displayed by way of well-thought-out dioramas and tableaux. Curiously enough, the corner of the high street and rue de la Gare, a few metres to the north of the museum, is the spot where US and British soldiers met on January 11, 1945, as their respective armies converged on the Bulge; a commemorative **plaque** depicts the wintry scene.

ARRIVAL AND INFORMATION
LA ROCHE-EN-ARDENNE

By train and bus La Roche is not on the rail network; the nearest stations are Marloie and Melreux on the Liège-Jemelle line, both around 30min away. Buses leave every two hours – catch the #13 from Melreux (30min) or the #15 from Marloie (2hr 35min) – and drop passengers off in the centre of town.

Tourist information The tourist office is at place du Marché 15 (daily 9.30am–5pm, 6pm during July & Aug;

☏ 084 36 77 36, ⓦ la-roche-tourisme.com). They have details of B&Bs and sell a selection of walking and cycling maps; the *La Roche-en-Ardenne* map costs €7 and features ten marked rambles.

Tourist train From March to Nov, Le P'tit Train (☏ 084 47 73 34, ⓦ petit-train.be) runs 40min tours of the town and surroundings. Trains depart from place du Bronze; tickets cost €6/4 adult/child.

ACCOMMODATION

Camping Benelux rue de Harzé 24 ☏ 084 41 15 59, ⓦ campingbenelux.be. Large, leafy site spread along a curve in the Ourthe River. There's a shop and, in high season, a bar. Easter to Sept. Pitch **€7.50**, per person **€3**

Camping de l'Ourthe rue des Échavées ☏ 084 41 14 59, ⓦ campingdelourthe.be. Situated 700m from the town centre, this family-orientated riverside site has a kids' corner, wi-fi and a shop. Mid-March to Oct. Pitch **€6**, per person **€2**

Clairefontaine rue Vecpré 64 ☏ 084 41 24 70, ⓦ clairefontaine.be. About 2km outside La Roche on the road to Marche-en-Famenne, this is the best option if you have a car; it's a lovely old lodge strewn with antiques with extremely well-appointed rooms set in an extensive garden. Sauna and massages available. **€98**

Les Genêts corniche de Deister 2 ☏ 084 41 18 77, ⓦ lesgenetshotel.com. Delightful, old-fashioned option a 10min climb up from the high street: take rue Clerue out of town from the bridge by place du Marché, and veer left again up rue St Quoilin. Has seven comfortable rooms, some offering views over the town, and a quaint restaurant with good-value three-course menus around the €30 mark. **€95**

Moulin de la Strument Petite Strument 62 ☏ 084 41 13 80, ⓦ strument.com. About 800m to the south of the town centre along the Val du Bronze. Has eight clean rooms, and a cosy on-site restaurant. It also has a huge campsite with a picturesque setting beside a stream. Hotel closed Jan; campsite closed Nov–Feb. Hotel: double **€95**; camping: pitch **€9**, per person **€2.50**

EATING

Chez Henri rue Chamont 8 ☏ 084 41 15 64. Rustic restaurant with wood-panelled walls serving traditional Ardennais cuisine in a variety of excellent-value menus ranging from €15–26. You can tuck into a pot of mussels in season for €17.50 too. Daily noon–2.30pm & 6–9.30pm.

La Stradella place du Marché 2 ☏ 084 41 11 34, ⓦ lastradella.be. Garish decor, but the hand-crafted, wood-fired Italian pizza (€13.50) is worth it and, if you're feeling hungry, then the two- and three-course menus (€20–30) will appeal. Very central. Daily 11am–3pm & 5–11pm.

Durbuy

A circuitous 25km northwest of La Roche (you'll need your own wheels to get here) lies inordinately pretty **DURBUY**. Tucked into a narrow ravine beside the River L'Ourthe, below bulging wooded hills – and billed as the smallest town on Earth – it inevitably attracts far too many day-trippers for its own good. But out of season and late in the evening it remains a delightful spot – not because of any specific attractions but because its immaculately maintained huddle of seventeenth- and eighteenth-century **stone houses**, set around a cobweb of cobbled lanes, is a treat to explore.

INFORMATION AND GETTING AROUND	DURBUY

Tourist information Durbuy's tourist office is on the main square at place aux Foires 25 (Mon–Fri 9am–12.30pm & 1–5pm, Sat & Sun 10am–6pm; ☎ 086 21 24 28, ⓦ durbuyinfo.be).

Tourist train A canvas-roof mini train (March–June, Sept

& Oct Sat & Sun; July & Aug daily; €4/1.50 adult/child) takes tourists up to Belvedere, Durbuy's panoramic point, and stops outside the Confiturerie Saint-Amour jam factory (ⓦ confitureriesaintamour.be) so travellers can enjoy a quick, free visit (and buy some jam).

ACCOMMODATION AND EATING

La Brasserie Ardennaise place aux Foires 22 ☎ 086 21 47 44. Modern brasserie with terrace offering soup and snacks from €3.50, croque monsier, pastas, or a wide range of meat and fish dishes from around €8. Daily 10am–midnight.

Clos des Récollets rue de la Prévôté 9 ☎ 086 21 29 69, ⓦ closdesrecollets.be. A charming stonewall house right in the centre that has slick, modern and very comfortable rooms with large bathrooms. Their respected restaurant (closed Tues and Wed) does fancy French and is fairly traditional, with main courses for around €20. Breakfast

€12.50 per person. €110

Ferme au Chêne rue Cote d'Ursel 36 ☎ 086 21 10 67. Belongs to the local Marckloff micro brewery, whose beer can be enjoyed on the premises, or on an outside terrace overlooking the river, with omelettes, salads and plates of ham and cheese. Mon, Tues, Fri–Sun 11am–9pm.

★**Victoria** rue des Récollectines 4 ☎ 086 21 23 00, ⓦ hotelvictoria.be. Has 15 equally charming, yet cheaper, rooms and their upmarket modern restaurant has a big open kitchen and mains from €16. Guests also benefit from discounted access to the Sanglier des Ardennes spa. €80

Grottes de Hotton

2km from the centre of Melreux-Hotton village • April–June, Sept & Oct daily 10am–5pm; July & Aug daily 10am–6pm; Nov–March Sat & Sun open at set times: noon, 2pm & 3.30pm • €9.50 • ☎ 084 46 60 46, ⓦ grottesdehotton.be • The caves are well signposted from Melreux-Hotton but only reachable on foot or by car; from the main riverside rue de la Roche, follow route de Speleo Club de Belgique

The deepest of the Ardennes cave systems, the **Grottes de Hotton** are well worth the short trip from La Roche. **Tours** last a little over an hour and take you 75m underground, where a fast-flowing river pours through a canyon almost 40m deep and just a few metres wide – an awesome sight. There are **stalactites** and **stalagmites** galore, including patches of rare and peculiar specimens that grow horizontally from the rock. It gets chilly, so take a jumper.

Bouillon and the Semois river valley

Beguiling **BOUILLON**, close to the French border on the edge of the Ardennes, is a fairly handsome resort town, enclosed in a loop of the River Semois and crowned by an outstanding **castle**. Be sure to mingle with the locals at the **weekly market** held every Sunday morning from April to October on boulevard Heynen and, if visiting in summer, at the **medieval market** held the second weekend of August. The town makes an excellent base for exploring the wildly dramatic scenery of the surrounding countryside, in particular the **Semois river valley** to the west, with quiet country roads climbing up into wooded hills before careering down to the riverside. Holidaying Belgians descend on this beautiful area in their hundreds, with many **old farmhouses** turned into gîtes and a wealth of opportunities for **outdoor activities**. You'll definitely need your own wheels – car or bike – for getting around or, for the likes of Poupehan, simply hop in a canoe.

The château

esplanade Godefroid 1 • April–June & Sept Mon–Fri 10am–6pm, Sat & Sun 10am–6.30pm; July & Aug daily 10am–7pm; March, Oct & Nov daily 10am–5pm; Dec–Feb Mon–Fri 1–5pm, Sat & Sun 10am–5pm; falconry shows March to mid-Nov 11.30am, 2pm and 3.30pm • €6.50, combined ticket with Musée Ducal & Archéoscope €14.50 • ☎ 061 46 42 02

Bouillon's highlight is its impossibly picturesque castle, set on a long and craggy ridge that runs high above town. The castle was originally held by a succession of

5

independent dukes who controlled most of the land hereabouts. There were five of these, all called **Godfrey de Bouillon**, the fifth and last of whom left on the First Crusade in 1096, selling his dominions (partly to raise the cash for his trip) to the prince-bishop of Liège, and capturing Jerusalem three years later, when he was elected the Crusaders' king. However, he barely had time to settle himself before he became sick – either from disease or, as was suggested at the time, because his Muslim enemies poisoned him, and he died in Jerusalem in 1100. Later, Louis XIV got his hands on the old dukedom and promptly had the castle refortified to the design of his military architect **Vauban**, whose handiwork defines most of the fortress today.

It's an intriguing old place, with three **drawbridges** to enter and then paths winding through most of its courtyards, along the battlements and towers, and through dungeons filled with weaponry and instruments of torture. Most visitors drive to the entrance, but walking there is easy enough too – either via rue du Château or, more strenuously, by a set of steep steps that climbs up from rue du Moulin, one street back from the river. Among the highlights, the thirteenth-century **Salle de Godfrey**, hewn out of the rock, contains a large wooden cross sunk into the floor and sports carvings illustrating the castle's history; there's also the **Tour d'Autriche** (Austrian Tower) at the top of the castle, with fabulous views over the Semois valley. From March to mid-November there are daily falconry shows.

Musée Ducal

rue Petit 1–3 · Easter–Sept daily 10am–6pm; Oct to mid-Nov daily 10am–5pm · €4, combined ticket with castle & Archéoscope €14.50 · ☏ 061 46 41 89, ⓦ museeducalbouillon.be

Below the castle, and accessible across the car park, the **Musée Ducal** exhibits a wide-ranging collection in an attractive eighteenth-century mansion. As you'd expect, there are lots of artefacts relating to the fifth Godfrey, plus assorted weaponry, exhibits on medieval daily and religious life, and a large-scale model of the town in 1690.

Archéoscope Godefroid de Bouillon

quai des Saulx 14 · Feb Tues–Fri 1–4pm, Sat & Sun 10am–4pm; March–April daily 10am–4pm; May–Sept daily 10am–5pm; Oct & Nov Tues–Sun 10am–4pm; Dec Tues–Fri 1–4pm, Sat & Sun 10am–4pm · €6.25, combined ticket with castle & museum €14.50 · ☏ 061 46 83 03, ⓦ www.archeoscopebouillon.be

The **Archéoscope Godefroid de Bouillon** should ideally be visited before exploring the castle: its exhibitions on the Crusades and Arab culture, plus a **multimedia show** on the duke and a half-hour film laying out the castle's history, really help to put everything in context, so when you do visit you can fully soak up the atmosphere.

Poupehan

Heading west from Bouillon along the N810, it's just 12km to **POUPEHAN**, an inconsequential village that straggles the banks of the River Semois. The target of the most popular **canoe trips** from Bouillon (see box, p.289), Poupehan's handful of cafés and restaurants makes a healthy living from its many visitors, most of whom are here to enjoy the peace and quiet and to mess around on the river.

Rochehaut

From Poupehan, it's a steep 4km drive up through the woods to **ROCHEHAUT**, a beguiling hilltop village whose rustic **stone cottages** amble across a gentle dip between two sloping ridges. Nowadays, most visitors come here to **hike** (see box, p.289), exploring the locality's steep forested hills and the valley down below by

5

ACTIVITIES AROUND BOUILLON AND THE SEMOIS RIVER VALLEY

The **River Semois** snakes its way across much of southern Belgium, rising near Arlon and then meandering west until it finally flows into the Meuse in France. The most impressive part of the **river valley** lies just to the west of Bouillon, the river wriggling beneath steep wooded hills and ridges – altogether some of the most sumptuous scenery in the whole of the Ardennes. For a really active day out, you could canoe to **Poupehan** and follow one of the walking routes back to Bouillon, walk to **Rochehaut** (see p.288) and back, or follow one of the circular routes around Bouillon.

WALKS

Before setting out, **walkers** should get hold of the *Promenades du Randonnée* (on sale at Bouillon's tourist office), with nine circular walks – ranging from 12km to 25km – that begin and end in town. The routes are well marked, but you need to study the map carefully if you want to avoid having to walk on major or minor roads. Note that the marked river crossings are not bridges, so you may well end up with wet feet. The tourist office also sells a map detailing suggested **cycling** routes, and **mountain-bikes** can be rented from Semois Kayaks (see below).

There's also a **half-day circular hike** from Rochehaut to Poupehan and back again. From Rochehaut, take the path out of the southern end of the village, which leads into thick forests high above the river, from where a series of **fixed ladders** helps you to negotiate the steep slopes down to the water. This is by far the hardest part of the walk, and once you're at the bottom you can follow the easy path to Poupehan; from there, take the path that follows the river north back up to a **quaint bridge** over the river to the hamlet of **Frahan**, a huddle of stone houses draped over a steep hillock and surrounded by meadows. From here various paths will deliver you back up to Rochehaut on its perch high above.

CANOEING

As regards canoeing, the riverscape is gentle and sleepy, the Semois slow-moving and meandering – and the whole shebang is less oversubscribed than, say, Dinant. Bouillon has two main **canoe rental** companies, both of whom provide transport either to the departure point or from the destination.

Les Epinoches Faubourg de France 29 (by the Pont de France) ☎ 061 25 68 78, ⓦ kayak-lesepinoches .be. Rents kayaks and canoes to go down to Saty (7km; 2hr), Dohan (14km; 3hr) and Cugnon (28km; 5hr). Prices range from €16 to €55.

Semois Kayaks Port de Liège ☎ 0475 24 74 23, ⓦ semois-kayaks.be. Oversees routes in the other direction down to Poupehan (15km; 3hr 30min), and from Poupehan to Frahan (4km; 1hr). Advance reservations are strongly advised. Single kayaks cost €15–18, doubles €25–36, depending on the distance.

means of a network of marked trails. There are superb views over the Semois from the village.

| ARRIVAL AND INFORMATION | BOUILLON AND THE SEMOIS RIVER VALLEY |

By train and bus Catch the train to Libramont, on the Namur–Luxembourg line, then take bus #8 (hourly; 40min) to Bouillon, which departs from outside the station. Taxis are scarce and expensive. No buses or trains run from Bouillon to Rochehaut, so a car or taxi is required.

Tourist information Bouillon's tourist office is central, at quai des Saulx 12 (Mon–Sat 10am–6pm, Sun 10am–5pm; ☎ 061 46 62 57, ⓦ bouillon-initiative.be). They can book accommodation at no extra cost, have a list of B&Bs, and sell local hiking maps.

ACCOMMODATION

BOUILLON

Auberge de Jeunesse route du Christ 16 ☎ 061 46 81 37, ⓦ lesaubergesdejeunesse.be. Large and well-equipped HI hostel with dorm beds and family rooms, plus kitchen, laundry and café. It's east across the river from the castle, on the hill opposite – a long walk by road, but there

is a short cut via the steps leading up from rue des Hautes Voies, just above place St Arnould. Reservations advised. Closed Jan and early Feb. Dorm €22, double €60

Hotel Cosy rue Au-Dessus de la Ville 23 ☎ 061 46 04 62, ⓦ hotelcosy.be. Perched on a hill overlooking the old town, the exterior of this place looks a little kitsch, but its

5

11 individually designed boutique-style rooms have bags of character – some have castle views, others a hot tub – as does the on-site restaurant and terrace. Check their website for weekend deals. €150

Halliru route de Corbion 1 ☎ 061 46 60 09. Nicely situated and reasonably well-equipped riverside campsite, some 1.5km southwest of the town centre on the road to Corbion. It's an easy walk – go through the tunnel by the Auberge d'Alsace, turn left and follow the path by the river. Open April–Sept. Cash only. All in €17.50

★ **Hôtel Panorama** rue Au-Dessus de la Ville 25 ☎ 061 46 61 38, ⚏ panoramahotel.be. A four-star that lives up to its name, with sweeping views of the Semois valley and Bouillon castle from each of its 22 high-spec rooms and terrace bar. A small wellness centre is also being added. €90

Hôtel de la Poste place St Arnould 1 ☎ 061 46 51 51, ⚏ hotelposte.be. There's been a hotel here, right by the Pont de Liège, since the 1730s. The present incarnation is nothing fancy, but it's pretty good value for what you get – and there's a nice, lively bar downstairs. There are great views of the castle from one side of the hotel, so be sure to get a west-facing room, preferably high up in the hotel tower – worth the extra money. €120

POUPEHAN

Auberge le Vieux Moulin rue du Pont 18 ☎ 061 46 61 29.

Spartan rooms in a peaceful setting. The superb, traditional restaurant, with menus starting at €19 and a huge stone open fireplace, – not to mention the pool (heated from May to mid-Sept) – all serve to sweeten the deal. €85

Île de Faigneul rue de la Chérizelle 54 ☎ 061 46 68 94, ⚏ iledefaigneul.com. Cosy campsite a 10min walk from the centre. If you don't have a tent there's a kooky red, wooden tepee you can stay in, or a boat. Frustratingly, showers for campers cost €1.50, but there is free wi-fi, plus washing machines and a shop. April–Sept. Pitch €15, per person €3.75, tepee €30, boat €60

ROCHEHAUT

Auberge de l'An rue du Palis 7 ☎ 061 46 40 60, ⚏ an1600.be. A first-rate alternative to the *Auberge de la Ferme*, with ten rooms and another top-quality restaurant in a charming whitewashed cottage. Closed Jan & late June to early July. €130

Auberge de la Ferme rue de la Cense 12 ☎ 061 46 10 00, ⚏ aubergedelaferme.be. Offers a range of comfortable rooms in a tastefully modernized old stone inn with outbuildings and a modern annexe, and an excellent restaurant (although you can also eat more informally – and just as well – in the bar). Rooms without hot tubs are about twenty per cent cheaper. Closed most of Jan. €90

EATING AND DRINKING

For a place of its size and popularity, Bouillon is surprisingly light on good places to **eat** – and its **nightlife** is more or less non-existent. The below represents the best of a rather uninspiring bunch. A couple of the accommodation options listed for **Rochehaut** and **Poupehan** also offer good eating.

★ **Hostellerie du Cerf** Pré Lamquin 1 ☎ 061 46 70 11, ⚏ hotelducerf.be. Drive or cycle the 3km south to dine at this B&B-cum-restaurant run by the Castenmillers. They're both well travelled, and Bart incorporates some of these world flavours into his lovingly prepared meals. His wife, Chrissy, looks after you in the dining room. Reservations recommended. Call ahead for hours.

Le Roy de la Moule quai du Rempart 42 ☎ 061 46 62 49.

A local favourite famed for its steaming pots of mussels cooked 35 different ways (€14). Wash them down with a glass of Ciney blonde beer. Daily 11.30am–2.30pm & 6–10pm.

La Vieille Ardenne Grand-rue 9 ☎ 061 46 62 77. Slightly old-fashioned restaurant near the Pont de Liège specializing in regional dishes, with main courses averaging around €18. Also has an extensive beer menu. Tues–Sun 10am–10pm.

Abbaye d'Orval

rue Orval, Florenville • Daily: March–May & Oct 9.30am–6pm; June–Sept 9.30am–6.30pm; Nov–Feb 10.30am–5.30pm • €6/3 adult/child • ⚏ orval.be • If driving, Orval is 8km from Florenville, in the direction of Virton; alternatively, take train to Florenville (direction Bertrix and Virton) then catch daily TEC bus (Mon–Fri 12.55pm, Sat 5.45pm, Sun 2.51pm) from station and alight at "Orval Carrefour"

Around 30km southeast of Bouillon, the **Abbaye d'Orval** is a place of legendary beginnings. It was founded, so the story goes, when Countess Mathilda of Tuscany lost a gold ring in a lake and a fish recovered it for her, prompting the countess to donate the surrounding land to God for the construction of a monastery – a fish with a golden ring is still the emblem of the monastery, and can be seen gracing the bottles of **beer** for which Orval is most famous these days. Most of the medieval abbey disappeared during an eighteenth-century revamp, but much of this was destroyed in turn by the

5

French Revolutionary army in 1793. Thereafter, the abbey lay abandoned until 1926, when the **Trappist order** acquired the property and built on the site to the eighteenth-century plans, creating an imposing new complex complete with a monumental statue of the Virgin.

Of the original twelfth- and thirteenth-century buildings, only remnants survive. You can see the ruins of the Romanesque-Gothic **church of Notre-Dame**, with the frame of the original rose window and Romanesque capitals in the nave and transept, and its attached **cloister** and surrounding buildings, including the almost-intact chapterhouse and the eighteenth-century **cellars**, which hold a small **museum**, and models and photos of the site over the years. The abbey has always been first and foremost a **working community**, making beer and cheese (samples of which are on sale in the abbey shop); unfortunately, the main, modern part of the complex isn't accessible to the public and it is only possible to visit the **brewery** on open days – see website for listings.

ACCOMMODATION AND EATING ABBAYE D'ORVAL

Orval Guesthouse ☎ 061 32 51 10. It is possible to stay in the abbey's guesthouse, which has a mixture of simple single and double rooms, but you'll need to bring your own sheets (or rent them for €8) or sleeping bag, and towels. Guests can stay for up to a week and are invited to participate in prayers, or seek guidance from the Brothers.

The free thrice-daily communal meals are taken in silence with background music. **€38**
Camping Alternatively, you can camp – very cheaply. You'll need to bring everything with you, although it's possible to pay a little for use of a fridge. Note that use of the shower costs €15. **€2.50**

Arlon

The capital of Luxembourg province, **ARLON** is one of the oldest towns in Belgium – a trading centre for the Romans as far back as the second century AD. These days it's an amiable country town, perhaps a little down on its luck, but with a relaxed and genial atmosphere that makes for a pleasant break in any journey – although there's not a lot to see. The modern centre is **place Léopold**, with the clumping Palais de Justice at one end and a World War II tank in the middle, commemorating the American liberation of Arlon in September 1944. A couple of minutes' walk from place Léopold, up a flight of steps, is the diminutive **Grand-Place**, where there are fragments from Roman times, namely the **Tour Romaine** (no public access), formerly part of the third-century ramparts. The principal sites are the **Musée Archéologique** (rue des Martyrs 13; Tues–Sat 9am–noon & 1–5.30pm, April–Sept also Sun 1.30–5.30pm; €4, €6 with Musée Gaspar; ☎063 21 28 49, ⏿ial.be), which is situated behind the Palais de Justice and has a good collection of Roman finds from the surrounding area; and the **Musée Gaspar** (rue des Martyrs 16; Tues–Sun 9.30am–noon & 1–5.30pm; €4, €6 with Musée Archeologique; ☎063 60 06 54, ⏿ial.be), which displays the works of nineteenth-century sculptor Jean-Marie Gaspar, who was a native of Arlon.

ARRIVAL AND INFORMATION ARLON

By train Arlon train station is a 5min walk from the south side of the town centre.
Destinations Jemelle (every 30min; 50min); Luxembourg City (every 25min; 20min); Namur (hourly; 1hr 40min).

Tourist information The tourist office is just off the main square at rue des Faubourgs 2 (Mon–Fri 8.30am–5pm, Sat & Sun 9am–5pm; ☎ 063 21 94 54, ⏿ arlon-tourisme.be).

EATING

Faubourg 101 rue des Faubourgs 101 ☎ 063 60 28 33. Trendy brasserie-cum-lounge bar with an invariably delicious *plat du jour* for €12, exceedingly good pasta and

dainty slivers of steak and duck for €20. Mon–Thurs 10am–1am, Fri 10am–3am, Sun 4pm–3am (kitchen closes 10pm).

5 Bastogne

BASTOGNE, some 30km north of Arlon, is a brisk modern town and important road junction, whose strategic position has attracted the attentions of just about every invading army that has passed this way. Indeed, the town is probably best known for its role in World War II, when the Americans held it against a much larger German force in December 1944 – a key engagement of the Battle of the Ardennes, or **Battle of the Bulge** (see box below). The American commander, General Anthony McAuliffe's, response to the German demand for surrender was "Nuts!" – one of the more quotable rallying cries. Nowadays, there's no strong reason to overnight here, but there are several sights, the more interesting of which are connected with the events of 1944.

Place McAuliffe

As a token of its appreciation for the Americans holding the town during the Battle of the Ardennes, the town renamed its main square after **General McAuliffe**, and plonked an American **tank** here just to emphasize the point. Wide and breezy, the square is the most agreeable part of town and very much the social focus, flanked by a string of busy cafés.

Église St-Pierre

place St-Pierre • Free

From the northeast corner of the central square, **Grand-rue** – the long main street – trails off to place St-Pierre, a ten-minute walk away, where the **Église St-Pierre** sports a sturdy Romanesque tower topped by a timber gallery. Inside, and more unusually, the vaulting of the well-proportioned Gothic nave is decorated with splendid, brightly coloured **frescoes**, painted in the 1530s and depicting biblical scenes, saints, prophets and angels. Also of note are a finely carved Romanesque baptismal font and a flashy Baroque pulpit.

THE BATTLE OF THE ARDENNES

The **Battle of the Ardennes** – also known as the **Battle of the Bulge** – was the site of some of the fiercest fighting in the latter stages of World War II. By September 1944, the Allies had liberated most of Belgium, after which they concentrated on striking into Germany from Maastricht in the north and Alsace in the south, leaving a lightly defended central section whose **front line** extended across the Ardennes from Malmédy to Luxembourg's Echternach. In December 1944, Hitler embarked on a desperate plan to change the course of the war by breaking through this part of the front, his intention being to sweep north behind the Allies, capture Antwerp and force them to retreat. It was virtually the same plan Hitler had applied with such great success in 1940, but this time he had fewer resources – especially fuel oil – and the Allied air force ruled the skies. **Von Rundstedt**, the veteran German general in command, was acutely aware of these weaknesses – indeed, he was against the operation from the start – but he hoped to benefit from the wintry weather conditions which would limit Allied aircraft activity. Carefully prepared, Von Rundstedt's offensive began on **December 16, 1944**, and one week later had created a "bulge" in the Allied line that reached the outskirts of Dinant (the Germans famously reached the so-called Rocher de Bayard, which still marks the spot today), although the American 101st Airborne Division held firm around Bastogne. The success of the operation depended on rapid results, however, and Von Rundstedt's inability to reach Antwerp meant failure. Montgomery's forces from the north and Patton's from the south launched a counterattack, and by the end of January the Germans had been forced back to their original position. The **loss of life** was colossal, however: 75,000 Americans and over 100,000 Germans died in the battle.

Bastogne War Museum and American Memorial

Colline du Mardasson 5, 2km north of town • Jan–June & Sept–Dec Tues–Sun 10am–6pm (Mon too during school/public holidays); July–Aug daily 10am–7pm • €12 • ☎ 061 21 02 20, ⓦ bastognewarmuseum.be

Built on the site of the former Bastogne Historical Centre, the superb new **Bastogne War Museum** relates the events of World War II with a special focus on the Battle of the Bulge. Similar in setup and style to Ieper's In Flanders Fields museum (see p.140), it's a dynamic layout of artefacts, interactive videos and sound pods, and 3D displays. Flanking the museum is the star-shaped **American Memorial**, inscribed with the names of all the American states, and side panels recounting different episodes from the battle. The **crypt**, with its three altars, is suitably sombre, and it's possible to climb up onto the **roof** for a windswept look back at Bastogne.

101st Airborne Museum

avenue de la Gare 11 • April–Sept Tues–Sun 10am–5pm; Oct–March Wed–Sun 10am–5pm • €8 • ☎ 061 50 12 00, ⓦ 101airbornemuseumbastogne.com

Housed in a 1930s former Belgian Army officers' mess that was used by the Germans during the World War II occupation, the **101st Airborne Museum** displays the belongings – via a series of dioramas – of the 101st Airbourne Division and other units involved in the Battle of Bastogne. The **basement** has been converted into a "bombing experience" bunker – parents might want to check it out first before coming in with children, as it can be quite noisy and intimidating.

ARRIVAL AND INFORMATION   BASTOGNE

By train and bus Bastogne is not on the train network, but there are connecting buses (40min) from the nearest train station, at Libramont, which stop at place McAuliffe; TEC bus #80 runs between Arlon and Bastogne.

Tourist information The tourist office is at place McAuliffe 60 (daily: mid-June to mid-Sept 9am–12.30pm & 1–6pm; mid-Sept to mid-June daily 9.30am–12.30pm & 1–5.30pm; ☎ 061 21 27 11, ⓦ bastogne-tourisme.be). It has free town maps and a variety of brochures on the Battle of the Bulge, and will book accommodation on your behalf for free.

ACCOMMODATION AND EATING

Café 1900 place McAuliffe 8–9 ☎ 061 21 48 88, ⓦ hotel-collin.com. A well-turned-out café in *Hotel Collin* with hints of Art Nouveau. Good for snacks and light meals, and beloved for its meatballs in tomato sauce. Mon–Wed, Sat & Sun 11.30am–9pm.

Léo Hotel at Home rue du Vivier 4–8 ☎ 061 21 14 41, ⓦ wagon-leo.com. Just off the central place McAuliffe, this place has twelve spacious – if unremarkable – a/c rooms, but their lively wood-panelled *Wagon Léo* restaurant inside an old 1940s train carriage (that was once used as a *frituur*) is a real experience, if a little pricey (€28 for steak). Check website for special offers. €80

Le Merceny Motel chaussée d'Arlon 4 ☎ 061 31 18 12, ⓦ lemerceny.be. This three-star's eight crisp, modern, soundproofed rooms have a/c and free wi-fi. They only serve a breakfast buffet and there's no on-site restaurant, but still this represents superb value for money. €59

Luxembourg

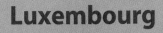

BRIDGE OVER ALZETTE RIVER, GRUND,
LUXEMBOURG CITY

Luxembourg

Often tacked on to a Belgium trip as an afterthought, Europe's seventh-smallest country – it's a mere 85km from tip to toe – shouldn't be underestimated. The Grand Duchy of Luxembourg is packed with intensely pretty hilltop villages, castles galore (over 130), deep forested valleys ideal for hiking and rivers ripe for canoeing. Add to this its proud culinary traditions, delicious home-produced Moselle Valley wines and a UNESCO-listed capital, and you'll understand why this ultra-clean, efficient and well-maintained duchy is Europe's best-kept secret.

The obvious place to start a visit is **Luxembourg City**, one of the most spectacularly sited capitals in Europe and home to a fifth of Luxembourg's population. Portions of its massive bastions and zigzag walls have survived in good shape, while its deep winding valleys and steep hills have restricted development, making the city feel more like a grouping of disparate villages than the world financial centre and administrative focus for the EU that it is. It's true that there is not an overabundance of sights here, but there's compensation in the excellent restaurants and plush hotels. In the southeast corner of the country but within easy striking distance of the capital, **vineyards** line the west bank of the **River Moselle**, which forms the border with Germany. Tours and tastings of the wine cellars (*caves*) are the big deal here, and best arranged in **Remich**. Further afield, the northeast corner of the Duchy boasts a patch of spectacular scenery known as **La Petite Suisse Luxembourgeoise**. The inviting town of **Echternach**, which boasts a fine old abbey, is easily the best base hereabouts.

Further to the north, in the **Luxembourg Ardennes**, is **Vianden**, a popular resort famous for its glowering castle. In between the two, more humdrum **Diekirch** has an extremely good museum dedicated to the Battle of the Bulge (much of which took place in the northern part of the country). Also worth visiting are the imposing castle of **Bourscheid** and the quaint village of **Esch-sur-Sûre**, clasped in the horseshoe bend of its river.

Brief history

Before **Napoleon** rationalized much of western Europe, Luxembourg was just one of several hundred small kingdoms dating back to medieval times, and perhaps the most surprising thing about the modern state is that it exists at all: you'd certainly think that Luxembourg, perilously sandwiched between France and Germany, would have been gobbled up by one or the other – and but for some strange quirks of history, it would have been.

Romans and counts

The **Romans** incorporated the region into their empire, colonizing Luxembourg City after the conquest of Gaul (including present-day Belgium) by Julius Caesar in 58–52

MULLERTHAL TRAIL

Highlights

❶ Chemin de la Corniche This panoramic walkway offers some fabulous views over the capital's bastions and bulwarks. **See p.305**

❷ Esch-sur-Sûre A postcard-perfect hamlet snuggled in a bend of the Sûre River. **See p.312**

❸ Vianden Site of an inordinately pretty castle atop a steep, wooded hill. **See p.313**

❹ Clervaux Home to "The Family of Man" – one of the world's most famous and moving photographic exhibitions. **See p.317**

❺ Moselle Valley Lined with vineyards producing the sparkling crémant – Luxembourg's affordable and delicious alternative to champagne. **See p.318**

❻ Echternach A lovely little town with a surprising archeological secret, not to mention some excellent hiking in the surrounding wooded hills and valleys. **See p.320**

❼ Mullerthal Trail A highly scenic 112km walking trail through Luxembourg's "Little Switzerland" region, home to castles and staggering rock formations. **See box, p.323**

HIGHLIGHTS ARE MARKED ON THE MAP ON P.299

6

BC. Roman control lasted until the middle of the fifth century, when the region was overrun by the **Franks**, who had absorbed the area into their **Merovingian** empire by 511. Four hundred years later, with no dominant power, middle Europe had broken up into dozens of small principalities, and one of these was Luxembourg, established by **Count Siegfried of Lorraine** when he fortified the site of what is now Luxembourg City in 963. Siegfried and his successors ensured that Luxembourg City remained – as it had been under the Romans – a major staging point on the trade route between German Trier and Paris, its strategic importance enhanced by its defensibility, perched high above the sheer gorges of the Pétrusse and Alzette rivers. These counts ruled the area first as independent princes and then as (nominal) vassals of the Holy Roman Emperor, but in the early fourteenth century, dynastic shenanigans united Luxembourg with **Bohemia**.

Medieval Luxembourg

In 1354 Luxembourg was independent again, this time as a **duchy**, and its first dukes – John the Blind and his son Wenceslas – extended their lands up to Limburg in the north and down to Metz in the south. This state of affairs was also short-lived; in 1443, Luxembourg passed to the dukes of Burgundy and then, forty years later, to the **Habsburgs**. Thereafter its history mirrors that of Belgium, successively becoming part of the Spanish and Austrian Netherlands before occupation by **Napoleon**.

A bid for independence

Things got really complicated in the early nineteenth century. In 1814 – following the final defeat of Napoleonic France – the Congress of Vienna decided to create the **Grand Duchy of Luxembourg**, nominally independent but ruled by **William I** of Orange-Nassau, who doubled as the newly appointed king of the newly created united Kingdom of the Netherlands (including Belgium). This arrangement proved deeply unpopular in Luxembourg, and when the **Belgians rebelled** in 1830, the Luxembourgers joined in. It didn't do them much good. The Great Powers recognized an independent Belgium, but declined to do the same for Luxembourg, which remained in the clutches of William. Even worse, the Great Powers were irritated by William's inability to keep his kingdom in good nick, so they punished him by giving a chunk of Luxembourg's Ardennes to Belgium – now that country's *province* of Luxembourg. By these means, however, Luxembourg's survival was assured: neither France nor Germany could bear to let the Duchy pass to its rival and London made sure the Duchy was **declared neutral**. The city was **demilitarized** in 1867, when most of its fortifications were torn down, and the Duchy remained the property of the Dutch monarchy until 1890 when the ducal crown passed to the House of Nassau-Weilburg – a (separate) Germanic branch of the House of Orange.

World War I and II

In the **twentieth century**, the Germans overran Luxembourg in 1914 and again in 1940, when the royal family and government fled to Britain and the USA. The second occupation was predictably traumatic. At first, the Germans were comparatively benign, but later they banned the Luxembourgish language, dispatched forced labourers to the

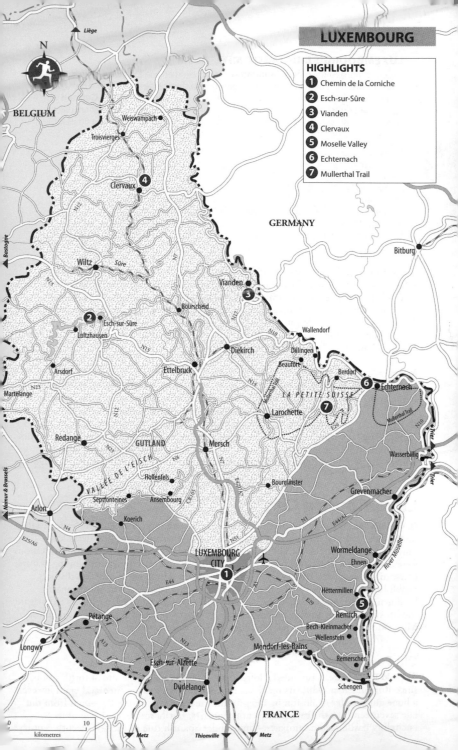

LUXEMBOURG'S LINGUISTIC MIX

Luxembourg has three **official languages**: French, German and **Luxembourgish** (Lëtzebuergesch), a Germanic language derived from the Rhineland. **French** is the official language of the government and judiciary, but many Luxembourgers speak **German** with equal ease. **English** is widely understood and spoken by the younger generation, but attempts by visitors to speak Lëtzebuergesch are well received – though sometimes locals are too surprised to seem exactly pleased.

Moien	Good morning/hello
Äddi or *a'voir*	Goodbye
Merci (villmols)	Thank you (very much)
Pardon	Sorry
Entschëllegt	Excuse me
Wann-ech-glift (pronounced as one word)	Please
Ech verstin lech nët	I don't understand you
Ech versti kee Lëtzebuergesch	I don't understand any Luxembourgish

---

Russian front and took savage reprisals against any acts of resistance. **Liberation** by US forces led by General Patton (see box, p.311) came in September 1944, but in December of that year the Germans launched an offensive through the Ardennes between Malmédy in Belgium and Luxembourg's Echternach. The ensuing **Battle of the Bulge** (see p.292) engulfed northern Luxembourg: hundreds of civilians were killed and a great swathe of the country was devastated – events recalled today by several museums (see p.317 and p.318) and many roadside monuments.

Modern-day Luxembourg

In the **postwar period**, Luxembourg's shrewd policy of industrial diversification has made it one of the most prosperous parts of Europe. It has also discarded its prior habit of neutrality, joining **NATO** and becoming a founding member of the EU, and remains a **constitutional monarchy**, ruled by Grand Duke Henri (b.1955), who succeeded his long-serving father, Jean, in 2000. Today, the tax-haven Duchy most often hits headlines on account of EU probes into questionable tax deals for **multinational corporations**. Disputes between the European Commission and Luxembourg government are ongoing.

Luxembourg City

LUXEMBOURG CITY is one of the most spectacularly sited capitals in Europe. Seated in the south of the country, it is spread across a series of sandstone plateaus and deep, leafy canyons carved by the rivers Alzette and Pétrusse. The city's Old Town and its fortifications were designated a **UNESCO** World Heritage Site in 1994 for being "an outstanding example of a fortified European city". This old centre is encircled by modern **business districts** established to service and house the European institutions and international banking headquarters that have brought the city its wealth. Compact and relatively easy to navigate, the city's charms will quickly become apparent: staggering views, smart hotels and more Michelin-starred restaurants per head than anywhere else on Earth.

Old Town

The **Old Town** plateau provided a lofty lookout and has been the site of fortifications since Roman times, while its mazy street plan dates back to the medieval era. However, a huge gunpowder explosion in 1554 meant the buildings had to be **rebuilt** from the late seventeenth to the early nineteenth centuries. Furthermore, over half of its encircling bastions and ramparts – built under Spanish rule in the seventeenth century

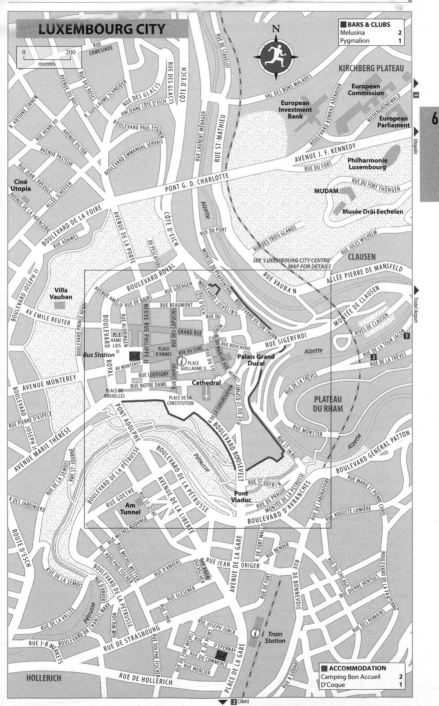

LUXEMBOURG CITY

BARS & CLUBS
Melusina **2**
Pygmalion **1**

ACCOMMODATION
Camping Bon Accueil **2**
D'Coque **1**

KIRCHBERG PLATEAU

European Commission

European Investment Bank

European Parliament

Philharmonie Luxembourg

MUDAM

Musée Dräi Eechelen

CLAUSEN

SEE 'LUXEMBOURG CITY CENTRE MAP FOR DETAILS

Ciné Utopia

Villa Vauban

Bus Station

Palais Grand Ducal

Cathedral

PLATEAU DU RHAM

Am Tunnel

Pont Viaduc

HOLLERICH

Train Station

6

Utopolis

Findel Airport

2 (3km)

6

LUXEMBOURG CITY ORIENTATION

Luxembourg has **four main districts** (*quartiers*), all of which can be visited on foot, but if time is tight, focus your footsteps pacing the streets of the Old Town and the Grund.

Old Town (La Vieille Ville) No more than a few hundred metres across, the Old Town (see p.300) sits on a tiny plateau forged by valleys of the rivers Alzette and Pétrusse. Almost all the sights and most of the best restaurants are located here and the area is largely pedestrianized.

Grund (Lower Town) The Lower Town – known as the Grund (see p.305) – sits at the base of the river valley. It's an attractive village-like enclave that once housed the city's working class, but is now partly gentrified with an engaging mix of old stone houses, medieval fortifications and parkland. It can be accessed from the Old Town via a lift (see box, p.305).

Clausen Situated north of the Grund, this district is an expat hotspot and the site of Rives de Clausen, a new nightlife "village" filled with bars, clubs and restaurants.

Kirchberg The fourth part of the city lies to the northeast of the Old Town, on the far side of the Alzette valley, and is reached by the imposing modern span of the Pont Grand-Duchesse Charlotte, usually known as the "Red Bridge" for obvious reasons. Kirchberg accommodates the Centre Européen, which is home to several EU institutions, while the new Musée d'Art Moderne Grand-Duc Jean (MUDAM) (see p.306) and Philharmonie (see p.310) have made the area slightly more alluring to visitors.

– were knocked down when the city was **demilitarized** in 1867. Boulevards Royal and Roosevelt are built on their foundations – though the more **easterly fortifications** have survived pretty much intact. These give a clear sense of the city's once formidable defensive capabilities.

Place d'Armes

Nicknamed the "Parlour of the City", **place d'Armes** forms the heart of the Old Town and is lined with pavement cafés and the sturdy **Palais Municipal** of 1907 – now a convention and exhibition centre. It's a delightful spot and throughout the summer there are frequent free concerts – everything from jazz to brass bands – as well as a small (and expensive) **flea market** every second and fourth Saturday of the month. Near the square are the city's principal **shops**, concentrated along Grand-rue and rue des Capucins to the north, rue du Fossé to the east, and rue Philippe II running south.

Place Guillaume II

Food market Wed and Sat 7.30am–1pm

A passage from the southeast corner of place d'Armes leads through to the larger and less immediately picturesque **place Guillaume II**, in the middle of which is a jaunty-looking equestrian statue of William II. The square, the site of Luxembourg's main fresh-food market, is flanked by pleasant old town houses as well as the solid Neoclassical **Hôtel de Ville**, adorned with a pair of gormless copper lions. There's also a modest stone water fountain bearing a cameo of the Luxembourg poet and writer **Michel Rodange** (1827–76), who created something of a stir with his best-known work, *Rénert the Fox*, a satirical exploration of the character of his fellow Luxembourgers.

Cathédrale Notre-Dame

rue Notre-Dame • Daily 7am–8pm • Free • ☎ 46 20 23, ⓦ cathol.lu

Steps lead down from place Guillaume II to rue Notre-Dame, where an ornate Baroque portico leads into the **Cathédrale Notre-Dame**, whose slender black spires dominate the city's puckered skyline. It is, however, a real mess of a building: the transepts and truncated choir, dating to the 1930s, are in a clumping Art Deco style and have been glued onto the (much more appealing) seventeenth-century nave. Items of interest are few and far between, but there is a **plaque** in the nave honouring those priests killed in World War II, and the Baroque **gallery** at the back of the nave, graced by alabaster angels and garlands of flowers and carved in 1622, is a likeable affair. In the apse is the country's most venerated **icon**, *The Comforter of the Afflicted*, a seventeenth-century lime-wood effigy of the Madonna and Child which is frequently dressed up in all manner of lavish gear with crowns and sceptres, lace frills and gold brocade.

The crypt

A door on the west side of the chancel leads through to the side entrance of the cathedral. Here, stairs lead down to the **crypt** and a barred chapel containing a number of ducal tombs. You'll also come across the Baroque **tomb** of John the Blind (Jean l'Aveugle), which depicts the Entombment of Christ in a mass of mawkish detail. John was one of the most successful of Luxembourg's medieval rulers, until he came a cropper at the Battle of Crécy in 1346.

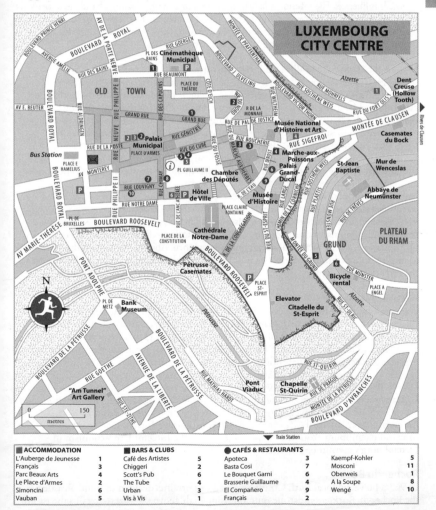

■ ACCOMMODATION		■ BARS & CLUBS		● CAFÉS & RESTAURANTS			
L'Auberge de Jeunesse	1	Café des Artistes	5	Apoteca	3	Kaempf-Kohler	5
Français	3	Chiggeri	2	Basta Cosi	7	Mosconi	11
Parc Beaux Arts	4	Scott's Pub	6	Le Bouquet Garni	6	Oberweis	1
Le Place d'Armes	2	The Tube	4	Brasserie Guillaume	4	A la Soupe	8
Simoncini	6	Urban	3	El Compañero	9	Wengé	10
Vauban	5	Vis à Vis	1	Français	2		

Casemates de la Pétrusse

place de la Constitution • Easter, Whitsun, July & Aug guided tours every hour daily 11am–4pm • €3 • ☎ 22 28 09

Across from the side entrance to the cathedral, **place de la Constitution** sits on top of one of the old bastions, whose subterranean depths – the **Casemates de la Pétrusse** – are entered via a stone stairway. The Spaniards dug these artillery chambers in the 1640s and they make for a dark and dank visit. Place de la Constitution also acts as the starting point for the **Pétrusse Express** (see box, p.308).

Palais Grand-Ducal

rue du Marché aux Herbes • Guided tours in English (45min) mid-July to Aug daily except Wed 4.30pm, departing from rue du Rost • €7; book a day in advance at the tourist office (see p.307)

Originally built as the town hall but adopted by the Luxembourg royals as their winter residence in the nineteenth century, the **Palais Grand-Ducal** has been remodelled on several occasions. The **exterior**, with its dinky dormer windows and spiky little spires, reveals a Moorish influence. The **interior** is lavish in the extreme, with dazzling chandeliers, Brussels tapestries, frescoes and acres of richly carved wood panelling. To the right of the palace, an extension of 1859 houses the Luxembourg Parliament, the **Chambre des Députés**, in slightly plainer but nevertheless still very opulent surroundings.

Musée d'Histoire de la Ville de Luxembourg

rue du St-Esprit 14 (you can also access it from rue Large) • Tues–Sun 10am–6pm, Thurs till 8pm • €5 • ☎ 47 96 45 00, ⓦ mhvl.lu

Converted from four historic houses, the excellent **Musée d'Histoire de la Ville de Luxembourg** features a series of wooden models of the city through the ages, plus displays (with plenty of information in English) on the city's royal dynasty and government, industry and also contemporary life for the Luxembourgers. The highlight, though, is the **360-degree panorama** showing city life in 1655 – it's a perfect example of a trompe-l'oeil, making you feel slightly giddy when you stand in the middle. A large part of the museum is also dedicated to **temporary exhibitions**.

Musée National d'Histoire et d'Art

place du Marché aux Poissons • Tues–Sun 10am–6pm, Thurs till 8pm • €5 • ☎ 47 93 30 1, ⓦ mnha.lu

The large and lavish **Musée National d'Histoire et d'Art** has a wide-ranging permanent collection, beginning in the basement with a **prehistoric** section and then working its way up chronologically to the **Middle Ages** and **Renaissance**. Above here are two floors devoted to **fine art**, mostly from Luxembourg and Belgium, and stretching from medieval times to the early twentieth century. There's also a floor devoted to **temporary exhibitions**.

The Gallo-Roman collection

The extensive **Gallo-Roman** section in the basement is a high point: southern Luxembourg has proved particularly rich in Roman artefacts, with archeologists unearthing literally truckloads of bronzes and terracottas, glassware, funerary objects, busts and mosaics. In particular, look out for a fine (albeit weathered) **marble bust** of Septimius Severus and a magnificent **mosaic** from Vichten.

The Middle Ages and the fine art galleries

Upstairs there are displays on the fortress and the **Middle Ages**, while the top-floor **fine art** galleries include the lively *Paysage de Cannes au Crépuscule* by Pablo Picasso, *La Montagna Sainte* by Paul Cézanne, and two paintings by Turner, who spent a lot of time in Luxembourg. You might also look out for the forceful Expressionism of Luxembourg's own Joseph Kutter (1894–1941).

Rocher du Bock

In 963 a powerful local lord, Count Siegfried of Lorraine, decided to build a castle on the **Rocher du Bock**, a sandstone outcrop rising high above the Alzette just to the east of today's Marché aux Poissons. The city of Luxembourg originated with this stronghold, but precious little survives of Siegfried's construction – it was incorporated into the much more impressive **fortifications** that were built round the city from the seventeenth century onwards. The only significant piece of masonry to survive is the so-called **Dent Creuse** (Hollow Tooth) stone tower on the north side of the rue Sigefroi/Montée de Clausen. This same road, linking the Old Town with the suburb of Clausen, makes it doubly difficult to appreciate the layout of the original castle, which in medieval times was linked to the Marché aux Poissons by a drawbridge. That said, the **views** looking out over the spires, outer fortifications and aqueducts of the Alzette valley are superb.

6

Casemates du Bock
Montée de Clausen • March–Oct daily 10am–5pm • €3

In 1745, the Spaniards began digging beneath the site of Siegfried's castle, eventually creating the **Casemates du Bock**, a honeycomb of tunnels and galleries within which they placed bakeries, kitchens, stables and all the other amenities necessary to support a garrison. At the entrance you'll find the archeological crypt housing the remains of Luxembourg's first **castle**, and then another flight of steps leads you down into the Casemates themselves, but nowadays only a tiny portion of the 20km of tunnels can be visited.

Chemin de la Corniche

From just above the Casemates du Bock on rue Sigefroi, you can follow the pedestrianized **chemin de la Corniche** along the ramparts that marked the eastern perimeter of the main fortress. The views are absolutely spectacular and there's no better way to get a sense of the strength of the city's fortifications. Several major European powers added to them over the years, but most notably the French who, after 1684, made Luxembourg into one of the continent's most strongly defended cities – the so-called "Gibraltar of the north". A few minutes' walking brings you to place St-Esprit and more fortifications in the form of the **Citadelle du St-Esprit**, a colossal, stone-faced bastion built in 1685. On the far side of the square you'll find the main **elevator** down to Grund (see box below).

Villa Vauban
ave Emile Reuter 18, Parc Municipal • Mon, Wed, Thurs, Sat & Sun 10am–6pm, Fri 10am–9pm • €5 • ☎ 47 96 49 00, ⓦ villavauban.lu

West of the Old Town, ten minutes' walk from place d'Armes, the nineteenth-century **Villa Vauban** is an elegant building that takes its name from the architect of the Luxembourg fortress, part of which served as the foundation of the building and can be seen in the **basement**. Back to its best after an extensive restoration, it makes a fitting backdrop for a small collection of eighteenth- and nineteenth-century **paintings** and is also used to stage rotating exhibitions.

The Grund
Take the lift on place St-Esprit (see box below) or go via Montée du Grund

Below and to the east of the Old Town, the Alzette river valley area is dominated by **the Grund**. Once a thriving working-class quarter, today it is dotted with ancient, pastel-painted **houses**, **cafés** and **art galleries**, and the battered remains of the outer **fortifications**. The walls of the main fortress rise steeply above the quarter, which is centred on a chunky

---

LIFT BETWEEN THE UPPER AND LOWER TOWNS
You can reach the Pétrusse and Alzette river valleys from the Old Town by road, steps or **elevator**: the main elevator runs from place St-Esprit to Grund (daily 7am–2am).

little **bridge** that spans the Alzette close to the elevator. The markers at **no. 14 rue St-Ulric** show how high the river has risen in flood years (the worst inundation was in 1756).

Église St-Jean Baptiste
rue Munster • Daily 10am–noon & 2–6pm • Free • ☎ 46 20 23

Seated next to the river, the pretty **Église St-Jean Baptiste** has a massive spire and a flashy Baroque portal. The interior boasts a whopping – and inordinately gaudy – high altar, while the side chapel holds a much-venerated **black Madonna**.

Abbaye de Neumünster – Centre Culturel de Rencontre
Next door to Eglise St-Jean Baptiste • Mon–Fri 8am–7pm, Sat & Sun 10am–6pm • ☎ 26 20 521, ⊛ ccrn.lu

The seventeenth-century **Abbaye de Neumünster**, used as a prison by the Nazis during World War II, has been entirely revamped and now houses the **Centre Culturel de Rencontre**, a cultural centre with temporary exhibitions and a nice brasserie which features live jazz on Friday and Sunday.

Pétrusse river valley

The pathway of **rue St-Quirin** threads its way west through the wooded parkland of the **Pétrusse river valley**. There's one specific sight here, the mostly fourteenth-century **Chapelle St-Quirin**, a tiny chapel chiselled out of the rock-face and equipped with a dinky little spire. Further along the valley, paths clamber up to both ends of the **Pont Adolphe**, from where it's the briefest of walks back into the Old Town.

"Am Tunnel" Art Gallery
rue Ste-Zithe 16 • Mon–Fri 9am–5.30pm, Sun 1.30–6pm • Free • ☎ 40 15 59 00

Tucked away in the basement of a branch of the Banque et Caisse d'Epargne de l'Etat Luxembourg, the elegant **"Am Tunnel" Art Gallery** houses the bank's private contemporary art collection. Some one hundred Luxembourgish artists are featured, as well as photos by **Edward Steichen**, the man behind the world-famous "The Family of Man" exhibition in Clervaux (see p.318).

Kirchberg

Until the 1960s, the **Kirchberg** district – on a plateau a couple of kilometres to the northeast of the Old Town – was nothing more than agricultural land, but the construction of Pont Grande-Duchesse Charlotte, or "The Red Bridge", in 1963 attracted a battery of European institutions and today the area is the site of the largest **urban development programme** in the country, with new roads, parks, shops and offices being created. Plus it's home to a clutch of first-rate museums.

Musée Dräi Eechelen
Park Dräi Eechelen 5 • Mon & Thurs–Sun 10am–6pm, Wed 10am–8pm • €5 • ☎ 26 43 35, ⊛ m3e.lu • Bus #1, #13 or #16 from the centre stops outside; ask for stop Philharmonie/MUDAM

Housed in the handsomely restored round-towered Fort Thüngen, Luxembourg City's newest museum, the **Musée Dräi Eechelen**, traces the history of the Grand Duchy and the fortress using over six hundred items – many of them never on show until now – from historical photographs, paintings and costumes to documents. A free and detailed **audio guide** available in English explains them all, and there's a film too to help set the scene.

Musée d'Art Moderne Grand-Duc Jean (MUDAM)
Park Dräi Eechelen 3 • Mon & Wed–Fri 11am–8pm, Sat & Sun 11am–6pm • €5 • ☎ 45 37 85 1, ⊛ mudam.lu

Across the way from Musée Dräi Eechelen, the **Musée d'Art Moderne Grand-Duc Jean (MUDAM)** is a huge glass structure designed by the architect I.M. Pei (more famous for the Louvre pyramid). The museum has a far-reaching and wide-ranging collection of **modern and contemporary art**, displayed through a programme of rotating temporary shows on the first floor alongside regular visiting exhibitions. Travellers with smartphones can download a free app guide. If your trip coincides, there are free guided tours in English every first Sunday of the month at 11am.

ARRIVAL AND DEPARTURE

LUXEMBOURG CITY

BY PLANE

Luxembourg's Findel airport (☎ 24 64 0, ⓦ lux-airport.lu) is situated 6km east of the city on the road to Grevenmacher. There are a number of ways of getting into town: the best is to take bus #16 (Mon–Fri 5.30am–11pm every 10min, Sat 5.25am–11.05pm every 20min, Sun 6am–11pm every 30min) to the bus station in the Old Town on place E. Hamilius, or to the train station – a half-hour journey that costs a flat-rate €2, plus a small extra charge for any large items of luggage. Travelling by taxi, expect to pay €30 to get into the city centre.

BY TRAIN

The train station is in the southern quarter, a ten- to fifteen-minute walk from the Old Town. It has a left-luggage office and coin-operated luggage lockers and many of the city's cheaper hotels are located nearby. The

CFL office in the station is located at place de la Gare 9 (☎ 24 89 24 89, ⓦ cfl.lu; Mon–Fri 8.30am–6pm).
Destinations Arlon (every 30min; 20min); Brussels (hourly; 3hr); Clervaux (hourly; 50min); Diekirch (hourly; 30–40min); Ettelbruck (every 20min; 20–25min); Liège (hourly; 2hr 30min); Namur (hourly; 2hr); Wasserbillig (every 30min; 30–40min).

BY BUS

Most long-distance buses stop beside the train station. Almost all of the city's buses are routed via the train station, and the vast majority go on to (or come from) the bus station on place E. Hamilius.
Destinations Diekirch (hourly; 1hr 20min); Echternach (hourly; 50min); Mondorf-les-Bains (hourly; 25min); Remich (hourly; 45min).

GETTING AROUND

BY BUS

Luxembourg City has an excellent public transport system (ⓦ mobiliteit.lu), with buses from every part of the city and its surroundings converging on the bus station on place E. Hamilius in the Old Town. Usefully, most services are also routed via the train station. Tickets cost a flat-rate €2 and are valid for two hours; a block of ten tickets costs €16 and you can also buy day-tickets for €4. Public transport is free with the Luxembourg Card (see p.298). The city also operates a night bus service every Fri and Sat (10pm–3am; every 15–30min). Bus #CN1 connects the centre with Hollerich, the train station and Rives de Clausen.

BY CAR

Driving in Luxembourg city centre can be slow and stressful: the inner streets are narrow and many of them are one-way – an up-to-date sat nav is invaluable.
Car rental Autolux ☎ 22 11 81, ⓦ autolux.lu; Avis (airport) ☎ 43 51 71, ⓦ avis.lu; Europcar ☎ 40 42 28, ⓦ europcar.lu; Hertz (airport) ☎ 43 46 45, ⓦ hertz.com.
Car parks There are four underground car parks in the Old Town (see map, p.301), though spaces can still be hard to find. All charge around €1.50/hr during the day, with cheaper rates in the evening and at weekends. For regularly updated information on which car parks have spaces

available, check ⓦ lcto.lu.

BY TAXI

Before collapsing into a taxi, bear in mind that they are expensive in Luxembourg – during the day there's a pick-up charge of €2.50, plus over €1 per kilometre, with a ten percent surcharge at night and a whopping 25 percent supplement on Sunday.

BY BICYCLE

If you're quite fit – there are lots of hills – cycling can be a good way to get around the city, which has a well-marked cycle trail.
Bike rental Véloh bikes (800 611 00, ⓦ www.veloh.lu) is a city bike-rental scheme whereby you can pick up and drop off a bike at 72 stations dotted around town. It's best to opt for the seven-day pass, which costs €1 to set up, after which the first 30min are free, then it's €5/24hr. Payment is by bank card. Vélo en Ville at rue Bisserweg 8 in the Grund (☎ 47 96 23 83; April–Sept Mon–Fri 8am–noon & 1–8pm, Sat & Sun 10am–noon & 1–8pm; Oct–March Mon–Fri 7am–3pm) charges €5 an hour, €12.50 for a half-day, €20 a day, and €75 for a week. They'll provide you with details of the cycle network (also available from the tourist office) and offer a repair service as well.

INFORMATION

Tourist offices The Luxembourg National Tourist Office (Mon–Fri 8.30am–5pm; ☎ 42 82 82 10, ⓦ visitluxembourg.com) is situated inside the train station concourse. It supplies free city maps, all manner

6

LUXEMBOURG CITY TOURS

BUS TOURS

The popular hop-on-hop-off double-decker bus tours with **City Sightseeing** (☎ 236 26 348, ⓦ city-sightseeing.com) run Jan–March Sat & Sun 10.30am–4pm, April–June & mid-Sept–Oct daily 9.40am–5.20pm, mid-June–mid-Sept daily 9.40am–7pm. Buses depart every 30min (low season) or 20min (high season) from place de la Constitution. Tickets can be bought online, cost €14 per adult, €7 per child, and are valid for 24 hours. Commentary in ten languages.

PÉTRUSSE EXPRESS

This **sightseeing train** runs fifty-minute city tours (April–Oct daily 10am–6pm) with departures every 30 minutes from place de la Constitution. Tickets cost €9 for adults, €5 for children. Combi-tickets with the hop-on-hop-off sightseeing bus are available when booked online: €19 adult, €10 child.

WALKING TOURS

The tourist office also organizes a series of **guided walks**, starting from the tourist office on place Guillaume II, including a two-hour "City Promenade" tour in English of the Old Town (Easter–Oct daily 2pm; Nov–Easter Mon, Wed, Sat & Sun 1pm; €9 adult, €4.50 child); and the excellent 2hr 30min "Wenzel Walk" (Wed & Sat 3pm; €10 adult, €5 child), which takes you right around the fortifications on the east side of the Old Town.

of glossy leaflets and details of guided tours (see box, above), and can advise on – and book – accommodation right across the Grand Duchy. The Luxembourg City Tourist Office (LCTO) at place Guillaume II 30 (April–Sept Mon–Sat 9am–7pm, Sun 10am–6pm; Oct–March Mon–Sat 9am–6pm, Sun 10am–6pm; ☎ 22 28 09, ⓦ lcto.lu) offers a similar service, though – as the name suggests – it deals only with the city.

ACCOMMODATION

HOTELS

★ **D'Coque** rue Léon Hengen 2 ☎ 43 60 60, ⓦ coque.lu; map p.301; buses #1 and #16 depart from Luxembourg Central Train Station. Part of one of Europe's best sport centres with 36 spacious, fresh, woodland-themed rooms, this superb wild-card option is located in the Kirchberg business district east of the city centre. Added perks include free access to an Olympic-size pool and discounted access to the Centre de Détente spa. €97

Français place d'Armes 14 ☎ 47 45 34, ⓦ hotelfrancais .lu; map p.303. This attractive, central, three-star has 24 smart and spotless rooms furnished in a crisp, modern style. Not surprisingly, the rooms at the back are a lot quieter. Free wi-fi throughout, and a nice café (see p.309). €125

★ **Parc Beaux Arts** rue Sigefroi 1 ☎ 26 86 761, ⓦ parcbeauxarts.lu; map p.303. Housed in one of the city's oldest mansions, right in the centre, this hotel has eleven fresh, bright suites each decorated with a unique piece of artwork and some with touches of the old building such as stone fireplaces and parquet floors. €235

Le Place d'Armes place d'Armes 18 ☎ 27 47 37, ⓦ hotel-leplacedarmes.com; map p.303. Regal five-star situated in the heart of the Old Town. The tasteful rooms are a seamless blend of modern and traditional decor, and there's a gourmet restaurant, brasserie, two wine bars and

snug wellness centre also on site. Website invariably has offers and online-only discounts. €350

Simoncini rue Notre Dame 6 ☎ 22 28 44, ⓦ hotelsimoncini.lu; map p.303. Sleek boutique hotel bang in the centre of the Old Town, just off place Guillaume II. Rooms are cool and stylish, the service is good and there's free wi-fi throughout. Good weekend deals, but not overpriced in any case. €140

Vauban place Guillaume 10 ☎ 22 04 93, ⓦ hotelvauban.lu; map p.303. Right in the thick of the action, opposite the town hall, this good-value option has sixteen small but spotlessly clean rooms with wooden floors and white bed linens. €100

HOSTEL AND CAMPING

L'Auberge de Jeunesse rue du Fort Olisy 2 ☎ 26 27 66 650, ⓦ youthhostels.lu; map p.303; bus #9 or #14 from the airport or train station; ask the driver to drop you off at "Plateau Altmunster". Modern, well-equipped, HI-affiliated hostel located down below the Bock fortifications 1km from the centre. It has 240 beds in all: 28 four-bed rooms, all with shower and toilet, and fifteen six-bed rooms, some with shower and toilet. Facilities include laundry, bar/café, free wi-fi and 24hr reception. Non-members pay €3 extra. Dorm €20.90, double €51.80

Camping Bon Accueil rue du Camping 2, Alzingen

☎ 36 70 69, ⓦ camping-alzingen.lu; map p.301; buses #192 and #194 depart from the city centre bus station and stop outside. Just 10km south of the city with a nice location on the banks of the River Alzette, off route d'Echternach in the village of Alzingen. Closed mid-Oct to March. Pitch €5, adult/child €4/2

EATING

The Old Town is crowded with cafés and restaurants, including **inexpensive places** where a filling *plat du jour* can cost as little as €10. **French cuisine** is popular, and traditional **Luxembourgish dishes** are found on many menus too, mostly meaty affairs such as neck of pork with broad beans (*judd mat gaardebounen*), black sausage (*blutwurst*) and chicken in Riesling (*hahnchen im Riesling*), not to mention freshwater fish from the River Moselle. Keep an eye out also for *gromperenkichelchen* (potato cakes, usually served with apple sauce) and, in winter, stalls and cafés selling **glühwein** (hot wine mulled with cloves). One of the great Luxembourg traditions is **coffee and cakes** in a salon or one of the city's numerous patisseries. As in Belgium, **pavement cafés** are thronged in the summertime, place d'Armes being the centre of the outdoor scene.

★ **Apoteca** rue de la Boucherie 12 ☎ 26 73 77, ⓦ www .apoteca.lu; map p.303. Perhaps the most fashionable restaurant in town, solidly booked at weekends, with two floors of dining and a nightclub-like bar downstairs. The menu is wide-ranging and imaginative with a fondness for Italian flavours. Mains are around €25 in the evening or €16 at lunch, when there are also good-value menus on offer. Ask for the wine list and you'll receive the key to the cellar, where bottles range from the entirely affordable (around €15) to the hideously expensive. Restaurant Mon–Fri noon–2pm & 7.30–10.30pm, Sat & Sun 7.30–10.30pm; bar Tues–Thurs 5pm–1am, Fri & Sat 5pm–6am.

Basta Cosi rue Louvigny 10 ☎ 26 26 85 85, ⓦ bastacosi .lu; map p.303. Stylish restaurant, with lots of dark wood and hints of purple and pink. The menu is traditional with Italian old-timers such as lasagne, saltimbocca and bruschetta dominating the list (mains from €14). Mon–Thurs & Sat noon–2.30pm & 7–10.30pm, Fri noon–2.30pm & 7.30–11pm.

Le Bouquet Garni rue de l'Eau 32 ☎ 26 20 06 20, ⓦ www.lebouquetgarni.lu; map p.303. Polished restaurant with old-beamed ceilings, exposed stone walls and starched tablecloths. The French cuisine, which features local ingredients, regularly wins a Michelin star and there's an excellent wine cellar too. Main courses from around €24. Mon & Sat 7–9.30pm, Tues–Fri noon–2pm & 7–9.30pm.

Brasserie Guillaume place Guillaume II 12–14 ☎ 26 20 20 20, ⓦ brasserieguillaume.lu; map p.303. This bright, modern brasserie is beloved for its lobster and carpaccio dishes. It's very affordable too, with *plats du jour* for €12.50 at lunch time; otherwise it's €20 or so for a main course. Reserve at weekends. Daily 11am–11.30pm.

El Compañero rue de l'Eau 26–30 ☎ 46 25 38, ⓦ companero.lu; map p.303. Fashionable place for Spanish tapas (€7), fajitas (€20) and wicked cocktails at reasonable prices. It's popular with the locals, and the bar, with bright pink walls, turns into a disco late at night. Mon 10am–7pm, Tues–Thurs 10am–1am, Fri 10am–3am, Sat 5pm–3am.

Français place d'Armes 14 ☎ 47 45 34, ⓦ hotelfrancais .lu; map p.303. The pavement café of the *Hôtel Français* offers tasty salads (€18) and an extensive menu including several Luxembourgish standbys at around €19, and sweet treats such as ice creams and pancakes too. Daily 7am–11pm.

★ **Kaempf-Kohler** place Guillaume 18 ☎ 26 86 861, ⓦ kaempff-kohler.lu; map p.303. This sumptuous upmarket deli-cum-café offers all manner of sandwiches and other picnic goodies, such as fancy cheeses and the like, plus it has a terrace overlooking the square. Mon–Sat 8am–6pm.

Mosconi rue Münster 13 ☎ 54 69 94, ⓦ mosconi.lu; map p.303. This smart Italian down by the river in Grund is regularly awarded two Michelin stars, and is a very sleek place with a waterside terrace. It's obviously not a budget option, but the set lunch menus can be a good deal, and it's a lovely place for a special night out. Tues–Fri noon–2pm & 7–10pm, Sat 7–10pm.

Oberweis Grand-rue 16 ☎ 47 07 03, ⓦ oberweis.lu; map p.303. There's a café-restaurant upstairs here, but the real deal is the mouthwatering patisserie section full of cakes, chocolates and tarts, and famous across the whole of the Duchy. Great sandwiches and wraps, too, and an outside terrace to enjoy it all from. Mon–Fri 7.30am–6.30pm, Sat 8am–7pm.

A la Soupe rue Chimay 9 ☎ 26 20 20 47, ⓦ alasoupe .net; map p.303. Good for breakfast and lunch, with porridge in the morning and inventive soups (served with bread, from €4.50) at lunch time – all consumed from swish stools in a cool, modern environment. Mon–Sat 9am–7.30pm.

Wengé rue Louvigny 15 ☎ 26 20 10 58; map p.303. Delicious cakes, chocolates and quiches are on sale in the front (patisserie) part of *Wengé*, while the restaurant upstairs offers a first-rate, French-style menu with mains from €15. Restaurant Mon–Sat noon–2.30pm & 7–10pm; tearoom Mon–Fri 2.30–6pm, Sat 9–11.30am & 2.30–6pm.

6

FESTIVALS IN LUXEMBOURG CITY

As the weather warms up, so does Luxembourg's social scene, and several spring and summer concerts and events are organized annually – most of them fairly high-brow.

Blues'n Jazz Rallye Annual July jazz event attracting fifty or so local and international bands who play on ten open-air city-centre stages.

Luxembourg City Film Festival A ten-day slew of films and documentaries made in or with Luxembourg.

Rock-A-Field ⓦrockafield.lu. A three-day rock festival at the end of June, which boasts big-name acts such as Kings of Leon and Ellie Goulding.

Schueberfouer ⓦfouer.lu. Held over the last week in August and first two weeks of September, this is the city's main knees-up, featuring one of the biggest mobile fairs in Europe.

Summer in the City ⓦfestivals.lcto.lu. An annual programme of free music concerts, fashion shows and parades, beginning in late June and ending in the middle of September.

NIGHTLIFE AND ENTERTAINMENT

On Wednesdays, Fridays and Saturdays Luxembourg City has a lively **bar and club** scene. Hotspots include place d'Armes and its surrounding streets, around the train station, Rue de Hollerich south of the city, and the Rives de Clausen bar/club "village" east of the centre – a **night-bus service** connects them all (see p.307). Opening hours are fairly elastic, but bars usually stay open till around 1am, clubs till 3am. Look out for local **Luxembourg beers** – Mousel, Diekirch or Bofferding. If you fancy a quieter night, there's a trio of **cinemas** dotted around town, the best of which are: Ciné Utopia (ave de la Faïencerie 16) and Utoplis (ave J F Kennedy 45). The city also boasts a sleek concert hall strongly resembling an ancient Greek temple in the **Philharmonie Luxembourg** (☏ 26 32 26 32, ⓦphilharmonie.lu) at place de l'Europe, Kirchberg.

BARS AND CLUBS

Café des Artistes Montée du Grund 22 ☏46 13 27; map p.303. Charming café-bar close to the bridge in Grund. From Wed–Sat they lay on *chanson* with piano accompaniment to a mixed crowd. Wed–Sun 9pm–late.

★ **Chiggeri** rue du Nord 15 ☏22 82 36, ⓦchiggeri.lu; map p.303. Cool first-floor bar in the Old Town, serving light bites and good wines to a mixed clientele beneath a funky painted ceiling. It also has a smarter restaurant on the ground floor. Daily noon–2.30pm & 7–11pm.

Melusina rue de la Tour Jacob 145, Clausen ☏26 00 89 75, ⓦmelusina.lu; map p.301. An expat favourite, with varied sounds from local and international DJs. Fri & Sat 10pm–3am.

Pygmalion rue de la Tour Jacob 19, Clausen ☏42 08 60; map p.301. Raucous Irish bar down in the depths of Clausen, serving all the Emerald Isle classics such as Guinness, Kilkenny and cider. Mon–Thurs & Sun 4pm–1am, Fri & Sat 4pm–3am.

Scott's Pub Bisserwée 4 ☏22 64 75, ⓦscotts.lu; map p.303. By the bridge in Grund, this pubby English bar is where expats congregate for draught Guinness and bitter. Daily 11am–1am.

The Tube rue Sigfroi 8, Old Town ☏27 28 058, ⓦthetube.lu; map p.303. Youthful bar/nightclub named after the London Underground. Live DJs most nights play varied sounds from techno through to soul, and there are screenings of sports events (and Formula 1), plus twice-monthly quiz nights. Mon–Fri 5pm–1am, Sat & Sun 5pm–3am.

★ **Urban** rue de la Boucherie 6 ☏26 47 85 78, ⓦurban .lu; map p.303. This bar-restaurant is popular with expats and local business folk for its retro-chic interior, good burgers and impressive cocktail list. Mon–Thurs & Sun 11am–1am, Fri & Sat 11am–2am.

Vis à Vis rue Beaumont 2 ☏46 03 26; map p.303. Laidback, comfortable bar with old posters and a relaxed feel – good for a drink or a snack at any time of day. Mon 8am–1am, Tues–Fri 7.30am–1am, Sat 8.30am–1am, Sun 3–9pm.

DIRECTORY

Embassies Belgium, rue des Girondins 4 ☏ 44 27 461; Ireland, route d'Arlon 28 ☏45 06 101; Netherlands, rue Ste-Zithe 6 ☏22 75 70; UK, blvd Joseph II ☏22 98 64; USA, blvd E. Servais 22 ☏46 01 23.

Emergencies Fire and ambulance ☏112; police ☏113.

Internet The city has a wi-fi cloud and access codes (€4.90/2hr, €8.90/5hr) can be bought from KIOSK outlets at place d'Armes 3 and on place du Théâtre.

Post office The main post office is at rue Aldringen 25

(☏47 65 44 51; Mon–Fri 7am–7pm, Sat 7am–5pm).

Newspapers English-language editions are sold at most newsagents from about 11am on the day of publication.

Pharmacies Central pharmacies include Goedert, place d'Armes 5 (Mon–Sat 9am–5.30pm). Duty rotas are displayed in pharmacy windows.

Police The main station is at rue Glesener 58–60 (☏49 97 45 00).

Luxembourg Ardennes

The rolling, thickly forested hills north of Luxembourg City are known as the **Luxembourg Ardennes** (D'Éisléck in Luxembourgish), and spread across the border with France, Belgium and Germany. It's an intensely pretty and peaceful region studded with ancient hilltop castles and quaint villages ensconced within river bends. Its forests and rivers are ideal for **sports**, with plentiful opportunities for kayaking, hiking and biking. Highlights include **Vianden Castle**, picture-perfect **Esch-sur-Sûre** and Clervaux's UNESCO-listed photography exhibition, **Family of Man**.

6

Ettelbruck

ETTELBRUCK, just 20km north of Luxembourg City, is a workaday crossroads town at the confluence of the rivers Alzette and Sûre. Badly damaged in the fighting of 1944, the only significant sight is dedicated to **General George Patton** (see box below), the American general who liberated the town on Christmas Day 1944.

Musée Général Patton

rue Dr Klein 5 • June to mid-Sept daily 10am–5pm; mid-Sept to May Sun 2–5pm • €5 • ☎ 81 03 22, ⓦ patton.lu

A rather dry affair, the **Musée Général Patton** focuses on the eponymous general's involvement in the Battle of the Bulge (see p.292 & below), with over 1000 photographs displayed alongside weapons and arms. A statue of Patton, presented to Ettelbruck by his son, sits just outside of town on the N7 back towards Diekirch.

ARRIVAL AND INFORMATION | **ETTELBRUCK**

By train There are direct trains from Luxembourg City (every 20min; 25min).

Tourist information The tourist office is located at rue Abbé Muller 5 (July & Aug Mon–Fri 9am–5pm, Sat 10am–5pm; Sept–June Mon–Fri 9am–5pm; ☎ 81 20 68, ⓦ ettelbruck.lu/tourisme). Has free town maps, plenty of regional info and can book accommodation.

Bourscheid

North of Ettelbruck, two equally appealing country roads – the CR348 and the CR349 – worm their way 10km through forested hills to the trio of villages known collectively as **BOURSCHEID**. Rambling along the bony ridge is Bourscheid village and down in the valley are Bourscheid-Moulin and Bourscheid-Plage. High on a hill above these is the massive **Bourscheid castle.**

GENERAL PATTON

Born in California to an affluent family with a strong military tradition, **General Patton** (1885–1945) was the American commander who, at the head of the US 3rd Army, drove the Germans out of Luxembourg in the later stages of the **Battle of the Bulge** (see p.292). He entered the Virginia Military Institute at the age of 18, transferring to the United States Military Academy a year later before seeing service in France during **World War I**. Badly wounded when a bullet ripped through his upper thigh, he would later joke about being a "**half-assed general**", regularly dropping his pants to prove it.

As a field commander, the charismatic, immaculately groomed Patton was among the best, but his **compulsiveness** was disruptive: he repeatedly berated British Commander Field Marshal Bernard **Montgomery** for being too cautious and, in an incident that almost wrecked his career, slapped the face of a battle-fatigued GI he was visiting in hospital, accusing him of cowardice. By comparison with his tumultuous life, Patton's **death** can't help but seem anticlimactic – he died from injuries sustained in a car accident. It was perhaps a blessing in disguise: peace could hold little for a man who declared "Compared to war, all other forms of human endeavour shrink to insignificance…God how I love it".

Château de Bourscheid

rue du Château • Daily: April to mid-Oct 9.30am–6pm; mid-Oct to March 11am–4pm • €5; free audio guide • ☎ 99 05 70, ⓦ chateau.bourscheid.lu

The first proper fortifications were erected on the site of the **Château de Bourscheid** around 1000 AD, when stone walls were substituted for a previous wooden structure. Predictably, little of this original stronghold has survived and most of what you see today – most memorably the castle's mighty **turrets** and thick **towers** – dates from the fourteenth century. By comparison, the interior is something of a disappointment, with precious little to see, though the gabled **Stolzembourg house** gamely displays a ragbag of artefacts unearthed during archeological digs, alongside occasional exhibitions of local artists' work.

ARRIVAL AND DEPARTURE
BOURSCHEID

By bus Bus #545 departs hourly from outside the station in Ettelbruck and stops on Groussgaass; then it's a 10min climb up to the castle.

Esch-sur-Sûre

From Bourscheid-Moulin, you can follow the River Sûre west along the N27 for about 15km to reach **ESCH-SUR-SÛRE**. This little place has a reputation out of all proportion to its size – mainly on account of its gorgeous situation, with the village draped over a hill within an **oxbow loop** in the river. Specific sights are in short supply, but wandering its old cobbled streets, lined with good-looking stone houses, is very enjoyable and you can scramble round the hilltop ruins of its medieval **château** (open access; free) and follow the walking trail off Rue de Kaundorf for aerial views of the village.

ARRIVAL AND INFORMATION
ESCH-SUR-SÛRE

By train and bus Trains from Luxembourg City travel as far as Ettelbruck (every 20min; 25min); bus #535 (every 30min; 30min) will take you to Esch-sur-Sûre.

Tourist information The tourist office has moved to the Naturepark, a 5min walk west of town towards the Haute-Sûre lake. The official address is route de Lultzhausen 12 (June & Aug daily 9am–6pm; Nov–April Mon–Fri 10am–noon & 2–5pm, Sat & Sun 2–5pm; ☎ 89 93 31, ⓦ esch-sur-sure.lu).

ACCOMMODATION

Hôtel de la Sûre Rue du Pont 1 ☎ 83 91 10, ⓦ hotel-de-la-sure.lu. Packed full of charm, this warren-like four-star hotel has fourteen standard rooms and ten luxury rooms, the latter with either hot tub or private hammam. Super restaurant, bar and bike rental too. Closed last two weeks of December. **€92**

Diekirch

The compact centre of **DIEKIRCH** hugs the north bank of the River Sûre, its encircling boulevard marking the path of the long-demolished medieval walls. The town took a pounding in 1944 – hence the modern buildings that characterize the centre – but bits and pieces of the old have survived. Today, Diekirch is a fairly bland place, with most of the action centring on the pedestrianized shopping street, **Grand-rue**, and the main square of **place de la Libération** at its far end. It's nowhere near as enchanting as other Luxembourgish towns, but if you're passing through it's worth wandering around for an hour or so.

Musée National d'Histoire Militaire

rue Bamertal 10 • Daily 10am–6pm • €5 • ☎ 80 89 99, ⓦ mnhm.lu

One of the best World War II museums in the region, the **Musée National d'Histoire Militaire** provides an excellent historical survey of the Battle of the Bulge (see box, p.292), with special emphasis on the US forces that liberated Diekirch. There's plenty of equipment on display but the **photographs** are the real testimony, showing both sets of troops in action and at leisure, some recording the appalling freezing conditions of December 1944, others the horrific state of affairs inside the medics' tents. There's also a variety of dioramas and a display entitled **Veiner Miliz**, detailing the activities of the Luxembourg resistance movement based in Vianden, and a room devoted to **Tambow**, the camp to which all the Luxembourgers captured by the Germans were sent.

Musée d'Histoire

rue du Curé 12 • Tues–Sun 10am–6pm • €5 • ☎ 80 87 901, ⓦ mhsd.lu

Situated next to St Lawrence Church, the bright and modern **Musée d'Histoire** is split over four floors. You're led through five themed rooms covering **local history** and then onto humankind's development through the ages and our impact on the environment. It's dry stuff, but they've made a valiant effort to liven things up.

6

ARRIVAL AND GETTING AROUND   DIEKIRCH

By bus Diekirch's combined bus and train station is less than a 10min walk southwest of the centre on ave de la Gare. Many buses also stop on or near place Guillaume. Bus no. 500 travels between Diekirch and Echternach (hourly; 35min); no. 570 serves Vianden (every 30min; 20min).

By bicycle Rent-A-Bike on rue Jean l'Aveugle 27 (daily April–Sept 10am–5pm; ☎ 26 80 33 76, ⓦ cigr-nordstad.lu) rents out city bikes (€7.50) and mountain-bikes (€15) for the day or longer.

INFORMATION

Tourist information The tourist office is in the centre, on place de la Libération 3 (July & Aug Mon–Fri 10am–12.30pm & 1–6pm, Sat 10am–12.30pm & 1–5pm, Sun 10am–2pm; Sept–June same hours except closed Sun;

☎ 80 30 23, ⓦ tourisme.diekirch.lu). It issues free town maps, free foldouts detailing local cycling routes, and will book accommodation free of charge.

ACCOMMODATION AND EATING

Hôtel Du Parc Ave de la Gare 28 ☎ 80 34 72, ⓦ hotel-du-parc.lu. A spick-and-span, modern three-star hotel facing the River Sûre. Bonuses are an on-site restaurant serving Luxembourgish cuisine and free wi-fi. **€93**

Camping de la Sûre Route de Gilsdorf ☎ 80 94 25, ⓦ camping.diekirch.lu. Leafy, modern three-star campsite,

just 250m southeast of town. Has 196 pitches, a spick-and-span laundry and a TV lounge. Adults charged €1 extra "eco tax". Closed mid-Oct to April. Pitch **€7.50**, adult/child **€6/2.25**

Restaurant du Commerce rue du Marché 1 ☎ 26 80 37 74. Very central option serving tasty, traditional Luxembourgish dishes at reasonable prices – mains for €17–20. Daily noon–2pm & 6–10pm.

Vianden

Mighty French poet Victor Hugo once wrote: "Vianden, embedded in a splendid landscape, will be visited one day by tourists from the whole of Europe" – and he was right. Hidden away in a deep, forested fold in the landscape, tiny **VIANDEN**, with its famous hilltop castle, is one of Luxembourg's most strikingly sited towns. Its main street, the **Grand-rue**, starts from the **bridge** and sweeps some 500m up a steep hill lined with ageing, pastel-coloured buildings to the **château**.

The bridge

Vianden's pint-sized **bridge** spans the River Our and is crowned with a **statue** of St John Nepomuk, a fourteenth-century Bohemian priest who was thrown into the River Vltava for refusing to divulge the confessional secrets of his queen – an untimely end that was to make him the patron saint of bridges. Also on the bridge is a fine bust of **Victor Hugo** (1802–85), who was expelled from France for supporting the French Revolutionaries of 1848 and spent almost twenty years in exile. He visited Vianden four times and spent the summer of 1871 here.

> ## THE VIANDEN TOURIST TRAIN
>
> "Benni" makes a 35min gambol round Vianden beginning at the town bridge (daily: May, July & Aug from 11am; Sept from 1.30pm; ⓦ benni-vianden.lu). Tickets (€7.50/3.50) sold inside Victor Hugo museum.

Victor Hugo museum

rue de la Gare 37 • Tues–Sun 11am–5pm • €4; free with Luxembourg Card • ☎ 26 87 40 88, ⓦ victor-hugo.lu

The *Les Misérables* author's former summerhouse has been turned into a modest four-floor **museum**. It's filled with many original salvaged items, including bedroom furniture, letters, copies of poems and manuscripts including his *Discourse on Vianden*, and sketches by the great man of local places of interest – the castles at Beaufort and Larochette, for example.

Église des Trinitaires

Grand-rue 55 • Easter–Oct daily 11am–5pm • Free

Located halfway up Grand-rue on the left, the **Église des Trinitaires** is a stunning Gothic church dating back to the thirteenth century that is praised for its vaulted ceiling, twin naves and elaborate **cloître** (cloister). Look for the fourteenth-century **statue** of Mary and Child above the interior entrance.

Musée Histoire de la Ville

Grand-rue 96 • Easter–Oct daily 11am–5pm • €3 • ☎ 83 45 91

Up the street from the church, the **Musée Histoire de la Ville** – previously known as the **Veiner Musée** – occupies an old and distinguished-looking house. It holds an enjoyable hotchpotch of rural **furniture**, fancy firebacks and old clothes, plus a sprawling display of **dolls**; on the top floor, a small room is devoted to old **photographs** of the town and castle.

The castle

Top of Grand-Rue • Daily: April–Sept 10am–6pm; March & Oct 10am–5pm; Nov–Feb 10am–4pm • €6/2, audio guide €2; medieval festival €7.50/2 (tickets available on day only) • ☎ 83 41 08, ⓦ castle-vianden.lu

Vianden's inordinately picturesque **castle** perches high above the town. Originally a fifth-century structure, what you see today mostly dates from the eleventh century, though bits and pieces were added much later – hence the mixture of Romanesque, Gothic and Renaissance features. The castle was the home of the **counts of Vianden**, who ruled the town and much of the area during the twelfth and thirteenth centuries, until they fell under the sway of the House of Luxembourg in 1264.

A sprawling complex, the castle is now open in its entirety following a very thorough and sensitive **restoration** – previously much of it was in ruins. Some rooms have been furnished in an approximation of period style – the **Salle des Banquets** (Banqueting Hall) being a case in point – while others display suits of armour and suchlike. Of particular architectural merit are the long **Galerie Byzantine** (Byzantine Room), with its high trefoil windows, and the **Chapelle Supérieure** (Upper Chapel) next door, surrounded by a narrow defensive walkway. For a bit of authentic mustiness, peek down the **well** just off the Grand Kitchen, its murky darkness lit to reveal profound depths in which, legend maintains, a former count can be heard frantically playing dice to keep the devil at bay and avoid being dragged off to hell.

Every year, in the last week of July, the castle hosts a **medieval festival** featuring costumed actors battling it out with swords and sticks, plus metalworkers, falconry displays and food and drink available in the castle's vaulted basement.

The télésiège

rue du Sanatorium 39 • April to mid-Oct daily 10am–5pm • €4.80 return • ☎ 83 43 23

If you'd prefer to forego the sweaty climb up the hill, there's a **télésiège** (chairlift) – the only one in the Grand Duchy – which takes you up a neighbouring hill. At the top

FROM TOP PHILHARMONIE LUXEMBOURG (P.310); MOSELLE VALLEY (P.318); THE FAMILY OF MAN, CLERVAUX (P.318) >

you'll find a **café** and extravagant views over Vianden. From there, it's just a five-minute walk along the ridge to the castle. Look for signs around the town bridge pointing you towards it.

ARRIVAL AND INFORMATION

By bus Vianden's tiny bus station is about a 5min walk east of the town bridge along rue de la Gare and its continuation rue de la Frontière.

Destinations Diekirch (every 30min; 15min); Ettelbruck (every 30min; 25min).

Tourist information The tourist office is on the castle side of the river, at rue du Vieux Marché 1A (☏ 83 42 57, ☜ tourist-info-vianden.lu; Mon–Fri 10am–noon & 1–5pm, Sat & Sun 10am–3pm). Issues hiking maps and sells a useful booklet describing around thirty walks in the vicinity of Vianden, ranging from a short ramble along the river to more energetic hauls up into the surrounding hills.

ACCOMMODATION

Auberge de Jeunesse Montée du Château 3 ☏ 26 27 66 800, ☜ youthhostels.lu. Modern hostel with ten rooms (all with shared facilities) set back from the road at the top of Grand-rue, on the left, near the castle. There's free wi-fi and the on-site kitchen can prepare packed lunches (€5.50) and evening meals (€7.50). Beware the late check-in time of 5pm; non-members pay €3 extra. Closed late Dec to Feb. Dorm €18.50, double €53

★ **Auberge de l'Our** rue de la Gare 35 ☏ 83 46 75, ☜ www.aubergevianden.lu. This riverside option right by the bridge offers smart, contemporary rooms with en-suite wet-room bathrooms. Their *LaJolla Lounge* right by the water is the best riverside café in town, even though service is slow in high season. €140

Camping de l'Our route de Bettel 3 ☏ 83 45 05, ☜ camping-our-vianden.lu. Top-notch campsite situated 1km south of town by the river. Has every conceivable facility, including free wi-fi, mini-golf, restaurant, shop and washing machines. Closed Nov to March. Pitch €5.50, adult/child €5.50/2.70

Hôtel Heintz Grand-rue 55 ☏ 83 41 55, ☜ hotel-heintz.lu. Traditional, even old-fashioned, family-owned hotel, whose workaday facade belies its thoroughly alpine interior, with lots of wood panelling and oodles of local bygones. The rooms are comfortable and well appointed and some have private balconies with views over the river. Closed April to early Nov. €100

EATING AND DRINKING

Café Club Ancien Cinema Grand-rue 23 ☏ 62 12 27 850, ☜ anciencinema.lu. Quirky café-bar filled with books, old cinema chairs and a large screen at the back (occasional film nights). Has a tasty please-all menu of pizza, pasta, tortillas for around €10, as well as fifty kinds of organic tea and a luscious array of cakes for €3.50 a slice. Wed–Sun 1pm–1/3am.

Om Maesgoort Grand-rue 43 ☏ 83 41 61. Respected bakery selling Luxembourgish almond-flaked, pretzel-shaped bretzel, as well as sandwiches, pizza slices and lasagne. Has a pleasant terrace overlooking the Église des Trinitaires. Daily 7am–5.30pm.

Veiner Stuff rue de la Gare 26 ☏ 83 41 74. Upmarket restaurant that takes real pride in serving traditional Luxembourgish food made only with seasonal products. The menu changes every week and features just three options for starters and mains (€20). There's also an excellent-value two-course lunch menu for €12.50. Reservations required. Mon–Wed & Fri–Sun noon–2pm.

Wiltz

WILTZ is a quiet hilltop town whose steep streets will give your legs plenty of exercise. It clusters around the elegant **Wiltz Castle**, which now serves as the impressive venue for the annual summer **Wiltz Festival** (☜ festivalwiltz.lu), Luxembourg's largest, combining theatre performances with classical music concerts. The town was caught up in intensive World War II battles throughout 1944 and its local airfield was used by both sides as the front line was pushed back and forth.

Wiltz Castle

rue du Château 35 • July & Aug daily 9am–6pm; Sept–June Mon–Sat 9am–noon and 2–5pm • €3.50 to all three museums • ☏ 26 95 00 32

A **castle** has stood on this site since the thirteenth century, but the current version dates from 1720 and was built for the Counts of Wiltz. Today, access is restricted to some areas because the white-walled château houses the city **university**, but there are **three museums** inside.

Battle of the Ardennes Museum

Reopened after renovation, this museum focuses on the bloody **Battle of the Bulge** (see p.292) that raged from December 16 1994 to January 21 1945. Collections of photos, uniforms, documents and other war paraphernalia sit alongside a few mocked-up scenes, such as a soldier receiving his orders. Despite the improvements it's still fairly bland viewing.

Tannery Museum

The **Tannery Museum** examines Wiltz's association with leather since the sixteenth century. By the mid-nineteenth century the town had over 28 tanneries and after World War II it was one of the premier leather manufacturers in western Europe. The last one, Lambert, closed its doors in 1953.

Beer Museum

Situated inside the castle's low vaulted-ceilinged old stables, the **Beer Museum** covers the 6000-year-old history of brewing in Luxembourg, but of more interest is the attached authentic wooden-floored **estaminet** and **microbrewery**, which produces just fifty litres of beer a year, making it the world's smallest – or so they claim.

ARRIVAL AND INFORMATION WILTZ

By train Direct trains to and from Luxembourg City depart every hour (1hr). The train station is an 8min walk northwest of the town centre.

Tourist office The tourist office is located inside the castle at rue du Château 35 (Jan–June & Sept–Dec Mon–Sat 9am–noon & 2–5pm; July–Aug daily 9am–6pm; ☎ 95 74 44, ⓦ tourisme.wiltz.lu).

Bike rental Mountain-bikes can be rented from *Camping Kaul* (see below) for €15/day with a €30 deposit per bike.

ACCOMMODATION AND EATING

Aux Anciennes Tanneries rue Joseph Simon 42A ☎ 95 75 99, ⓦ auxanciennestanneries.com. North of the river, this friendly three-star has seventeen floral, Mediterranean-style rooms, a leafy terrace and an atmospheric breakfast room/restaurant set beneath a vaulted stone ceiling. €125

Camping Kaul rue Joseph Simon 46B ☎ 95 03 59, ⓦ kaul.wiltz.lu. Superb, central, riverside, four-star campsite offering wooden Hobbit-style pods and cabins for families, as well as camper sites. Heated open-air swimming pool with slide and bike rental just some of the perks. Closed Nov–March. Camping for two people with car or camper €25, pod €53, two-bed cabin €105

Le Croquant rue G D Charlotte 4 ☎ 26 95 33 63. A simple affair, close to the castle, that serves a tasty array of freshly prepared sandwiches. Mon–Fri 9am–6pm, Sat 10am–3pm.

Du Vieux Château Grand-rue 1–3 ☎ 95 80 18, ⓦ hotelvchateau.com. Very central, quaint dining room. While mains such as the pigeon-and-mushroom ragout and their gourmet hamburger are pricey at €34, they're invariably quite delicious. Wed–Sun noon–2pm & 7–9pm.

Clervaux

In the far north of Luxembourg, pretty **CLERVAUX** – the site of intense fighting during World War II – snuggles into a tight, forested loop of the River Clerve and is an instantly likeable village, with meandering lanes that are especially pleasant to just wander about. Don't miss the first-rate **Family of Man** photo exhibition in the castle.

Château de Clervaux

Seated on a hill in the heart of the village, the white-walled **Château de Clervaux**'s oldest section – the west wing – dates from the twelfth century, while the impressive "Witch Tower" in the main courtyard was added later. It sustained considerable damage during World War II and large sections had to be rebuilt. Its courtyard hosts a trio of **museums**, including the eminently missable **Models of Luxembourg Castles** exhibition (May–Oct Tues–Sun 10am–6pm; Nov–April Sat & Sun 10am–6pm; €3.50 or €5 with Battle of the Bulge Museum, under 18s free; ☏92 96 86).

The Family of Man

March–Dec Wed–Sun noon–6pm • €6, including iPad guide; under 21s free • ☏ 92 96 57, ⓦ steichencollections.lu

The village and castle's prime attraction, **The Family of Man**, is a really remarkable collection of 503 photographs compiled by Edward Steichen (1879–1973) as a manifesto for peace and to celebrate "how marvellous people are". Steichen, formerly Director of Photography at the **Museum of Modern Art** in New York, where the show was first exhibited in 1955, made his selection from no fewer than two million entries, with the final cut depicting life, love and death as captured by 273 photographers from **68 countries**. They range from TIME magazine covers to the snapshots of little-known photographers, but the overall collection is very raw and moving. Steichen bequeathed it to the country of his birth in his will and in 2003 it was classified by **UNESCO** as a "Memory of the World".

Battle of the Bulge Museum

May–Oct Tues–Sun 10am–6pm; Nov–April Sat & Sun 10am–6pm • €3.50, under 18s free, combi ticket with Models of Luxembourg Castles museum €5 • ☏ 26 91 069, ⓦ ceba.lu

Across the courtyard, the **Battle of the Bulge Museum** is a simple collection of glass display cases crammed with artefacts from the battle, including foot-powder bottles, bullets, uniforms and **battlefield plans**. There's not much explanation of the items, but those with a World War II interest will enjoy spending half an hour here.

ARRIVAL AND INFORMATION

CLERVAUX

By train Clervaux is on the Luxembourg City-Liège train line (hourly; 50min), which bisects northern Luxembourg. From Clervaux train station, it's a good 10min walk south into the town centre, straight down rue de la Gare and its continuation, Grand-rue.

Tourist information The tourist office is at Grand-rue 11, tucked away up a flight of steps off place Princesse Maria Teresa (daily 10am–noon & 2–4pm; ☏ 92 00 72, ⓦ destination-clervaux.lu). It has details of local accommodation and issues free town maps.

ACCOMMODATION

Camping Reilerweier 2km out of town on the Vianden road ☏ 92 01 60, ⓦ reilerweier.lu. Verdant riverside campsite with laundry, shower and wi-fi facilities. Table tennis and playground too. Closed Nov–March. Pitch €6, adult/child €6/3

★ **Le Clervaux** Grand-rue 9 ☏ 92 11 05, ⓦ le-clervaux .com. New, central five-star boutique hotel with 22 individually styled, opulent suites. Cocktails concocted in the on-site *Cabana Lounge* and posh Italian grub served at the *Da Lonati* restaurant. €180

Hôtel du Commerce route de Marnach 2 ☏ 92 10 32, ⓦ www.hotelducommerce.lu. Offers 49 smart-ish, value-for-money rooms with free wi-fi and parking, plus an indoor pool, sauna and fitness centre. €46

Hotel International Grand-rue 10 ☏ 92 93 91, ⓦ www.interclervaux.lu. Backing onto its sister hotel, *Le Clervaux*, this four-star has crisp, updated rooms as well as the shared on-site sauna, pool and fitness studio. Check website for good deals. €111

EATING

Au Chocolat Grand-rue 13 ☏ 26 90 47 07. Dishes up indulgent, home-made cakes, crêpes (€2.90) and ice creams (€6.50) with good coffee. Nice terrace too, when the weather is warm enough. Tues–Sat 8.30am–6pm, Sun 9am–6pm.

Rhino Steakhouse Grand-rue 10 ☏ 92 11 05 161, ⓦ rhino-steakhouse.com. Part of the *Hotel International* (see above), this smart dining room rustles up sizzling steaks and stone-baked pizzas. Daily 11.30am–9.30pm.

Moselle River Valley

The region to the east of Luxembourg City is shaped by the **Moselle River**, which forms a watery border with Germany. Its waters have made the soils rich and the area is famous for its vineyards. **Remich** and **Grevenmacher** are good bases from

6

CRUISING THE MOSELLE RIVER

Cruise boats to Schengen, Wormeldange, Grevenmacher and Wasserbillig are operated by **Entente Touristique de la Moselle Luxembourgeoise** (☎ 75 82 75, ⓦ entente-moselle .lu). As a sample fare, a single from Remich to Grevenmacher costs €11 (€15 return), and they also operate short cruises on the river from Remich (€5.50 per person; 30min). Alternatively, **Navitours** (Quai de la Moselle ☎ 75 84 89, ⓦ navitours.lu) offer a one-hour cruise daily (€9) between March and October with the first sailing at 11am and the last at 5.45pm.

---

which to sample the wares of the various *caves*, and further indulgences can be had at **Mondorf-les-Bains** spa.

Remich

Around 25km east of Luxembourg City, **REMICH** is a likeable, riverside town and the touristic hub of the wine-growing **Moselle Valley**. Germany lies just across the bridge and **cruise boats** (see box above) ply the Moselle River from Easter to October, connecting Remich with Schengen to the south and Wormeldange, Grevenmacher and Wasserbillig to the north. Several local **wineries** offer tours and tastings (see box, p.321).

ARRIVAL AND INFORMATION   REMICH

By bus From Luxembourg City bus #175 serves Remich (every 30min; 40min).

Tourist information The tourist office is located at rue Enz 5 (daily 9am–noon & 1–6pm; ☎ 23 69 84 88, ⓦ si-remich.lu).

ACCOMMODATION AND EATING

Mosel-Camping Dreiländereck Sinzer Strasse 1, Nennig, Germany ☎ +49(0)68 66 322, ⓦ mosel-camping .de. A 5min walk just across the bridge into Germany, this riverside campsite has 110 pitches, a kid's play area across the road with mini-golf and an open-air swimming pool over the river, plus the on-site *Moselbrück* restaurant. Closed Nov–March. Tent **€6.50**, per person **€3.20**

Hôtel St-Nicolas Esplanade 31 ☎ 26 66 3, ⓦ saint-nicolas.lu. Smart four-star that occupies a distinguished old building dating back to the 1880s. Forty classical-style rooms, plus sauna, fitness suite and French restaurant. **€130**

Hôtel des Vignes route de Mondorf 29 ☎ 23 69 91 49, ⓦ www.hotel-vignes.lu. Rustic three-star on the edge of town, surrounded, as the name suggests, by vines. Their smart restaurant serves Luxembourgish specialities. **€117**

Ehnen

Just 10km north of Remich, the hamlet of **EHNEN** is a huddle of old and very quaint stone buildings tucked away in a wooded dell just off the main road.

Musée du Vin

route du Vin 115 • April–Oct Tues–Sun 9.30–11.30am & 2–5pm • €3.50 • ☎ 76 00 25, ⓦ museevin.lu

The **Musée du Vin** is an old-fashioned exhibit housed in an eighteenth-century home detailing the various aspects of the wine-making process, past and present. English-language explanation sheets can be picked up from reception and there's usually a glass

---

MONDORF-LES-BAINS

Around 8km southwest of Remich, the old spa town of **Mondorf-Les-Bains** has attracted health tourists since the 1840s, when an underground spring was discovered here. Visitors still come from all around to wallow in the mineral waters of its **Domaine Thermal** (Avenue des Bains 52; daily Mon–Thurs 9am–10pm, Fri 9am–11pm, Sat 9am–9pm, Sun 9am–8pm; ☎ 23 66 66 00, ⓦ mondorf.lu), a series of indoor and outdoor **pools** heated to 36ºC, and no fewer than nine themed **saunas**. There's also an on-site **spa** offering all manner of treatments and massages. It costs €16 for two hours or €35 for a day pass, but check the website for deals.

of something offered at the end of your visit. There are lovely walking trails through the vineyards, which end views over the Moselle Valley.

ARRIVAL AND DEPARTURE	EHNEN

By car By far the easiest option, you follow the N10 north for 10km.
By train There's a station in Nennig, Germany – 1km east of Remich – which travels to the village of Wincheringen. From there it's a 2km walk to Ehnen. Trains depart hourly Mon–Sat 8am–10pm.

Grevenmacher

GREVENMACHER, about 20km upriver from Remich, is the pint-sized official capital of the Luxembourg Moselle. It's a pleasant old town, with a comely set of stone houses, but the main pull is the Bernard Massard and Domaine de Vinsmoselle **wineries** (see box, p.321). It also hosts the annual **Fête du Raisin et du Vin** – one of Luxembourg's biggest wine festivals – on the second weekend of September.

ARRIVAL AND INFORMATION	GREVENMACHER

By bus Bus #450 departs from outside the Remich tourist office and serves Grevenmacher (hourly Mon–Sat). Moving on, there is an hourly bus service north along the river to Wasserbillig and Echternach. At Wasserbillig, you can pick up the train back to Luxembourg City (hourly; 40min).
Tourist office Route du Vin 10 (☎75 82 75, ⓦ grevenmacher.lu; Mon–Fri 8am–noon & 1–5pm, May–Aug also Sat 10am–3pm). Hands out free town maps.

Echternach and around

ECHTERNACH, snuggled right up against the German border, is Luxembourg's **oldest town**, founded in 698 by St Willibrord, a Yorkshire missionary-monk who was said to cure epilepsy. Today, Willibrord is commemorated by a renowned **dancing procession**, held annually on Whit Tuesday, in which the participants, holding white handkerchiefs, cross the town centre in leaps and jumps (to signify epilepsy) to the accompaniment of polka music. Heavily damaged during World War II, the city – with a stone bridge across the Sûre River to connect it to Germany – was lovingly **restored** to its ancient style and its central squares are very pretty indeed. The surrounding landscape supports a plethora of **activities** (see box, p.323) and boasts not one, but two, **castles**.

Palais de Justice

place du Marché

The central **Place du Marché** is flanked by an elegant mix of old buildings, but the jewel among them is the fifteenth-century **Palais de Justice**, or Denzelt (Law Courts), which juts out on the northern side. This striking, turreted structure has an elegant **Gothic arcade** at its base and, at each corner, statues of local, ecclesiastical and biblical figures – although these were only added in the 1890s. The Denzelt is now tacked onto the eggshell-yellow **Hôtel de Ville**, which stands to its right, and was completed in a pleasing French-Empire style in the nineteenth century.

Basilique St-Willibrord

parvis de la Basilique • Daily 9.30am–6.30pm • Free • ⓦ willibrord.lu

The forceful **Basilique St-Willibrord**, equipped with two sets of turreted towers, is the fifth version to stand on this site. The first structure, built in 706, was a relatively modest affair, but as the Benedictine monastery grew richer, so the monks had it extended, stuffing it with all sorts of holy treasures. The monastery later served as a **pottery factory**, but the Benedictines returned a few years later and promptly restored the abbey to an

LUXEMBOURG'S WINERIES

Whether or not the Romans introduced **wine** to the Luxembourg region is still the subject of much debate, but one thing is certain: the fertile banks of the River Moselle have been nourishing the vine for a very long time. **Rivaner** and **Elbling** (one of the oldest wines in the world) used to dominate the area, but nowadays **Riesling**, **Auxerrois**, **Pinot Gris** and **Pinot Blanc** make a strong presence. Standards are generally very high, so it's still surprising that Luxembourgish wine is largely overshadowed by that of its neighbours, France and Germany. Its champagne-like sparkling wine – known as **crémant** – is particularly praiseworthy and costs half the price of the French stuff.

Bernard Massard rue du Pont 8, Grevenmacher ⏹75 05 451, ⓦbernard-massard.lu. Bernard Massard is known for its sparkling, *méthode champenoise* wine, but visitors usually see the modern production process, making it a less interesting (and shorter) tour than it might be. Included is a short introductory film and a tasting in the slick hospitality suite. The *cave* is on the south side of town, right next to the main street and river. €5. April–Oct Tues–Sun 9.30am–6pm; other times by appointment.

★**Caves St Martin** route de Stadtbredimus 53, Remich ⏹23 61 991, ⓦcavesstmartin.lu. The house speciality here is sparkling wine, and the 45min tours are arguably the pick of the bunch, showing the traditional *méthode champenoise* process in which the bottles are turned by hand every other day. The *caves* are located a 15min walk north along the river from the centre of Remich, on the left of the main road (the N10).

€5. April–Oct Tues–Sun 10–11.30am & 1.30–5pm.

Cep D'Or Waistrooss 15, Stadbriedemes ⏹76 83 83, ⓦcepdor.lu. Designed by the Austrian architect François Valentiny, everything in this unusual, bunker-style *cave* is functional – even the artificial lake on top of the roof is there to keep the cellar cool. A family-owned winery, it's known for its Chardonnay and Gewürztraminer, and has a comfortable bar and terrace where you can sample them. No tours though. April to mid-Dec Mon–Fri 8am–noon & 2–7pm, Sat & Sun 3–7pm; mid-Dec to March Mon–Fri 8am–noon & 2–7pm, Sat 11.30am–7pm.

Domaines de Vinsmoselle rue des Caves 12, Grevenmacher ⏹23 69 661; ⓦvinsmoselle.lu. Founded in 1966, Vinsmoselle works as a cooperative for wine cellars in five surrounding towns that are famous for their crémant. They arrange one-hour tours of the Caves des Vignerons in Wellenstein or Wormeldange. €3.50.

6

approximation of its medieval layout. Bombing during the Battle of the Bulge meant another rebuild; skilfully executed, today's basilica has all the feel of a medieval church, most notably in its yawning, dimly lit **nave**. That said, the furnishings are in themselves pretty pedestrian, and the only significant piece to have survived the bombing is a part of the exquisite **crucifix** on the nave's left-hand wall. Downstairs, its whitewashed walls decorated by several faded frescoes, the **crypt** dates back to the original eighth-century foundation and accommodates the primitive **coffin** of St Willibrord, though this is enclosed within a hideously sentimental marble canopy of 1906.

The abbey

The huge **abbey** complex spreads out beyond the church, its crisply symmetrical, mainly eighteenth-century buildings now used as offices (including the **tourist office**) and a school. At the far end of the courtyard, through an arch, are the manicured abbey **gardens** and a Rococo pavilion.

Musée de l'Abbaye

parvis de la Basilique 11 • Daily: April, May & Oct 10am–noon & 2–5pm; June & Sept 10am–noon & 2–6pm; July & Aug 10am–6pm • €2 • ⏹72 74 72, ⓦ willibrord.lu

Next door to the church, in the right corner of the Abbey Pavilion, are the vaulted cellars of the former Abbot's Palace, now the **Musée de l'Abbaye**. There's an excellent collection of **illuminated manuscripts** here, organized chronologically to explore an artistic development that began in the eighth century and continued through to the scriptorium's eleventh-century, German-influenced heyday. Two of the finest are the tenth-century *Codex Caesareus Upsaliensis* and the book of Pericopes (a selection of biblical texts) made for the Holy Roman Emperor Henry III (1017–56). Many of the manuscripts are illustrated and explained at some length (in French and German), though all are facsimiles. The rest of the museum holds a few incidental bits and pieces, including a couple of seventh-century **sarcophagi**, and a piece of **mosaic flooring** from a Roman villa discovered just outside town.

The Roman estate

Site rue des Romains 47a • April to mid Oct Tues–Sun 10am–noon & 1–5pm • €1.50 • ☎ 26 72 09 74, ⓦ mullerthal.lu/en/100-culture?item=275 • **Tours** 1hr 30min • €60 • Book through the Musée National d'Histoire et d'Art on ☎ 47 93 30 214

Echternach's trump card is the sprawling **Roman estate** – the biggest Roman village north of the Alps – that lies an 850m walk southwest of town. The foundations of a seventy-room manor house have been excavated alongside some ten other buildings. A modern **visitor centre** brings it all to life and (expensive) **guided tours** can be arranged.

ARRIVAL AND INFORMATION   ECHTERNACH

By bus The bus station is 500m from the main square, place du Marché, straight down rue de la Gare.
Destinations Beaufort (9 daily; 20min); Diekirch (hourly; 35min); Ettelbruck (16 daily; 45min); Grevenmacher (hourly; 40min); Larochette (every 45min; 1hr); Luxembourg City (hourly; 1hr); Wasserbillig (hourly; 30min).

Tourist information The tourist office is opposite the entrance to the basilica at Parvis de la Basilique 9–10 (Mon–Fri 10am–4pm, Sat 10am–noon; ☎ 72 02 30, ⓦ echternach-tourist.lu). It supplies free town maps, and sells the Mullerthal trail (see box, p.323) hiking map, which also includes local walking routes.

ACCOMMODATION

L'Auberge de Jeunesse chemin vers Rodenhof ☎ 26 27 66 400, ⓦ youthhostels.lu. This sporty hostel – with indoor climbing wall and bike rental – has 118 beds in two- to fourteen-bed rooms. It's a 15min walk southwest from the town centre. Coming from Luxembourg City, take bus #110 or #111 and get off at the Nonnemillen/Lac stop, from where it's a 5min walk. Non-members pay €3 extra. Dorm **€20.50**, double **€57**
★ **Hostellerie de la Basilique** place du Marché 7–8 ☎ 72 94 83, ⓦ hotel-basilique.lu. The nicest hotel in the centre, this four-star, family-owned establishment has fourteen well-appointed, modern rooms, some of which

overlook the main square. **€110**
Kulturhaff Millermoler rue Girsterklaus 13, Hinkel ☎ 53 27 73, ⓦ kulturhaffmillermoler.lu. Situated on the 38km Mullerthal Trail route (see box, p.323), this delightful B&B has simple rooms with countryside views. Breakfast is entirely organic and taken at the attached tearoom and shop that sells local goodies. **€110**
Le Petit Poète place du Marché 13 ☎ 72 00 72, ⓦ lepetitpoete.lu. Bang in the centre of town, and very cheap, with just twelve plain but perfectly adequate modern rooms above a café on the main square. Closed Dec & Jan. **€65**

EATING AND DRINKING

Café De Philo'soff rue de la Gare 31 ☎ 27 76 28 68. Student bar serving light bites with an Art Nouveau-style entrance, leafy terrace and a tank of terrapins out the back. Busy on Fri nights. Tues–Sun 11am–1am.
GriMouGi rue du Pont 34 ☎ 72 00 26, ⓦ grimougi.com. Opposite the river and the old customs tollhouse, this lively restaurant is very popular with locals, particularly for the inventive salads (€16), good fish dishes and brochettes. Mon, Wed–Fri, Sun 11.30am–2pm & 6–10pm, Sat

6–10pm.
Oktav Amadeus rue de la Gare 56 ☎ 26 72 15 18, ⓦ oktav-amadeus.lu. Italian restaurant with smart-if-curt waiters, pleasant outdoor terrace and lavish interior dining room. Menu is comprised of authentic Italian classics, wood-fired pizzas (€10) and refined pastas (€14). June–Sept daily 10.30am–11.30pm; Oct–March 10.30am–2.30pm and 6–11.30pm, closed Wed lunch time.

Larochette Castle

rue de Medernach 4 • Daily: mid-March to May, Sept & Oct 10am–6pm; June–Aug 10am–7pm • €3 • ☎ 83 74 97, ⓦ larochette.eu • You can walk here from Larochette village; otherwise you'll have to drive

Lying 25km west of Echternach, the ruins of the imposing **Larochette Castle** sprawl along a rocky ridge. There's been a fortress here since the tenth century, but the most

ACTIVITIES AROUND ECHTERNACH

WALKING

Echternach sits in the heart of Luxembourg's "**Little Switzerland**" region and is the best base for tackling the very scenic 112km **Mullerthal Trail**, commonly split into three shorter routes: a 38km trail that loops east, starting and finishing in Echternach, leading walkers through open meadows, forest and a **Tudor castle**, which can be broken with an overnight stay at the charming *Kulturhaff Millermoler* (see p.322); a 37km trail that loops west from Echternach, taking in the Wolfsschlucht ("Wolves Canyon") and the almighty Goldfralay and Goldkaul **rock formations**; and another 37km trail that starts and ends not in Echternach but in the town of Mullerthal and encompasses Hallerbauch Valley, **Larochette Castle** (see p.322) and more rock formations. The trail is steep in places, but paths are well marked and suitable for children. **Maps** can be picked up from the Echternach tourist office (see p.322), or ordered in advance via email (Ⓦ mullerthal-trail.lu).

The Mullerthal Trail map details other **local walks**. One popular, much shorter route, taking in some fine rugged scenery, is the 6km walk west from Echternach to the plateau hamlet of **Berdorf**, up the dramatic **Gorge du Loup**. At the top of the gorge are grottoes – which may have been where the Romans cut millstones – and an open-air theatre. There's a fairly frequent bus service between Berdorf and Echternach, or you can extend the hike by returning down the next valley to the south, with the path weaving through the **woods** across the valley from the N11, the main road back into Echternach.

CYCLING

There are three official **cycling routes** departing from Echternach: Echternach-Luxembourg City (37km); Echternach-Wasserbillig (22km); and the Echternach-Vianden/Diekirch option (30km). The tourist office can supply more information.

Bike Mëllerdall Ⓦ rentabike-mellerdall.lu. Rents mountain-bikes (€15/day) and trekking bikes (€7/day) from twelve bike stations dotted around the region. In Echternach, they can be picked up from *Hotel Bel-Air* at route de Berdorf 1 (☎ 72 93 83, Ⓦ hotel-belair.lu).

CANOEING AND KAYAKING

You can **kayak** or **canoe** down the River Sûre to Echternach from Dillingen. In the high season (mid-July to Sept) the Dillingen-Echternach route is 14km; in low season you can choose a 12km or a 16km route.

Outdoor Freizeit rue de la Sûre 10, Dillingen ☎ 86 91 39, Ⓦ outdoorfreizeit.lu. Rents out single (€22.50) and double kayaks (€30) and Canadian canoes (€40). Advance booking is essential; rates cheaper in low season.

---

significant remains date from the fourteenth century, when the local lords controlled a whole swath of Luxembourg. Allow a good thirty minutes to explore the fortress before popping down to the **village**, which strings along the valley below, its attractive medley of old houses harbouring a fine nineteenth-century **church**.

Beaufort Castle

rue du Château 24, Beaufort • Easter–Oct daily 9am–5.30pm • €5 • ☎ 72 04 57, Ⓦ chateau-beaufort.lu

From Larochette Castle, it's about 15km northeast along pretty country roads to the humdrum agricultural village of **BEAUFORT** and its rambling, mostly medieval **château**, whose stern walls and bleak towers roll down a steep escarpment. The most impressive part of a visit is the climb up the **stone stairway** into the fortress, past a series of well-preserved gateways. There's not much to look at inside, though the **torture chamber** is suitably grim and the old well authentically stinky.

MUSÉE DE LA TAPISSERIE, TOURNAI

Contexts

History

Jumbled together throughout most of their history, the countries now known as Belgium, Luxembourg and the Netherlands didn't define their present frontiers until 1830. Before then, their borders were continually being redrawn following battles, treaties and alliances, a shifting pattern that makes it impossible to provide a history of one without frequent reference to the others. To make matters more involved, these same three countries were – and still are – commonly lumped together as the "Low Countries" on account of their topography, though given the valleys and hills of southern Belgium and Luxembourg, this is more than a little unfair. Even more confusing is the fact that the Netherlands is frequently called "Holland", when Holland is actually a province in the Netherlands. In the account that follows we've used "Low Countries" to cover all three countries and "Holland" to refer to the province. In addition, we've termed the language of the northern part of Belgium "Flemish" to save confusion, though "Dutch" and even "Netherlandish" are sometimes the preferred options among Belgians themselves.

Beginnings

Little is known of the **prehistoric** peoples of the Low Countries, whose various tribes only begin to emerge from the prehistoric soup after Julius Caesar's conquest of Gaul (broadly France) in 57–50 BC. The **Romans** found three tribal groupings living in the region: the mainly Celtic **Belgae** (hence the nineteenth-century term "Belgium") settled by the rivers Rhine, Meuse and Waal to the south and, further north, two Germanic peoples, the **Frisians** and the **Batavi**. The Romans conquered the Belgae and incorporated their lands into the imperial province of **Gallia Belgica**, but the territory of the Batavi and Frisians was not considered worthy of colonization. Instead, these tribes were granted the status of allies, a source of recruitment for the Roman legions and curiosity for imperial travellers. In 50 AD Pliny observed, "Here a wretched race is found, inhabiting either the more elevated spots or artificial mounds…When the waves cover the surrounding area they are like so many mariners on board a ship, and when again the tide recedes their condition is that of so many shipwrecked men."

The **Roman occupation** continued for nigh on five hundred years until the legions were pulled back to protect the heartland of the crumbling empire. Yet, despite the length of their stay, there's a notable lack of material evidence to indicate their presence, an important exception being the odd stretch of city wall in Tongeren (see p.215), one of the principal Roman settlements.

c.1750 BC	c.750 BC	c.50 BC
Beginnings of the "Belgian" Bronze Age.	"Belgian" Iron Age kicks off with dramatic improvements in tools.	The Romans subdue the Belgae, whose territory is incorporated within the Roman Empire.

The Merovingians

As the Roman Empire collapsed in chaos and confusion, the Germanic **Franks**, who had been settling within Gallia Belgica from the third century, filled the power vacuum to the south, and, along with their allies the Belgae, established a **Merovingian** kingdom based around their capital in Tournai. A great swath of forest extending from the Scheldt to the Ardennes separated this predominantly Frankish kingdom from the more confused situation to the north and east, where other tribes of Franks settled along the Scheldt and Leie – a separation which came to delineate the ethnic and linguistic division that survives in Belgium to this day. North of the Franks of the Scheldt were the **Saxons**, and finally the north coast of the Netherlands was settled by the **Frisians**.

Towards the end of the fifth century, the Merovingians extended their control over much of what is now north and central France. In 496 their king, **Clovis**, was converted to **Christianity**, a faith which slowly filtered north, spread by energetic missionaries like St Willibrord, first bishop of Utrecht from about 710, and St Boniface, who was killed by the Frisians in 754 in a final act of pagan resistance before they too were converted. Meanwhile, after the death of the last distinguished Merovingian king, Dagobert, in 638, power passed increasingly to the so-called "mayors of the palace", a hereditary position whose most outstanding occupant was **Charles Martel** (c.690–741). Martel ruled a large but all too obviously shambolic kingdom whose military weakness he determined to remedy. Traditionally, the Merovingian (Frankish) army was comprised of a body of infantry led by a small group of cavalry. Martel replaced this with a largely mounted force of trained knights, who bore their own military expenses in return for land – the beginnings of the **feudal system**.

The Carolingians

Ten years after Martel's death, his son, Pepin the Short, formally usurped the Merovingian throne with the blessing of the pope, becoming the first of the **Carolingian** dynasty, whose most famous member was **Charlemagne**, king of the west Franks from 768. In a dazzling series of campaigns, Charlemagne extended his empire south into Italy, west to the Pyrenees, north to Denmark and east to the Oder, his secular authority bolstered by his coronation as the first **Holy Roman Emperor** in 800. The pope bestowed this title on him to legitimize the king's claim to be the successor of the emperors of imperial Rome – and it worked a treat. Based in Aachen, Charlemagne stabilized his kingdom and the Low Countries benefited from a trading boom that utilized the region's principal rivers. However, unlike his Roman predecessors, Charlemagne was subject to the divisive inheritance laws of the **Salian** tribe of Franks, and after his death in 814, his kingdom was divided between his grandsons into three roughly parallel strips of territory, the precursors of France, the Low Countries and Germany.

The growth of the towns

The **tripartite division** of Charlemagne's empire put the Low Countries between the emergent French- and German-speaking nations, a particularly dangerous place to be – and one that has defined much of its history. This was not, however, apparent amid

406 AD	450	496
Barbarians cross the River Rhine in numbers; the Roman Empire recedes.	Merovingian kingdom coalesces around Tournai.	Clovis, the Merovingian king, becomes a Christian; the new faith filters north.

the cobweb of local alliances that made up early feudal western Europe in the ninth and tenth centuries. During this period, French kings and German emperors exercised a general authority over the Low Countries, but power was effectively in the hands of **local lords** who, remote from central control, brought a degree of local stability. From the twelfth century, feudalism slipped into a gradual decline, the intricate pattern of localized allegiances undermined by the increasing strength of certain lords, whose power and wealth often exceeded that of their nominal sovereign. Preoccupied by territorial squabbles, this streamlined nobility was usually willing to assist the growth of towns by granting charters, which permitted a certain amount of autonomy in exchange for tax revenues, and military and labour services. The first major cities were the **cloth towns of Flanders**, notably Ghent, Bruges and Ieper, which grew rich from the manufacture of cloth, their garments exported far and wide and their economies dependent on a continuous supply of good-quality wool from England. Meanwhile, the smaller towns north of the Scheldt concentrated on trade, exploiting their strategic position at the junction of several of the major waterborne trade routes of the day.

The **economic interests** of the urbanized merchants and guildsmen often conflicted with those of the local lord. This was especially true in **Flanders**, where the towns were anxious to preserve a good relationship with the king of England, who controlled the wool supply, whereas their count was a vassal of the king of France, whose dynastic aspirations often clashed with those of his English rival. As a result, the history of thirteenth- and fourteenth-century Flanders is punctuated by endemic conflict, as the two kings and the guildsmen slugged it out, but though the fortunes of war oscillated between the parties, the underlying class conflict was never resolved.

The Burgundians

By the late fourteenth century the political situation in the Low Countries was fairly clear: five lords controlled most of the region, paying only nominal homage to their French or German overlords. Yet things began to change in 1419, when **Philip the**

THE BÉGUINAGES

One corollary of the urbanization of the Low Countries was the establishment of **béguinages** (**begijnhoven** in Flemish) in almost every city and town. These were semi-secluded communities, where widows and unmarried women – the **béguines** (*begijns*) – lived together, the better to do pious acts, especially caring for the sick. In **construction**, *béguinages* followed the same general plan, with several streets of whitewashed, brick terraced cottages hidden away behind walls and gates, and surrounding a central garden and chapel. The **origins** of the *béguine* movement are somewhat obscure, but it would seem that the initial impetus came from a twelfth-century Liège priest, a certain Lambert le Bègue (the Stammerer). The main period of growth came a little later when several important female nobles established new *béguinages*, such as the ones in Kortrijk, Ghent and Bruges. *Béguine* communities were different from convents in so far as the inhabitants did not have to take **vows** and had the right to return to the secular world if they wished. At a time when hundreds of women were forcibly shut away in convents for all sorts of reasons (primarily financial), this element of choice was crucial.

768	**c.1000**	**1200s onwards**
Charlemagne becomes the king of the Franks and subsequently extends his control over the whole of the Low Countries.	The monks of St-Hubert breed the first bloodhound.	Growth of the cloth towns of Flanders.

Good, Duke of Burgundy, succeeded to the countship of Flanders and by a series of adroit political moves gained control over the southern Netherlands, Brabant and Limburg to the north, and Antwerp, Namur and Luxembourg to the south. Philip consolidated his power by establishing a strong central administration based in Bruges and by curtailing the privileges granted in the towns' charters. Less independent it may have been, but **Bruges** benefited greatly from the duke's presence, becoming an emporium for the **Hanseatic League**, a mainly German association of towns which acted as a trading group and protected its interests with a system of trading tariffs.

Philip died in 1467 to be succeeded by his son, **Charles the Bold**, who was killed in battle ten years later, plunging his father's carefully crafted domain into turmoil. The French took the opportunity to occupy Arras and Burgundy and, before the people of Flanders would agree to fight the invading French, they kidnapped Charles's successor, his daughter **Mary**, and forced her to sign a charter that restored the civic privileges removed by her grandfather.

The Habsburgs

After her release, Mary married the Habsburg **Maximilian of Austria**, who assumed sole authority when Mary was killed in a riding accident in 1482. A sharp operator, Maximilian continued where the Burgundians had left off, whittling away at the power of the cities with considerable success. When Maximilian became Holy Roman Emperor in 1494, he transferred control of the Low Countries to his son, **Philip the Handsome**, and then – after Philip's early death – to his grandson **Charles V**, who then became king of Spain and Holy Roman Emperor in 1516 and 1519 respectively. Charles ruled his vast kingdom with skill and energy but, born in Ghent, he was very suspicious of the turbulent Flemish burghers. Consequently, he favoured **Antwerp** at their expense and this city now became the greatest port in the Habsburg Empire, part of a general movement of trade and prosperity away from Flanders to the cities further north. As part of the process, the Flemish cloth industry had, by the 1480s, begun its long decline, undermined by England's new-found cloth-manufacturing success.

By sheer might, Charles V systematically bent the merchant cities of the Low Countries to his will, but regardless of this display of force, a spiritual trend was emerging that would soon question the rights of the Emperor and rock the power of the Catholic Church.

The Reformation

An alliance of church and state had dominated the medieval world: pope and bishops, kings and counts were supposedly the representatives of God on Earth, and they worked together to crush religious dissent wherever it appeared. Much of their authority depended on the ignorance of the population, who were entirely dependent on their priests for the interpretation of the scriptures, their view of the world carefully controlled. The **Reformation** was a religious revolt that stood sixteenth-century Europe on its head. There were many complex reasons for it, but certainly the development of **typography** was a crucial element. For the first time, printers were able to produce

1302	1419	c.1430
Battle of the Golden Spurs; French knights come a cropper against the Flemings outside Kortrijk.	Philip the Good, the Duke of Burgundy, consolidates his control over most of the Low Countries, including "Belgium".	Ghent's celebrated altarpiece, *The Adoration of the Mystic Lamb*, completed.

relatively cheap Bibles in quantity, and the religious texts were no longer the exclusive property of the priesthood. The first stirrings of the Reformation were in the welter of debate that spread across much of western Europe under the auspices of theologians like **Erasmus of Rotterdam** (1465–1536; see box below), who wished to cleanse the Catholic Church of its corruptions, superstitions and extravagant ceremony; only later did many of these same thinkers – principally **Martin Luther** – decide to support a breakaway Church. In 1517, Luther produced his 95 theses against indulgences, rejecting – among other things – Christ's presence in the sacrament of the Eucharist, and denying the Church's monopoly on the interpretation of the Bible. There was no way back, and when Luther's works were disseminated his ideas gained a European following among reforming groups branded as **Lutheran** by the Church, while other reformers were drawn to the doctrines of **John Calvin** (1509–64). Luther asserted that the Church's political power was subservient to that of the state; Calvin emphasized the importance of individual conscience and the need for redemption through the grace of Christ rather than the confessional.

These **Protestant** seeds fell on fertile ground among the merchants of the Low Countries, whose wealth and independence had never been easy to accommodate within a rigid caste society. Similarly, their employees, the guildsmen and their apprentices, had a long history of opposing arbitrary authority, and were easily convinced of the need to reform an autocratic, venal Church. In 1555, **Charles V abdicated**, possibly on account of poor health, transferring his German lands to his brother Ferdinand, and his Italian, Spanish and Low Countries territories to his son, the fanatically Catholic **Philip II**. In the short term, the scene was set for a bitter confrontation, while the dynastic ramifications of the division of the Habsburg Empire were to complicate European affairs for centuries.

ERASMUS, THE ITINERANT GENIUS

By any measure, **Desiderius Erasmus** (1466–1536) was a remarkable man. Born in Rotterdam, the illegitimate son of a priest, he was orphaned at the age of 13 and defrauded of his inheritance by his guardians, who forced him to become a monk. He hated monastic life and seized the first opportunity to leave, becoming a student at the University of Paris in 1491. Throughout the rest of his life Erasmus kept on the move, travelling between the Low Countries, England, Italy and Switzerland, and everywhere he went his rigorous scholarship, sharp humour and strong moral sense made a tremendous impact. He attacked the abuses and corruptions of the Church, publishing scores of polemical and satirical **essays** which were read all over western Europe. He argued that most monks had "no other calling than stupidity, ignorance . . . and the hope of being fed". These attacks reflected Erasmus's determination to reform the Church from within, both by rationalizing its doctrine and rooting out hypocrisy, ignorance and superstition. He employed other methods too, producing **translations of the New Testament** to make the scriptures more widely accessible, and co-ordinating the efforts of like-minded Christian humanists. The Church authorities periodically harassed Erasmus but generally he was tolerated, not least for his insistence on the importance of Christian unity. Luther was less indulgent, bitterly denouncing Erasmus for "making fun of the faults and miseries of the Church of Christ instead of bewailing them before God". The quarrel between the two reflected a growing schism among the reformers that led directly to the Reformation.

1482	1517	1555
Mary of Burgundy killed in a riding accident; Belgium and Luxembourg absorbed into the Habsburg empire.	Luther nails up his 95 theses against the sale of indulgences by the Catholic Church; the Reformation starts in earnest.	The resolutely Catholic Philip II of Spain prepares to weed out his Protestant subjects in the Low Countries.

The revolt of the Netherlands

After his father's abdication, **Philip II** decided to teach his heretical subjects a lesson they wouldn't forget. He garrisoned the towns of the Low Countries with Spanish mercenaries, imported the **Inquisition** and passed a series of anti-Protestant edicts. However, other pressures on the Habsburg Empire forced him into a tactical withdrawal and he transferred control to his sister **Margaret of Parma** in 1559. Based in Brussels, the equally resolute Margaret implemented the policies of her brother with gusto. In 1561 she reorganized the Church and created fourteen new bishoprics, a move that was construed as a wresting of power from civil authority, and an attempt to destroy the local aristocracy's powers of religious patronage. Protestantism – and Protestant sympathies – spread among the nobility, who now formed the "**League of the Nobility**" to counter Habsburg policy. The League petitioned Philip for moderation but was dismissed out of hand by one of Margaret's Walloon advisers, who called them "*ces geux*" (those beggars), an epithet that was to be enthusiastically adopted by the rebels. In 1565 a harvest failure caused a winter famine among the urban workers across the region and, after years of repression, they struck back. The following year, a Protestant sermon in the tiny Flemish textile town of Steenvoorde incited the congregation to purge the local church of its papist idolatry. The crowd smashed up the church's reliquaries and shrines, broke the stained-glass windows and terrorized the priests, thereby launching the **Iconoclastic Fury**. The rioting spread like wildfire and within ten days churches had been ransacked from one end of the Low Countries to the other, nowhere more so than in Antwerp. The ferocity of this outbreak shocked the upper classes into renewed support for Spain, and Margaret regained the allegiance of most nobles – with the principal exception of the country's greatest landowner, Prince William of Orange-Nassau, known as **William the Silent**. Of Germanic descent, he was raised a Catholic, but the excesses and rigidity of Philip had caused him to side with the Protestant movement. A firm believer in religious tolerance, William became a symbol of liberty for many, but after the Fury had revitalized the pro-Spanish party, he prudently slipped away to his estates in Germany.

The Duke of Alva and the sea-beggars

Philip II was keen to capitalize on the increase in support for Margaret following the Iconoclastic Fury, and in 1567 he dispatched the **Duke of Alva** (and an army of ten thousand men) to the Low Countries to suppress his religious opponents absolutely. Margaret was not at all pleased by Philip's decision and, when Alva arrived in Brussels, she resigned in a huff, initiating what was, in effect, military rule. One of Alva's first acts was to set up the Commission of Civil Unrest, which was soon nicknamed the "**Council of Blood**", after its habit of executing those it examined. No fewer than twelve thousand citizens were polished off, mostly for taking part in the Fury.

Initially the repression worked: in 1568, when William attempted an invasion from Germany, the towns, garrisoned by the Spanish, offered no support. William waited and conceived other means of defeating Alva. In April 1572 a band of privateers entered Brielle on the Meuse and captured it from the Spanish. This was one of several commando-style attacks by the so-called **Waterguezen** or **sea-beggars**, who were at first obliged to operate from England, although it was soon possible for them to secure bases in the Netherlands, whose citizens had grown to loathe Alva and his Spaniards.

1566	1567	1576
Rebellious Protestants smash up hundreds of Catholic churches in the Iconoclastic Fury.	In Brussels, Philip II establishes the "Council of Troubles" to punish his Protestant subjects; locals soon rename it the "Council of Blood".	In the Spanish Fury, Antwerp's Spanish garrison turns on the city, slaughtering thousands.

Luis de Resquesens, the Spanish Fury and the Union of Brussels

After the success at Brielle, the revolt spread rapidly: by June the rebels controlled the province of Holland and William was able to take command of his troops in Delft. Alva and his son Frederick fought back, but William's superior naval power frustrated him and a mightily irritated Philip replaced Alva with **Luis de Resquesens**. Initially, Resquesens had some success in the south, where the Catholic majority were more willing to compromise with Spanish rule than their northern neighbours, but the tide of war was against him – most pointedly in William's triumphant relief of Leiden in 1574. Two years later, Resquesens died and the (unpaid) Habsburg garrison in Antwerp mutinied and attacked the town, slaughtering some eight thousand of its inhabitants in what was soon known as the **Spanish Fury**. Though the Habsburgs still held several towns, the massacre alienated the south and pushed its inhabitants into the arms of William, whose troops now swept into Brussels, the heart of imperial power. Momentarily, it seemed possible for the whole region to unite behind William and all signed the **Union of Brussels**, which demanded the departure of foreign troops as a condition for accepting a diluted Habsburg sovereignty. This was followed, in 1576, by the **Pacification of Ghent**, a regional agreement that guaranteed freedom of religious belief, a necessary precondition for any union between the largely Protestant north (the Netherlands) and the predominantly Catholic south (Belgium and Luxembourg).

The United Provinces break free

Despite the precariousness of his position, Philip II was not inclined to compromise, especially after he realized that William's Calvinist sympathies were giving his new-found Walloon and Flemish allies the jitters. The king bided his time until 1578 when, with his enemies arguing among themselves, he sent another army from Spain to the Low Countries under the command of Alessandro Farnese, the **Duke of Parma**. Events played into Parma's hands. In 1579, tiring of all the wrangling, seven northern provinces agreed to sign the **Union of Utrecht**, an alliance against Spain that was to be the first unification of the Netherlands as an identifiable country – as the **United Provinces**. The assembly of these United Provinces was known as the **States General** and it met at The Hague. The role of **Stadholder** was the most important in each province, roughly equivalent to that of governor, though the same person could occupy this position in any number of provinces. Meanwhile, in the south – and also in 1579 – representatives of the southern provinces signed the **Union of Arras**, a Catholic-led agreement that declared loyalty to Philip II and counter-balanced the Union of Utrecht in the north. Parma used the south as a base to recapture Flanders and Antwerp, which fell after a long and cruel siege in 1585. But Parma was unable to advance any further north and the Low Countries were, de facto, divided into two – the Spanish Netherlands and the United Provinces – beginning a separation that would lead, after many changes, to the creation of three modern countries.

The Spanish Netherlands (1579–1713)

With his army firmly entrenched in the south, Philip was now prepared to permit some degree of economic and political autonomy, exercising control over the **Spanish Netherlands** through a governor in Brussels, but he was not inclined to tolerate his

1579	1584	1599
The seven provinces of the Netherlands break with Habsburg Spain, establishing the United Provinces, but Belgium and Luxembourg remain Habsburg fiefdoms as the Spanish Netherlands.	A Catholic fanatic assassinates the Protestant hero, William the Silent.	Anthony van Dyck born in Antwerp.

newly recovered Protestant subjects. As a result, thousands of weavers, apprentices and skilled workers – the bedrock of Calvinism – fled north to escape the new Catholic regime, thereby fuelling an economic boom in Holland. It took a while for this migration to take effect, and for several years the Spanish Netherlands had all the trappings – if not the substance – of success, its mini-economy sustained by the conspicuous consumption of the Habsburg elite. Silk weaving, diamond processing and tapestry- and lace-making were particular beneficiaries and a new canal was cut linking Ghent and Bruges to the sea at Ostend. This commercial restructuring underpinned a brief flourishing of artistic life centred on **Rubens** and his circle of friends – including Anthony van Dyck and Jacob Jordaens – in Antwerp during the first decades of the seventeenth century.

Habsburg failure

Months before his death in 1598, Philip II had granted control of the Spanish Netherlands to his daughter and her husband, appointing them the **Archdukes Isabella and Albert**. Failing to learn from experience, the ducal couple continued to prosecute the war against the Protestant north, but with so little success that they were obliged to make peace – the **Twelve-Year Truce** – in 1609. When the truce ended, the new Spanish king **Philip IV** proved equally foolhardy, bypassing Isabella – Albert was dead – to launch his own campaign against the Protestant Dutch. This was part of the **Thirty Years' War** (1618–48), a devastating conflict that spread across most of western Europe in a mix of dynastic rivalry and religious (Catholic against Protestant) hatred. The Spanish were initially successful, but they were weakened by war with France and Dutch sea-power. Thereafter, from 1625 onwards, the Spaniards suffered a series of defeats on land and sea and in 1648 they were compelled to accept the humiliating terms of the **Peace of Westphalia**. This was a general treaty that ended the Thirty Years' War, and its terms both recognized the independence of the United Provinces and closed the Scheldt estuary, an action designed to destroy the trade and prosperity of Antwerp. By these means, the commercial pre-eminence of Amsterdam was assured.

The Spanish Netherlands paid dearly for its adherence to the Habsburg cause. In the course of the Thirty Years' War, it had teetered on the edge of chaos – highwaymen infested the roads, trade had almost disappeared, the population had been halved in Brabant, and acres of fertile farmland lay uncultivated – but the peace was perhaps as bad. Denied access to the sea, Antwerp was ruined and simply withered away, while the southern provinces as a whole spiralled into an **economic decline** that pauperized its population. Yet the country's ruling families seemed proud to appear to the world as the defenders of the Catholic faith; those who disagreed left.

The Counter-Reformation

Politically dependent on a decaying Spain, economically ruined and deprived of most of its more independent-minded citizens, the Spanish Netherlands turned in on itself, sustained by the fanatical Catholicism of the **Counter-Reformation**. Religious worship became strict and magnificent, medieval carnivals were transformed into exercises in piety, and penitential flagellation became popular, all under the approving eyes of the **Jesuits**. Indeed, the number of Jesuits was quite extraordinary: in the whole of France, there were only two thousand, but the Spanish Netherlands had no fewer than 1600. It

1604	**1609**	**1610 onwards**
Ostend wins the admiration of Protestant Europe by enduring a three-year siege, albeit unsuccessfully.	Rubens sets out his artistic stall in Antwerp.	A veritable army of Jesuit priests settles over the Spanish Netherlands.

was here that they wrote their most important works, exercised their greatest influence and owned vast tracts of land. Supported by draconian laws that barred known Protestants from public appointments, declared their marriages illegal and forbade them municipal assistance, the Jesuits and their fellow Catholic priests simply overwhelmed the religious opposition; in the space of fifty years, they transformed this part of the Low Countries into an introverted world shaped by a mystical faith, where Christians were redeemed by the ecstasy of suffering.

The visible signs of the change were all around, from extravagant Baroque churches to Crosses, Calvaries and shrines scattered across the countryside. Literature disappeared, the sciences vegetated and religious orders multiplied. In **painting**, artists – principally Rubens – were used to confirm the ecclesiastical orthodoxies, their canvases full of muscular saints and angels, reflecting a religious faith of mystery and hierarchy; others, such as David Teniers and the later Bruegels, retreated into minutely observed realism.

French interference

In 1648, the **Peace of Westphalia** (see p.332) freed the king of France from his fear of Germany, and the political and military history of the Spanish Netherlands thereafter was dominated by **Louis XIV**'s efforts to add the country to his territories. Fearful of an over-powerful France, the United Provinces, England and Sweden, among others, determinedly resisted French designs and, to preserve the so-called balance of power, fought a long series of campaigns beginning with the **War of Devolution** in 1667 and ending in the **War of the Spanish Succession**. The latter was sparked by the death in 1700 of **Charles II**, the last of the Spanish Habsburgs, who had willed his territories to the grandson of Louis XIV of France. An anti-French coalition refused to accept the settlement and there ensued a haphazard series of campaigns that dragged on for eleven years, marked by the spectacular victories of the **Duke of Marlborough** – Blenheim, Ramillies, Malplaquet and Oudenaarde. Many of the region's cities were besieged and badly damaged during these wars, and only with the **Treaty of Utrecht** of 1713 did the French abandon their attempt to conquer the Spanish Netherlands. The latter were now passed to the Austrian Habsburgs in the figure of the Emperor Charles VI.

The Austrian Netherlands (1713–94)

The transfer of the country from Spanish to **Austrian control** made little appreciable difference: there were more wars and more invasions, and a remote central authority continued to operate through Brussels. In particular, the **War of the Austrian Succession**, fought over the right of Maria Theresa to assume the Austrian Habsburg throne, prompted the French to invade and occupy much of the country in 1744, though Austrian control was restored four years later by the **Treaty of Aix-la-Chapelle**. Perhaps surprisingly, these dynastic shenanigans had little effect on the country's agriculture, which survived the various campaigns and actually became more productive, leading to a marked increase in the rural population, especially after the introduction of the **potato**. But intellectually the country remained vitrified and stagnant – only three percent of the population were literate, workers were forbidden to change towns or jobs without obtaining permission from the municipal authorities, and skills and crafts were tied to particular families. As **Voltaire** quipped:

1648	1700	1708
More warfare; the Dutch win and force the closure of the River Scheldt; Antwerp hits the economic skids.	The last of the Spanish Habsburgs, the pathetic Charles II, dies without issue; more warfare.	The Duke of Marlborough wins a spectacular victory over the French at Oudenaarde.

In this sad place wherein I stay,
Ignorance, torpidity,
And boredom hold their lasting sway,
With unconcerned stupidity;
A land where old obedience sits,
Well filled with faith, devoid of wits.

Progress at last

This sorry state of affairs began to change in the middle of the eighteenth century as the Austrian oligarchy came under the influence of the **Enlightenment**, that belief in reason and progress – as against authority and tradition – that had first been proselytized by French philosophers. In 1753, the arrival of a progressive governor, the **Count of Cobenzl**, signified a transformation of Habsburg policy. Eager to shake the country from its torpor, Cobenzl initiated an ambitious programme of public works. New canals were dug, old canals deepened, new industries were encouraged and public health was at least discussed, one result being regulations forbidding burial inside churches and the creation of new cemeteries outside the city walls. Cobenzl also took a firm line with his clerical opponents, who took a dim view of all this modernizing and tried to encourage the population to thwart him in his aims.

The Brabant Revolution

In 1780, the **Emperor Joseph II** came to the throne, determined, as he put it, to "root out silly old prejudices" by imperial decree. His reforming zeal was not, however, matched by any political nous and the deluge of edicts that he promulgated managed to offend all of the country's major groups – from peasants, clerics and merchants right through to the nobility. Opposition crystallized around two groups – the liberal-minded **Vonckists**, who demanded a radical, republican constitution, and the conservative **Statists**, whose prime aim was the maintenance of the Catholic status quo. Pandemonium ensued and, in 1789, the Habsburgs dispatched an army to restore order. Against all expectations, the two political groups swallowed their differences to combine and then defeat the Austrians near Antwerp, in what became known as the **Brabant Revolution**. The rebels promptly announced the formation of the United States of Belgium, but the uneasy alliance between the Vonckists and Statists soon broke down, not least because the latter were terrified by the course of the revolution which had erupted across the border in France. Determined to keep the radicals at bay, the Statists raised the peasantry to arms and, with the assistance of the priests, encouraged them to attack the Vonckists, who were killed in their hundreds. The Statists now had the upper hand, but the country remained in turmoil, and when Emperor Joseph died in 1790, his successor, **Léopold**, was quick to withdraw many of the reforming acts and send in his troops to restore imperial authority.

French rule and its aftermath (1794–1830)

The new and repressive Habsburg regime was short-lived. French Republican armies brushed the imperial forces aside in 1794, and the Austrian Netherlands was annexed the following year, an annexation that was to last until 1814. The **French** imposed radical reforms: the Catholic Church was stripped of much of its worldly wealth; feudal

1713	1794	1814
Belgium and Luxembourg are passed to another branch of the Habsburg family as the Austrian Netherlands.	The French Revolutionary army occupies the Austrian Netherlands, which ceases to exist.	French control of Belgium disintegrates; local leaders argue things out.

privileges and the guilds were abolished; and a consistent legal system was formulated. **Napoleon**, in control from 1799, carried on the work of modernization, rebuilding the docks of Antwerp and forcing the Netherlanders, whose country the French had also occupied, to accept the reopening of the Scheldt. Unrestricted access to French markets boosted the local economy, kick-starting the mechanization of the textile industry in Ghent and Verviers and encouraging the growth of the coal and metal industries in Hainaut, but with the exception of a radical minority, the French occupation remained unpopular with most of the populace. Looting by French soldiers was commonplace, especially in the early years, but it was the introduction of **conscription** which stirred the most resistance, provoking a series of (brutally repressed) peasant insurrections.

The United Kingdom of the Netherlands (1815–30)

French rule in the Low Countries began to evaporate after Napoleon's disastrous retreat from Moscow in 1812, and had all but disappeared long before Napoleon's final defeat just outside Brussels at the **Battle of Waterloo** in June 1815. At the **Congress of Vienna**, called to settle Europe at the end of the Napoleonic Wars, the main concern of the Great Powers – including Great Britain and Russia – was to create a buffer state against any possible future plans the French might have to expand to the north. With scant regard for the feelings of those affected, they decided to establish the **United Kingdom of the Netherlands**, which incorporated both the old United Provinces and the Spanish (Austrian) Netherlands. On the throne they placed Frederick William of Orange, crowned **King William I**. The Great Powers also decided to give Frederick William's German estates to Prussia and in return presented him with the newly independent **Grand Duchy of Luxembourg**. This was a somewhat confused arrangement. The duchy had previously been part of both the Spanish and Austrian Netherlands, but now it was detached from the rest of the Low Countries constitutionally and pushed into the German Confederation at the same time as it shared the same king with the old United Provinces and Austrian Netherlands.

Given the imperious way the new Kingdom of the Netherlands had been established, it required considerable royal tact to make things work. William lacked this in abundance and indeed some of his measures seemed designed to inflame his French-speaking (Belgian) subjects. He made Dutch the official language of the whole kingdom and, in a move against the Catholics, he tried to secularize all Church-controlled schools. Furthermore, each of the two former countries had the same number of representatives at the States General despite the fact that the population of the old United Provinces was half that of its neighbour. There were **competing economic interests** too. The north was reliant on commerce and sought free trade without international tariffs; the industrialized south wanted a degree of protectionism. William's refusal to address any of these concerns united his opponents in the south, where both industrialists and clerics now clamoured for change.

Independent Belgium: 1830–1900

The **revolution** against King William began in the Brussels opera house on August 25, 1830, when the singing of a duet, *Amour Sacré de la Patrie*, hit a nationalist nerve and

1814	1815	1830
Belgium and Luxembourg passed to the Dutch king, William I, as part of the new United Kingdom of the Netherlands.	Battle of Waterloo fought just outside Brussels; Napoleon famously defeated.	The Belgians revolt against the Dutch; creation of an independent Belgium with Léopold I as king.

the audience poured out onto the streets to raise the flag of Brabant in defiance of the king. At first the revolutionaries only demanded a scaling down of royal power and a separate "Belgian" administration, but negotiations soon broke down and in late September the insurrectionists proclaimed the **Kingdom of Belgium**. William prepared for war, but the liberal governments of Great Britain and France intervened to stop hostilities and, in January of the following year, they recognized an independent Belgian state at the **Conference of London**. The caveat – and this was crucial to the Great Powers given the trouble the region had caused for centuries – was that Belgium be classified a "**neutral**" state, that is one outside any other's sphere of influence. To bolster this new nation, they ceded to it the western segments of the Grand Duchy of Luxembourg and dug out Prince Léopold of Saxe-Coburg to present with the crown. William retained the northern part of his kingdom and even received the remainder of Luxembourg as his personal possession, but he still hated the settlement and there was a further bout of sabre-rattling before he finally caved in and accepted the new arrangements in 1839.

Léopold I

Shrewd and capable, **Léopold I** (1830–65) was careful to maintain his country's neutrality and encouraged an industrial boom that saw coal mines developed, iron foundries established and the rapid expansion of the railway system. One casualty, however, was the traditional linen-making industry of rural Flanders. The cottagers who spun and wove the linen could not compete with the mechanized mills, and their pauperization was compounded by the poor grain harvests and potato blight of 1844–46. Their sufferings were, however, of only mild concern to the country's political representatives, who were elected on a strictly limited franchise, which ensured the domination of the middle classes. The latter divided into two loose groups, the one attempting to undermine Catholic influence and control over such areas as education, the other profoundly conservative in its desire to maintain the status quo. Progressive elements within the bourgeoisie coalesced in the **Liberal party**, which was free trade and urban in outlook, whereas their opponents, the **Catholic party**, promised to protect Belgian agriculture with tariffs. The political twist was that the Catholic party, in its retreat from the industrialized and radicalized cities, began to identify with the plight of rural Dutch-speaking Belgians – as against the French-speaking ruling and managerial classes.

Léopold II

Léopold II's long reign (1865–1909) saw the emergence of Belgium as a major industrial power. The 1860s and 1870s also witnessed the first significant stirrings of a type of **Flemish nationalism** which felt little enthusiasm for the unitary status of Belgium, divided as it was between a French-speaking majority in the south – the Walloons – and the minority Dutch-speakers of the north. There was also industrial unrest towards the end of the century, the end results being a body of legislation improving working conditions and, in 1893, the extension of the **franchise** to all men over the age of 25. The Catholic party also ensured that, under the Equality Law of 1898, Dutch was ratified as an official language, equal in status to French – the forerunner of many long and difficult debates. Another matter of concern was the

1860s onwards	1885	1907
Belgium becomes a major industrial power, but one with striking inequalities.	Léopold II becomes the owner of a vast tract of Africa, the Congo Free State.	Georges Prosper Remi, the future Hergé – and creator of Tintin – is born in a suburb of Brussels.

Belgian Congo. Determined to cut an international figure, Léopold II had decided to build up a colonial empire. The unfortunate recipients of his ambition were the Africans of the Congo River basin, who were effectively given to him by a conference

A ROYAL MISCELLANY: BELGIUM'S KINGS

Léopold I (1831–65). Foisted on Belgium by the Great Powers, Léopold, the first king of the Belgians, was imported from Germany, where he was the prince of Saxe-Coburg – and the uncle of Queen Victoria. Despite lacking a popular mandate, Léopold made a fairly good fist of things, keeping the country neutral as the Great Powers had ordained.

Léopold II (1865–1909). Energetic, crafty and forceful, Léopold – son of Léopold I – encouraged the urbanization of his country and promoted its importance as a major industrial power. He was also the man responsible for landing Brussels with such pompous monuments as the Palais de Justice and for the imposition of a particularly barbaric colonial regime on the peoples of the Belgian Congo (now the Democratic Republic of the Congo).

Albert I (1909–34). Easily the most popular of the dynasty, Albert's determined resistance to the German invasion of World War I made him a national hero, and his untimely death, in a climbing accident, traumatized the nation. Albert was the nephew of Léopold II and the father of Léopold III.

Léopold III (1934–51). In contrast to his father, Léopold III had the dubious honour of becoming one of Europe's least popular monarchs. His first wife died in a suspicious car crash; he nearly lost his kingdom by remarrying (then anathema in a Roman Catholic country); and he was badly compromised during the German occupation of World War II. During the war, Léopold remained in Belgium rather than face exile, fuelling rumours that he was a Nazi collaborator – though his supporters maintained that he prevented thousands of Belgians from being deported. After several years of heated postwar debate, during which the king remained in exile, the issue of Léopold's return was finally put to a referendum in 1950. Just over half the population voted in his favour, but there was a clear French/Flemish divide, with opposition to the king concentrated in French-speaking Wallonia. Mercifully for Belgium, Léopold abdicated in 1951 in favour of his son, Baudouin.

Baudouin I (1951–93). A softly spoken family man, Baudouin did much to restore the popularity of the monarchy, not least because he was generally thought to be even-handed in his treatment of the French- and Flemish-speakers. He also hit the headlines in April 1990 by standing down for a day so that an abortion bill (which he as a Catholic had refused to sign) could be passed. Childless, he was succeeded by his brother.

Albert II (1993–2013). Born in 1934, Albert (Baudouin's younger brother) was impeccably royal, from his Swiss finishing school to his aristocratic Italian wife, Queen Paola. A steady chap, who looks distinctly avuncular, he proved a safe pair of hands, becoming a national figurehead in the manner of his predecessor and steering a diplomatic course through the shoals of Flemish-Wallonian antagonisms. Albert abdicated in 2013 on the grounds of poor health and old age, though his decision may well have been influenced by a long-running paternity suit that dogged his last years as king.

Philippe I (2013–). Born in 1960, the son of Albert II, Philippe I has inherited his father's banker-like looks, but without the avuncular air (few would accuse him of being charismatic). A carefully assembled CV, including an international education, military training, marriage to Mathilde, a Walloon aristocrat, and four children, has ticked most of the Belgian Royal boxes, but as yet the country has not really taken to him – and, given his reputation for awkward aloofness, there's no certainty it ever will.

1908	1912	1914
Belgian government takes over the Congo after the savagery of the king's colonial rule becomes a national disgrace; no one asks the Congolese, who benefit not at all.	René Magritte's mother commits suicide when he is just 13.	The Germans invade Belgium at the start of World War I; only a pocket of territory around De Panne is spared occupation.

of European powers in 1885. Ruling the Congo as a personal fiefdom, Léopold established an extraordinarily cruel colonial regime – so cruel in fact that even the other colonial powers were appalled and the Belgian state was obliged to end the embarrassment (if not the brutal exploitation of the Congolese) by taking over the region – as the Belgian Congo – in 1908.

The twentieth century to 1939

At the beginning of the twentieth century, Belgium was an industrial powerhouse with a booming economy and a rapidly increasing workforce – 934,000 in 1896, 1,176,000 in 1910. It was also determined to keep on good terms with all the Great Powers, but could not prevent getting caught up in **World War I**. Indifferent to Belgium's proclaimed neutrality, the Germans had decided as early as 1908 that the best way to attack France was via Belgium, and this is precisely what they did in 1914. They captured almost all of the country, the exception being a narrow strip of territory around De Panne. Undaunted, **King Albert I** (1909–34) and the Belgian army manned the northern part of the Allied line, and the king's refusal to surrender made him a national hero. The **trenches** ran through western Flanders, and all the towns and villages lying close to them – principally Ieper (Ypres) and Diksmuide – were simply obliterated by artillery fire. Belgium also witnessed some of the worst of the slaughter in and around a bulge in the line, which became known as the **Ypres Salient** (see pp.143–146). The destruction was, however, confined to a narrow strip of Flanders and most of Belgium was relatively unscathed, though the local population did suffer during the occupation from lack of food and outbursts of cruel treatment from the occupying army, while hundreds of Belgians were forced to work in German factories.

Political change in the 1920s and 1930s

After World War I, under the terms of the **Treaty of Versailles**, Belgium was granted extensive reparations from Germany as well as some German territory – the slice of land around Eupen and Malmédy and, in Africa, Rwanda and Burundi. Domestically, the Belgian government extended the franchise to all men over the age of 21, a measure that subsequently ended several decades of **political control** by the Catholic party. The latter was now only able to keep power in coalition with the Liberals – usually with the Socialists, the third major party, forming the backbone of the opposition. The political lines were, however, increasingly fudged as the Catholic party moved left, becoming a Christian Democrat movement that was keen to cooperate with the Socialists on such matters as social legislation. The political parties may have been partly reconciled, but the **economy** staggered from crisis to crisis even before the effects of the Great Depression hit Belgium in 1929.

The political class also failed to placate those **Flemings** who felt discriminated against. There had been a widespread feeling among the Flemish soldiers of World War I that they had borne the brunt of the fighting and now an increasing number of Flemings came to believe – not without justification – that the Belgian government was overly Walloon in its sympathies. Only reluctantly did the government make Flanders and Wallonia legally unilingual regions in 1930, and even then the linguistic boundary was

1914–18	1915	1918
Trenches are dug right across Flanders from the North Sea to Switzerland; mass carnage ensues.	A British nurse, Edith Cavell, is shot by German firing squad in Brussels for helping Allied prisoners escape.	End of World War I: Belgium revives and recovers.

left unspecified in the hope that French-speakers would come to dominate central Belgium. Furthermore, changing expectations fuelled these **communal tensions**. The Flemings had accepted the domination of the French-speakers without much protest for several centuries, but as their region became more prosperous and as their numbers increased in relation to the Walloons, so they grew in self-confidence, becoming increasingly unhappy with their social and political subordination. Perhaps inevitably, some of this discontent was sucked into **Fascist** movements, which drew some ten percent of the vote in both the Walloon and Flemish communities, though for very different reasons: the former for its appeal to a nationalist bourgeoisie, the latter for its assertion of "racial" pride among an oppressed group.

World War II

The Germans invaded again in **May 1940**, launching a blitzkrieg that overwhelmed both Belgium and the Netherlands in short order. This time there was no heroic resistance by the Belgian king, now **Léopold III** (1934–51), who ignored the advice of his government and surrendered unconditionally and in such great haste that the British and French armies were, as their Commander-in-Chief put it, "suddenly faced with an open gap of twenty miles between Ypres and the sea through which enemy forces might reach the beaches". It is true that the Belgian army had been badly mauled and that a German victory was inevitable, but the manner of the surrender infuriated many Belgians, as did the king's refusal to form a government in exile. At first the occupation was relatively benign and most of the population waited apprehensively to see just what would happen next. The main exception – setting aside the king, who at best played an ambivalent role – was the right-wing edge of the **Flemish Nationalist movement**, which cooperated with the Germans and (unsuccessfully) sought to negotiate the creation of a separate Flemish state. Popular opinion hardened against the Germans in 1942 as the occupation became more oppressive. The Germans stepped up the requisitioning of Belgian equipment, expanded its forced labour schemes, obliging thousands of Belgians to work in Germany, and cracked down hard on any sign of opposition. By the end of the year, a **Resistance** movement was mounting acts of sabotage against the occupying forces and this, in turn, prompted more summary executions of both Resistance fighters and hostages.

The summer of 1942 witnessed the first roundups of the country's **Jews**. In 1940, there were approximately 50,000 Jews in Belgium, mostly newly arrived refugees from Hitler's Germany. Much to their credit, many Belgians did their best to frustrate German efforts to transport the Jews out of the country, usually to Auschwitz: the Belgian police did not cooperate, Belgian railway workers left carriages unlocked and/ or sidelined trains, and many other Belgians hid Jews in their homes for the duration. The result was that the Germans had, by 1944, killed about half the country's Jewish population, a much lower proportion than in most other parts of occupied Europe. With the occupation hardening, the vast majority of Belgians were delighted to hear of the D-Day landings in June 1944. The **liberation** of Belgium began in September with American troops in the south and the British and Canadian divisions sweeping across Flanders in the north.

1940	1944	1944–45
Invasion: the Germans occupy Belgium and Luxembourg in double-quick time.	Hardy Amies, future dressmaker to Queen Elizabeth II, responsible for Special Operations against the Germans in occupied Belgium.	Liberation: Belgium and Luxembourg are liberated piece by piece, with Brussels welcoming the Welsh Guards in September 1944.

1945–2010

After the war, the Belgians set about the task of economic **reconstruction**, helped by aid from the United States, but hindered by a divisive controversy over the wartime activities of **King Léopold**. Inevitably, the complex shadings of collaboration and forced cooperation were hard to disentangle, and the debate continued until 1950 when a **referendum** narrowly recommended his return as king from exile. Léopold's return was, however, marked by rioting across Wallonia, where the king's opponents were concentrated, and Léopold **abdicated** in favour of his son, **Baudouin**.

Otherwise, the development of the **postwar Belgian economy** followed the pattern of most of western Europe: boom in the 1960s; recession in the 1970s; retrenchment in the 1980s and 1990s; and a severe jolt during the financial crash of 2008. Significant events included the belated extension of the franchise to women in 1948; an ugly, disorganized and hasty evacuation of the Belgian Congo in 1960 and of Rwanda and Burundi in 1962; and the transformation of Brussels from one of the lesser European capitals into a major player when it became the home of the EU and NATO (the latter organization was ejected from France on the orders of de Gaulle in 1967). There was also acute **labour unrest** in the Limburg coalfield in the early 1980s, following plans to close most of the pits; a right royal pantomime when Catholic King Baudouin abdicated for the day while the law legalizing **abortion** was ratified in 1990; and public outrage in 1996 when the Belgian police proved itself at best hopelessly inefficient, at worst complicit, in the gruesome activities of the child murderer and pornographer **Marc Dutroux**, who finally received a life sentence in 2004. The Euro currency was introduced in 1999; the legalization of same-sex marriages came in 2003 and the same year saw the government formally opposing the invasion of Iraq; 2005 witnessed a nationwide strike over proposals to reform pensions; and in 2008 the government felt obliged to invest huge sums of public money to shore up the banking sector, thereby increasing the public debt from 84 percent of GDP in 2007 to 99.6 percent in 2012. In 2010, the official **Adriaenssens Commission** published a detailed report outlining several hundred cases of alleged child abuse by Catholic priests – a body blow to the church's reputation; and in 2013 Delphine Boel launched proceedings to oblige King Albert to acknowledge her as his daughter.

Communal tensions take centre stage

Above all, the postwar period was dominated by increasing **tension** between the Walloon and Flemish communities, a state of affairs that was entangled with the economic decline of Wallonia, formerly the home of most of the country's heavy industry, as compared with burgeoning Flanders. One result of the tension was that every **national institution** became dogged by the prerequisites of bilingualism and at the same time all the main political parties created separate Flemish- and French-speaking sections. Bogged down by these inter-communal preoccupations, the federal government often appeared extraordinarily cumbersome, but there again much of the political class came to be at least partly reliant on the linguistic divide for their jobs and, institutionally speaking, had little incentive to see the antagonisms resolved. **Regional government** was also transformed by this communal rivalry. The country had long been divided into provinces, but superimposed on

1946	1959
Retribution: in Belgium, 56,000 alleged Nazi collaborators are prosecuted and 250 executed, including August Borms, one of the leading Flemish nationalists.	Albert, the future king of Belgium, marries an Italian aristocrat, Paola, who soon shocks the establishment by being snapped in a bathing costume – and a bikini to boot.

this, in 1962, was the **language divide** (see box below), which recognized three linguistic communities – French-, Flemish- and German-speaking. This was supplemented, in 1980, by the division of the country into three **regions**, one each for the French and Flemish, with Brussels, the third, designated a bilingual region. The transfer of major areas of administration from the centre to the regions followed.

THE BELGIAN LANGUAGE DIVIDE

There are almost eleven million Belgians, divided between two main groups. The **Flemings** (Dutch- or Flemish-speakers) are concentrated in the north of the country, and form about sixty percent of the population; to the south are the **Walloons**, French-speakers, who account for around forty percent. There are also, in the far east of the country, a few pockets of **German**-speakers around the towns of Eupen and Malmédy.

The Flemish–French **language divide** has troubled the country for decades, its significance rooted in deep class and economic divisions. When the Belgian state was founded in 1830, its ruling and middle classes were predominantly French-speaking, and they created the new state in their linguistic image: French was the official language and Flemish was banned in schools. This Francophone domination was subsequently reinforced by the way the economy developed, with Wallonia becoming a major coal-mining and steel-producing area, while Flanders remained a predominantly agricultural, rural backwater. There were nationalist stirrings among the Flemings from the 1880s onwards, but it was only after World War II – when Flanders became the country's economic powerhouse as Wallonia declined – that the demand for linguistic and cultural parity became irresistible. In the way of such things, the Walloons read Flemish "parity" as "domination", setting the scene for all sorts of inter-communal hassle.

As a response to this burgeoning animosity, the **Language Frontier** was formally drawn across the country in 1962, cutting the country in half from west to east. The aim was to distinguish between the French- and Flemish-speaking communities and thereby defuse tensions, but it didn't work. In 1980, this failure prompted another attempt to rectify matters with the redrafting of the constitution and the creation of a federal system, with three separate **communities** – the Flemish North, the Walloon South and the German-speaking east – responsible for their own cultural and social affairs and education. At the same time, Belgium was divided into three **regions** — the Flemish North, the Walloon South and bilingual Brussels, with each regional authority dealing with matters like economic development, the environment and employment.

In hindsight, the niceties of this partition have done little to calm troubled waters, and right across Belgium discontent on almost any matter – but especially pay, immigration and unemployment – smoulders within (or seeks an outlet through) the framework of this linguistic division; even individual neighbourhoods can be paralyzed by language disputes, with **Brussels-Halle-Vilvoorde** (BHV; see p.342) being a case in point. All this said, it would be wrong to assume that Belgium's language differences have gone beyond the level of personal animosity and institutionalized mutual suspicion. Belgian **language extremists** have been imprisoned over the years, but very few, if any, have died in the fight for supremacy. Indeed, some might see a bilingual nation as a positive thing in a Europe where trading – and national – barriers are being increasingly broken down. Suggesting this to a Belgian, however, is normally useless, but there again the casual visitor will rarely get a sniff of these tensions. It's probably better to speak English rather than Flemish or French in the "wrong" part of Belgium, but if you make a mistake, the worst you'll get is a look of glazed indifference.

1960	1962	1980
Belgium pulls out from the Congo, which becomes an independent state, amid bloody chaos and confusion.	Entrenching animosities: creation of the Belgian "Language Frontier" distinguishing French- from Flemish-speaking Belgium.	More communal entrenchment: Belgium adopts a federal form of government with three regions – the Flemish North, Walloon South and bilingual Brussels.

Political stalemate

In 1999, **Guy Verhofstadt**, the leader of the Liberal VLD, cobbled together a centre-left coalition and repeated this political feat after the federal elections of 2003. Matters might then have proceeded fairly smoothly had it not been for a bitter conflict between French- and Flemish-speaking politicians over the electoral arrangements pertaining to **Brussels-Halle-Vilvoorde** (BHV for short). This extraordinarily complex dispute sapped the strength of the national government and, after the **federal elections of 2007**, no politician was able to construct a ruling coalition and the country was left rudderless for several months. Eventually, a government was formed, but the new Prime Minister – **Yves Leterme** – was soon struggling to keep his coalition afloat and as a result he tendered his resignation to the king in July 2008. It was rejected and Leterme soldiered on, but the instability at the heart of the national government remained, with a political carousel of resignations and changing party alliances. There were new federal elections in June 2010, but the results did nothing to hold the centre: the largest party in Flanders was the right-wing, separatist **Nieuw-Vlaamse Alliantie** (NVA; New Flemish Alliance), under the controversial leadership of Bart de Wever, while Wallonia went left with the winners being the **Parti Socialiste** (PS; Socialist Party) led by Elio Di Rupo.

Belgium today

After the federal elections of 2010, it took the politicians over a year to hammer out a governing coalition, but finally in December 2011 **Elio Di Rupo** became the new prime minster – and the first Francophone to hold the position since the late 1970s. Of Italian extraction and openly gay, Rupo has had to draw on all his considerable negotiating skills: in the **2014 federal election**, Rupo's Parti Socialiste lost seats, while Wever's Nieuw-Vlaamse Alliante picked up a few more, making it the largest party. The king asked Wever to rustle up a coalition government and, at time of writing, the political horse-trading has begun. Not for the first time, the breakup of Belgium seems a distinct possibility, but there is one intractable problem: who gets Brussels – and this may in itself be enough to hold things together.

This political stalemate reflects deep inter-communal tensions. In essence, the **Walloons** fear that the wealthier and more numerous Flemings will come to dominate the state, and indeed they may make this a self-fulfilling prophecy with their reluctance to learn Flemish – bilingualism being a prerequisite for any national job. The **Flemings**, on the other hand, want political and cultural recognition, and many bristle at what they perceive as Wallonian cultural and linguistic arrogance. These tensions can, however, be exaggerated. In 2006, a Belgian TV station, RTBF, mounted an elaborate spoof, saying that the Dutch-speaking half of the country had declared independence. There were pictures of cheering crowds waving the Flemish flag and of trams stuck at the new international border, but few Belgians were jubilant and instead there was widespread alarm, bordering on horror. Polls indicate that a clear majority of Belgians want their country to survive, though few would give the same reason as the country's most popular writer, **Hugo Claus** (1929–2008), who wrote "I insist on being Belgian. I want to be a member of the pariah nationality, the laughing stock of the French and the object of contempt of the Dutch. It's the ideal situation for a writer."

1996	1998	1999	2007
Threatened with blackmail, Elio di Rupo, one of Belgium's leading politicians, comes out of the closet.	Noël Godin, Belgium's famous cream-pie flinger (*entarteur*), sticks one on Bill Gates.	Belgium's finest film-makers, the Dardenne brothers, win their first Palme d'Or.	Belgium is without a national government for 100 days: a signpost to the future?

The Grand Duchy of Luxembourg from 1830

At the Congress of Vienna in 1815, Luxembourg had been designated a **Grand Duchy** by the Great Powers and given (as personal property) to King William I of Orange-Nassau, the ruler of the United Kingdom of the Netherlands (see p.335). After Belgium broke away from William's kingdom in 1830, Luxembourg remained the property of the Dutch monarchy until 1890 when the ducal crown passed to another (independent) branch of the Nassau family, who have ruled there ever since. In 1867, the Great Powers made further decisions about Luxembourg: the **Treaty of London** reaffirmed the duchy's territorial integrity and declared it neutral in perpetuity, thereby – it was hoped – protecting it from the clutches of both Germany and France. Following this declaration, Luxembourg City's fortifications were largely demolished.

The second half of the nineteenth century saw Luxembourg's agricultural economy transformed by the discovery, and then the mining, of **iron ore deposits**, which led to the foundation of what was soon one of Europe's largest steel industries. In 1914, the Grand Duchy confirmed its neutrality, but was still occupied by the Germans – as it was again in **World War II** when the Luxembourgers put up a stubborn resistance, leading to many brave acts of defiance and considerable loss of life. In particular, the Battle of the Bulge (see p.292) was a major disaster for Luxembourg – and as the war ended in 1945, one-third of the country's farmland lay uncultivated, the public transportation system was in ruins, and some sixty thousand people were homeless.

In the **postwar years**, reconstruction was rapid, though there was a major crisis in the mid-1970s when the iron and steel industry hit the economic buffers, obliging the government to pursue a policy of industrial diversification, with the main area of growth being the **financial sector**, which now accounts for almost one third of the duchy's tax revenues. Luxembourg also forsook its policy of neutrality, opting to join both NATO and the EC (EU), where it has often played a conciliatory role between the larger countries. In striking contrast to its neighbour, the duchy has also been extremely stable politically, with the **Christian Social People's Party** (CSV) the dominant force since 1945. Nonetheless, the long-serving leader of the CSV, **Jean-Claude Juncker**, who had been the prime minister since 1995, managed to lose the 2013 election: a scandal involving SREL, the Grand Duchy's intelligence service, and its cavalier attitude to legality (especially in the matter of wire-tapping), showed Juncker in a poor light and, although the CSV remained the largest party, it lost power to a three-party coalition, including the Greens.

2008	2008–10	2010
Luxembourg: Grand Duke Henri threatens to block a bill legalizing euthanasia; Parliament responds by (further) restricting his powers.	Fortis, Belgium's largest bank, engulfed in the banking crisis and only saved with government (ie tax payers') money.	Political failure: after Belgium's federal elections, it takes over a year (yes, a year) to create a ruling coalition.

Belgian art

From medieval times, the Low Countries and its successor states – the Netherlands, Belgium and Luxembourg – have produced some of Europe's finest artists, whose work has been digested and analysed in countless art books, some of which are reviewed in the "Books" section on p.350. This Guide doesn't have the space to cover the subject in any great detail, but the text below provides some background on ten of the country's most important painters. You'll see their work in museums across Belgium, but especially in Antwerp, Ghent, Brussels and Bruges. The one major omission here is René Magritte (see box, p.64).

Jan van Eyck (1335–1441)

Medieval Flanders was one of the most artistically productive parts of Europe, with each of the cloth towns, especially Bruges and Ghent, trying to outdo its rivals with the quality of its religious art. Today, the works of these early Flemish painters, known as the **Flemish Primitives**, are highly prized and an excellent sample is displayed in Ghent, Bruges and Brussels. **Jan van Eyck** is generally regarded as the first of the Flemish Primitives, and has even been credited with the invention of oil painting itself – though it seems more likely that he simply perfected a new technique by thinning his paint with (the newly discovered) turpentine, thus making it more flexible. His fame partially stems from the fact that he was one of the first artists to sign his work – an indication of how highly his talent was regarded by his contemporaries. Van Eyck's most celebrated work is the *Adoration of the Mystic Lamb*, a stunningly beautiful altarpiece displayed in St-Baafskathedraal in Ghent (see pp.155–160). The painting was revolutionary in its realism, for the first time using elements of native landscape in depicting biblical themes, and was underpinned by a complex symbolism which has generated analysis and discussion ever since.

Rogier van der Weyden (1400–64)

Apprenticed in Tournai and one-time official painter to the city of Brussels, **Rogier van der Weyden** turned his hand to both secular and religious subjects with equal facility. His serene portraits of the bigwigs of his day were much admired across a large swathe of western Europe, their popularity enabling him to set up a workshop manned by apprentices and assistants, who helped him with his work (and have often made authentication of his paintings problematic). In 1450, Weyden seems to have undertaken a pilgrimage to Rome, and although contact with his Italian contemporaries does not appear to have had much effect on his paintings, it did bring him several rewarding commissions. Perhaps, above all, it's his religious works that are of special appeal: warm and emotional, sensitive and dramatic, as in *St Luke painting the Portrait of Our Lady*, now displayed in Bruges (see p.109).

Hans Memling (1440–94)

Born near Frankfurt, but active in Bruges, **Hans Memling** was almost certainly a pupil of van der Weyden (see above), from whom he learnt an exquisite attention to detail. Memling is best remembered for the pastoral charm of his landscapes and the quality of his **portraiture**, producing restrained and impeccably crafted works that often survive on the rescued side-panels of triptychs. His **religious paintings** are similarly delightful, formal compositions that still pack an emotional punch – as exemplified by his *Moreel Triptych* (see p.109). The Memling collection in Bruges (see p.114) has a wonderful sample of his work.

Hieronymus Bosch (1450–1516)

One of the most distinctive of the early Netherlandish painters, **Hieronymus Bosch** lived in the southern Netherlands for most of his life, though his style is linked to that of his Flemish contemporaries. About forty examples of his work survive, but none is dated and no accurate chronology can be made. Nonetheless, it seems likely that his more conventional religious paintings, such as *The Crucifixion* in the Musées Royaux in Brussels (see p.60), were completed early on. Bosch is, however, much more famous for his **religious allegories**: frantic, frenetic paintings filled with macabre visions of tortured souls and grotesque beasts. At first glance, these works seem almost unhinged, but it's now thought that they are visual representations of contemporary sayings, idioms and parables. While their interpretation is far from resolved, Bosch's paintings draw strongly on subconscious fears and archetypes, giving them a lasting, haunting fascination.

Quentin Matsys (1464–1530)

Following Flanders' decline at the end of the fifteenth century, the leading artists of the day migrated to the booming port of Antwerp, where they began to integrate the finely observed detail that characterized the Flemish tradition with the style of the Italian painters of the Renaissance in what is sometimes called the **Antwerp School**. A leading light of this school was **Quentin Matsys**, who was born in Leuven but spent most of his working life in Antwerp. Matsys introduced florid classical architectural details and intricate landscapes to his work, influenced perhaps by Leonardo da Vinci. As well as religious pieces, he also painted portraits and **genre scenes**, all of which have recognizably Italian facets and features, thereby paving the way for the Dutch genre painters of later years.

Pieter Bruegel the Elder (c.1525–69)

The greatest Netherlandish painter of the sixteenth century, **Pieter Bruegel the Elder** remains a shadowy figure, but it seems probable he was born in Breda in the Netherlands, and he certainly travelled widely, visiting France and Italy (where he was impressed by the Alps rather than the Italian painters) and working in both Antwerp and Brussels. Many of his early works were landscapes, but in the 1560s he turned his skills to the gruesome **allegories** (and innovative interpretations) of religious subjects for which he is now most famous – as in *The Fall of the Rebel Angels* and *The Fall of Icarus* (see p.62). Pieter also turned out a number of finely observed **peasant scenes**, genre paintings that influenced generations of Low Country artists. Bruegel's two sons, **Pieter Bruegel the Younger** (1564–1638) and **Jan Bruegel** (1568–1625) were lesser painters: the former produced fairly insipid copies of his father's work, though Jan developed a style of his own, producing delicately rendered flower paintings and genre pieces that earned him the nickname "Velvet".

Pieter Paul Rubens (1577–1640)

Easily the most important exponent of the Baroque in northern Europe, **Rubens** was born in Siegen, Westphalia, but raised in Antwerp, where he entered the painters' guild in 1598. He became court painter to the Duke of Mantua in 1600, and until 1608 travelled extensively in Italy, absorbing the classical architecture and the art of the High Renaissance. By the time of his return to Antwerp he had acquired an enormous artistic vocabulary: the paintings of **Caravaggio** in particular were to influence his work strongly. His first major success was *The Raising of the Cross*, painted in 1610 and displayed today in Antwerp cathedral (see p.182). A large, dynamic work, it caused a sensation at the time, establishing Rubens' reputation and leading to a string of commissions. *The Descent from the Cross*, his next major work (also in the cathedral), consolidated this success; equally Baroque, it is nevertheless quieter and more restrained. Thereafter, he was able to set up his own **studio**, where he gathered a team of talented artists (among them Anthony van Dyck and Jacob Jordaens). The subsequent division of labour ensured a high rate of productivity and a degree of personal flexibility; the degree to which Rubens personally worked on a canvas would vary – and would determine its price. From the early 1620s onwards Rubens turned his hand to a plethora of themes and subjects – religious works, portraits, tapestry designs, landscapes, mythological scenes, ceiling paintings – each of which was handled with supreme vitality and virtuosity. From his Flemish antecedents he inherited an acute sense of light, using it not to dramatize his subjects (a technique favoured by Caravaggio and other Italian artists), but in association with colour and form. The drama in his works comes from the vigorous animation of his characters. His **large-scale allegorical works**, especially, are packed with heaving, writhing figures that appear to tumble out from the canvas. The energy of Rubens' paintings was reflected in his **private life**. In addition to his career as an artist, he also undertook diplomatic missions to Spain and England, and used these opportunities to study the works of other artists and – as in the case of Velázquez – to meet them personally. In the 1630s, gout began to hamper his activities, and from this time his painting became more domestic and meditative. **Hélène Fourment**, his second wife, was the subject of many portraits and served as a model for characters in his allegorical paintings, her figure epitomizing the full, well-rounded women found throughout his work.

Anthony van Dyck (1599–1641)

Anthony van Dyck worked in Rubens' studio for two years from 1618, often taking on the depiction of religious figures in his master's works – the ones, that is, which required particular sensitivity and pathos. Like Rubens, van Dyck was born in Antwerp and travelled widely in Italy, though Rubens influenced his initial work much more than his Italian contemporaries. Eventually, van Dyck developed his own distinct style and technique, establishing himself as court painter to Charles I in England from 1632, and creating **portraits** of a nervous elegance that would influence portraiture there for the next hundred and fifty years. Most of his great portrait paintings remain in England, but his best religious works – such as the *Crucifixion* in Mechelen's cathedral (see p.204) – can be found in Belgium.

James Ensor (1860–1949)

Born to an English father and a Belgian mother, **James Ensor** lived in Ostend for almost all of his long life, and was one of Belgium's most original artists. His early works were bourgeois in tone and content, a mixed bag of portraits and domestic interiors that gave little hint as to what was to follow. In the 1880s, he was snubbed by the artistic elite in Brussels and this seems to have prompted a major rethink, for shortly afterwards he picked up on the subject matter which was to dominate his paintings thereafter: macabre, disturbing works of skeletons, grotesques and horrid **carnival masks**, whose haunted style can be traced back to Bosch and Bruegel. As such, Ensor was a formative influence on the Expressionists and was claimed as a forerunner by several leading Surrealists.

Marcel Broodthaers (1924–76)

Born in Brussels, **Marcel Broodthaers** is one of Belgium's most celebrated modern artists, a witty and multi-talented man who doubled as a film-maker and journalist. He also tried his hand as a poet, but in 1964, after twenty largely unsuccessful years, he gave up, symbolically encasing fifty unsold copies of his poetry in plaster and thereby, somewhat accidentally, launching himself as an artist. Initially, Broodthaers worked in the Surrealist manner with found objects and collage, but he soon branched out, graduating from cut-paper geometric shapes into both the plastic arts and the sharp and brightly coloured **paintings** of everyday artefacts, especially casseroles brimming with mussels, for which he became famous. Broodthaers summed himself up like this: "I wondered whether I could not sell something and succeed in life . . . Finally the idea of inventing something insincere crossed my mind and I set to work straight away".

Books

Most of the books listed below are in print and in paperback, and those that are out of print (o/p) should be easy to track down either in secondhand bookshops or online. Titles marked with the ★ symbol are especially recommended. Popular Belgian authors in print, but not in English, include Serge Delaive, Stefan Hertmans and Caroline Lamarche.

Travel and general

Noah Charney *Stealing The Mystic Lamb*. Ghent's "Mystic Lamb" altarpiece (see p.155–160) has had a wild, weird and wonderful history with parts or all of it being stolen time and again. This easy-to-read book charts its many adventures, though the story is a tad tarnished by some lacklustre writing and the occasional dubious assertion.

Hilde Deweer & Jaak van Damme *All Belgian Beers*. This is the most comprehensive guide on the market, with 1568 pages covering its subject in extravagant (alphabetical) detail. Everything you ever wanted to know about Belgian beer and then some.

Sue Lonoff (ed), Charlotte & Emily Brontë *The Belgian Essays* (o/p). The Brontë sisters left their native Yorkshire for the first time in 1842 to make a trip to Brussels; and Charlotte returned to Brussels the following year. This handsome (and expensive) volume, published by Yale in 1997, reproduces the twenty-eight essays they penned (in French) during their journey and provides the English translation opposite. A delightful read with particular highlights being *The Butterfly*, *The Caterpillar* and *The Death of Napoleon*. Can be difficult to locate.

Bruce McCall *Sit!: The Dog Portraits of Thierry Poncelet*. This weird and wonderful book features the work of Belgian Thierry Poncelet, who raids flea markets and antique shops for ancestral portraits, then restores them and paints dogs' heads over the original faces.

Philip Mosley *The Cinema of the Dardenne Brothers: Responsible Realism*. The brothers Jean-Pierre and Luc Dardenne are arguably the finest Belgian film-makers of today, composing hard-hitting, emotionally charged films set amid the post-industrial landscape of Wallonia. Mosley analyses the brothers' career from documentary beginnings to their six major films, from *The Promise* of 1996 through to *The Kid with a Bike* (2011). By the same author, there is also the authoritative *Split Screen: Belgian Cinema and Cultural Identity*, which tracks through the development of Belgian cinema in lucid detail; the "Split Screen" refers to the Walloon/Flemish cinematic/cultural division.

Luc Sante *The Factory of Facts* (o/p). Born in Belgium but raised in the US, Sante returned to his native land for an extended visit in 1989, at the age of 35. His book is primarily a personal reflection, but he also uses this as a base for a thoughtful exploration of Belgium and the Belgians – from art to food and beyond.

Emma Thomson & John Ruler *World War I: A Travel Guide to the Western Front*. Slim, easy-to-read book covering the war in Flanders and northern France with oodles of practical details.

Marianne Thys *Filmography of Belgian Movies, 1896–1996*. This authoritative hardback volume has reviews of every Belgian film ever made. Published in 2000, it's 992 pages long, as is reflected in the price.

★**Tim Webb** *Good Beer Guide to Belgium*. Belgium produces the best beers in the world; Webb is one of the best beer writers in the world – and the result is the best book on its subject on the market: cheeky, palatable and sinewy, with just a hint of fruitiness. Belgium's best bars, beers and breweries are covered in loving, liver-drowning detail. Webb's *100 Belgian Beers to Try Before You Die!* (2008) is similarly excellent.

Tintin

Michael Farr *Tintin: The Complete Companion*. This immaculately illustrated book – written by one of the world's leading Tintinologists – explores every aspect of Hergé's remarkably popular creation. It's particularly strong on the real-life stories that inspired Hergé, but you do have to be seriously interested in Tintin to really enjoy it. Farr has written a string of books on Tintin, and this was published in 2011.

Hergé *The Calculus Affair* and *Tintin: Explorers on the Moon*. Tintin comic strips come in and out of print at a rapid rate, usually in anthologies; there's a wide selection of audio cassettes too. The two anthologies listed here are as good a place as any to start. Both were recently published by Egmont (ⓦ egmont.co.uk).

Benoit Peeters *Tintin and the World of Hergé: An Illustrated History* (o/p). Examines the life and career of Hergé, particularly the development of Tintin, and the influences on his work, with no fewer than three hundred illustrations.

History and politics

★**J.C.H. Blom (ed.)** *History of the Low Countries*. Belgian history books are thin on the ground, so this incisive, well-balanced volume is very welcome. A series of historians weigh in with their specialities to build a comprehensive picture of the region from the Celts and Romans through to the 1980s. Hardly deckchair reading, but highly recommended nonetheless.

Nicholas Crane *Mercator*. Arguably the most important map-maker of all time, Gerard Mercator was born in Rupelmonde near Antwerp in 1512. This book details every twist and turn of his life and provides oodles – perhaps too many oodles – of background material on the Flanders of his time.

Pieter Geyl *The Revolt of The Netherlands 1555–1609* (o/p). Geyl presents a detailed account of the Netherlands during its formative years, chronicling the uprising against the Spanish and both the formation of the United Provinces and the creation of the Spanish Netherlands (the Belgium of today). First published in 1932, it has long been regarded as the classic text on the subject, though it's a hard and ponderous read.

Craig Harline and Eddy Put *A Bishop's Tale*. An unusual book based on the journals of Mathias Hovius, who was Archbishop of Mechelen in the early seventeenth century. It is, perhaps, a little too detailed to enthral the average reader, but it does provide a real insight into the period – its preoccupations and problems.

Samuel Humes *Belgium: Long United, Long Divided*. A welcome addition to the limited number of books on this subject, Humes has written a concise and well-considered account of Belgium from early times, with special reference to the Walloon-Flemish schism that so troubles the country today.

Lisa Jardine *The Awful End of Prince William the Silent*. Great title for an intriguing book on the premature demise of one of the Low Countries' most acclaimed Protestant heroes, who led the revolt against Habsburg Spain and was assassinated in 1584 for his pains. The tale is told succinctly, but – unless you have a particular interest in early firearms – there is a bit too much information on guns.

Philip Mansel *Prince of Europe: the Life of Charles Joseph de Ligne (1735–1814)*. The Habsburg aristocracy, which dominated the Austrian Netherlands (Belgium) in the eighteenth century, has rarely come under the historical spotlight, but this weighty tome partly remedies the situation. This particular aristocrat, the priapic Charles Joseph, was a multifaceted man, a gardener and a general, a curious traveller and a diplomat and the owner of the château of Beloeil (see p.233). Mansel explores his life and milieu thoroughly and entertainingly.

★**Geoffrey Parker** *The Dutch Revolt* (o/p). Compelling account of the struggle between the Netherlands and Spain. Quite the best thing you can read on the period, even if it is out of print. Additionally, Parker's *The Army of Flanders and the Spanish Road 1567–1659* may sound academic, but gives a fascinating insight into the Habsburg army that occupied the Low Countries for well over a hundred years – how it functioned, was fed and moved from Spain to the Low Countries along the so-called Spanish Road.

Andrew Wheatcroft *The Habsburgs: Embodying Empire*. An excellent and well-researched trawl through the dynasty's history, from its eleventh-century beginnings to its eclipse at the end of World War I. Enjoyable background reading.

The Belgian Congo

Neal Ascherson *The King Incorporated: Leopold the Second and the Congo*. Belgium's King Léopold II was responsible for one of the cruellest of colonial regimes, a savage system of repression and exploitation that devastated the Belgian Congo. Ascherson details it all.

★**Adam Hochschild** *King Leopold's Ghost*. Harrowing account of King Léopold's savage colonial regime in the Congo, explaining, exploring and assessing all its gruesome workings. Particularly good on Roger Casement, the one-time British consul to the Congo, who publicized the cruelty and helped bring it to an end. Hochschild's last chapter, *The Great Forgetting*, is a stern criticism of the Belgians for their failure to acknowledge their brutal colonial history.

Jules Marchal *Lord Leverhulme's Ghosts: Colonial Exploitation in the Congo*. In his later years, Jules Marchal, who had been a Belgian diplomat in the Congo, became incensed by the suppression of information on the cruelties inflicted by his countrymen on the Congolese. After he retired in 1989, he spent fourteen years researching this same colonial history, producing seven extremely detailed books on the subject, four on the Léopold regime and three on forced labour from 1910 to 1945. Only one has been translated into English, and this is it, with the spotlight falling on the British entrepreneur Lord Leverhulme, who came to the Congo to exploit its rubber and was perfectly happy to take advantage of King Léopold's system of forced labour. Marchal died in 2003.

David van Reybrouck *Congo*. Born in Bruges in 1971, Reybrouck has travelled extensively in the Congo and this well-composed and very detailed book examines the country's troubled history with special reference to the hundreds of Congolese Reybrouck has interviewed over the years. The account ends in 2010.

Waterloo

Malcolm Balen *A Model Victory: Waterloo and the Battle for History*. Some twenty years after Waterloo, the British government asked Lieutenant William Siborne, a great fan of the Duke of Wellington, to prepare a scale model of the battle. They assumed that he would depict the start of the engagement, but he chose the crisis instead – and this is where he came unstuck. Based on interviews with scores of Waterloo veterans, Siborne's model had the Prussian army arriving on the battlefield earlier than the duke claimed, thereby taking some of the glory from the British army. Siborne felt the full fury of Wellington's ire – and this much-praised book details it all.

Basil Henry Liddell Hart (ed.) *The Letters of Private Wheeler 1809–1828*. A veteran of World War I, Liddell Hart writes with panache and clarity, marshalling the letters penned by the eponymous private as he fought Napoleon and the French across a fair slice of Europe. Wheeler fought at Waterloo, but the section on the battle is surprisingly brief. As a whole, the letters are a delight, a witty insight into the living conditions and attitudes of Wellington's infantry.

★**Christopher Hibbert** *Waterloo*. For many years, Hibbert (who died in 2008) was one of Britain's leading historians, an astute commentator who wrote in a fluent and easily accessible style. This three-part book examines Napoleon's rise to power; Wellington and his allies; and the battle itself. Hibbert was also responsible for editing *The Wheatley Diary*, the journal and sketchbook of a young English officer who fought his way across Europe during the Napoleonic Wars.

Geoffrey Wootten *Waterloo 1815: The Birth of Modern Europe*. About one-third of the length of Hibbert's *Waterloo* (see above), this 96-page book focuses on the battle, providing a clear, thorough and interesting account.

World War I

William Allison & John Fairley *The Monocled Mutineer* (o/p). An antidote to all those tales of soldiers dying for their country in World War I, this little book recounts the story of one Percy Toplis, a Nottinghamshire lad turned soldier, mutineer, racketeer and conman who was finally shot by the police in 1920. Includes an intriguing account of the large-scale mutiny that broke out along the British line in 1917.

Paul Fussell *The Great War and Modern Memory*. Intriguing take on World War I, giving prominence to the rants, epistles, poems and letters of those British soldiers who were caught up in it – and, by implication, the effect it had on British society as a whole.

★**Martin Gilbert** *The First World War*. Highly regarded account of the war, focused on the battles and experiences of the British army. Very thorough – at 640 pages – and hard to beat.

Robert Graves *Goodbye To All That*. Written in 1929, this is the classic story of life in the trenches. Bleak and painful memories of World War I army service written by Graves, a wounded survivor.

Basil Henry Liddell Hart *The History of the First World War*. No armchair general, Liddell Hart (1895–1970) fought in the trenches in World War I – and had the wounds to prove it. After the war, he became a well-known military expert and he always claimed (with some justification) that he foresaw the potential importance of tanks – a voice crying in the British military wilderness before Hitler unveiled his blitzkrieg on, among many others, the poor old Belgian army. First published in 1930 and last republished in 2014, his *History of the First World War* is lucidly written, well researched and good on military strategy and tactics. If you take a shine to it, then you can also try Hart's *The History of the Second World War*. See also Hart's *The Letters of Private Wheeler 1809–1828* (see above).

Janet Morgan *The Secrets of Rue St Roch*. Intriguing account of British spy operations in occupied Luxembourg during World War I. Drawn from the assorted documents of a certain Captain George Wellington, a Paris-based intelligence officer who ran several agents, including a Belgian soldier who began by landing behind enemy lines in a balloon.

Siegfried Sassoon *The Memoirs of an Infantry Officer*. Sassoon's moving and painfully honest account of his experiences in the trenches of World War I. A classic, and infinitely readable.

★**A.J.P. Taylor** *The First World War: An Illustrated History*. First published in 1963, this superbly written and pertinently illustrated history offers a penetrating analysis of how the war started and why it went on for so long, plus a fine section on events in the Ypres Salient. Many of Taylor's deductions were controversial at the time, but such was the power of his arguments that much of what he said is now mainstream history.

Art and architecture

Ulrike Becks-Malorny *Ensor*. Eminently readable and extensively illustrated account of the life and art of Ostend's James Ensor, one of the country's finest painters, though often neglected. A Taschen art book.

Kristin Lohse Belkin *Rubens* (o/p). Too long for its own good, this book details Rubens' spectacularly successful career both as artist and diplomat. Belkin is particularly thorough in her discussions of technique and the workings of his workshop, while extensive reference is made to Rubens' letters. Excellent illustrations.

Robin Blake *Anthony van Dyck*. Whether or not van Dyck justifies a book of this considerable length is a moot point, but he did have an interesting life and certainly thumped out a fair few paintings. This volume explores every artistic nook and cranny.

Till-Holger Borchert *Van Eyck: Renaissance Realist*. Not much is known about van Eyck, but Borchert has done his best to root out every detail in this nicely balanced and attractively illustrated 96-page Taschen book. Borchert has also written *Van Eyck to Dürer: The Influence of Early Netherlandish Painting on European Art, 1430–1530*, a beautifully illustrated tome, which covers its subject with academic rigour (it's 552 pages long). Published in 2010, this book is already something of a collector's item and can be extremely expensive. The same caution applies to Borchert's similarly detailed *Bruegel: The Complete Paintings, Drawings and Prints*, which he co-authored with Manfred Sellink in 2007.

Walter Bosing *Bosch: The Complete Paintings*. Attractive little book in the Taschen art series that covers its subject in just the right amount of detail (it's 96 pages long). Well conceived and well illustrated.

Aurora Cuito (ed) *Victor Horta*. Concise and readily digestible guide to the work of Victor Horta, Belgium's leading exponent of Art Nouveau (see p.73). Since its publication in 2002, the book has become something of a collector's item, so unless you have a special interest – or lots of money – you'll probably want to settle for a secondhand copy.

★ **Rudi H. Fuchs** *Dutch Painting* (o/p). As complete an introduction to the subject as you could wish for, in just a couple of hundred pages. Particularly good on the early Flemish masters. Published in the 1970s, so an update would be welcome. Can be hard to track down.

Suzi Gablik *Magritte*. Gablik lived in Magritte's house for six months in the 1960s and this personal contact

informs the text, which is lucid, perceptive and thoughtful. Most of the illustrations are, however, black and white. At 208 pages, it's also very manageable – and very readable.

Walter S. Gibson *Hieronymus Bosch* (o/p) and *Bruegel* (o/p). Two wonderfully illustrated titles on these two exquisite allegorical painters. The former contains everything you wanted to know about Bosch, his paintings and his late fifteenth-century environment, while the latter takes a detailed look at Pieter Bruegel the Elder's art, with nine well-argued chapters investigating its various components.

Rachel Haidu *Absence of Work*. Haidu, an American art professor, clearly has a real respect for the Belgian artist Marcel Broodthaers, and it shows in this detailed exploration of his life and times, work and philosophy.

Stephan Kemperdick *Rogier van der Weyden* (o/p). Van der Weyden is something of a shadowy figure, but Kemperdick does well to muster what information there is – and the analysis of the paintings is first-rate.

Mark Lamster *Master of Shadows: The Secret Diplomatic Career of Peter Paul Rubens*. Detailed investigation of Rubens' work as a spy and diplomat – it's a wonder he ever got round to the painting.

Alfred Michiels *Hans Memling*. Thorough and very workmanlike investigation of the life and times of Hans Memling with a particularly good chapter on his major works. Extensively illustrated.

Susie Nash *Northern Renissance Art*. Erudite, 368-page book which examines how art was made, valued and viewed in northern Europe from the late fourteenth to the early sixteenth centuries. All the leading Netherlandish figures are examined – van Eyck, Memling, der Weyden and so forth – and by these means Nash argues that it was these painters who set the artistic tone of the Europe of their day, rather than the Italians.

Gilles Neret *Rubens*. This Taschen art book is a well-composed and concise introduction to the great man, his times and his art.

Marcel Paquet *René Magritte*. This well-written and attractively illustrated Taschen book examines Magritte's life, times and artistic output. At just 96 pages, it's concise, too.

Literature

★ **Bernardo Atxaga** *Seven Houses in France*. A simply wonderful novel set in the Congo among the members of its Force Publique (gendarmerie) in 1903. The enigmatic Chrysostome joins the garrison of a remote town, leading to a series of puzzling encounters and weird events. Rarely has the cruel brutality of the Belgian Congo been thrown into sharper/subtler relief – with never an anti-colonial rant in sight. Perhaps surprisingly, the author is a Spaniard.

Mark Bles *A Child at War* (o/p). This powerful book

describes the tribulations of Hortense Daman, a Belgian girl who joined the Resistance at the tender age of fifteen. Betrayed to the Gestapo, Daman was sent to the Ravensbruck concentration camp, where she was used in medical experiments, but remarkably survived. This is her story, though the book would have benefited from some editorial pruning.

Hugo Claus *The Sorrow of Belgium*. Claus (1929–2008) was generally regarded as Belgium's foremost

Flemish-language novelist, and this was his finest novel, charting the growing maturity of a young boy living in Flanders under the Nazi occupation. Claus' style is dense to say the least, but the book gets to grips with the guilt, bigotry and mistrust of the period, and caused a minor uproar when it was first published in the early 1980s. His *Swordfish* is a story of an isolated village rife with ethnic and religious tensions which precipitate a boy's descent into madness, while *Desire* is a strange and disconcerting tale of two drinking buddies who, on an impulse, abandon small-town Belgium for Las Vegas, where both of them start to unravel.

Alan Hollinghurst *The Folding Star*. Not a Belgian novel, but a British writer's evocation of a thinly disguised Bruges, in a compelling novel of sex, mystery and obsession. The enthusiastic descriptions of gay male sexual encounters make this a climactic book in more ways than one.

Barbara Kingsolver *The Poisonwood Bible: A Novel*. In 1959, an American Baptist missionary and his family set out to convert souls in the jungly depths of the Belgian Congo. They are unprepared for the multiple disasters that befall them – from great, stinging ants to irregular Congolese soldiers.

Amelie Nothomb *Hygiene and the Assassin*. English-language translations of modern Belgian books are a rarity, but Nothomb, one of Belgium's most popular novelists, has made the linguistic leap. This particular novel deals with a terminally ill prizewinning author, who grants deathbed interviews to five journalists. A deeply unpleasant man, the protagonist is only unpicked by his last interviewer – to stunning effect. Other Nothomb novels in translation include the controversial *Sulphuric Acid*, where a Big

Brother-style show turns into a blood-fest in the manner of a concentration camp – hence the furore; and *The Stranger Next Door* (o/p), featuring weird and disconcerting happenings in the Belgian countryside.

Jean Ray *Malpertuis*. This spine-chilling Gothic novel was written in 1943 by Ghent's own Raymundus de Kremer, who adopted the pen name Jean Ray for his novels – he also turned out comic strips under the guise of John Flanders. The novel is set in Flanders, where the suffocating Catholicism of the Inquisition provides a suitably atmospheric backdrop.

★**Georges Rodenbach** *Bruges la Morte*. First published in 1892, this slim and subtly evocative novel is all about love and obsession – or rather a highly stylized, decadent view of it. It's often credited with starting the craze for visiting Bruges, the "dead city" where the action unfolds.

Georges Simenon *The Hanged Man of Saint-Pholien* and *Pietr the Latvian*. There can be no dispute that Simenon (1903–89) was Belgium's most famous crime writer, his main creation being the Parisian detective Maigret. There are dozens of books to choose from – and these two (recently reprinted) ripping yarns can get you started.

Emile Zola *Germinal*. First published in 1885, and the inspiration for a whole generation of Belgian radicals, *Germinal* exposed the harsh conditions of the coal mines of northeast France. It was also a rallying call to action with the protagonist, Etienne Lantier, organizing a strike. A vivid, powerful work, Zola had a detailed knowledge of the mines – how they were run and worked – and makes passing reference to the coalfields of southern Belgium, where conditions and working practices were identical.

Flemish and French

Throughout the northern part of Belgium, in the provinces of East and West Flanders, Antwerp, Limburg and Flemish Brabant, the principal language is Dutch, which is spoken in a variety of distinctive dialects commonly (if inaccurately) lumped together as Flemish. Flemish-speakers have equal language rights in the capital, Brussels, where the majority of Belgians speak a dialect of French known as Walloon, as they do in the country's southern provinces, known logically enough as Wallonia. Walloon is almost identical to French, and if you've any knowledge of the language, you'll be readily understood. French is also the most widely spoken language in Luxembourg, along with German – although most Luxembourgers also speak a local and distinctive German dialect, Lëtzebuergesch (see p.300).

Flemish

Flemish, or Dutch, is a Germanic language, and although Dutch-speakers are at pains to stress the differences between the two, if you know any German you'll spot many similarities. Many Flemish-speakers also speak English to varying degrees of excellence, especially in the larger cities, and partly as a result any attempt you make to speak Flemish may be met with bewilderment – though this can have as much to do with pronunciation (Dutch is very difficult to get right) as their surprise that you're making an effort. The following words and phrases serve as an introduction to the language, and we've included a basic **food and drink glossary** too, though menus are often multilingual, and where they aren't, ask and one will almost invariably appear.

Pronunciation

Flemish is **pronounced** much the same as English. However, there are a few Dutch sounds that don't exist in English, which can be difficult to get right without practice. **Double-consonant** combinations generally keep their separate sounds in Flemish: **kn**, for example, is never like the English "knight". Note also the following:

j is an English y, as in yellow

ch and **g** indicate a throaty sound, as at the end of the Scottish word loch. The Dutch word for canal – gracht – is especially tricky, since it has two of these sounds – it comes out along the lines of khrakht. A common word for hello is Dag! – pronounced like daakh

ng as in bring

nj as in onion

y is not a consonant, but another way of writing **ij**

For **vowels** and **diphthongs**, doubling the letter generally lengthens the vowel sound:

a is like the English apple

aa like cart

e like let

ee like late

o as in pop

oo in pope

u is like the French tu if preceded by a consonant; it's like wood if followed by a consonant

uu is the French tu

au and **ou** like how

ei and **ij** as in fine, though this varies strongly from region to region; sometimes it can sound more like lane

oe as in soon

eu is like the diphthong in the French leur

ui is the hardest Dutch diphthong of all, pronounced like how but much further forward in the mouth, with lips pursed (as if to say "oo").

The basics

yes	ja
no	nee
please	alstublieft
(no) thank you	(nee) dank u or bedankt
hello	hallo, dag or hoi
good morning	goedemorgen
good afternoon	goedemiddag
good evening	goedenavond
goodbye	tot ziens
see you later	tot straks
Do you speak English?	Spreekt u Engels?
I don't understand	Ik begrijp het niet
women/men	vrouwen/mannen
children	kinderen
men's/women's toilets	heren/dames
I want…	Ik wil…
I don't want to…	Ik wil niet… (+verb)
sorry	Sorry

Travel, directions and shopping

How do I get to…?	Hoe kom ik in…?
Where is…?	Waar is…?
How far is it to…?	Hoe ver is het naar…?
How much is…?	Wat kost…?
far/near	ver/dichtbij
left/right	links/rechts
airport	luchthaven
post office	postkantoor
postbox	postbus
money exchange	geldwisselkantoor
cash desk	kassa
railway platform	spoor or perron
ticket office	loket
here/there	hier/daar
good/bad	goed/slecht
big/small	groot/klein
open/closed	open/gesloten
push/pull	duwen/trekken
new/old	nieuw/oud
cheap/expensive	goedkoop/duur
hot/cold	heet or warm/koud
with/without	met/zonder
north	noord
south	zuid
east	oost
west	west

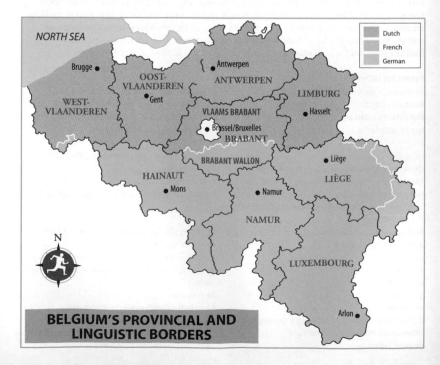

BELGIUM'S PROVINCIAL AND LINGUISTIC BORDERS

Signs and abbreviations

alle richtingen	all directions (road sign)	heren/dames	men's/women's toilets
A.U.B.	*Alstublieft*: please (also shown as S.V.P., from French)	open	open
		rechtdoor	straight ahead
		T/M	*Tot en met*: up to and including
BG	*Begane grond*: ground floor	toegang	entrance
geen toegang	no entry	uitgang	exit
gesloten	closed	V.A.	*vanaf*: from
ingang	entrance	Z.O.Z.	please turn over (page, leaflet, etc)
K	*kelder*: basement		
let op!	attention!		

Useful cycling terms

tyre	band	pump	pomp
cycle	fiets	brake	rem
cycle path	fietspad	handlebars	stuur
broken	kapot	pedal	trapper
chain	ketting	wheel	wiel
puncture	lek		

Days of the week

Sunday	zondag	yesterday	gisteren
Monday	maandag	today	vandaag
Tuesday	dinsdag	tomorrow	morgen
Wednesday	woensdag	tomorrow morning	morgenochtend
Thursday	donderdag	week	week
Friday	vrijdag	day	dag
Saturday	zaterdag		

Months

year	jaar	June	juni
month	maand	July	juli
January	januari	August	augustus
February	februari	September	september
March	maart	October	oktober
April	april	November	november
May	mei	December	december

Time

hour	uur	What time is it?	Hoe laat is het?
minute	minuut		

Numbers

When saying a number, Dutch speakers generally transpose the last two digits: for example, €3.25 is drie euro vijf en twintig.

0	nul	8	acht
1	een	9	negen
2	twee	10	tien
3	drie	11	elf
4	vier	12	twaalf
5	vijf	13	dertien
6	zes	14	veertien
7	zeven	15	vijftien

16	zestien	70	zeventig
17	zeventien	80	tachtig
18	achttien	90	negentig
19	negentien	100	honderd
20	twintig	101	honderd een
21	een en twintig	200	twee honderd
22	twee en twintig	201	twee honderd een
30	dertig	500	vijf honderd
40	veertig	525	vijf honderd vijf en twintig
50	vijftig	1000	duizend
60	zestig		

A FLEMISH MENU READER

Basic terms and ingredients

belegd	filled or topped, as in belegde broodjes (bread rolls topped with cheese, etc)	koud	cold
		nagerechten	desserts
		peper	pepper
		sla/salade	salad
boter	butter	stokbrood	french bread
boterham/broodje	sandwich/roll	suiker	sugar
brood	bread	vegetarisch	vegetarian
dranken	drinks	vis	fish
eieren	eggs	vlees	meat
gerst	barley	voorgerechten	starters/hors d'oeuvres
groenten	vegetables	vruchten	fruit
honing	honey	warm	hot
hoofdgerechten	main courses	zout	salt
kaas	cheese		

Cooking terms

doorbakken	well done	geraspt	grated
gebakken	fried/baked	gerookt	smoked
gebraden	roasted	gestoofd	stewed
gegrild	grilled	half doorbakken	medium done
gekookt	boiled	rood	rare

Starters and snacks

erwtensoep/snert	thick pea soup with bacon or sausage		and perhaps soup
		patat/friet	chips/French fries
huzarensalade	potato salad with pickles	soep	soup
koffietafel	light midday meal of cold meats, cheese, bread,	uitsmijter	ham or cheese with eggs on bread

Meat and poultry

biefstuk (hollandse)	steak	kip	chicken
biefstuk (duitse)	hamburger	kroket	spiced veal or beef in hash, coated in breadcrumbs
eend	duck		
fricandeau	roast pork		
fricandel	frankfurter-like sausage	lamsvlees	lamb
gehakt	mince	lever	liver
ham	ham	ossenhaas	beef tenderloin
kalfsvlees	veal	rookvlees	smoked beef
kalkoen	turkey	spek	bacon
karbonade	a chop	worst	sausages

Fish and seafood

forel	trout	**paling**	eel
garnalen	prawns	**schelvis**	haddock
haring	herring	**schol**	plaice
kabeljauw	cod	**tong**	sole
makreel	mackerel	**zalm**	salmon
mosselen	mussels	**zeeduivel**	monkfish
oesters	oysters	**zeewolf**	wolf fish/cat fish (Atlantic)

Vegetables

aardappelen	potatoes	**sla**	salad, lettuce
bloemkool	cauliflower	**stampot andijvie**	mashed potato and endive
bonen	beans		
champignons	mushrooms	**stampot boerenkool**	mashed potato and cabbage
erwten	peas		
knoflook	garlic	**uien**	onions
komkommer	cucumber	**wortelen**	carrots
prei	leek	**zuurkool**	sauerkraut
rijst	rice		

Sweets and desserts

appeltaart/ **appelgebak**	apple tart or cake	**poffertjes**	small pancakes/fritters
gebak	pastry	**(slag) room**	(whipped) cream
ijs	ice cream	**speculaas**	spice- and cinnamon-flavoured biscuit
koekjes	biscuits	**stroopwafels**	waffles
pannenkoeken	pancakes	**taai-taai**	spicy Dutch cake
pepernoten	Dutch biscuits	**vla**	custard

Fruits and nuts

aardbei	strawberry	**hazelnoot**	hazelnut
amandel	almond	**kers**	cherry
appel	apple	**kokosnoot**	coconut
appelmoes	apple purée	**peer**	pear
citroen	lemon	**perzik**	peach
druiven	grape	**pinda**	peanut
framboos	raspberry	**pruim**	plum/prune

Drinks

anijsmelk	aniseed-flavoured warm milk	**appelsap**	apple juice
		bessenjenever	blackcurrant gin

FLEMISH SPECIALITIES

hutsepot – a winter-warmer consisting of various bits of beef and pork (including pigs' trotters and ears) casseroled with turnips, celery, leeks and parsnips.

konijn met pruimen – rabbit with prunes.

paling in 't groen – eel braised in a green (usually spinach) sauce with herbs.

stoemp – mashed potato mixed with vegetable and/or meat purée.

stoofvlees – cubes of beef marinated in beer and cooked with herbs and onions.

stoverij – stewed beef and offal (especially liver and kidneys), slowly tenderized in dark beer and served with a slice of bread covered in mustard.

waterzooi – a delicious, filling soup-cum-stew, made with either chicken (*van kip*) or fish (*van riviervis*).

chocomel	chocolate milk	**met ijs**	with ice
warme chocolade melk	hot chocolate	**met slagroom**	with whipped cream
		pils	Dutch beer
citroenjenever	lemon gin	**proost!**	cheers!
droog	dry	**sinaasappelsap**	orange juice
frisdranken	soft drinks	**thee**	tea
jenever	Dutch gin	**tomatensap**	tomato juice
karnemelk	buttermilk	**vruchtensap**	fruit juice
koffie	coffee	**wijn**	wine (white/red/rosé)
koffie verkeerd	coffee with warm milk	**(wit/rood/rosé)**	
kopstoot	beer with a jenever chaser	**vieux**	Dutch brandy
melk	milk		

French

Most **Walloons** (French-speaking Belgians) working in the business and tourist industries have at least some knowledge of English, but beyond that, and especially in Wallonia's small towns and villages, you'll need at least a modicum of **French** to have any sort of conversation at all. Differentiating words is the initial problem in understanding **spoken Walloon** – it's very hard to get people to slow down. If, as a last resort, you get them to write it down, you'll probably find you know half the words anyway – French and English share many words. Of the available **phrasebooks**, Rough Guides' own *French Phrasebook* – as an ebook or print version – should sort you out better than most.

Pronunciation

Consonants are pronounced much as in English, except:

c is softened to the **s** sound when followed by an "e" or "i", or when it has a cedilla (ç) below it

ch is always **sh**

g is softened to a French **j** sound when followed by e or i (eg gendarme)

h is silent

j is like the **s** sound in "measure" or "treasure"

ll is like the **y** in yes

qu is normally pronounced like a **k** as in key (eg quatre)

r is growled (or rolled)

th is the same as **t**

w is **v**

Vowels are the hardest sounds to get right:

a as in hat

e as in get

é between get and gate

è between get and gut

eu like the **u** in hurt

i as in machine

o as in hot

o, au as in over

ou as in food

u as in a pursed-lip version of use

More awkward are the combinations below when they occur at the ends of words, or are followed by consonants other than *n* or *m*:

in/im like the an in anxious

an/am, en/em as in don when said with a nasal accent

on/om like the **don** in Doncaster said by someone

with a heavy cold

un/um like the u in understand.

Basics

yes	oui	**good morning**	bonjour
no	non	**good afternoon**	bonjour
please	s'il vous plaît	**good evening**	bonsoir
(no) thank you	(non) merci	**goodnight**	bonne nuit
hello	bonjour	**goodbye**	au revoir
how are you?	comment allez-vous? /ça va?	**see you later**	à bientôt
		now/later	maintenant/plus tard

sorry	pardon, Madame, Monsieur/je m'excuse	men	hommes
do you speak English?	parlez-vous anglais?	children	enfants
I (don't) understand	je (ne) comprends (pas)	I want…	je veux…
women	femmes	I don't want	je ne veux pas
		OK/agreed	d'accord

Travel, directions and shopping

how do I get to…?	comment est-ce que je peux arriver à…?	railway station	gare
where is…?	où est…?	ticket office	le guichet
how far is it to…?	combien y a-t-il jusqu'à…?	here/there	ici/là
		behind	derrière
how much is…?	c'est combien…?	good/bad	bon/mauvais
when?	quand?	big/small	grand/petit
far/near	loin/près	push/pull	pousser/tirer
left/ right	à gauche/à droite	new/old	nouveau/vieux
straight ahead	tout droit	cheap/expensive	bon marché/cher
through traffic only	voie de traversée	hot/cold	chaud/froid
airport	aéroport	with/without	avec/sans
post office	la poste	a lot/a little	beaucoup/peu
stamp(s)	timbre(s)	East	est
money exchange	bureau de change	North	nord
cashier	la caisse	West	occidental/ouest
quay, or (railway) platform	quai	South	sud

Signs and abbreviations

S.V.P.	*S'il vous plaît*: please	fermé	closed
acces interdit	no entry	fermeture	closing period
Attention!	attention!	hommes/femmes	men's/women's toilets
entrée	entrance	ouvert	open
étage	floor (of a museum, etc)	sortie	exit

Useful cycling terms

cycle	bicyclette	pedal	pédale
broken	cassé	puncture	pneu crevé
chain	chaîne	tyre	pneu
brake	frein	pump	pompe
handlebars	guidon	wheel	roue

Days of the week

Monday	lundi	evening	soir
Tuesday	mardi	night	nuit
Wednesday	mercredi	yesterday	hier
Thursday	jeudi	today	aujourd'hui
Friday	vendredi	tomorrow	demain
Saturday	samedi	tomorrow morning	demain matin
Sunday	dimanche	day	jour
morning	matin	week	semaine
afternoon	après-midi		

Months

month	mois	February	février
year	année	March	mars
January	janvier	April	avril

May	mai	**September**	septembre
June	Juin	**October**	octobre
July	juillet	**November**	novembre
August	août	**December**	décembre

Time

minute	minute	**What time is it...?**	Quelle heure est-il...?
hour	heure		

Numbers

0	zéro	18	dix-huit
1	un	19	dix-neuf
2	deux	20	vingt
3	trois	21	vingt-et-un
4	quatre	30	trente
5	cinq	40	quarante
6	six	50	cinquante
7	sept	60	soixante
8	huit	70	soixante-dix (local usage is septante)
9	neuf		
10	dix	80	quatre-vingts
11	onze	90	quatre-vingt-dix (local usage is nonante)
12	douze		
13	treize	100	cent
14	quatorze	101	cent-et-un
15	quinze	200	deux cents
16	seize	500	cinq cents
17	dix-sept	1000	mille

A FRENCH MENU READER

Basic terms and ingredients

beurre	butter	**oeufs**	eggs
chaud	hot	**pain**	bread
crème fraîche	sour cream	**poisson**	fish
dégustation	tasting (wine or food)	**poivre**	pepper
escargots	snails	**riz**	rice
frappé	iced	**salade**	salad
fromage	cheese	**sel**	salt
froid	cold	**sucre/sucré**	sugar/sweet (taste)
gibier	game	**tourte**	tart or pie
hors d'oeuvres	starters	**tranche**	slice
légumes	vegetables	**viande**	meat

Cooking terms

à point	medium done	**grillé**	grilled
au four	baked	**mijoté**	stewed
bien cuit	well done	**pané**	breaded
bouilli	boiled	**rôti**	roast
frit/friture	fried/deep fried	**saignant**	rare (meat)
fumé	smoked	**sauté**	lightly cooked in butter

Starters and snacks

assiette anglaise	plate of cold meats	**bouillabaisse**	fish soup (originally from Marseilles)
bisque	shellfish soup		

bouillon	broth or stock	au plat	fried eggs
consommé	clear soup	à la coque	boiled eggs
croque-monsieur	grilled cheese and ham sandwich	durs	hard-boiled eggs
		brouillés	scrambled eggs
crudités	raw vegetables with dressing	omelette…	omelette…
		nature	plain
potage	thick soup, usually vegetable	au fromage	with cheese
		salade de…	salad of…
un sandwich/une baguette…	a sandwich…	tomates	tomatoes
		concombres	cucumbers
de jambon	with ham	crêpes…	pancakes…
de fromage	with cheese	au sucre	with sugar
de saucisson	with sausage	au citron	with lemon
à l'aïl	with garlic	au miel	with honey
au poivre	with pepper	à la confiture	with jam
oeufs…	eggs…		

Meat and poultry

agneau	lamb	foie	liver
bifteck	steak	gigot	leg of venison
boeuf	beef	jambon	ham
canard	duck	lard	bacon
cheval	horsemeat	porc	pork
cuisson	leg of lamb	poulet	chicken
côtelettes	cutlets	saucisse	sausage
dindon	turkey	veau	veal

Fish and seafood

anchois	anchovies	maquereau	mackerel
anguilles	eels	morue	cod
carrelet	plaice	moules	mussels
crevettes roses	prawns	saumon	salmon
hareng	herring	sole	sole
lotte de mer	monkfish	truite	trout

Vegetables

aïl	garlic	laitue	lettuce
asperges	asparagus	oignons	onions
carottes	carrots	petits pois	peas
champignons	mushrooms	poireau	leek
choufleur	cauliflower	pommes (de terre)	potatoes
concombre	cucumber	tomate	tomato
genièvre	juniper		

SOME WALLOON AND BRUSSELS SPECIALITIES

carbonnades de porc Bruxelloise – pork with a tarragon and tomato sauce
chicorées gratinées au four – chicory baked with ham and cheese
fricadelles à la bière – meatballs in beer
fricassée Liégois – fried eggs, bacon and sausage or blood pudding
le marcassin – young wild boar, served either cold and sliced or hot with vegetables
pâté de faisan – pheasant pâté
truite à l'Ardennaise – trout cooked in a wine sauce

Sweets and desserts

crêpes	pancakes	madeleine	small, shell-shaped sponge cake
crêpes suzettes	thin pancakes with orange juice and liqueur	parfait	frozen mousse, sometimes ice cream
glace	ice cream	petits fours	bite-sized cakes or pastries

Fruits and nuts

amandes	almonds	noisette	hazelnut
ananas	pineapple	pamplemousse	grapefruit
cacahouète	peanut	poire	pear
cerises	cherries	pomme	apple
citron	lemon	prune	plum
fraises	strawberries	pruneau	prune
framboises	raspberries	raisins	grapes
marrons	chestnuts		

Drinks

bière	beer	thé	tea
café	coffee	vin...	wine...
eaux de vie	spirits distilled from various fruits	rouge	red
		blanc	white
jenever	Dutch/Flemish gin	brut	very dry
lait	milk	sec	dry
orange/citron pressé	fresh orange/lemon juice	demi-sec	sweet
		doux	very sweet

Glossary

Flemish terms

Abdij Abbey.

Begijnhof Convent occupied by beguines (*begijns*), ie members of a sisterhood living as nuns but without vows, retaining the right of return to the secular world (see box, p.327).

Beiaard Carillon (ie a set of tuned church bells, either operated by an automatic mechanism or played by a keyboard).

Belfort Belfry.

Beurs Stock exchange.

Botermarkt Butter market.

Brug Bridge.

Burgher Member of the upper or mercantile classes of a town, usually with certain civic powers.

Gemeente Municipal, as in *Gemeentehuis* (town hall).

Gerechtshof Law Courts.

Gilde Guild.

Gracht Canal.

Groentenmarkt Vegetable market.

(Grote) Markt Central town square and the heart of most Flemish communities.

Hal Hall.

Hof Courtyard.

Huis House.

Jeugdherberg Youth hostel.

Kaai Quay or wharf.

Kapel Chapel.

Kasteel Castle.

Kerk Church; eg Grote Kerk – the principal church of the town.

Koning King.

Koningin Queen.

Koninklijk Royal.

Korenmarkt Corn market.

Kunst Art.

Lakenhal Cloth hall: the building in medieval weaving towns where cloth would be weighed, graded and sold.

Molen Windmill.
Onze Lieve Vrouwekerk or **OLV** Church of Our Lady.
Paleis Palace.
Plaats A square or open space.
Plein A square or open space.
Polder An area of land reclaimed from the sea.
Poort Gate.
Raadhuis Town hall.
Rijk State.
Schatkamer Treasury.
Schepenzaal Alderman's Hall.
Schone Kunsten Fine arts.

Schouwburg Theatre.
Sierkunst Decorative arts.
Stadhuis The most common word for a town hall.
Stedelijk Civic, municipal.
Steeg Alley.
Stichting Institute or foundation.
Straat Street.
Toren Tower.
Tuin Garden.
Vleeshuis Meat market.
Volkskunde Folklore.
Weg Way.

French terms

Abbaye Abbey.
Auberge de jeunesse Youth hostel.
Beaux arts Fine arts.
Beffroi Belfry.
Béguinage Convent occupied by beguines, ie members of a sisterhood living as nuns but without vows and with the right of return to the secular world (see box, p.327).
Bourse Stock exchange.
Chapelle Chapel.
Château Mansion, country house, or castle.
Cour Court(yard).
Couvent Convent, monastery.
Église Church.
Fouilles Archeological excavations.
Gîte d'étape Dormitory-style lodgings situated in relatively remote parts of the country, which can house anywhere between ten and one hundred people per establishment.
Grand-place Central town square and the heart of most Walloon communities.
Halle aux draps Cloth hall. The building in medieval weaving towns where cloth would be weighed, graded, stored and sold.

Halle aux viandes Meat market.
Halles Covered, central food market.
Hôpital Hospital.
Hôtel Hotel or mansion.
Hôtel de ville Town hall.
Jardin Garden.
Jours feriés Public holidays.
Maison House.
Marché Market.
Moulin Windmill.
Municipal Civic, municipal.
Musée Museum.
Notre Dame Our Lady.
Palais Palace.
Place Square, marketplace.
Pont Bridge.
Porte Gateway.
Quartier District of a town.
Roi King.
Reine Queen.
Rue Street.
Syndicat d'initiative Tourist office/information.
Tour Tower.
Trésor Treasury.

Art and architectural terms

Ambulatory Covered passage around the outer edge of the choir of a church.
Apse Semicircular protrusion (usually) at the east end of a church.
Art Deco Geometrical style of art and architecture especially popular in the 1930s.
Art Nouveau Style of art, architecture and design based on highly stylized vegetal forms. Especially popular in the early part of the twentieth century.
Balustrade An ornamental rail, running, almost invariably, along the top of a building.

Baroque The art and architecture of the Counter-Reformation, dating from around 1600 onwards. Distinguished by extreme ornateness, exuberance and by the complex but harmonious spatial arrangement of interiors.
Basilica Catholic church with honorific privileges.
Carillon A set of tuned church bells, either operated by an automatic mechanism or played on a keyboard.
Carolingian Dynasty founded by Charlemagne; mid-eighth to early tenth century. Also refers to art, etc, of the period.
Caryatid A sculptured female figure used as a column.

Chancel The eastern part of a church, often separated from the nave by a screen (see "rood screen", p.364). Contains the choir and ambulatory.

Classical Architectural style incorporating Greek and Roman elements – pillars, domes, colonnades etc – at its height in the seventeenth century and revived, as Neoclassical (see below), in the nineteenth.

Clerestory Upper storey of a church with windows.

Diptych Carved or painted work on two panels. Often used as an altarpiece – both static and, more occasionally, portable.

Expressionism Artistic style popular at the beginning of the twentieth century, characterized by the exaggeration of shape or colour; often accompanied by the extensive use of symbolism.

Flamboyant Florid form of Gothic (see "Gothic" below).

Fresco Wall painting – durable through application to wet plaster.

Gable The triangular upper portion of a wall – decorative or supporting a roof – which is a feature of many canal houses.

Gallo-Roman Period of Roman occupation of Gaul (including much of present-day Belgium), from the first to the fourth centuries AD.

Genre painting In the seventeenth centuries the term "genre painting" applied to everything from animal paintings and still lifes through to historical works and landscapes. In the eighteenth century, the term came only to be applied to scenes of everyday life.

Gobelin A rich French tapestry, named after the most famous of all tapestry manufacturers, based in Paris, whose most renowned period was during the reign of Louis XIV; also loosely applied to tapestries of similar style made in Belgium.

Gothic Architectural style of the thirteenth to sixteenth centuries, characterized by pointed arches, rib vaulting, flying buttresses and a general emphasis on verticality.

Grisaille A technique of monochrome painting in shades of grey.

Merovingian Dynasty ruling France and parts of "Belgium" from the sixth to the middle of the eighth century. Refers also to art, etc, of the period.

Misericord Ledge on choir stall on which the occupant can be supported while standing; often carved with secular subjects (bottoms were not thought worthy of religious subject matter – quite right too).

Mosan Adjective applied to the lands bordering the River Meuse – hence Mosan metalwork.

Nave Main body of a church.

Neoclassical A style of classical architecture (see above) revived in the nineteenth century; popular in the Low Countries during and after French rule in the early nineteenth century.

Neo-Gothic Revived Gothic style of architecture popular in the late eighteenth and nineteenth centuries.

Pediment Feature of a gable, usually triangular and often sporting a relief.

Pilaster A shallow rectangular column projecting, but only slightly, from a wall.

Renaissance The period of European history marking the end of the medieval period and the rise of the modern world. Defined, among many criteria, by an increase in classical scholarship, geographical discovery, the rise of secular values and the growth of individualism. Began in Italy in the fourteenth century. Also refers to the art and architecture of the period.

Retable Altarpiece.

Rococo Highly florid, light and intricate eighteenth-century style of architecture, painting and interior design, forming the last phase of Baroque.

Romanesque Early medieval architecture, distinguished by squat, heavy forms, rounded arches and naive sculpture.

Rood loft Gallery (or space) on top of a rood screen.

Rood screen Decorative screen separating the nave from the chancel.

Stucco Marble-based plaster used to embellish ceilings, etc.

Transept Arms of a cross-shaped church, placed at ninety degrees to nave and chancel.

Triptych Carved or painted work on three panels. Often used as an altarpiece.

Tympanum Sculpted, usually triangular and recessed, panel above a door/facade.

Vauban Seventeenth-century French military architect whose fortresses still stand all over Europe and the Low Countries; hence the adjective Vaubanesque.

Vault An arched ceiling or roof.

Small print and index

A ROUGH GUIDE TO ROUGH GUIDES

Published in 1982, the first Rough Guide – to Greece – was a student scheme that became a publishing phenomenon. Mark Ellingham, a recent graduate in English from Bristol University, had been travelling in Greece the previous summer and couldn't find the right guidebook. With a small group of friends he wrote his own guide, combining a highly contemporary, journalistic style with a thoroughly practical approach to travellers' needs.

The immediate success of the book spawned a series that rapidly covered dozens of destinations. And, in addition to impecunious backpackers, Rough Guides soon acquired a much broader readership that relished the guides' wit and inquisitiveness as much as their enthusiastic, critical approach and value-for-money ethos.

These days, Rough Guides include recommendations from budget to luxury and cover more than 120 destinations around the globe, as well as producing an ever-growing range of ebooks.

Visit **roughguides.com** to find all our latest books, read articles, get inspired and share travel tips with the Rough Guides community.

Rough Guide credits

Editor: Neil McQuillian
Layout: Ankur Guha
Cartography: Deshpal Dabas
Picture editor: Raffaella Morini
Proofreader: Jan McCann
Managing editors: Natasha Foges, Alice Park
Assistant editor: Sharon Sonam
Production: Janis Griffith

Cover design: Nicole Newman, Raffaella Morini,
Ankur Guha
Photographer: Lydia Evans
Editorial assistant: Rebecca Hallett
Senior pre-press designer: Dan May
Programme manager: Gareth Lowe
Publisher: Joanna Kirby
Publishing director: Georgina Dee

Publishing information

This sixth edition published March 2015 by
Rough Guides Ltd,
80 Strand, London WC2R 0RL
11, Community Centre, Panchsheel Park,
New Delhi 110017, India
Distributed by Penguin Random House
Penguin Books Ltd,
80 Strand, London WC2R 0RL
Penguin Group (USA)
345 Hudson Street, NY 10014, USA
Penguin Group (Australia)
250 Camberwell Road, Camberwell,
Victoria 3124, Australia
Penguin Group (NZ)
67 Apollo Drive, Mairangi Bay, Auckland 1310,
New Zealand
Penguin Group (South Africa)
Block D, Rosebank Office Park, 181 Jan Smuts Avenue,
Parktown North, Gauteng, South Africa 2193
Rough Guides is represented in Canada by Tourmaline
Editions Inc. 662 King Street West, Suite 304, Toronto,
Ontario M5V 1M7
Printed in Singapore

Help us update

We've gone to a lot of effort to ensure that the sixth edition of **The Rough Guide to Belgium & Luxembourg** is accurate and up-to-date. However, things change – places get "discovered", opening hours are notoriously fickle, restaurants and rooms raise prices or lower standards. If you feel we've got it wrong or left something out, we'd like to know, and if you can remember the address, the price, the hours, the phone number, so much the better.

Please send your comments with the subject line "**Rough Guide Belgium & Luxembourg Update**" to mail @uk.roughguides.com. We'll credit all contributions and send a copy of the next edition (or any other Rough Guide if you prefer) for the very best emails.

Find more travel information, connect with fellow travellers and plan your trip on ⊚roughguides.com.

Readers' updates

Thanks to all the readers who have taken the time to write in with comments and suggestions (and apologies if we've inadvertently omitted or misspelt anyone's name):

John Akhurst; John Allen; Rob Andrews; Anthony Neil Ashworth; Richard Barker; Tom Baxter; Johan Bergstromallen-Allen; Otto Beuchner; Alexsandra Bilos; Lianne Bissell; Julia Bomken; Nawal Boulyou; Chris Burin; Piroja Bustani; Dick Butler; Richard Butler; Martin Connors; David Cox; Emmanuel David; John & Frances Davies; Nele Depoorter; Mike Dobson; Simon Evans; Franck Faraday; Anthea Finlayson; Sheina Foulkes; Catherine Froidebise; Patrick Gardinal; Eric Van Geertruyden; Johan De Geyndt; Pieter Van der Gheynst; Mike Gingell; Kareen Goldfeder; J. Goodfellow; Sally Gritten; David Gruccio; Katrien Gysen; Tony Hallas; John Hammond; Helen Harjanto; Lucy Hartiss; Pat Hindley; Herman Hindricks; Nick Howard; Jay Jones; Adam Kramer; John & Angela Lansley; Peter & Vivien Lee; Simon Loveitt; Heather McCann; Richard Madge; Fab

Marsani; Loes Maveau; Claudia Merges; Slávi Metz; Deirdre & David Mills; William Milne; Paul Mitchell; Bernadette & Michael Mossley; Ros Murphy; Mary Murray; B. E Neale; Stuart Newman; Barry Newsome; Delphine Nizet; Adolphe Nzeza; Maureen O'Keefe; Marc Oris; Isabel Payno; Melissa Perry; Susan Plowden; Johnny Pring; David Reeves; Barbara Reid; Kiron Reid; John A Rosenhof; Chris Serle; Dennis Simmonds; Ed Silverman; Pascale Slagmulders; Roel Smeyers; Christine Smith; Tim Smith; William Smith; Phyllis Snyder; Zoe Spyvee; K. Tan; Colin Tattersall; Warren Thomas; Christina Thyssen; Robin Tilston; Elisabeth Timenchik; David Trussler; Frederik Vlieghe; Mary Whitham; Brian & Suzanne Williams; James Williams; Jim Williams; Steve Willis; Stephen Wills; Melanie Winterbotham; Glenda Young.

ABOUT THE AUTHORS

Phil Lee has been writing for Rough Guides for well over twenty years. His other books in the series include Canada, Norway, Norfolk & Suffolk, Amsterdam, Mallorca & Menorca, and England. He lives in Nottingham, where he was born and raised.

Martin Dunford is one of the founders of Rough Guides and has worked in travel publishing for over 25 years. He is the author of more than ten guidebooks and works as a freelance travel writer and as a publishing and digital consultant to the travel industry. When not on the road, he lives in Blackheath, London, with his wife and two daughters, where he also spends time making soup and watching his local football team, Charlton Athletic.

Emma Thomson is an award-winning freelance travel writer and a member of the British Guild of Travel Writers. She lives in Aalst, Belgium, and writes about the country for international newspapers, magazines and publishers (print and online) and, as a country specialist, is consulted regularly on everything ranging from where to find the best chips to booking the hippest hotels.

Acknowledgements

Phil Lee would like to thank his editor, Neil McQuillian, for his enthusiastic attention to detail during the preparation of this new edition of the *Rough Guide to Belgium & Luxembourg*. Special thanks also to the charming and superbly efficient Anita Rampall of Visit Flanders; the ever helpful Ellen Hubert of Antwerpen Toerisme; and the super diligent Rebekka Koch of Toerisme Mechelen. Thanks also to Katalin Chovanetz from Visit Gent; Pieters Hens of Toerisme Oostende; Sabine Palmans of the Jenevermuseum, Hasselt; and Nathalie Standaert of the *Hotel Adornes*, Bruges. Thanks also to my co-authors, my old friend Martin Dunford and the enthusiastic Emma Thomson.

Index

Maps are marked in grey

Map symbols

The symbols below are used on maps throughout the book

Main road	Wall	⊙ Statue	▲ Mountain peak	Ⓜ Metro
Minor road	Railways	◆ Point of interest	✈ Airport	Church
Motorway	◄— One way	♣ Museum	★ Bus stop	Building
Pedestrianized road	✉ Post office	🏛 Abbey	🅿 Parking	Park
Steps	ⓘ Information office	🏛 Monument	🚹 Race circuit	Beach
---- Path	⊠ Gate	♜ Castle	Ⓣ Tram stop	⊞ Cemetery

Listings key

● Café/restaurant

■ Accommodation

■ Bar/club/live music venue

● Shop